Dear Nathan,

This book is given to you with love and appreciation for your tremendous support of the soldiers of Israel through the years.

Brig. Gen. Eliezer Hamel:

Sep. 25 98

ISRAEL

Editors-in-Chief:
Yehuda Shiff, Danny Dor

Editors:
Ben Caspit, Ilan Kfir

Photography Editor:
Moshe Milner

MetroBooks

MetroBooks

An Imprint of Friedman/Fairfax Publishers

Published in 1998 by Michael Friedman Publishing Group, Inc.
by arrangement with Alfa Communication, Ltd.

©1998 Alfa Communication, Ltd.

Library of Congress Cataloging-in-Publication Data available upon request.

ISBN 1-56799-678-7

English Text: Liora Barash-Morgenstern, Ph.D. - BonUse International
Executive Editors: Liora Barash-Morgenstern, Ph.D., Angela Godfrey, Tali Barash-Gottlieb
Editors: Jennifer Balick, Shelly Medello, Tony Berris
Translators: Paloma Reichbart, Bernice Keren, Dedy Barak, Noya Shilo
Columns: David Weil, Nitzan Sandor
Research: Hani Lerner, Guy Leshem
Jacket Design: Yehuda Salomon

Printed in Israel by Alfa Communication, Ltd.

1 3 5 7 9 10 8 6 4 2

For bulk purchases and special sales, please contact:
Friedman/Fairfax Publishers
Attention: Sales Department
15 West 26th Street
New York, NY 10010
212/685-6610 FAX 212/685-1307

Visit our website:
http://www.metrobooks.com

Photographers:

Governmental Press Office photographers:
Ya'acov Sa'ar, Avi O'Hayon, Moshe Milner, David Eldan, Fritz Cohen,
Moshe Fridan, Ilan Brunner, Zvi Israeli, Nati Hernick, Maggie Ayalon, Hanania Herman,
Hans Pin, Kluger Zultam, Teddy Brauner, Paul Goldstein, Hugo Mendelson, Werner Braun,
Benny Tel-Or, Nissim Gabbay, Nathan Alpert, Ziv Koren, Micha Perry.

"Ba'Mahaneh" photographers:
Avi Simchoni, Avraham Vered, Micha Bar'Am, Mickey Zarfati, Uzi Keren, Shlomo Arad, Alex Gal, Uri Dan.

Ma'ariv photographers:
Ruby Castro, Shmuel Rachmani, Yossi Aloni, Naor Rahev, Eli Dassa, Adi Avishai, Noam Wind,
Yonatan Sha'ul, Gary Abramowitz, Motti Kimchi, "Koko."

The Photographers:
Zoom 77, Shalom Bartal, Yossi Roth, Yossi Greenberg,
Shabtai Tal, David Rubinger, Assaf Kutin, Danny Rosenblum, Herzl Kunzari,
Oscar Tauber, Yigal Tumarkin, Micha Han, Rami Lachover, Kobi Kantor,
Government Press Office archives, "Ba'Mahaneh" archives, Ma'ariv archives,
IDF archives, Lavon archives.

Thanks to:
Ya'acov Sa'ar, director of the photography department at the Government Press Office;
Mickey Zarfati, photography editor of Ma'ariv;
Avi Simchoni, photography editor of "Ba'Mahaneh;" Ilan Dayan and Einat Anker,
the photography archives, Government Press Office.

Fifty Years

"Every now and then in this arena of historical forces a great historic opportunity presents itself - as in the Jewish legend, according to which once every year the Heavens open for a single moment and your every wish is granted."

The above words were spoken by David Ben-Gurion on January 19, 1933, some fifteen years before his voice rose once again to announce the establishment of the State of Israel.

Yet even when the Heavens opened, and the great historic opportunity was granted, 600,000 people surrounded by enemies, haunted by infiltrators, lacking an economy and natural resources, had to be unified into one state. Fifty years later, the result is a nation of five and a half million people, a well-trained army, a developed economy, national health care and continuing immigration.

This is the story of the first fifty years. The wars, the waves of immigration, the economy, construction, settlement. The historic wonder that grew out of nothing and thrived.

Hundreds of thousands of events have taken place during the course of these fifty years. Most of them are not included in this album. Our goal has been to try and bring together those events which have had the greatest influence on the life of Israel. Thus, in addition to the history unfolding here, we have not ignored significant international events taking place at the same time which have also affected the Israeli people.

These are the stories we wished to focus upon. These are the stories we have chosen to portray the story of our State. An unending story. A never ending story.

The Editors

PRESIDENTS OF ISRAEL

Ephraim Katzir: 1973-1978

Fourth president of the State of Israel. Professor of bio-chemistry and an internationally known scientist. His brother, Professor Aharon Katzir, was murdered in 1972 during a terrorist attack at Lod – now Ben-Gurion – Airport. Decided to resign upon completion of his first term of office.

Yitzhak Navon: 1978-1983

Fifth president of the State of Israel. Prior to his election he was secretary to David Ben-Gurion and a member of the Israeli *Knesset*. After one term of office he returned to the Labor party to become minister of education in the government of Shimon Peres.

Zalman Shazar: 1963-1973

Third president of the State of Israel. Prior to his election upon the death of President Shazar he was one of the leaders of the *Mapai* labor movement and minister of education in the first Israeli government, led by David Ben-Gurion. Died in 1974.

Chaim Weizmann: 1948-1952

First president of the State of Israel. Prior to his election he was one of the leading personalities in the Zionist Movement, and a world-renowned scientist in his own right. It was to a considerable extent due to him that Great Britain in 1917 issued the Balfour Declaration on the establishment of a Jewish national home. Died in 1952.

Chaim Herzog: 1983-1993

Sixth president of the State of Israel. Earlier he served as a General in the Israeli Defense Forces, as an outstanding military spokesman and commentator, a member of *Knesset* and Israeli delegate to the United Nations. He was the son of Israel's chief rabbi. Died in 1996, three years after completing his final term of office.

Yitzhak Ben-Zvi: 1952-1963

Second president of the State of Israel, elected as the successor to President Weizmann following the latter's death. Before this he was one of the leading activists in the *Mapai* labor movement and a long-standing political partner of David Ben-Gurion. Died in 1963.

Ezer Weizman: 1993 –

Seventh president of the State of Israel. Some of his earlier positions were commander-in-chief of the Israeli Air Force, General in the Israeli Defense Forces, member of *Knesset* and government minister. He is a nephew of Chaim Weizmann, the first president of the State.

PRIME MINISTERS OF ISRAEL

Yitzhak Rabin: 1974-1977; 1992-1995

Fifth prime minister of Israel, who earlier served as chief of staff and Israeli ambassador to the United States. He served as minister of defense in the governments of Shimon Peres and Yitzhak Shamir from 1984-1990. On November 4, 1995, soon after having signed a peace agreement with Yasser Arafat, he was assassinated by an Israeli youth at the close of a mass peace rally in the center of Tel Aviv.

Menachem Begin: 1977-1983

Sixth prime minister of Israel, and the first to head a government with a rightist signature. He was elected after leading the opposition in the *Knesset* for 29 years. In 1978 he signed the historic peace agreement with Egypt – the first with any Arab country. Resigned in 1983 and withdrew entirely from public life. Died in 1992.

Golda Meir: 1969-1974

Fourth prime minister of Israel, and the only woman so far to occupy this high office, appointed following the death of Levi Eshkol. She was prime minister during the *Yom Kippur* War, but was forced to resign in 1974 following severe public criticism about the conduct of the war. Died in 1978.

Yitzhak Shamir: 1983-1984; 1986-1992

Seventh prime minister of Israel, who was elected following the resignation of Menachem Begin. Previously he was foreign minister and speaker of Israel's parliament – the *Knesset*. During the elections in 1992 he lost to the Labor Party, and was succeeded by Yitzhak Rabin.

David Ben-Gurion: 1948-1953; 1955-1963

First prime minister, and responsible for the fateful decision about the establishment of the State. He led the country during the War of Independence and the first difficult years of mass immigration and austerity. Died in 1973.

Levi Eshkol: 1963-1969

Third Israeli prime minister. Earlier occupied the influential position of minister of finance in the government of David Ben-Gurion, to succeed him following the latter's final resignation. Died in 1969 while still in office.

Shimon Peres: 1984-1986; 1995-1996

Eighth Israeli prime minister. One of the oldest and most senior Israeli Labor politicians with an international reputation. After two years as prime minister he gave up his position to Yitzhak Shamir under an existing rotation agreement. In 1992 he became foreign minister in the government of Yitzhak Rabin, and following the latter's assassination took his place as prime minister until defeated in the elections of 1996.

Moshe Sharett: 1953-1955

Second prime minister, appointed following Ben-Gurion's decision to retire temporarily to Kibbutz Sde Boker in the Negev. He was foreign minister in the first Israeli cabinet. Died in 1965.

Binyamin Netanyahu: 1996 –

Ninth prime minister of Israel, chosen at the age of 47 following the first direct elections for prime minister. Previously he was Israel's representative at the United Nations and deputy minister of foreign affairs in the Shamir government. In 1993 he was chosen as head of the rightist *Likud* Party, in which capacity he contended with Shimon Peres in the 1996 elections. winning – against most forecasts – by a mere percentage point.

ISRAEL 1948-1997

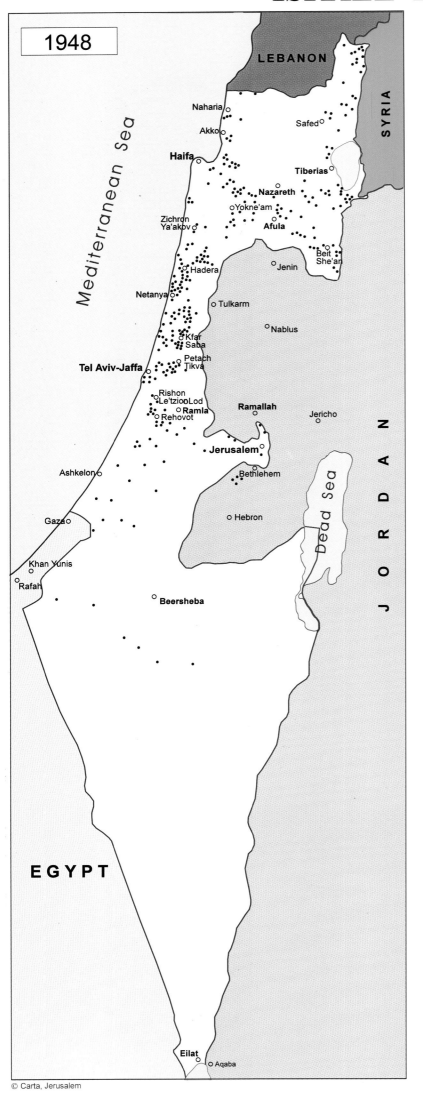

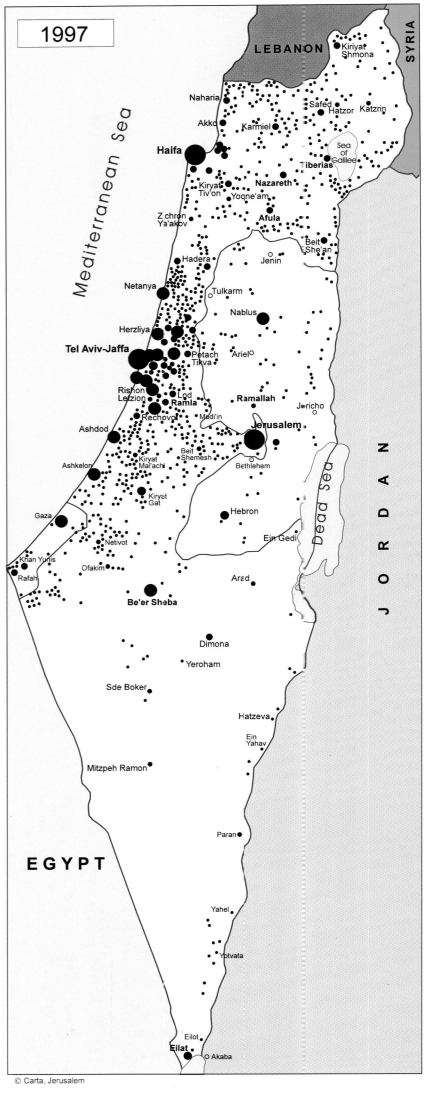

© Carta, Jerusalem

© Carta, Jerusalem

POPULATION DENSITY 1948-1997

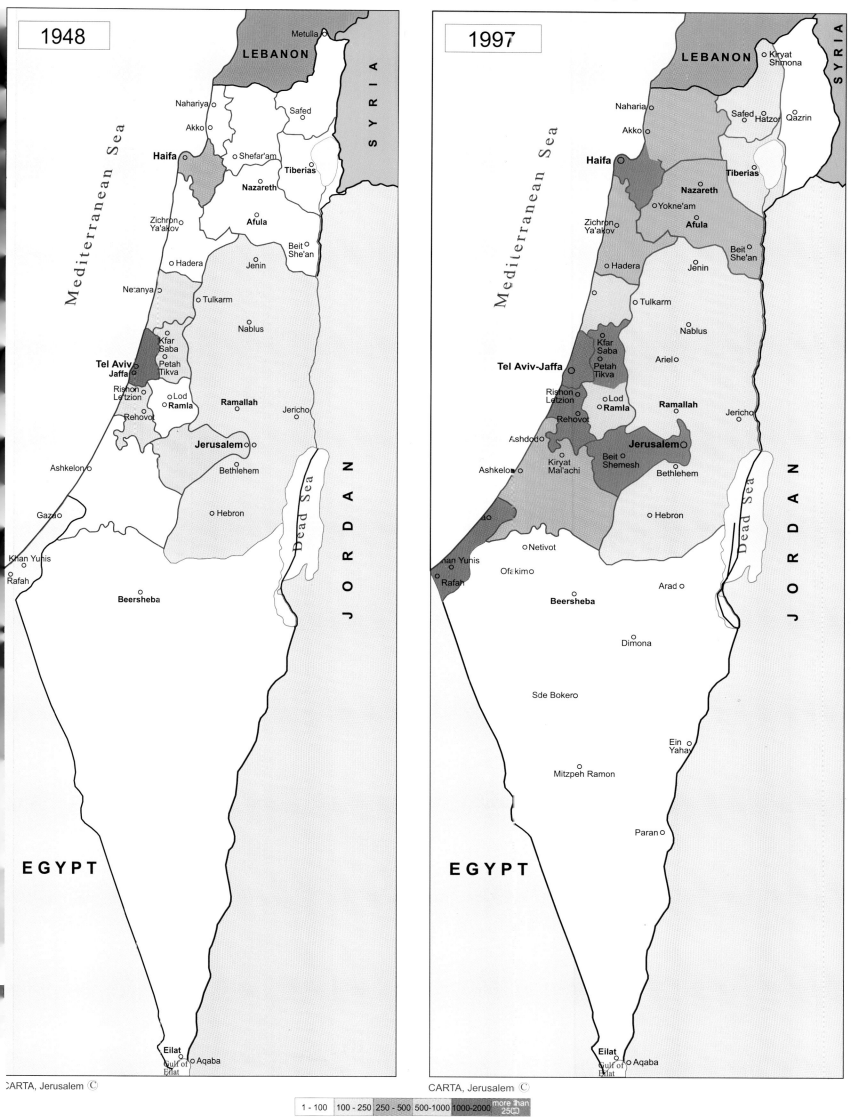

Population density per km²

1 - 100 | 100 - 250 | 250 - 500 | 500-1000 | 1000-2000 | more than 2500

Black

ITALY

YUGOSLAVIA **BULGARIA**

ALBANIA

• Istanbul

GREECE

TURK

• Athens

• Tunis

TUNISIA

M e d i t e r r a n e a n   S e a

• Nicosia

CYPRUS

• Tripoli

LEBANO

Beiru

ISRAEL

Jerusalem

Cairo •

LIBYA

EGYPT

NIGER

CHAD

SUDAN

• Khartoum

• N'Djamena

MIDDLE EAST

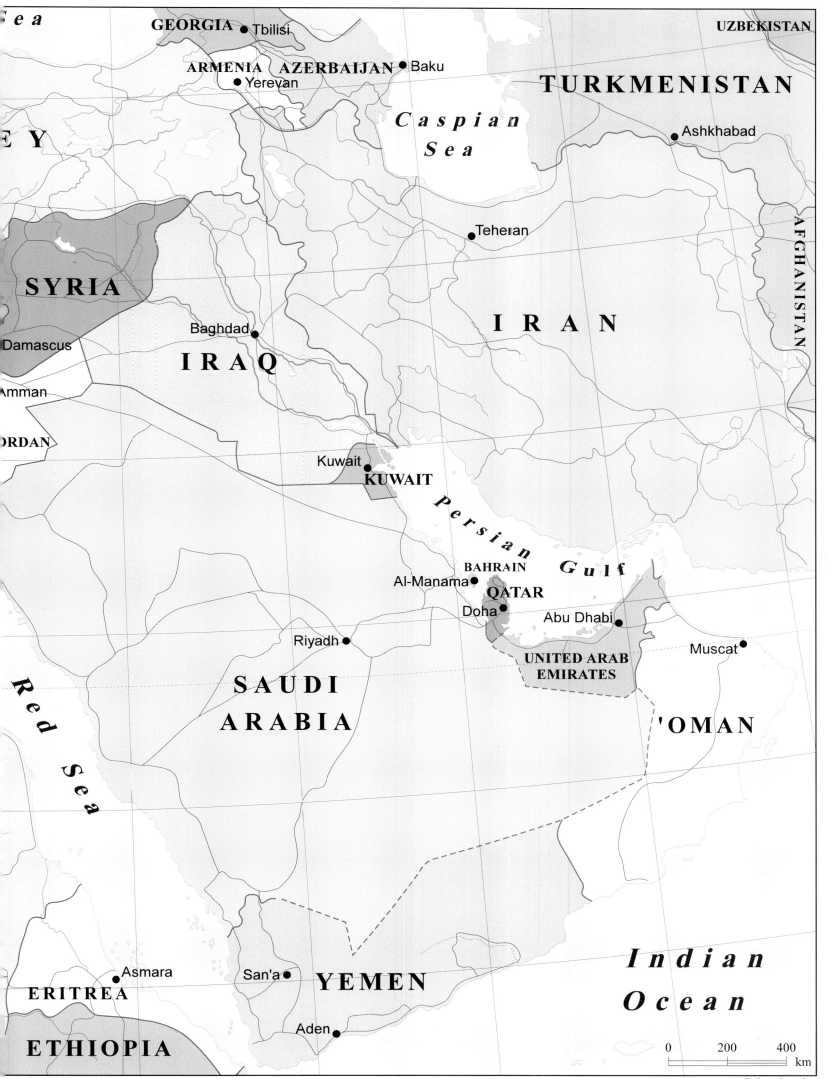

S e a

GEORGIA · Tbilisi

UZBEKISTAN

ARMENIA AZERBAIJAN · Baku

· Yerevan

TURKMENISTAN

Caspian Sea

EY

· Ashkhabad

AFGHANISTAN

· Teheran

SYRIA

I R A N

Damascus

Baghdad ·

Amman

I R A Q

ORDAN

Kuwait ·
KUWAIT

Persian Gulf

BAHRAIN

Al-Manama ·
QATAR

Doha ·

Abu Dhabi ·

Muscat ·

Riyadh ·

UNITED ARAB
EMIRATES

Red Sea

**SAUDI
ARABIA**

'OMAN

*Indian
Ocean*

Asmara ·

San'a ·

YEMEN

ERITREA

Aden ·

ETHIOPIA

0   200   400

km

© Carta, Jerusalem

NO MAN KNEW WHO SHE WAS

*No man knew who she was
From whence she had come
and whither she was headed
But as she appeared
Every eye blazed aflame.*

*From a foreign land
From a distant country
She came like a bird
With her joy and laughter.*

Chaim Nachman Bialik

The Magic Carpet, 1950.

Israel is Established

Hours after David Ben-Gurion declared the establishment of the State of Israel, Arab armies invaded the borders of the new state. Egypt from the south, Iraq and Jordan from the east, and Lebanon from the north joined local forces and threatened to conquer the newly-formed country.

The declaration was made in a special hour-long National Council meeting. Hundreds of thousands of people were glued to their radios, listening excitedly to the live broadcast. The country burst into celebration. City residents danced in the squares. Thousands came to Rothschild Boulevard in Tel Aviv to witness the historic moment with their own eyes.

The excitement peaked with a spontaneous rendering of 'Hatikva,' Israel's national anthem. Ben-Gurion approached the singers with the generals of the newly-formed army at his side: Chief of Staff Ya'akov Dori and his deputy, General Yigael Yadin. Afterwards, the

The historic moment. Ben-Gurion announces the establishment of the State of Israel.

three headed to an emergency meeting of the new army's commanders to prepare for the imminent invasion of the newborn State.

Jerusalem Under Siege. Egyptians Approach Tel Aviv

Several hours after the declaration of the State, it seemed that the new country would be crushed in battle when it had barely been established. Egyptian armored forces succeeded in severing the Negev from the rest of Israel, conquering Ashkelon and advancing towards Ashdod. Dozens

of people were killed by an Egyptian aerial attack on Tel Aviv.

The most critical problem, however, remained Jerusalem. The Jordanian army cut the city off from the center of the country, conquered the Old City and isolated Mt. Scopus. The only contact with Jerusalem was

achieved through convoys, some of which did not make it through.

The Syrian army crossed the Jordan River, and the Lebanese army took over the Lower Galilee and Nazareth in the northern part of the State. In the east, the Iraqi army took over most of Judea and Samaria.

Battles in the Negev. Egyptian forces near Ashdod.

1948 MAY

154 alleged guerrillas and communists executed in Greece after the assassination of the minister of justice. Hundreds arrested in connection with the investigation. (May 4)

•

Italy's first president elected. He had a strong influence on Italy's inclusion in the Marshall Plan. (May 13)

•

Etzion settlers taken prisoner; fighting stopped with Red Cross intervention. The terms of surrender: all able-bodied soldiers to be taken prisoner and kept in camps supervised by the Red Cross. Women, non-combatants and wounded to be brought to Jerusalem by the Red Cross. (May 14)

•

The Israeli Air Force, formerly known as the Jewish Aviation Force, is established. On the first day of its existence the force downs an Egyptian airplane near Rehovot and strafes Syrian forces in the area of Zemach in the Jordan Valley. All our aircraft return home safely. (May 21)

•

American consul general in Jerusalem and communications officer die from wounds after being shot by Arab snipers. (May 23)

•

'Herald Tribune' editorial says that United States should lift Middle East arms embargo for Israel. (May 24)

•

Hundred million dollar loan given to Israel. President Truman and Dr. Chaim Weizmann meet to discuss the possibility of a US loan to Israel; it was granted in February, 1949. (May 25)

•

USSR has agreed to exchange diplomatic missions with Israel. (May 26)

•

The government has issued an order for the formation of the IDF. All armed forces operating outside the IDF are outlawed. David Ben-Gurion disarmed the undergrounds and united them in one army. The IZL was the first to announce that it would join the army; the Lehi followed 24 hours later. (May 28)

1948

JUNE - JULY

Air force 'planes bombed military targets in Jordan's capital as well as troop concentrations in the Tulkarm and the Tira areas. (June 1)

•

The American Defense Department has instructed occupation authorities in Europe to name the Jewish Agency as the official organization to transport Jewish displaced persons to Israel. (June 7).

•

Foreign minister Shertok met mediator Bernadotte today and charged that the Syrians had violated the cease-fire. (June 13).

•

Today, the IDF will pledge allegiance to the State of Israel. Chief commanders were sworn in last night. The oath of allegiance was issued by the IDF's first Chief of Staff, Ya'acov Dori (Dostrovsky) soon after the 'Altalena' incident. (June 28)

•

The evacuation of British forces was completed upon the entry of the Israeli fleet to Israel at Haifa port. David Ben-Gurion attended the ceremony, raised the flag at the port and was applauded when he said: "We are prepared to meet our enemy, whether on land, sea or air." (July 1)

•

The army staff did not want to accept a truce as Israel's offensive drove ahead of schedule, said Yigael Yadin, Israeli army chief of operations. In the nine days between the truces, the Arab armies suffered over 5,000 casualties. (July 21)

•

Explosive issues before the UN General Assembly: Korea, Greece, atomic energy and the veto are on the agenda. Possible additional items: Palestine and the Berlin blockade. The Assembly is to open in Paris on September 21. (July 24)

•

More cease-fire violations by Arabs. Egyptian forces attack Israel supply convoys to the Negev . Israel replied by attacking enemy lines. Still no peace in Jerusalem. Arab Legion soldiers fired on Jewish positions from the police school on Mt. Scopus. (July 31)

Arms Ship 'Altalena' Sunk Off the Tel Aviv Coastline

The 'Altalena' on fire off the Tel Aviv coast. Thirteen men died on the ship.

On June 22, troops of the Israel Defense Forces sank the arms ship 'Altalena,' which had arrived on Israel's shores. The ship transported weapons for the IZL - *Irgun Zvai Leumi (National Military Organization)* despite the fact that its members had announced that they would join the IDF.

The provisional government claimed that the independent attempt to import weapons represented a division that endangered the unity of the people. The IZL refused the government's demand to hand over the weapons and insisted on allocating 20 percent to their own IZL fighters stationed in Jerusalem.

The provisional government sent a special military force to the village Kfar Vitkin, on the Sharon coast, where the ship had anchored. The IZL members there refused to carry out the government's clear instructions, which were designed to prevent the unloading of the weapons - by force if necessary.

The ship reached the Tel Aviv coast, where a military confrontation between IDF forces and the IZL took place. The ship was bombarded, at Ben-Gurion's command, and set on fire. Thirteen men were killed, and 48 injured.

The IDF forces were commanded by Yitzhak Rabin, later to become the IDF's chief of staff and Israel's prime minister, who was tragically assassinated in 1995.

Tel Aviv Bombed. Among the Victims: Women and Children

Egyptian *Spitfire* combat airplanes flying at low altitude bombed several areas of Tel Aviv on June 10. Most of the damage sustained was in streets located far from army bases. Among those killed were many women and children. Tel Aviv's citizens were enraged that the emergency alarm system was not activated in advance of the attack. Some told Mayor Israel Rokach that they had heard the sound of the 'planes long before they heard the alarm.

The IDF Liberates Lod and Ramla

The cities of Lod and Ramla were conquered by the Israel Defense Forces, and thousands of Arab citizens fled towards the state's eastern border. Beit Nabala and Ben Shemen were also conquered after a rapid military operation known as 'Operation Danny,' named for Danny Mas, who commanded the Lamed Hey convoy to Gush Etzion. The military commander of the operation was Lieutenant Colonel Moshe Dayan, Israel's future chief of staff, minister of defense and foreign minister.

Battles on other fronts continued as well. On the southern front, two Egyptian attempts to conquer Julis failed. Kibbutz Ruhama was bombed seven times during the course of one day, and one of its defenders died. On the central front, the battles continued in the Sha'ar Hagai area. The Jordanian army bombarded several settlements and the city of Afula, and maintained pressure on Mishmar Hayarden and Mt. Gilboa.

'Operation Danny' for the conquest of Lod and Ramla. Named after Danny Mas.

Count Bernadotte is Murdered in Jerusalem

On Sept. 7, United Nations Security Council mediator Count Folke Bernadotte was assassinated in Jerusalem. Only six hours had passed since he had arrived for the latest visit in his ongoing shuttle diplomacy. His personal assistant, Colonel Andre Sareau of France, was also shot dead.

At 5:30 p.m. Bernadotte was on his way to a meeting with the Israeli Military Governor of Jerusalem, Dr. Dov Yosef. The convoy, comprising three cars flying UN flags, made its way from the office of the high commissioner to the city center. At an intersection in the Katamon quarter, the cars were stopped by four young men in uniform. Two approached the car, numbered 873, in which Berna-

dotte, Sareau and Bernadotte's secretary were riding.

One of the soldiers opened the car door and emptied a submachine gun magazine into the passengers. Sareau was killed instantly. Count Bernadotte was fatally wounded and died soon afterwards.

An underground group calling itself 'Chazit HaMoledet' (The Homeland Front) took responsibility for the assassination because Bernadotte was urging a division of both Jerusalem and *Erez Israel*. Immediately after the Sept. 17 murder, the provisional government issued arrest warrants for 170 members of the *Lehi (Lohamei Herut Israel - Freedom Fighters of Israel)* in Jerusalem.

Bernadotte's murderers were never caught. *Years later, the name of Yitzhak Shamir, Lehi commander and future Israeli prime minister, was linked to the incident, but in interviews he refused to be drawn.*

Shamir.

First Population Census

The first population census was carried out on Sept. 8, in order to prepare for the upcoming general elections to the Founding Assembly. The results of the census would aid in issuing identity cards and regulating the elections. A countrywide general curfew was declared from 5.00 p.m that evening until midnight. During that time, 15,000 census takers went from house to house and registered the citizens of the state. The census comprised approximately 600,000 citizens from the age of 15 and up, including soldiers on active service.

Count Bernadotte. A burst of submachine gun fire into the car.

Pogrom in Cairo, Jews are Arrested

In early August, the first details came to light of pogroms against Cairo's Jewish population, that had occurred during the month of July.

According to eyewitness accounts, at least three rabbis were murdered in the Jewish slaughterhouse, and 120 wounded were brought to Cairo's Jewish Hospital.

In late July, all Jews living near the royal palace and government buildings were evacuated. The Jews were ordered to leave their houses within 48 hours; many were searched and looted during these evictions. Any person found in possession of books or any other material in Hebrew was sent to one of Cairo's most notorious prisons.

Bernadotte urged the Security Council to affirm the right of between 250,000-300,000 Arab refugees to return to Israeli controlled areas of Palestine. The Israeli Government has refused to discuss their return in large numbers except as part of a lasting peace settlement. (August 7)

•

Recruiting for the Women's Corps has begun. All women born between 1920-1930, who are unmarried or who are married but do not have children, must join the corps. Mothers will be exempt. The Women's Corps' first commander, Lieutenant Colonel Mina Rogozchik, reported that the women were filling various roles: nurses, drivers, cooks, secretaries, military policewomen, quartermasters, and land jobs in the airforce and navy. (August 18)

•

Israel's envoy to Moscow, Mrs. Golda Meyerson, left for Prague on her way to Moscow. (August 29)

•

Juliana becomes Queen of the Netherlands. The 39-year-old succeeded to the throne on Queen Wilhelmina's abdication. (September 4)

•

Czechoslovakia mourns Eduard Benes, former president and one of the founders of the republic, who died at 64 from a stroke, after being unconscious for four days. (September 4)

•

Mohammed Ali Jinna, founder of Pakistan, has died at 72. Karachi mourns his death. India advances into Hyderabad, the largest of India's states that did not elect to join India or Pakistan. (September 12)

•

Trygve Lie asks for UN force of 5,000, as mediator's final report is published. Bernadotte proposed recognizing a smaller Israel. The UN should set the boundaries with the following revisions: the Negev should be defined as Arab territory; Haifa port and refineries and the Lod airport as free areas; reparation for those Arab refugees that chose not to return; Jerusalem requires special treatment due to its religious and international significance. (September 20)

1948

OCTOBER - DECEMBER

Leonard Bernstein opened the Israel Philharmonic Orchestra's season as soloist and conductor. (October 3)

•

US favors Negev to Israel. US delegation in Paris takes a serious view of the breaches of the truce made by the Egyptians in the Negev. There is also good reason to believe that they are opposed to the plan - attributed to the British - to divide the Negev between Egypt and Trans-Jordan. (October 10)

•

US will talk but keep A-bomb. The US is willing to talk about the Bomb but will maintain its stockpile until Russia raises the Iron Curtain, says Warren Austin, United States delegate to the UN. (October 18)

•

Cease-fire from 3.00 p.m. today; Beersheba falls, Egyptian army pockets in the Negev doomed. Dr. Bunche, acting mediator, asks both sides to confirm cease-fire. (October 22)

•

Truman elected president as Democrats regain majorities in the Senate and House. Dewey says he won't run again. (November 2)

•

Security Council adopts armistice resolution. The Security Council called on the Jews and Arabs to negotiate a permanent armistice in Palestine, and ordered the Jews to leave the Negev. (November 16)

•

Preliminary figures of the first Israeli census show a total of 782,000: 713,000 Jews and 69,000 Arabs and others. (November 18)

•

Elections in Israel planned for Jan. 25, credentials to be issued to about 427,000 voters in early January. (November 25)

•

Chinese Communists edging southward. The Communists outnumber the Nationalist by more than two to one where it counts. Chiang Kai Shek's wife to visit the US to appeal for increased aid for the Chinese government. (November 28)

•

Israel submitted an official request to become a member of the UN. (November 30)

Beersheba Taken. Dramatic Operation Liberates Galilee

Egyptian forces, who had nearly reached the outskirts of Tel Aviv, were pushed back from the majority of their footholds in the south. In seven hours of heavy fighting, the last Egyptian stronghold blocking the main road to Beersheba was overrun. Israeli forces also attacked the city of Gaza.

In a surprise attack on Oct. 22, the Israel Defense Forces took Beersheba. They found the town practically deserted, because the Arab population had fled several days before.

In the north, successes continued. On Nov. 1, most of the Galilee was liberated in a daring lightning operation. It began at the end of the week with a pincer movement: one force advanced from Safed, a second moved from Tarshiha and a third from Lubia. The heaviest fighting occurred in Sasa, Tarshiha and Jish (Gush Halav).

Circassian and Druze soldiers,

The IDF takes Beersheba.

deserters from Kaukji's army, reported that the commander of the Arab forces in the north had barely escaped from the IDF.

Menachem Begin Establishes *Herut*

Begin. A comprehensive attack.

On Oct. 20 IZL leader Menachem Begin announced the establishment of *Herut*, a new political movement. Begin declared that he would run for office in the coming elections.

Begin promised that if *Herut* won the public's confidence and received a majority of the vote, his government would not disappoint its constituency. He did not rule out the possibility of joining the current ruling coalition headed by David Ben-Gurion.

Begin demanded the nullification of the partition agreement and the launching of an all-out offensive against the Arab countries on all fronts.

He urged against signing a separate peace agreement with King Abdallah and against engaging in talks with leaders of the Arab countries, until their armies retreated unilaterally from Israeli territory.

From 1949 to 1977, Begin failed to gain a majority in all his election campaigns. It was only in 1977 that he succeeded in defeating Shimon Peres and finally becoming prime minister.

Chaim Weizmann Arrives in Israel

Weizmann. Choked by tears.

Chaim Weizmann, president of Israel's Temporary Council, arrived in the country and took part on Oct. 1 in a festive council meeting. During the event, he recited the *Shehechianu* blessing in a voice choking with emotion. Although no advance notice was given of Weizmann's participation in the meeting, thousands had gathered to await his arrival.

The president arrived from Rehovot with his wife and members of his entourage. As he entered the hall, the large audience cheered.

Cease-fire Agreements Signed with both Egypt and Lebanon

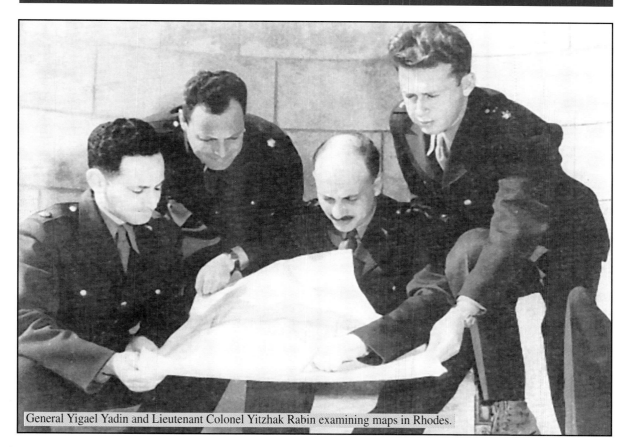

General Yigael Yadin and Lieutenant Colonel Yitzhak Rabin examining maps in Rhodes.

On Jan. 13 negotiations began for a cease-fire agreement between the delegations of Israel and Egypt. The talks took place on the Mediterranean island of Rhodes. Members of the Israeli delegation included Foreign Ministry Director-General Major-General Yigael Yadin and the head of the ministry's Middle Eastern department. The Egyptian delegation was headed by Colonel Mohammed Ibrahim Saif a-Din.

The two delegations were authorized by their respective heads of state to sign cease-fire agreements.

Syria announced initially that it would not participate, but in early February it joined the talks.

The agreement on the cease-fire lines with Egypt was signed after four days. Egypt pledged to withdraw its forces from Kis Faluja. Ten days later, a cease-fire agreement was signed with Lebanon.

First Elections Held. Ben-Gurion Forms a Government. Chaim Weizmann Elected President

Israel's first elections took place on Jan. 25. On election day, which was declared a public holiday, 427,000 citizens voted out of a possible half million. The counting of the ballots took two days. The results were: *Mapai (Erez Israel Workers' Party)* - 36% of the vote, *Mapam (United Workers' Party)* - 15%, the religious bloc - 12%, *Herut* - 12%, the General Zionists' party - 5% and the Progressive party - 4%. Five thousand ballots were counted a second time because of suspected irregularities.

Three weeks later, on Feb. 15, the first sitting of the Founding Assembly was opened in Jerusalem, in the presence of Temporary President Chaim Weizmann, the chief rabbis, IDF generals, judges, and representatives of the Jewish Agency. Flags decorated the Jerusalem streets and the police orchestra played 'Hatikva' twice. Before the

Weizmann - pledging allegiance.

elected representatives were sworn in, two memorial candles were lit in memory of all the victims of the Holocaust and the War of Independence casualties.

One month later, David Ben-Gurion, as both prime minister and minister of defense, presented his government's Cabinet: Moshe Sharett as foreign minister, Golda Meyerson as minister of labor, Rabbi Fishman as minister of religious affairs, Rabbi Levin as minister of welfare, Moshe Shapira as minister of immigration and the interior, Bechor Shetreet as minister of police, Pinhas Rosen as minister of justice, David Remez as minister of transport, Zalman Shazar as minister of education, Dov Yosef as minister of rationing and supply, and Avraham Kaplan as minister of finance.

On Feb. 17, Chaim Weizmann was elected as the first president of the State of Israel.

Shanghai asks for cease-fire. Shanghai city council went over the head of the government and asked the Chinese Communists for a cease-fire. (January 3)

●

Five British 'planes shot down over Israel as cease-fire goes into effect in the Negev. Two RAF pilots captured well inside border. (January 7)

●

It was announced that meat will be distributed to the citizens of the State during the course of the week. The ration will include frozen chicken and fillet of fish. 250 grams (half a pound) of fish will cost 70 Mil, 200 grams clean and butchered chicken will cost 220 Mil. The meat will be supplied on presentation of voucher 13 in the ration book. (January 12)

●

Chinese Communists occupy Tiansin. (January 15)

●

Chiang Kai-Shek resigns as the president of Nationalist Party. (January 21)

●

Chinese government willing to negotiate peace on the basis of Mao Tse-Tung's offer of last week. (January 22)

●

Clothes rationing discontinued in Great Britain, as wartime clothes rationing become no longer necessary. (February 1)

●

Martial law in Persia. The Tudeh left wing party outlawed. The party was accused of fomenting revolution and unrest throughout Persia, culminating in the assassination attempt on the Shah. (February 5)

●

Communists cross over the Yangtze River into Nationalist China. (February 6)

●

Gandhi's killers are to hang. N.V. Godse, the man who assassinated Mahatma Gandhi on January 30, 1948 and N. Apte were sentenced to death. Five other men were given sentences of life imprisonment. (February 10)

●

Five states will talk peace if refugees taken back. Syria, Lebanon, Iraq, Yemen and Saudi Arabia will agree to armistice talks with Israel, providing there is a prior understanding that Israel take back Arab refugees. (February 13)

Non-stop flight around the world. A US Air Force B-50 bomber completed the first non-stop flight around the world Wednesday. The flight took 94 hours and required four mid-air refuelings. (March 2)

•

Israel's flag was raised on the beach of the Red Sea. Um Rashrash, later to become Eilat, was conquered without a shot being fired. It was this conquest which determined Israel's southern border. (March 8)

•

12 Western nations signed the 20-year North Atlantic Pact. These nations seek an insurance policy against aggression and the possibility of a third world war. The signing nations: Belgium, Canada, Denmark, France, Iceland, Italy, Luxembourg, The Netherlands, Norway, Portugal, UK, and USA. (April 4)

•

New constitution for Germany. The foreign ministers of Britain, United States and France announce the approval of occupation statute for Germany, defining the powers of the occupation authorities upon the establishment of the German Federal Republic. (April 9)

•

Ireland declares itself a republic, Dublin its capital. Northern Ireland remains British, with Belfast as its capital. (April 18)

•

Stephen Wise dies in New York at 75. Founder and first secretary of the Federation of American Zionists, he played a major role in the creation of the World Jewish Congress. (April 19)

•

Two more British ships shelled, 42 sailors killed on four warships. Yangtze crossed in force. The Chinese communist armies opened a showdown battle with forces one and a half million strong, in order to crush nationalist China. Shanghai may fall soon. A million converge on the city. (April 21)

•

Russia ready to lift Berlin blockade if the West lifts its counterblockade and arranges a Big Four foreign ministers' meeting to thrash out all issues on Germany. (April 26)

Austerity Regime in Israel. Campaign Waged Against the Black Market

On Apr. 27 the government announced a policy of austerity and rationing to begin in May. The decision was announced in the *Knesset*, after Prime Minister David Ben-Gurion rejected proposals to restrict immigration to allow the country to cope with its economic problems.

Since January, 210,000 new immigrants from 50 countries had arrived in Israel. Fifty-three thousand immigrants were housed in immigrant camps because of the serious housing shortage.

Minister Dov Yosef explained that

"Eliminate the Black Market Or else - it will eliminate you."

the government would provide citizens with daily rations of 2,700 calories, giving preference to local produce. A special budget was drawn up to allow each citizen provisions totaling IL6 *(six Israeli lira)* a month: 360 gr (13 oz) of bread per day, 60 gr of cornflour, 60 gr of white flour, 17 gr of rice, 58 gr of sugar, and a monthly allowance of 750 gr of meat, 200 gr of lean cheese, 12 eggs and 3.5 kg (8 lb) of potatoes.

After a stormy debate in the *Knesset*, the austerity plan was approved on May 12.

'Operation Magic Carpet' Set in Motion

Marching in the desert, on the way to the Land of Israel: Yemenite immigrants going to Aden.

Under a thick cloak of secrecy, Israel carried out 'Operation Magic Carpet,' which achieved the transfer of practically the entire Jewish community of Yemen to Israel. British and American planes operated an airlift between Aden and Israel for the Yemenite Jews, most of whom had never seen an airplane before.

The Jews were first led on a long and dangerous journey to Aden.

They had to pass through territory controlled by hostile tribes and were forced to pay a ransom more than once before being allowed to continue. In Israel, the new immigrants were housed in *ma'abarot*, mainly in the center of the country.

Another half a year would pass before the massive undercover operation would be partially revealed.

Ironically, while the dramatic air- *lift was underway, there were press reports about new immigrants demanding to return to their countries of origin. Most of these immigrants were Moroccan Jews, who turned up every morning at the French Consulate, which was then representing Morocco. It is estimated that about 500 newly arrived immigrants went back to Morocco during the first months of 1949.*

Cease-fire Agreement with Jordan Signed

Jordan became the third country to sign a cease-fire agreement with Israel. The agreement with King Abdullah, signed on Apr. 4, was similar in format to the agreements signed with Egypt and Lebanon.

Wadi Ara and the railroad between Rosh Ha'Ayin and Hadera came under Israeli sovereignty. The Triangle was returned to Arab Legion control. King Abdullah was promised financial compensation for the

Tulkarm road which remained in Israeli hands.

East Jerusalem and the Old City remained under Jordanian rule for 19 more years until the end of the Six-Day War.

Israel is Admitted to UN

On May 13, exactly one year after the State of Israel had been declared, Israel was admitted as the 59th member of the United Nations. After the first request had been defeated in the Security Council, the General Assembly considered Israel's second request for admission. Thirty-seven members voted in favor, 12 against and nine abstained. Following the vote, the Israeli flag was raised on the UN building in New York to the sound of 'Hatikra.'

Israeli Foreign Minister Moshe Sharett was present during the vote and pledged allegiance to the UN charter on behalf of Israel.

The General Assembly admits Israel as its 59th member.

The Tubiansky Affair Exposed. Wrongly Executed for Treason

On July 5, about one year after he had been executed for treason, the incident involving a senior *Haganah* commander falsely accused of turning over information to the enemy came to light.

Meir Tubiansky, who had been *Haganah* commander in Jerusalem and CO of Camp Shneller, was executed on June 30, 1948, following a special court-martial.

During the first lull in the fighting, two soldiers had come to Tubiansky's house, asking him to accompany them to general headquarters.

They took him to the Arab village of Bet Giz near the Burma Road.

Tubiansky was brought before a special court-martial and tried by officers of the *Palmach*.

The presiding officers gave him no opportunity to appeal their verdict. He was found guilty, sentenced to death and executed on the spot by a firing-squad. He was buried at the site of his execution.

A few days later, Tubiansky's widow contacted David Ben-Gurion and lawyer Ya'acov Levitzky. Ben-Gurion ordered an investigation into Tubiansky's disappearance. Quite soon after, Tubiansky's body was found near an orchard not far from Kibbutz Harel.

Issar Be'eri a *Haganah* commander and chief of military intelligence, was arrested as a suspect in causing Tubiansky's death. Be'eri requested that he be tried by a military tribunal, but his request was denied.

A long line of respected public and military figures testified at the trial. Be'eri was found guilty and sentenced to one day in jail. Tubiansky's name was cleared.

Syria Too has Now Signed a Cease-fire Agreement

Syria has become the last Arab country to sign a cease-fire agreement with Israel. The agreement was signed on July 20, following talks that began in April in no-man's-land between the two countries.

The agreement stated that the Syrian army would pull back from all the territories it then controlled. Mishmar Hayarden would be released, and the Syrians would allow overland passage to besieged Ein Gev. The evacu-ated area would be demilitarized.

The signing of the treaty with Syria completed Israel's cease-fire agreements. The country's borders were now fixed and remained in effect until the Six-Day War in June 1967.

1949
MAY - JULY

Russia will lift Berlin blockade on May 12. Big Four foreign ministers to meet in Paris May 22. The US Air Force announced that the Allies' air lift to Berlin, which began June 26 1948, had flown 1,510,466 tons of supplies. 27 Americans lost their lives and 27 'planes were lost. America's share of the airlift's cost was $157,490,000. (May 5)

Siam changes its name to Thailand. (May 11)

Russia rejects West's proposal for a unified Germany and accuses the West of trying to avoid an overall solution of the German problem. East Germany votes on a constitution. Only one of the 2,000 delegates to the Russian-controlled German people's congress abstained. (May 30)

The Vatican declares a global ban on communism. (June 13)

Twenty four tons of wheat purchased from Russia have arrived in Israel. An additional 6,000 tons, given to Israel by the Emergency Council for Wheat Distribution in Washington, are expected to arrive soon. (June 19)

The Palestine Conciliation Commission announces an 18-day recess in Lausanne talks, hoping that the delegations would receive new instructions to solve the fundamental problems of territories and refugees. The Arabs still have to decide on policy towards Israeli territory, and the Israelis must still decide on policy towards Arab refugees. (June 25)

Bahai group returns to Israel. 85 year-old Mirza Baha'ulla, his wife and a group of 80 Persian followers returned to Haifa after 15 months in Lebanon. Haifa and Acre are holy cities to the Bahai faith. (July 16)

The president awards 12 medals for valor at the Army Day parade in Tel Aviv. Forty thousand spectators gathered to pay tribute to the victorious army. (July 17)

Lausanne PCC talks re-open, both sides assure commission of their desire to reach a just and permanent peace in Palestine. (July 28)

Israel's offer to admit 100,000 Arab refugees is tabled at PCC parley. Reuven Shiloah, head of Israel's delegation, said there were two conditions that must be accepted by the Arabs - any repatriation of Arab refugees should be also accompanied by simultaneous resettlement of a large number of Arab refugees to Arab countries. Any repatriation project undertaken would be an integral part of a final peace settlement. (August 3)

•

Security Council votes to lift its Middle East arms embargo, and that the armistice supersede the various UN truces. (August 11)

•

Right wins German elections in the country's first chance to form a federal government since Hitler took power in 1933. 78.56% of 31,179,422 voters cast their ballots. The anti-socialists expected to form coalition. Dr. Konrad Adenauer is likely to become chancellor. (August 15)

•

Seven mothers who have given birth to ten or more children,were invited to the Prime Minister's Office in Jerusalem. Ben-Gurion praised the women for their great assistance to the advancement of Israel, and awarded each one a prize of 100 Lira and a personal letter. (September 23)

•

The watchword for this year (by the Jewish calendar) as far as land and settlements are concerned is 'Go South.' Plans to bring water from the Yarkon River were being made. The bulk of financing for these plans will come from the UJA (United Jewish Appeal) and the United States. (October 11)

•

Leaders of the American Communist Party are indicted for conspiracy. (October 14)

•

Communist Chinese near Hong Kong after Canton falls. 32,000 British troops guard the colony's borders. (October 16)

•

One hundred thousand new arrivals, almost ten percent of Israel's population, are going to have to winter in immigration camps; about 20,000 will do so in tents. (October 20)

Herzl's Remains Brought to Israel

Honor guard of government ministers awaits Herzl's coffin at Lod airport.

On Sept. 18, after two months of preparation, the coffin of Theodor Herzl was brought to Israel. The visionary father of the Jewish state was buried on Har Hamenuchot (*Mount of Quietudes*), from then on known as Mount Herzl.

The aircraft carrying the coffins of Herzl, his parents and sister flew low over Haifa, accompanied by the thunder of artillery fire in his honor. A few minutes later, the aeroplane landed at Lod Airport, where it was received by Prime Minister David Ben-Gurion, *Knesset* Speaker Yosef Sprinzak, Cabinet ministers, the chairman of the Jewish Agency and members of the Israel Defense Forces' general staff. Herzl's coffin, draped in black, was transported by military convoy to Tel Aviv, where it lay in state in the *Knesset* square. Thousands of people came from all over the country to pay their final respects to Herzl.

The coffin was moved to Jerusalem the next day. The funeral motorcade came to a halt at the entrance to the city, where the public stood at attention for a minute of silence.

Tel Aviv and Jaffa United

On Oct. 15, after more than a year of deliberations, the government approved plans for the unification of Tel Aviv and newly liberated Jaffa. The unified city numbers 300,000 inhabitants. Tel Aviv Mayor Israel Rokach sent an urgent message to the government, asking for an explanation of the unification plans; neither he nor the City Council had been consulted.

The government acceded to Rokach's request to postpone the municipal elections until the city was prepared for unification. The new city would have 150,000 people holding voting rights.

Tel Aviv Municipal Council. From now on - one city.

Assassination Attempt on Prime Minister and Ministers

A disaster was averted on Sept. 13, when two *Knesset* ushers overpowered Avraham Zarfati, who had entered the *Knesset* building and aimed a submachine gun, intending to open fire on the government benches.

Zarfati, a new immigrant from Teheran, succeeded in entering the building with a suitcase containing the *Sten* submachine gun, by telling the guards that he was carrying a manifesto to give to government officials.

Upon entering the plenary hall, he pulled out the gun and aimed it at the government table. At that point, the two ushers overpowered him and handed him over to the police. Police Minister Bechor Shetreet and senior police officers who had been present in the hall interrogated Zarfati. The *Knesset* session was not interrupted.

Jerusalem is Declared the Capital of Israel

On Nov. 7, in a moving speech in the *Knesset*, Prime Minister David Ben-Gurion declared Jerusalem the capital of Israel. The *Knesset* unanimously endorsed the announcement. In his speech, Ben-Gurion stated that Jerusalem was an inseparable part of the State of Israel, just as it is of Israeli history and the Jewish faith: "Jerusalem is the very heart of the State of Israel," he said.

A week later, following the passage of a resolution in the United Nations General Assembly that Jerusalem be declared an international city, Israel decided unilaterally to move all its government offices to Jerusalem. On Dec. 14 the government passed a resolution designating Jerusalem as the capital of Israel. The seat of the *Knesset*, it was also decided, would move to the new capital. The signing of the armistice agreements between Israel and Jordan did not solve the problem of Jerusalem. The UN suggested several resolutions, all revolving around the principle of turning Jerusalem into an international city. Throughout the discussions, Israel and Jordan abstained from making any declarations regarding the city's future. Up

Jerusalem in 1949. An integral part of the State of Israel.

until David Ben-Gurion's surprising announcement.

Most countries still maintain their embassies in Tel Aviv, in order to avoid being seen as taking a position on the issue.

El Al Carries 750 Passengers per Month

On Nov. 6, El Al Israel Airlines announced the opening of two new passenger routes to London and Geneva. The new routes would be a continuation of the airline's current two weekly flights to Europe, to Paris and Rome. The flight to Rome would continue to Geneva, and the flight to Paris continue to London.

The airline estimated that it could fly 750 passengers per month with its four *Skymaster* airliners, which had 44 seats each.

Yigael Yadin is Named the Second IDF Chief of Staff

Major-General Yigael Yadin was appointed chief of staff of the Israel Defense Forces on Nov. 9, replacing Lieutenant-General Ya'akov Dori.

Dori was relieved of the post, which he had held for approximately 18 months, due to serious illness requiring treatment abroad.

Yadin's first decisions were to lift the veil of secrecy surrounding the identities of senior army officers and to disclose his new appointments: Mordechai Maklef as deputy chief of staff, Shimon Mazeh as chief of the manpower division, Mordechai Green as chief of logistics and Majors-General Moshe Dayan and Yosef Avidar as staff generals.

Yadin held the post of chief of staff for two years and then retired due to cuts in the army's budget. After his retirement, he concentrated on his true passion - archeology. In 1977, after establishing the Dash (Democratic Movement for Change) party, he was appointed as deputy to Prime Minister Menahem Begin.

Chief of Staff Yigael Yadin.

Entire Yemen Jewish community being transferred to Israel. In an operation that began weeks ago, 25,000 Jews have arrived in 'Operation Magic Carpet.' The immigrants reached Aden on foot or donkey and were taken to a camp run by the Joint from where they were flown to Lod. (November 7)

●

The first meeting of the European Community. (November 7)

●

Naturam Godse is hanged in India, for Mahatma Gandhi's assassination. (November 15)

●

The Shah in the US to ask for more military aid. He will follow Moslem line regarding Israel. He said that Persia is important to world peace and the security of the Middle East. (November 17)

●

The Director General of the Ministry of Immigrant Absorption reported at an official press conference that there were currently more than one million Jews living in Israel. On the day the state was established, the Jewish Yishuv numbered only 550,000 Jews. Forty percent of the immigrants have emigrated from the east. (November 21)

●

India remains in the British Commonwealth, as a federal republic. (November 26)

●

Chiang Kai-Shek fled mainland China for Formosa where the Nationalists have set up their government. (December 11)

●

Indonesia ratifies its new constitution. The Indonesian parliament ratified the Hague Agreement and the Constitution: 226 voted in favor, 62 against, with 19 abstentions. (December 14)

●

Germany is made a full member of Marshall Plan. (December 15)

●

Japanese diplomats to be trained in the US. The State Department disclosed that it will begin training Japanese diplomats as part of its policy to speed up Japan's readmission to the family of nations. (December 18)

●

Einstein publishes his theory of relativity. (December 26)

Russia boycotts UN Council as move to expel Chinese nationalist delegate fails. (January 14)

•

A thirty-year alliance between Russia and China signed. China to receive $300 million credit to buy industrial and railway equipment in the USSR. (February 15)

•

Israel asks for US, British arms. The request was aimed at offsetting the shipment of British arms to Arab countries. (February 26)

•

Swedish report blames Israel in Bernadotte crime. The Swedish report accused the Israeli authorities of negligence in their search for the assassins of UN mediator Bernadotte. (March 9)

•

The coffin of paratrooper Hanna Szenes was brought to Israel from Hungary. The coffin was placed in Beit Hanna in Kibbutz Sdot Yam. (March 28)

•

Chancellor Adenauer demands Western Europe accept West Germany as full, equal partner to ensure the balance of power necessary for world peace. (April 18)

•

Senators protest UK shipments of arms. Senator Herbert O'Connor called for Anglo-American action to control arms shipments to the Middle East. (May 18)

•

Arabs refuse talks unless Israel takes back refugees. Four states reject PCC request for a new Geneva meeting. (May 20)

•

Abba Eban was appointed Israel's ambassador to the US, in addition to his role as Ambassador to the UN. Eban, who was Israel's foreign minister between '66-'74, has served as Israel's main spokesperson around the world. (May 28)

•

Northern forces invade S. Korea, Security Council meets. Fall of Seoul expected; S. Korean defenses crumble. Truman sends forces to Korea and Formosa; world crisis intensifies following Truman's order. (June 2)

•

El Al makes first flight to US today. The DC 4 will touch down at Rome, Lisbon, the Azores, Newfoundland, and New York. (June 18)

Crisis between Veterans and Immigrants over Education. Riots in Immigrant Camps

Three people were wounded and seven arrested in riots at the Ein Shemer immigrants' camp. In light of the serious crisis that had emerged between immigrants and veterans on the subject of education, these figures were only the tip of the iceberg.

The riots broke out on Jan. 17, when two young representatives of *Agudat Israel* arrived at the camp to find out whether or not the immigrant children were getting a traditional religious education.

The camp manager called in two policemen, who detained the visitors in the camp offices. The immigrants, who thought the men were rabbis, came out in their defense. About a thousand people assembled at the offices and began throwing stones. They freed the two fake 'rabbis' and helped them get away. Police reinforcements were called in to disperse the demonstrators.

Two state committees were set up to investigate complaints about the education of immigrant children in the camps after immigrants complained about the forced cutting off of sidelocks.

Ha'Poel Ha'Mizrahi representatives claimed that *Mapai* had banned religious education in order to eradicate religion among the newly arrived immigrants.

Several weeks later, the minister of religious affairs resigned over the issue of the education of children in camps. The crisis resulted in the resignation of Prime Minister David Ben-Gurion and the forming of a new government. The new government did not complete its term in office, either, and resigned for exactly the same reasons.

The rift between religious and secular elements has been part of the Israeli landscape for the entire 50 years of its existence, causing the fall of governments and dividing the nation into two camps.

Great Britain Recognizes State of Israel

On Apr. 28, nearly two years after the end of the British Mandate, Britain's home secretary has announced that Great Britain recognizes the State of Israel. Following the United States, the USSR and France, Britain was the last world power to recognize Israel.

In the same statement, the home secretary also announced recognition of the new Jordanian kingdom. Great Britain did not recognize Israel's rights to Jerusalem, but only the need to preserve the holy places for all faiths.

Britain also announced that it would not establish military bases on Israeli or Jordanian soil.

Polio Epidemic in Israel

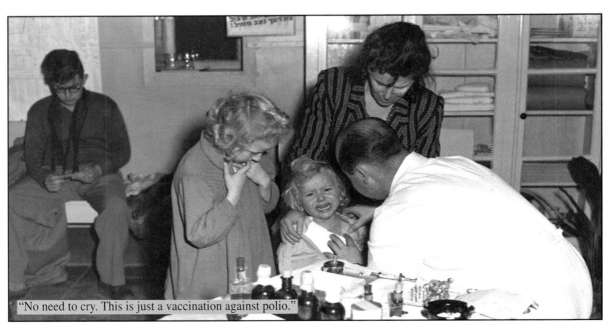

"No need to cry. This is just a vaccination against polio."

Following 12 cases of infantile paralysis in the Haifa area, the director-general of the Ministry of Health stated publicly that there was no cause to fear an outbreak of an epidemic in the coming summer. The director-general revealed the following statistics: 25 cases of polio had been diagnosed in the Yemenite *ma'abara (transit camp for immigrants)*, in Rosh Ha'Ayin, with another 11 cases in a *kibbutz* in the Sharon area. He said, however, that this number of cases did not constitute an epidemic.

In the Haifa region, there were two fatalities among polio patients - a child and an adult. Most patients were toddlers below kindergarten age. The director-general stated that in cases of high fever, it was imperative to keep children in bed and call a doctor.

'Operation Magic Carpet' Completed

'Operation Magic Carpet' immigrants await their 'plane to Israel. Journey's end.

1950

JULY - SEPTEMBER

Thirteen thousand tourists have visited Israel in the first six months of 1950. Only 7,867 visited the state during the first six months of 1949. (July 2)

•

The Cabinet's statement supporting the Security Council's action against North Korea does not imply that Israel is abandoning its policy of neutrality in the Cold War. (July 2)

•

North Korea scores further gains as MacArthur is given UN command. (July 8)

•

Senate ends McCarthy's investigations. The Senate Foreign Relations Committee voted unanimously to end Republican Senator McCarthy's investigation of communists in the American government. (July 20)

•

Rationing of clothing, footwear and textiles had become necessary because there was only half the foreign currency available for these goods than had been available last year. An important factor in this decision was the rise in the number of consumers, said Dr. Dov Joseph, Minister of Supply and Rationing. (July 31)

•

Leopold III of Belgium abdicates in favor of his son, Baudouin. (August 1)

•

Motions in the *Knesset* to debate the government's promise of medical aid to UN forces in Korea were defeated. (August 8)

•

Prime Minister Ben-Gurion called upon Jews throughout the world to raise $1,500 million by 1953 to cover the cost of rescuing Jews in the Middle East and East Europe while they were still free to move to Israel. (August 16)

•

All religious orders in Hungary are dismantled by the Communist government. (September 7)

•

As Seoul falls back to American hands MacArthur says US may begin peace talks. The US forces from north and south link up almost at the same spot where the first Americans were overrun by the Communists three months ago. (September 26)

On Sept. 19, six months after 'Operation Magic Carpet' came to an end, the government released the first details of the dramatic rescue that had brought the Jews of Yemen to Israel.

The operation had lasted for 15 months; 50,000 Jews immigrated to Israel from Yemen on 378 flights. Before the last flight took off from Aden on Feb. 11, a ceremony was held in memory of the 700 Jews who had died in the transit camp in Aden, while waiting to emigrate.

The operation had been carried out in three stages with the full cooperation of the 'Joint' *(JDC - American Jewish Joint Distribution Committee)*. During the first stage, beginning in 1948, 3,000 Yemenite Jews who had been living in a transit camp since 1942 were flown to Israel. In the second stage, in early 1949, 1,500 immigrants were flown to Israel. The third stage, lasting from June, 1949 to February, 1950, brought 40,000 immigrants to Israel. Twelve babies were born in-flight. The oldest immigrant was a 108-year-old rabbi.

The operation cost $5 million, and maintaining the transit camp in Aden had cost $50,000 a month.

Law of Return Ratified by *Knesset*

On the symbolic date of Tammuz 20 (July 4), the anniversary of the death of the founder of the state, Theodor Herzl, the *Knesset* ratified the Law of Return. Only 30 *Knesset* members were present at the important plenary session. The law, which was passed unanimously, determined that every Jew was entitled to come to Israel and receive Israeli citizenship.

At the same session, the *Knesset* passed several more, far-reaching resolutions: the flogging law was abolished, and a bill to abolish the death sentence was passed.

David Ben-Gurion objected to the repeal of the death sentence, but Justice Minister Pinhas Rosen brought up examples of many countries where the death sentence had not resulted in a decrease in the number of serious crimes.

The Law of Return has been a controversial subject ever since, because it did not determine who is a Jew.

Law Passed on the Punishment of Nazis and their Collaborators

On Aug. 13 the *Knesset* passed the Law on the Punishment of Nazis and their Collaborators.

A problem had arisen when it appeared that the existing law did not allow for prosecution of a person who had committed a crime in a foreign country. The new law redressed this problem, making it possible to prosecute such a person.

The law generated a flood of accusations against Jews and those pretending to be Jewish who had collaborated with the Nazis in their murderous deeds and then immigrated to Israel.

The first person to be prosecuted under the new law was Andre Bunik, a 31-year-old Slovak, who was tried in several courts. Bunik was accused of being a member of the Slovak Nazi Guard.

According to the charge sheet, Bunik had been the secretary of the 'Linka Guard' organization, in the Mikalovozka area, and had used his position to register property in his own name which had been owned by Jews who had been sent to the death camps.

South Koreans cross the 38th Parallel; China warns against American invasion. General MacArthur calls on the North to lay down their arms in surrender or suffer total defeat. (October 1)

•

Trans-Arabian Pipeline completed. Construction of the longest pipeline in the world completed last week. (October 8)

•

UN forces enter North Korea's capital Pyongyang. (October 20)

•

The Dalai Lama, 15 year-old spiritual and temporal ruler of three million Tibetans has asked the Indian government for asylum for himself and his government. (October 31)

•

Chinese troops in Korea are volunteers and have a moral duty to back North Korea, says China. UN line is holding. (November 5)

•

Due to shortage of milk, the government has decided to stop distributing milk to adults. The entire milk supply will be allocated to children only. (November 30)

•

Use of atom bomb under consideration says Truman, adding that if aggression "is successful in Korea we can expect it to spread throughout Asia and Europe to this hemisphere." (November 30)

•

Great Britain ceases to receive post-war aid under the Marshall Plan. (December 13)

•

Salvador Dali completes his painting 'The Madonna of Port Ligat.' (December 31)

GET YOUR SHEKEL

All-out War on the Black Market

On Oct. 1 Prime Minister David Ben-Gurion came to the studios of Kol Israel *(Voice of Israel)* and set in motion 'Operation Black Market Eradication.'

The ministries of justice, police and rationing cooperated in the major operation, and special courts were established to dispense summary justice to black marketeers. Punishment ranged from revoking of commercial licenses to the passing of prison sentences.

Deputy Inspector-general of Police Yosef Nahmias headed the operation. Ben-Gurion announced on the radio that, if necessary, the army would aid the police. On the fourth day of the operation, military police blocked all entrances to Tel Aviv, checking all incoming vehicles. At the checkpoints, large amounts of vegetables, poultry and other unlicensed goods were confiscated.

By the end of the operation, the government was in possession of six tons of leather, 30 tons of iron, five km *(three miles)* of woven fabric, 15,000 meters *(16,114 yards)* of

Searching cars for unlicensed goods. A smuggled chicken.

cloth, 10 tons of all kinds of foodstuffs, 12,000 Virginia cigarettes, tens of thousands of eggs and 35 tons of olive oil.

First Reserve Mobilization

On Oct. 16, the Israel Defense Forces held its first reserve mobilization exercise. The mobilization code words, *'Passover Seder,' 'Sleeping Beauty,' 'Counting of the Omer,' 'Wig'* and *'Raging Sambatyon,'* were broadcast on the radio, and reserve soldiers began streaming to their respective bases.

As part of the exercise, hospitals, public transportation, postal services and the telephone and telegraph systems came under army control. The police were authorized to arrest deserters and draft-dodgers. The commander of the navy was put in charge of all the country's ports, and the army mobilized a large number of civilian vehicles.

At the start of the exercise, Chief of Staff Yigael Yadin issued the order of the day, saying: "Last night at

Reserve soldiers came immediately after hearing their code words.

midnight the IDF began its first extensive maneuvers since the founding of the state."

"We cannot permit ourselves to lessen our efforts to strengthen the security of the state in the light of the arming of our enemies, who have yet to make peace with us. All the work invested over the past year by all the IDF soldiers in the organization of the army and all its divisions will now be put to the test."

Education Crisis: Prime Minister Resigns

In a letter dated Oct. 16, David Ben-Gurion notified the president of his resignation and proposed assigning the forming of a new government to one of the *Knesset* members.

The prime minister presented a transitional government to the *Knesset*. The *Mizrahi* party left the government and did not participate in the transitional government. The president did not accept Ben-Gurion's recommendations, and charged him with forming a new government.

The new government was approved by the *Knesset*: 69 in favor, 42 against.

Ben-Gurion closed the Ministry of Rationing in the new government. The government was headed by Ben-Gurion as prime minister and minister of defense.

At a Cabinet meeting of the new government, Ben-Gurion criticized two ministers, Meyerson and Shertok, for still not having Hebraized their surnames.

Israel Demands Compensation for Nazi Crimes from West

For the first time, Israel's demand for compensation for Nazi crimes came to light. On Jan. 16 a formal communication from the Israeli government was sent to the governments of the United States, the Soviet Union, France and Great Britain. The message made mention of the enormous damage inflicted on German Jewry, of the six million victims and of entire Jewish communities that had been destroyed throughout Europe.

Israel registered a complaint about the fact that six years after Germany's surrender to the Allies, no solution to the issue of compensation had yet been found. Israel demanded that the issue of reparations remain the responsibility of the Allies, even if the government in Germany was to be transferred back to the Germans.

In the message, the government claimed that many Israeli citizens had claims against Germany, and that a legal mechanism should therefore be established in Germany to enable the swift handling of these outstanding demands.

That same year, the matter of German reparations provoked a serious - sometimes violent - confrontation between the government and the opposition, headed by *Herut* leader Menachem Begin.

It was not until late 1952 that the Knesset approved the Reparations Agreement.

1951
JANUARY - JUNE

Government Falls. Early Elections Expected

The ballots for the second elections are ready. The education crisis brought down the government.

The Minister of Religious Affairs, Rabbi Yehuda Maimon, resigned on Feb. 14 in protest against education in immigrant camps and secular coercion being carried out there.

Following his resignation, a crisis ensued in the *Knesset*, leading to the resignation of the government and to early elections for the second *Knesset*.

The government lost a vote of no-confidence, and David Ben-Gurion announced his resignation. That same day, he made one of his most scathing speeches in the *Knesset* on the issue of religion and state.

"No one will have a monopoly on religion in this country. We will not permit the religious parties to hold sole custodianship of religious education... For three years I have done my best" he said.

Ultra-orthodox Attempt to Attack *Knesset* Foiled

On May 14, as *Knesset* members were discussing work and rest hours, guards noticed suspicious movements outside the building. Two young men dressed in outmoded military uniforms were detained by *Knesset* ushers and were interrogated by the police minister. As a result of the interrogation, 35 more *yeshiva* students, calling themselves 'The Secret Alliance of Zealots' and suspected of intending to act against the drafting of religious girls into the army, were then arrested.

That night, police raided the Me'a She'arim and Bet Israel sections of Jerusalem. At the Sinai house of learning in the Abu Tor area, a large cache of outdated arms was discovered, along with leaflets against desecration of the Sabbath, cans of kerosene and homemade explosives.

The chief of police was personally involved in the interrogation of suspects, who were immediately moved to a special prison camp at Jalami, under emergency regulations carried out on the prime minister's orders.

The suspects included *yeshiva* students who were members of the *Agu-dat Israel* party among them the son of a Jerusalem City Council member.

Another detainee was Israel Soroka, a member of the Bnei Brak City Council.

Menashe Levy, the leader of the underground cell, gave himself up one week after his associates had been arrested.

An intensive interrogation revealed that the members of the alliance had planned to break into Defense Ministry offices and to destroy all documents relating to the drafting of girls into the Israel Defense Forces.

Prime Minister David Ben-Gurion told a tense and crowded *Knesset* that a totally mobilized Israel could maintain its independence if there is a global war. He also said that the Jewish people's fate depended upon the existence and independence of Israel. (January 2)

•

The Electricity Corporation has requested the public not to use electrical appliances between 4:30 - 8:00 p.m. and on Fridays between 9:00 to 11:00 a.m. The request followed the total collapse of the electricity system on Friday morning, due to the excessive use of ovens. (January 16)

•

According to the Central Bureau of Statistics, 169,000 people immigrated to Israel in 1950, which is 70,000 fewer than in 1949. (February 13)

•

National service for women attacked by Chief Rabbinate. Friction between the prime minister and religious parties reached a new height due to Defense Ministry's plan to recruit orthodox girls for national service. (February 27)

•

Iran parliament votes to end foreign control of oil. London concerned about oil interests. (March 8)

•

Hula reclamation Israel's right, says a spokesman for the Ministry of Foreign Affairs, after the Security Council ordered Israel to halt its drainage project until an agreement is reached with the Syrians. (May 19)

•

Ice shortage in Israel. Manufacturers have curtailed ice production due to the government's refusal to allow them to raise their prices. Long lines can be seen at all ice shops. (May 21)

•

Seventy thousand in Iran next on list to emigrate to Israel. The resurgence of nationalism has strengthened the feeling of insecurity among most of the 100,000 Jews still there. (June 25)

•

After strict examination for contamination the Ministry of Health has permitted swimming at Tel Aviv's beaches. This was the first summer since '48 that swimming is allowed in Tel Aviv. (June 26)

One hundred and fifty immigrant children suffering from ringworm were brought to a military base for treatment. During the course of the summer, 9,000 additional children, aged two to 13, were afflicted by the disease; they remained in the bases for six weeks, their hair was shaved and they were treated with ointments and X-rays. In the late Eighties, a secret report disclosed that these X-rays exposed most of the patients to cancer. (September 6)

The United States of America signs a peace treaty with Japan, at San Francisco. (September 8)

West ignores Israel in Middle East defense plans. There is no mention of Israel in any forecasts concerning the projected mid-East defense organization. (October 7)

Ben-Gurion forms new government. (October 9)

The four powers ask Egypt to join mid-East defense, and Britain would then leave the Suez Canal. Egypt rejected the Four's offer. The Egyptian parliament unanimously approved the abrogation of the 1936 Anglo-Egyptian treaty. (October 13)

Professor Albert Einstein bought the 20th bond of Israel's independence loan for the amount of $500. Einstein bought the bond from Yael, daughter of Minister of Foreign Affairs Moshe Sharett, who is selling the bonds in the US. (October 30)

President Chaim Weizmann was elected for a second term. Weizmann was the only candidate, and *Herut* was the only party who voted against him in the *Knesset*. (November 19)

Colonel Adib Shishakli takes over as dictator of Syria. (December 1)

Libya is declared an independent republic. (December 14)

The question of direct negotiation talks with the German government regarding reparations will be put before the *Knesset* this week. (December 31)

King Abdullah has been Assassinated in Jerusalem

King Abdullah, center.

On July 20, King Abdullah was assassinated as he left Friday morning prayers at the al-Aqsa Mosque on the Temple Mount. A state of emergency has been declared in Jordan. General Glubb Pasha, commander of the Arab Legion, tried to calm the flaring passions in his country. Abdullah's son, Crown Prince Talal, escaped from a psychiatric hospital in Geneva, where he had been hospitalized after opening fire on the king's ministers in June.

Members of the underground to which the assassins belonged, including 100 Arab residents of the Old City of Jerusalem, were arrested. A curfew was declared in the Old City. The assassin, Mustafa Shikri Ushu, was a member of the extermination squads of the *Jihad* fighters in the Jordanian army. These squads had been disbanded after the War of Independence.

On Sept. 5, Talal was crowned at a festive session of both houses of the Jordanian Parliament.

The king's assassination had ended any chances for peace between Israel and Jordan. King Abdullah's secret meetings with Golda Meir and Moshe Dayan had been among the reasons for the murder.

It was not long before the Jordanians came to the conclusion that King Talal was incapable of ruling, and his son, 17-year-old Hussein, replaced him.

King Hussein is still in power today, 46 years after he was crowned.

Ma'abarot Flooded. Thousands of Children and Adults Evacuated

The *ma'abarot* flooded. Sixty thousand immigrants evacuated.

New immigrants living in *ma'abarot* (transit camps for immigrants) were the primary victims of stormy weather that hit in the third week of December. Twenty-three out of 136 camps in the country were completely evacuated by the army and police. Approximately 60,000 children and adults were transferred to public institutions near the camps. The worst hit was the Nahariya camp, where all 350 families had to be evacuated. Hundreds of volunteers joined in the effort to help evacuate children and to supply food and warm clothing.

Knesset Approves Reparations Agreement

"Our honor is not for sale; our blood will not be redeemed by goods. Let us wipe out the shame !" Begin speaks against the agreement.

On Jan. 9 the *Knesset* approved the Reparations Agreement with the government of West Germany by a large majority. The results of the vote were 60:50 and six abstentions. *Herut* and *Maki* (Israeli Communist Party) opposed the measure.

Under the agreement, West Germany would transfer funds to Israel as compensation for the destruction of European Jewry. The German government would pay both personal compensation to families of Holocaust victims as well as reparations to the state.

Stormy weeks of political protest preceded the agreement, led by *Herut* leader Menachem Begin, who accused Prime Minister David Ben-Gurion of selling the memory of the six million victims for profit.

On Jan. 6 in Jerusalem, 2,000 demonstrators tried to breach police barricades, and the police responded using fire hoses and tear gas. The demonstrators wielded iron bars and threw stones. The confrontation lasted five hours, until 8 pm.

In all, 396 people were arrested, with 75 taken to a special prison camp for 48 hours.

Two hundred demonstrators and 140 police were wounded. Shmuel Hanagid, Be'eri, Ben-Yehuda and King George Streets looked more like battlefields than city streets.

At one point before the agreement was approved, the government considered outlawing *Herut*, and Begin was expelled from the *Knesset* for three months. The *Knesset* session in which the agreement was ratified was marked by a sharp confrontation between Begin and Ben-Gurion, which planted seeds of the long-lasting animosity existing between the two.

The reparations agreement helped Israel and many individuals cope with economic difficulties in the early years of statehood.

The *Knesset* in a dramatic session defeated an opposition motion designed to prevent the government from taking up the West German government's offer to discuss reparations with Israel. (January 9)

●

Anti-British demonstrations take place in Egypt. (January 18)

The distribution of meat has been renewed after two months. The ration: 100 grams a day per person. (January 20)

●

King George VI is dead; Elizabeth II is Queen. (February 6)

Uproar, riots in Bonn on German rearmament. Chancellor Adenauer's policy opposed. Bonn votes for rearmament on conditions. The Bundestag gave its conditional approval to West Germany making a contribution to Western defense by a 204:156 vote. Among the conditions: adequate representation in NATO until Germany becomes a full member, democratic conditions in the Saar, settlement with the Western allies on release of war criminals and a reasonable contribution to European defense. (February 7)

●

Pundit Nehru wins the first elections held in newly independent India. (March 1)

●

Steps against 'draft dodgers' - any citizen who cannot prove he has served in the army will not be granted food coupons. IDF headquarters requested jurisdiction over the dodgers. (March 11)

●

Curtain is raised on reparation parley in The Hague. The Israeli delegation has been instructed to outline the government's case as follows: "No indemnity, however large, can make good the loss of human life and cultural values or atone for the suffering of men women and children put to death." (March 20)

●

Samuel Beckett's play 'Waiting for Godot' is written. (March 21)

●

Tornadoes rip through five states in America. (March 22)

●

President Truman retires from the presidential race in the United States. (March 29)

Thousands tried to force their way into the *Knesset*.

Two Jews Hanged in Baghdad

On Jan. 22, Yosef Avraham Bazri and Shalom Zallah were hanged in Iraq after being convicted of throwing bombs in order to spur Jews to emigrate to Israel. Another 70 Iraqi Jews were imprisoned. The two victims' families emigrated to Israel, and the government announced its intention to pay them compensation for their suffering.

The two Jews were executed in Baghdad by royal decree.

The UN Statistics Office has estimated the world population at 2,400 million. (April 19)

•

Condemned atomic spies Julius and Ethel Rosenberg appeal to the US Supreme Court. (April 20)

•

The government announces that all tourists staying in Jerusalem will be invited to lunch at the Tourist Club in Talbieh on Independence Day. (April 30)

•

Giant locust plague threatens the Middle East. The UN Food and Agricultural Organization (FAO) announced today that the plague threatens the entire food supply of agricultural nations from Africa to Asia. (May 13)

•

Medical school graduates its first class of doctors. Sixty three young physicians were awarded the first degrees issued by Hebrew University-Hadassah Medical School at a colorful ceremony in the still incomplete Binyaney Ha'Uma in Jerusalem. (May 13)

•

Blind author Helen Keller arrived in Jerusalem through the Mandelbaum Gate. Blind children greeted the author and gave her a greeting written in Braille. (May 19)

•

The US, Britain and France signed conventions with West Germany under which 48 million West Germans get most of their sovereignty. The Germans pledge to rearm and provide 12 divisions, totaling 300,000 men, to serve in a six-nation European army. The *Knesset* protests about the rearmament and restoration of Germany into the family of nations. (May 26)

•

Jordan's cabinet strips King Talal of powers. Ministers returned from Paris with medical documents indicating the dangerous psychiatric condition of the king. (June 4)

•

Heavy fighting reported from the Korean front, for the fifth consecutive day,along the invasion route to Seoul. (June 11)

•

Moshe Sharett said today that the West German restitution offer of $714 million is an advance over previous offers. (June 18)

Locusts Swarm over Israel

Fighting the locusts. Swarms every few years, threatening the crops.

Swarms of locusts were first sighted on Apr. 8 in the Hebron area, 20 km *(13 miles)* east of Beersheba. The police, army, and industrial plants in the Negev were alerted. The Operations Center Against Locusts distributed anti-locust poison to settlements all over the country. The United States announced that it had 25 locust-fighting 'planes that could be at Israel's disposal if the swarms moved westwards. The locusts reached as far as Ramla, Rehovot, the B'not Ya'acov Bridge, Beit Nabalah and Gedera.

Thousands of people were mobilized to fight the locusts before they caused irreversible damage to crops. In Rosh Ha'Ayin, where the approaching swarms could be seen from a distance, people lit huge bonfires and made loud noises.

No Fuel. Cars Grounded

After talks with Britain on supplying gasoline failed, gasoline supplies were so low, the government moved to cut consumption by 20 percent.

On May 15, a new regulation went into effect, stipulating that all equipment must be transported by Israel Railways.

A week later, the ministerial committee on gasoline matters grounded all cars in the country for two days a week. Every car got a sticker indicating the days on which it was not allowed on the roads.

A new ministerial committee was appointed to classify all industrial plants according to necessity. The activities of non-essential plants were restricted.

On June 8, the government began limiting the use of 'buses and shutting down 'bus services at 11.00 p.m.

All Currency Exchanged

In a special radio broadcast at 8.30 a.m. on June 9, Minister of Finance Eliezer Kaplan announced that a new compulsory loan to the state was in effect immediately. Only senior Treasury officials knew in advance about the new plan, which had been drafted within the context of emergency regulations. The loan was applied only on cash and bank deposits, but the Treasury announced its future intention of imposing a property tax of one percent.

At 12 noon banks began exchanging currency. Ten percent of all money exchanged at banks was transferred to the Treasury. For every lira brought to the bank, customers received a new lira, worth 900 prutot. The compulsory loan was to last for eight years, at a rate of four percent annual interest.

Bank Leumi prepared in advance the reserves of new money required by the banks. One thousand two hundred policemen were mobilized to secure the transfer of the new money to the banks. Armed police guarded the Bank of Israel building on Herzl Street in Tel Aviv, from where trucks loaded with money spread across the country. The currency exchange operation lasted two weeks.

In a special broadcast on national radio, the finance minister estimated that the loan would add 25 million lirot to the state's coffers.

A line at a bank.

Reparations Agreement Signed

Despite protest demonstrations, the Reparations Agreement between West Germany and Israel was signed.

After lengthy negotiations, the Reparations Agreement between Israel and West Germany was signed in Luxembourg on Sept. 10. The agreement was signed by West German Chancellor Konrad Adenauer and Israeli Foreign Minister Moshe Sharett. The main part of the agreement stipulated that over the next 12 years, West Germany would transfer a total of 3.45 billion marks. This sum was to serve as compensation for the injustice perpetrated against the Jewish people and as participation in the absorption of half a million refugees from the Nazi regime.

Under a separate agreement, diaspora Jewry would receive 450 million marks from West Germany.

Israel would receive an annual grant of gasoline worth 18 million marks, vehicles worth 11 million, goods worth 8 million and steel products worth 5 million.

President Weizmann Dies

Chaim Weizmann, Israel's first president, died in Rehovot on Nov. 9 following a heart attack. He had been seriously ill for about a year. The government declared an official state of mourning, and the flag was flown at half-mast.

Weizmann's last request had been to be buried near his residence in Rehovot. The Chief Rabbinate consecrated a burial plot in Rehovot with the blowing of the *shofar*. The coffin lay in state in the Weizmann residence, and 250,000 citizens came to Rehovot to pay their last respects. United States President Harry Truman eulogized Weizmann before the United Nations General Assembly. "The human race has lost a many-talented leader," he said.

A commission formed by the government determined that a new president should be elected within one month, as indicated by law.

On Nov. 18, the name of Profes-

Chaim Weizmann.

Itzhak Ben-Zvi.

sor Albert Einstein was submitted as a possible presidential candidate. Einstein said he would accept the post if it were proposed to him officially. It is said that because he received only an unofficial letter from the Israeli government, he refused.

On Dec. 10, Itzhak Ben-Zvi was sworn in as the second president of Israel. The blowing of the *shofar* and a 21-gun salute accompanied his acceptance of the post.

The chief of Naguib's cabinet was asked to comment on Lt. Col. Gamal Abdel Nasser's statement that unless the British evacuate the Suez Canal Zone, Egypt will wage guerrilla war against them. He said Nasser's statement was the embodiment of the entire nation's aspirations. (January 5)

•

Arabs invited to join the new Anglo-American Middle East Defense Treaty Organization. (January 8)

•

Soviet Union says nine leading doctors, five of them Jews, had 'confessed' to the murder of Andrei Zhdanov, the secretary of the Communist Party's Central Committee, and to the murder of General Alexander Shcherbakov, the secretary of the Communist Party's Moscow Committee. (January 22)

•

Top East Germans escape as the communists isolate Jews: two prominent East German Christian Democratic Party officials have fled to West Berlin to avoid the purge taking place in East Germany. (January 22)

•

President Eisenhower rejected Ethel and Julius Rosenberg's plea for pardon. The Jewish couple was sentenced to death after giving the Soviet Union the formula of the American atomic bomb. (February 12)

•

Jewish Communist purge takes place in Hungary. Israeli and Soviet envoys are on their way home. Thirty of the top Jewish Communists are reported to have committed suicide or fallen victim to the spreading wave of anti-semitism behind the Iron Curtain. (February 21)

•

Easing of military rule in the Galilee, elections in Nazareth, promised by Minister of Interior. (February 26)

•

The remains of Naftali Herz Imber, who wrote the words for the national anthem, 'Ha'Tikva,' were brought to Israel in accordance with his will. Imber died in 1909 and was buried in a New York cemetery. (March 4)

Stalin is Dead

"The sun of the peoples has set."

Josef Stalin, leader of the Soviet Union, died on Mar. 5 after suffering a brain hemorrhage and lying in a coma for 24 hours. Millions of people all over the world mourned the death of the dictator. Among the mourners were the leftist parties in Israel - Mapam (United Workers' Party), Ahdut Ha'Avoda and the Communist parties. Al Ha'Mishmar, Mapam's newspaper, came out with a front page headline: "The sun of the peoples has set."

In Moscow, millions of people escorted Stalin's coffin during his funeral on Red Square, near the burial site of Vladimir Lenin, the founder of the Communist party. Nikita Khrushchev was in charge of funeral arrangements.

The Soviet Union Severs its Relations with Israel

On Feb. 12 the Soviet Union severed diplomatic relations with Israel, within months veering from enthusiastic support for the young state to extreme opposition. Relations between Israel and the USSR deteriorated rapidly. On Jan. 13, TASS, the official Soviet news agency reported that a conspiracy had been discovered to assassinate top Soviet leaders. The conspirators were said to be a terrorist organization of Jewish doctors with American Jewish links.

On Feb. 9 a powerful bomb was thrown into the grounds of the Soviet embassy in Tel Aviv. Most of the damage occurred in the embassy kitchen, where the ambassador's wife had been sitting. Three were hospitalized. Two days later, the Soviet Union severed relations with Israel and accused Israel of fostering hostile anti-Soviet acts. Simultaneously, Israel demanded that all holders of Soviet diplomatic passports leave the country.

A bomb thrown into Soviet embassy grounds led to severing of volatile relations.

Commando Unit 101 Set Up

As infiltrations and acts of terror against civilians and soldiers escalated, Israel sent a message to the United States, Italy, Great Britain and France, warning that its military would soon be forced to take strong measures. The latest occurrences were the murder of two soldiers in Tel Mond, the murder in March of a couple in Zippori and the murder of two young people in Kfar Hess.

The Israel Defense Forces general staff decided to set up a special commando unit to undertake special guerrilla operations and exercises in retaliation for terror attacks. Unit 101 would be better able to cope with these hostile actions. Moshe Dayan, regional commander of the Southern District, initiated the move.

A young reserve officer, Major

'Arik' Sharon instructing the fighters of Unit 101.

Ariel ('Arik') Sharon commanded it *(later to be Defense Minister incurring the Lebanon War and a minister in the Netanyahu government).*

The Soviet Embassy's Bombers are Arrested

In June, a new Israeli underground was uncovered and its members arrested. They were brought before a military court presided over by Judge Binyamin Halevi. The 15 men, most of whom were revisionist activists, were accused of bombing the Soviet embassy in Tel Aviv three months earlier and of forming an underground organization with the intent of harming the security of the State of Israel.

On the first day of the trial, ten of the accused declared that they did not recognize the legitimacy of the military court and demanded to be tried before a civil court. Given that the accused were not soldiers, it was unclear why a military court had been chosen.

The lawyers representing the accused, headed by Advocate Shmuel Tamir, argued before the presiding judge that their power of attorney to represent the accused was limited to a civil trial and requested a civil hearing. When prosecutor Chaim Cohen read the charges, the accused disrupted the hearing by singing *'Hevenu Shalom Aleichem.'*

The defendants' request for a civil trial was denied. During the course of the trial, which was conducted in closed session, the defendants repeatedly burst into song. This was also their response when the prosecutor presented the judges with weapons and ammunition which had been found in large milk containers.

Ya'acov Heruti.

Thirteen of the 15 suspects were convicted of taking part in an underground organization, and thus placing the security of the state at great risk, and given sentences of up to ten years' imprisonment.

Infiltration Attacks Increase

Infiltrators increased their attacks on civilians and soldiers. On June 7, a youth was killed and three wounded in shootings in Jerusalem. Two days later, infiltrators attacked a moshav near Lod, murdering one resident, throwing hand grenades, and shooting in all directions. That night, a different group attacked a house in Hadera. On June 10, a house in Mishmar Ayalon was destroyed. The following day, a home in Kfar Hess was also attacked, and a young woman was killed.

These attacks were carried out some hours after a treaty was signed between Israel and Jordan, under UN mediation. Jordan agreed not to allow terrorists to use its territory. The Israeli Cabinet went into emergency session.

Home bombed by cell of infiltrators.

1953

JUNE - JULY

Queen Elizabeth II of Great Britain crowned at Westminster Abbey. (June 2)

•

The cornerstone for the university named after Rabbi Meir Bar-Ilan has been laid in Ramat Gan. The first four buildings will be completed in '54. The university's special feature: all students will be required to study Judaic Studies. (June 3)

Following Secretary of State Dulles' statement last week, informed quarters anticipate America will pressure Israel to accept at least a token number of refugees. (June 13)

Ethel and Julius Rosenberg, found guilty of spying for USSR, went to the electric chair in America, in Sing Sing prison. They were buried in the Jewish plot. (June 21)

•

Secret police chief Lavrenti Beria, second in command in communist leadership in Russia, jailed. He is charged with treason, a crime punishable by death. (July 11)

•

Thirty thousand Chinese troops attacked a 12-mile sector of the central front. This was the heaviest Communist attack in Korea in more than two years. (July 13)

•

USSR renews diplomatic ties with Israel after a five month break. (July 20)

•

First shipment of German goods under the reparations agreement, (iron and fertilizer), sailed for Haifa. (July 21)

•

'Under Milk Wood' is written by Dylan Thomas. (July 31)

Remember the *'Altalena'*!

Soviet Premier Georgi Malenkov told the joint session of the Supreme Soviet that the US no longer enjoys a monopoly on the hydrogen bomb. (August 8)

•

Three islands vanish in the worst earthquake in Greek history. One thousand islanders are reported dead, as international ships rush to save victims; the Israeli navy goes to the scene. Four Israeli ships, on maneuvers in Ionian Sea, assist the inhabitants of Kephallnia, as do American cruiser, British destroyer, Greek minesweeper and three cargo vessels. (August 11)

•

The Persian army overthrows Mossadeq in a bloody revolt. General Fazlollah Zahedi was appointed prime minister by the Shah before he fled to Iraq. The Shah said that the differences with the British remain, but any nation recognizing Persia's supreme interests and sovereignty, would have no problem establishing normal relations with his country. (August 19)

•

The sweeping victory of Konrad Adenauer's Christian Democrats in West German elections will probably wreck all chances for German unity in the future and tie West Germany more closely to the West. (September 7)

•

The fourth Maccabia International Jewish Games opened in Ramat Gan. (September 20)

•

The *Knesset* decided to establish offices to deal with the submission of civil claims for reparations from Germany. The offices will instruct citizens how to fill out forms and will examine the entitlement for personal compensation. The deadline for the submission of requests - October 1955. (September 21)

Five People Killed on Road to Petra

Three young men and two young women on their way to the ancient Jordanian city of Petra (known as the 'Red Rock') were killed by Jordanian soldiers on Aug. 29.

The five, two students from Haifa, a member of Kibbutz Sde Boker and two members of Moshav Kfar Yehoshua, were hitchhiking south of Ein Hozov in the northern Arava.

Having been warned of the dangers lurking in Petra, which had become a notorious attraction for Israelis, the five asked for a ride to Eilat.

At a certain point they hitchhiked with a civilian vehicle. Another group of five youngsters wishing to join them was delayed.

Relatives of the five claimed that the young travellers did not intend to reach the Red Rock at all, and probably got lost on the way from Ein Hozov to Eilat.

All five were shot dead by the Jordanian army. No signs of mutilation were found on the bodies, which were returned to Israel on Aug. 30.

This was the first incident in which young Israelis were killed on the road to Petra.

In the following years, many more young victims illegally venturing there were to die.

Following the Peace Treaty signed by Yitzhak Rabin and King Hussein in 1995, Petra has become a tourist spot much favored by many Israeli visitors.

The 'Red Rock.' An attraction for dozens of young Israelis in the 1950's. Many were brought back in coffins.

Head of *Betar* Movement in Israel is Arrested

Ptachya Shamir, head of the *Betar* movement in Israel, was suspected of attempting to sabotage '*Rimon*,' the ship that brought the first reparations cargo from Germany.

Shamir, 30, was arrested on Sept. 7 at his home in Tel Aviv after returning from a *Herut* committee meeting. Ben-Zion Hartman, another *Herut* activist, had been arrested by police while trying to smuggle a 3-kg (7 lb) bomb into the port. The bomb was made of a clock, a battery and explosives.

Hartman claimed that he had been following Shamir's instructions, with the intention of causing damage to the reparations ship.

According to the assessment of the police, he intended to sneak into one of the cargo holds on the ship and put the bomb there.

Herut, led by Menachem Begin, was opposed to all reparations from Germany. They furiously refused to allow Germany to 'compensate' for the Holocaust victims.

The Korean War has Ended

After three years and three months, the Korean War - the first armed conflict between East and West since World War II - has ended.

The war, which had nearly swept the world into a nuclear conflagration, ended exactly where it began, with the Thirty-eighth Parallel being recognized as the border between North and South Korea.

During the course of the war, 24,000 American soldiers were killed, 98,000 injured and 11,000 declared 'MIA;' 546 British soldiers were killed, and 2,000 injured.

It is estimated that the joint losses of North Korea and China, which came to North Korea's rescue and sent millions of soldiers to join the war, disguised as volunteers, reached about three million casualties.

Ben-Gurion Resigns to Sde Boker

Ben-Gurion and Paula admire a lamb on Sde Boker. At age 67, the prime minister settled on a *kibbutz* of young idealists.

On Dec. 7, the ministers of David Ben-Gurion's Cabinet, as well as the public, were taken by surprise when Ben-Gurion submitted his resignation to the president. Moshe Sharett was appointed prime minister in his place, and Pinhas Lavon was appointed minister of defense.

Rumors of the prime minister's astonishing resignation had spread earlier. On Oct. 4, Ben-Gurion extended his leave by three additional weeks. Ten days later, a delegation of ministers visited him to clarify rumors he was moving to the Negev.

On Oct. 18, photos of the bungalow built for Ben-Gurion on Kibbutz Sde Boker were published. Ben-Gurion informed his Cabinet of his imminent resignation and requested they make it possible for him to retire from his post in a month's time. In an act of solidarity, Haifa's workers announced their intent to strike in an effort to dissuade Ben-Gurion from retiring.

Ben-Gurion first offered the position of prime minister to Levy Eshkol, who declined. Two days after Ben-Gurion's retirement the president instructed Moshe Sharett to form a government. Ben-Gurion did not retire from the Knesset. Yitzhak Navon, Ben-Gurion's personal secretary, moved with him to Kibbutz Sde Boker.

Moshe Dayan Becomes Israel's Fourth Chief of Staff

Moshe Dayan.

General Moshe Dayan has been appointed Israel's fourth chief of staff. Upon his appointment, Dayan resigned from the central committee of *Mapai*. Dayan's appointment was David Ben-Gurion's final decision as minister of defense. The appointment was approved despite much debate.

A year before, Moshe Dayan had been offered the position of deputy chief of staff. He had declined the offer and been sent abroad as part of a delegation participating in hearings at the United Nations Security Council. On his return, Dayan was appointed minister of defense by Ben-Gurion.

Dozens of Women and Children Killed in Kfar Kibya

On Oct. 14, the IDF completed its first reprisal mission in Jordan. The mission resulted in tragedy. The target, Kfar Kibya, was known as a hiding place of infiltrators who had penetrated into Israel and murdered a mother and her two children in Kfar Yehud. The Unit 101 commandos who took over Kfar Kibya and prepared to blow up its houses did not know that dozens of civilians, mainly women and children, were hiding inside the homes.

Jordan complained to the UN, and the Security Council condemned Israel for the operation. For a long period, Israel denied any connection to the operation and claimed it had been executed by vigilantes unconnected with the IDF.

In the aftermath of the operation, regulations on the army's duty towards civilians present in a battle area were changed.

1953

OCTOBER - DECEMBER

Salazar wins all seats in Portugal's elections. (October 8)

•

The Israel Jordan Combined Armistice Committee charged that Israeli forces raided Kibya causing 42 deaths and destroying 41 houses. UN Security Council accepts Arab demand to debate Kibya. UNTSO chief Bennike reports Middle East tension near breaking point. (October 13)

•

British Prime Minister Winston Churchill was awarded the Nobel Prize for Literature and said he hoped to go to Stockholm to receive the award. (October 15)

•

US releases $26 million in aid to Israel after work near B'not Ya'acov on the Jordan River is suspended. (October 28)

•

The first oil drilling is started near Sdom. (November 3)

•

Ibn Saud has died; his son, Said Emir Saud, 52, is new monarch of Saudi Arabia. (November 10)

•

Former President Truman in a nationwide radio and television broadcast blasted McCarthyism as a cancer consuming life in the US. (November 17)

•

The UN Security Council approved the Western resolution calling for the strongest censure of Israel for the attack on Kibya on October 15. (November 24)

•

Eugene O'Neill, the playwright, has died. (November 27)

•

Supervision over cookies, candies and halva has been canceled. The head of the food department at Ministry of Trade and Commerce promised that cancellation of the tax would become valid within the next few days, but would not apply to chocolate. (November 29)

•

Ho Chi Minh, leader of the northern Vietminh regime, sees peace in Vietnam only if France quits. (November 29)

•

Moshe Sharett given mandate to form new Cabinet. (December 9)

•

Arthur Miller writes play, *"The Crucible."* (December 23)

The Indo-China War enters its seventh year. This marks the final stage of the long and bitter confrontation between the French and Vietnamese forces. (January 1)

•

The Ministry of Foreign Affairs requested that foreign embassies be strict with Israelis wishing to leave the country. The Swiss announced that they would not grant visas to Israelis. The Austrians will grant visas to Israelis only on the presentation of a return ticket. (January 5)

•

British *Comet* passenger jet, crashes over the Mediterranean. (January 11)

•

First atom powered submarine, the USS *'Nautilus'* was launched. The development of the submarine was not without controversy, and even today the navy is not sure whether it is a milestone in naval history, or just a guinea pig. Hyman G. Rickover, the spirit behind the project, promoted by President Eisenhower, to the permanent rank of Rear-Admiral. (January 21)

•

Moshe Sharett and *Mapai* form a new government coalition in Israel. (January 24)

•

Egypt claims the entrance to the Gulf of Aqaba as Egyptian territorial waters. Israel will complain to the Security Council on the Suez blockade and Egypt's interference with Israeli shipping. (January 27)

•

An amendment to the Law of Return would bar known criminals from automatically receiving the right of entry under the current law. (February 2)

•

The minister of transportation objects to the air route between Israel and Germany. The minister claims that there is no need for such a route. (February 4)

•

Knesset votes to abolish death penalty for all but Nazi collaborators. (February 16)

•

Syrian and Egyptian officers simultaneously overthrow their respective heads of state. Shishakli flees Syria, Nasser grabs power in Egypt. (February 25)

Private Elbaz Sacrifices His Life for Fellow Soldiers

Nathan Elbaz. Embraced the grenade and saved his friends.

An act of heroism on the part of Private Nathan Elbaz has earned the admiration of the Israel Defense Forces. On Feb. 11, Elbaz, a new immigrant from Morocco serving in the infantry, was given the task of taking apart hand-grenades. Elbaz took the grenades to his tent. While at work, he realized by its sound that the safety catch of one of the grenades had come loose.

He ran outside with the grenade and called to soldiers there to run to the nearby *wadi*. Realizing that it would be impossible for him to throw the grenade without injuring other soldiers, Elbaz embraced the grenade and jumped into a nearby ditch. The grenade exploded and he was blown up.

After Elbaz's death, Chief of Staff Moshe Dayan honored him with a medal for "having sacrificed his life for his friends in an extraordinary act of heroism."

Nasser Becomes the New Leader of Egypt

Nasser. Nationalized the canal and brought about the Sinai Campaign.

A year and a half after the 'Free Officers' Revolution' and the deposition of King Farouk, Egypt has a new leader. On Feb. 25, President and Prime Minister Mohammed Naguib was dethroned and replaced by Colonel Gamal Abdul Nasser.

Nasser had been the real leader of the coup, but preferred to stay out of the limelight and allow General Naguib to appear as the leader. When Naguib was no longer willing to follow their instructions, Nasser and his colleagues decided to depose him and have Nasser assume his place.

Nasser was one of Egypt's most gifted officers in the War of Independence and belonged to the large Egyptian force that was besieged in Kis Faluja from October, 1948 until February, 1949.

Government Buys Electricity Corp.

On Jan. 11 a bill was passed in the *Knesset* known as the Electricity Corporation Law. The corporation, until then privately owned, passed to the state's control despite disagreements within the government. The General Zionists party voted against the purchase, and other factions abstained. The law was passed after lengthy negotiations with the corporation's owner, Lord Nathan of England. The government had initially offered Nathan partnership in the corporation, but after his refusal, the government decided to buy him out.

Infiltrators Slaughter 'Bus Passengers at Ma'ale Aqrabbim

Bodies of passengers next to the 'bus at Ma'ale Aqrabbim. Infiltrators from Jordan ambushed the 'bus.

1954
MARCH - APRIL

Passengers of an Egged 'bus on their way from Eilat to Tel Aviv were slaughtered on Mar. 17. When the 'bus arrived at Ma'ale Aqrabbim in the northern Negev, it came under attack at close range. The infiltrators ambushed the 'bus at a point in the road where the driver was forced to slow down because of dangerous curves.

The first shots killed the driver and injured many of the passengers. Once the 'bus had come to a halt, the murderers entered and shot each passenger. Eleven people were killed. Survivors reported that the murderers spat on the bodies and abused them.

The infiltrators' footsteps led to the Jordan border 20 km *(13 miles)* from the incident. Prime Minister Moshe Sharett, Defense Minister Pinhas Lavon and Minister of Police Bechor Shetreet arrived at the scene shortly afterwards. A week later, Israel resigned from the Israeli-Jordanian Armistice Committee when its chairman, Colonel Hutchinson of the United States, refused to condemn Jordan for the murders. On Mar. 30, Jordan began concentrating forces at its border with Israel and in the area of the Jerusalem mountains.

Grinwald is Accused of Defaming Israel Kastner

A simple libel trial against an eccentric Jerusalem Jew has become one of the most famous trials in the history of the State.

The state prosecuted Malkiel Grinwald for words he had written against Dr. Israel Kastner, a senior clerk at the Ministry of Trade and Commerce.

During the 1940's, Kastner had been one of the heads of the committee engaged in efforts to save Budapest Jews. Kastner developed a relationship with Kurt Becker, an SS officer, and with Adolf Eichmann, who was responsible for the extermi-

Grinwald. Accused Kastner.

nation of the Jews of Hungary. Grinwald accused Kastner of having abandoned Hungary's Jews in order to save his own life and the lives of hundreds of his friends.

The trial began in February before Judge Binyamin Halevi. Grinwald was represented by Advocate Shmuel Tamir, and the state was represented by Advocate Amnon Tal, who was later replaced by Chaim Cohen, the attorney general.

The aftermath of this case led to the downfall of the government and to a political murder. Its echoes can still be heard today.

The nuclear arms race has entered a new and frightening stage, with the atomic test carried out in the Bikini Islands in the Pacific Ocean, by the United States. The effect of the blast was 500 times greater than that of the A-bombs dropped on Hiroshima and Nagasaki in 1945. (March 1)

•

US and Japan sign mutual defense treaty. (March 8)

•

The British arrest 700 *'Mau Mau'* activists in Kenya, including Jomo Kenyatta, who remains imprisoned for many years, later to become Kenya's first president. (March 12)

•

Charlie Chaplin thanked the Soldiers' Welfare Committee for inviting him to perform on Independence Day, but declined the offer saying that he was too busy. The Committee did not have Chaplin's address, and addressed his invitation: "Charles Chaplin, Switzerland." (March 15)

•

Jordan claims nine soldiers killed and 17 wounded by 200 Israelis at Nahalin. The foreign minister said Nahalin was a local affair and a reaction to a murder that took place two days earlier at Kesalon. (March 17)

•

Israel leaves the United Nations armistice committee. (March 23)

•

The Soviet Union asks to become a member of NATO. (March 31)

•

The remains of Baron de Rothschild and his wife Adelaide were brought to Israel for burial. In accordance with the baron's will, the couple was buried in a plot close to Zichron Ya'acov. The plot is now called Ramat Hanadiv. (April 6)

•

President Nasser takes full control of the United Arab Republic of Egypt. (April 18)

•

Gyorgy Malenko is elected prime minister of the United Soviet Socialist Republic. (April 27)

•

Dr. Robert Oppenheimer, the head of the team which developed the nuclear bomb, is declared a security risk by the McCarthy Committee investigating non-American activities. (April 29)

The British sprinter, Roger Banister, ran the mile in under four minutes, (3 mins. 59.4 seconds), setting a new world record, at Oxford. (May 6)

President Eisenhower's personal representative to the Middle East, Mr. Eric Johnston, optimistic as Israel and Arabs reply on cooperative use of Jordan River waters. (May 7)

Dien Bien Phu falls after a 57-day siege. (May 7)

France proposes a cease-fire in Vietnam, between France and the VietMinh. (May 8)

Prime Minister Sharett, in a policy statement opening the summer session of the Knesset, said that US policy of wooing the Arabs endangers Israel. (May 10)

The United States' Supreme Court outlaws racist separation in American schools. (May 17)

Charles Ives, the American composer, dies. (May 19)

Israel tells UN that Jordan caused 37 border incidents in 43 days from March 30 to May 11, including an attack on a train and sending armed bands into Israel's territory. (May 22)

President Tito of Yugoslavia makes an official visit to Greece. (May 31)

Hebrew University dedicates new permanent home for university in Jerusalem after six years of exile from Mount Scopus. (June 2)

Three weapons manufactured by Israel are being used by the IDF. The Uzi, which has replaced the Sten sub-machine-gun, the Bazooka, which is an anti-tank missile, and a grenade projector. (June 10)

Pierre Mendes France is elected as the prime minister in France. (June 18)

Israel was insulted by the American demand that Israel finance Chief of Staff Moshe Dayan's tour of the US, but did so. Dayan visited the Pentagon, meeting the US Chief of Staff. (June 30)

Death Sentence to Israelis Acting Against Israel in War

On June 14 the Knesset ratified an amendment to the penal code to allow for the sentencing to death of any Israeli citizen during wartime. The amendment extended the penal code to Israeli citizens who had acted to bring about any of the following situations: Israel ceasing to be a sovereign state; a certain area ceasing to be under Israel's sovereignty or control; or anyone who intentionally acted to bring about war against Israel.

The amendment also included anyone disclosing information to the enemy or assisting the enemy in engaging in war against Israel; and anyone trying to change the orders of Israel's government by engaging in acts of violence or by using arms. The amendment was presented to the minister of justice and it faced strong opposition from members of all Opposition factions, who argued that such laws would run the risk of the government exploiting its authority to suppress criticism.

Katarina Szenes: Not Enough was Done to Save her Daughter

Katarina Szenes, mother of paratrooper Hanna Szenes, testified in the libel trial against Malkiel Grinwald on June 14.

For the first time, Szenes talked about her encounters with her daughter at the Hungarian prison in Budapest, shortly before she was executed. Szenes, who had seen her daughter battered, tortured and toothless, testified on behalf of Grinwald and claimed that the committee headed by Kastner to save Hungary's Jews did not do enough to save her daughter.

The mother's dramatic testimony shocked the courtroom. Katarina Szenes had lived in Budapest during the Second World War and had not known that her daughter, who had emigrated to Israel some years earlier, was stationed in Hungary as an Israeli paratrooper sent to save the country's Jews. The first words Szenes had heard from her daughter were: "Forgive me, Mother."

Hungarian investigators arranged a meeting between mother and daughter, in the hope that the Israeli prisoner would give away details of her missions. Hanna Szenes did not utter a word.

Hanna Szenes. Her first words were "Forgive me, Mother."

The Herd was Stolen and so Kibbutz Ein-Gedi Retaliated

Ten young members of Kibbutz Ein-Gedi, next to the Dead Sea, crossed the border into Jordan on May 26 after the kibbutz's herd of cows had been stolen. The kibbutz received information that the cows were near Chirbat El Geneva in the Hebron mountains. The young kibbutzniks arrived there, armed, and encountered four Bedouin who were guarding the herd. One of the Bedouin tried to escape and was fatally shot. The remaining three were tied and left at the site. On their way back to Israel with the herd, the kibbutz members were attacked by Jordanian soldiers. All three soldiers were killed and the Israelis returned unharmed to Ein-Gedi. Jordan protested against the operation.

On June 20, three civilians from Mevo Beitar, in the Jerusalem mountains, were killed. The bodies of the three were torn to pieces by their killers. On June 27, Jordanian infiltrators killed a farmer from Ra'anana.

On June 30, Jordanian snipers fired from the Old City walls on civilians walking in Mamilla Road in West Jerusalem at the Jaffa Gate entrance, killing one woman and wounding 17. All children were evacuated from their homes on Mamilla Road. The next day, a soldier was shot dead on Mount Zio.

Seventeen Killed in a *Piper* Crash on Kibbutz Ma'agan

On July 29, a *Piper* aeroplane crashed amidst a crowd of 2,500 people during the unveiling of paratrooper Perez Goldstein's memorial at Kibbutz Ma'agan. Seventeen people were killed and 25 injured, most of them seriously.

The *Piper* was circling above the ceremony in order to release the president's congratulatory note to the crowd. The pilot released the note but it was caught between the 'plane's wheels. At this point, the pilot tried to release the small parachute, by leaning out of the cockpit, and so losing control of the 'plane which crashed within seconds.

The area on which the aeroplane had crashed had originally been designated for the gathering of Kibbutz Ma'agan's children. Since the children were late to arrive, police directed them elsewhere and thus saved their lives. Shortly before the crash, the paratroopers' guard of honor arrived at the site. Their commander, Lieutenant Simcha Levy was killed instantaneously.

On Sept. 9, the investigation committee publicized its findings and determined that the tragedy was caused by the pilot's carelessness and irresponsibility.

Women's Corps Marches

Marching with an *Uzi*, a long skirt and a flashy hat.

Five years after its establishment, the Women's Corps has become an integral part of the IDF. The percentage of 'draft dodgers' among Israeli-born women is relatively low. The new wonder, an armed woman soldier (the *Uzi* had been introduced a month earlier), has become an object of admiration all over the world.

Fear for Fate of Tens of Thousands of Moroccans

Moroccan immigrants.

The battle between the Moslem Nationalists and the sultan's followers in Morocco hurt Morocco's Jews severely, particularly those in the city of Fez.

On Aug. 5, riots broke out in the town of Petit Jean. A speech by a Moslem preacher incited 900 Moslems to break into the town's Jewish quarter, where they murdered and looted. In a village next to the city of Meknas, six Jewish merchants were murdered after they refused to comply with the Moslems' demands to close their shops.

Israel was concerned about the fate of Morocco's Jews, who were estimated to number 250,000.

Twenty-five thousand Moroccan Jews registered in August to emigrate to Israel, and thousands crossed Morocco in order to reach the transit camps in Casablanca. One thousand Moroccan Jews managed to reach Israel during this month. In September, this number was doubled.

Ambassador Eric Johnston: Israel, Jordan, Syria and Lebanon accept the principle of sharing the Jordan River waters and working with the US on a mutually acceptable program to develop the irrigation and hydro-electric potentials of the basin. Israel stated that Johnston expressed personal views, not those of the Israeli Government. (July 7)

The maiden flight of the American made Boeing 707 takes place. (July 15)

Theodore Heuss is made chancellor of West Germany. (July 17)

Britain and Egypt initial pact on evacuation of Suez Canal zone. British troops to leave in 20 months. (July 27)

The chief topic of Israel-U.S. discussions is the possible effects of the Anglo-Egyptian agreement on Israel's security, and for the first time the existence of this problem is recognized by the State Department. (August 11)

Fifteen hundred people are killed and thousands are made homeless in an earthquake in Aurelienville, Algeria. (September 9)

In a formal letter to the Swiss government, Israel expressed interest in the deposits made by Jews who died in the Holocaust. The Swiss were requested to transfer the money to the heirs or to international Jewish institutions. The Swiss government's response was: we will address the issue and get back to you. (September 10)

The People's Republic of China convenes its congress in Peking (Beijing). (September 15)

Israeli embassy in London said that if arms are supplied to Arab states then Israel must insist on receiving arms in the same measure so that the balance of power will be maintained and not be to the advantage of those who continue to threaten Israel's annihilation. (September 18)

1954

OCTOBER - DECEMBER

Hanoi has been conquered by communist forces. (October 8)

Ambassador Abba Eban declares to Security Council that Suez Canal blockade violates Israel's international rights, and also the armistice agreement. (October 14)

Britain and Egypt sign Suez pact. 72 years of British occupation of Suez Canal ended. Israel watchful. (October 19)

Terrorism erupts in Algiers, as anti-French violence, the most threatening since World War II, takes over. Many are killed in terror attacks of the nationalist group MTLD, seeking democratic freedom from French imperialism. (November 3)

Burma and Japan sign a peace treaty. (November 5)

Colonel Chaim Herzog, son of the chief rabbi of Israel, is appointed commander of the Jerusalem area. His brother Ya'acov is the advisor on matters relating to Jerusalem at the Ministry of Foreign Affairs. (November 17)

Gamal Abdel Nasser becomes the official head of state of Egypt. (November 17)

Sir Winston Churchill is presented with a birthday book and a portrait painted by Graham Sutherland. The painting was commissioned by both houses of Parliament. Unfortunately, Lady Clementine Churchill disliked the painting intensely, and it was later destroyed. (November 30)

The US signs an agreement with the nationalist Republic of China (Taiwan). (December 1)

The United States Senate condemns Senator Joseph McCarthy. (December 2)

20,000 French soldiers are being sent to Algeria. (December 23)

William Golding's famous novel, 'The Lord of the Flies' is published in England. (December 31)

Elia Kazan makes the film 'On the Waterfront' with a young Marlon Brando. (December 31)

Egypt Arrests Jewish Espionage Network

Marcelle Ninio.

Philip Nathanzon.

Robert Dassa.

On Dec. 8, Egypt announced the arrest of 13 Egyptian Jews suspected of spying for Israel. The discovery exposed the 'Lavon Affair.'

The arrested were from Cairo and Alexandria. The network was exposed in July, when improvised explosives exploded in the pocket of one of the men, at the entrance to an Egyptian cinema. Prior to this incident, the network's members had blown up the American Library in Cairo, in an attempt to damage Egypt's relations with the US.

On Dec. 10 the trial of the suspects began. The men were accused of having been recruited by Israel and sent to sabotage various sites in Cairo and Alexandria. Some of the suspects had been caught in possession of radio transmitters.

The Lavon Affair, also known as the 'security mishap,' influenced the country's politics for 20 years. Details of the episode remained secret. Years later it became clear that the network had been operated by senior army officers, not the government.

The intelligence officer who had been sent from Israel to operate the network escaped from Egypt. The Israeli public only knew him as 'The Third Man.' Eventually, his name was disclosed - Avri Elad, who carried a German passport in the name Paul Frank. Elad, brought to Israel undercover in 1958, was accused of having been a double agent, and exposing the network to the Egyptians. He was convicted and sentenced to 12 years in prison; his sentence was later commuted to ten years.

'Bat Galim' Sailors Released After Three Months in Prison

On Dec. 13, after spending three months in an Egyptian prison, the ten sailors of the ship 'Bat Galim' were released and the Egyptians retracted their accusation that the ship's crew had shot local fishermen.

'Bat Galim' had been captured by Egyptian soldiers at the entry to the southern portion of the Suez Canal, and the sailors had been placed in an Egyptian prison.

Throughout their imprisonment, the sailors maintained contact with their families by mail.

Israel complained about the situation to the United Nations Security Council, which transferred the issue to its cease-fire committee.

The Egyptians eventually succumbed to international pressure and agreed to release the crew. The UN spectators also determined that there was no factual basis for the Egyptians' accusations. The fishermen who were allegedly shot by the sailors were not found.

'Bat Galim' and its captain, Zvi Shidlo, had been instructed to cross

The ten sailors are welcomed with flowers.

the Suez Canal as part of the Israeli effort to prevent the closure imposed by Egypt on the passage of Israeli ships and goods.

Before their departure, 'Bat Galim's' sailors had been insured by the ship's owners, the Poseidon company, for IL *(Israeli lira)* 100,000.

Even after the crew's release, the Egyptians continued to hold the boat and its cargo of leather, meat and timber.

Upon their return to Israel, the sailors received a hero's welcome.

Each sailor was awarded IL 500 as compensation for his arrest.

Moshe Marzuk and Shmuel Azar are Hanged in Cairo

Moshe Marzuk's mother at her son's funeral in Israel.

Marzuk, on the left. Death by hanging.

Dr. Moshe Marzuk and engineer Shmuel Azar, two central activists of the Jewish community in Egypt, were hanged on Jan. 31 in Cairo's central prison after the city's military court had convicted them of belonging to an Israeli espionage network. The two were apprehended by the Egyptian security services after the exposure of the spy network set up in Egypt by Israeli intelligence, operating mainly in Cairo and Alexandria.

On Aug. 10 of last year, the Egyptian police announced that it had arrested 13 suspects. Among them was Meir (Max) Bennett, a major in Israeli intelligence, accused of being the head of the network.

Bennett was severely tortured and committed suicide shortly after the trial began. After his suicide, the Egyptian media claimed that Marzuk was the head of the Zionist group in Cairo, and that Azar was responsible for the espionage and sabotage network in Alexandria.

The network's members sabotaged English and American facilities in an attempt to frustrate the agreement between Britain and Egypt concerning the evacuation of the Suez zone by the British.

The espionage incident in Cairo and the executions of Marzuk and Azar stirred up a political storm in Israel. Minister of Defense Pinhas Lavon claimed that he did not know of the network. David Ben-Gurion

Azar. Death by hanging.

demanded that an investigation committee be established to investigate Israel's role in the incident.

Uri Ilan Commits Suicide in Prison in Damascus

Uri Ilan, a soldier in the *Golani* brigade *(one of Israel's elite commando units)*, committed suicide on Jan. 12 in a Damascus prison. Notice of his death was given to the Chairman of the Israeli-Syrian armistice committee by Syria's government in the early morning.

Uri Ilan, member of Kibbutz Gan Shmuel, was one of five IDF soldiers to have crossed the border on Dec. 9, 1954 who were all taken captive by the Syrians while installing a bugging device on telephone lines in Syria.

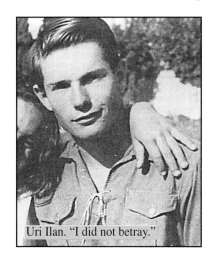

Uri Ilan. "I did not betray."

It was reported that the five Israeli soldiers who had penetrated Syria were armed with *Uzis*, hand grenades and commando knives. They were also carrying ropes and communications devices. When Uri Ilan's body was transferred to Israel on Jan. 14 a note in his handwriting was found in his clothes: "They are killing us. Revenge." In another note hidden between his toes, Uri Ilan wrote: "I did not betray..."

Many generations of IDF fighters have been brought up on the myth of Udi Ilan.

Two hikers go missing in the Judean Desert, Oded Wegmeister of Kibbutz Deganya and Shoshana Har-Zion from Bet Alpha, the sister of the famous paratrooper, Meir Har-Zion. (January 2)

•

The Tel Aviv municipality is taking measures against shops selling pork. Licenses to sell pork were given to two shops only: one, in the Jewish city of Tel Aviv, is intended for diplomats, and the second, in Jaffa, intended for Christians. (January 4)

•

Israel's budget for 1955 causes a government crisis between MAPAI and the General Zionists, who demanded a lowering of income tax and a cutting of the State Budget by IL 15.5 million. (January 12)

•

Two tractor drivers from Moshav Mevo Hamma in the Jerusalem Hills were murdered by infiltrators. Footsteps of the murderers led across the Jordanian border. (January 15)

•

The government of Kenya proposes a settlement with the *'Mau Mau'* fighters. (January 18)

•

The Soviet Union formally ends its state of war with West Germany. (January 25)

•

Haim Elbaz, a member of Moshav Ein HaShlosha in the Negev, is murdered by infiltrators while ploughing his farm. Israel reports the incident to the United Nations, as an example of the significant growth in *fedayeen* attacks. (January 25)

•

Talks between Israeli and American teams on Eric Johnston's plans for the development of the Jordan River waters began today. (January 27)

•

The Ministry of Transport takes measures to punish bicyclists who drive at night without lights, because of an increase in road accidents in the dark. (January 28)

•

The postal bank announces that special savings plans are to be introduced. Investors may open a savings account with a minimum of IL3 in cash, or with savings stamps. (January 30)

Hardly a day passes recently without two or three violent attacks on Tunis Jews; the attackers use a variety of weapons. In every 30 cases reported, 26 are against Jews. (February 1)

Mendes France resigns as prime minister of France. (February 5)

Malenkov resigns. Nikolai Bulganin is appointed as head of the Soviet government, with Nikita Khrushchev remaining as president. (February 8)

The Israeli Consulate in New York published an ad in the major newspapers: 'If you are planning to send packages to your relatives in Israel, why not send cash instead. Your relatives will enjoy it more.' (February 11)

Ben Gurion back in Cabinet as Defense Minister; Lavon out. The prime minister published a statement that Mr. Lavon had asked for an inquiry to be held. (February 17)

Jordan accepts new plan for the division of Jordan and Yarmuk Rivers between the four Middle East countries. (February 19)

Turkish-Iraqi defense treaty signed in Baghdad. Egyptian army ordered to stand ready because the developments were aimed at forcing Egypt to join the pact. (February 24)

Cairo alerts army and air force after 38 killed and 45 wounded in Gaza clash February 28. Egypt calls for urgent UN meeting. (February 28)

West Germany, Italy and France confirm the European Community Agreement. (March 11)

Egypt woos the West, but demands the Negev as its wedding dowry. (March 20)

Pakistan declares a state of emergency. (March 27)

The UN Security Council unanimously approved a resolution condemning Israel for the attack on Egyptian forces in the Gaza Strip on February 28. (March 29)

Purge of Chinese communist party takes place. (March 31)

42 Egyptian Soldiers Killed in Reprisals in the Gaza Strip

The raiding soldiers enter the Egyptian base. The most extensive operation in Egypt since the War of Independence.

Forty two Egyptian soldiers were killed and 36 were injured by a reprisal carried out by a paratroopers unit, commanded by Ariel Sharon. The IDF suffered eight fatalities.

The reprisal, one of the most extensive in its scope, came as a reaction to the numerous attacks carried out by the *fedayeen*, Palestinian terrorists, against Israeli settlements in the south.

Radio Cairo reported heavy casualties on the Egyptian side, after a force comprised of hundreds of Is-raeli soldiers penetrated an Egyptian military base in north-east Gaza and opened fire.

An Egyptian force which rushed to the attacked camp's help, encountered an ambush and was almost totally wiped out.

An Egyptian spokesperson said that this was the most severe attack on the Israeli-Egyptian border since the cease-fire agreements were signed in 1949.

The Israeli forces retreated to Israel, after blowing up military instal-lations at the Egyptian base.

The attack on Gaza was the first in a series of reprisals that the IDF executed against military targets in Egypt, Jordan and Syria during 1955-1956.

Following the reprisal and the Egyptian defeat, Nasser signed an agreement with the Soviet Union for the supply of arms, and for military and economic collaboration. So began 30 years of the USSR's close involvement in the Middle-East.

Dead Sea Scrolls Arrive in Israel

Thousands of years after their writing, and many years after their discovery in the Judean Desert, the Dead Sea Scrolls were returned to their natural home, the State of Israel. The scrolls had been discovered by a Bedouin, at Qumran.

Former Chief of Staff Yigael Yadin, who had dedicated his civilian life to Israel's archeology, was told of the opportunity to buy the scrolls back. He recruited an American investor, Sam Gottesman, to purchase them without Israel being identified as the buyer. Gottesman paid more than $250,000 for the scrolls. The sellers did not know that the scrolls had been purchased by Israel until the very last moment. The Dead Sea Scrolls, the writings of a sect from the Judean Desert, are among the most significant archeological finds of the 20th century.

The Dead Sea Scrolls. One of the most significant archeological finds.

Albert Einstein Dies. His Brain Donated to Science

Professor Albert Einstein, one of the world's top scientists, died in a New York hospital on Apr. 18. The official announcement of his death was made seven hours afterwards.

The hospital reported that the delayed announcement of Einstein's death was due to the fact that no one had phoned to inquire about him. Einstein was 76 at the time of his death. He was born in Germany and emigrated to the United States in 1933 when the Nazis took control.

Einstein, considered to be one of the world's leading physicists, instructed that his body be cremated. His son, Dr. Hans Einstein, said that his father had requested on numerous occasions that his brain be given to Princeton University for research.

Dr. Robert Oppenheimer, the Jewish scientist, had made discoveries which Einstein then used to produce the first nuclear deterrent.

In his will, Einstein asked the leaders of the world powers to treat Israel in a sincere and just manner. At the time of Israel's establishment, David Ben-Gurion had hoped that the great scientist would consent to assume the position of president of the state. At an emotional meeting between the two, Einstein thanked Ben-Gurion for the great honor, but declined. The position was then given to another great scientist, Chaim Weizmann.

Albert Einstein. Requested that countries treat Israel in a sincere and just manner.

IDF Reveals the *Uzi*

At the military parade in Tel Aviv on Apr. 27, commemorating Israel's seventh Independence Day, the Israel Defense Forces unveiled the *Uzi* for the first time.

The *Uzi* is a new submachine gun used by elite infantry units.

The *Uzi* was developed by Uzi Gal, an employee of the Military Industries, and has revolutionized the field of light weapons.

Due to its small size and close-range efficiency, it became a popular weapon, still used by numerous countries and organizations. Within a short time, it became one of the Military Industries' largest export items, exported mainly to Third-World countries.

Through all its various stages - with a short barrel and folding butt - the Uzi has always been used by the IDF, although not by soldiers on the front line.

The Uzi became quickly famous in the world when photographs were published of young Israeli women soldiers carrying it. Outside Israel, the Uzi is still a popular and efficient close-range weapon used by many organizations operating outside the law.

Uzi Gal. A real revolution.

The *Uzi*.

The Accadia Hotel in Herzliya, Israel's most luxurious hotel, was opened. 3,000 people took part in the opening gala. The price of a room per night - 28 lira, per suite - 75 lira. The great attraction: each room has an external telephone. (June 2)

A serious accident occurs at the French Formula One Grand Prix held at Le Mans. A Mercedes sports car crashes into spectators killing 70, and injuring over 100 people. This tragedy led to formal restrictions being introduced for the first time in the rules of motor racing. (June 11)

The United States and Great Britain sign a treaty for atomic energy. (June 15)

Golda Meyerson, *Mapai's* candidate to be mayor of Tel Aviv, is not even entitled to vote in Tel Aviv. Meyerson appears in Jerusalem's list of voters, having moved to Jerusalem where she served as a minister. (June 25)

For the first time in hundreds of years, the Jordanians cleaned the ancient tombs in the Cave of the Patriarchs in Hebron. The Moslems are proud of the fact that since the crusades, no one but Moslems have entered the cave. (July 9)

Disneyland, the world's most sophisticated amusement park, is opened in California. (July 15)

Israel Navy buys two British 'Z' class destroyers. The ships are to be renamed 'Jaffa' and 'Eilat.' (July 16)

Water starts flowing from the Yarkon River to the Negev. The 62-mile line means another 3,750 acres of irrigated land in the Negev. (July 19)

Donald Campbell breaks the speedboat racing record, reaching 325 kph *(203 mph)*. (July 23)

Nikita Khrushchev and Nikolai Bulganin make an official visit to East Germany. (July 24)

Israel lodges a 'vehement protest' at the shooting down of El Al airliner on July 28, by Bulgaria. All passengers and crew dead. (July 28)

The Judge's Verdict: Israel Kastner Sold his Soul to the Nazi Satan

Binyamin Halevi.

Kastner with his wife and daughter.

President of the district court in Jerusalem, Binyamin Halevi, issued his verdict on Kastner on June 21.

The judge ruled: "Israel Kastner, the head of the life-saving committee during the Nazi reign, sold his soul to the Nazi Satan, abandoned the majority of Hungary's Jews and left them at the Nazi's mercy, so that he could save prominent members of the community, and amongst them, his own family."

"Kastner," wrote Halevi, "knew that his collaboration with the Nazis facilitated the extermination of the majority of Hungary's Jews. Kastner was aware of his role in their destruction."

"The Nazis would not have been able to mislead the Jews had it not been for the false rumors spread through certain Jewish channels."

Kastner's trial turned from a simple libel trial to a political one which stirred the nation and involved Israel's top echelon.

Elections '55: *Herut* Doubles its Power

Despite *Mapai's* victory in the elections for the third *Knesset* on July 27, it lost 11% of its power and received only 40 mandates versus the 45 mandates it had previously enjoyed. The true surprise was *Herut*, which almost doubled its power, and enjoyed an increase of seven mandates, bringing it to a total of 15. This change was mainly on account of the seats lost by the General Zionists who had only 13 mandates, instead of their previous 20.

58 Killed in El Al Airplane Shot Down over Bulgaria

Families by the coffins of their loved ones.

In the early morning hours of July 27, an El Al airplane was shot down over Bulgaria. All 58 passengers and the entire crew were killed. The airplane, on its way from Paris to Israel, flew over Yugoslavia through international airspace and was attacked by Bulgarian Air Force jets.

For unknown reasons, the aircraft had deviated from its route and entered Bulgarian air space, where it was attacked by combat aircraft. The 'plane was hit immediately, and its rear wings burst into flame. The pilot tried to carry out a forced landing at an old German air base. Three hundred meters *(330 yards)* from the ground, the airplane was again attacked by the Bulgarians and this time exploded in mid-air.

All the passengers were killed, among them three children. After the crash, Bulgaria tried to cloud the details surrounding the incident and blamed the aircraft pilot for entering Bulgarian air space without appropriate authorization.

80 Egyptians Killed in IDF Mission in Khan Yunis

1955
AUGUST - SEPTEMBER

Three paratroopers preparing for the Khan Yunis bombing.

In retaliation for recent murderous activities, paratroopers of the Israel Defense Forces raided the Egyptian army base in Khan Yunis, in the Gaza Strip. The base, a large police building, had become the *fedayeen* exit point for terror attacks on Israel. According to Israeli intelligence, the base contained many Egyptian troops and also served as headquarters for the Palestinian Brigade, which acted as a branch of the Egyptian army.

In the daring raid, the Israeli paratroopers bombed the police building. One paratrooper was killed, and eight were injured. Approximately 80 Egyptian soldiers were killed, which was the highest number of fatalities in one operation since the War of Independence. The Egyptians admitted that the number of casualties in Khan Yunis was higher than that of the operation in Gaza seven months earlier.

Chief of Staff Moshe Dayan awaited the Israeli force at the border between Israel and Egypt. Two of the force's commanders, 'Motta' Gur, the operation's commander, and Lieutenant Moshe Peles (Stempel), were awarded a commendation for their role in the battle.

Oil Found in the Negev

Oil, oil, oil! Gusher at Heletz. Disappointed ever since.

On Sept. 29, commercial quantities of oil were found at the drilling site Heletz 1 in the northern Negev. The discovery of oil caused much excitement in Israel and was reported on every newscast that day. The drilling site's chief geologist, Dr. Herman Tzop, claimed that the field seemed to be extremely rich in high-quality oil, and that its diameter was estimated at several kilometers.

The news of oil in the Negev spread quickly, and many Israelis interrupted their day's work and ventured out to the site to see the oil gush from the wells.

Despite this optimism, Sde Heletz was the first and last field in which commercial quantities of oil were found. Several years later, the field dried up, and no other well since then has measured up to that first, promising discovery.

A rightist Moslem government has come to power in Indonesia. (August 11)

●

German author, Thomas Mann, dies. (August 12)

●

The third *Knesset* was declared in session by President Yitzhak Ben-Zvi. Ben-Gurion agrees to try and form a broad coalition. (August 15)

●

Following the riots in Morocco, the Jewish Agency discussed an emergency operation for the evacuation of 20,000 Moroccan Jews. Street battles against the French army have been going on continuously. Israel received information that the Moroccan Jews are suffering from serious harassment due to anti-Semitism. (August 26)

●

Egypt raiders murder seven people in Israel and wound eight others since Monday. US and UK ask for end to border fighting. (August 30)

●

Israel accepts cease-fire terms. Two Egyptian jets shot down inside Israel. The Security Council unanimously approved a Western resolution calling on Egypt and Israel to bring about order and tranquillity to the Gaza Strip. (September 10)

●

Egyptian units destroy Nitzana border posts. The Ministry of Foreign Affairs spokesman said that this action was a culmination of a long series of violations of the armistice agreement in the demilitarized zone along the Egyptian-Israeli border. Israel and Egypt are ready for withdrawal from Nitzana. Israel wants assurances that Egypt will comply with the armistice agreement. (September 20)

●

Czechs to barter arms for Egyptian cotton and rice. Nasser says Egypt took the step after repeated failures to secure arms from the West. US and Britain prepare a joint approach to Russia, warning of the serious consequences of a mid-East arms race. Israel presses for US arms because of Egyptian purchase from the Soviets. (September 27)

1955

OCTOBER - DECEMBER

Prime Minister Sharett appeals for arms. In the *Knesset* foreign policy debate, Sharett also said that Israel would not hesitate to obtain arms from any possible source. (October 18)

•

A European test for sub-machineguns ranked the Israeli *Uzi* in first place. In second place was the Swedish Karl Gustav which is being used by the *fedayeen*. (October 20)

•

An official announcement stated that the purpose of Sharett's Geneva discussions would be to draw the attention of the representatives of the four powers to the grave danger threatening Israel as a result of Czech arms sales to Egypt. (October 23)

•

UN tells Egypt to quit Nitzana after her attack on the Israeli position in the demilitarized zone. Israel retaliates by raiding Kuntilla, an Egyptian army camp seven kilometers *(four miles)* inside Egypt. (October 29)

•

Prime Minister Ben-Gurion declares that the problem is not simply the security of our independence, territories, frontiers or regime, but the security of our physical survival. (November 2)

•

Egyptians driven from Nitzana. Enemy loses 50 dead and 49 prisoners.(November 3)

•

75,000 people are still living in *ma'abarot*, despite the government's undertakings to evacuate all *ma'abarot* by the end of '55. Apparently the majority of their residents are unwilling to leave. (November 7)

•

Curfew imposed in Jordanian cities. Parliament dissolved as rioters protest joining the Baghdad pact. (December 11)

•

One hundred and forty seven people emigrated from Israel to the US, more than the number of American immigrants who have come to Israel. (December 18)

•

UN Security Council postpones Galilee debate. Israeli Ambassador Eban stated Syria had established bridgeheads in Israeli territory along north-west shore of the Sea of Galilee. (December 22)

Egypt - Czechoslovak Arms Deal is Signed

Nasser. Invaded Nitzana.

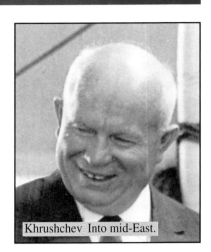
Khrushchev. Into mid-East.

The extensive arms deal between Czechoslovakia and Egypt signed in October caused deep concern to Israel and the West. The details of the deal, which was signed after the Israel Defense Forces' reprisals in Khan Yunis and Gaza, were leaked to the press and shed new light on the arms race in the Middle East.

Czechoslovakia was to supply Egypt with weapons from the Eastern Bloc valued at hundreds of millions of dollars. These weapons included hundreds of *Stalin* tanks and modern *MiG* aircraft. Since Israel had relatively fewer heavy weapons and airplanes, this deal injected a new element of danger into the Middle East arena.

The United States and Britain made a futile attempt to eliminate the Middle East from the arms race. Minister of Foreign Affairs Moshe Sharett met with his American counterpart and the US undertook to supply Israel with defensive weapons in response to the Soviet arms, so that parity would be maintained.

IDF Raid Syrian Posts near the Sea of Galilee

Soldiers of the raiding force depart from Kibbutz Ein Gev on the operation.

On Dec. 11, at least 50 Syrian soldiers were killed and 30 taken prisoner during an Israel Defense Forces' retaliatory operation against Syrian army units overlooking the Sea of Galilee. The IDF's most extensive reprisal was executed by Paratroop Battalion 890, a *Golani* squadron and artillery units. According to sources, more than 300 soldiers took part in the operation.

The IDF took the Syrian forces by surprise after they had crossed the Sea of Galilee and the area near the mouth of the River Jordan. The paratroopers attacked the fortified posts and conquered them in hand-to-hand battle. Four IDF soldiers were killed, and 12 injured.

Yitzhak Ben-Menachem, known as 'Gulliver,' died in the operation. He had commanded Squadron D in place of 'Motta Gur, who had been injured in the Khan Yunis operation.

Action to Wipe Out Illiteracy

On Jan. 26, Education Minister Zalman Aranne initiated a new initiative to eradicate illiteracy in Israel. Four hundred thousand Israeli residents can neither read nor write in Hebrew.

Since the Ministry of Education and Culture had no budget to fund the operation, it was decided to rely on volunteers to teach Hebrew in the workplace. The volunteer workers were to teach their co-workers during lunch breaks throughout February and March.

The workers who knew Hebrew would teach their co-workers simple tasks, such as signing their name, identifying street names and understanding their salary slips. To aid the project, a book by Ben-Zion Reich called 'Hebrew for the People' was distributed, and included reading and writing exercises and guidelines for the volunteers.

Learning Hebrew. 400,000 citizens cannot read or write in Hebrew.

Four Israeli Prisoners of War Return from Syrian Captivity

Four soldiers return from Syrian captivity after 15 months. The fifth, Uri Elan, took his own life in prison.

On Mar. 29 four Israel Defense Forces soldiers returned to Israel after 15 months of captivity. In return, Israel freed 41 Syrian POW's.

The four soldiers - Meir Moses, Ya'acov Lind, Gad Kastelanitz and Meir Ya'acobi - had been captured on Dec. 8, 1954, during a mission to plant wiretapping devices near a Syrian army camp in Syrian territory. The squad had a fifth member, Uri Elan, who committed suicide in captivity after he had been tortured and made to believe that all his friends had been executed.

The POW exchanges took place on the B'not Ya'acov Bridge. Thirty-five of the Syrian prisoners had been captured in two border-crossing missions aimed at capturing hostages for negotiation purposes. Six others had been captured after they had infiltrated across the border into Israel.

The liberated soldiers were awarded a short vacation with their families, after which an investigation was held regarding the circumstances of their capture and their long term of captivity. They had been severely tortured in the Syrian prison.

1956
JANUARY - MARCH

French elections fail to break the political deadlock. President Rene Coty named socialist Guy Mollet as prime minister and charged him with the formation of France's 22nd post-war government. (January 3)

•

The dissolution of parliament ruled illegal in Jordan. Jordan's caretaker government quits. Riots against Jordan joining the Baghdad pact continue, curfew is imposed and military censorship is proclaimed. Prime Minister Samir Rifai warns Egypt and Saudia to cease anti-Jordanian propaganda. 2,000 British paratroopers sent to Cyprus as reinforcements due to the situation in the Middle East. (January 4)

•

President Eisenhower and Secretary of State Dulles called on the United States as a whole to wake up to the necessity of countering the efforts of the Soviet Union to penetrate the Middle East. Dulles went on to say that the United States must counter these measures not by outbidding Communism in sheer amounts of economic aid, but by making new independent peoples and states feel that they can best satisfy their wants by becoming and remaining part of the community of free nations. (January 11)

•

The British may delay their formal military withdrawal from the Suez Canal because of the general situation in the Middle East. (January 12)

•

An increase in the egg ration. The ration in January is ten eggs per person, whereas in December it was nine. As a result, the price of eggs on the free market has been lowered. (January 12)

•

The first Hebrew prayer book to be published in the Soviet Union, since the Russian Revolution is being printed. Permission to produce the prayer book follows the earlier allocation of paper to the Russian Orthodox Church for the first printing of the Bible since the revolution. (January 16)

•

The UN Security Council unanimously adopts a Western resolution condemning Israel for her December 11 attack on Syria. (January 19)

Eisenhower rules against sale of arms to Israel at the present time. France, Italy and Canada are mentioned unofficially in London as potential suppliers. (April 2)

•

Memorial day for the victims of the Nazis was held for the first time at the site of the memorial center, Yad Vashem, which is still in the early stages of construction. (April 8)

•

President Rene Coty to put seal of approval on plan to send 100,000 reinforcements for the army in Algeria by early May. 70,000 are reservists. (April 11)

•

Eight French *Mystere-IV* 'planes, with four more to follow, arrive in Israel. The *Mysteres* are the first modern war-planes Israel has received since she began to press for arms from the West. (April 12)

•

A stern warning that the nation may face in the ninth year of its statehood "A supreme test graver and more difficult than that which we faced successfully eight years ago" was issued by the Prime Minister in Independence Day broadcast. (April 15)

•

Dissolution of Cominform officially confirmed. The Cominform: Communist Information Bureau was set up at a secret meeting in Poland by nine nations in 1947. (April 17)

•

UNICEF ambassador, the actor Danny Kaye, arrived in Israel from Istanbul. (April 26)

•

Dr. Nahum Goldmann, Chairman of the Jewish Agency Executive, warned that within a generation or two, it is possible that three million Jews would be wiped out in Eastern Europe. Generally speaking the East Europeans cannot be accused of anti-Semitism but without Jewish schools, ties with other Jews, and Zionism which is considered counter-revolutionary, despite egalitarianism the death sentence is a fact. "It's our solemn duty and right to ask East European governments to make it possible for Jewish communities to exist and survive." (April 29)

Fedayeen Claim 17 Dead in Attacks on Settlements

Dozens of attacks by Egyptian soldiers and *fedayeen* gangs took place against settlements in the south. On Apr. 4, five soldiers were killed by Egyptian soldiers, who attacked IDF posts near Kibbutz Nirim. The IDF retaliated with cannon shots aimed at the Dir el-Balah refugee camp in the Gaza Strip.

On Apr. 5, the Egyptians retaliated by shelling hundreds of settlements along the Gaza Strip border. Four soldiers and two members of Kibbutz Nahal Oz were injured. In Ein Ha'Shlosha, severe damage was caused to the *kibbutz* infirmary. It was only thanks to the evacuation of the children to the shelters a few minutes earlier that no one was injured. Severe damage was also caused to houses and property in Nirim, Kisufim and Kfar Gaza.

Additional attacks took place in Ashkelon, Kibbutz Giv'at Haim, Kibbutz Nitzanim, Ketziot, Shapir, Tekuma, Achiezer, and many other settlements. The terrorists' method was similar: in most cases hand grenades were thrown into houses late at night while the victims were sleeping peacefully. The terrorists also shot at cars and exploded pipe lines, water wells and lighting posts. Life in the south became unbearable. Despite IDF efforts, the terrorists usually returned to Gaza unharmed.

On Apr. 11, terrorists penetrated into Moshav Shafrir, near Ramla. They entered the synagogue and fired at children and their minders who were praying there, killing three children and one adult; five other children were injured.

Bodies of infiltrators in the south. Terror in southern Israel and in the center became unbearable.

On Apr. 29, Egyptian soldiers murdered 21-year-old Roi Ruthenberg, a member of Kibbutz Nahal Oz. Roi was trying to chase away Egyptian solders who had penetrated into Israel. He was shot, wounded, and dragged by the Egyptian soldiers to the Gaza Strip, where he was tortured and murdered.

When Ruthenberg's body was returned to Israel, his eyes had been pierced and his body was severely mutilated.

Chief of Staff Moshe Dayan emotionally eulogized Ruthenberg at the funeral. *Some of Ruthenberg's murderers were caught after 'Operation Kadesh,' in April when the IDF raided several Egyptian posts in the Gaza Strip and Sinai.*

The IDF chief of staff is also digging trenches.

War Alert in Egypt, Syria and Israel

All Arab countries bordering Israel have declared a high-level military alert. Soldiers there have received orders to "drive back any Israeli acts of aggression." Public and private shelters are being constructed in all Israeli cities and settlements, including those that are not near the borders.

Meanwhile, the arms race in the region continues. Syria has received Soviet weapons, and Israel has received fighter 'planes from France and Canada.

The situation in the Middle East headed the agenda in the meeting between Prime Minister Nikolai Bulganin of the Soviet Union and Prime Minister Anthony Eden of Great Britain, in London. The Soviet Union called upon Israel and the Arab countries to adhere to the cease-fire agreements, but continued to arm the Arab countries with modern weapons.

On Apr. 19, Egypt agreed to adhere to the cease-fire in the region, but ten days later Egyptian soldiers murdered Roi Ruthenberg from Kibbutz Nahal Oz.

Sharett Resigns. Golda Meir to Head Foreign Ministry

Minister of Foreign Affairs Moshe Sharett resigned on June 18, following a dispute with Prime Minister David Ben-Gurion. Relations between Sharett and Ben-Gurion had deteriorated on political, security and personal levels. In opposition to Ben-Gurion's activist approach, Sharett preferred the moderate policy that has characterized his actions since he first served in directing Israel's foreign policy after the murder of Chaim Arlozorov in 1933.

Sharett and Ben-Gurion worked side by side in the leadership of the nation-to-be, and later, the State of Israel. Their dispute was aggravated following 'Operation Sea of Galilee' against Syrian army posts on the eastern shore of the Sea of Galilee.

Sharett, who was in the United States at the time, defined the operation as a "stab in the back of the foreign minister." He claimed that Ben-Gurion had undermined his efforts to obtain arms from Washington.

Golda Meir, formerly labor minister, was appointed to replace Sharett. The new labor minister was to be Mordechai Namir, who resigned his post as head of the *Histadrut* in order to make way for Pinhas Lavon.

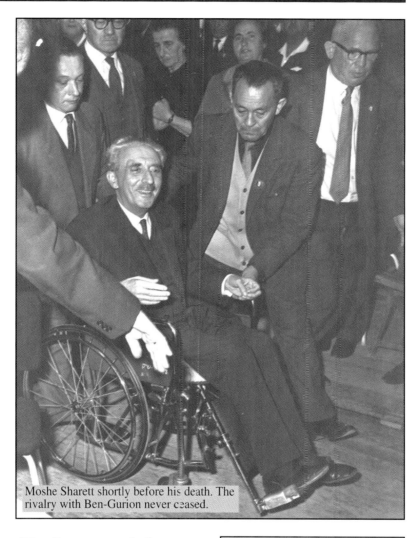

Moshe Sharett shortly before his death. The rivalry with Ben-Gurion never ceased.

Israel is anxious to resume work on the Jordan River project, Minister of Foreign Affairs Moshe Sharett stated. (May 5)

●

Israeli stamps have captured the fancy of American collectors. Among reasons stated for collectors' interest in Israel's stamps are interest in the land of the bible and the fact that Israel is only eight years old so collectors feel they can make entire collections. (May 6)

●

Japan and Russia sign a fishing pact to end dispute over salmon fishing in the Pacific, and agree to resume peace talks which were broken off in March. (May 15)

●

An Egyptian journalist spent 12 days touring Israel this month, with the permission of Israeli and Egyptian governments. Ibrahim Izzat of the Cairo weekly '*Rose el-Yossef*' had stated at an international journalists' meeting in Europe that Israel is a dictatorship. Members of the Israeli press invited him to come and see for himself. (May 20)

●

President Tito of Yugoslavia is in Moscow. Diplomats said the Russians are determined to show the extent of changes that have taken place since Stalin's death in March 1953. (June 2)

●

Argentine government forces crush Peronist revolt; 33 insurgents executed. (June 10)

●

US still prepared to offer any practical assistance to help Britain and Greece find a solution for the problem of Cyprus. (June 14)

●

Chancellor Adenauer says negotiations are underway between West Germany and Israel on the establishment of diplomatic relations. (June 14)

●

Destroyers '*Jaffa*' and '*Eilat*' reach Haifa. The two ships would have redressed the naval balance in the Middle East had not the Soviets upset it by supplying two destroyers to Egypt. (June 20)

●

Lenin's famous 'testament,' the letter he sent to the 13th Communist Party Congress in 1923, in which he expressed his distrust of Stalin, is made public for first time. (June 30)

Mordechai Oren Released from Czechoslovak Prison in Prague

On May 13, after four and a half years of imprisonment, Mordechai Oren, one of *Mapam's* leaders, was released from Czechoslovak prison. Oren had been arrested on Dec. 31, 1951, on his arrival in Prague in order to locate his relative, Shimon Orenstein, who had been arrested by Czechoslovakia's authorities a few months earlier.

Despite being a guest of the unions and a close friend of Czechoslovakia's communist leaders, Oren was put on trial and convicted of espionage. After being severely tortured by his investigators, Oren confessed to spying on the Czech government, and was sentenced to 15 years in prison.

As a result of Israel's continuous diplomatic efforts, Oren was finally released and ordered to leave the country immediately. He joined his wife in Zurich, and the two returned to Israel two days later.

Speaking at the airport, Oren said that despite the great injustice he had suffered he was still loyal to revolutionary socialism. On his return he resumed his positions in *Mapam*.

It was Oren's admission that he had spied that served Czechoslovakia years later in the show trial which took place against deposed cabinet leaders.

Mordechai Oren. Homecoming.

New Taxes to Fund Arms Purchase

In light of the economic situation, the *Knesset* legislated the Yahav-Magen law on May 16, in order to raise the 50 million Israeli lira needed for the purchase of weapons and construction of shelters. The law levied new taxes, including a fixed salary tax deduction for the forthcoming ten months. A special tax was also levied on radios (3 IL), telephone bills (10%), electricity bills (20%), automobiles (20 - 75 IL), beverages, movie tickets and various other items.

British Foreign Secretary Selwyn Lloyd says Britain must maintain its force on Cyprus. The Cyprus bases guard Middle East oil: "We cannot therefore accept any doubt about their availability." (July 7)

•

An agreement for the supply of oil was signed between Israel and the USSR in Moscow. This is seen around the world as proof of the USSR's recognition of Israel's status in the Middle East. (July 17)

•

America's adherence to the Baghdad Pact seen likely in London after the US withdraws loan offer for the Aswan Dam to Egypt. (July 21)

•

Egyptian Embassy in Paris says King Saud of Saudi Arabia has decided to approach the US on behalf of Egypt about the status of the Suez Canal, thus sending a warning about the status of oil supplies in the eventuality that the situation between Egypt, the Arab nations and the West deteriorates. (August 23)

•

Tanks of the National Guard face white race-rioters in the US over the admission of 12 Negro pupils to the local high school, in accordance with a Federal Court order. (September 3)

•

Abba Eban: Egypt's troubles do not ease ours. As the target of Arab national enmity, Israel's paramount interest is still to adjust the arms imbalance between herself and her Arab neighbors. The Suez Crisis has made the world more aware of Israel's rightful claim to receive arms. (September 4)

In a letter sent to the five nation committee in Cairo, headed by Australia's Prime Minister Robert Menzies, Nasser flatly rejects the London Conference proposals on Suez. (September 9)

•

Algerian rebels victimize Jews. Police sources in Algiers disclosed that local Jewish merchants have been victimized by a widespread extortion plan to finance the Algerian rebellion. (September 13)

•

"Of all the beautiful gifts and birthday greetings, I enjoyed Canada's gift the most," said Ben-Gurion, referring to Canada's decision to sell 24 Saber jets to Israel. (September 21)

Nasser Nationalizes Suez Canal

Gamal Abdul Nasser announced the nationalization of the Suez Canal before a crowd of 300,000 excited supporters in Alexandria on July 27. Nasser moved to nationalize the stock company of the canal, registered in Egypt, whose capital was mostly owned by British, French and American investors. The nationalization came in response to those countries' governments' refusal to fund the construction of the Aswan Dam.

Nasser's speech was the main event celebrating the fourth anniversary of the 'Free Officers' Revolu-

Nasser. Confiscated British property.

tion' and the removal of King Farouk. Nasser attacked Great Britain and the United States, as well as Israel, for having refused to fund the dam and declared a naval embargo on Israeli ships in the Suez Canal.

The West was shocked. Great Britain, France and America attempted to forge a joint plan against the nationalization. France and Britain drafted thousands of soldiers, and forces were deployed to the Middle East and the canal zone. Britain froze all Egyptian-owned foreign currency held in British banks.

Fatal Incidents on Jordanian Border. IDF Swiftly Retaliates

The climax of the retaliatory actions. Paratroopers preparing to blow up Kalkilya police station.

Bloody incidents on the Jordanian border continued. At the beginning of September four people were shot dead on the road to Eilat; the shots came from the direction of the Jordanian border.

King Hussein announced a state of emergency and amassed a large military force near the border, following Israel's declaration that aggressors would be punished.

On Sept. 10, seven soldiers were killed by machine gun and mortar shelling in the Dwema area opposite the Hebron mountains.

The next day, Israel Defense Forces' troops stormed A-Rahawe, the Jordanian National Guard headquarters.

On Sept. 12, the Jordanians murdered three Druze guards in the Arava. The IDF responded with an assault on the Arrandal police station in the Arava, where they had followed the tracks of the murderers.

On Sept. 23, Jordanians opened fire into a crowd during an archeological gathering in Kibbutz Ramat Rachel, leaving four dead and 17 injured. Fearing an Israeli response, the Jordanian government tried to convince Israel that it had been the act of an insane soldier.

On the following day two more Israelis were killed: a tractor driver was kidnapped and murdered near the Sheikh Hussein Bridge, and a young girl from Aminadav was mur-

dered while picking figs in the fields of the moshav.

The IDF responded immediately. On Sept. 25 Jordanian Legion outposts in the Hussan area, southwest of Jerusalem, were attacked. A force of IDF paratroopers took over the Hussan police station, killing 39 legionnaires and blowing up the building. Ten paratroopers were killed in the assault, three of them members of Kibbutz Zikim.

Two weeks later, an IDF force executed the largest retaliatory raid to date. The raid on the Kalkilya police station was the largest military action since the War of Independence: 88 Jordanian legionnaires were killed, and the IDF suffered 18 fatalities.

The IDF Conquers Sinai

The ceremony celebrating the end of fighting. Chief of Staff Moshe Dayan. On his left, Brigadier-General Assaf Simhoni. On his right, Colonel Avraham Yaffe.

On Oct. 29 at 9.00 p.m. the IDF spokesman announced that IDF forces had penetrated Egyptian territory and conquered Kuntila, 60 km (38 miles) northwest of Eilat, and Ras-el-Nakeb, 10 km (6 miles) from Eilat. Parachuted forces took over an important crossroads near the canal.

So began the largest military operation carried out by Israel since the War of Independence. Within seven days, the IDF had conquered the entire Sinai Peninsula, had taken control of Tiran (from which Egyptian forces had blocked the shipping route to Eilat) and the Gaza Strip, from where most of the *fedayeen* entered Israel. The Suez Canal was conquered in a joint operation with the armies of France and Britain.

One hundred and seventy-one IDF soldiers were killed in action, including Brigadier General Assaf Simhoni, commander of the southern command.

The 'Kadesh Operation' was initiated when paratroopers, commanded by 'Raful' (Raphael Eitan), landed in the Mitla Pass near Suez. They waged a bloody battle against Egyptian forces entrenched in the narrow mountain pass. Meanwhile, ground forces entered Sinai, heading towards the canal. the Gaza Strip. and Sharm el-Sheikh.

On the following day, Oct. 30, France and Britain declared an ultimatum, ordering Egypt and Israel to stop the fighting, to retreat ten miles from the Suez Canal and to allow the positioning of a French-British force in the canal zone.

Israel accepted the ultimatum, but Nasser rejected it and ordered a national mobilization. France was willing to take immediate action against Egypt. Great Britain hesitated.

Unprecedented havoc broke loose in London; the Labor party tried to overthrow Eden's government. In the US, Israel and the two superpowers were accused of conspiracy.

Next day, IDF forces overran all Egyptian posts near Rafiah and El-Arish, the undeclared capital of the Sinai Peninsula. Over the next two days, El-Arish was captured, followed by the entire Gaza Strip. The IDF held more than 5,000 POW's, including many senior officers. The Egyptian army collapsed, and its soldiers, thirsty and barefoot, made their way towards the Suez Canal.

Hitler's successor leaves jail today. Germany's FBI strengthening its watch on the neo-Nazi movement in anticipation of the release from Spandau prison of ex-Grand Admiral Karel Doenitz. He is the first of seven blacklisted Nazis imprisoned in Spandau after the Nuremberg war crimes trials to be freed, having served his full ten-year sentence. (October 1)

•

Israel's largest passenger ship, the 9000 ton 'Theodor Herzl' slides down the shipyard slip in Hamburg. (October 2)

•

"If the UN has not the strength to force the Arabs to keep the peace, we will have no other choice than to see to it that everyone who raises a hand against us will pay dearly for his action," says Foreign Minister Golda Meir. (October 4)

•

Mary Frances Hagen, an American citizen, was convicted of spying for Syria and sentenced to one year's imprisonment. Hagen worked as a secretary in the Syrian delegation to the UN and was arrested ten days after her arrival in Israel. A romantic relationship with a Syrian intelligence soldier was the basis for her spying activity. (October 11)

•

A detachment of border guard soldiers killed 43 inhabitants of Kafr Kassem. The inhabitants returned to the village on the eve of war, not knowing a curfew had been imposed on all Arab villages in the northern region on the first day of the Sinai Campaign. Two years later, eight of the soldiers were convicted of murder. Among them was the unit's commander who had instructed his soldiers to kill anyone who violated the curfew. (October 29)

•

Suleiman Nablus, the pro-Egyptian leader of the National Socialist Party, completed the formation of a new Jordanian Cabinet, which was sworn in by King Hussein. (October 29)

•

UK and France bomb Egyptian army targets, using Cyprus bases. Egyptian destroyer captured and towed to Haifa, after shelling the city. (October 30)

Egyptian cannon facing the Straits of Tiran. The danger has passed.

A paratrooper at the Mitla Pass.

Egypt's Sinai army in full flight. Israel forces seal off the Gaza Strip. UK and French navies converging on Suez. (November 1)

•

Red Army crushes Hungary as Nagy is held. The UN calls on the Soviet Union to halt its armed attack on Hungary and withdraw. President Eisenhower asks Premier Bulganin to withdraw Soviet forces from Hungary. (November 4)

•

Israel's flag flies over the Tiran Straits. UN gets general ceasefire pledges. 177 Israeli soldiers were killed during the campaign. (November 6)

•

Eisenhower wins 41 states, but Democrats control Congress. First job: to replace Dulles and find someone who will command the confidence and respect of the US's allies. The fact that Dulles is hospitalized for at least another month offers the opportunity to request his resignation. (November 6)

•

Israel is ready to withdraw from Egyptian territory after the arrival of a UN force at the Canal. The UN General Assembly emergency session calls on Israel once again immediately to withdraw all its forces behind the 1949 armistice lines. (November 8)

•

Soviets repeat 'volunteers' warning. US declares it will oppose the move. A Tass statement today said government circles expressed their satisfaction at the decision of France, Britain and Israel to cease their aggression in Egypt, at the same time they will not prevent Soviet citizens from joining Egyptian defense forces if the three powers do not withdraw. (November 10)

•

Ben-Gurion refutes USSR 'aggression' charge, rejects Egypt's right for compensation and calls for direct negotiations. (November 18)

•

US Ambassador to the UN, Henry Cabot Lodge says that the US possesses information that since November 14 at least 16,000 Hungarians have been deported to the USSR. Israel backs move at the UN to halt deportations from Hungary. (November 19)

Superpowers Confront Israel. Demand Immediate Withdrawal

Egyptian prisoners of war. The IDF captured more than 5,000 Egyptian POW's. The Egyptians captured one pilot.

On Nov. 8, only a day after Prime Minister David Ben-Gurion's declaration in the *Knesset* that the previous joint border with Egypt was a thing of the past, he announced that Israel was ready to withdraw its troops from Sinai. He also stated that Israel agreed to a multinational police force presence in the Sinai Peninsula. At the same time, Ben-Gurion emphasized that Israel would not allow any foreign force to enter its territories.

The purpose of the second announcement was to avoid a deterioration of the situation in the Middle East. The Soviet Union had threatened to interfere directly in the crisis by sending 'volunteers' to Egypt.

The Soviet Union had severed its diplomatic relations with Israel during the Sinai Operation, and now demanded that Israel pay compensation to Egypt. Ben-Gurion refused this demand.

Ben-Gurion. Forced to announce that Israel agrees to withdraw.

Egypt Deports the Jews

In mid-November, less than a month after Egypt's defeat at the hands of Israel, Egypt started to expel a large number of its Jews, holding many of them in concentration camps. Dozens were indicted, charged with treason. The Egyptian authorities issued deportation orders to all 50,000 Jewish citizens of the country, revoking their citizenship. Deportation orders were also issued to all British and French residents.

The Jewish community's property was abandoned and confiscated; among the assets confiscated by the Egyptian Government were factories and large department stores. Egyptian masses were incited to injure Jewish convoys passing through city centers. The Jews were bound and massively squashed on trucks.

Heavy Restrictions on Use of Electricity and Gas

Restrictions on the use of vehicles were also introduced on Dec. 2. The government restricted the use of gas and electricity, fearing a gas shortage. Similar restrictions were imposed in France following the interruption to the supply of gas as a result of the Middle East crisis.

The drivers of all privately owned automobiles and taxis were ordered to ground their vehicles for one day each week. The country was divided into five regions and car owners were not allowed to travel outside the region where they lived. The scope of public transportation was reduced, as was the number of buses in service.

Major restrictions were also placed on electricity use. Lighting in private homes was limited to one light bulb of no more than 60 watts per room, and the total monthly consumption of electricity was restricted according to apartment size. Water boilers were allowed to be used for two nights per week, and neon lights in store windows and on billboards were banned. Electricity use in industry and offices was also reduced.

Tens of thousands protest Ben-Gurion's decision to withdraw from Sinai.

Israeli Archeological Discoveries in the Sinai

On Dec. 6, delegations of archeologists from the Israeli Antiquities Department and the Hebrew University discovered important archeological finds in the Sinai Desert. The delegations toured the Sinai for two and a half weeks and reached certain sites even before the Israel Defense Forces.

One of the delegations excavated in the Kadesh-Barnea area, which was one of the important sites of the Israelites who had wandered in the Sinai on their way to Canaan.

The other delegation researched St. Catherine's Monastery and discovered an ancient library containing 3,200 manuscripts and artique documents as well as 7,000 books in various languages. These findings were proof of the cultural wealth of the monks in the ninth and tenth centuries.

The archeologists stated that this was the first time that historic sites in the Sinai had been thoroughly researched.

1956
DECEMBER

Jewish refugees arrive from Hungary and Egypt, in Israel. (December 4)

●

In a statement to the *Knesset*, Prime Minister Ben-Gurion expressed his profound regret at the killing of a number of Arabs at Kafr Kassem by members of the border police on October 29. Ben-Gurion appointed a three-man committee to investigate the matter. He continued: "I feel it my duty on behalf of the government, the police force and myself to express profound anxiety that such an act was possible - an act which strikes a blow at the most sacred foundations of human morality drawn from Israel's *Torah*." (December 8)

●

Chief of Staff Moshe Dayan said that the Egyptians had quality weapons but not the men to use them effectively, and that Nasser's plan to build a powerful Arab army had been shattered in the Sinai Campaign. Dayan also said one of the principal causes of the IDF's success was the equipment supplied to us by the friendliest nation toward us today - France. (December 15)

●

Beersheba's residents decided to ostracize the city resident who charged 2 lirot to a soldier returning from Sinai for the use of her shower. (December 15)

●

7,000 residents left Israel in 1956, including many new immigrants from Morocco who decided to return to their homeland because of social and economic difficulties which they encountered in Israel. (December 20)

●

The 47-day occupation of Port Said ends as the last Anglo-French forces leave under the umbrella of UN forces. Israel is to withdraw from Egypt in two phases: to El-Arish by the first week of January and completely later. (December 23)

●

Salvage operations begin at the southern end of the Suez Canal with six UK ships under the UN flag, mines being the main obstacle for resuming full-scale clearing operations. (December 27)

Egypt revokes the 1954 treaty with Britain on Suez Canal bases. Britain does not accept the right of the Egyptian government to unilaterally abrogate the agreement. (January 1)

•

Notables of Kafr Kassem write to the prime minister about their appreciation of the government's stand and efforts to investigate the murders of 47 villagers by the border police, on the day the Sinai Campaign began. (January 1)

•

Nasser declares he will not allow British and French ships to pass through the canal as long as Israel does not withdraw from the Gaza Strip. (January 6)

•

Harold Macmillan became Britain's prime minister in succession to Sir Anthony Eden, who resigned due to ill heath. (January 9)

•

Israel will approach the UN with a proposal to begin negotiations aimed at securing freedom of shipping in the Gulf of Aqaba, as a prerequisite for her withdrawal from the eastern coast of the Sinai Peninsula. (January 15)

•

Exchange of prisoners between Israel and Egypt. In exchange for 5,850 Egyptian prisoners, Egypt released only four Israeli prisoners. Only one of the prisoners was captured during the Sinai Campaign, the others had been imprisoned for over a year. (January 27)

•

The Soviet Union states that Raoul Wallenberg, a Swedish diplomat who saved many Jews during World War II and who disappeared after Soviet troops entered Budapest in 1945, died two years later in a Moscow prison. (February 10)

•

State Department officials said that the US is willing to use moral pressure but not force to carry out its proposed move to support Israel's right to free navigation in the Gulf of Aqaba. (February 14)

•

Six European nations: France, West Germany, Italy, Holland, Belgium and Luxembourg announce their agreement to create a free European 'Common Market' (EEC). (February 20)

IDF Withdraws from Sinai

A picture of the 'Rais' Nasser also returns to Israel with the withdrawing troops.

On Jan. 15, two months after reaching the Suez Canal, the Israel Defense Forces withdrew from most of the territory they had occupied in the Sinai Peninsula. This completed the second phase of the withdrawal from the territories which Israel had occupied as a result of the 'Kadesh Operation.'

IDF forces evacuated El-Arish, the capital of the peninsula, and transferred it to newly arrived United Nations forces. Two hours later, Egyptian units entered the city. The IDF retained a narrow strip between Eilat and Sharm el-Sheikh, and the Gaza Strip.

At this stage, Israel intended to continue occupying the Gaza Strip. The residents of the area joined forces with Israeli taxpayers and during January various taxes were collected in the Gaza Strip.

The government proposed the 'Gaza Plan' to the United Nations, in which all military forces would be evacuated from the area, while civil and social services would be super-

From the Suez Canal - back to the Negev.

vised by the UN. According to the plan, Israeli police were to remain in the area and assist UN forces in maintaining order. In response, the UN condemned Israel for not retreating to the cease-fire lines. Only in March did Israel finally bow to international pressure, and Ben-Gurion,

almost in tears, addressed a Cabinet meeting. "I am the one who gave our young men the order to stand and fight, and now I have to explain to them why we must retreat..." Five days later, the IDF evacuated the Gaza Strip in a quiet operation carried out at night.

25,000 Polish Jews have made Application for Aliya

Twenty-five thousand Polish Jews, almost half the country's Jewish population, have applied to emigrate to Israel. The main reason was the poor economic situation, but the renewal of anti-Semitic activity was

also a factor. For instance, many Jews from the Lodz medical school received anonymous letters demanding they give up their jobs and leave the country. In contrast, in the February edition of the Communist Party

newspaper, articles and letters were published which condemned anti-Semitism and called on Jews to stay in the country.

In 1957, Poland first allowed Jewish emigration to Israel.

Terror on Borders. Syria Targets Kibbutz Gadot

The result of a direct hit on Kibbutz Gadot. The Syrians selected this kibbutz as their favorite target.

The attacks on border areas continued.

At the beginning of May, one man was killed and three injured in three separate attacks on Israeli vehicles near Be'er Menuha, on the road to Eilat.

On June 16 an engineer was killed near the Jordan River by a Syrian sniper. The engineer was performing a routine check of the River Jordan hydrometric stations.

A week later, a member of Kibbutz Gadot was killed by Syrian forces firing on the *kibbutz*.

Machine-gun fire targeted the *kibbutz* when most of the members were in the dining room or returning from work in the fields. Raya Goldschmidt, a paramedic, was shot on her way to the clinic and died shortly afterwards.

On the border of the Gaza Strip, several Israelis were injured by mines planted on dirt roads.

The cattle herds of Kibbutz Nir Yitzhak were stolen several times.

In years to come, Kibbutz Gadot would become a favorite target for Syrian army shelling and sniper fire.

Eilat Port is Re-opened

On Mar. 22, five months after the Kadesh Operation, Eilat's port again became operational.

The first cargo ship to enter the port was heartily welcomed. Three days later, the Danish ship *'Birgitte Toft'* became the first foreign ship since the Kadesh Operation to cross the Straits of Tiran and enter Israel. Despite Arab threats, the closure of the Straits of Tiran was not renewed.

The removal of the naval closure benefited the southern city; Eilat's hotels were full. Plans for developing the city and expanding the port were accelerated, and a road to Beersheba was paved.

Many people specifically requested to move to Eilat but were refused and most of the city's residents were new immigrants.

The construction of an oil pipeline from Eilat to Beersheba was completed in April. The country's longest oil pipeline, it transported oil from Eilat's port to Beersheba and from Beersheba to the oil refineries in Haifa.

Eilat's port.

Last Israeli contingents move out of the Gaza Strip. Mob rules Gaza as *fedayeen* lead reprisals. Israel warns Gaza situation heading for explosion if *fedayeen* not checked. Israel informs the UN of renewal of raids from Gaza. (March 7)

•

Four young men between the ages of 19-22 were shot in Jordan when trying to get to Petra. Their bodies were brought to Israel two days later. Petra attracted many young people, most of whom did not return to Israel alive. *In 1994, after the signing of the peace treaty between Israel and Jordan, Petra opened its gates to Israeli tourists.* (March 22)

•

Bermuda conference urges quick enactment of UN decisions on the Gulf of Aqaba and Gaza. Israel can expect strong British and American pressure for UN forces to be stationed on Israel's side of the border. (March 24)

•

The trial has begun of 11 members of the border police for the murder of 47 villagers at Kafr Kassem on Oct. 29. (March 25)

•

First tanker brings 16,700 tons of oil from Persian Gulf to Eilat. The French have taken a decision to help build the long Eilat-Haifa pipeline. (April 6)

•

Suez Canal cleared for maximum draught shipping following the towing of the last frigate blocking the canal to the Bitter Lakes. (April 8)

•

Hussein bans political parties, imposes martial law. These steps were taken against the pro-Egyptian opposition threatening his overthrow. US Sixth Fleet to the E. Mediterranean to prevent Jordan's carve-up. (April 25)

•

Yael Dayan, daughter of Moshe Dayan, who was chief of staff during the Sinai Campaign, has completed the IDF officers' course. Her parents and brothers, Ehud and Assaf, attended the graduation ceremony. *In 1992, Yael Dayan was elected to the 13th Knesset, and thus created history: three generations of MK's - grandfather Shmuel, father Moshe, and granddaughter Yael.* (May 24)

US arms to Jordan for internal security only. The State Department said the $20 million was allocated in accordance with the US desire to see Jordan remain independent. (July 1)

•

One killed, seven wounded in a ten-hour attack by Syrians at Kibbutz Gonen. Three cease-fire calls by the UN Truce Supervision Organization were ignored by the Syrians. Israel has expressed its concern to the US over the increase of unprovoked incidents by Syria. Contact was also understood to have been made by Israel with Britain and France. (July 9)

•

British troops and aircraft have moved towards Muscat and Oman to aid the Sultan quell the rebels, now in control of the interior around the Nizwa area. (July 21)

•

Six million Israeli pounds have been made available by the Rothschild family for the erection of the new *Knesset* building in Jerusalem. (July 22)

•

Cairo allows Haifa-bound Danish cargo vessel *'Birgitte Toft'* into the canal but seizes Israeli sailor. The sailor was later released but no reason was given for his detention. (July 22)

•

A record in the history of Israel - 8,000 Israelis left the country in July. Only 870 declared outright that they will not be returning to Israel. On the other hand, more than 5,000 new immigrants arrived in July. (August 1)

•

Syrian security chiefs sacked in a coup and a member of the Communist party is appointed chief of staff. Syria's metamorphosis into a Soviet satellite is not expected to cause flare-ups along Israeli border now. Concern in Jerusalem over the long-term results of this political upheaval. Secretary of State Dulles said that Syrian officials controlling arms shipments seem to be influenced by international Communism. Moscow feels confident of being able to counterbalance the US in doubtful areas such as the Middle East. (August 17)

Amos Ben-Gurion Defeats the 'Line of Volunteers'

On July 17, Amos Ben-Gurion, deputy chief of police and son of David Ben-Gurion, won a libel action against four members of the 'Line of Volunteers' - Dr. Appelbaum, Elyakim Ha'etzni, Dr. Simonson and Hanan Rappaport.

Ben-Gurion sued the four for having published a brochure called 'A Danger Lurking from Within,' in which bribery and favoritism among the State's upper echelon had been condemned.

The defense attorney of the four, Shmuel Tamir, attacked Amos Ben-Gurion and the heads of police, and demanded that police investigation documents be disclosed. Senior police officers had refused to disclose those documents.

Shmuel Tamir accused Amos Ben-Gurion of violating both police and municipal regulations, of conduct contradicting public morality, abuse of his position in order to purchase assets at a minimal price, and of having accepted gifts with and without permission.

The judges ruled in Amos Ben-Gurion's favor and ordered the four defendants to pay IL5,300 to Ben-Gurion in damages.

Amos Ben-Gurion had been mentioned as a friend of Yeshayahu Yarkoni and as his partner in the Kurim company. Yarkoni had been involved in a police investigation, and the brochure stated that a high ranking police officer had closed his file at Yarkoni's request.

In the published letter, the four wrote that the friendship between

Amos Ben-Gurion. IL 5,300 damages.

Yarkoni and Amos Ben-Gurion implied moral legitimacy in their business dealing, which might influence an investigator or police officer.

The hearings were a source of public interest for months.

Triangle Villages' Curfew Eased

During a meeting with the five Arab *Knesset* members on July 5, the prime minister announced steps to relieve the plight of the Arab residents of Israel and a program to develop their villages.

Among other items, it was decided to shorten the night curfew that had been in effect in the Arab villages in the Triangle area since the end of the War of Independence. It was also decided that the Arabs of the Galilee would no longer need special permits in order to enter Nazareth, Acre and Afula.

In addition, a special fund was announced by the Ministry of Agriculture for the development of agriculture in the Arab districts.

At that time, there were 115,000 Arabs living in the Galilee and some

Military government. Night curfew shortened.

35,000 in the Triangle region. The easing of the military government regulations represented a change in government policy, which since the founding of the State had neglected

the Moslem minority in favor of the Druze and Christians.

The military government in the Arab villages in the Galilee and the Triangle area was ended in 1967.

Stormy Sabbath Demos Take Place in Tel Aviv

On the eve of Aug. 3, hundreds of *haredim* gathered in the Shapira neighborhood, next to the central 'bus station, for the first demonstration of *haredim* against the 'Dan' company, who had been operating its 'bus services before the end of the Sabbath.

The demonstrators maintained that policemen called to disperse them had hit and injured many, and had even used dogs against them.

The complaints of the Orthodox caused a storm in the Knesset; as a result, the police decided to refrain from using dogs to break up demonstrations.

At the beginning of September, Minister of Transport Moshe Carmel gave his backing to the secular

demand to bring forward the time of the Sabbath 'bus schedule. The Orthodox threatened to resign from the coalition.

A prolonged dispute over public transport also took place in Jerusalem, where Orthodox leaders demanded the cessation of organized Sabbath transport from Jerusalem to the beach.

Grenade in the Knesset. Ben-Gurion is Injured

On Oct. 29 a grenade was thrown into the *Knesset*, injuring the prime minister and three ministers. Minister of Religious Affairs, Moshe Shapira, was severely injured. He underwent several operations and was hospitalized for about two months. Prime Minister David Ben-Gurion, Foreign Minister Golda Meir and Transportation Minister Moshe Carmel were lightly injured in the blast. They were all hospitalized in Hadassah Hospital for several weeks.

Dozens of citizens gathered in front of the hospital daily to hear about the medical condition of the injured ministers.

The assailant, Moshe Dweik, 26, was mentally ill, and his act was not politically motivated. Although the grenade was thrown on the anniversary of the Sinai Operation, Dweik had no connection with any particular political group.

Dweik had come to Israel from Syria as a child and served in the Israel Defense Forces. After finishing his army service, he demanded money from the Jewish Agency on the basis of his poor health.

After sending a threatening letter to the president of the Supreme Court, Dweik was ordered to be given a psychiatric examination and was then hospitalized in the Be'er Ya'acov psychiatric hospital.

A few days after the attempted assassination, Prime Minister David Ben-Gurion sent a personal letter to Dweik's parents, who lived in poverty in the *ma'abara* in Pardessia. He acknowledged their regret regarding the action of their son and promised them that they would suffer no harm.

The Russians launch the first satellite into space, beating the Americans in the space race. *'Sputnik'* orbits the earth every 95 minutes. (October 4)

●

Steel-helmeted militiamen used tear-gas grenades in Warsaw for the third consecutive night of disorders over the banning of the student newspaper *'Po Prostu.'* (October 5)

●

Signals from *'Sputnik'* were picked up today by the Post Office radio services. (October 6)

●

UN Secretary-General Dag Hammarskjold warns that the present quiet and generally satisfactory conditions along the Gaza Strip border could erupt at any moment. (October 12)

●

Albert Camus, the 43-year-old French novelist, was awarded the 1957 Nobel Prize for Literature. Camus is one of a group of postwar French writers calling themselves 'Existentialist.' During the war, he was a founder of the underground resistance publication *'Combat.'* (October 17)

●

In a festive ceremony, the blockage which had stopped the flow of the Hula waters to the River Jordan was freed. Over the past five years the Jordan's channel has been widened to enable the flow of water into the Sea of Galilee. 60,000 dunams (14,826 acres) were gained as the Hula swamp reclamation project entered its final stage. (October 31)

●

40,000 tons of material arrived for the Sinai War. The director-general of the Ministry of Defense revealed that early in 1956 Messrs. Guy Mollet, Bourges Maunoury and Christian Pineau of France decided to meet Israel's demands for military assistance because they understood she was right. "These ties were maintained with a minimum of diplomatic formality and a maximum of personal confidence. Orders for equipment worth millions of dollars were handled by a small group of men who had decided to trust one another." Shimon Peres went on to say this friendship still exists and we will do our best to maintain it. (October 31).

Hey, Let's Go South to Eilat

A final layer of tar. In the background - the Ramon Crater, through which the new road to Eilat passes.

The paving of the new road to Eilat was progressing at full speed. Workmen had already completed the road's foundations and were currently coating it with asphalt and tar.

The new road was intended to open in 1958, to replace the old road to Eilat that went through Ma'ale Akkrabim.

Israeli Diplomat Kidnapped and Tortured in USSR

Israeli diplomat Eliyahu Hazan returned to Israel on Sept. 17, after three days of interrogation in KGB cellars. Hazan was kidnapped and tortured by the Soviet secret police in Odessa.

Hazan, an attache in the Israeli embassy in Moscow, had traveled with his wife to Odessa on Aug. 30, on vacation. A week later, when he was visiting a Jewish acquaintance in the city, secret-police officers burst into the house and arrested the two. The investigators ignored Hazan's diplomatic immunity and interrogated him under threats for three days. They claimed that his wife, who had been hospitalized due to stomach illness, was in their hands.

The Jewish acquaintance was brought into the room, after having undergone severe torture. The secret-police investigators tried to extract information about Israel's embassy, and demanded that Hazan work for the Soviet security forces.

After three days of investigation, the couple was allowed to return to Moscow, where they related what had happened.

Ben-Zvi for Second Term

Ben-Zvi.

The President of Israel, Itzhak Ben-Zvi, was elected on Oct. 28 for a second term. There were no objections to his re-election.

Former defense minister Marshal Georgi Zhukov is expelled from the Communist Party Central Committee and its all-important Presidium. Khrushchev strengthened by the move. The big question in Washington is what will Khrushchev do with the power if he can hold it? (November 2)

•

Eisenhower says America must meet the Soviet challenge by spending substantially more on new weapons. He recalled the days of Nazi Germany, and said not enough people took Hitler at his word. "We shall not make that mistake again," he asserted. He said there should be an accelerated program of education to train more scientists, and in view of Soviet developments, an increase in basic research in the United States. (November 14)

•

Soviets grant Egypt $170 million in economic aid to be repaid in instalments over a 12-year period. (November 20)

•

Starting tomorrow, the Indonesian government has banned all publications in Dutch, circulation of films with Dutch sub-titles and is prohibiting the Dutch royal airlines (KLM) from operating its services in the country. This action is regarded as retaliation to UN inaction to consider Indonesia's claim to Dutch New Guinea. (December 1)

•

Members of the Hebrew Encyclopedia's editorial board complained that the *Histadrut* is trying to influence the encyclopedia's contents. The *Histadrut* claims the editorial board is minimizing the Labor Party's accomplishments and contribution to the State of Israel. Most of the criticism is directed against the sixth volume of the encyclopedia, which is dedicated to 'Eretz Israel,' and its editor in-chief, Dr. Ben-Zion Netanyahu, a revisionist and father of Binyamin Netanyahu. (December 6)

•

El Al *Britannia* aircraft cracks 16 commercial air records, including longest and fastest passenger aircraft, in a non-stop flight from New York to Lod. The 5,900 mile flight took 14 hours 56 minutes. (December 19)

Prime Minister's Military Secretary Commits Suicide

Nehemia Argov with David Ben-Gurion. Committed suicide after injuring a cyclist.

On Nov. 2, Col. Nehemia Argov, the Prime Minister's military secretary, took his own life, after seriously injuring a cyclist on his way from Jerusalem to Tel Aviv. Testifying at the police station, Argov said he had lost control of the car when a bee had stung him in the eye.

Argov wrote in a letter that even if the cyclist was to live, he himself found no reason to continue his life. He donated all his property to the victim of the accident, David Kadosh, who lived in a shed in the *ma'abara* in Ramla.

Argov, 43, Ben-Gurion's military secretary since the State was established, left a long, personal, farewell letter to the prime minister.

On that day, David Ben-Gurion was in hospital, recovering from the injuries caused by a grenade that had been thrown into the *Knesset*. To prevent Ben-Gurion from finding out about the death of Argov, one of the closest people to him, special editions of the newspapers were printed omitting the report about the suicide. Three days later, the sad truth was revealed to Ben-Gurion.

Rumors spread at the time that Argov had either committed suicide or had been executed because of his involvement in espionage on behalf of the Soviet Union. This wave of rumors was only much later disproved.

Soviets Send Dog into Orbit

The Soviet Union has beaten the Americans yet again.

On Nov. 3 they sent *'Sputnik-2'* into space. Inside was the first living creature ever to travel in space - a dog named Laika. She circled the planet at an altitude of 900 km (560 miles).

The dog had to be poisoned to death after a week, when it was discovered that there was no way to return her to earth safely.

Ben-Gurion Resigns over Connection with Germany

On Dec. 30, Prime Minister David Ben-Gurion handed President Itzhak Ben-Zvi a letter of resignation and dissolved the government. The crisis had begun two weeks earlier, when the decision to send a senior official to West Germany on a mission regarding national security issues came to light.

The Cabinet members from the *Ahdut Ha'Avoda* and *Mapam* parties objected to the mission and any contact between Israel, or the Israel Defense Forces, and Germany. The decision was approved in the government by a majority of one vote: the seven *Mapai* members voted in favor and six members voted against the decision.

Following the outcry that arose when the decision was made public, Ben-Gurion canceled the special envoy's mission, and decided to send two official messengers instead.

Ben-Gurion raged at the members of *Ahdut Ha'avoda* who had exposed the affair and damaged the Cabinet's confidentiality. He declared that he could no longer cooperate with a party that would publicly expose such an important political and security issue.

In order to settle the crisis, Ben-Gurion outlined his demands.

He demanded legislation that would enforce the secrecy of Cabinet meetings. He insisted on complete discipline within the coalition with no option of objecting to or even abstaining from votes in the *Knesset*. Ben-Gurion also required a pledge by newspapers owned by political parties to avoid defamation of coalition members.

Skirmishes in North. Tanks Target Syrian Outposts

On Mar. 30, heavy tank combat and mortar shelling broke out between the Israel Defense Forces and Syrian troops in the Galilee hills and Sea of Galilee region. One man was killed - Binyamin Krieger, 23, of Kibbutz Gadot. Krieger was the third casualty in Gadot in six months. Two other residents were slightly injured.

The battle began when Syrian soldiers opened fire on a group of Israeli workers digging a drainage canal for water springs, south of the Hula. The Syrians claimed the work was being carried out in the demilitarized zone, violating ceasefire agreements.

Syria and Egypt Unite. Security Threat to Israel

On Jan. 31 Syria and Egypt announced their unification into one federation: the United Arab Republic. The united nation would have one flag, one parliament, one capital - Cairo, and one president - Gamal Abdel Nasser.

In response, Jordan and Iraq also declared unification. King Hussein of Jordan and his cousin, King Faisal of Iraq, declared their unification on Feb. 15. It was decided that Amman and Baghdad would serve alternately as capitals, each for half a year. Both countries would continue to maintain separate governments.

Six months later, a military revolution took place in Iraq, and the 'free officers' took control of the country, with the support of the Egyptian-Syrian federation. After a few days of fighting, Faisal surrendered. King Faisal and his prime minister were both murdered.

King Hussein appealed to the West for help. America and Britain shipped military forces through Aqaba and airlifted arms supplies to Amman.

Despite Hussein's objections, the Americans and British eventually acknowledged the new regime in Iraq and decided to cut down their military involvement in the Middle East. The United Arab Republic broke up in 1961.

Fifth IDF Chief of Staff

Haim Laskov.

Lt.-Gen. Haim Laskov has replaced Moshe Dayan as the IDF chief of staff. The new chief of staff, who assumed his position on Jan. 1, was commander of the armored forces during the Sinai Campaign and later the commander of the Southern Region.

Tension Rises in Anticipation of IDF Parade in Jerusalem

Tension rose in anticipation of the Israel Defense Forces' parade to take place in Jerusalem on Apr. 24, the tenth anniversary of the State of Israel. Following Jordanian protests, it was decided to station United Nations observers on both sides of the border in Jerusalem during the parade. Jordan declared a state of emergency in the Old City.

The United States feared a military incident following the parade and at a certain stage considered evacuating American citizens from the country.

However, the parade ended peacefully. The IDF displayed its modern weapons, as well as tanks and guns captured both in 'Operation Kadesh' and a recent attack on a Syrian army outpost near the Hula.

During the last few weeks, terrorist attacks from the Jordanian border increased. In February, a police offic

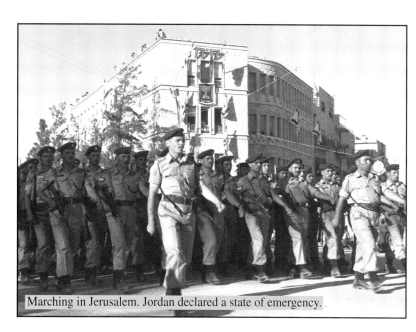

Marching in Jerusalem. Jordan declared a state of emergency.

er was killed in the Gilboa region, and in the Sharon a member of Moshav Yanuv was murdered. On Passover eve, Avraham Zahavi and Nahum Shmuel were murdered while driving a Jeep in the Lachish region.

1958
JANUARY - APRIL

The first US satellite, *'Alpha'* successfully launched into orbit with a *Jupiter-C* rocket, developed from the World War II German V-2 rocket. (January 31)

•

Ya'acov Hodorov, Israel's soccer goalkeeper, was given a hysterical welcome on his return from London. Hodorov hurt his nose playing against Wales and despite the 0:2 defeat, Israel's team received much praise. Hodorov, the team's star player, was given a special treat: a photograph taken with the glamorous movie star, Marilyn Monroe. (February 10)

•

The US and Britain signed an agreement to establish ballistic missile bases in Britain. Four bases will be constructed on British soil and will be equipped with American weapons. (February 22)

•

Khrushchev replaces Bulganin as premier and also retains his position as secretary of the Communist Party. (March 27)

•

The United States applies an embargo on the shipment of weapons for Cuba. (April 2)

•

Israel wins a tentative vote on Aqaba at the UN Conference on the Law of the Sea. (April 2)

•

The Ministry of the Interior is distributing new identity cards. Instructions to state 'nationality: Jewish' angered the religious parties and caused the National Religious Party to resign in June from the coalition. (April 15)

•

The second decade of independence ushered in with a parade in the capital attended by dignitaries, including the president, the prime minister, the chief of staff, cabinet members and nearly 20,000 spectators. Jordan protests the presence of heavy armaments in Jerusalem. (April 24)

1. 'Voice of Israel.'

The population of Israel officially passes two million. There were 650,000 Jewish residents on the day of the State's proclamation. Another 160,000 minorities were added to that number after the 1949 armistice. 70% of the 1.2 million increase derives from immigration from Arab countries. The other 30% - natural increase. (May 1)

•

Israel's Security Prize was awarded to Major Uziel Gal, inventor of the *Uzi*, four years after he invented what has become the IDF's standard sub-machine gun. (May 15)

•

Communal riots take place between Greek and Turkish Cypriots, in Nicosia and Famagusta. In London the War Office announces that a battalion of paratroops is being sent as a precautionary measure. (June 12)

•

British transports still ferrying more men into Jordan in response to the urgent request for aid sent by King Hussein. (July 17)

•

Colonel Ezer Weizman is made commander of the Air Force. Weizman, who coined the phrase "the best to the air force," served as commander for eight years, was responsible for the absorption of the French *Mirages,* and made the force one of the best in the world. *Weizman was a politician for many years, and since May 1993, has been Israel's seventh president.* (July 24)

•

Voice of Israel forbids broadcast of the songs 'Ha'Sela Ha'Adom' *(the Red Rock)* and 'Anaksh,' a song describing the life of a prostitute. The songs were banned due to their negative influence on young people. (July 30)

•

The United States nuclear submarine *'Nautilus'* completes a submerged passage beneath the North Pole ice cap, pioneering a new sea lane between the eastern and western hemispheres. She sailed from Honolulu July 23, traveled through the Bering Straits, went under the ice pack at Point Barrow, and emerged in the Atlantic off Greenland and Spitzbergen 96 hours and 1,830 miles later. (August 8)

Four Dead in Attack on Mount Scopus

Four Israeli policemen were killed and two injured, one seriously, during a Jordanian attack on Mt. Scopus in Jerusalem on May 26. Colonel Flint, the chairman of the Israeli-Jordanian Committee, was also killed in the assault, during an attempt to rescue the wounded Israeli policemen.

The Jordanians claimed that an Israeli unit crossed the cease-fire line, headed towards the Arab village of Iswiya and opened fire in the direction of Jordanian soldiers. In a telegram sent by King Hussein to the chief United Nations observer, Hussein claimed that Flint had been killed by Israeli fire.

Following the Jordanian assault, the Israel Defense Forces blocked the road leading from Iswiya to the Old City of Jerusalem.

Coalition Crisis over 'Who Is a Jew' Issue

The National Religious Party dropped out of the coalition on June 24, following a dispute regarding the 'Who is a Jew' issue. The episode began when new regulations were published, stipulating that a child could be registered as a Jew on his Israeli identification card if both his parents declared that the child was Jewish. Religious circles claimed that the new regulations allowed those considered by *Halacha* as non-Jews to register as Jewish.

At the end of the month, the National Religious Party ministers - Minister of Religious Affairs Moshe Shapira, and Minister in Charge of the Postal Services Yosef Burg - resigned from the government. After all attempts to find a compromise had failed, a committee of ministers was set up. The committee's goal was to define criteria for determining 'Who is a Jew.'

Yosef Burg, minister in charge of postal services, with President Shazar. Resigning from the coalition.

Marines Land in Lebanon

On July 14 a military revolution took place in Iraq, headed by Abed el-Karim Kasem. The next day, 5,000 American marines landed on the shores of Beirut.

The Americans wished to signal to Iraq and Syria that the States and the West would not tolerate any aggression against Lebanon. The American forces were also prepared to assist King Hussein if Syria and Iraq threatened the independence of Jordan.

Amos Hacham Wins Bible Contest

Amos Hacham, a clerk who had suffered from paralysis since childhood, won the first International Bible Contest. The contest was held on Aug. 19 in the amphitheater of the university in Jerusalem, as part of celebrations marking Israel's tenth anniversary. Hacham, a clerk from the Educational Institution for the Blind in Jerusalem, became one of the cultural heroes of the young nation overnight.

Hacham overcame fifteen competitors from different countries worldwide.

Amos Hacham.

Accused in Kafr Kassem Case Guilty of Murder

A few months after the massacre, a large reconciliation rally was held in Kafr Kassem.

Malinky. 17 years.

On Oct. 16, eight of the 11 defendants in the Kafr Kassem trial were convicted of murdering 43 residents of the village two years earlier. Three of the defendants in the case were acquitted.

Among the convicted were Major Shmuel Malinky, commander of a Border Patrol regiment, Deputy Gabriel Dahan, a platoon commander and six Border Patrol soldiers.

The massacre in Kafr Kassem occurred on Oct. 29, 1956, the first day of the 'Kadesh Operation.'

Malinky had been ordered by the brigade commander, Colonel Issachar Shadmi, to institute a curfew on the villages of the Triangle area, including Kafr Kassem.

The orders were to enforce the curfew and shoot offenders. Malinky passed on the orders. The curfew was set for 5.00 p.m. Within an hour, 43 people completely unaware of the curfew, including women and children, were killed.

The three judges determined that Malinky was obeying a clearly illegal order and convicted him on the charge of soliciting of murder.

Furthermore, they concluded that Col. Shadmi should also be brought to justice.

Malinky was sentenced to 17 years in jail.

Cornerstone Placed for New *Knesset* Building

Dorothy de Rothschild delivers speech.

On Oct. 14 the cornerstone was laid for the new *Knesset* building in Jerusalem, by Dorothy de Rothschild, widow of Edward de Rothschild, who left money for the *Knesset* construction.

Fear of War Between US and China

On Sept. 1, the United States deployed dozens of fighter airplanes and thousands of troops to the Taiwan-controlled Camay Islands, after China had shelled the islands for nine days.

China, supported by the Soviet Union, demanded the annexation of the islands. At one point, the US delivered nuclear missiles to Formosa.

After all communication efforts between the parties failed, the president of the US decided to withdraw from a threat of war.

Nearly 800,000 people, approximately 40% of Israel's population, live in government-built housing. (September 12)

•

India leads bid at UN to give China (Peking) a seat. Israel abstains. In recent assembly sessions, Israel voted to back the American view against unseating Nationalist China (Taiwan) in favor of Peking. (September 22)

•

Israel buys two *S-class* submarines from Britain. At the Portsmouth ceremony, the 715 ton *'Springer'* will raise the Israeli flag and become the *'Tannin,'* to be joined by the *'Rahav'* before the end of the year. (October 7)

•

Soviets extend United Arab Republic credit for Aswan Dam project. Khrushchev pledges $100 million. (October 23)

•

Shimon Peres, director-general of the Ministry of Defense, has announced his intention to resign from office in 1959 to dedicate his time to politics. Peres said that he would like to appear on *Mapai's* list for the next elections. (November 11)

•

One of the largest spy networks uncovered in Israel has been liquidated with the arrest of ten Israeli Arabs alleged to have worked for Syrian intelligence. (November 12)

•

Shots from a Syrian position kill the wife of the British air attache, who was about 26m (78 feet) inside Israel. (November 16)

•

Heaviest artillery duel in the Galilee region since the War of Independence. Israel calls for a Security Council session after the Syrian attack; Ambassador Eban asks UN to help avert need for major reprisals. Cairo steps up threats. (December 3)

•

One of the largest locust invasions to be recorded in a decade was reported in the Negev. Plant protection workers and air spraying crews are fighting the locusts. (December 16)

•

Israeli jets shoot down one Egyptian *MiG-17* from a group that crossed into Israel's air space. (December 20)

Four Cabinet ministers will probably visit the US during the next few months to boost fund drives which are now urgent in view of the rising wave of immigration. (January 19)

•

Knesset Speaker, Yosef Sprinzak, succumbs to a heart attack at 74. (January 28)

•

At *Mapai* party headquarters, David Ben-Gurion disclosed that before the elections for the third *Knesset* a "group of people" proposed to "achieve leadership by use of force." Almost all the opposition factions submitted proposals for the agenda and questions. (February 1)

•

The Shama'a family, who came to Israel in 'Operation Magic Carpet,' demands information on the fate of their son, Paltiel, who disappeared ten years earlier from a children's home in Jerusalem. The family claims that the boy was adopted by a German family currently living in Kiryat Ono. The claim was rejected but the police were unable to locate the missing boy. (March 2)

•

Tel Aviv lights up to greet its 50th year. Starting out as a garden suburb of Jaffa with 60 families, Tel Aviv today is a metropolitan center with 400,000 inhabitants. (March 10)

•

Eleanor Roosevelt, the American president's widow, visited Israel and bought a camel in the Beersheba market for 40 lirot. The camel was transported to the US by ship and was given to Mrs. Roosevelt's granddaughter, who raises exotic animals. (March 26)

•

Official sources in Washington revealed that the termination of grant-in-aid to Israel arose from a political decision by the State Department to disengage to some extent from American identification with Israel. (April 1)

•

OC Northern Command General Yitzhak Rabin has been appointed chief of the General Staff. General Chaim Herzog has been appointed chief of intelligence. (April 2)

•

President Eisenhower accepts Dulles' resignation. Mr. Christian Herter is nominated secretary of state. (April 15)

Near-war Situation Following Mistake in Mobilization Exercise

Ben-Gurion. Formed a committee to investigate the 'Night of the Ducks,' as the episode was named.

Yehoshafat Harkabi, head of intelligence.

Meir Zorea, head of operations.

Prime Minister and Minister of Defense David Ben-Gurion dismissed Brigadier-General Meir Zorea, head of operations, and Brigadier-General Yehoshafat Harkabi, head of intelligence, following a drill in the mobilization of reserves that threatened to drag the Middle East into another full-scale war.

It all began on Apr. 1, when Voice of Israel dramatically broadcast the reserve forces' call to duty.

The announcement, in eight different languages, was broadcast several times and caused immediate panic in Arab countries.

The broadcast actually referred to a minor draft exercise affecting three units. It turned into a communications farce because of a series of technical mistakes and the faulty conduct of two senior officers.

Following the broadcast, Syria and Egypt declared high-level alerts and began to mobilize their forces. In both Europe and the United States, the news about Israel's 'general mobilization' and the fear of war was broadcast dramatically.

The broadcasts on Israeli radio were interpreted by the West and the Arab countries as a general mobilization of forces. The immediate denial that came from Jerusalem was ignored, and the worldwide media reported on the "unexpected and dangerous developments in Israel."

Ben-Gurion immediately formed a committee to investigate the episode. The opposition demanded the resignation of the government, and a long list of no-confidence motions were tabled in the *Knesset*.

The investigation revealed that the public and the press had not been prepared in advance for the drill, that Voice of Israel had received conflicting reports from military officials and the word 'drill' had somehow been omitted from the broadcast.

Egypt Confiscates Israeli Goods in the Suez Canal

In March, Egypt began to stop ships carrying Israeli exports from traveling through Suez. The Egyptians stopped two cargo carriers, one Liberian and the other German, which were loaded with cement, citrus fruits, potassium and canned foods. The merchandise was bound for Ceylon, Hong Kong and other destinations.

On Apr. 16 an Alexandria court issued an order confiscating all Israeli merchandise on shipping traveling through the canal, and confiscating an Israeli fishing boat captured 18 months previously far from Egyptian territorial waters. The Egyptians claimed that they were confiscating the goods for the benefit of Arab refugees, and that the goods or their value would be used for the refugees' rehabilitation.

Israel's Arms Deal with Germany is Revealed

Begin. No words to describe.

On June 25 the revelation of an arms deal caused a local and international storm. The deal involved large quantities of weapons and ammunition sold by Israel to the West German army, who only a few years earlier had murdered six million Jews. It led to the resignation of the government and new elections in Israel.

Director-general of the Ministry of Defense Shimon Peres justified its importance to Israel's security; the Arab countries were being equipped with modern weapons, so Israel was forced to improve its balance of payments and increase its foreign currency reserves.

"I will not accept advice from anyone in matters of national security," said an irritated David Ben-Gurion.

The arms deal included *Uzi* submachine guns, grenade launchers and ammunition. The Germans expressed satisfaction with the quality and low price of the Israeli weapons.

Peres. Important deal.

The public outcry in Israel spread to Europe, and the episode received much publicity. On July 5 Ben-Gurion submitted his resignation to the president, not for the first time.

Ambassador to US Does Not Have Israeli Citizenship

The Ministry of the Interior granted the request of Israel's ambassador to Washington, Abba Eban, and issued him with Israeli citizenship on May 20. So ended an embarrassing episode, in which it was revealed that the ambassador, formerly the ambassador to the United Nations, was not an Israeli citizen.

The first doubts regarding Eban arose at the beginning of 1959, when the *Mapai (Erez Israel Workers' Party)* party decided that Eban was to return from the UN and join the leadership of the party.

At this stage, it became clear that the South African-born ambassador, was not a citizen of Israel.

Investigation revealed that Eban had never registered in Israel as a new *oleh (immigrant)*, and had therefore never officially received citizenship. The fact that he had fulfilled many high-level diplomatic

Abba Eban, with David Ben-Gurion and US former President, Harry S. Truman.

posts since the establishment of the country did not change the peculiar situation.

Eban was on the list of *Mapai* candidates for *Knesset* membership in the fourth elections, so it was decided that he should request Israeli citizenship. Abba Eban then became a citizen of Israel, both entitled to vote and be elected to the *Knesset*.

Wadi Salib, Haifa Burns

On July 8 an unruly drunk caused havoc in a downtown Haifa coffee shop. Police arriving at the scene fired shots into the air. In the ensuing panic, one man was injured by a bullet; rumors spread he had been killed by police, hundreds of North African-born citizens gathered, a mass riot broke out, at the end of which 15 policemen were hospitalized.

The riots in Wadi Salib spread to other places most populated by newcomers from Morocco, placing the distress of the North African immigrants on the public agenda. Following the riots, the government decided to set up a committee to investigate claims of discrimination.

More weapons including *Uzis* and mortars sold to Bonn. A German army mission to Cairo reported disappointment in the quality and price of Arab arms and advised against purchasing them. (September 3)

•

Jerusalem's municipality closes off an entire street due to author S.Y. Agnon's complaints that he is unable to concentrate because of the noise in his neighborhood, Talpiyot. Cars are not allowed in the street between 10.00 p.m. and 7.00 a.m. (September 14)

•

At a press conference held during his visit to the US, Russian leader Nikita Khrushchev was asked why his country is not friendly towards Israel, despite the fact that Israel is the most socialist country in the Western world. Khrushchev replied: "The microscope that can detect socialism in Israel is yet to be invented." (September 15)

•

There are about 12,082,000 Jews in the world, according to a survey published by the World Jewish Congress. (October 1)

•

According to the editor of Al-Gomhouriyya, who has just returned from Russia, Premier Khrushchev declared his support in principle for the UAR's Suez Canal boycott of Israel. He also expressed his readiness to supply the UAR with the latest Soviet weaponry. (November 1)

•

The country goes to the polls today: 1,216,000 citizens are eligible to vote. 82% turnout is recorded in the elections for the fourth *Knesset*. Prime Minister Ben-Gurion says all but *Herut* and the Communists are welcome in coalition. (November 3)

•

Eleven Yemenite immigrants who had wandered through deserts to Israel, died on their way. Another 26 managed to reach Israel. The members of this underground immigrant group had wandered over half the earth to Israel: they walked across the desert, crossed the sea to Africa, from there to southern Europe, and finally came to Israel by air. (December 2)

Great *Mapai* Victory. Dayan, Eban and Peres Join the Government

Ben-Gurion led *Mapai* to a great victory in Israel's fourth elections. *Mapai's Knesset* seats grew from 40 to 48. The General Zionists, *Ahdut Ha'Avoda* and *Maki* significantly declined. *Herut*, led by Menachem Begin, increased its number of mandates from 15 to 17.

The elections, held on Nov. 3, resulted in the election of 30 new members, including former chief of staff, Moshe Dayan, former director of the ministry of defense, Shimon Peres, and former ambassador to Washington, Abba Eban.

The left wing parties had initially refused to join the government, in light of the new 'Discipline Law,' obligating ministers voting against the Cabinet to resign.

In its negotiations to join the Cabinet, *Agudat Israel* presented hardline conditions: exempting *yeshiva* students from military service, main-

Ben-Gurion's government: minister of agriculture - Dayan, minister without portfolio handling foreign affairs - Eban.

taining the status quo with respect to the military service of women and the observation of the Sabbath.

The new government presented by Ben-Gurion in mid-December was comprised of *Mapai*, the Progressives, NRP, *Ahdut Ha'avoda*, and *Mapam*.

First Submarine Docks in Haifa

The *'Tannin'* arrives at the port of Haifa. The era of submarines.

The *'Tanrin'* (*crocodile*), the Israeli navy's first submarine, arrived in Haifa on Dec. 16.

The *'Tanrin'* was a British submarine from the early 1950's, which had been renovated in shipyards in Great Britain. It entered the Haifa harbor in a solemn naval review, accompanied by airplanes and destroyers, and was received with great ceremony.

Prime Minister Ben-Gurion declared the day to be one of celebration in Israel and emphasized the new dimension added to the abilities of the Israel Defense Forces.

A resident of Bat Yam present at the ceremony decided to name his child Tannin after the submarine.

The arrival of the *'Tannin'* marked the beginning of a new era for the Israeli navy.

Renault Car Company Surrenders to Arab Boycott

On Oct. 16, long after spare parts for Renault automobiles had stopped arriving, the French company confirmed that shipments to Israel had been halted. At the same time, the firm was no longer on the Arab Boycott's blacklist.

Israel blamed Renault for surrendering to the dictates of the Arab Boycott, and decided to postpone the renewal of its commercial agreement with France.

The French government intervened, assuring Israel of its deep friendship and trying to persuade Israel that Renault's decision was based on the particulars of the issue and not linked to the Arab Boycott.

Interpol Seeks Eichmann

Newspapers in Israel reported that Adolph Eichmann had been traced to Kuwait, so revealing the name of the man who would become a symbol of the Holocaust. *Eichman was not living in Kuwait, but hiding in Argentina, where he was kidnapped by the Israeli Mossad six months later.*

Historic Meeting between Israeli and German Leaders

Fifteen years after the end of the Second World War and the discovery of the Holocaust's horrors, and 12 years after the establishment of the State of Israel, a historic meeting was held between Prime Minister David Ben-Gurion and West Germany's Chancellor Konrad Adenauer. News of the meeting was the headline on every American news report. The meeting was especially important because of the tension with the Eastern Bloc about the status of the divided Berlin.

The meeting between the two men paved the road to diplomatic relations between Israel and Germany and led eventually to full normalization of relations.

Prime Minister Ben-Gurion with Chancellor Adenauer.

"Where is our Yossele?"

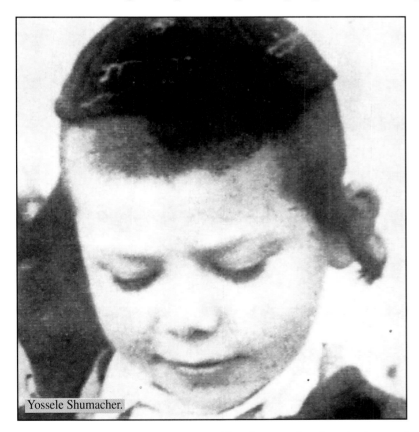

Yossele Shumacher.

Ruth Ben-David smuggled Yossele abroad.

An Orthodox grandfather refused to return his grandson to the child's secular parents. So began, on Jan. 18, the 'Yossele Shumacher Affair.'

The Shumacher family immigrated to Israel in 1958. Due to financial hardship and the family's absorption, Yossele's parents, Alter and Ida Shumacher, turned for help with their children's upbringing to the mother's parents, a wealthy Orthodox couple living in Me'a She'arim in Jerusalem. The daughter was sent to a boarding school in Kfar Habad, and

Yossele was taken into the home of his grandparents, Nachman and Miriam Shtarks.

Shortly afterwards, when Yossele's father was employed and the family's financial situation improved, the parents wanted their children to come home. The grandfather agreed to send the daughter back, on the condition that she receive a religious education, and promised to return Yossele to his parents at the beginning of the school year. He did not, however, keep his word.

Yossele's father repeatedly asked for his son back but the grandfather refused. Nachman Shtarks told the father that in order to get Yossele back the family would have to move to Me'a Sh'earim.

The parents, fearing that Yossele would be sent to his uncle in London, turned to the courts to issue a court order. At the first court hearing, on Feb. 10, the grandfather refused to give Yossele back to his parents. The court ruled that he must do so within four days. The Shtarks did not obey the court order and hid their grandson.

Yossele's parents once again turned to the courts, and demanded that the grandfather be found in contempt of court. The parent's lawyer also demanded that the police enforce the court's ruling. The court instructed the police to search for the missing boy. The police carried out a search, mainly in Jerusalem, but had no success.

No one imagined that Yossele was already out of the country.

Bonn claims appearance of swastikas is a bid to defame the state. Anti-Semitic incidents reported in ten countries. Nahum Goldmann, President of the World Zionist Organization says the outbreak should not be exaggerated but warned against the complacency that had resulted in Hitler and a world war. (January 2)

Two American soldiers decided to search for the cities of Sodom and Gomorrah, which were destroyed in 1900 BC. The search, which was conducted mainly along the bottom of the Dead Sea, stopped after several days when it became evident that diving was impossible in the Dead Sea. (January 11)

Syrian artillery backs border crossings. OC Northern Command states: "We will resist border change." The Syrian positions in Khirbet el-Tawfik were completely wiped out at 3.30 a.m on Monday. (January 29)

Scrolls are found in caves on the Israeli side of the Dead Sea shore. The caves are believed to have served as refuge for rebels following the defeat of the Bar Kokhba revolt of 135 AD. (February 7)

Metulla is connected to the electricity network encompassing the entire area from Sedom to the Galilee panhandle. A record in electricity consumption was registered in the summer, due to the pumping of water. (February 21)

An earthquake in Agadir, Morocco claims 12,000 lives, among them 3,000 foreigners and 2,000 Jews. The Jewish quarter of Agadir was destroyed. (February 29)

The 'New York Times' reported that the Soviet government is refusing to permit the baking of *matzo* in some western areas of the Soviet Union. The paper says its information came from foreigners who recently visited Kiev, Odessa, Kishinev and Riga. (March 20)

American dockers refused to unload the cargo of the Egyptian vessel 'Cleopatra,' in protest against the attacks on Israeli shipping. (April 13)

UAR, Lebanon, Saudi Arabia and Jordan have begun to boycott American shipping in retaliation for the picketing of *'Cleopatra'* in New York. The combined US trade union federation refused to bow to government pressure and pledged support to the New York dockers who were boycotting the Egyptian ship *'Cleopatra.'* They protested against the blacklisting of US flag ships which the Arab League was trying to implement. (May 2)

•

The State Department pledges action on Arab Boycott, picketing of the *'Cleopatra'* ends. (May 7)

•

The USSR may free the pilot of the U-2, Francis Gary Powers, as a gesture towards the Eisenhower-Khrushchev summit. (May 7)

•

The Cabinet approves the appointment of Gideon Hausner as new attorney general, to take effect on July 1. (May 8)

•

Colonel Moshe Ben-Isaac was one of the anti-aircraft team which downed the American spy flight in USSR. The officer was awarded a medal of honor. The Soviet team included two other Jewish officers. (May 8)

•

Professor Yigael Yadin announced to David Ben-Gurion the discovery of letters dispatched by Bar Kokhba, leader of the Jewish revolt against the Romans in the Second century AD. Yadin said he had managed to decode the letters which were discovered in caves in the Judean Desert. (May 10)

•

Minister of Justice Francois Erasmus tells the South African parliament that the state of emergency is indefinite. (May 18)

•

Israel's first farming and agricultural school 'Mikve Israel' celebrates its 90th birthday. The school was founded by the French Jewish organization *Alliance Israelite.* (May 25)

•

The Turkish army sets up a nonparty cabinet after bloodless coup. Freedom of the press is restored, and journalists who had been arrested because of what they had written about the Menderess administration are to be released. (May 27)

Adolf Eichmann Brought to Israel

Adolf Eichmann, one of Hitler's closest advisors and the man responsible for carrying out the 'Final Solution,' was captured in Argentina after a long search and brought to trial in Israel for crimes against the Jewish people. This dramatic announcement was made by Prime Minister David Ben-Gurion in the *Knesset.* News of Eichmann's arrest was published on May 23, stunning the entire nation. No details of Eichmann's capture were disclosed.

Tel Aviv Chief Magistrate Emanuel Halevi came to Eichmann's secret remand cell in Jaffa and extended the arrest by 14 days. Eichmann did not deny his identity. His line of defense, to which he adhered throughout his trial, was that he had operated as a soldier in an army, had obeyed his commanders' instructions, and did not know of the extermination of the Jews.

Minister of Justice Pinchas Rosen and Inspector-General of Police, Yosef Nahmias, informed the press that if Eichmann was convicted he would be sentenced to death under the Nazi and Nazi Collaborators (Punishment) Law of 1950.

After World War II, Eichmann had escaped from Germany and hid in Buenos Aires, Argentina's capital, under the assumed name Ricardo Klement. His wife and sons had joined him there, and lived with him in difficult financial conditions. He was found in the suburb where he was living, and abducted at the beginning of May while on his way home from work.

Mossad agents were responsible for the kidnapping, under the supervision of Isser Harel, head of the *Mossad.* Eichmann was hidden in Buenos Aires for ten days after his

Adolf Eichmann. Lived in Argentina under assumed name - Ricardo Klement.

capture. He was then flown to Israel with his captors on an El Al aircraft.

The incident created a crisis in Israel's diplomatic relations with Argentina. Argentina demanded that Eichmann be returned and requested that the United Nations Security Council condemn Israel for its actions. The Argentine ambassador left Israel in protest, and Israel's ambassador in Buenos Aires was recalled to Israel. Israel's explanations were by no means accepted by the Argentine government.

At the beginning of August, the countries issued a joint notice of their renewed relations, thus ending the crisis.

Soviets Shoot Down American *U-2* 'plane

Gary Francis Powers. Shot down over Russia.

On May 8, the Soviet Union announced it had shot down a *U-2* American spy 'plane that had flown over Soviet skies at high altitude. This created an unprecedented crisis between the USSR and the US.

The pilot of the American 'plane, Gary Francis Powers, managed to parachute to the ground safely, but was then captured by Soviet troops. In its announcement of the incident, the USSR disclosed for the first time that it possessed anti-aircraft *SAM*

missiles capable of shooting down aircraft flying at high altitudes. The American 'plane, which crossed the USSR from south to north while carrying out a photographic mission, was shot down from an altitude of 20.000m. The Soviets publicized details of the American pilot's equipment, including a suicide needle to be used in the event of capture.

As an initial reaction to the incident, President Eisenhower canceled his imminent visit to Russia.

First Photograph of Eichmann in Israel

Eichmann as an SS officer.

The first photograph published of Adolf Eichmann in Israel.

Security reasons and the diplomatic crisis between Israel and Argentina delayed publication of a photograph of Adolf Eichmann in Israel. The photo was first published by the Israeli government on June 8, three weeks after Eichmann had been brought to Israel.

Eichmann's interrogators reported that the Nazi murderer was being questioned for approximately five hours a day by a team of 20 men and was cooperating, disclosing information about his activity in the Nazi army and party.

Air Contact with Israel Paralyzed

All flights to and from Israel were paralyzed.

On July 15, El Al Israel Airline's air crew declared a labor dispute and froze all El Al flights to and from Israel. The strikers demanded a raise in wages, a raise in daily allowances, a pension fund, an increase in disability payments and a reduction in the number of flight hours.

In order to maintain air transport, El Al leased aircraft from six foreign airlines. At the same time, the *Histadrut* received the International Aviation Authority's approval to operate El Al aircraft using foreign crews.

The strategy worked, and the strike concluded after ten days.

Ten Jordanian Ministers Killed in Explosion

A meeting of the Jordanian cabinet on Aug. 29 turned into a horrifying tragedy. A powerful bomb exploded at the office of Jordanian Prime Minister Hajali, where the meeting was taking place. The results were fatal: the prime minister and nine ministers were killed, and the entire building collapsed.

The meeting had convened in order to discuss the results of the Arab foreign ministers' assembly, which had met that week in Beirut to discuss the situation of Palestinian refugees and the granting of independence to the West Bank.

Jordanian King Hussein, who was supposed to take part in the meeting, had canceled his participation at the last moment.

'Exodus' team leaves Israel to film scenes in Cyprus. Before going, Paul Newman said: "During my ten weeks here I have become convinced that the facts of Israel's reality are far more striking than what had been fictionalized in the book *'Exodus.'* (June 5)

Informed diplomatic quarters in Tel Aviv are hopeful that the excellent relations between Argentina and Israel will not be affected by the Eichmann case. (June 7)

De Gaulle and Ben-Gurion commence their talks. French sources revealed that General de Gaulle assured Ben-Gurion that Israel could count on France's opposition to any change in the *status quo* in the Middle East. (June 14).

The first *Fouga Magister (C-170)* to be assembled by Israel Aircraft Industries (IAI) will be ceremonially handed over to the air force today. (July 6)

El Al refused to comply with the chief rabbinate's demand that it place *kashrut* supervisors on its 'planes. El Al claimed that the demand was superfluous as the 'planes are equipped with separate dishes for meat and dairy and the crews were given a special course on *kashrut*, which was passed by a rabbi and approved by the rabbinate. (July 7)

American U-2 pilot, Gary Francis Powers, shot down over Soviet territory, will be put on trial August 17. He is charged with espionage, the maximum penalty for which is execution. (July 18)

Argentina and Israel state the Eichmann rift is healed, with a joint 70-word announcement published simultaneously in Jerusalem and Buenos Aires. (August 3)

A new medical center was inaugurated in the Jerusalem Hills: 30 million lira was invested in the establishment of Hadassah Ein Karem, the largest medical center in the Middle East. (August 3)

Gary Francis Powers pleaded guilty in open court to spying for the US against Russia and said he made his U-2 flight under military orders. (August 16)

1960

SEPTEMBER - DECEMBER

Pakistan and India sign the Indus Treaty, resolving a 13-year dispute, which has continued ever since the founding of both countries, over the waters of the Indus River basin. (September 19)

•

The Commission of Inquiry headed by Justice Haim Cohen to reexamine the conduct of two officers in connection with their testimony before the Olshan-Dori Committee five and a half years ago, concluded its investigation and submitted its conclusions. A recent civil court decision gave reason to believe some testimony of the two had been falsified. In his testimony before the Knesset Foreign Affairs and Security Committee, Moshe Sharett, prime minister at the time of the affair, said that it involved grave security matters. The main question was: who gave the order to activate a Jewish spy ring in Egypt in 1954. (October 16)

•

New American Identikit system resulted in the arrest of a criminal. The police investigators succeeded in composing a precise sketch of the criminal's face, who was surprised by his speedy identification. (November 1)

•

1960 Nobel Prizes for Chemistry and Physics go to American scientists Dr. Willard F. Libby and Dr. Donald A. Glasher. Dr. Libby won for his method to use *Carbon 14* for age determination in archeology, geophysics and other branches of science. Dr. Glasher won for his invention of a 'bubble bath chamber' for the photographing of atomic particles. *Carbon 14* was to be used to date the Dead Sea Scrolls. (November 13)

•

Clark Gable, the American film star, dies of a heart attack, aged 59. During his career, Gable appeared in 90 films, most successfully in *'Mutiny on the Bounty,' 'San Francisco'* and *'Gone with the Wind.'* (November 16)

•

The first instalment of Eichmann's memoirs published in the current issue of *'Life'* magazine. Eichmann, who herded millions of Jews to their death, now awaiting trial in Israel, says: "I carried out orders," and that he was "merely a small cog in the machinery." (November 23).

Israel Admits it has Built Atomic Energy Reactor

On Dec. 21, Prime Minister David Ben-Gurion admitted that Israel was building a nuclear reactor in the Negev, but denied that the reactor would be used to develop an atomic bomb. The issue of the nuclear reactor damaged the relationship between Israel and the United States, because the US claimed that Israel was secretly developing an atomic bomb with the assistance of French expertise.

At the beginning of December, the US had demanded information from Israel regarding its ability to manufacture an atomic bomb. The demand came, following intelligence information the US had received which included satellite photographs showing that Israel was building a nuclear reactor capable of manufacturing plutonium. Israel insisted that the facility was nothing but a textile factory. Israel's ambassador in London stated that Israel did not manufacture atomic bombs and had no intention to do so.

Israel's elusive responses angered the heads of the American security departments and the American president demanded clear answers.

At this point Israel complied and gave the US government authorities extensive information about the nuclear reactor.

The United States found the Israeli explanations satisfactory, and expressed support of the establishment of such plants for the purpose of promoting peace.

On Nov. 1, Abba Eban inaugurated Israel's first golf course, in Caesarea.

New President in White House: John F. Kennedy

New American president: John F. Kennedy.

After a close race, which reached its peak during the world's first televised debate, Democrat John Fitzgerald Kennedy was elected president over Republican Richard M. Nixon, thus becoming the youngest president ever to enter the White House.

In his victory speech, Kennedy promised a new era for America. He rapidly became the most admired president of the twentieth century.

Born to a prominent Boston family, Kennedy brought a new spirit ('Camelot') to the White House. Americans came to love his young wife Jacqueline and their two young children, and mourned with them when he was assassinated.

Extensive Search in Argentina for Mengele

After the acclaimed success of Adolf Eichmann's capture, Israelis tried to locate the murderous doctor, Josef Mengele, in Argentina. News of the search was published by foreign newspapers on March 16.

From Buenos Aires, Argentina's capital, it was reported that at least five countries were taking part in the search for Mengele, who was proclaimed as the world's most wanted criminal. Argentina's police authorized two German observers as well

Josef Mengele. The next target after Eichmann.

as American and Soviet agents to take part in the search.

During World War II, Mengele served as physician to the concentration camps. He was also responsible for performing the selection of Jews who were to go to the gas chambers, deciding with a flick of his finger who would live and who would die. Mengele personally carried out horrifying physical experiments on humans. After World War II, he fled to South America.

'Egoz' Sinks on its Way to Spain

Only in 1994 were the bodies brought for burial in Israel.

The ship 'Egoz,' carrying dozens of Jewish refugees from Morocco, sank in the Mediterranean Sea on Jan. 10. The ship was on its way from Morocco to Spain when it hit a reef and sank within seconds. During the rescue searches that followed, 23 bodies were found in the sea. Three survivors, including the ship's captain, were brought to shore by lifeboat.

The 23 bodies were buried in Morocco. David Ben-Gurion tried to bring the bodies to Israel but was not successful. The newly-crowned king, King Hassan the Second,

feared that collaboration with Israel would result in an unfavorable reaction by Arab countries.

Only after the Madrid conference in 1991 was it agreed that an Israeli representative would be sent to Morocco to locate the bodies and send them to Israel. In 1994, the exumed bodies were brought to Israel and were buried with state ceremony in various cemeteries.

An investigation of the incident concluded that the captain of the boat had been drunk and that no life vests or other means of rescue were available to the passengers.

Ben-Gurion Resigns Over Lavon Affair

Walked to the president.

On Jan. 31, during a special Cabinet meeting, David Ben-Gurion tendered his resignation as prime minister.

The background for his resignation was the Lavon Affair, the Jewish espionage network which had been exposed in Egypt seven years earlier.

The government which Ben-Gurion left was the widest coalition in the history of the State. It encompassed 89 *Knesset* members, from *Mapam* to the religious party, *Po'alei Agudat Israel*.

During its term, the government had numerous important accomplishments, including the capture of Eichmann in Argentina.

The specially convened Cabinet meeting was very short. Ben-Gurion read his resignation letter, bid the ministers goodbye, and left the room less than ten minutes later. He did not bother waiting for his driver and walked to the President's Residence to submit his resignation.

1961
JANUARY - MARCH

The United States accuses Castro of deliberately forcing a break in US-Cuban relations by strategy of harrassment. (January 5)

•

On its maiden flight from New York, El Al's first *Boeing-707* jet sets a record of 230 minutes from Paris to Tel Aviv. (January 6)

•

A special booth made of Belgian security glass has been built especially for the trial of Adolf Eichmann. Bullets fired from close range, to check the resistance of the glass, do not penetrate the booth. (January 13)

•

Deputy Chief of Staff Yitzhak Rabin, 38, is chosen by Chief of Staff Zvi Zur as his deputy. General Zur referred to Rabin as one of the defense forces' most brilliant officers. (January 24)

•

The attorney general indicts Adolf Eichmann. He stands accused of crimes against the Jewish people and against humanity, war crimes and membership of a Nazi organization declared by the Nuremberg Tribunal to have been criminal. (February 1)

•

Russia has launched an earth satellite which itself will launch an 'interplanetary' station, on a journey to Venus during the second half of May. (February 12)

•

The coffin of David Raziel, first commander of the IZL, which had been transferred 12 years earlier from Iraq to Cyprus, finally arrives in Israel. Raziel had been sent on British intelligence missions to Iraq, and was killed there by German aerial bombardment. (February 15)

•

Moroccan King Mohammed V dies during a tonsillectomy and nose operation. He was 51; his son Moulay Hassan 31, succeeds him as Hassan II. (February 26)

•

Pres. Kennedy establishes Peace Corps, enlisting US students and graduates to volunteer on international aid projects. (March 1)

•

Peace talks to take place in Evian-les-Bains between French government and Algerian insurgents aimed at bringing peace to war-torn Algeria. (March 19)

The trial of Adolf Eichmann begins. This was Eichmann's first public appearance since he was brought to Israel last May. One spectator said: "But he looks like an ordinary person." "That's what's so terrible," is the reply. (April 11)

•

The State's *Bar Mitzva* marked, thousands cheer military parade in Jerusalem. (April 20)

•

Anti-Castro rebels, backed by US, land in three places on Cuba and engage in heavy fighting with government forces. Castro announces that the incursion has been crushed. Washington reveals that CIA plan was formed by the previous Eisenhower administration. The affair became known as 'The Bay of Pigs.' (April 22)

•

The film actor Gary Cooper dies of cancer, aged 60. (May 13)

•

One of President Kennedy's recommendations to a joint session of Congress was that the US "should commit itself to achieving the goal, before the decade is out, of landing a man on the moon and returning him safely to earth." (May 23)

•

Prime Minister Ben-Gurion and President Kennedy meet for 90 minutes in New York. The two discussed the common aims of the US and Israel. (May 30)

•

Ben-Gurion returned from a 16-day, four-nation tour of Canada, US, Britain and France. He said he met appreciation for Israel's needs as well as a great deal of friendship. (June 6)

•

Premier Kassem announces that Kuwait is part of Iraq's territory and it would be annexed by peaceful means. Independence will be defended, says Kuwait. British to quit Kuwait as soon as Iraqi threat is over. (June 25)

•

The movie *'Exodus'* was screened in Tel Aviv cinema. The movie, based on a screenplay by Leon Uris, stars Paul Newman. The movie became one of Israel's best promotional devices. Ben-Gurion, who attended the screening, said the film was: "long and imprecise, but definitely leaves its mark." (June 25)

Eichmann's Trial Begins

Adolf Eichmann facing the judges from his glass booth.

The trial of Adolf Eichmann, the Nazi criminal responsible for 'the final solution,' the extermination of Europe's Jews during the Second World War, commenced on Apr. 11 at the Beit Ha'Am building in Jerusalem. The tense atmosphere on the first day of the trial peaked when hundreds arrived at the court wearing yellow stars.

The trial was conducted by Judge Moshe Landau. The prosecutor was Attorney General Gideon Hausner and the defense attorney was a German lawyer named Robert Servatius. Until the very last moment, Servatius had attempted to prevent the trial by claiming that Eichmann's abduction from Argentina was illegal.

Hausner touched the hearts of hundreds of people in his opening speech when he said that he was speaking as the representative of six million Jews who had not lived to see that day.

The trial was covered by the international media, including 50 German reporters. The famous American broadcaster Walter Cronkite broadcast the first hearing live, as the accused stated distinctly, "Ich bin Adolf Eichmann" (*'I am Adolf Eichmann'*).

The trial was significant not only because it sentenced a mass murderer to death, but also because it exposed an entire generation, which was born in Israel and did not experience the Holocaust, to a painful chapter in Jewish history.

Israeli Caught Spying for Russia

The most severe spy case ever to occur in the history of Israel was exposed on Apr. 15 with the arrest of Dr. Israel Be'er, a military commentator and the minister of defense's advisor for military history.

Be'er, an intelligence officer and lieutenant-colonel, served as the Israel Defense Forces' military historian.

Be'er was also a close friend of the prime minister and the minister of defense.

Dr. Be'er was arrested on Mar. 30 at his home.

The announcement of Be'er's arrest and of his role as a Soviet spy stunned Prime Minister David Ben-Gurion. The prime minister's re-

Dr. Israel Be'er spied for Russia.

sponse was: "I was deceived."

Be'er was arrested after an East German agent, with whom he had met several times, was followed.

Be'er was accused of contact with a foreign agent and with transferring confidential information to a foreign state. His arrest took Israel's leaders by surprise.

Be'er's trial was conducted in closed session. He was sentenced to ten years' imprisonment; he appealed the sentence and the court extended his imprisonment to 15 years.

Only after his death was it discovered that Be'er had been a Soviet intelligence officer who had penetrated Israel many years before his arrest.

Russian is First Man in Space

The first astronaut in history to complete a full orbit of the earth was a Russian cosmonaut, 27-year-old Major Yuri Gagarin. Gagarin completed his mission in the spaceship *'Vostok 1.'* It was the first manned flight in space. Gagarin was in space for a total of 108 minutes.

This was the second time that the Soviet Union had prevailed over the United States in the space race. Four years earlier, the Soviet Union had preceded the US in launching a spaceship to orbit the earth.

The success of Gagarin's mission encouraged the Americans to send American astronaut Alan Shepard into space. Shepard did not orbit the earth but went to an altitude of 180 kilometers (113 miles) and back.

Eight months later, on Feb. 20, the United States succeeded in sending the astronaut John Glenn into space. He was the first American astronaut to orbit the world, which he did three times.

The space race between the US and the USSR continued until '69, when the US succeeded in putting a man on the Moon for the first time.

Missile *'Shavit-2'* Launched

Ben-Gurion and Peres examining the missile.

On July 6, Israel launched the *'Shavit-2,'* the first experimental meteorological missile manufactured by Israel. The launch's purpose was to examine Israel's ability to manufacture strategic missiles bearing explosive heads, intended to protect the State in the future.

Israel's achievement received worldwide recognition. The international press published a photograph of Prime Minister David Ben-Gurion and Deputy Minister of Defense Shimon Peres standing next to the missile before the launch.

The Arab world was enraged by the launch and demanded that the United States condemn Israel's act. The launch prompted Egypt's leader, Gamal Abdel Nasser, to try to catch up to Israel in the ballistics race. Nasser asked the Soviet Union to supply Egypt with Russian ground-to-ground missiles and employed German scientists who had worked for the Nazi regime to develop ballistic missiles for Egypt.

The American government refused to condemn the launching of *'Shavit-2'* but hinted Israel should invest its development funds in more positive projects. Ben-Gurion's rivals called the launch an election gimmick.

First *Mirages* Arrive

The best: the *Mirage* in Israel.

Israel has bought *Mirage* combat jets from France. The *Mirage* is considered the best combat 'plane in the world.

The Israeli Air Force's acquisition was first disclosed on Aug. 27 in an interview held between Egypt's leader, Gamal Abdel Nasser, and an American broadcaster. Nasser said that Israel's purchase was a direct response to Egypt's purchase of Russian *MiG-19* jets.

The Mirages were Israel's main combat 'planes in the 1960's, and they served as the front line 'planes for Israel's victory during the Six-Day War. Their pilots participated in numerous aerial battles and shot down many enemy 'planes.

Only at the end of the Sixties, following the French embargo on weapons supply to Israel, did the American Phantom take the place of the French Mirage in the air force.

Mapai Loses Seats in Elections

On Aug. 15, elections for the fifth *Knesset* were held, influenced by a background of the Lavon Affair (the affair surrounding an Israeli spy network exposed in Egypt) and the rift between David Ben-Gurion and his party.

The results were not surprising: *Mapai* lost five seats and decreased from 47 *Knesset* members to 42. *Herut* maintained its 17 seats.

Many *kibbutz* members expressed their dissatisfaction with Labor by inserting blank voting papers in the ballot boxes.

Ten weeks of intense discussions took place, in an effort to form a coalition. David Ben-Gurion finally managed to form a coalition based on 68 *Knesset* members from four parties. Among new ministers was General (res.) Yigal Allon, a hero of the War of Independence.

1961
JULY - SEPTEMBER

Iraq's leader, General Kassem, announced his intent to annex Kuwait. Britain sends 2,000 commandos to Kuwait. (July 2)

•

Ernest Hemingway, Nobel Prize winner, accidentally kills himself while cleaning a gun. (July 2)

•

Khrushchev increases Soviet defense budget by $3,500 million. Kennedy asks for same increase in preparation for a showdown over Berlin. (July 26)

•

Gherman Titov, second Soviet cosmonaut, landed today after 25 hours in orbit. He slept in orbit for seven and a half hours. (August 7)

•

Jomo Kenyatta, convicted in 1953 for leading the *Mau Mau* rebellion against the British in Kenya, is freed. In his first speech, he appeals for peace and unity, so that "we will get our independence faster." (August 14)

•

Thirty thousand see President Ben-Zvi open the Fifth Maccabia Games. Twenty-seven countries are represented. (August 20)

•

The US and Britain urge Russia to agree to prohibit nuclear tests in the atmosphere which could produce fallout. (September 3)

•

The US detects Soviet nuclear blast 24 hours after test ban offer. It is the second detonation since Friday. (September 4)

•

President Kennedy announces he has ordered the resumption of tests "in the laboratory and underground with no fallout." Moscow sets off third explosion in the atmosphere. (September 5)

•

Secretary General of the United Nations, Dag Hammarskjold, is killed in a 'plane crash in Congo. The accident occurred during Hammarskjold's attempt to bring peace to Congo. Hammarskjold was a great friend of Israel and assisted the State greatly in the UN. (September 17)

•

Syrian army revolts against Gamal Abdul Nasser. The new Syrian regime to deport all Egyptians from Syria. The Syrian premier declares Syria independent from the UAR. (September 28)

The United States and Russia agree on appointment of U Thant of Burma as the UN Secretary General. (October 15)

●

Adlai Stevenson terms the Soviet atomic tests "A great leap backward towards anarchy and disaster." (October 30)

●

The *Knesset* confirmed the new Cabinet 78 days after the August 15 elections and nine months after David Ben-Gurion's resignation. (November 2)

●

A special UN political committee recommends economic sanctions be imposed against South Africa and that her expulsion from the UN be considered. In a reply to motions from the opposition, Prime Minister Ben-Gurion said that Israel would have been untrue to the moral imperatives of Judaism and her vital interests had she failed to support condemnation of apartheid. However, opposition members pointed out that this was a vote against a friendly nation, with those countries who wanted to destroy Israel. (November 13)

●

Several thousand East German workers, guarded by over 1,000 heavily armed soldiers, toiled all day raising a massive concrete wall and tank barriers on East Berlin's border with West Berlin. East German Communist leader, Mr. Walter Ulbricht, declared the wall dividing Berlin will go only when West Germany leaves NATO. West Berlin's deputy mayor, Franz Amrehn, describes the walls as 'The Thousand Year Wall.' (November 20)

●

The first communal city was established in Mitzpe Ramon. A group of young men and women, organized by the *Nahal's (pioneering combatant youth)* headquarters and the *Histadrut*, settled in temporary residences above the Ramon Crater. The attempt failed. The group was unable to sustain its population and its sources of income, and abandoned the site a few years later. (November 28)

●

After the huge success of hit musical 'West Side Story' on Broadway, a spectacular film is made. The music - Leonard Bernstein, the story - William Shakespeare. 'Romeo and Juliet' comes to New York. (November 30)

Eichmann Sentenced to Death

A rare photograph. A doctor examining Eichmann to determine whether he was fit to stand trial.

On Dec. 15, after an eight-month trial, Adolf Eichmann's judges took only 13 minutes to decide on the most severe sentence possible: death. The three judges, presided over by Chief Justice Moshe Landau, wrote that their decision reflected "a deep sense of responsibility to punish the accused and deter others."

Eichmann was brought into his glass booth in the courtroom only a minute before the sentence was read.

Upon hearing the translation of the sentence, Eichmann's whole body shuddered and his face revealed much emotion, contrary to the apathy displayed by him throughout the trial. Eichmann's defense counsel, German lawyer Robert Servatius, announced that he would appeal the sentence and ask the Israeli president for clemency.

The sentence was much discussed throughout the world. German newspaper reports did not express surprise at the sentence. Many important public figures stated that Eichmann had received a fair trial, much fairer than the fate Eichmann himself had meted out to so many innocent victims.

British academic figures contended that a death sentence was unjustifiable, and that Eichmann should be sentenced to life imprisonment as a lesson to the world.

Herut, Liberals Negotiate to Unify

Initial negotiations were conducted for the unification of *Herut* and the Liberal party. The negotiations were initiated by *Herut*, and were aimed at creating an alternative to *Mapai*. *Herut* knew it would only gain power in coalition with another liberal party. *The negotiations between the two parties continued until 1965.*

The Orthodox Demand Observance of Sabbath

On Nov. 21, Orthodox citizens held demonstrations to pressure the Cabinet to pass a law enforcing the observance of the Sabbath. The demonstrations were initiated by the 'National Committee for the Sabbath.' Thousands of religious representatives took part in the demonstrations, which were held throughout the country.

In opposition to the Orthodox demonstrators, hundreds of citizens who objected to religious coercion carried signs with words such as: "We are against Me'a She'arim in Dizengoff" and "Observe the Sabbath in your own home."

The police feared a violent encounter and did not allow secular demonstrators to demonstrate in front of the Mann Auditorium. Despite pressure from the Orthodox, a law enforcing observance of the Sabbath was never passed.

Eichmann is Hanged and His Body is Cremated

The Israeli Supreme Court unanimously rejected Adolf Eichmann's appeal of his death sentence, and Israeli President Itzhak Ben-Zvi refused to grant him clemency. On May 31, at 4:35 a.m., Eichmann was hanged at the Ramla prison. His body was cremated, and his ashes scattered at sea, far from Israel's territorial waters.

Eichmann was completely apathetic before his execution and told the wardens who were setting up the execution chamber, "In a little while, gentlemen, we will meet again. For this is everyone's fate." The last

Eichmann. Human and legal justice.

thing Eichmann said before he was hanged was that he had always obeyed his superiors and was therefore not guilty.

During Eichmann's last meeting with a clergyman, the clergyman tried to read to him from the Bible. Eichmann refused to listen, claiming that he did not believe in God or in the Bible, and that he did not need any support.

Eichmann's last request was for a bottle of wine. He drank half the bottle and asked to read, for the last time, the two letters he had received that day from his brothers.

The three power nuclear test ban conference is suspended in utter failure after more than three years of negotiations. Soviet Union insists the talks are all over, and that they had been wrecked by the West. The West maintains the talks are only adjourned, not ended. No communique is issued after the 353rd meeting, because delegates cannot agree on what had taken place. (January 29)

Kennedy announces a total embargo on US trade with Cuba. The White House says the loss of income to Castro's regime will "reduce the capacity of the Soviet-tied Havana government to engage in any subversion or other activities endangering the Western hemisphere's security." The step was taken after Cuba was ousted from the Organization of American States (OAS). (February 3)

Washington confirms that American pilots are flying with South Vietnamese pilots on combat missions against Communist guerilla forces. (March 10)

Syrian positions at Nukeib destroyed in move to end Sea of Galilee raids. Foreign Minister Golda Meir said attack necessary to safeguard security. "During the past month the Syrians, without cause or provocation, have made three attacks on Israeli fishermen and police patrol boats, wounding two Israelis." (March 16)

France abstains as the UN Security Council censures Israel over the attack on Nukeib on the night of March 16. The French delegate explained prior to the vote that the draft was not impartial and did not take into account Syrian provocations that preceded Israel's attack. (April 9)

Coin operated public telephone booths operating at three post offices in Israel. (May 14)

Three hundred and ten people accused of plotting to overthrow the Lebanese government in a coup d'etat, which failed last December 31, went on trial today. (June 1)

The IDF Raids Nukeib

Evacuating injured soldiers from Nukeib.

On Mar. 17, *Golani* units, elite commandos of the Israel Defense Forces, raided Syrian posts located in Nukeib, a village north of Kibbutz Ein Gev. The raid came following a long series of incidents along the Syrian-Israeli border.

The raid was executed late at night. The Israeli forces were immediately detected, and heavy fire erupted from the Syrians, who also shelled Kibbutz Ein Gev.

The difficult battle at Nukeib lasted 70 minutes.

Seven IDF soldiers were killed, and many more were injured. Two soldiers were taken captive and were later returned to Israel.

The Syrian soldiers did not flee, as they had in previous battles, but instead they fought stubbornly for every position.

The Syrians continued to shell the IDF. Armored trucks sent to assist the IDF drove into a minefield and were destroyed.

Towards the morning hours, Israeli combat 'planes entered the arena and shelled and destroyed several Syrian gun emplacements.

President Charles de Gaulle proclaims Algeria's independence in Paris. (July 3)

•

United States sets off first high shot hydrogen test, between 200 - 500 miles in space, above the Pacific Rim. The flash was seen in New Zealand and Hawai. (July 9)

•

US launches an orbiting space relay station. Satellite 'Telstar' makes worldwide television possible and opens a new era in human communications. (July 10)

•

After Egypt succeeds in launching four 600 km (375 miles) missiles from a base in the Western desert, Pres. Nasser announces: "Our missiles can hit anywhere south of Beirut." Military circles in Israel are not surprised. They say that Nasser had planned to fire the rockets last year to celebrate the ninth anniversary of the Egyptian Revolution. However, the firing by Israel of the *Shavit* rocket just a few days before the anniversary had caused Nasser to postpone his demonstration, as it would have been an anti-climax. (July 21)

•

Marilyn Monroe, 36, takes her own life. The coroner declares that she died from an overdose of sleeping pills. (August 5)

•

Ten thousand feared dead in Persian earthquake. Israel sends aid. First shipment left Lod for Teheran on board a BOAC flight. A further six tons of medical supplies, food, clothing and blankets were flown by El Al to Teheran in response to an appeal by Persian authorities. (September 1)

•

The American State Department states that Soviet construction of a fishing port in Cuba will be watched closely to see whether it poses a threat to American safety. The port in Havana Bay could also be used as an auxiliary base for submarines and torpedo ships. (September 26)

•

Yemen ruler killed, republic is declared. Egyptian troops guard airfields in capital to secure revolt. Saudia cuts ties with Egypt as its warships and 'planes raid villages. Egypt and Yemen sign a defense agreement. (September 27)

Yossele Shumacher is at Last Found in New York

Isser Harel found Yossele in US.

"Mama'le, mama'le."

On July 1, two and a half years after his disappearance from Jerusalem, Yossele Shumacher was located in America. Yossele had been smuggled from Israel with the assistance of missionary Ruth Ben-David, who had dressed him up as a girl and supplied him with a false passport.

Yossele was found in New York, in a grocery shop owned by *Satmar Hassidim*. Two days after he was found by the *Mossad*, he was united with his mother, Ida Shumacher. His first words to her were, "Mama'le, mama'le."

Jewish Spy Deported from Israel Commits Suicide

Dr. Robert Soblen, who was arrested and deported from Israel, poisoned himself on Sept. 11 while on his way to the airplane that was supposed to send him from London back to the United States. Soblen, an American Jew, had been convicted in the US of spying for Russia and was sentenced to life imprisonment. He escaped to Israel with a forged passport, and in Israel requested political asylum.

The United States then submitted an application for Soblen's extradition, which led Israeli police to locate and arrest the fugitive spy. The Israeli court approved his arrest and he was held for ten days.

On July 1, Soblen was taken from the Israeli prison by security services, transported to the airport, and forcefully put on the airplane. During the flight, Soblen seized the opportunity, when his bodyguards fell asleep, to try to commit suicide. He was taken off the 'plane in London and hospitalized.

After months of legal battles and an attempt to revoke the extradition, Soblen was taken to the airport in London to fly to America.

On his way to the 'plane, Soblen swallowed poison which he had managed to smuggle past his guards. He died ten days later as a result of the poisoning.

On Sept. 27, after three years of discussion and delays, the United States agreed to sell *Hawk* missiles to Israel. The awaited approval was obtained only after the Minister of Foreign Affairs, Golda Meir, visited the US.

Attorney General Hausner Resigns

Gideon Hausner.

Gideon Hausner, who will be remembered forever as the prosecutor in the trial of Nazi murderer Adolf Eichmann, announced his resignation as attorney general.

The *Knesset*: Arab Refugees Will Not be Returned to Israel

Before Minister of Foreign Affairs Golda Meir left Israel to participate in talks at the United Nations, the *Knesset* decided on Nov. 13 that Palestinian refugees would not be allowed to return to Israel. Furthermore, the *Knesset* decided that the burden of finding a solution to the Palestinian problem should be assumed by the Arab countries. Sixty-three *Knesset* members from the coalition voted in favor of the decision. Surprisingly, *Herut* members abstained in the hope that the Cabinet would not enjoy a majority.

From 1959 on, international pressure was put on Israel to solve the problem of the Palestinian refugees. Western countries especially feared an oil embargo by the Arab countries. The United States appointed a special representative, Joseph Johnson, to examine the problem in the Middle East and report to the US government. Israel tried to influence Johnson's report, but in the end the report called on Israel to rapidly solve the problem of the hundreds of refugees who had fled from Israel in 1948 and were residing in temporary camps in the West Bank and Gaza Strip.

New City in Arava – Arad

On Nov. 21, the city of Arad was established in a formal ceremony attended by the prime minister, ministers, and *Knesset* members. The first family of settlers arrived at the city and was greeted by David Ben-Gurion.

Cuban Missile Crisis

On Oct. 22, the United States imposed a naval closure on Cuba after spy 'planes discovered that the Soviet Union had turned Cuba into a missile base. The Soviet Union refused to remove the missiles, and American President John F. Kennedy instructed the American navy to search any ship sailing toward Cuba.

Confrontation between the US and the USSR seemed inevitable as American combat ships approached the Soviet ships headed towards Cuba. Finally, Nikita Khrushchev, leader of the Soviet Union, proposed a summit meeting under the auspices of Secretary General to the United Nations, U Thant.

Israel Fails in Bid to Join the Common Market

After many unsuccessful attempts, a representative delegation of countries in the European Common Market finally met with Minister of Finance Levi Eshkol in Brussels on Nov. 26. Eshkol explained to the delegation that, to secure Israel's economic future, the countries must grant it special customs rights on merchandise manufactured in Israel. "Fifteen years ago, our political infrastructure was laid," said Eshkol, "but now we must lay the foundations for our economic future."

A land of olive oil and honey.

The delegation's members expressed sympathy for Israel but rejected Eshkol's terms. Their opposition stemmed from the considerable pressure applied by Arab countries on France, the central pillar of the European Common Market.

Eventually, Eshkol managed to reach a compromise with the Market's countries, which granted Israel limited rights for certain goods.

1962

OCTOBER - DECEMBER

The new Yemen republic prime minister visits Cairo. Four days later Egyptian troops guard an oil-field in the Yemeni capital as the revolt is secured. (October 4)

•

Sana warns of war with Saudi Arabia if Saudia aids the Imam. Egypt offers full backing to the republic. (October 11)

•

Two Britons and an American share the Nobel Prize for Medicine for their discovery of DNA (deoxyribonucleic acid). The discovery has far-reaching consequences in both medicine and biology. The winners are James Dewey Watson, Professor of Biology at Harvard, Francis Compton Crick, a molecular biologist at the Cavendish Institute, Cambridge UK and Maurice Wilkins, Deputy Director of Physics at Kings College London. (October 18)

•

Ukrainian Supreme Court sentences six Jews, including an 81-year-old, to be shot for currency speculation. Alter Bronstein, 81, was described as the ring-leader. (October 23)

•

The *Knesset* elected President Itzhak Ben-Zvi for a third term. (October 30)

•

Foreign Minister Golda Meir: Israel is "shocked and dismayed" by the world's unwillingness to expose Egypt's military intervention in Yemen. (November 12)

•

The *Knesset* rejected the proposal to establish an educational television channel. The discussion was instigated by the opposition and some coalition members supported the initiative. (November 21)

•

Syrian attack on a tractor east of Tel Katzir sets off a prolonged exchange of fire. Ben-Gurion warns of retaliation: "If the UN cannot maintain quiet on the Syrian border we will have to do so with all the force at our command." (December 4)

•

US extends diplomatic recognition to Yemeni republic in wake of an announcement in Cairo that Egypt is willing to withdraw its troops from Yemen, if Saudi Arabia and Jordan stop backing the Imam of Yemen. (December 19)

1963

JANUARY - JUNE

Nasser opens next stage in Aswan Dam construction. (January 9)

•

The *Knesset* decided to raise the president's salary from 540 to 1500 lira a month. President Ben-Zvi objected to the raise and announced that he would donate half his salary to the Foundation for the Research of Israel. (January 21)

•

Lord Samuel, a leading British Jew and former parliamentary leader of the Liberal Party, died at 92. Lord Samuel served as the first High Commissioner for the British Mandate in Palestine after the First World War. (February 5)

•

Syrian military junta appoints Salah e-Din Bitar, co-founder of the Socialist Ba'ath party, as prime minister and defense minister. (March 10)

•

Soviet Jews have been told again this year that state-run bakeries will not supply them with *matzo* for Passover. The ban was first enforced last year. (March 18)

•

Swiss see no early trial for two Israeli agents arrested March 2. Foreign Minister Golda Meir, in a *Knesset* statement on behalf of the government, demanded that the West German government take action to stop the activity of German scientists in developing offensive weapons aimed at the destruction of Israel. (March 18)

•

Security services' chief Isser Harel quits in a rift with Ben-Gurion, who was understood to have been concerned with assessments regarding the German scientists in Egypt. (March 25)

•

US President John F. Kennedy announces that America supports Israel's security and will intervene in its favor in the event of violence. Britain supports the announcement. (May 8)

•

Detachment of paratroopers from Congo arrived in Israel for military training. The soldiers were trained as paratroop instructors for Congo's independence day. Israel has established a parachuting school in Congo. (May 17)

•

Large crowds cheer President Kennedy on an official visit to Berlin, as he makes his famous speech: "Ich bin ein Berliner" *("I am a Berliner").* (June 26)

Germany Helps Egypt to Manufacture Weapons

On Mar. 2, Swiss police arrested an Israeli citizen and an Austrian scientist on suspicion of spying for Israel. After the arrest, Golda Meir exposed shocking details about the assistance Egypt had received from German scientists in the manufacturing of long-range guided missiles capable of destroying Israel.

The two suspects, Yosef Ben-Gal and Dr. Otto Uclik, belonged to an Israeli intelligence ring working to disrupt Egypt's efforts to recruit German scientists to develop Egyptian weapons. Uclik had at first worked for the Egyptians, but guilt and heavy pressure applied by Israel convinced him to take part in the struggle against the German scientists' aid to Egypt.

Uclik and Ben-Gal were arrested in Basel after they tried to persuade the daughter of one of the Germans to convince her father to stop assisting Egypt.

The arrest of the two exposed the activities of the *Mossad's* Swiss branch, responsible for the disappearance of several senior scientists who had worked for Egypt.

Ben-Gurion Resigns. Eshkol Forms New Government

David Ben-Gurion and his successor, Levi Eshkol.

On June 16, David Ben-Gurion, prime minister and minister of defense, resigned from all his positions in the Israeli Cabinet and in the *Knesset,* stating that his resignation was for personal reasons.

He appointed Minister of Finance Levi Eshkol as his successor, and asked the ministers to form a new Cabinet within a week, comprised of the same coalition members.

Eshkol, the new prime minister, also assumed the defense ministry. Pinchas Sapir was appointed minister of finance, Zalman Eran was made minister of education, and Abba Eban became deputy prime minister.

After his resignation, Ben-Gurion returned to his home on Kibbutz Sde Boker and announced that he would be devoting his time to his hobbies: studying philosophy and the Bible, writing articles, playing with his grandchildren and doing Feldenkreis

Ben-Zvi Dies. Shazar is made Israel's Next President

On Apr. 23 Israel's second president, Itzhak Ben-Zvi, died of a terminal illness at the age of 78.

Ben-Zvi had kept his illness secret from the public, and news of his death shocked the nation. Voice of Israel interrupted its broadcast at 7:05 a.m. to announce the president's death.

Ben-Zvi's coffin lay in state at the Binyanei Ha'Uma building in Je-

Zalman Shazar.

rusalem, and tens of thousands of citizens came to pay their last respects. Leaders from all over the world attended the funeral which took place on Mount Herzl.

Many countries announced official days of mourning in memory of the president.

On May 21, one month after Ben-Zvi's death, Zalman Shazar was elected Israel's third president.

President Kennedy Assassinated

President Kennedy. After his assassination in Dallas, prime ministers stopped traveling in convertible cars.

On Nov. 22, President John F. Kennedy was assassinated during a visit to Dallas, Texas.

The assassin, a young man named Lee Harvey Oswald, was arrested and he himself was assassinated two days later. Vice President Lyndon Johnson took the oath of office on the same 'plane in which Kennedy's body was returned to Washington for a full state ceremonial burial.

The entire world was stunned with grief. Radio and television around the world interrupted their broadcasts to report the assassination. The United States was in deep mourning, and the flags of many countries were flown at half-mast.

Rabin Appointed Chief of Staff

Levi Eshkol handing Yitzhak Rabin the chief of staff's pennant.

On Dec. 25 the Cabinet approved the appointment of Yitzhak Rabin, deputy chief of staff and chief of operations, as chief of staff. Rabin assumed his position a week later, entering the history books as the chief of staff who led Israel to one of its greatest victories, the Six-Day War.

Ben-Gurion had objected to Rabin's appointment for many years due to Rabin's affiliation with Ahdut Ha'Avoda and his opposition to the break-up of the Palmach (which had originally been set up to repel a possible German invasion from Egypt).

Israel Told to Ensure Return of Palestinian Refugees

On Dec. 4, the UN General Assembly approved the American proposal that Israel must compensate Palestinian refugees or allow their immediate return to Israel. Israel was the only country at the assembly that objected to the proposal.

The vote was the result of a process of several years, during which immense pressure was placed on the other UN member countries by the Arab world.

After John F. Kennedy had been elected president of the United States, American pressure on Israel had lessened. In its place came the demands of other Western countries that Israel compensate the Palestinian refugees.

After much discussion, a committee headed by American Joseph Johnson had been established to examine the issue. Johnson recommended that a limited number of refugees be allowed to return to Israel, but Israel rejected his proposal. The Arab Bloc said that as long as the refugee problem remained unre-solved, they would not cooperate with companies from countries that did not exert pressure on Israel. The Arab Boycott resulted in a new wave of pressure and eventually led to the UN resolution.

Despite the resolution, Israel's attitude remained unchanged until the early 1990's, when Israeli leaders first agreed in Madrid talks and later in the Oslo Accords, to meet with Palestinian representatives to try to find a political solution to the problem of the refugees.

1963
JULY - DECEMBER

Philby revealed as third man to Burgess and Maclean. Kim Philby had warned the three diplomats that the British secret service was on to them, so enabling them to disappear behind the Iron Curtain in 1951. (July 3)

●

British journalist returns from Yemen to report he saw Egyptian 'planes drop gas bombs on village in north Yemen. This is the first confirmation that Egypt is using poison gas in the war. (July 20)

●

Russia, America and Britain initialed a treaty to ban all nuclear tests except those underground. July 28: Israel expected to join Moscow test ban pact. August 6: the big three sign partial atom test ban in Moscow. August 13: 49 nations had signed the British text of the partial test ban treaty by last night. (July 25)

●

Third Buddhist monk burns himself to death at Hue, 700 kilometers (438 miles) north of Saigon, to protest alleged religious discrimination by the South Vietnamese government. August 21: President Ngo Dinh Diem declared martial law throughout South Vietnam and sent troops storming through the Pagoda centers of the Buddhist opposition. (August 13)

More than 200,000 negroes and white friends stage a giant orderly 'march for jobs and freedom' in Washington. Demonstration organizers hope it will lead to a historic breakthrough all along the American civil rights front. Speakers demanded the passage of President Kennedy's Civil Rights Bill and more. (August 28)

President Kennedy orders Secretary of Defense Robert McNamara and General Taylor to fly to Saigon. Kennedy said that it would not be wise to cut off South Vietnam, but the government there has lost touch with the people. Mr. McNamara's and General Taylor's recommendations will have a major bearing on the extent of future collaboration with Diem's government, as they tell Kennedy they believe major American involvement in South Vietnam's campaign against the Communist guerrillas will be ended by December 1965. (September 21)

US State Department spokesman says that as far as the US government knows, Israel's National Water Carrier subscribes to the overall blueprint of the Johnston plan approved on the technical level by Israeli and Arab experts. Prime Minister Eshkol declared that Israel will protect her vital rights if Arab states should attempt to divert the Jordan headwaters with the aim of sabotaging the water carrier. (January 13)

●

Minister of Finance Pinhas Sapir accompanied his wife to the airport and discovered a new tax had been instituted: a port tax of five lira. (February 6)

●

A team of 33 scientists at the Brookhaven National Laboratory has confirmed the theory of grouping of elementary atomic particles worked out eight years ago by Dr. Yuval Ne'eman, Professor of Physics at Tel Aviv University. (February 21)

●

The first *matzo* is baked in Moscow. Rabbi Yehuda Levin inaugurated a private bakery and produced the first *matzo* for Passover. (March 11)

●

Jack Ruby is convicted and sentenced to death by electric chair for the murder of President Kennedy's accused assassin, Lee Harvey Oswald. (March 14)

●

The remains of Revisionist leader Ze'ev Jabotinsky, who died in New York in 1940, will be transferred to Israel to be re-interred in Jerusalem on the 24th anniversary of his death. (March 15)

●

Yehuda Unterman and Yitzhak Nissim are chosen as chief rabbis. Unterman was elected chief Ashkenazi rabbi of Israel, a post vacant since Rabbi Isaac Halevi Herzog's death in July 1959. (March 17)

●

Crown Prince Faisal is in full control of Saudi Arabia. (March 30)

●

US Jewish leaders see President Johnson and Secretary of State Rusk. The US government was urged to express its concern over discrimination against Jews in the Soviet Union. (April 7)

Pope Paul VI in Israel

Pope Paul VI in Israel.

On May 1, Pope Paul VI arrived in Israel for an 11-hour visit, on his way from Jordan. The pope and his entourage were officially welcomed in Megiddo by an Israeli delegation led by President Zalman Shazar, who arrived from Jerusalem by helicopter. Before stopping in Megiddo, the pope visited East Jerusalem, Bethlehem and Jericho, where he was welcomed by King Hussein.

During his visit to the Church of the Holy Sepulcher, fire broke out due to a short-circuit on a television camera being used to film the visit. The fire put at risk the masses who came to receive the Pope's blessing and delayed his departure.

For the pope's arrival, Prime Minister Levi Eshkol published an official greeting, calling on the pope to try to bring peace to the area on behalf of its 500 million Christians. Both in Jordan and in Israel, the pope was transported in an armored car, a result of the painful lesson learned from the assassination of American President John F. Kennedy.

The international media covered the historic event extensively. *Since then, the leading figure in the Christian world has never visited Israel. However, at the beginning of 1997, Pope John Paul II assured Prime Minister Netanyahu that he would visit Israel before the year 2000.*

An Egyptian Pilot Defects with 'Plane

On Jan. 19, an Egyptian pilot, Captain Mahmoud Abbas Hilmi, landed his Soviet-made *Yak-11* airplane at a military airport in southern Israel and requested political asylum. Hilmi had successfully escaped the Egyptian air force 'planes that had pursued him.

When Hilmi entered Israeli air space, he requested permission to land, which was immediately granted. Upon landing, he was transferred to a remand cell on the Israeli base, where he was interrogated.

During the course of the interrogation, Hilmi was visited by Chief of Staff Yitzhak Rabin and Air Force Commander Ezer Weizman. The two did not identify themselves to him.

Eventually, Hilmi asked to leave Israel and he settled in Argentina under a false identity. Six months later, he was found dead in his apartment in Buenos Aires.

Egyptian pilot Hilmi defected to Israel.

Eshkol Weds *Knesset* Librarian

Miriam and Levi Eshkol.

Prime Minister and Minister of Defense Levi Eshkol, 69, married the Knesset's librarian, 34-year-old Miriam Zelikovich on Jan. 3.

The Palestine Liberation Organization is Formed

The *Palestine Liberation Organization* was established at a summit conference held on May 27. Ahmed Shukeiry was appointed head of the organization, and a young man named Yasser Arafat was appointed head of the organization's military division.

The founding conference was held at the Intercontinental Hotel on the Mount of Olives in East Jerusalem. The organization received the blessing of most Arab countries, who also promised to help by supplying it with weapons and other equipment. The Palestinian Covenant was also approved. It defined the Palestinians' right to all of Israel, their denial of Israel's right to exist and their right to self-determination. It was decided that the organization would include two military branches comprised of volunteers from the Arab states.

In 1968, Arafat became leader of the PLO and said that he viewed military action as the only way to achieve independence and obtain a state for the Palestinian people.

US Bombs North Vietnam

Johnson, after the war.

On Aug. 5, responding to an attack by North Vietnamese torpedo vessels on a United States destroyer, United States President Lyndon Johnson ordered the bombing of North Vietnamese military targets.

Until the bombing, American intervention in Vietnam had been relatively small-scale and had been defined primarily as an operation of military observers sent to train and instruct South Vietnam's army.

Ze'ev Jabotinsky Interred in Israel

Menachem Begin and a guard of veterans alongside Jabotinsky's coffin.

Ze'ev Jabotinsky and his wife Johanna were reinterred in a state funeral on Mount Herzl in Jerusalem on July 9.

The coffins of Jabotinsky and his wife were flown from the United States where they had been buried since Jabotinsky's death in 1940.

The *Herut* leader, Menachem Begin, arranged for the body of the founder of the Revisionist movement and spiritual father of the *Likud* political party to be buried in Israel. In his will Jabotinsky had requested that this be carried out if so ordered by the future Jewish state's government. Prime Minister David Ben-Gurion had always refused permission to bring over the remains of Jabotinsky, his enemy from before the founding of the state. It was Levi Eshkol, Ben-Gurion's successor, who granted permission.

Jabotinsky's coffin first lay in state in Herbert Samuel Square in Tel Aviv, where thousands of people filed by to pay their last respects. From there, it was driven in a state procession through the city's main streets. The president of the State of Israel and the heads of all the political parties were present at the funeral. The flag of Israel was flown at half-mast.

At the press of a button Nikita Khrushchev inaugurated the Aswan Dam in Egypt. The Soviet leader took the opportunity to attack Israeli imperialism. This was one of Khrushchev's last public appearances before his death several months later. (May 14)

•

Pandit Nehru, 74, prime minister since India's 1947 independence, dies of a heart attack. India's new premier, Lal Bahadur Shastri, is to continue Nehru's policy of non-alignment. (May 27)

•

President Zalman Shazar presented Nahum Stelmach, Israel's soccer captain, with the Asia Cup, after Israel's 2-1 victory over South Korea. (June 3)

•

Israel and the US agreed to build a nuclear reactor in Israel which will be used to produce electricity. American Secretary of State, Dean Rusk, emphasized that the US has an interest in a strong and secure Israel. (June 5)

•

Nelson Mandela is given life sentence in South Africa. (June 12)

•

American Reform rabbis declare that Israel must separate religion from the State. This declaration enrages Israeli Orthodox circles, who demand that all ties with Reform Jews be severed. (June 15)

•

President Shazar proposed a solution to the dispute between the *Bnei Israel* community and the Chief Rabbinate. He proposed a statement which would be issued by the rabbinate containing an interpretation of its directives concerning the *Bnei Israel* status as Jews, which would be acceptable to both sides. The *Knesset* affirms that the *Bnei Israel* are 'Jews in all respects,' and calls on the Chief Rabbinate to find a way of removing the causes of any feeling of discrimination among the *Bnei Israel*. (July 31)

•

Turkish jets strafe Cyprus as Greek Cypriots conquer three Turkish Cypriot villages. The Greek, Turkish and Cypriot governments agree to a general ceasefire in the ongoing Cyprus conflict. (August 8)

Water Flows from Galilee to Negev

On June 10 the pipeline running from the Sea of Galilee to the Negev was inaugurated, and water started to flow over a length of 94 miles. Many pumping stations, equipped with new and sophisticated, state-of-the-art instruments, were built along the length of the pipeline.

The operation of the National Water Carrier caused a furore in Arab countries, whose armies went on high alert, anticipating war against Israel. *In fact, the first terror attack which Fatah undertook in Israel was against the national water pipeline.*

The Arab Summit debated the Palestine question. They discussed military aspects related to Arab diversion schemes of the River Jordan waters. The Israeli Cabinet reaffirmed Israel's determination to repel any aggression and to act for the preservation of Israel's rights should the Arab states attempt to implement their plans for the diversion of the Jordan River's tributaries. (September 5)

•

The Warren Report on President John F. Kennedy's assassination is published. "The commission discovered no evidence that the Soviet Union or Cuba were involved in the assassination of President Kennedy, nor did the commission's investigation of Jack Ruby produce any grounds for believing that Ruby's killing of Oswald was part of a conspiracy." (September 28)

•

A Japanese student, Yoshinori Sakai, who was born on the day on which Hiroshima was bombed, lights the Olympic flare and opens the 18th Olympic Games, in Tokyo. Ninety five countries participate. (October 10)

•

Twenty-three animals from Kenya, including zebras, giraffes, ostriches and elephants, arrived at Ramat Gan's Safari Park, Israel's largest zoo. (October 12)

•

Dr. Martin Luther King, Jr., the civil rights leader, wins the 1964 Nobel Peace Prize. (October 15)

•

The Soviet Communist Party's general secretary was surprisingly ousted and placed under house arrest. The *troika* of Brezhnev (the strong man), Kosygin and Podgorny was appointed in Nikita Khrushchev's place. (October 15)

•

King Saud is dethroned and his brother Faisal, 59, becomes the Saudi monarch. (November 2)

•

Lyndon Johnson sweeps the US election by the greatest margin in history. (November 4)

•

Jordanian troops wound three Israeli police guards at the Israeli enclave on Mount Scopus. Israel protests to UNTSO Chief of Staff, General Odd Bull, over Mount Scopus shooting. (December 23)

First Dogfight Between *Mirage* and *MiG* Fighters

The first battle of its type between a *Mirage* and a *MiG-21* ended in a clear victory for the Israeli Air Force. A *MiG-21* was downed in the confrontation.

On Nov. 13, after heavy shelling of the She'ar Yashuv and Kibbutz Dan settlements, the air force was called into action against Syrian positions in the north. Four Syrian *MiG's* were scrambled against four Israeli *Mirages*. This clash, which took place over the Sea of Galilee, was the first of its kind between the world's two best jet fighters. One Syrian *MiG* was downed, and the three others returned to Syria.

In the Syrian shelling of settlements and border positions, three soldiers were killed and many soldiers and civilians were wounded. Israeli fire killed seven Syrian soldiers and wounded twenty-six.

A United Nations initiative brought about a cease-fire between the two sides.

Ben-Gurion Leaves *Mapai*

Yesterday's friends became the most bitter enemies in the history of the Labor movement. Eshkol faces Ben-Gurion's threatening hands.

On Nov. 15, after the *Mapai* (Erez Israel Workers' Party) central office approved the proposal of Prime Minister Levi Eshkol to unite *Mapai* with *Ahdut Ha'Avoda*, the former prime minister, David Ben-Gurion, announced that he could no longer continue to be a party member. Eshkol's proposal was approved by an overwhelming majority, with 182 votes in favor and eight against.

Ben-Gurion's resignation, which was based on the party's handling of the notorious 'Mishap,' caused much embarrassment in the party's central office and an exchange of bitter recriminations among key members. Moshe Dayan, who had resigned from the Ministry of Agriculture ten days earlier, called on the party to accept Ben-Gurion's demands for further handling of the 'Mishap' in the future.

Foreign Minister Golda Meir was obliged to interrupt her speech because of Ben-Gurion's repeated heckling. Meir announced that she was unwell and left the rostrum.

After Ben-Gurion's resignation on December 8, other key members including Moshe Dayan, Shimon Peres, Teddy Kollek and Yitzhak Rabin, resigned from the party.

'Suitcase Spy' Extradited to Israel

Mordechai Lock, an Israeli citizen, crossed the border into Egypt in 1961, was recruited by Egyptian intelligence as a spy, and was extradited to Israel on Nov. 25. Lock, who underwent intelligence training in Egypt, was sent to work as an intelligence operative in Italy. When his Egyptian handlers suspected him of trying to establish contact with Israel, they decided to forcibly return him to Egypt.

Lock was kidnapped and taken to the Egyptian embassy in Rome, where he was drugged and placed in a large diplomatic bag bound for Cairo. He woke at Rome airport and was taken from the bag, after an Italian porter heard shouts from inside.

Lock was extradited to Israel and sentenced to 13 years in jail.

Official Relations with Germany

Seventeen years after the founding of the State of Israel, the *Knesset* decided on March 16 to establish diplomatic relations with West Germany. Sixty-six *Knesset* members supported the decision, with 29 voting against it.

During the preceding six months, the Arab states had exerted heavy pressure on Germany not to establish relations or enter into any economic or security transactions with Israel. A month before the vote, Germany had succumbed to Arab pressure and decided to postpone the establishment of diplomatic relations with Israel, but counter-pressure from the United States brought about a reversal of the decision.

Prime Minister Levi Eshkol and Foreign Minister Golda Meir declared that in view of the change in Germany's official position, there was no alternative but to establish relations, which would greatly assist Israel's economic and security situation. In addition, they claimed that if Israel did not agree to full diplomatic relations, it would be interpreted as a victory for Nasser and those who wished for Israel's continued international isolation.

Leading the opponents of the decision was the *Herut* leader, Menachem Begin, who made an emotional speech condemning Germany. Many *Knesset* members abstained from the vote in order to avoid voting against their party.

First *Fatah* Terrorist Act

After the terrorist attack, motorized patrols were introduced along the pipelines of the National Water Carrier in the Galilee.

On Jan. 3, *Fatah*, the military wing of the PLO, attempted to carry out its first terrorist attack in Israel. The target selected was the National Water Carrier which had recently started operation. The attempt was thwarted and security forces managed to arrest one of the members of the terrorist team which had planted the device. This was the first time that the name of *Fatah* was linked to a military operation. After the attempted attack, the organization published victory announcements in Cairo and Damascus.

Churchill Dies

Churchill, the last leader.

Winston Churchill, the British statesman who, more than anyone else, symbolized Britain's struggle during World War II, died on Jan. 24. The 90-year-old Churchill was the last surviving Allied leader; Roosevelt had died in 1945, Stalin in 1953.

Throughout the long war years, Churchill was the only leader of his generation to assist the British in withstanding the German bombardments. His broadcast speeches inspired British civilians and soldiers alike with patriotic fervor. His "blood, sweat and tears" speech, which promised the Nazis that the British would fight for every inch of their soil, has been inscribed in the pages of history and quoted on countless occasions.

Churchill was a good friend of Israel and among the most enthusiastic supporters of its founding. Despite his longstanding illness, his death came as a shock to Britons and people throughout the world.

1965
JANUARY - APRIL

The four-day Arab Summit ended in Cairo. All countries involved agreed to continue the implementation of the Jordan River diversion project to subvert Israel's National Water Carrier. Chief of Staff Yitzhak Rabin said it would be better for Israel to rely on deterrent ability than on Lebanon's efforts to withstand Arab pressure on diverting one of the sources of the Hasbani. (January 12)

•

The movie 'Salah Shabbati' directed by Ephraim Kishon won the prestigious Hollywood Golden Globe award in the 'Best Foreign Movie' category. (January 31)

•

Prime Minister Kosygin pledged Soviet support for North Vietnam in its struggle against imperialism. (February 6).

•

Syrian tractors working on the diversion of the River Jordan headwaters were hit in an exchange of fire which started when the Syrian army fired on an Israeli patrol inside Israel. (March 17)

•

Soviet cosmonaut, Lt. Col. Alexei Leonov, steps out of the 'Vikshod-2' craft to become the first man to stand alone in the great vacuum of outer space. (March 18)

•

The first delegation of young Israelis to visit the death camps in Poland marked the 20th anniversary of the liberation of the camps by Allied Forces. (April 4)

•

Chief of the Arab Unified Command, General Amer and Secretary General of the Arab League, Abdul Khalek Hassouna are expected to tour Syria, Jordan and Lebanon next week in an attempt to settle the military and political problems confronting these countries in connection with the diversion of the River Jordan headwaters. (April 7)

•

Over 12,000 students demonstrate outside the White House, urging an end to the Vietnam War and an American withdrawal. (April 17)

•

The Shrine of the Book, a semi-subterranean museum housing the Dead Sea Scrolls and other ancient manuscripts and relics, will be ceremonially opened in Jerusalem tonight. (April 20)

Two hit as *Fatah* cell blasts house in Afula; tracks traced from Jordan and back. Israel's note to the UN lists six incidents issuing from Jordan. The IDF raids Jenin, blowing up a flour mill and ice factory. In Kalkilya two main fuel stations are destroyed. Chief of Staff Rabin says the raids are a warning to Jordan for its aid to *Fatah*. (May 27)

•

A 14-year-old girl and a man were killed and four people wounded after Jordanian soldiers opened fire on houses in Jerusalem's Musrara neighborhood. (May 31)

•

Prof. Martin Buber dies in Jerusalem at 87. (June 14)

•

Israel mourns Israel's first foreign minister, and second prime minister, Moshe Sharett, after a long and painful illness. (July 7)

•

'Mariner 4' relays first close-up photos of Mars. Transmission of 21 photos expected to take a week. Scientists hope pictures will be 100 times better than from Earth. They may show objects as small as 1.5 miles in diameter. (July 15)

•

Ben-Gurion, who decided to resign from *Mapai* and found the *Rafi* party, returned the car and chauffeur which had been placed at his disposal by *Mapai*. (July 19)

•

President Johnson announces an increase in conscription, to boost American forces in Vietnam from 75,000 to 125,000 (July 28)

•

Seventh Maccabia Games opens in Tel Aviv with a parade of Jewish athletes who have come from 27 countries, before a crowd of 50,000. (August 23)

•

King Faisal and Pres. Nasser decide to give people of Yemen the right to decide the government they wish, in a popular plebiscite, and form a transitional conference with all factions. (August 24)

•

American astronauts Gordon Cooper and Charles Conrad return to Earth after setting a new record of 190 hours and 56 minutes in space aboard the spaceship 'Gemini 5.' (August 29)

Eli Cohen Hanged in Damascus

The Israeli spy who succeeded in infiltrating the highest levels of the Syrian government.

Israeli spy Eli Cohen, 40, was hanged on May 18 in the central square of Damascus, after being convicted of espionage. Cohen, who succeeded in infiltrating the highest levels of the Syrian government, was described in state newspapers as the person who caused the most serious espionage damage in Syria's history.

Cohen, born in Egypt, was recruited by the *Mossad* and for three years operated in Syria under the name Kamal Amin Taabeth. He managed to become friendly with all key government members, including the Syrian leader.

He had succeeded in entering Syria in the guise of a Syrian emigre who had made money in Argentina. Helped by recommendations from the Argentine community's leaders, he contacted the heads of the Syrian government and joined the ranks of the governing party's bosses.

Cohen would make his wireless broadcasts to Israel every morning from his apartment close to Syrian military headquarters in Damascus. He was caught after arousing the suspicion of the Syrian security services and being identified as a Cairo-born Jew by a Damascus resident. In order to trace him, the Syrians silenced all the nation's radio broadcasts, thus enabling his broadcast signals to be clearly received.

During the trial, Israel tried to propose exchange deals to Syria, but the Syrians rejected them all. They also rejected requests for a pardon that arrived from many countries worldwide, even from the Pope.

Israel Museum Opened in Jerusalem

On May 11 the Israel Museum was opened in Jerusalem's Valley of the Cross. Israel's president, Zalman Shazar, and the prime minister, Levi Eshkol, were present at the opening and bestowed golden keys of honor to the four principal donors.

The ceremony was organized by the chairman of the board of directors of the museum, Teddy Kollek, who had recently retired from his post as director-general of the Prime Minister's Office.

The leaders of the city's religious community bitterly opposed the placing of statues on the museum grounds and attempted until the last minute to prevent the opening. The press also attacked the project and asked whether this was the time to invest millions in imported marble.

At the museum's opening, works of art worth some IL 40 million and brought from forty museums around the world were displayed. The most expensive items, which included Rembrandt's 'Moshe,' were protected by many security officers. *The museum continues to attract major international exhibitions.*

West German Ambassador Presents Credentials

Against a backdrop of stormy demonstrations in Jerusalem, the first West German ambassador to Israel presented his credentials to President Zalman Shazar. The largest demonstration was held in Herbert Samuel Square in Tel Aviv. In front of 5,000 people, Menachem Begin made one of his most impassioned speeches, accusing the Israeli government of betraying the 1.5 million children slaughtered in the Holocaust. At the same time, thousands of Holocaust survivors and supporters of the opposition carrying signs against the decision to establish diplomatic relations with West Germany

Ambassador Pauls presents his credentials to President Shazar.

arrived in the capital.

Pauls' first act as ambassador was to visit the Yad Vashem memorial in Jerusalem. Five days later, Israel's first ambassador to West Germany presented his credentials in Bonn.

Eshkol Wins the Elections – Crushing Defeat for Ben-Gurion

Victorious – Levi Eshkol.

Defeated – David Ben-Gurion.

Incoming – Uri Avneri.

The elections for the sixth Knesset, held on Nov. 2 in the shadow of the serious rift between *Mapai (Erez Israel Workers' Party)* and the newly founded *Rafi*, ended in a decisive victory for Prime Minister Levi Eshkol. The alignment of *Mapai* with *Ahdut Ha'Avoda* won 45 mandates. David Ben-Gurion's *Rafi* party won only ten seats.

The result dealt a cruel blow to the 'Old Man' from Sde Boker who had believed that he could win the elections with the assistance of the young team led by Moshe Dayan and Shimon Peres.

Gahal (the joint list of *Herut* and the Liberals), managed to achieve only 26 seats, in comparison with the 17 members that each of the partners had in the previous *Knesset*.

The big surprise of the elections was the entry of Uri Avneri who ran in order to fight the Libel Law. Over 80% of the population voted in the elections: a typical Israeli turnout.

Eshkol was formally invited to form a Cabinet by President Shazar on November 28; he did so within two weeks.

Mayor Teddy Kollek Wins in Jerusalem

Teddy Kollek defeated incumbent Mordechai Ish-Shalom to become Jerusalem's mayor. Kollek, a protege of Ben-Gurion, served as director general of the Prime Minister's Office, where his close relationship with Ben-Gurion made him highly influential.

In his inaugural speech, he called on the capital's residents to be tolerant of the beliefs and values of their fellow citizens.

Kollek inherited a small city, whose borders ended beside the walls of the Old City, but in 1967 Jewish Jerusalem was united with East Jerusalem.

Kollek served as its mayor until 1993, becoming the person most identified with the city.

During Kollek's term as mayor, Jerusalem's population doubled and it became one of the world's most important cities.

Teddy Kollek: mayor for 27 years.

Journalists Strike Against Libel Law

All Israeli newspapers went on strike for one day on Nov.16, following the *Knesset* adoption of the Libel Law, fearing that freedom of the press would be curtailed. The bill, submitted by members of *Knesset* from the center and the right, gained much support from government ministers, led by Prime Minister Levi Eshkol. Eshkol was determined to pass the law despite many requests from members who requested he reconsider the bill. Before the final vote, some members threatened to bolt the coalition if the law was passed. Members of the religious parties raised additional problems: in return for their support of the law, they demanded the adoption of the Sabbath Law which would require businesses and places of entertainment to be closed on the Sabbath.

The Tel-Aviv Hilton opened its doors, with Prime Minister Levi Eshkol expressing the wish for Israeli-Arab peace talks in the near future - perhaps even in a Hilton hotel "be it in Tel-Aviv, Cairo, or any other place." (September 14)

●

Pakistan seizes Indian strongholds in Kashmir. India then invades Pakistan 500 km southwest of Kashmir, in order to forestall Pakistan attack. On Sept. 9, U Thant starts UN brokered talks as Pakistan strikes back. Decisive tank battles in Pakistan. UN cease-fire agreed to, but five days later fighting flares on the Indo-Pakistani border. India's prime minister is under much pressure to authorize manufacture of atomic weapons. (September 14)

●

The port of Jaffa is closing after 3,000 years. Ashdod Port is to open on November 25. Thus ends an era in the history of Mediterranean ports. Jaffa is mentioned in 1468 BC by Pharaoh Thutmosis IV of Egypt as a conquest. Jonah the prophet started his journey there which ended inside a whale. Tel Aviv port, inaugurated in 1937 when Jaffa was closed after the outbreak of 1936-'39 disturbances, will also close. (October 10)

●

A report from the British Institute for Strategic Research has determined that Israel is capable of producing one atomic bomb per year and that Israel's defense expenses were the highest in the world for this year. (November 19)

●

First French satellite launched into orbit from launchpad in the Sahara Desert. (November 27)

●

President Joseph Mobutu takes over in the Congo in a bloodless coup. He tightens his grip by assuming the power to rule by decree. (December 1)

●

The screening of the James Bond movie *'Goldfinger'* was halted following complaints that the German actor, Gert Frobe, was a former Nazi. The screening was resumed only after presentation to a court of affidavits from people stating that during the Second World War, Frobe had saved them from the Nazis. (December 15)

President Johnson promises to pursue peace, but says: "We will stay *[in Vietnam]* until the aggression is stopped." (January 12)

•

Knesset approves Levi Eshkol's new Cabinet. After almost ten years as foreign minister, Mrs. Golda Meir handed over the 'keys of office' to her successor, Abba Eban. (January 12)

•

The Russian spacecraft *'Luna-9'* landed on Venus and transmitted strong and clear signals to Earth. *This achievement spurred the Americans to begin sending astronauts on space flights, and in the end they were the first to land a man on the Moon.* (February 3)

•

Two Russian authors, Andrei Sinyavsky and Yuli Daniel, tried for writing anti-Communist books, are condemned to labor camp. (February 14)

•

'Maoz,' the association set up to help Soviet Jews, called on people to leave an empty chair at the Passover table as a sign of solidarity with the refuseniks. Tens of thousands complied. (March 23)

•

Classroom TV to start in Israel on a regular basis. (March 24)

•

American F-104 *Starfighter* jets sold to Jordan. In a statement, a Foreign Ministry spokesman said: "Israel notes the statement of the US concerning the sale of *Patton* tanks to Jordan, indicating the US desire to avoid destabilizing factors and the creation of an arms imbalance in the Middle East." (April 2)

•

Ben-Gurion informed all ministers that he had decided not to watch the IDF parade in Haifa on Independence Day, and said that Prime Minister Levi Eshkol should have decided that the parade be held in Jerusalem. As a gesture of protest, Ben-Gurion returned the two tickets he had received for the parade. (April 20)

•

Major-General Ezer Weizman, commanding officer of the Air Force for the past eight years, is appointed Head of General Staff Branch. (April 26)

Abie Nathan Flies to Egypt to Meet Nasser

Abie Nathan with his 'plane. All the newspapers announced his death.

Abie Nathan, owner of Tel Aviv's 'California' restaurant, flew to Cairo on Feb. 28 in his private 'plane. He left Lod airport and crossed the border without requesting an exit permit and without advance coordination with Egyptian authorities. Information that he had crashed reached Israel, but the following day Egypt informed Israel that Nathan was safe and well, and would be deported.

After he had crossed the Sinai Desert, Nathan landed in Port Said.

He met the airfield commander and told him he had come from Israel to meet the Egyptian president. He emphasized that he did not represent the Israeli government and intended to present President Nasser with a peace petition that had been signed by 100,000 people.

Nathan did not meet with the Egyptian president. Thirty-five hours after taking off from Lod, he was returned to Israel. Scores of police waited for him at all airports in

the south of the country to arrest him for illegally leaving the country.

Nathan continued his extraordinary activities to promote peace for many years, even trying some years later to fly to Syria to meet with Assad. At the beginning of the 1980's he founded a pirate radio station, the Voice of Peace, that broadcast "from somewhere in the Mediterranean," and used a banner ID of Sadat's world famous declaration: "No more war. No more bloodshed."

First Pictures of Atomic Reactor

On Apr. 17 pictures of the atomic reactor in Dimona were broadcast for the first time. The photographs, which were shown on American TV, were taken secretly with telescopic equipment.

It was stated on the television program that in spite of American opposition, Israel intended to produce a nuclear bomb. France was depicted in the program as having provided Israel with considerable technical and scientific assistance in developing the reactor.

Coca-Cola Opens a Plant in Israel

In mid-April, Coca-Cola capitulated to enormous pressure from United States dealers and businessmen and announced that it would open a plant in Israel. Hundreds of American restaurant owners, associations and dealers had threatened to stop marketing the company's soft drinks if Coca-Cola continued to bow to the Arab Boycott of Israel.

The fact that Coca-Cola had caved in to the Arab Boycott was advertised in Israel by the owners of the Tempo soft drink company, after

it had failed in all its attempts to purchase the franchise to produce Coca-Cola in Israel.

Coca-Cola announced in response that it had not established a plant in Israel up to that point for purely economic reasons. However, it did hasten to sell the franchise some weeks later. Following the company's decision, the Arab Boycott office gave instructions for Coca-Cola to be added to its blacklist and threatened to close down all the company's plants in Arab countries.

Israel: Syria is Heightening Tension on Northern Border

In one day, July 14, two people were killed and two were seriously wounded in four terrorist operations carried out by *Fatah* with the assistance of Syrian soldiers.

Near Moshav Almagor, a soldier and a Jewish National Fund employee, a father of five children from Tiberias, were killed when their vehicle drove over a mine. Near Kibbutz Mahanayim, a 15-year-old youth was wounded when a tractor detonated a mine.

In response, Israeli Air Force combat aircraft shelled Syrian targets on the eastern shore of the Sea of Galilee. The fighter jets aimed at the region where work to divert the river was in progress and hit six tractors and motor vehicles. In a dogfight north of the lake, a Syrian *MiG-21* was shot down. Five days later, *Fatah* terrorists who had infiltrated from Lebanon planted nine explosive devices in Moshav Margaliot in the Upper Galilee.

In mid-August, fighting with Syria resumed. Four Syrian *MiG's* opened fire on an Israeli patrol vessel that had run aground on a rock close to the northeastern border of the Sea of Galilee. In a dogfight, two Syrian aircraft were downed, a *MiG-17* and a *MiG-21*. One of the Syrian aircraft plunged into the lake.

Chief of Staff Yitzhak Rabin said he had explicitly ordered pilots to cross the Syrian border to attack the aircraft that had entered Israeli air space. He said: "We had no alternative but to speak to the Syrians in the only language they understand "

Knesset Building Inaugurated

Knesset building. Beacons lit on all the hills for the inauguration ceremony.

The new *Knesset* building was inaugurated on Aug. 30.

The ceremony was held in the presence of 47 representatives of overseas Jewish communities, 44 heads of foreign governments, 5,000 invited guests and representatives of all Israel's diverse communities.

At the end of the ceremony, a beacon was lit, followed by beacons on the hills of Jerusalem and throughout the country, to symbolize the festive event.

The new building was inaugurated 20 days after the closing session of the *Knesset* in Bet Froumine, the former *Knesset* building in the center of Jerusalem.

The *Knesset*'s large *menorah*, which had been donated by British Jewry, was also moved and placed in the President's Park opposite the new building.

The first session in the new building took place the following day, and the members discussed The Basic Law: The Government.

Students Against Adenauer's Visit

On May 5, scores of students were wounded when police violently dispersed demonstrations against Germany's former chancellor, Konrad Adenauer, who had come to visit Jerusalem's Hebrew University.

The disturbances began when some students who had requested permission to demonstrate against the expected visit of the former chancellor, mingled with masses of students who wanted to get a close view of Adenauer. The police, fearing that matters would get out of hand, used force to disperse them. Next day, thousands of students demonstrated opposite the Prime Minister's Office.

Paris firm on deadline for ouster of NATO headquarters; France is determined to withdraw from NATO command July 1. (May 4)

•

American 'planes for Israel a step towards stability, balancing the *F-104* deal with Jordan. This is the first time the US has offered 'planes to Israel. (May 19)

•

Six Buddhist leaders press demands for military government in Saigon to resign. (May 31)

•

Prime Minister Levi Eshkol returns from three week tour in Africa, after visiting Senegal, Ivory Coast, Liberia, Congo, Malagasy, Uganda and Kenya. (June 17)

•

Knesset member Moshe Dayan, the former chief of staff, visited Vietnam as a guest of the US army. En route, Dayan stopped over in London, Paris and Washington. (July 3)

•

Thousands participated in the dedication ceremony of the Kennedy Forest and Memorial in the Jerusalem Hills. The circular monument, whose shape resembles felled trees, symbolizes the life of John Fitzgerald Kennedy, the assassinated president of the United States. (July 4)

•

Dozens of US pilots are paraded through the streets of Hanoi as thousands shout "Down with the American aggressors!" (July 6)

•

Vice President Abdul Hakim Amer, at a two-hour parade marking the 14th anniversary of the revolution in Egypt stated: "Egypt's battle to wipe out Israel is a duty every Arab dreams of." (July 23)

•

An Iraqi pilot who defected with his aircraft, landed at an IDF base. The *MiG-21* aircraft, the most advanced in the service of the Eastern Bloc and the defense forces of Egypt, Syria and Iraq, is the first to fall into the hands of the West. At a press conference with the pilot, Munir Radfah, Air Force chief, Maj.-Gen. Mordechai Hod noted that he had received a letter from the pilot stating his intention to defect. (August 16)

Dr. Hendrik Verwoerd, prime minister of South Africa and architect of apartheid policy, assassinated in parliament by a white parliamentary messenger. (September 6)

•

OC Northern Command, Major General David Elazar, said Israel will not allow the diversion of the Jordan headwaters to continue. (September 20)

•

Following the statement by Chief of Staff Rabin that Israel should strike a blow at the Syrian government for encouraging anti-Israel conspiracies, Prime Minister Levi Eshkol forbids IDF staff officers to make statements on political and military matters, and is compelled by the outcry to distance himself from the words of the chief of staff. (September 28)

•

Albert Speer, former Nazi armaments minister, released from Spandau Prison after 20 year sentence completed. (October 1)

•

Five people slightly injured when infiltrators from Jordan blast two houses in Romema, Jerusalem. Prime Minister Eshkol said Israel "would take steps" to make clear the gravity of the deteriorating situation on the borders. (October 7)

•

Haile Selassie of Ethiopia and de Gaulle confer on the potentially explosive situation that may arise if French Somaliland becomes independent. (October 21)

•

China successfully fires fourth nuclear weapon with guided missile. (October 27)

•

The Arab League countries have decided to boycott Ford and Coca-Cola for trading with Israel. (November 2)

•

The *Knesset* votes to end military government of border and Arab-populated areas. (November 8)

•

Minister of Finance Sapir calls on the public to accept the severe recession. "You are deluding yourselves if you believe that what we have already achieved, and what we still have to achieve, will be at no cost. It will be a painful process." (December 20)

Nobel Prize for Literature for Writer S.Y. Agnon

Writer S.Y. Agnon won the 1966 Nobel Prize for Literature. On Oct. 18 he was sent a special announcement by the Swedish Academy in Stockholm. Agnon won the prize together with a Jewish writer who lived in Sweden, Nelly Sachs.

Shmuel Yosef Agnon (Czaczkes) was born in 1888 in the village of Buczacz in Eastern Galicia. During his childhood, he studied in *heder*, but acquired most of his knowledge from reading books on Judaism and philosophy.

His first Hebrew poem was published on the Jewish holiday of *Lag Ba'Omer*, 1904, in the journal *Ha' Mitzpeh* in Cracow. He joined Zionist organizations and later emigrated to Israel in 1908.

S.Y. Agnon. The first Israeli to win a Nobel Prize. After him came Begin, Rabin and Peres.

Between 1913 and 1924, he lived in Germany where he married. He first used his literary name 'S.Y. Agnon' when his story *'Agunot'* (Forsaken Wives) was published in the journal *'Ha Omer.'* In 1924 this name became his official one.

Agnon is the only Israeli to receive a Nobel Prize for Literature. Twelve years later, another Israeli received the prestigious Nobel Prize - Prime Minister Menachem Begin received the Nobel Prize for Peace, together with Anwar Sadat, after signing the peace agreement with Egypt.

In December, 1994 the Nobel Prize for Peace was again awarded to an Israeli prime minister, Yitzhak Rabin, this time together with the foreign minister Shimon Peres.

Maccabi Tel Aviv Debut

Tal Brody in action.

Thousands of spectators crammed into *Maccabi's* grounds in Tel Aviv's Maccabi Street to watch Jewish-American basketball star, Tal Brody, make his first appearance for *Maccabi Tel Aviv*. In a game against *Maccabi Petah Tikva*, Brody scored 31 points and displayed remarkable ability. He accompanied *Maccabi Tel Aviv* to a string of victories, culminating in the European Basketball Championship in 1977.

Operation Kills Jordanians

IDF troops penetrated into Jordan on Nov 13, blowing up many houses in Kfar Samoa in the Hebron hills, in response to a series of terrorist attacks which had taken place against Israeli targets, climaxing two days before when three soldiers were killed and six wounded in a military command car that drove over a mine planted by infiltrators close to the Jordanian border in the Hebron region.

In the Kfar Samoa operation the parachute battalion commander, Lt.-Col. Yoav Shacham, was killed and ten soldiers wounded.

In contrast to the night attacks the IDF had previously mounted, the operation began at 6.00 a.m., when parachute and armored forces invaded the area and blew up the Jordanian police station in Kfar Samoa. When the Jordanians sent in reinforcements, the IDF requested aerial assistance.

In a dogfight, a Jordanian *Hunter* aircraft was downed. Scores of Jordanian Legion soldiers were killed in the attack and three were taken prisoner.

After the raid, West Bank inhabitants rioted against King Hussein.

6 Syrian *MiG's* Downed in Dogfight in the North

After a year's cease-fire, Syrian tanks opened fire on northern settlements on Jan. 8. Two members of Kibbutz Shamir were wounded in the shelling.

Throughout January, there were exchanges of fire almost every day between the Israel Defense Forces and the Syrians, who shelled the settlements and agricultural fields of the Upper Galilee.

Six Syrian *MiG* warplanes were downed on Apr. 7 in dogfights on the northern border. Since the early morning hours, the Syrians had been firing on tractors as they were plowing the fields of Kibbutz Ha On to the east of the Sea of Galilee. The IDF responded to the Syrians with heavy tank fire.

The Syrians used heavy mortars to shell Kibbutz Gadot near the B'not Ya'acov bridge for many hours. One officer was killed in the shelling and three *kibbutz* members were wounded.

In the afternoon, an aerial dogfight commenced over Kibbutz Shamir and parts of Jordan and Syria. Two of the Syrian 'planes were downed close to Damascus. Three more fell into Jordanian territory. Israeli Air Force pilots received permission to chase the Syrian aircraft as far as Damascus.

The clashes concluded in the evening. Some days later, the Syrians resumed firing on *kibbutzim* in the Upper Galilee.

What, You Didn't Bring a Towtruck?

The *Gashashim* make an entire country smile.

In 1967 *Hagashash HaHiver*, created four years earlier. managed to express the mood of an entire nation. A short time after the Six-Day War, the three performers, Polly, Shaike and Gavri came out with a sketch about the mobilized car, and even those civilians who had given the IDF their cars in good condition and had a wreck returned to them ("Was there an engine?") couldn't avoid smiling together with the three.

Thousands of *Haredi* Jews Demonstrate Against Autopsies

There were stormy demonstrations of *haredim* in Jerusalem on Mar. 14 to protest the continuation of autopsies. Seventeen policemen and 40 demonstrators were wounded. Fifteen *haredim* were arrested.

The demonstrations began as a quiet procession of 4,000 *haredim* beside the city's Mahane Yehuda market. The demonstrators prayed and the disturbances began immediately afterwards. Stones were thrown and there were clashes with police.

One month later, on Apr. 18, more than 10,000 Bnei Brak residents demonstrated after sitting *shiva* for the *rebbetzin* Rachel Nadel. They had discovered, while her body was being washed prior to burial, that her heart had been excised.

The demonstrators, headed by the mayor of Bnei Brak, rabbis and other religious leaders, demanded legislation that would permit only family members of the dead to approve that autopsies be carried out.

The demonstrators demanded the cancellation of the hospital directive which ruled that patients who demanded that their bodies should not be autopsied must not be hospitalized. The demonstration was quietly dispersed.

In Jerusalem's Me'a She'arim district, abusive slogans against the state and autopsies appeared.

The demonstrations continued to be a focus of controversy in Israel until the Six-Day War broke out.

Israel and Syria "reaffirmed their commitment to refrain from all kinds of hostile or aggressive action" at the conclusion of a five-hour extraordinary meeting of the Israeli-Syrian MAC. On the agenda was the cultivation of 12,500 acres in the demilitarized zone. (January 6)

●

According to Hanoch Smith, director of the Ministry of Labor Manpower Planning Authority, 11,000 Israelis left the country in 1966, 3,000 more than in 1965. Since the establishment of the State, a total of 165,000 Israelis have emigrated. (January 9)

●

Two new IDF Majors-General: Rehavam ('Gandhi') Ze'evi, 40, and Ariel ('Arik') Sharon, 38. Sharon gained fame as the founder of Unit 101, as the paratroop commander in the large-scale reprisals carried out in the 1950's, and as the commander of the paratroop brigade in the Sinai Campaign. Ze'evi, who was in the first *Palmach* brigade, served as OC Southern Command in the Sinai Campaign. (February 20)

●

Svetlana, Stalin's daughter, requested political asylum from the US embassy in India. From there she was secretly flown to Rome. Shortly afterwards, the dictator's daughter began writing memoirs of her childhood for which an American publisher paid her $325,000. (March 10)

●

The government decided to cancel the prohibition on the screening of German-language movies. The prohibition on the screening of movies made during the Nazi era, those that express sympathy for Nazis and those starring actors with Nazi pasts, remained in force. (April 9)

●

Over 100,000 at the unveiling of the Auschwitz memorial. Many of those attending were former prisoners. (April 16)

●

Cosmonaut Vladimir Komarov was killed when the Soviet spaceship *Soyuz-1* crashed on its way back to Earth. The crash was caused by a complication with the landing parachute cords. Three months ago, three American astronauts died during training on the ground. (April 24)

Middle East Heads for War

Reserve soldiers during the waiting period before the fighting.

Eshkol and Begin with soldiers.

The major powers are to boycott the Independence Day parade in Jerusalem. (May 14)

•

Two hundred thousand people watched the scaled-down IDF parade in Jerusalem to celebrate Israel's 19th Independence Day. Many expressed disappointment with the few weapons on display. Two groups of young people displayed cardboard models of tanks in protest against the lack of heavy weaponry in the parade. (May 15)

•

Prof. Yigael Yadin founded a non-political movement to change the electoral system. Maj.-Gen. Chaim Herzog also participated in the founding conference. (May 17)

•

Prime Minister Levi Eshkol called on the world powers "to act without delay to maintain the right of free passage" to Eilat and declared that "international support for these rights is determined and widespread." (May 23)

•

Expressions of support continue to pour into Israeli missions abroad. One man delivers 1,500 first-aid battle dressings. In Berne the consulate reports dozens of offers from Jews and non-Jews alike to enlist in the army. In Bonn, young Germans who have recently finished national service offer to enlist in the Israeli army, and young girls volunteer as nurses. (May 26)

•

President Johnson has asked Israel to act with restraint until international action has been organized to settle the Middle East crisis. (May 28)

•

King Hussein and President Nasser sign a defense pact. America is shocked by Amman's act, which is another blow to a basic assumption of American foreign policy. The US had helped to arm Jordan, while giving assurances to Israel's friends that those arms would never be used against Israel. Hussein may be loosening his ties with the US. (May 30)

•

The first of ten Soviet warships passes through the Dardanelles. The US Sixth Fleet in the Mediterranean has been on the alert since the flare-up in the Middle East began. (May 31)

On May 15, during the Independence Day parade in Jerusalem, heads of state received an urgent message: Egyptian President Gamal Abdel Nasser was deploying large military forces in the Sinai Desert because of increased border tension between Israel and Syria.

The Egyptian army declared an alert, and Israel began to call up its reserve forces. Two days later, Nasser demanded that the 3,000 United Nations troops evacuate their positions along the Sinai border. Egyptian and Palestinian soldiers immediately took their place.

The Middle East crisis intensified. The United States sent its Sixth Fleet to the danger zone. At the same time, the Israel Defense Forces increased its mobilization of reserve forces. Israel entered into a waiting period, on the eve of war.

Army commanders pressed the government to initiate an immediate military operation against Egypt, but Prime Minister Levi Eshkol preferred to wait, in order to exhaust all political options and enlist the support of Western nations for an Israeli military operation.

On May 28 Jordan announced a

defensive military alliance with Egypt. According to the terms of the agreement, signed by Nasser and King Hussein in Cairo, the two armies would have a joint command and during war the commander of the Egyptian army would head the armed forces of both nations.

Egypt signed a similar agreement with Syria and at the beginning of June also signed one with Iraq.

Another such agreement was signed between Iraq and Jordan. Iraqi military units entered Jordan and established positions on the West Bank and in the Hebron region.

Nasser Closes Straits of Tiran

The President of Egypt, Gamal Abdel Nasser, announced on May 22 that he was closing the Straits of Tiran to Israeli vessels and to vessels taking military supplies to Israel.

This delivered a clear message to

Israel and to the world: Egypt was heading for war.

Nasser announced the closing of the Straits of Tiran in a speech to Egyptian air force pilots stationed in the Sinai Desert.

"The Gulf of Eilat represents our territorial waters," he said. "We will not allow the Israeli flag to cross the gulf. The Israelis are threatening war. *Ahlan Wasahlan (Welcome)*. We are prepared."

Home Front Prepares for War

Digging ditches at the rear on the orders of the Civil Defense.

As soon as the military alert was announced, civilians began to buy and hoard vast quantities of food and commodities. Within a short period, there was a food shortage in most stores. Israelis were called upon repeatedly to reduce their hoarding.

Food warehouses, flour mills and oil factories began to work around the clock to supply the demand.

In banks, a shortage of cash was created following huge withdrawals by panicking citizens.

Most of the nation's men were called up for reserve duty.

Those left behind at the rear were given instructions by the Civil Defense to prepare the bomb shelters and dig ditches as emergency shelter from attacks.

A National Unity Government. Moshe Dayan Minister of Defense

Unity government. Moshe Dayan is the new minister of defense. Menachem Begin and Yosef Sapir – ministers without portfolio.

After ten days of discussion, the *Rafi (Israel Labor list)* and *Gahal (Herut/Liberal bloc)* parties joined the coalition on June 1, and a national unity government was formed.

Three new ministers joined the government: Moshe Dayan – minister of defense, and Menachem Begin and Yosef Sapir - ministers without portfolio.

Moshe Dayan joined the government despite the opposition of Golda Meir, the *Mapai (Erez Israel Workers' Party)* general secretary.

Meir had demanded that Yigal Allon be appointed minister of defense. Most of the *Mapai* ministers supported her. The prime minister, Levi Eshkol, also found it difficult to accept the fact that Moshe Dayan would take the defense portfolio from him. However, the National Religious Party threatened to leave the coalition if a national unity government with Dayan as defense min-

Army commanders. Chief of Staff Yitzhak Rabin with Ezer Weizman and Chaim Bar-Lev.

ister was not formed.

The appointment of Dayan was received with great joy by the public and mainly by the army, which be-

lieved that the appointment would signify the conclusion of the protracted waiting period and the commencement of hostilities.

Last-ditch French Attempt to Prevent All-out War

In a last-ditch attempt to prevent war, France tried on June 1 to convene a meeting of the four superpowers. The mediation failed because of Soviet opposition.

After that failure, Charles de Gaulle, the French president, announced on June 2 that his country would remain neutral in the Middle East conflict: France did not view itself as being linked to either side in

the Middle East, and it wished to avoid the use of force. De Gaulle went on to declare that the first to use weapons would lose France's support. The French announcement was received with great disappointment in Israel.

The US and Britain drew up a draft declaration on behalf of the maritime nations concerning the freedom of navigation in the Straits

of Tiran. Israel announced its readiness to sign a declaration stipulating that the gulf was an international sea route and passage should not be blocked. On June 2 an American aircraft carrier crossed the Suez Canal on its way from the Mediterranean Sea to the Red Sea. Two Egyptian submarines followed it. On June 4, Israel stated it still sought a solution to the tension by diplomatic means.

American casualties in South Vietnam climbed to peak level last week with 313 servicemen killed and 2,616 wounded. (June 1)

•

Two US Air Force helicopters landed before a cheering crowd at Le Bourget, after a non-stop flight from New York. This was the first non-stop helicopter flight across the Atlantic. The flight took 29 hours and 48 minutes, and retraced the route of Charles Lindbergh's solo flight across the Atlantic. (June 1)

•

China celebrates the first anniversary of the appearance of the first poster of the cultural revolution. There were warnings that some wrong slogans were being put up, which could refer to recent attacks on the Prime Minister Chou En-lai; many slogans have been put up defending the Prime Minister. (June 1)

•

The Federal Communications Commission orders that hearings be held to find out what effect the construction of the twin 110-story towers at the World Trade Center would have on television reception. (June 2)

•

Opposition to de Gaulle's neutral stance in the Middle East grows in political and private circles in France. The daily *'L'Aurore'* runs a head-line: "De Gaulle spectator, he says that no one has opened fire in the Middle East, as if the blockade of Aqaba Gulf was not an act of aggression." (June 3)

•

Attempt made in Bonn to ram the Shah of Iran's motorcade with a remote-controlled Volkswagen failed when it hit a parked car. The Shah is on a nine-day visit to Germany. Anti-Shah demonstrations during the visit resulted in one death. (June 3)

•

Alexander Solzhenitsyn addresses a letter to the Congress of Soviet Writers, denouncing what he calls "[the] oppression no longer tolerable that our literature has been enduring from censorship." He called on the writers union to demand the abolition of controls over the publication of fictional literature. (June 4)

Air and armor battles at the border. The IDF engage battle with an Egyptian force moving towards Israel. The battle starts after a period of tension over two weeks that manifests itself in the concentration of large Egyptian forces along the border estimated at 100,000 men, including armored and air force components. The tension escalates after Iraqi forces enter Jordan, and Egyptian units are sent to Jordan.

•

Voice of Israel in Arabic announces 120 Egyptian 'planes have been destroyed. Israeli settlements along the Gaza Strip are under artillery shelling. A grand total of 277 Egyptian 'planes are destroyed on the ground, most during the first three hours of the war. Another 61 Egyptian 'planes have been shot down. The grand total of destroyed planes for Egypt, Jordan, Syria, Iraq and Lebanon for the Six-Day War: 452. The IAF has lost 46 planes during the war, all to ground fire.

•

Moscow says its response depends on that of the White House. The White House has been informed of the fighting but initially refrains from comment. London is also silent.

•

Blackout enforced from tonight, from sunset to sunrise.

•

UN Security Council recessed after 12 hours of futile efforts to frame a cease-fire resolution in the Middle East. The failure was a result of Egypt's refusal with Soviet backing to return its force to lines it held on June 4th.

•

In Washington, the administration seeks a neutral stance in the Middle East without formally committing itself to being neutral. The White House only warns of the "tragic consequences" that would result if fighting continues. The administration calls on both sides to accept an immediate cease-fire. The dominant reaction in Congress is that the US should not act unilaterally in the Middle East.

•

In Vietnam, US 'planes downed three *MiG's* near Hanoi while bombing North Vietnam's Thainguyen industrial complex.

War! Hundreds of Enemy War-Planes Destroyed in a Morning

At 7.45 a.m. Israeli Air Force 'planes began attacking Egyptian airfields in waves, and within three hours the Egyptian air force had been destroyed. The afternoon saw the destruction of the Jordanian air force, and within one hour, two thirds of the Syrian air force.

In an attack on an Iraqi airfield, ten aircraft were destroyed. The Isareli Air Force destroyed a total of 400 enemy aircraft, most of them on the ground and some in dogfights, thus achieving absolute aerial superiority for the Israel Defense Forces for the duration of the war.

Ground fighting started in the morning on the Egyptian front, when IDF troops broke through the Gaza Strip and into the Sinai Peninsula.

Air-raid sirens sounded throughout the country, and civilians rushed into shelters. Thousands of shells fell on Jerusalem. The Syrians and Jordanians shelled settlements along the border. In Tel Aviv, 12 shells fell. An Iraqi warplane managed to penetrate the center of the country and drop bombs on both Tel Aviv and Netanya. It was shot down.

At 8.00 a.m. the IDF spokesman made the first announcement of fierce battles between IDF troops and Egyptian air and armored forces that were moving towards Israel.

Enemy warplanes on the ground. Their destruction gave the IAF total control of the air.

It was not until the end of the first day of war that the battle fog began to disperse, and the true picture became clear to the public.

The principal struggle was on the southern front. The IDF captured Khan Yunis, and tanks advanced to El-Arish. Aerial supremacy enabled armored forces to advance and to destroy the Egyptian divisions.

Heavy Shelling of both Jerusalem and Tel Aviv

Jerusalem burning from Jordanian army shells.

Since the morning, there had been heavy Jordanian shelling of Jerusalem and all settlements along the border. Twelve shells fired from Kalkilya fell on Tel Aviv and Tel Baruch. Homes were damaged, but no one was injured. In the evening, Tirat Zvi, the town of Lod and other settlements were shelled.

The inhabitants of those settlements spent long hours in the shelters.

There were some civilians fatalities in the shelling of Jerusalem, which continued throughout the night. Most of the damage was in the neighborhoods of Nahalat Shimon, Musrara and Me'a She'arim.

Syrian Warplanes Attack North

During the first day of fighting, there were no land battles with Syria. The Syrians refrained from shelling Israel, except for a single shell that fell on Rosh Pina.

During the afternoon, Syrian aircraft attacked the northern settlements: Rosh Pina, Ilavon, Megiddo, Efar Ha'Horesh, Talmon and Kurdani. A Syrian warplane managed to reach the Haifa Bay and damaged Kibbutz Ein Ha'Mifratz. Israeli Air Force aircraft attacked Syrian airfields and destroyed most of the Syrian fighter aircraft.

Old City Surrounded. Kalkilya and Ramallah are Captured

'Motta' Gur and paratroop commanders overlooking the Old City and Temple Mount. The paratroopers surrounded East Jerusalem.

A paratroopers brigade summoned to Jerusalem from the south, commanded by Colonel 'Motta' Gur, together with the Jerusalem Brigade, surrounded the Old City of Jerusalem. Most Arab villages around Jerusalem: Shuafat in the north, Zur Bahar in the south and the French Hill, were already in the hands of the Israel Defense Forces. The IDF also controlled Sheikh Jarrah, on the road to Mount Scopus.

The paratroopers in the fortified area of Ammunition Hill were involved in heavy fighting and lost many men. The IDF was instructed to preserve the holy places.

During the morning, Latrun, Nebi Samuel and Beit Iksa were captured. A number of Egyptian officers, who had been sent to Jordan after the signing of the defense agreement between Jordan and Egypt, were taken prisoner in Latrun.

The IDF also began to operate in the Triangle area. By around noon, Jenin was overrun, and in the afternoon there was a heavy armored battle in Emek Dotan. Kalkilya was captured, and the IDF entered the town with no opposition from its inhabitants, who had flown white flags on their houses. At 7.30 p.m. Ramallah was captured.

By the afternoon, 12 civilians had been killed in Jerusalem, and some 5,000 wounded had been transferred to hospitals. The central municipal kitchen prepared 10,000 meals for the children of families evacuated from damaged areas. In the shelling of the capital, many public institutions had been hit, among them the university, the Israel Museum, synagogues and Hadassah Hospital.

Gaza Surrenders. IDF Rushes to Canal

Gaza governor surrenders.

For the second time in nine years, the Israel Defense Forces conquered the Gaza Strip.

In the Sinai Peninsula, the fortified area of Abu-Agila was conquered after paratrooper forces executed a brilliant encircling operation and outflanked the fortification in an exhausting night maneuver. Armored forces also defeated the Egyptians in Jebel Libni and continued their westward advance to the Suez Canal. The Egyptian army collapsed and began its retreat westward.

Syrian Shelling in North

A Syrian force tried to capture Tel Dan and attacked Kibbutz Dan. Armored and infantry forces repelled the attack. The Syrian tanks withdrew and some sank in the River Jordan. The Syrians continued to shell Upper Galilee settlements. Inhabitants of the north feared that the fighting would end without an incursion into Syrian territory. They exerted heavy pressure on the commander of the northern front, Maj.-Gen. David ('Dado') Elazar, to convince the government to capture the Golan Heights.

Radio Damascus announces that heavy Syrian forces have flooded the Hula Valley and are rapidly advancing in the direction of Nazareth, while repelling IDF troops blocking their path.

•

A Jordanian shell hits the President's Residence in the center of Jerusalem. President Shazar was not in residence at the time.

•

In Washington, Secretary of State Dean Rusk says he wished to clarify the State Department's neutrality. "The word does not mean indifference," he said. The States was concerned the conflict would lead to world crisis in oil. Half US petrol for the Vietnam War came from the Persian Gulf.

•

Egypt, Iraq, Syria, Yemen, Algeria and Sudan sever diplomatic relations with the US, as a result of its active military support of Israel. Syria and Iraq also severed relations with Great Britain.

•

Arab oil producers cut off supplies to US and Britain, charging that the two countries were giving air cover to Israel during Monday's hostilities.

•

Spectacular victory on the first day of the war. Rafiah, El-Arish, Khan Yunis, Deir el-Ballah captured. Artillery bombardment begun along the Jordanian border.

•

Amman radio has reported this morning that King Hussein called Nasser saying he had proof that British and American 'planes are involved in the fighting. British and Americans issue denials.

•

Egypt closes the Suez Canal. US and British embassies attacked in Arab states. *(The canal was to remain blocked to all vessels until the mid-70's.)*

•

One killed and 21 wounded when an Iraqi aircraft bombed Netanya shortly after 6.00 a.m. The 'plane was shot down.

•

French government announces its embargo on military shipments to Middle East is to include weapons and spare parts. The embargo is severely criticized in the French press, and seen as stabbing Israel in the back.

Chief of Staff Rabin said the Straits of Tiran are open, Sharm el-Sheikh and most of Sinai have fallen, and Israeli forces are near Suez. The IDF controls most of the West Bank including the Old City of Jerusalem, Nablus, Ramallah, Jericho and Bethlehem.

●

A *'Jerusalem Post'* editorial says: "Israel had an account of its own with Jordan since 1948, for its failure to observe the armistice agreements. (...) Free access to the Western Wall, which was part of the agreement, has never been implemented and scarcely ever debated. Access to the old Hadassah Hospital and Hebrew University buildings on Mt. Scopus has not been free but limited to fortnightly convoys. (...) The Old City itself is a very much more delicate issue, for although some fire came from positions inside the city, Israel was not prepared to shell this close-packed warren of old buildings containing some of the most treasured religious monuments of the three faiths."

●

Prime Minister Eshkol announced that arrangements at the holy places in the Old City would be determined by the councils of the three religions.

●

Israel Railways started its preparations to establish a railway line from Ashdod to Gaza City. According to experts, the works can be completed within several weeks. The trip from Ashdod to Gaza will take approx. one hour.

●

UN Security Council unanimously adopts a Soviet resolution calling for a complete cease-fire in the Middle East war at 10.00 p.m. last night (Israel time). The Soviet Union issued a statement threatening to break diplomatic relations with Israel if it did not obey "immediately." The Soviets made no such threat to the Arabs although Egypt and Iraq have refused to obey the cease-fire. The resolution was passed at 8.40 p.m. This request is impractical even if it had been accepted, since there has not been time to transmit the orders to commanders in the field. Observers believe the Soviet move was a desperate attempt to save Syria from the same military debacle that Egypt and Jordan have suffered.

The Western Wall is Ours

Paratroopers beside the Western Wall.

A historic moment. The Israeli flag over the Western Wall.

In the morning, a reserve paratroop brigade commanded by Col. 'Motta' Gur broke through the Lions' Gate on the eastern side of the Old City and liberated the Western Wall and Temple Mount. This was the climax of the war. Israelis trembled when they heard the unforgettable words uttered by 'Motta' Gur, "The Temple Mount is ours."

Maj.-Gen. Shlomo Goren, the army's chief rabbi, was with the paratroopers who advanced to the Western Wall. Those arriving at the Wall prayed with dust-covered soldiers. Goren blew the *shofar*, soldiers recited psalms, and later *kaddish* and *hallel* prayers, and a special *yizkor* memorial prayer in memory of fallen comrades in arms.

The photograph of tearful paratroopers against the background of the Western Wall became one of the symbols of the war. An Israeli flag was unfurled over the Wall.

Shortly afterwards, Prime Minister Levi Eshkol, Defense Minister Moshe Dayan, the Chief of Staff, Lt.-Gen. Yizhak Rabin, and CO of the Central Region, Maj.-Gen. Uzi Narkiss all visited the Western Wall. Rabin said, "I was born in Jerusalem, I fought the War of Independence here, and today my arrival with the minister of defense through the Lions' Gate into the Old City expresses for me, more than anything else could, what has happened during the past 55 hours."

IDF Takes Sharm el-Sheikh

On the Egyptian front, Israel Defense Forces armored and infantry columns continued their advance through the Sinai on three central axes, capturing *en route* thousands of thirsty, exhausted Egyptian soldiers.

On the northern axis, the troops advanced to Romani, some 34 km (21 miles) from the Suez Canal. On the central axis, the IDF advanced from Jebel Libni in the west to Bir Gafgafa, and along the way overran Bir Hama.

On the southern axis, the forces advanced to Bir Hasaneh, and from there to Bir Tamada, fighting the entire way.

Naval forces, who had sailed

The Israeli flag at an Egyptian position in Sharm el-Sheikh.

south from Eilat, reached Sharm el-Sheikh in the afternoon and gained control of the Straits of Tiran, which had been abandoned.

Armored Forces Cross from Southern Front to North

Syrian guns continued to shell border settlements from the Galilee panhandle to the southern end of the Sea of Galilee. Two people were killed and 16 injured. All the roads from the center of the country to the north were crowded with military vehicles and personnel.

The general feeling was that with the conclusion of the fighting in the Sinai and on the West Bank, it was the Syrians' turn to pay the price for their aggression, despite international pressure being exerted on Israel to call a halt to the combat.

IDF Reaches Golan Heights

After four days of waiting, the signal finally came through. The army began to ascend the Golan Heights.

On June 8 the Syrians continued their shelling of northern settlements. The OC of the Northern Region, David ('Dado') Elazar, who feared that Israel might yield to international pressure for a cease-fire, demanded an operation against the Syrian army to conquer the Golan. In preparation for an IDF attack on the Syrians, the Israeli Air Force struck a severe blow to the Syrian formation.

On the morning of June 9 the minister of defense gave the order to begin the attack on the Golan. During the first moments, notorious positions fell which for many years had rained heavy fire on Israeli Galilee settlements. The hardest battle took place at Tel Fahar, and the *Golani* Brigade suffered heavy losses.

Jerusalem Returns to Normal

The cease-fire with Jordan was maintained except for small local pockets of resistance. The main problem was the supply of services and food to the large population of the West Bank, most of whom did not flee east to Jordan.

In Jerusalem, life was beginning to return to normal. All the municipal 'bus lines were functioning normally. Schools had prepared for a resumption of studies after inhabitants of shelled neighborhoods had been evacuated. Volunteers from Tel Aviv and Haifa streamed in to help the city resume normal services. The removal began of tens of thousands of mines scattered between the east and west of the city.

At a press conference in Amman on June 8, King Hussein admitted that his army had sustained heavy losses, mainly during the Israeli aerial bombardments. The king complained that the Arab states had abandoned him and had not come to his aid when he remained isolated.

On the Banks of the Suez Canal

On the fourth day, the first soldiers arrived at the Suez Canal.

On June 8 the Israel Defense Forces completed their capture of the Sinai Peninsula. IDF troops succeeded in blocking all passages to the Suez Canal. Thousands of Egyptian soldiers were left in the Sinai Desert, cut off from supply sources of fuel, water, food and weapons.

On the northern axis, Israeli forces reached eastern Kantara on the bank of the Suez Canal. On the central axis, the IDF arrived opposite Ismailiya on the shores of Lake Timsah, and further south they captured the Egyptian oil town of Ras Sudar at the north of the Gulf of Suez. The Egyptians managed to set fire to the many oil fields in the vicinity of the town before they retreated.

Fierce tank battles took place to the west of Bir Gafgafa and Mitla. The Egyptians attempted to open a route in the direction of the canal. At the end of the day's fighting, the IDF finally closed the way to the canal and cut off the Egyptian army remaining in the Sinai.

On June 9 the Egyptians made one final attempt to attack from the canal to save the forces who were stranded in the desert. The attack was repulsed.

1967

JUNE
8 – 9

Egypt has informed UN Secretary General U Thant that it is ready to accept a cease-fire. The move came after a major tank battle in the Sinai in which Israeli forces seem to have broken the back of Egypt's armored forces. Nasser announced his resignation, following Egypt's defeat. (June 8)

•

34 killed and 75 wounded on US intelligence vessel *'Liberty,'* attacked by Israeli aircraft and three Israeli torpedoes, near El-Arish shores. The ship was in no danger of sinking, and steamed north to meet US vessels moving to her aid. The Americans had not coordinated the arrival of the ship with Israel despite Israeli warnings not to approach the battle arena. Israel's Ambassador Avraham Harman told US Secretary of State Dean Rusk that Israel was prepared to "make amends for the tragic loss of lives and material damage" resulting from the mistaken attack on the US communications ship. An officer on board was quoted: "To put it bluntly she was there to spy for us. Russia does the same thing. We moved in close to monitor the communications of both Egypt and Israel. We have to. We must be informed of what's going on in a matter of minutes." Questions remain as to the circumstances. Didn't the ship receive an order sent by the CIA to leave the fighting zone? Was the ship taken to be an Egyptian vessel, leading to the error? (June 8)

•

Egyptian and Jordanian attempts to pin the blame for their military defeat on alleged American and British air intervention were given the lie by Israel army intelligence, with a recording of a radio-telephone conversation in which Nasser and King Hussein agreed to blame Arab defeat on "intervention." (June 8)

•

The Soviet Union announced its intention to break off relations with Israel, accusing this country of failing to observe the cease-fire on the Syrian border. (June 9)

•

Nasser retracts his resignation, following demonstrations in Cairo in his support. The commander of Egyptian forces, Abed el-Hakim Amer, and the minister of defense resign. (June 9)

The IDF spokesman published the number of wounded in the war: 679 killed, 2,563 wounded, of whom 255 were wounded seriously or moderately. (June 10)

•

Alitalia, Sabena and Swissair, which had halted flights to Israel when war broke out, announced their resumption. (June 10)

•

The commanders of Egyptian air, sea and land forces have all resigned. Four other high ranking officers have been pensioned off by Nasser. (June 10)

•

Foreign Minister Abba Eban stated on his return from the UN that Israel's foreign policy must now emphasise "viable agreements directly arrived at between the governments of our region in order to establish a peaceful and stable order." (June 11)

•

The SS 'Dolphin,' flying the Israeli flag, passes through the Straits of Tiran en route to Eilat. (June 11)

•

The government has yet to formulate its position on the question of territorial concessions. In view of the complexity of the question, this may take some time. The 1949 armistice agreements and demarcation lines are no longer recognized by Israel, since they have been invalidated by Egyptian, Syrian and Jordanian aggression. (June 11)

•

Israel is not prepared to return to the situation that reigned a week ago. Prime Minister Eshkol told the Knesset in a special address: "Alone we fought for our existence and security. We are entitled to determine what are the true and vital interests of our country and how they should be secured." The Prime Minister went on to say: "The position that existed up to now will never again return. The territory of Israel shall no longer be a no-man's-land, open to acts of sabotage and murder." (June 12)

•

The Soviet Union announces its intention to break off relations with Israel, and threatens sanctions, if Israel fails to observe the cease-fire on the Syrian border. (June 12)

Quneitra is Captured, Cease-fire in the North

The Rescue Corps arriving in Quneitra six hours after Radio Damascus announced its fall.

The Golan Heights were captured on June 10. The Israel Defense Forces completed the second stage of the fighting, and after capturing the first line of emplacements, the tanks broke through in the direction of Quneitra and the missiles stationed on the Golan Heights.

During the morning the Syrian defenses collapsed and their forces began the retreat to the east which turned into a rout. At 8.30 a.m. Radio Damascus announced that Quneitra was in the hands of the IDF, six hours before its actual capture. On the same day the Israelis captured

positions in the towns of Tawfiq, Khirbet Batin, Mazat A'Din, and Kufr Harib on the south bank. From the Galilee settlements which had suffered for years from Syrian fire it was possible to see IDF soldiers clambering up the steep incline and taking over the notorious positions. IDF forces took control of the eastern shores of the Sea of Galilee. At 5:30 p.m. they captured Butamiya and at 6.00 p.m. Mas'ada. The cease-fire took effect at 6.30 p.m.

Thus was the end of the Six-Day War.

The Syrian sector was the scene of the hardest battles experienced by the IDF during the war. Syrian soldiers fought with determination. The mountainous region, the rocks and the location of their positions made it difficult to break through. The Engineers Corps had to pave new access routes through the many minefields that covered the heights.

Thirsty Egyptian Soldiers Try to Reach the Canal

Such scenes occurred both in the Sinai and on the Golan Heights: enemy soldiers surrendering in masses.

After six days of fighting, thousands of exhausted, hungry and thirsty Egyptian soldiers marched in the direction of Suez. They left behind vast quantities of equipment, weapons and ammunition.

After taking their weapons from them, IDF soldiers made it possible for the Egyptians to move freely in the direction of the canal. Officers were taken prisoner. For more than a week the Red Cross occupied itself tracing and rescuing all Egyptian soldiers abandoned in Sinai.

Israel and the world gradually began to realize the magnitude of the victory. The southern region commander, Maj-Gen. Gavish summarized the fighting on the Egyptian front: 600 Egyptian tanks were destroyed and some 100 captured. 10,000 Egyptian soldiers were killed and more than 5,000 taken prisoner. During the crossing of the Mitla Pass a base of Soviet-manufactured ground-to-air missiles containing gas containers was discovered. It had not previously

been known that such missiles were in the possession of a state outside the Communist bloc.

Fifteen IDF soldiers were taken prisoner: 11 in Egypt, one in Syria, two in Iraq and one in Lebanon. About 6,700 Egyptian, Jordanian, and Syrian soldiers were held prisoner in Israel, among them nine Egyptian generals. A few weeks later all were returned. The Jordanians and Iraqis also abandoned huge amounts of tanks, cannon, armored vehicles and weapons.

200,000 People Visit the Western Wall in One Day

Maj.-Gen. Uzi Narkiss, Moshe Dayan and Yitzhak Rabin entering the Old City of Jerusalem.

The Western Wall was first opened to the public on June 14, the festival of *Shavuot* - the Jewish Pentecost; 200,000 visitors made their way to pray at the Wall by a guarded route through the alleys of Jerusalem's Old City: the first pilgrimage since the Dispersion. The inhabitants of the Old City were under curfew. Emotional and excited, hundreds of thousands moved about the courtyard in front of the Western Wall, with no separation between men and women. During subsequent weeks, tens of thousands came every day to pray in the city which lies at the heart of Judaism, and give thanks for Israel's unbelievable war success.

On June 27 the *Knesset* almost unanimously passed three laws annexing the areas captured during the war, among them a law enabling the interior ministry to unite new Jerusalem with the eastern city, and the appointment of citizens from the eastern city to the united city council.

The next day the minister of the interior published an order annexing the Old City of Jerusalem. Expanded Jerusalem also included the areas of Zur Bahar, Sheikh Jarrah, Kalandia airfield, Mt. Scopus and Shufat.

One day after the official annexation, the barriers separating the two parts of the city were opened and inhabitants were allowed to move freely in both directions.

Many Houses Next to the Western Wall Evacuated

First visit to the Western Wall.

Scores of Arab families from the Old City who had been living close to the Western Wall, and in synagogues in the Jewish Quarter, were evacuated from their houses by the military governor and housed in nearby Arab villages.

Most moved to Silwan village, and the rest to Abu Dis and Hebron. The evacuation was observed by Israeli and international journalists, and care was taken to ensure that the evacuees were suitably housed. The military government confiscated hundreds of vacant and abandoned apartments. Immediately after the evacuation, bulldozers arrived and cleared the entire area along the length of the Western Wall.

1967
JUNE 13 — 30

Reports from informed sources in Cairo say the Soviet Union will send 200 *MiG* fighters to replace the war losses. (June 14)

•

At the United Nations, Foreign Minister Abba Eban accused the Soviet Union of being greatly responsible for the crisis in the Middle East and rejected as "totally unacceptable" Soviet demands that Israel withdraw from Arab lands conquered in the Six-Day War. He defined as "frivolous" the charge made by Soviet Premier Alexei Kosygin that Israel had started the war with the Arabs. Mr. Eban said the USSR has played a provocative role in spreading alarmist and incendiary reports among Arab governments as to the intentions of Israel. Since 1955, he said, the USSR had supplied the Arabs with 2,000 tanks, 700 fighter jets, ground-to-air missiles, seven destroyers, 14 submarines, 46 torpedo boats, including missile boats, and numerous field guns. (June 19)

•

Since the beginning of the fighting, 3,600 volunteers have arrived in Israel. 200 doctors and nurses were sent to work in hospitals and the remainder were sent to work in the fields and to rebuild what was destroyed during the war. (June 23)

•

Two Israeli pilots were returned from Iraqi jails. Capt. Yitzhak Glanz and Capt. Gidon Dror had been captured when attacking H-3 military airfield. In exchange, Israel returned 428 Jordanian prisoners. (June 27)

•

The Old-New Jerusalem border is abolished, with free movement in the newly united city from noon today. A State Department spokesman told a press conference that "hasty administrative action cannot be regarded as determining the future of the holy places or the status of Jerusalem in relation to them." (June 29)

•

Minister of Defense Moshe Dayan stated that the occupied territories should be held until peace agreements were signed with the Arab states. (June 29)

1967

JULY

Five hundred dignitaries from Bethlehem submitted a demand to the military governor that their city be recognized as part of the State of Israel. Moslem representatives and heads of the city's church signed a petition. (July 3)

•

Congo government claims that loyal government troops completely control the cities of Kisangani, Bukavu and Kindu after defeating white missionaries who revolted five days ago. (July 9)

•

Egypt has agreed to the stationing of UN observers along the Suez Canal to supervise the cease-fire with Israel. (July 10)

•

The US government expressed its concern over Soviet shipments of warplanes and other arms to Egypt and other Arab countries, to replace their losses in the Six-Day War. The State Department made a new call for Soviet cooperation in limiting military shipments to the Middle East to avoid a new arms race there. (July 11)

•

Six Egyptian jets downed in 48 hour Sinai fighting. Dayan tells UN that canal open to all or none. The UN observers begin supervising cease-fire along Suez Canal. (July 15)

•

Foreigners quit Nigeria's east as war advances. The Nigerian government allows an international evacuation operation for hundreds trapped in the secessionist eastern region of the country. (July 17)

•

Twenty-nine killed, thousands injured as race riots spread to 12 US cities. 11,500 federal troops in Detroit. Civil rights leaders condemn violence sweeping the country as unjustified. A statement issued by Dr. Martin Luther King and others says "killing, arson, looting are criminal acts and should be dealt with as such." President Johnson proclaims an official day of prayer for racial peace. (July 25)

•

Abie Nathan again flew to Egypt. He took off from Cyprus in the old Auster that had belonged to King Hussein of Jordan. After two hours in Port Said he was deported back to Israel where, on landing in Herzliya, he was arrested and questioned. (July 28)

Tank Battles and Commando Raids in Suez Canal Zone

Guns in the canal. Minor exchanges of gunfire turned into an artillery duel on both sides of the canal within minutes.

On July 1, three weeks after the end of the Six-Day War, the Egyptians began again to fire on Israel Defense Forces positions. An Egyptian command force that had crossed the Suez Canal encountered a patrol. Fire broke out and gradually evolved into a full-scale tank battle. Seven soldiers were wounded.

In the weeks that followed, the Egyptians tried almost every night to cross the canal and fire on IDF soldiers. Heavy artillery fire was often exchanged in the region.

On July 8 five soldiers were killed and three were wounded as a result of Egyptian gun and tank fire in the Port Said area. One week later eight soldiers were killed, 40 were wounded and two were taken prisoner in a combined Egyptian commando and artillery attack. Three Egyptian aircraft were shot down in aerial battles that same day.

Refugees in Jordan to Return to the West Bank

They escaped during the battles and returned after the war.

On July 2, the government decided to allow West Bank inhabitants who had moved to Jordan after the Six-Day War to return to their houses. Those wishing to return had to do so by Aug. 10. The decision, announced on Arab radio and also disseminated via the Red Cross, was made following a wave of rumors, ignited by Arab states, that the Israel Defense Forces were evicting all West Bank inhabitants from their houses.

After the war, each day hundreds of Palestinians had fled from the West Bank to Jordan. Only after six weeks, on July 18, did the first refugees begin to return to the areas captured during the war.

Ammunition Warehouse Explodes

Three were killed and dozens wounded on July 3 in the explosion of a huge ammunition warehouse at an Israel Defense Forces base close to Acre. The ammunition burned for three hours. Shells blew up and landed on western Galilee, mainly along the lakeshore. Inhabitants of the area went down to the bomb shelters. Many thought that the Syrians were carrying out a surprise attack.

The ammunition dump had been in an open area. The soldiers on the base tried at first to extinguish the fire themselves. When they were not successful they escaped. The leaders of all the nearby settlements were informed of the explosion and they in turn told the local residents to go down to the shelters.

Hundreds of shells fell on nearby Acre. Fortunately, most did not explode, but scores of houses were damaged. Hundreds of shells also landed on Nahariya.

Strike in the Old City

After houses near the Western Wall had been destroyed, a vast square capable of holding hundreds of thousands of worshippers was created.

A general strike was declared in the Old City of Jerusalem on Aug. 7 to protest the unification of the city. The strike lasted for a day and was planned by 'The Committee for the Defense of Arab Jerusalem.' An additional reason for the strike was the decision of the military governor to banish four Arab dignitaries who were accused of incitement and subversive activity. The four had announced a week earlier they did not recognize Jerusalem's unification.

An outcome of the strike was the decision to take aggressive measures in order to deter the activities of nationalistic young people living in the eastern part of the city. As a result, two dignitaries and a number of young people were arrested for incitement and for distributing anti-Israel pamphlets.

Despite deteriorating relations between the inhabitants of East Jerusalem and the military governor, Jewish tourists continued to pour into the Old City.

Rabbis Disagree about Praying on Temple Mount

The army's chief rabbi, Maj.-Gen. Shlomo Goren, on Aug. 18 canceled his plan to hold prayers on the Temple Mount. One week earlier Goren had held public prayers in the area, but the Waqf *(Arab religious trust)* representatives threatened to close all mosques for an unlimited period of time if more prayers were held.

The subject of prayers was a point of contention for the rabbis. At a meeting convened at the end of the month, Rabbi Ovadia Yosef, a member of the Rabbinical High Court, claimed that Jews are forbidden to enter the Temple Mount and that the

Ovadia Yosef: Forbidden to pray.

Shlomo Goren: Permissible to pray.

divine presence inhabits the area for eternity. In a lecture to guests, among them President Zalman Shazar, Rabbi Yosef proclaimed that it is forbidden even to circle the Temple Mount in a helicopter because the divine presence extends high above the surface of the ground.

Four Shot Dead at Disco

On Aug. 2, an inhabitant of Kiryat Shmona murdered four people in the town's *'Martef' (Basement)* discotheque. Six other people were injured in the shooting. The episode continued for six hours. Among the dead was the commander of the local police station who had tried to overpower the gunman.

Eliahu Amar, 27, had entered the discotheque, closed its doors, and for six hours shot at anyone who tried to approach the place.

Only after some hand-grenades had been thrown in by the police did they succeed in overcoming him.

During questioning, Amar revealed that he had decided to take control of the nightclub because a few days earlier he had lost about IL 3,000 in a game of cards.

Arab Foreign Ministers open Khartoum parley with a call by Sudan for a united Arab front against "Zionist imperialist aggression." Summit policy on Israel is vague. (August 1)

•

Only peace talks can settle border issue, says Foreign Minister Eban. (August 1)

•

President Johnson asks for higher taxes to pay for accelerated troop buildup in Vietnam, bringing the number of troops to 525,000 by next June. (August 3)

•

Israeli and Jordanian representatives agree on arrangements for the return of West Bank residents who have crossed to the East Bank of the Jordan; the deadline for return is set for August 31. People whose permanent residence was on the West Bank on June 5, and who crossed to the East until July 4, will be allowed to return. (August 6)

•

It was officially disclosed that the US Air Force has been bombing Communist targets in Laos for the past three years, since May 1964. The main target: the Ho Chi Minh trail that runs from North Vietnam through Laos to South Vietnam. The Air Force spokesman in Saigon said the bombings were at the "request of the Royal Laotian government." (August 12)

•

After much deliberation by the Ministry of Defense and the government, it was decided that the official name of the war would be the "Six-Day War," the name already bestowed on it both in Israel and overseas. (August 24)

•

Israel has accepted a proposal by General Odd Bull to extend the ban on the passage of ships through the Suez Canal indefinitely. This has also been accepted by Egypt until a permanent agreement can be worked out. (August 27)

•

Heads of 13 Arab states open summit in Khartoum to agree policy in attempt to recuperate from the defeats of the June war. (August 29)

•

Only 14,056 Arab refugees wished to return from Jordan to the West Bank during 'Operation Refugee.' (August 31)

Khartoum summit ended with the following resolution regarding Israel: no recognition, no peace, no negotiations. Prime Minister Eshkol described it as an irresponsible move diminishing the chances of peace. (September 1)

•

Gur Sharon, 11, the son of Maj.-Gen. Ariel Sharon, was killed by a bullet fired accidentally while he and his friends were playing with an old rifle that had hung on the wall of the family home in Zahala. Sharon, who was at home at the time, rushed his son to hospital, but the boy died on the way. (September 4)

•

US casualties in the Vietnam War near the 100,000 mark. 13,365 dead, 83,433 wounded, 749 missing in action. (September 21)

•

Cuban revolutionary leader, Ernesto ('Che') Guevara was killed in a clash between Bolivian army troops and guerillas. (October 10)

•

Prime Minister Levi Eshkol awards the Six-Day War Ribbon to Chief of Staff Yitzhak Rabin and IDF generals. (November 15)

•

The Security Council unanimously adopted Resolution 242 requiring withdrawal of Israeli forces from occupied Arab territories and an end to all belligerency in order to establish a "just and lasting peace in the Middle East." (November 22)

•

The world's first heart transplant. In Cape Town, South Africa, Prof. Christiaan Barnard implanted the heart of a young girl into the body of a 55 year-old man. The operation was a success, but after 18 days the patient died from pneumonia. (December 3)

•

The first of 48 *Skyhawks* sold to Israel before the Six-Day War are now being delivered. The US State Department refused to confirm or deny that Israel had asked for *Phantoms*. (December 21)

•

Measures against Syria's 3,500 Jews, reported by French newspaper *'Le Monde,'* include dismissal from the civil service and a travel ban. All Syrian Jews' identity cards bear the word "Jew" in red ink. (December 28)

Destroyer *'Eilat'* is Sunk. 47 Sailors are Killed

The *'Eilat'* a short time before her fateful voyage. Four missiles sank the destroyer

The Israeli destroyer *'Eilat'* was sunk on Oct. 21 outside Port Said to the north of the Suez Canal by four sea-to-sea missiles fired from two Egyptian missile boats. The destroyer was carrying 202 crew members. Many of those rescued were seriously wounded.

Two missiles, each of which contained half a ton of explosives, scored direct hits on the center of the vessel and the engine room. The destroyer was paralyzed and its central section began to burn. The crew succeeded in containing the fire; they assembled the wounded and made plans to abandon ship. For two hours the *'Eilat'* leaned at an angle, with no electricity, unable to communicate her condition.

It was during this period that a third missile hit the stern, causing the explosion of the ammunition and the sinking of the vessel. The crew jumped into the water and then a fourth missile exploded in the water. Many were wounded by the underwater blast.

Israeli Air Force aircraft and helicopters were summoned to rescue the crew after a military shore-based unit reported sparks and explosions in the water. Many sailors spent several hours in the water until help came. Crew members displayed heroism in exposing themselves to great danger in order to save the wounded and some were commended for valor.

In response to the sinking of the *'Eilat,'* the Israel Defense Forces on Oct. 24 shelled the town of Suez, south of the canal.

Jordan River Becomes Firing Line

On Nov. 21 Jordanian tanks opened fire on Israeli troops from across the Jordan river in the Um-Shurt Bridge area. IDF soldiers responded with gun and tank fire which developed into the most serious battle on the Jordanian border since the end of the Six-Day War. Israel had no option but to call in the air force whose 'planes silenced the Jordanian positions. Three servicemen were killed in the battles, one of whom was the pilot of a downed *Mystere* 'plane.

Exchange of fire with the Jordanians had increased on both sides of the river. On one occasion, at the beginning of November, the Jordanians had provided cannon fire to cover the activity of terrorists while they planted explosives on Kibbutz Sde Eliahu in Bet She'an Valley to blow up its granary and crop warehouse. Jordanian forces at the same time directed artillery fire at Kibbutz Ma'oz Haim and at the Kfar Ruppin region

Children from a Bet She'an Valley kibbutz hurry to bomb shelters during Jordanian shelling.

in the Bet She'an Valley. A number of buildings were hit and one person was lightly wounded. IDF guns silenced the Jordanian fire.

Shelling and terrorist attacks on Jordan Valley and Bet She'an Valley settlements continued until the mid-1970's.

The 'Dakar' Submarine Disappears

On Jan. 26 the submarine 'Dakar' disappeared with 69 crew members on board. The submarine had left the British port of Portsmouth on Jan. 9 after some weeks of renovations and crew training. At the end of a series of training exercises the submarine sailed for Israel. The 'Dakar' sailed on the water's surface until Gibraltar. After a brief stop, she entered the Mediterranean where she was supposed to make her way under water in order to avoid being tracked by Egyptian radar. The planned route kept her far from Egyptian territorial waters. The last contact with her was on Jan. 24 when her commander received an instruction to reach Israel on Jan. 29 for a planned reception in Haifa port.

Searches began as soon as contact with the submarine was lost. The destroyer 'Jaffa,' which had been participating in training exercises in the region of Sicily, and its sister ship, the submarine 'Dolphin' were summoned to take part in the search. The entire navy and air force cooperated in efforts to trace the submarine or her remains. Sixth Fleet vessels sailing in the area and Greek and British vessels also all participated in the search. Even Lebanon announced a search in her waters.

On Jan. 28, Egypt announced that her navy had no connection with the disappearance and that they had not sunk the submarine. Large forces scanned hundreds of thousands of square kilometers but were unable to solve the riddle. No remains or signs were found.

In February 1969, approximately one year after the submarine's dis-

Sailing to death. The 'Dakar' crew on board the submarine.

appearance, one of her buoys was found on the Gaza shore. Experts who examined the buoy used the depth of its tear and the vegetation marks on it to make estimates concerning the area in which the 'Dakar' sank and the depth of the water there, but even these findings could not help them solve the puzzle.

The disappearance of the 'Dakar' and its entire crew shocked Israel. The army and the navy declared that they would not rest until the mystery was solved.

Martin Luther King Murdered

The black leader Martin Luther King was murdered on Apr. 5 in the American city of Memphis. King had been prominent in the struggle for equal rights for blacks in the United States, and it was thanks to his many years of campaigning that discrimination against blacks was outlawed.

A young white man shot King while he was standing on the balcony of his hotel room. King had arrived in the southern town of Memphis in order to organize a black solidarity march.

The murder caused disturbances throughout the entire US. Tens of thousands rioted in many cities.

Israeli Spy Wolfgang Lotz is Released from Egyptian Jail

The Israeli spy Wolfgang Lotz, the so-called 'Spy on Horseback,' was released at the beginning of March in return for nine Egyptian generals who had been captured by Israel during the war.

In 1965, Lotz had been sentenced in Cairo to life imprisonment on charges of spying for Israel. He was accused of having gathered information in Egypt for three years beginning in May 1962 and transferring it by wireless to his Israeli handlers.

Lotz had owned a riding club near Cairo, and among his customers were police and army officers. There he formed the initial relationship with them which he cemented at the parties and other social events he hosted at his home.

Lotz passed on to Israel information about the Egyptian army's missile systems. He was also accused of sending letter bombs to German scientists working in Egypt.

Throughout the period of his trial and imprisonment the true identity of Lotz was not disclosed.

Under questioning he said that avarice had prompted him to spy. Egypt, believing that he was a German citizen, did not execute him because it did not wish to harm the country's delicate relations with West Germany.

Only after his release and arrival in Israel as part of a prisoner-exchange deal was it revealed that Lotz was in fact a major in the Israel Defense Forces.

Lieutenant General Chaim Bar-Lev became Israel's eighth chief of staff. The US agreed to the appointment of former Chief of Staff Yitzhak Rabin as Israel's new ambassador to the US. (January 1)

●

The chief topic of President Johnson's and Prime Minister Eshkol's talks was the balance of arms in the Middle East. (January 10)

●

New ambassador to the United States: after four years of commanding the army, Yitzhak Rabin left for Washington where he will serve as ambassador until 1973. (February 20)

●

In 1967 there were 53,430 private automobiles in Israel, double the number of 1960, and 3,200 more than in 1966. (February 26)

●

Submarine 'Dakar' officially declared lost and 69 crew perished. (March 6)

●

The High Court of Justice rejected the request of a young Ethiopian to be recognized as Jewish so that he could marry. The rabbinate refused to register him as a Jew on the grounds that the *Falashas* are not Jews and therefore he would have to convert. (March 7)

●

Four killed, 28 wounded in Bet She'an *Fatah* raid and Negev road mining. Israel wipes out *Fatah* bases in Jordan, killing at least 150 terrorists and taking prisoners. Israeli losses: 21 dead and 70 wounded. (March 18)

●

During archeological excavations in the town of Azor, a soft limestone wall collapsed on Defense Minister Moshe Dayan who was seriously injured and hospitalized for a number of weeks. This was the first time that the public had heard of the minister's not-so-legal hobby. (March 20)

●

The sixth high-ranking Jewish official is sacked in Warsaw since student clashes with authorities began on March 6. (March 25)

●

Cosmonaut Yuri Gagarin, the first man in space, was killed when the training 'plane he was piloting crashed. (March 31)

Israel's 20th Independence Day parade broke all records of attendance with about 600,000. (May 2)

•

Abraham Malk, a Jewish youth from Brooklyn, was this year's winner of the Bible Quiz. Malk was the first non-Israeli Bible Quiz winner. (May 3)

•

A general strike is called in France, with at least ten million workers disrupting the country, in support of the students whose demand for educational reforms incurs the worst peacetime rioting in Paris this century. One million march on Paris, while strikes disrupt industry. (May 12-13)

•

The UN Security Council is called into session at midnight, Israel time, to consider Jordan and Israel's charges arising out of Tuesday's clash across the Jordan River. (June 5)

•

Democrat Senator Robert Kennedy, brother of John F. Kennedy, the assassinated American president, was shot and killed some minutes after his announcement of victory in the party primaries. Kennedy was considered a sure candidate for the presidency and his assassination returned the entire nation to the traumatic days of his brother's assassination. The assassin, Sirhan Sirhan, was born in Taibeh near Ramallah. (June 5)

•

A Syrian spokesman said yesterday that the Syrian-trained *Fatah* organization has been operating against Israel during the last year with a 90% loss rate. (June 5)

•

Police break into the Sorbonne University in Paris. Student leader 'Danny the Red' wins international fame as student spokesman. (June 16)

•

Dr. Spock, the famous pediatrician, whose writings are the bible of parents throughout the world, is arrested in the US for anti-war activities. (July 10)

•

Israeli 'Peace Pilot' Abie Nathan left Lisbon for Biafra by air to help organize relief aid for the Biafran people. (July 25)

El Al Airplane Hijacked to Algeria

The Algerian hostages return home after 39 days of imprisonment.

An El Al airplane flying from Rome to Tel Aviv was hijacked July 23 by Palestinian terrorists. An hour after take-off, a message stating that the aircraft was being diverted to Algeria was received. Aboard the Boeing 707 were 38 passengers and ten crew members. Immediately after landing, the Jewish passengers were separated from the non-Jews. The latter, a large group of pilgrims on their way to visit the Holy Places, were released a short time after the hijacking.

The released pilgrims recounted details of the hijacking: immediately after take-off, five Palestinians armed with hand-grenades broke into the cockpit and instructed the crew to fly to Algeria. The *'National Front for the Liberation of Palestine'* claimed responsibility, and demanded that the Algerian government not release the Israeli hostages.

The Algerian government acceded to the demand of the hijackers. Countries around the world condemned Algeria, but the aircraft and the Israelis were not released. Algeria announced that the hostages were being kept under house arrest.

Various countries, including Arab states fearing Israeli retaliation, began to exert heavy pressure on the Algerian government to release the Israeli hostages. On July 30 the United States threatened to boycott Algerian ships and aircraft.

On Aug. 31, after 39 days of imprisonment, Algeria released the aircraft and hostages. The 'plane landed in Rome; the hostages were flown from there directly to Israel.

Mossad Chief Petitions High Court of Justice

Isser Harel, the former *Mossad* chief, on May 14 petitioned the High Court of Justice for a conditional ruling against the government because the censor had decided not to permit the publication of Harel's book on the capture of Adolf Eichmann.

After the petition, David Ben-Gurion and Levi Eshkol withdrew their opposition to the publication. The book was published and it revealed all the details of the complicated hunt, the kidnapping and the trial of the notorious murderer. After some time the book was turned into a successful movie.

Shells Fall on Jerusalem's Mamilla Neighborhood

Jerusalem's Mamilla neighborhood was shelled on May 7. No one was wounded, but all residents were evacuated from their homes. Kibbutz Manarah, Kibbutz Kfar Ruppin and Kibbutz Ashdot Ya'acov were also shelled that night.

On May 9 an armored car drove over a landmine beside the Yarmuk river. Three soldiers were killed by shelling in the northern Sinai on the same day. Seven other soldiers were seriously wounded when their vehicle rode over a mine beside Kibbutz Tirat Zvi. On May 10 Moshav Mar-galiot in Upper Galilee was shelled.

On May 14 the terror attacks reached Tel Aviv for the first time. A large terrorist device was discovered by urban Civil Defense personnel in the *Merkaz* cinema in the 'bus station. A composite photograph of the terrorist was published in all the daily newspapers.

On May 27 a group of children from Bet-She'an succeeded in foiling a terrorist attack in town when they discovered a device close to the old Bet-She'an amphitheater. The device was later dismantled.

Isser Harel. Against the government.

14 Dead in Suez Canal Battle

Fourteen Israel Defense Forces soldiers were killed and 31 were wounded on Oct. 26 in artillery and tank battles on both sides of the Suez Canal. Almost all of those killed were paratroopers who were playing soccer in Kantara when Egyptian shells started falling.

The IDF said that this was the largest battle to take place since the end of the Six-Day War. On the Egyptian side hundreds of guns and tanks took part. The first shells landed without warning in Kantara and within minutes there was shooting along the entire canal. After some two months of quiet along the canal the heavy shelling caught the soldiers unprepared. Precious minutes passed until the Israelis were in position for battle.

IDF guns responded to the artillery ambush with a barrage and set fire to the large Egyptian fuel stores close to the town of Suez.

A Terrorist Attack in the Cave of the Patriarchs

Defense Minister Moshe Dayan at the entrance to the Cave of the Patriarchs. The confrontations have not ended.

A hand grenade was hurled at the entrance to the Cave of the Patriarchs on Oct. 10. There were some 4,000 visitors to the cave at the time, 47 of whom were wounded. On the same day Israel announced that it would confiscate the Cave of the Patriarchs from the Moslem *kadi* of Hebron. The government announced that Arabs would be able to pray in the cave but that security measures would be tightened.

In response to the terrorist attack, a special prayer was held that same evening in the Cave of the Patriarchs. Spokesmen for the Jews who lived in Hebron demanded that the town's Jewish settlement be enlarged. A curfew was imposed on the town's Arab inhabitants. Fourteen suspects were arrested on Oct. 11.

One of the first decisions taken after the attack was to found Kiryat Hebron, modeled on Upper Nazareth. It was initially decided to build 100 residential units in the neighborhood immediately north of Hebron, to be called Kiryat Arba.

Friction between Jews and Arabs in the vicinity of the Cave of the Patriarchs increased as the years passed, and none of the attempts to find a solution by scheduling separate prayer times for the two religions proved to be successful.

Soviets Invade Czechoslovakia

On Aug. 21, following a short period of liberalization in Czechoslovakia in which the new leadership canceled censorship, released political prisoners and instituted a program of action called 'human socialism,' Warsaw Pact forces invaded Czechoslovakia and put an end to the regime of Alexander Dubcek and the spirit of liberalism in the country.

Polish, Hungarian, East German and Bulgarian forces crossed the border and over-ran the besieged nation. Soviet forces were flown in to take rapid control of large urban centers.

The 'Prague Spring,' as the short period of liberalism was called, was crushed with an iron fist.

Prague leaders called on civilians and soldiers not to fight the invaders, but despairing students, who tried to block the Soviet tanks in Prague with their bodies, were shot by soldiers. Tens of thousands were imprisoned.

After the conquest, Czech leader Alexander Dubcek and State President General Swoboda were transported to the Soviet Union where they were forced to sign an agreement approving the conquest. Swoboda continued his tenure as president, but Dubcek was overthrown as first secretary of the party and his place was taken by Gustav Husak.

Two Syrian pilots land their *MiG-17's* at airstrip in western Galilee. The pilots told interrogators they had mistaken the airstrip for an airfield near Latakia in northern Syria. (August 12)

•

The International Federation of Airline Pilots announced that it would boycott Algeria until the crew of the El Al Boeing 707 which was hijacked on July 23 and held in Algeria, was released. (August 12)

•

Hundreds of American Jews were requested to postpone their emigration to Israel because of a housing shortage. (August 15)

•

Algeria frees 12 Israelis held 39 days since hijacking of El Al airliner. Israel frees 16 Arabs held on infiltration charges before the Six-Day War as 'humanitarian gesture,' as agreed with Italian Government. (September 1)

•

Nigerian and Biafrans fought in the streets of Aba. The federal government announced it would allow the International Red Cross to fly mercy missions to refugees in Biafra for ten days; the Red Cross says ten days is inadequate and states the need for land and water mercy corridors to aid war victims in Biafra. (September 3)

•

In a market research survey on the public's preferred candidate for the premiership, 33.4% chose Moshe Dayan; 17%, Levi Eshkol; 6.3%, Yitzhak Rabin; 4.1%, Menachem Begin; 1.9% Ben-Gurion. (October 23)

•

Nine Israeli soldiers killed and 20 wounded in an artillery clash across the Suez Canal. Defense Minister Dayan warns Egyptians they will be hit where it hurts if incidents like last Saturday's assault are repeated. (October 26)

•

Mexico City Olympics opened in Latin America. More than 7,600 athletes from 110 nations took part in the games. US long-jumper Bob Beamon improved the world long jump record by 55 cm (22"), with a record jump of 8.9 metres (10 yards). Some of the Negro American team-mates manifested exhibitions of black power. (October 28)

Republican Richard Nixon beats Democrat Hubert Humphrey and is elected president of the United States. Nixon pledges to unite the nation and include Democrats in his administration. (November 4)

•

Paris peace talks are postponed, following Saigon's refusal to sit down at the same table with the Vietcong. (November 6)

•

King Hussein of Jordan says that Israel may have been behind the shooting incidents in Amman earlier that week which led to a military action against the Palestinian guerilla group. (November 6)

•

The heaviest bombardment ever launched by the *Fatah* hits Sdom Potash Works on the Dead Sea, but there are no casualties. The IDF struck deep into Jordanian territory during the night, cutting the main communication lines between Amman and Ma'an in the south. (November 30)

•

Minister Menachem Begin submits a proposal to Prime Minister Levi Eshkol to settle the occupied territories. Begin requests that Jews be allowed to settle in all areas and towns occupied after the Six-Day War, including Hebron, Jenin and Nablus. (December 16)

•

'Apollo 8' soars into space. Its astronauts are the first men to orbit the Moon. They report that it looks gray and colorless. The orbit ranges from 60.5 to 169 nautical miles. *'Apollo 8'* splashes down successfully in the Pacific. (December 27)

•

UN Security Council approves resolution condemning Israel's raid on Beirut airport, but the council chooses to ignore the attack on El Al's 'plane in Athens. Prime Minister Eshkol and the Knesset reject UN condemnation, implying it is a double standard. (December 28)

•

An agreement to supply US *Phantom* jets was signed by Israel and the United States following the personal commitment of the outgoing president, Lyndon Johnson. *The Phantom became the IDF's principal warplane during the Seventies.* (December 29)

'Raful' and Paratroopers in Beirut

A 'plane that was blown up at Beirut Airport. Legend has it that while the operation was on, 'Raful,' who commanded the amazing operation, ordered coffee at the air terminal cafeteria, drank it, paid for it, and left.

On Dec. 29 IDF troops took control of the international Beirut airport in a daring raid. A parachute unit commanded by Raphael 'Raful' Eitan, commander of the Paratroopers Brigade, captured the entire airport area and blew up the 14 'planes on the ground. In addition, the unit damaged the various airfield hangars and installations. The damage to the airport and aircraft was estimated at $100 million.

After taking control of the airport, the paratroopers attached explosive devices to all the aircraft in the airport. The soldiers took care not to harm the runways or the airport structures. During the operation, not one of the thousands of passengers who were in the airport building was injured.

Beirut airport had been chosen the target of the raid in order to make absolutely clear to the Arab states that Israel would not tolerate damage to its own aircraft. Pilots had recently been reporting instances of attempts to harm El Al Israel Airlines 'planes that were parked at overseas airports.

The raid on Beirut airport came in response to a terrorist attack on Dec. 26 on an El Al aircraft carrying 41 passengers, on their way from Israel to Paris and New York, who had made a transit stop at Athens airport. Two Palestinian terrorists threw hand grenades at the aircraft.

One passenger was killed in the attack and another was wounded.

The two terrorists were arrested by Greek police.

The *'National Front for the Liberation of Palestine'* claimed responsibility for the attack.

First Heart Transplant

Levy: Performed first heart transplant.

A team at Beilinson Hospital headed by heart surgeon Maurice Levy on Dec. 5 performed the first heart transplant in Israel. The surgery took eight hours. The patient, Yitzhak Sulam, a bank clerk from Jaffa, received the heart of Abraham Sadgat. Sulam recovered immediately after the operation but died two weeks later.

Daring Commando Operation in Egypt

On Oct. 31 an Israeli commando unit blew up two bridges over the River Nile and destroyed a large power station near Luxor. The destroyed power station was 230 kilometers (144 miles) from the Aswan Dam. The Egyptians understood that Israel could also hit the dam, a source of national pride for them.

The destruction of the power station cut off all southern Egypt from the electricity supply.

One month later, on Dec. 2, IAF 'planes attacked long-range gun batteries east of the River Jordan, in response to the firing on Bet She'an Valley settlements. Two days later IAF planes hit an Iraqi radar station.

Security Officer Saves El Al Passengers in Zurich

Warm reception for security officer Mordechai Rahamim upon his return to Israel after the trial in Zurich.

On Feb. 18 four terrorists opened fire on an El Al Israel Airlines 'plane that was preparing to land at Zurich airport. The attack was thwarted thanks to Mordechai Rahamim, a security officer on board the aircraft. Israel admitted for the first time that El Al flights are accompanied by security personnel in order to frustrate hijacking and terrorist attempts.

All the 'plane's passengers lay on the floor, while Rahamim pulled himself out of one of the windows and began firing at the terrorists. He subsequently jumped from the aircraft and began to chase them. He succeeded in killing one; the three others tried to escape and were captured. One of the pilots, Yoram Peres, was severely wounded when the entire cockpit was sprayed with machine-gun fire and he later died from his wounds.

Mordechai Rahamim, whose resourcefulness and courage saved all the aircraft's passengers, became a hero. He was arrested by the Swiss police and only after a number of days did he admit that he was an Israeli security officer. Rahamim was tried for murder under mitigating circumstances. In his court testimony he quoted, "If anyone comes to kill you, kill him first!" He was acquitted and returned to Israel.

Nine Jews Hanged in Baghdad

On Jan. 27 Israel and the rest of the world was shocked by the hanging of nine Jews in the central square of Baghdad, Iraq's capital. The nine had been convicted of committing espionage on behalf of Israel. The president of Iraq signed the order for the hanging.

Iraqi radio announced immediately after the hanging that the authorities had proclaimed a holiday and called on hundreds of thousands of citizens to witness the fate that befell enemies of the regime.

Levi Eshkol Dies

Levi Eshkol.

On Feb. 26, at eight o'clock in the morning, Prime Minister Levi Eshkol died of a heart attack. Three weeks earlier, on Feb. 3, he had suffered a slight heart attack, but had recovered and kept the attack a secret. The second attack was fatal.

Eshkol was the first prime minister to die while in office.

Eshkol had emigrated from Russia to Israel in 1914. In 1918 he was recruited to the Jewish Brigade. After the First World War he joined the group of pioneers who founded Kibbutz Deganya Bet. He served in David Ben-Gurion's governments as minister of finance and minister of agriculture.

When Ben-Gurion retired from the Cabinet in 1963, he recommended Eshkol as his successor.

For the first time in its history Kiryat Shmona was hit by *Katyusha* rockets. The town was unprepared, bomb-shelters were flooded, and two people were killed and many wounded. (January 1)

•

Sirhan Sirhan, the killer of Senator Robert Kennedy goes on trial. (January 7)

•

France confirms its ban on all military supplies to Israel in reaction to Israel's raid on Beirut's international airport. French political, cultural and religious leaders denounce General de Gaulle's decision to ban all arms supplies to Israel. (January 7)

•

The four main parties in the Vietnam War reach an agreement on procedure for their peace talks after 28 preliminary sessions, opening the way to top level talks between the US, South Vietnam and North Vietnam together with the National Liberation Front (NLF), the political arm of the Vietcong. (January 18)

•

Flowers pile up on the grave of Jean Palach, a 21-year old student of philosophy who committed suicide by setting himself on fire in Prague, to protest the Soviet invasion of Czechoslovakia. More than 500,000 people paid him their last respects. (January 25)

•

The distress buoy from the lost Israeli submarine *'Dakar'* *(Swordfish)* is found on a Northern Sinai beach, at Khan Yunis. (February 12)

•

A terrorist bomb exploded in the Supersol supermarket on Jerusalem's Agron Road, killing two students. (February 21)

•

World Jewish Congress seeks international backing to obtain permission for some 8,500 Jews to leave their homes in Iraq, Syria and Egypt because of persecution there. Dr. Nahum Goldmann cabled ten international bodies and non-aligned governments, including UN Secretary General U Thant, Yugoslavia's President Tito, Ethiopia's Emperor Haile Selassie and Indian premiere Indira Gandhi. (February 23)

General Hafez el-Assad takes control of Syria in a quiet coup, ousting President Nur A-Din Atassi. *Assad, one of the founders of the Ba'ath party, continues to rule over Syria today.* (March 3)

•

Defense Minister Moshe Dayan agrees to establish a Jewish enclave adjacent to the Cave of the Patriarchs in Hebron and notifies Moshe Levinger, head of the settler group, that he may open a coffee shop and souvenir shop beside the cave. (March 23)

•

Dwight Eisenhower, former president of the United States from 1953-1961 and commander of the Allies in Europe in World War II, dies at 78 from heart disease. He had suffered seven heart attacks in 13 years, four of them in the last year. (March 29)

•

Ten injured in Eilat after *Fatah Katyusha* bombardment from Aqaba. The IAF hit the *Katyusha* emplacements in the northern suburbs of Aqaba. The Chief of Staff commented that "the Jordanians should bear in mind that Aqaba is much more vulnerable than Eilat." Aqaba being Jordan's only port. (April 8)

•

Sirhan Sirhan is convicted of first degree murder in the assassination of Senator Robert ('Bobby') Kennedy. (April 17)

•

Alexander Dubcek, the man who defied Moscow with reforms and indirectly caused the Soviet invasion of Czechoslovakia is replaced as Communist Party First Secretary by Dr. Gustav Husak. (April 17)

•

Israeli commandos blast three strategic targets in Egypt. The government announcement stated the raid was to remind the Egyptians of their responsibility for cease-fire violations. (April 30)

•

Trans-Arabian Pipeline sabotaged in Golan by the *'Popular Front for the Liberation of Palestine'* (PFLP). Extensive efforts are made to keep 10,000 tons of crude oil from spilling over into the Sea of Galilee. The pipeline runs 1,750 kilometers (1,094 miles) from Daharan in Saudi Arabia to Sidon in Lebanon. (May 31)

War of Attrition in the Canal

Soldiers in one of the bunkers along the Bar-Lev Line. The protected bunkers saved the lives of many soldiers.

A long, hard day of battle on Mar. 8 symbolized the beginning of the War of Attrition in the Suez Canal. The war, declared that evening by Egyptian ruler Gamal Abdel Nasser, continued until August 1970.

Following an artillery duel that day, Israeli Air Force airplanes were scrambled and hit hard at oil installations to the west of the canal. In addition, the cities of Ismailiya and Suez were also bombed. One soldier was killed and nine were wounded. One Egyptian *MiG-21* was downed

and its pilot taken prisoner. The next day, on Mar. 9, the Egyptian Chief of Staff, Abdul Munaim Riyad, was killed by IDF shelling. Nasser placed the Egyptian army on highest alert and blacked out all towns in the region. Tens of thousands participated in the funeral of the chief of staff and called on Nasser to avenge his death.

Shooting on both sides of the canal continued until Apr. 15. In accordance with the instructions of the government, the IDF at first adopted a policy of restraint, but on Apr. 15,

Maj.-Gen. Avraham 'Bren' Adam, the commander of IDF armored forces in the Sinai, declared that his troops would respond to any breach of the cease-fire agreement.

On Apr. 24, following a series of Egyptian commando raids that killed three soldiers, UN Secretary General U Thant announced that a "war situation" prevailed in the Suez Canal zone. Next day, an Egyptian spokesman declared that the cease-fire agreement was canceled and no longer valid.

Golda Meir – Prime Minister

On Mar. 4 the Labor Party Cabinet elected Golda Meir as prime minister, to replace Levi Eshkol who had died one week earlier.

Golda Meir was elected in an attempt to block the route of Moshe Dayan, a *Rafi (Israel Labor List)* member and hero of the Six-Day War, to the position of prime minister. The candidacy of the popular Yigal Allon was also rejected by the *Mapai (Erez Israel Workers' Party)* leadership. The strong man of the Alignment, Pinchas Sapir, declined the appointment and was elected secretary of the Labor Party.

Meir's appointment was a sur-

Golda Meir, prime minister, despite slim chances.

prise and within a short period of time she gained the public's affection. During her five-year term of office she had to make extremely difficult decisions.

Immediately after her election she said: "I would have been happier if Moshe Dayan or Yigal Allon had challenged for the position."

Despite the fact that he was not elected, Minister of Defense Dayan continued to manipulate Meir, who was elected as a compromise candidate between hawks Allon and Dayan. Dayan refused to halt the activity of the 'Committee for Moshe Dayan as Prime Minister.'

Man Lands on the Moon

"One small step for a man, one giant leap for humanity." Neil Armstrong walks on the moon.

"That's one small step for a man, one giant leap for mankind." Neil Armstrong, commander of 'Apollo 11,' on July 21 summed up the historic moment in those words. The first human had landed on the Moon - the first landing of mankind on any celestial body whatsoever.

'Apollo 11' left Earth with three astronauts: Neil Armstrong, Edwin 'Buzz' Aldrin, Jr. and Michael Collins. The first two left the spaceship to pilot a small landing craft and a few minutes later landed on the Moon.

Neil Armstrong, the spaceship commander, went down the ladder first and placed the flag of the United States on lunar soil.

Immediately after landing, Armstrong picked up a small pebble and put it in his pocket so that he would have a small memento of the landing in case the two men suddenly had to leave the Moon.

The landing was broadcast live to many countries throughout the world. Television spectators were clearly able to see Armstrong detach his foot from the ladder and place it on the Moon. The two astronauts remained on the Moon approximately three hours. They performed some drilling, took soil and stone samples and made various measurements. Television viewers were able to see how ponderously and slowly they moved on the surface of the Moon.

In addition to the American flag, the two astronauts left on the Moon a small metal plaque bearing the following inscription: "We have come in peace in the name of humanity."

Al-Aqsa Mosque Set on Fire

A fire broke out at 7.30 a.m. in the al-Aqsa Mosque on the Temple Mount, on Aug. 29. The southern wing of the mosque, the third most important site in the Moslem world, went up in flames. It was assumed that the fire was caused by an electrical fault. Only the following day did it become apparent that a Jewish tourist from Australia, Dennis Rohan, was responsible for the blaze.

Immediately after the fire was discovered, stormy demonstrations broke out in east Jerusalem and on the West Bank. Police blocked all entrances to the Temple Mount and mobilized thousands of police officers to deal with rioters. In the afternoon a general curfew was declared in east Jerusalem. The fire was put out in the afternoon, but rumors spread of Israeli responsibility.

Dennis Rohan on trial for setting fire to the al-Aqsa Mosque.

The entire roof of the mosque, the central praying area and the seat of the kadi were totally burned, but only slight damage was caused to the famed silver dome.

Rohan told investigators that he had tried, on divine instructions, to destroy the al-Aqsa Mosque in order to rebuild the Jewish Temple on Temple Mount. He was found to be mentally insane and was later deported from Israel.

1969
JUNE - SEPTEMBER

Jordanians shell Dead Sea beach, killing one tourist and wounding four. (June 17)

•

Israel raids Green Island at the southern entrance of the Suez Canal. Anti-aircraft guns and radar destroyed, six Israeli soldiers killed. (June 19)

•

Edward Kennedy pleads guilty to leaving the scene of an accident. Mary-Jo Kopechne, 29, dies in the accident at Chappaquiddick. (July 26)

•

The air force bombs the Ghor irrigation canal, Jordanian army and Fatah entrenchments. The raid follows intensified Jordanian army and terrorist attacks in the area. (August 10)

•

British troops move into Londonderry in N. Ireland. Catholics and police battle on the streets for three consecutive days. 1,050 British troops sent to enforce the peace will remain in Belfast "as long as the situation demands," says British PM. (August 14)

•

TWA Flight 840 on its way from Rome via Athens to Lod is hijacked by the PFLP. Syria frees all passengers except six Israelis. (August 29)

•

The first shipment of Phantom aircraft arrives in Israel. The US announces that Israel has received the Phantoms in response to Soviet arms shipments to Arab states. (September 5)

•

A small Israeli taskforce raids Egypt, 40 kms south of Suez, stays for 12 hours, destroys a SAM-2 missile base and two radar tracking stations. Golda Meir says raid was aimed at bringing home to the Egyptians that aggression would evoke appropriate action. If the Arabs keep the peace "they will find full reciprocity on our part." (September 8)

•

Eleven Egyptian warplanes are downed in one long day of battle in the Suez Canal zone. Five of the 'planes were downed during attempts to attack IDF positions. One Israeli pilot was captured. (September 11)

Rockets blast the Beirut offices of the PLO. (October 15)

•

Samuel Beckett wins Nobel Prize for Literature. (October 23)

•

Over 80% vote in the elections for Israel's seventh Knesset. The Labor Party: 57 mandates, *Gahal*: 26, the National Religious Party: 12, and Ben-Gurion's party: 4 mandates. (October 28)

•

According to the Central Bureau of Statistics, one Israeli family in three has a TV set. By the end of December 500,000 sets have been bought. (November 3)

•

Powerful time bombs explode in three New York skyscrapers. The 70-story RCA building, the 60-story Chase Manhattan building and the 50-story building housing General Motors. One man injured. A letter sent to UPI blames giant American corporations for the Vietnam War, air pollution and the mindlessness of middle class life and racial inequality. (November 11)

•

250,000 march in Washington in protest march against the war in Vietnam. (November 15)

•

The *Arava*, the first Israeli-designed plane manufactured by Israel Aircraft Industries makes its maiden flight. It is is a multipurpose transport with short takeoff and landing capabilities. *It became one of the most popular executive aircraft in the world.* (November 27)

•

Knesset approves Prime Minister Golda Meir's new national government. The prime minister appeals to the Arab States to accept "a peace among equals" in which national honor might be preserved and national sovereignty respected. (December 15)

•

Anwar Sadat is made Egypt's vice-president. (December 21)

•

Rabin returns from Washington, officially to take part in discussion of US proposal for peace settlement with Egypt, but in fact to take part in important discussions of issue of in-depth bombing of Egypt. (December 21)

Five Missile Boats Abducted from Cherbourg Harbour

While the French were celebrating Christmas Eve on Dec. 24, five missile boats built for the Israeli navy in the shipyards of the French fleet in Cherbourg, France, disappeared, at 2.00 a.m. This operation, which represented a response to the French embargo on arms shipments to Israel, was one of the Israel Defense Forces' most amazing exploits.

The 72 crew members who had been training on the new vessels, as well as their families living in Cherbourg, disappeared together with the five boats.

During the three weeks before the operation, the boats' engines had been run at full power every night in order to accustom the citizens of Cherbourg to the noise so that on the day of the escape this noise would not attract any undue attention.

The five boats left Cherbourg harbour on a stormy night with no lights and no identifying flag. Their disappearance was discovered only 24 hours later, and from that moment until their entry into Haifa harbour on Dec. 31 they were the focus of world media attention.

The affair of the five missing boats caused a severe crisis in Israeli-French relations, and Maj.-Gen. Mordechai Mocca' Limon, head of the ministry of defense delegation in Paris, was declared *persona non grata* in France.

In order to allay French anger, Foreign Minister Abba Eban arrived in Paris and explained to the French that the boats had been handed over to a Norwegian company named 'Starboat and Weil,' and that they would be used to search for oil in the Middle East

The boats in the French port of Cherbourg. One morning they disappeared from the wharf.

Egyptian Radar Conveyed to Israel

A daring raid was carried out by an IDF *Nahal* division of paratroopers on Ra's A'arab past the Gulf of Suez during the night of Dec. 26. Israel Defense Forces troops succeeded in taking an Egyptian army radar base and conveying its entire radar system to Israel.

The modern Soviet radar, which tracked low-flying aircraft, was

The height of *chutzpah*. The Egyptian radar.

loaded on to a large *Frelon* helicopter which managed to cross the border by flying at low altitude.

Only a few days later did the first details of the operation, which impressed the whole world, become public. United States army personnel declared that the modern Soviet-made radar was of paramount strategic importance.

Israel Television to Broadcast on Sabbath

After a precedent-setting verdict handed down on Nov. 7 by High Court Judge Zvi Berenson, television entered a new era of Sabbath broadcasting. The verdict was delivered despite the prime minister's decision to cancel Sabbath broadcasts.

During coalition negotiations, the National Religious Party had claimed that Sabbath broadcasts should be canceled and Golda Meir had agreed. The heads of the Broadcasting Authority then threatened to resign, so an agreement was reached with the minister responsible for these matters, Israel Galili, that a caption stating "filmed on a weekday" would be added to the programs. However, Galili went abroad and Golda Meir, who had taken on responsibility for the Broadcasting Authority, canceled the broadcasts.

One Saturday evening two young people, Adi Kaplan and lawyer Yehuda Ressler, arrived at the house of the judge on duty and requested a conditional ruling that would instruct the Broadcasting Authority to begin Sabbath broadcasts. With the injunction in hand, the pair arrived at 7.00 p.m. at the Broadcasting Authority building in Romema, and two hours later TV anchor Chaim Yavin televised the News.

Several government ministers demanded the immediate dismissal of the high court judge who had allowed the injunction because he had agreed to discuss a petition on the Sabbath that was not, according to them, urgent.

Defense Minister's Son Saves El Al Passengers

Smiling despite her amputated leg, Hanna Meron returns from Munich to Israel

The alertness of Assaf "Assi" Dayan, the son of Defense Minister Moshe Dayan, on Feb. 10 prevented a murderous terrorist attack on El Al Israel Airlines passengers at Munich airport.

El Al passengers were in transit at Munich, on their way from Lod to London. While they were in a bus that was taking them from the airport building to the aircraft, three terrorists attacked them.

Dayan, who was among the passengers, noticed the approaching terrorists, and a few seconds before they opened fire he pointed them out to Uriel Cohen, the aircraft captain.

The terrorists were captured after a short battle. Cohen was wounded when he hurled himself onto one of the terrorists. The terrorist exploded a hand grenade, blowing off his own hand, and wounding Cohen. One passenger was killed in the attack and 11 were wounded, among them the Israeli actress Hanna Meron who was shot in the leg. A few days later doctors in Munich had to amputate her leg.

Swissair 'Plane Blown Up En Route to Israel

A Swissair 'plane on its way to Israel exploded in the air only minutes after taking off from Zurich airport. All 38 passengers and nine crew members were killed. Fifteen were Israelis.

Fifteen minutes after take-off the pilots announced to the Zurich control tower that there had been an explosion in the freight compartment. Immediately afterwards communication with the aircraft was cut off and the 'plane crashed in a forested area, 35 kilometers (22 miles) north of Zurich. The *'National Front for the Liberation of Palestine'* claimed responsibility for the attack. It was suspected that one of the Front members had managed to become friendly with a Swiss tourist and persuade her to send a suitcase to Israel for him. The tourist was killed along with all the other passengers.

Twelve Children from Moshav Avivim Murdered in a Terrorist Attack

Twelve children were killed and 19 wounded, most of them aged six to nine, in a terrorist ambush on May 22 on a 'bus carrying 35 children from Moshav Avivim to the regional school in Moshav Dovev. The terrorists stationed themselves on a hill across the border, in an area overlooking the 'bus route, and when the 'bus arrived at a bend in the road they fired three 82 millimeter *Bazooka* rockets.

Inhabitants of nearby Kibbutz Bar'am were the first to arrive on the scene. Traces of the terrorists led to Kefar Yar'un, and on that same day the Israel Defense Forces shelled villages in South Lebanon.

Those killed in the attack were buried in a joint funeral at a cemetery in Safed. The photographs of the dead children shocked hundreds of thousands of people in Israel and abroad. This was the most serious attack Israel had experienced on its northern border, and the fact that all the victims were children of the

OC Northern Command Mordechai 'Motta' Gur in the burnt 'bus.

same age and from the same moshav only intensified the shock.

After the massacre of the Moshav Avivim children, the IDF changed travel procedures in the area. For a long time people were forbidden to travel along the road unless driving in a convoy and accompanied by military vehicles.

Attempt by 12 Russian Jews to hijack 'plane in Leningrad fails. Searches carried out in Jewish homes in Leningrad, Moscow, Riga, Kharkov and Lobzovaya. Under Soviet law, fleeing abroad is considered treason. (June 21)

●

President Nasser concludes talks with Soviet leadership in Moscow, they together formulate demand that Israel must withdraw from all occupied Arab territory. USSR promises "all possible aid to Egypt." (July 17)

●

Five *MiG-21's* flown by Soviet pilots shot down over the Suez Canal, as they try to intercept Israeli fighter jets. (July 30)

●

Michael Rohan, who set fire to the al-Aqsa Mosque in Jerusalem, escapes from hospital for the mentally ill in Be'er Ya'acov. Rohan traveled to Tel Aviv and from there made his way to Mishmar Hayarden where he was arrested a day later. He was declared mentally incompetent and was sent to a Jerusalem hospital for the mentally ill. (September 1)

●

El Al crew and passengers on the way to New York via Amsterdam foil hijack attempt, first steward and four passengers wounded, one terrorist killed, female companion is caught. (September 6)

●

A hijacked Pan Am *Jumbo* from Amsterdam is blown up at Cairo airport, 154 passengers and crew of 23 safe. 100 TWA and Swiss Air passengers are released at Zarka, Jordan. The West German and Swiss governments agree to release six terrorists jailed for previous attacks on airliners and passengers. (September 7)

●

Hijacked BOAC joins two others at Zarka. Terrorists blow up all three 'planes at Zarka, but 40 hostages are released. (September 7)

●

Israel sends 200 tons of food to Amman as relief. (September 25)

●

The release of the last 40 hijack hostages opens the way for the repatriation of seven Arabs held in Switzerland, West Germany and Britain. Israel releases two Algerian officials who were on a transit flight that arrived in Israel last month. (September 29)

Cease-Fire in the Canal. *Gahal* Withdraws from the Government

Beginning in August it was possible to raise one's head - still cautiously - above the sandbags.

On Aug. 4 *Gahal* ministers submitted their resignation to Prime Minister Golda Meir and withdrew from the national unity government in protest at the Suez Canal cease-fire talks.

The government was at that time conducting indirect talks with the Egyptian government by means of mediator Gunnar Jarring. *Gahal* representatives in the government were opposed to the talks.

Minister without Portfolio Menachem Begin claimed that the Jarring document, on the basis of which the cease-fire negotiations were being conducted, was no different from the document of surrender signed in 1938 in Munich.

Three days later the canal cease-fire agreement was signed. The day after that, the War of Attrition which had lasted for one year and four months was brought to an end.

Prime Minister Golda Meir announced the agreement in a special radio broadcast.

Five days after the signing, the Egyptians breached the agreement when they advanced anti-aircraft tank batteries close to the canal.

'Black September'- Fierce Battles between Jordan, Syria and PLO

More than 8,000 fighters of the PLO were killed and tens of thousands were wounded in battles during which the Palestinians tried to topple King Hussein of Jordan and take control of the country. The Syrian army invaded north Jordan, conquering Irbid, the largest city in the north. The IDF went on alert and concentrated large forces, including reserves, along the Jordan river.

On Sept. 1 the PLO newspaper openly called for the ousting of King Hussein. Within 24 hours the king was saved from an assassination attempt while traveling to the airport. Amman, Jordan's capital, was cut off from the rest of the country and ten were killed in the ensuing battles.

A week later, on Sept. 9, the Jordanian army began to attack. During the first day of battles, 90 PLO fighters were killed by Jordanian air force shelling of bases in the Irbid region.

On Sept. 17, the Palestinians shelled Amman. At the same time the Jordanian army began to attack *Fatah* bases throughout the country. The following day, Syrian tanks began crossing the border to Jordan, and within two days a Syrian invading force had increased to two armored brigades and captured Irbid. The next day the Jordanian air force attacked the Syrian armored columns inflicting serious losses. The Syrians retreated. *Fatah* announced that 8,000 of its fighters had been killed in the previous five days of fighting.

On Sept. 23 the battles ended. King Hussein and Abu Iyyad, Arafat's deputy, called for a reconciliation between Jordan and the Palestinians. Hussein then completed the task. He expelled the terrorists and saved his kingdom.

Nasser Dead. Sadat His Successor.

Anwar Sadat.

Egyptian President Gamal Abdel Nasser died on Sept. 28 from a heart attack. Nasser, born in 1918, was behind the 1952 uprising of Free Officers who ousted King Farouk and turned Egypt into a republic. Within two years he had ousted General Mohammed Naguib and become the country's omnipotent ruler.

Nasser's deputy, Anwar Sadat, also a leader of the Free Officers and subsequently his successor, was elected to take his place.

Refuseniks Who Hijacked Aircraft Sentenced to Death

In response to the anti-Semitic campaign in the Soviet Union, public awareness of the struggle of Soviet Jews began to grow.

Twenty-one Jews, most of them *refuseniks* and among them ten doctors, were convicted on Dec. 25 of an attempt to hijack a Russian aircraft on June 16 in order to emigrate to Israel. There was a wave of protest demonstrations in Israel and throughout the world in response to the Leningrad trial verdict.

Two of the hijackers were sentenced to death and nine were sentenced to life imprisonment with hard labor. The harsh sentences inflamed passions around the globe and protests streamed into Moscow from various world capitals.

The Leningrad trial represented the height of a renewed campaign against Soviet Jews who were trying in vain to leave the country and emigrate to Israel. Soviet newspapers had adopted an extremely hard line against the refuseniks.

The hijackers had planned the operation for a long time. They had intended to take control of the aircraft at Leningrad airport and take off with their families for Israel. One of the hijackers was a former pilot in the Soviet air force. The mission was foiled by one of the activists who was an agent of the Soviet secret police. All the hijackers were arrested when they were already on board the aircraft. On Dec. 16 they were accused of treason.

Following the harsh sentence, the *Knesset* convened on Friday afternoon for its first special meeting. Mass protest demonstrations were organized in Tel Aviv and Jerusalem.

Following public protests, the sentences were deferred. *The Leningrad hijackers all eventually emigrated to Israel.*

Three Air Accidents in One Week

On Nov. 30, a TWA freight 'plane that had received approval for take-off and was running its engines on the runway at Lod airport collided with a tractor that was transporting an Israel Air Force *Stratocruiser*.

The captain of the American 'plane, which was on the airport's central runway, saw the military aircraft and tried to divert his 'plane at the last minute, but a wing of the Boeing hit the military aircraft.

The enormous explosion terrified everyone in the area and both aircraft went up in flames. Two were killed and two wounded in the tragedy. The American 'plane was loaded with vegetables, antiques and nylon stockings. The damage caused was estimated at $5 million.

On Dec. 7, a *Cessna* aeroplane crashed on its way from Jerusalem to Eilat. Four people perished in the crash on Mount Hebron. On the same day, another air tragedy occurred. The pilot of a *Cessna* crop-sprayer, on his way to seed clouds (to encourage rainfall) in the north of the country, crashed next to Kfar Beit Jann in the Upper Galilee.

De Gaulle Dead

General Charles de Gaulle, the leader of Free France during World War II and president of France from 1959 to 1969, died of a heart attack on Nov. 9 at the age of 79. He had escaped from Occupied France to England where he organized revolts against the attacking German army.

De Gaulle is considered to have been one of the world's leading statesmen. His relations with Israel were characterized by peaks and troughs: from enthusiastic support at the beginning of the Sixties to the serious rift and arms embargo after the Six-Day War.

De Gaulle and Ben-Gurion.

1970
OCTOBER - DECEMBER

The 1970 Nobel Prize for Literature is awarded to Russian author Alexander Solzhenitsyn. (October 8)

●

North Vietnam and the Vietcong reject President Nixon's peace plan as propaganda, saying basic issues in the Vietnam War should be settled before any cease-fire. Nixon proposes an immediate stand-still cease-fire, an exchange of all prisoners of war in order to establish good faith, and a broadened peace conference to seek a settlement of the Indo-China conflict. (October 8)

●

The largest single stone in the Western Wall is discovered; 11 meters (12 yards) long, 3.40 meters (4 yards) wide, it weighs 300 tons. (October 14)

●

The Immigrant Absorption Ministry decides to cancel the substantial assistance granted to returning emigrants after it is known that those returning after the Six-Day War number 7,000 out of a total of 100,000 immigrants. (November 1)

●

The US drops its opposition to a UN seat for Communist China, but demands that Taiwan stay a member of UN. (November 12)

●

Lieutenant-General Hafez el-Assad leads a bloodless coup d'etat in Syria. The ruling Ba'ath party has been in a state of turmoil since the abortive Syrian invasion of Jordan last September during the civil war there. (November 13)

●

Minister Yigal Allon meets with King Hussein of Jordan in the Arava Desert. The meeting is revealed following overseas publication of the news. Israel and Jordan do not react to the disclosure. (November 16)

●

The Sixth Asian Games end with Israel taking sixth place out of 18 countries that participated. Hana Shezifi took first place in the 800 and 1500 meter races. Esther Shachamorov took the gold in the pentathlon and 100 meter hurdles events. Israeli marksmen brought in the last two gold medals. (December 20)

IDF helicopters raid terrorist bases in Lebanon south of Sidon. Five Palestinian commandos, arrested at the beginning of January, supplied the information regarding the location of the bases. (January 15)

•

Damage was caused by fire at the Tel Aviv Hilton Hotel, costing hundreds of thousands of lira; no one injured. (January 27)

•

UN emissary Gunnar Jarring presents his Israel-Egypt peace plan: Israel would retreat to the June 4 border and sign a peace agreement, the Suez Canal would be opened to Israeli shipping, and the UN force would quit Sharm el-Sheikh. Egypt accepts the plan, Israel rejects it. (February 11)

•

At the World Congress of Conservative Rabbis in Jerusalem, Prime Minister Golda Meir said that Israel will not pull back to the pre-Six-Day War borders or rely for its security on guarantees from other nations. (March 20)

•

The United States supplies Israel with more *Phantom* aircraft. 12 were scheduled for delivery in May. (April 20)

•

Israel agrees in principle to consider proposals for a token presence of Egyptian police on the eastern bank of the Suez Canal. (May 8)

•

El Al's first Boeing 747 *Jumbo* Jet lands at Lod airport after flying from Seattle via London. (June 2)

•

The tanker *'Coral Sea'* bound for Eilat is attacked in the narrow Bab el Mandeb straits at the entrance to the Red Sea. The ship suffered minor damage. (June 11)

•

Hanna Meron returned to the stage in the title role of *'Medea,'* two years after losing her leg in a terrorist attack on El Al passengers at Munich. (June 19)

•

A malfunction on the Soviet spacecraft *Soyuz-11*, which had been in space for 25 days, causes the death of three cosmonauts upon its reentry to the atmosphere. (June 30)

Struggle for Soviet Jews is Intensified

On Jan.1 the high court of justice of the Soviet Federation remitted the sentences of the Leningrad hijackers, one week after their death sentence had been announced, commuting them to 15 years' imprisonment.

At the same time, Soviet pressure on Jews continued unabated, as did the pressure of the western world on the Soviet authorities to permit Jews to emigrate to Israel.

On Jan. 4, a Jewish youth from Riga was sentenced to four and a half years in prison after he publicly set fire to the Soviet flag. Forty young people were arrested in Leningrad, accused of learning Hebrew.

On the same day, 6,000 Americans demonstrated outside the building of the Soviet delegation to the UN with the call "Let my people go!"

Thousands of Soviet Jews who had submitted requests to emigrate to Israel received threatening letters which read, "Filth, get out of our holy country." Many Jews in Vilna were summoned for questioning by the KGB, and were told that they would lose their jobs if they continued their emigration initiatives.

Beate Klarsfeld, who with her husband became famous for an all-out campaign against Nazi war criminals, was arrested in Prague after a demonstration protesting the suppression of Soviet Jews, and deported to Austria.

'Black Panthers' Demonstrate

Charlie Biton heading the *'Black Panthers'* demonstration in Jerusalem.

For the first time since the large wave of immigration in the Fifties, massive demonstrations were held by Sephardic Jews and residents of poor neighborhoods to protest their disadvantaged situation as opposed to the benefits being given to Jews immigrating from the USSR. Five hundred people participated in the *'Black Panthers'* demonstration, which was the first of its kind in Israel. One of the most memorable moments came when Jerusalem Mayor Teddy Kollek shouted at the demonstrators, demanding that they get off the municipality lawn immediately, lest they destroy the grass.

On Mar. 26, hundreds of young people demonstrated in the Ha'Tikva neighborhood in Tel Aviv protesting the police decision to disallow street gambling booths. The youngsters threw bottles, broke shop windows, and threw stones at the police. Seven were arrested. The demonstrators complained that they were deprived compared to residents of north Tel Aviv, the level of education in their neighborhood was low, and the street lighting was insufficient.

Israeli Consul in Istanbul Kidnapped and Shot Dead

Ephraim Elrom, the Israeli consul in Istanbul, was kidnapped from his apartment on May 17 by an underground Turkish organization. In return for his release the kidnappers demanded that the Turkish government release prisoners from Turkish jails. The Turkish government said that it would not surrender to the demands of the kidnappers. A curfew was imposed on the city of three million inhabitants and Turkish policemen and soldiers made a house-to-house search for the consul and his kidnappers.

Five days later Elrom's body was found in an apartment only 500 meters (547 yards) from the site of the kidnapping. The body was flown to Israel.

The drama continued in Turkey when the police succeeded in tracing the three kidnappers, who had locked themselves in an apartment with a young girl they had taken hostage.

Israeli Spy 'Plane Shot Down in Sinai Desert

An Egyptian missile ambush in the Sinai Desert on Sept. 17 caused an Israeli *Stratocruiser* spy 'plane to crash. The aircraft, used as a mobile intelligence base, was flying over the Suez Canal.

The Egyptians fired a number of ground-to-air missiles at the *Stratocruiser* which crashed in the Sinai sands. Only one of the eight crew members survived.

The attack resulted in a warlike atmosphere between Israel and Egypt. Israel declared a state of alert in the region of the canal and dispatched large forces. The Egyptians also declared an alert, but after a few days the tension eased.

Ambassador Yitzhak Rabin - Another Washington Term

Ambassador Yitzhak Rabin and Prime Minister Golda Meir.

Foreign Minister Abba Eban announced on Aug. 9 to Prime Minister Golda Meir that Yitzhak Rabin had agreed to extend his tenure as Israel's ambassador to Washington by one year.

In return, Rabin was promised that in 1972 he would be appointed a minister in Meir's government. In the event, Yitzhak Rabin had to wait for that Cabinet appointment until December 1973.

Kahane Immigrates to Israel

Kahane in Israel. 'The Defender of Jews' makes *aliyah*.

A spokesman for the Jewish Defense League in the United States announced on July 2 that Rabbi Meir Kahane, who for years had headed the JDL, was immigrating to Israel with his family. *Kahane arrived with hundreds of his supporters and within a short time became the representative of the extreme right in Israel. He surrounded himself with extremists from the fringes of society and became the most extreme anti-Arab spokesman. In 1984 Kahane was elected to the Knesset.*

1971

JULY - SEPTEMBER

Louis 'Satchmo' Armstrong, who blew and sang his way into the hearts of millions, dies aged 71. (July 6)

Prof. Yeshayahu Leibowitz resigned his post as editor of the Hebrew Encyclopedia following a dispute with the Massada publishing house which demanded that he accelerate publication of the books. Leibowitz claimed that that would prejudice their quality. (July 7)

President Anwar Sadat said at the opening session of the newly formed National Congress of the Arab Socialist Union, Egypt's only party, that he "will not let the year 1971 pass" without resolving the Middle East crisis either by peace or war. He said Egypt was prepared to go to war even if it cost a million casualties. Sadat also stated that "The no war, no peace situation will not last and the current battle must be decided by the end of 1971." (July 23)

Twenty Jews from Kiev and Vilna in the USSR are arrested when they try to commemorate Tisha Be'av *(ninth of Av)*, August 1, by visiting the mass graves at Babi Yar. They were sentenced to 15 days in prison on charges of 'hooliganism.' (August 4)

Fires and bullets in Belfast claimed 17 lives in the worst riots in Northern Ireland in 50 years. Ten of the dead were civilians, among them a priest, two women and a 15-year-old boy. (August 10)

Bahrain declared its independence. Bahrain applied for membership in the UN and the Arab League. (August 14)

Nikita Khrushchev, former premier of the Soviet Union, dies aged 77. (September 11)

A delegation of Soviet Jews, petitioning for the right to emigrate, are told by head of the administrative section of the governing central committee, that there will never be free Jewish emigration to Israel because if all those who wanted to leave for Israel were to do so, it would lead to a colossal 'brain drain.' (September 20)

Sadat arrives in Moscow. President Nikolai Podgorny pledges to continue for a political settlement in the Middle East coupled with energetic measures to strengthen the defenses of the Arab countries. Immediately afterwards President Sadat says that "force and only force" should be used when dealing with Israel. Secretary of State William Rogers says after meeting with Foreign Minister Eban that the US must carefully reconsider its military commitments to Israel, because of the new Soviet promise of military aid to Egypt. (October 11)

•

German Chancellor Willy Brandt is awarded the Nobel Peace Prize, for his policies of reconciliation with former World War II enemies in Communist Eastern Europe. (October 20)

•

The UN General Assembly admits Communist China and expels Taiwan. The vote was 76-35 with 17 abstentions. This was the first expulsion of a country from the UN in its 26-year history. (October 25)

•

British Parliament votes to join the European Common Market (EEC) by 356-244. (October 28)

•

Three hundred and fifty 'planes make biggest US raids on North Vietnam since the halt of full-scale bombings. (November 1)

•

Two Soviet-piloted *MiG-25's* over-flew Israeli positions in Northern Sinai. This was the first direct violation of Israeli airspace by Soviet pilots, as well as an unprecedented Soviet involvement in the Middle East conflict. IAF interceptors were sent out but did not make contact with the *MiG-25's*. (November 6)

•

Jordan's Prime Minister is assassinated in Cairo by Palestinian terrorists. (November 28)

•

Iran seizes strategic islands in the Straits of Hormuz in the Persian Gulf. (November 30)

•

India and Pakistan at war, full scale battles rage on the borders. India strikes at East Pakistan in a bid to crush the 80,000 Pakistani army based there. (December 5)

Government Decides to Deport Black Hebrews

The Black Hebrews. Image of a racist country.

A family of Black Hebrews was deported from Israel on Oct. 5 one hour after landing at Lod airport. The Richardson family requested to be sent to Dimona where a large group of Black Hebrews was already living. The border police deported the family, claiming that they had arrived in Israel with no money and without return tickets to the US.

On Oct. 6, one day after the deportation, the Black Hebrews announced that a group of 45 people from their community was due to arrive in Israel, and that they would wage a public battle for their right to continue living in Israel.

The next day, 21 Black Hebrews arrived in Israel. The border police refused to permit them to enter Israel and they were returned to the aircraft that had brought them. The Black Hebrews forcibly opposed their deportation and attacked the policemen. The sect's leader declared that Israel was their homeland.

On Oct. 27 the government discussed the matter and heard reports from the minister of the interior and the minister of justice; both decided not to continue to push for deportation of the Black Hebrews lest Israel be viewed as a racist country by the international community. *The Black Hebrews continue to live in Dimona.*

African Heads Visit Israel

African presidents in Israel. Possible mediators between Israel and the Arabs.

As part of the effort to improve Israel's world standing, on Nov. 3 a conference was held in Israel with the presidents of Senegal, Nigeria, Zaire and Cameroon.

The objective of the conference was to discuss regional problems and explore whether the African leaders would be able to mediate in the Arab-Israeli dispute.

The four presidents were guests for three weeks, and traveled around the country. They left without committing themselves to assisting Israel in finding any solution.

Sadat: Ready to Sacrifice One Million Soldiers

In a speech delivered to soldiers in Cairo, President of Egypt Anwar Sadat declared that he was ready to sacrifice one million soldiers to liberate the territories captured from Egypt by Israel. Throughout the year the Egyptian president repeated this declaration a number of times. In a speech in September he declared that if Israel did not withdraw from the Sinai Peninsula it would pay a very heavy price.

Israel did not take these declarations of the Egyptian president seriously, and viewed them as a form of lip service to, and symbol of, the splendor of Arab culture. The Egyptian president was portrayed as someone stirring up war and as a person who could not be relied upon to achieve peace.

Letter Bombs in Israel

After numerous letter bombs had reached Israel at the beginning of the year, on Jan. 4 the police asked the public to be on the alert and carefully examine any suspicious packages arriving in the mail.

Thirteen booby-trapped packages were sent to Israel from Austrian and Yugoslav post offices at the beginning of January. The packages, usually 20x10 cm., contained note-books packed with explosives which were detonated by light contact. The packages were wrapped in floral paper and included New Year greetings cards.

Special equipment to detect explosives was installed at airports, and customs and post offices, after the discovery of the first packages. Extra security precautions were implemented at government offices and public institutions. The public was warned not to open any thick envelopes with unfamiliar foreign addresses. The police received dozens of calls, most of which were false alarms, from alarmed citizens.

All the envelopes were deactivated, and none of the recipients was injured. A sapper, however, was seriously injured while detonating one of the envelopes.

Northern Border Heats Up

An armored column in a 'Fatahland' raid.

The Israel Defense Forces attacked terrorist bases three times in southern Lebanon in January and February. The first raid took place on Jan. 10, when soldiers blew up four houses in the village of Bint Jebayel in the central sector, and in Kafr Hama'am in central 'Fatahland.' Two Israeli soldiers were killed in the attack.

The assault came in retaliation for a long list of terrorist activities since the beginning of December against border settlements. This was Chief of Staff David 'Dado' Elazar's first operation since his appointment at the beginning of January.

Two days later, a *Katyusha* rocket hit a kindergarten, fortunately unoccupied, in Kiryat Shmona. The following day, a couple was killed when a *Bazooka* missile scored a direct hit on their car. Six border police and two soldiers were injured in two other incidents.

On Feb. 25, the IDF initiated a major operation on the border of the Hermon. A huge taskforce took control of a number of villages from where most of the terrorist actions against Israel originated.

The operation continued for four continuous days, with the Israeli Air Force pounding many villages in southern Lebanon.

After four days of confrontation, and after roads from Israel into the heart of Lebanon had been paved, the soldiers returned to Israel.

'Dado' - Ninth Chief of Staff

Maj.-Gen. David ('Dado') Elazar, replaced Chaim Bar-Lev as the IDF's ninth Chief of Staff, on Jan. 1.

'Dado' (47) served in the *Palmach*, and after the Kadesh campaign in Sinai, transferred to the armored corps.

The president, prime minister, minister of defense and outgoing chief of staff congratulate 'Dado' (l).

1972

JANUARY - FEBRUARY

President Nixon authorizes $5.5 billion for the development of a space shuttle, which will land like a plane after completing its mission in space, then be sent into space again. (January 5)

•

Golda Meir refuses to meet with professors and intellectuals who had criticized her policies. The 35 associates had written her a letter saying that all options for preventing another war had not been exhausted. The group included writer A.B. Yehoshua and Amnon Rubinstein. (January 11)

•

Egypt's President Anwar Sadat says that the armed forces were on alert at the beginning of last month, but the order had been canceled when the Indo-Pakistan war broke out. Sadat also said that the only way to solve the Middle East crisis was through war. (January 13)

•

1,000 Jerusalem high-school students send a petition to the prime minister expressing support of her and her Cabinet. They commend Golda Meir for not giving in to Arab extortion. (January 13)

•

Record 300 immigrants land at Lod Airport. 14,000 new arrivals in 1971, increasing Israeli immigration by 1400%. (January 18)

•

Leadership of Zionist Congress prevents Meir Kahane from speaking at its assembly. Kahane gathers 500 people in Jerusalem, calling for increased immigration in light of the rising anti-Semitism in the US. (January 24)

•

Israel's French ambassador, Asher Ben-Natan, signs an agreement with France reimbursing Israel for 50 *Mirage-V* planes held due to the June 3, 1967 embargo imposed by President de Gaulle. The total payment was $74.5 million. Ben-Natan said Israel would have preferred the 'planes to the money. (February 15)

•

Member of *Knesset* Yosef Sapir, chairman of the Liberal party and the management of *Gahal*, dies of a heart attack, aged 70, while in Australia on behalf of the *Knesset*. (February 26)

Moshe Sneh dies after a short illness. He was one of the heads of the *Haganah* and was among the founders of *Maki (Israeli Communist Party)*. (March 1)

•

Two Austrian architects, Walter Dejaco and Fritz Ertl, who helped design and construct the crematoria at Auschwitz, were acquitted of complicity in the murder of Jews and set free. (March 10)

•

Charlie Chaplin, 82, receives honorary 'Oscar.' *'The French Connection'* wins five 'Oscars.' Gene Hackman, Jane Fonda ('Klute') win best actor awards. (April 10)

•

Apollo-16 blasts off to the Moon with astronauts John Young, Charles Duke and Thomas Mattingly aboard. Young and Duke spent a total of 20 hours 14 minutes on the Moon's surface, and drove a Moon buggy at a record speed of 11 mph. (April 17)

•

The four sides at the Vietnam peace talks in Paris agree that they will resume talks after a five-week suspension. (April 27)

•

In attempt to end the Vietnam War, President Nixon instructs the US Air Force to start heavy aerial bombardment ('carpet bombing') of North Vietnam. Hundreds of thousands evacuated from Vietnam's capital, Hanoi. (May 11)

•

Two hundred Soviet immigrants end their hunger strike at the Western Wall to support Soviet Jewry. The prime minister, president, ministers, members of *Knesset* and leaders of Zionist organizations came to the Wall in support of the demonstrators. (May 24)

•

President Nixon arrives in Iran to express the United States' support and reassure the Shah of Iran of the continued interest of the US in this region. (May 30)

•

The military public prosecutor in Beirut charges middle-aged Englishman and two Iraqis with spying on behalf of Israel, and refers them to a military investigating magistrate for further questioning. The Beirut police are still searching for an American, a Swiss and two Lebanese Jews. (May 30)

Sabena Hostages Rescued by IDF

IDF commandos in white overalls. Left, the commander, Ehud Barak.

In an audacious mission, IDF commandos rescued all 100 passengers and crew of a hijacked Sabena airliner at Lod Airport on May 9.

Four *Fatah* terrorists had taken control of the Belgian Sabena Boeing 707, after its departure from Brussels to Lod, the day before. The hijacked airliner landed at Lod in the evening and was immediately surrounded by security forces; at 2.00 a.m. that night the airliner's fuel tanks were emptied and its tires deflated, to prevent its take-off.

Defense Minister Moshe Dayan and Transport Minister Shimon Peres negotiated all night and into the following morning with the terrorists, who demanded the release of 317 *Fatah* terrorists detained in Israel. The hijackers threatened to blow up the airliner with its passengers if their demands were not met.

During the entire time, elite commandos, commanded by Lt.-Col. Ehud Barak, underwent training exercises in order to release the passengers. At 4.00 p.m., the soldiers, disguised as technicians, approached the airliner, opened its doors, and after a brief exchange of fire took control of the airliner.

Two male terrorists were killed and two female terrorists were taken captive. Three passengers were wounded, one of whom later died.

Ehud Barak, Benjamin Netanyahu and Danny Yatom participated in the operation. Yatom was appointed Mossad chief in 1996.

Massacre at Lod Airport

Twenty five people were killed and 72 injured by three Japanese terrorists, in a murderous attack at Lod.

The terrorists, who had arrived on an Air France airliner from Paris on May 30 at 9.55 p.m., passed through passport control, removed *Kalashnikovs* and hand grenades from their suitcases, and started spraying passengers in the thronged arrivals hall.

Scores of passengers were injured in the attack. A terrorist rushed onto the runway, lobbing hand grenades and shooting at an El Al airliner which had just arrived from Paris, wounding the passengers who were disembarking.

Sixteen of the murdered and 27 of the wounded were Puerto Rican pilgrims; six Israelis were killed, among them a prominent Israeli scientist, Prof. Aharon Katzir. *His brother, Ephraim Katzir, was elected President of Israel one year later.*

Two terrorists were killed by one

Kozo Okamoto in court. The Japanese terrorist was released in 1984.

of their own grenades. A third, Kozo Okamoto, was seized by an El Al staff member. Okamoto, 24, a member of the *'Japanese Red Army,'* trained with his comrades in Lebanon with the *'National Front for the Liberation of Palestine.'* He was court martialed and sentenced to life imprisonment.

The Japanese Government apologized for the atrocity carried out by its citizens, agreeing to pay 1.3 million dollars' compensation to the families of victims. Okamoto was released in a prisoner exchange deal after the Lebanon War.

Shapira. Political Storm.

Minister of Justice Shapira Resigns from Government

Justice Minister Ya'acov Shimshon Shapira resigned on June 11, following a public outcry which developed over the Netivei Neft (Oil Lines) Company. The conclusions of the Vitkin Committee were published in May.

The committee investigated the actions of the government company, and interrogated its general manager, Mordechai Friedman, after suspicions had arisen of negligence.

The committee determined that Friedman had acted correctly, but after concluding its investigations it became apparent that the director-general of the Finance Ministry had set exorbitant legal fees for its members. Justice Minister Shapira accepted responsibility for the mistake.

Golda Invites Sadat to Attend Direct Negotiations

On July 26, Golda Meir called on Egyptian President Anwar Sadat to attend a face-to-face meeting with her. In her *Knesset* speech, the prime minister addressed Sadat as the leader of a great nation, coming from an ancient heritage, and with the future ahead of him, and suggested that Egypt and Israel meet in a combined effort to solve their disputes.

The speech came in response to Sadat's decision to expel Soviet soldiers and military advisors from Egypt. On July 18, Sadat had announced that all military experts would leave the country, and that all factories, equipment and projects erected by them on Egyptian soil after 1967 would be considered Egyptian property.

Within weeks, 17,000 Russian military personnel, including those in strategic units and fighter pilots, had left Egypt.

Golda Meir was severely criticized for her tough stand in preventing negotiations with Arab leaders, and for her rejection of all attempts to close the gap with the enemy. She prevented Nachum Goldmann, president of the World Jewish Congress, from meeting with President Nasser, the previous Egyptian president.

Prime Minister Golda Meir inspecting female troops before her departure abroad.

Although Golda and Sadat met in Jerusalem, the meeting only took place five years later, in 1977, when Sadat came to Israel to end the state of war between the two countries. Golda did not then hold public office, but her administration had laid the groundwork for Sadat's visit.

Russia Claims Tariff from Jewish Academic Emigres

The Soviet Union announced on Aug. 3 that all Jewish academics wanting to leave the country must pay a tariff of up to 14,000 *rubles*, depending on their field of specialty. A number of Jews applying for exit visas in Vilna were informed of the new decree. Prior to the new edict, those emigrating had paid only 900 *rubles* for a passport.

For the same reason, a number of exit permits for Jews from Moscow was delayed during the first week of August.

The Soviet Union justified the high levy as a means of recouping the investment made in providing those Jews with an academic education.

The prime minister has admitted, for the first time, that Israel was the first to attack when fighting with Egypt in the Six-Day War. Golda Meir read the Cabinet's decision of 1967 to the Knesset, confirming the intent to attack Egypt. (June 4)

Most international airlines were inactive for 24 hours when 45,000 pilots went on strike in protest at the ineffectiveness of the battle against airline hijackers. The demonstration followed the murderous attack at Lod Airport where 24 passengers were slaughtered. (June 19)

Kozo Okomoto was sentenced to life imprisonment by a military court for his part in the Lod Airport massacre of May 30. (July 8)

Eleven were injured by an explosion at the Tel Aviv Central Bus Station. The bomb was placed on the window of the public bathroom; 200 Arabs were detained for interrogation. (July 11)

Ugandan President Idi Amin accuses the United States of sending Israelis disguised as American tourists into Ugandan territory. Amin warned that American-Ugandan relations would suffer should this alleged practice continue. (July 18)

The Soviet government withholds immediate comment on President Sadat's request that Russia withdraw its military advisers from Egypt. (July 19)

President Nixon has instructed Commerce Secretary Peter Peterson to try to reach a comprehensive new trade agreement with the Soviet Union before the end of the year. (July 20)

A booby-trapped phonograph exploded in an El Al airliner's cargo hold shortly after takeoff from Rome to Israel. The airliner, carrying 140 passengers, returned to Rome and landed safely. Two young British women had received the phonograph from terrorists at the airport and did not know that it was booby-trapped. (August 16)

Bobby Fischer of the United States is the new chess champion of the world. Fischer took the title in 21 games and a four point margin against his Russian opponent, Boris Spassky. (September 1)

•

Chief of Staff David Elazar said Israel expects a lull in the military situation, and as a result is considering cutting compulsory military service. (September 2)

•

Forty-seven Soviet Jews protest in an open letter to Soviet President Nikolai Podgorny, calling the tax on those Jewish professionals wishing to emigrate to Israel unconstitutional. (September 2)

•

Mark Spitz sets an Olympic record winning seven gold medals in the swimming events. (September 4)

•

Jordan's King Hussein initiated an unprecedented gesture by expressing his condolences to the families of the Israeli Olympic athletes who had been murdered in Munich. The king also sent a telegram to Germany's chancellor, expressing his deep shock at the atrocity. (September 6)

•

Zadok Ofir, an Israeli embassy worker in Brussels, was shot and severely wounded while sitting in a coffeeshop in Brussels. Ofir was shot by two terrorists who managed to escape. The main suspect, a member of *Fatah*, fled Belgium. (September 11)

•

Israel's agricultural attache, Ami Shehori, was killed as he opened a letter bomb addressed to him at the London embassy. The police warn the Israeli public to be on the alert as 26 more letter bombs addressed to Israelis are discovered throughout Europe, the US and Israel. (September 19)

•

25,000 Soviet Jews emigrated to Israel during the first half of 1972. This is the largest number of Soviet immigrants since the Fifties. (September 22)

•

In a BBC interview, Golda Meir says that Israel has nothing to discuss with the Palestinians, and will speak only to independent Arab states. (September 28)

Massacre of Athletes in Munich

The coffins of the Israeli athletes arrive in Israel. While the country was in a state of shock, the Olympic Games in Munich continued.

Eleven athletes, members of the Israeli Olympic team, were massacred on Sept. 5 in Munich. Nine of the athletes were killed during a rescue attempt made by German police.

Eight terrorists affiliated with the *'Black September'* terrorist group broke into the accommodations of the Israeli delegation in the Olympic Village at 4.30 a.m. Two athletes were killed on the spot.

The terrorists demanded the release of 200 terrorists imprisoned in Israel, in exchange for the release of nine Israeli athletes.

Israel stated that it would not yield to terror by releasing the prisoners. The deadline expired at noon, but West German Federal Interior Minister Heinrich Genscher continued negotiating with the terrorists until 9.00 p.m. An hour later, the terrorists and nine hostages left the Olympic Vil-

lage by bus, and then boarded a helicopter which took them to a military airfield near Munich. An aircraft was waiting to take them to Tunis, where they were offered asylum.

German sharpshooters opened fire at terrorists who left the helicopter to examine the aircraft. Despite the close range, the would-be rescuers missed their targets completely. All nine Israeli athletes, who were tied to each other in the two helicopters, were massacred in cold blood by the kidnappers.

Five terrorists were killed at the airfield during the failed rescue attempt, and three who had been injured were captured. A German police officer was killed during the attack, and a helicopter pilot was seriously injured.

During the first hours after the bungled rescue attempt, Germany an-

nounced that all the hostages had been safely released; only at 3.00 a.m was the tragic outcome made public.

The Israeli delegation withdrew from the Olympic Games and returned to Israel with the bodies of the athletes. Israel declared a day of national mourning.

The massacre shocked the world. In spite of this, the Olympic Committee resumed the Games after a one-day suspension, during which a memorial ceremony took place. Numerous athletes withdrew from the Games in protest.

The *Mossad* succeeded in tracking down the masterminds of the massacre over the years, on the instructions of Prime Minister Golda Meir. Although nearly all the terrorists involved in the conspiracy were eliminated, Israel never claimed responsibility for their deaths.

200 Killed in Lebanon Bombing

In retaliation for the murder of the athletes in Munich, on Sept. 8 the IDF attacked 11 terrorist bases in Syria and Lebanon. Dozens of fighter jets took part in the strike, which was defined as the most serious in over two years. More than 200 terrorists were killed in the bombings; three Syrian jets were downed, and the navy sank terrorist vessels outside Tyre. The IDF suffered no casualties.

A few days later, two soldiers were killed in an encounter with terrorists in the Mount Dov region, near

Arafat. Retaliation.

the Lebanese border.

In response, the IDF again penetrated 16 Lebanese villages, destroying 130 buildings. Three IDF soldiers were killed. Scores of terrorists were eliminated.

Battles in Lebanon continued for many months. The scenario was more or less uniform: terrorists carried out sabotage or shelled northern Israeli settlements, and the IDF retaliated, raiding villages and bombing terrorist strongholds in southern Lebanon and Syria.

Espionage Network Exposed

Udi Adiv, the *kibbutznik* from Gan Shmuel, second from left, with members of the network in court.

For the first time in Israel, on Dec. 8, police arrested a Jewish-Arab espionage and sabotage network. The network had been collaborating with Syrian terrorist organizations and intelligence agents. Those arrested were 20 Arabs and four Jews, who had all been trained in Syria in the use of weapons, communications, sabotage and equipment. The four Jews were Udi Adiv, 26, a *kibbutz* member from Gan Shmuel, Dan Vered, 28, and Yehezkel Cohen, 30, both from Tel Aviv, and David Coper, 28, from Bat Yam.

The unprecedented involvement of Jews in a hostile sabotage network astounded Israeli society. Adiv, born on Kibbutz Gan Shmuel, was a corporal in the reserve paratroopers. He was accused of providing the Syrians with details of IDF paratrooper units, training bases and weaponry used along the border for the prevention of terrorist penetration. During his investigation, Adiv admitted to visiting terrorist bases in Syria.

West Germany Releases the Killers of Munich Athletes

On Oct. 30, West Germany capitulated to the demands of Palestinian terrorists, who threatened to blow up a German airliner, by releasing the three *'Black September'* killers of the Israeli athletes in Munich.

On Oct. 29, three terrorists hijacked a Lufthansa Boeing 727 passenger airliner flying from Beirut to Frankfurt.

The hijackers took control of the airliner and its 20 passengers and crew, demanding in exchange the freedom of the three Munich killers.

The hijacked airliner refueled in Cyprus and eventually landed in Zagreb, Yugoslavia. Despite Israel's resolute stand, West Germany surrendered to the hijackers' demands and flew the three killers to Zagreb in a private aircraft.

Mamzer Episode Closed

Chanoch and Miriam Langer, the brother and sister who had been proclaimed illegitimate by the Rabbinical Court, married in a double wedding ceremony on Nov. 19, after the Rabbinical Court canceled its definition of illegitimacy.

The country was involved in the episode for years. Defense Minister Moshe Dayan, who had helped to find a solution to the problem, attended the weddings of the two.

The Langers were declared illegitimate by the Rabbinical Court in Tel Aviv in 1955, when they were children. Their mother, Hava, had been married when another man fathered the children. The Rabbinical Court authorized the decree in 1970.

Chief Rabbi Shlomo Goren, who supported the Langers, convened a special session of religious judges to arbitrate the matter. Despite vehement opposition from the Chief Sephardic Rabbi Ovadia Yosef, the religious judges concluded that the brother and sister were not illegitimate because their mother's husband was not Jewish.

Immediately after the verdict, Chief Rabbi Goren rushed to conduct the ceremony, in order to prevent any possibility of an appeal.

Dr. Henry Kissinger, President Nixon's national security adviser, returns to Washington after four days of secret talks in Paris with North Vietnam's Le Duc Tho. The White House maintains total blackout on talks. (October 12)

●

Egypt's Prime Minister Aziz Sidky concludes talks with Soviet leaders, intended to normalize relations with the Soviet Union after President Sadat expelled Soviet advisers from Egypt in July. (October 18)

●

Landslide victory for Republican Richard Nixon over Democrat George McGovern in the presidential elections. Nixon takes 49 States and loses Massachusetts and the District of Columbia. The Democrats retain control of Congress. (November 7)

●

Six *MiG-21's* shot down, an Israeli farmer killed during daylong air, armor and artillery duel along the 40 km front with Syria. 15 Syrian *T-54* and *T-55* tanks destroyed in heaviest fighting in over two years. (November 21)

●

Chad cuts its ties with Israel. President Francois Tombalbaye says the presence of Israeli representatives in Chad jeopardized his country's security and other African nations. (November 28)

●

Nixon resumes full-scale bombing of North Vietnam and warns there would be no respite until the Communists agree to a settlement of the Indo-China War. (December 18)

●

Ezer Weizman resigns from his position as *Herut* administrative chairman owing to his dissatisfaction with party chairman, Menachem Begin. Begin's response: "It's a pity. Weizman has made a mistake." Weizman only resumed party activity before the 1977 elections. (December 20)

●

President Harry S. Truman dies aged 88. Former Prime Minister David Ben-Gurion said: "I never knew a single president who revealed such a sympathetic attitude to Zionism and the birth of the State of Israel as did President Truman." (December 26)

Niger cuts relations with Israel. Congo Brazzaville and Chad had already severed; Chad after receiving a major loan from Libya. (January 5)

•

Cease-fire agreement is signed by the United States and North Vietnam after eight years of war. (January 27)

•

Israel Shipyards launches the first Israeli-made missile ship. The *'Reshef' (flash)* has twice the firepower and three times the range of the Cherbourg missile boats. The decision to build these ships in Israel had been taken due to the French embargo that led to the 1969 missile boat drama. (February 19)

•

'Black September' took US and other diplomats hostage at Saudi embassy in Khartoum; 2 Americans and a Belgian were murdered by the terrorists. The eight terrorists surrendered after nightlong negotiations. (March 1)

•

Soviets drop head tax on emigrants with higher education. A majority in Congress had threatened to vote against American Soviet trade agreement if the law was not replaced. (March 22)

•

Ten letter-bombs mailed in Turkey are discovered by alert postal employees in Israel. (April 3)

•

The government decided to continue the ban on land acquisition by Jews in Judea and Samaria. The debate was initiated a year ago by Defense Minister Moshe Dayan who supported private investors interested in buying plots in the area. (April 8)

•

A high state of alert in the IDF following the advance of Egyptian troops towards the Suez Canal. The alert was canceled after it became clear that the Egyptians were not preparing for war. (May 27)

•

Minister of Defense Moshe Dayan marries Rachel Korem at the home of the army's chief rabbi. Six months earlier, Dayan had left his wife Ruth for Rachel, ex-wife of Advocate Pinchas Rabinovitch. *Rachel Dayan is known today for her work with immigrant artisans.* (June 26)

Libyan Airliner Shot Down in Sinai. 105 Passengers Killed. 7 Survive

105 passengers were killed on Feb. 21 when the IAF fired at a Libyan passenger airliner flying in the area of Sinai; among the seven survivors, three were seriously injured.

The airliner was on a routine flight from Benghazi, Libya to Cairo when, due to pilot error, it flew off course, crossed the Suez Canal and continued east over the Sinai Peninsula. The Cairo air traffic control tower failed to warn the pilots that they had crossed the border.

Two Israeli *Phantoms* which intercepted the airliner signaled to the pilot to land at Refidim airbase. The airliner's 'black box' showed that until the last moment the Libyan pilot believed the jets to be Egyptian *MiG's*, and tried to evade them.

By international aviation regulations, the air force jets had to shoot down the airliner after their warnings had been disregarded. Chief of Staff David Elazar authorized Air Force Commander Maj.-Gen. Mordechai Hod to order the pilots to open fire and lightly damage the airliner, thus

Remains of the Libyan airliner in the Sinai.

forcing it to land. The Libyan pilot's attempt to make an emergency landing failed, and the airliner crashed and burst into flames.

After the tragedy, Elazar said that the decision to open fire on the airliner was one of the hardest decisions he had ever made. Defense Minister Moshe Dayan determined that under the circumstances the decision was correct, after intelligence warnings

had been received of plans to hijack an airliner and crash it over Tel Aviv in a suicide attack.

Most countries were outraged by the shooting down, condemning Israel. Dayan suggested a hot-line between Israel and its Arab neighbors be set up to prevent similar tragedies. Cairo rejected the suggestion. The Libyans accused Egypt of not having attempted to save the passengers.

Terrorists Killed in Beds

Palestinians terrorists attacked the residence of Israeli Ambassador Rahamim Timor in Cyprus on Apr. 9. The terrorists also attempted to attack an Arkia airliner at Nicosia Airport. In reprisal, the IDF executed one of its most daring missions, named *'Aviv Neurim,'* during the night of Apr. 9. Arafat's deputy, Abu Yussuf, and PLO spokesman Kamal Nasser, were killed in the operation.

Israeli paratroopers, and land and marine commandos landed on the beaches of Beirut, where they were met by *Mossad* agents who had arrived in Beirut the previous day and had rented cars for the invading force. The soldiers headed towards their target - the organization leaders' seven-floor headquarters and apartment building. The buildings were guarded by armed terrorists. One of the commanders was Lieut.-Col. Amnon Lipkin. According to various sources, the commander of the elite unit, Ehud Barak, arrived in Beirut disguised as a woman, in ad-

Remains of the bombed building in Beirut. High ranking terrorists were killed in the daring mission.

vance of the invading unit.

The operation continued for two-and-a-half hours. The terrorist leaders were caught by surprise in their beds and killed before they had a chance to open fire. Shots were fired in the direction of the Israeli force from a nearby Lebanese army vehi-

cle, killing two marine commandos. The raiding party seized documents and significant information on the organization's activities in Israel and this later led to the capture of terrorist leaders in the territories.

Amnon Lipkin was appointed the IDF's chief of staff 20 years later.

Ephraim Katzir, Israel's Fourth President

On May. 24 Israel's fourth president, Prof. Ephraim Katzir (Kachalski), was sworn in. The president was elected one-and-a-half months

earlier by 66 *Knesset* members. Katzir, a professor of biochemistry from Rehovot and one of Israel's prominent scientists, is the brother of

the late Aharon Katzir, a brilliant scientist killed a year earlier in the murderous attack by Kozo Okamoto and his comrades at Lod Airport.

Mistaken Assassination in Lillehammer, Norway

The Israeli *Mossad*, reputed to be the best secret service in the world, mistakenly killed Ahmed Boushiki, a waiter, in Lillehammer, Norway on July 27. Boushiki was mistaken for Ali Salameh, the *'Black September'* leader responsible for the massacre of Israeli athletes in Munich.

All six *Mossad* agents were arrested in Oslo shortly after Boushiki's assassination, and the operation was labeled as one of the *Mossad's* greatest failures. Boushiki, who emigrated from Morocco seven years earlier, was killed near his house shortly after he had finished his shift at a nearby restaurant.

Eye witnesses recorded the license number of the getaway car. This information led the Norwegian police to the house of Yigal Eyal, a security officer at the Israeli Embassy in Oslo, who had rented the car.

Norwegian police arrested two *Mossad* agents at Eyal's house, two others were arrested at the airport, and another two were arrested at the house of one of the agents. All the detainees admitted that they were *Mossad* agents. Yigal Eyal was declared *persona non grata* and deported from Norway.

Israel sent the Foreign Office legal advisor to Norway to handle the release of the Israeli detainees and to protest the search of an embassy employee's residence. Norway refused to release the agents; they were sentenced, but released soon after.

'Arik' Sharon Forms Likud Party

Two months after his retirement from the IDF as OC Southern Command, on Sept. 11, Ariel ('Arik') Sharon formed the *Likud* party, a coalition of *Gahal*, the Free Center and the National list. For the first time, a right-wing alternative was established to the left-wing *Mapai*, *Mapam*, *Rafi* and Labor Alignment bloc. Behind the initiative were 'Arik' Sharon, who joined the Liberal party immediately after his release from the IDF, and former Air Force Commander, Ezer Weizman.

The agreement was preceded by lengthy negotiations and heavy pressure applied by Sharon and Weizman on *Gahal's* veteran leadership, headed by Menachem Begin.

For some weeks, *Gahal* leaders refused to allow Shmuel Tamir, Free Center chairman, who had left the *Herut* party six years earlier, to join the new party.

'Arik' Sharon. Two months after shedding his uniform.

Miracle Saves Habash from Capture

The Israeli Air Force intercepted a Lebanese passenger aircraft en route from Beirut to Baghdad on Aug. 10. Immediately after take-off, two Israeli combat aircraft ordered the airliner to land at a military airfield in north Israel. The 74 passengers were interrogated and released once their identities had been checked. George Habash, leader of the *'Popular Front,'* was saved from Israeli captivity after changing his plans at the last minute.

Defense Minister Moshe Dayan said that the forced landing of the airliner was one of Israel's means of combating terrorism and preventing murderous acts.

1973

JULY - SEPTEMBER

Assistant air attache at the Israeli embassy is murdered outside his home in Washington DC. (July 1)

•

Major General Shmuel Gonen ('Gorodish') took over as OC Southern Command and Major General Ariel Sharon left the army for politics. (July 15)

•

Senate Watergate committee votes unanimously to sue President Richard Nixon, after he defies their demands to produce Watergate tapes and documents. (July 26)

•

The Arab member states of OPEC meet in Kuwait to discuss a joint policy towards the West and possible use of oil as a weapon to pressure the West in the Israel-Arab conflict. (September 4)

•

Five terrorists who had planned to use anti-aircraft missiles to shoot down an El Al airliner were arrested in Rome following a warning from Israel to the Italian security forces. (September 5)

•

Marxist President Salvador Allende commits suicide after being deposed in a military coup, headed by Chile's army commander, General August Pinochet. Allende had been the first freely-elected Marxist president in the West. (September 11)

•

Thirteen Syrian *MiG-21's* shot down as IAF reconnaissance patrol is attacked over international waters, 25 kilometers north-west of the Syrian port of Latakia. One IAF *Mirage* was shot down; the pilot was rescued together with a Syrian pilot. (September 13)

•

Henry Kissinger became the first foreign-born nationalized American citizen to be sworn in as a Secretary of State. Kissinger's family fled Nazi Germany in 1938. (September 22)

•

Two Arab terrorists hijacked a train with Soviet Jewish emigrants, taking three hostage to Vienna Airport. Chancellor Kreisky announced that the emigrant transit camp would be closed in exchange for the hostages, and the terrorists were given free passage. (September 28)

Informed sources stated that they did not expect a Syrian military initiative along the Golan front in the foreseeable future, despite the increase of troops in the area. The troop movements were seen as redeployment of forces from the Jordanian border due to the detente between the two countries. (October 1)

•

In an interview in *'Time'* magazine, King Hussein said that unless Israel withdraws from the territories held since the Six-Day War in exchange for a guarantee of peace, "a fresh disaster of great magnitude" could not be avoided. (October 2)

•

President Mobutu announced that Zaire was severing its diplomatic relations with Israel, making it the eighth African country to do so since 1967. (October 4)

•

Foreign Minister Abba Eban met US Secretary of State Henry Kissinger and discussed Austria's decision to shut down transit facilities for Soviet Jewish emigrants. The preliminary reaction to Mr. Eban's General Assembly speech of October 3 was that the speech was conciliatory in tone, but no change was seen in Israeli policy that would encourage the Arabs to come to the conference table. (October 4)

•

The Soviet Union evacuated hundreds of Soviet advisors and their families from Egypt and Syria. The Soviets were aware of the imminent attack on Israel, and wanted no part of the impending war. (October 4)

•

In a special cabinet session on *Yom Kippur* Eve, it was decided not to declare a full mobilization of reservists to avoid international accusations of initiating war against the Arab states. *The question "Why didn't you mobilize the reserves?" became the leading question in the campaign against Golda Meir's government.* (October 5)

•

Watergate tapes battle continues. Judge orders Nixon to submit nine subpoenaed tapes so he may judge if their contents should be kept secret. (October 5)

Israel Prepares for *Yom Kippur* - but Egypt and Syria for War

Still smiling. Chief of Staff 'Dado' (r) and OC Central Command 'Hofi' (l), a few days before the outbreak of the war.

Almost inconspicuously, Syria and Egypt on Oct. 1 declared a state of high alert along their borders. Syria moved troops from the Jordanian border to the Golan Heights. The next day the Syrian army commenced wide-scale mobilization of reserve units.

Israel interpreted the Syrian deployment as a retaliation for the 13 Syrian fighter jets that had been shot down the previous month. The IDF took limited action, redeploying the Seventh Brigade to the Golan Heights. This step was completed by Friday, the eve of *Yom Kippur*.

Three days before *Yom Kippur*, while touring the Golan Heights, the Defense Minister said that the IDF would respond forcefully to any Syrian attempt to conspire against Israel. Opinions were divided within the government and the upper IDF echelons on the need to mobilize reserve units. The Chief of Staff's demand for mobilization was supported by the Prime Minister, but opposed by the Defense Minister. Reserve soldiers meanwhile remained at home, enjoying their *Rosh HaShana (Jewish New Year)* trips and preparing for *Yom Kippur*

The Egyptian Army declared a state of full alert at the Suez Canal, along Israel's border, but the IDF estimated that Egypt's deployment was only a show of moral support for Syria.

Israel was almost completely unaware of the border activity. A serene Israel considered itself, on *Yom Kippur* Eve, to be an invincible military force, secure at its borders from the Golan Heights in the north to the Suez Canal in the south.

Austria Closes Immigrant Transit Camps

On Oct. 2 Prime Minister Golda Meir failed in her attempts to persuade Austrian Chancellor Bruno Kreisky to change his decision to close Camp Schonau, a transit camp for Soviet Jews traveling to Israel. Kreisky had surrendered to the demands of Palestinian terrorists, who had kidnapped three Soviet Jews and an Austrian tax official.

The four were kidnapped on Sept. 28 from a train transporting emigrants from the Soviet Union to the Schonau transit camp, which has, in the last decade, housed 50,000 Jews. The Palestinians, members of the *'Palestinian Eagle Revolution,'*

transferred the hostages to an airport in Vienna. They threatened the Soviet Union that they would attack its

Golda and Kreisky.

embassies if it did not stop the emigration of Jews to Israel.

The following day the Austrian government agreed to terminate all its services to Jewish emigrants on their way from the USSR to Israel, and allowed the terrorists to leave Vienna in a light aircraft in exchange for the release of the four hostages.

Jerusalem and the rest of the world regarded Kreisky's decision as capitulation to the demands of Arab terrorists.

Golda Meir left for Vienna to try to persuade Kreisky to reconsider his decision, but her attempt met with failure.

War in the North and South

The beginning of the war caught thousands of soldiers in the Sinai and Golan Heights unprepared.

At 2.00 p.m. on *Yom Kippur*, the Egyptian and Syrian armies commenced a general, coordinated offensive against Israel in the Sinai and Golan Heights. Some 200 Egyptian jets crossed the Suez Canal and bombarded camps, installations, airports, radar stations and artillery batteries. Simultaneously, massive artillery bombardments were aimed at front-line strongholds and at secondary line forts. Egyptian troops crossed the Suez Canal, attacking IDF positions along the canal and the Israeli armored corps which rushed to their assistance. Some 20,000 Egyptian soldiers crossed the canal in the initial wave and captured the eastern bank, which had been under Israeli control.

On the first day of the war, the Egyptian army succeeded in building bridges across Suez, over which their armored and infantry forces passed, taking control of IDF strongholds.

At the same time, Egyptian helicopters landed large numbers of troops on the canal's eastern bank.

Syrian 'planes attacked IDF units and installations, and artillery batteries bombarded civilian settlements.

Immediately after the first airborne attack, the Syrian army landed three helicopters with scores of commandos close to the Hermon position. Within a few hours, the Syrians succeeded in capturing the important intelligence position, striking a blow to IDF morale. Scores of IDF soldiers on the Hermon surrendered and were captured, and electronic intelligence equipment was taken to Syria.

Hundreds of Syrian tanks flooded over the Golan Heights in a swift movement to the west, with little interference from the IDF. The Israeli Air Force, which took off to cover the assaulted troops, discovered the enemy's secret weapon, anti-aircraft missiles, which became the terror of Israeli pilots.

The picture of the battle in the evening was bleak: almost the entire Suez Canal was controlled by Egyptian forces. All Israeli positions were cut off. Huge armored forces had crossed the canal and had started to move eastwards.

The Syrian armored forces could have swept on to the Sea of Galilee and the Hula Valley. Nothing stood in their way. The regular army awaited reserve army forces.

Reserve Soldiers Mobilized

In an emergency meeting in Tel Aviv on *Yom Kippur*, the government decided on an immediate mobilization of all reserve units. Intelligence had arrived in the morning supporting the assessment that Egypt and Syria would attack at 6.00 p.m.

Israel, in the middle of the *Yom Kippur* fast, found itself in the midst of a bitter battle. Despite the holy day, hundreds of vehicles drove through the streets collecting reserve soldiers. Some reservists arrived directly from synagogues and after changing into uniform hurried to assembly points.

Orthodox Jews in Jerusalem and Bnei Brak did not hinder the mobili-

Twenty four hours after mobilization, reservists reach the front.

zation, and even helped the IDF to locate addresses of those called up to the front lines.

At 2.00 p.m., radio broadcasts, which had ceased at the start of *Yom Kippur*, were renewed. The broadcasts opened with an announcement of the attacks in the north and south.

The Cabinet met in extraordinary session before the attack. Prime Minister Golda Meir informed US Ambassador Kenneth Keating that the attack was imminent, and that the Cabinet had decided not to preempt the Arab assault for political, not military reasons.

●

Commercial flights to and from Israel ceased, following the emergency situation and Lod Airport closed down. Two flights from Bucharest and Vienna, carrying hundreds of Soviet immigrants, were also canceled.

●

American Secretary of State Kissinger sought an immediate ceasefire in the Middle East. He contacted the Israeli, Egyptian and Syrian foreign ministers and Soviet ambassador Anatoly Dobrinin. During Kissinger's meetings with Arab and Israeli ministers and diplomats during UN sessions before the war, the State Department said Kissinger received no indications that military action was intended by any of the governments.

●

Five Syrian ships were sunk near the port of Latakia. Four were missile ships and the other a torpedo boat. The Israeli navy suffered no losses. The Soviet-built *Komar* and *Ossa* class ships were sunk with Israeli-made *Gabriel* missiles. The battle was the first of its kind as missile boats battled each other for the first time.

●

Prime Minister Meir addressed the nation on radio and television at 6.00 p.m., describing the state of the war. "The IDF is prepared to beat back the offensive. The enemy has suffered grave losses... For several days now our intelligence services had been apprised that the armies of Egypt and Syria were massing for a joint offensive. IDF patrols discovered that large forces were massing in offensive deployment in the vicinity of the Suez Canal and on the Golan Heights... We have no doubt that we shall be victorious."

●

Civil defense measures were enforced. These included a total blackout, the taping of windows and avoiding the use of cars or telephones unless in emergency. Schools were closed.

Two Israeli POW's were interviewed on Egyptian television. One, the son of a family which had immigrated from Afghanistan 40 years ago, complained of ethnic discrimination in Israel. The second reported that he had been captured after the Egyptians hit his tank and three others.

●

The United Jewish Appeal in New York raised 30 million dollars in one day. Increased sales of bonds were reported in the US and Canada.

●

Egypt and Syria applied heavy pressure on King Hussein of Jordan to join the war against Israel. The King declared that the massing of Jordanian forces on the eastern bank of the River Jordan would be sufficient.

●

President Nixon instructed Secretary of State Kissinger to request a UN Security Council meeting to discuss the fighting in the Middle East.

●

"Israel will not cease fighting until all invading enemy forces have been driven back across the borders" is the Cabinet policy that was conveyed to the US and other friendly governments.

●

All parties agree to suspend electioneering for October 30 *Knesset* elections until hostilities end.

●

El Al resumes its flights. Operations give priority to immigrants, especially Soviet Jews awaiting transportation in Vienna, and to agricultural exports. Pressure is reported, with hundreds of Israelis, volunteers and newsmen seeking urgent flights to Israel.

●

Israel regroups along the canal, abandoning some fortifications as reserve units arrive and bolster the regular forces. Nine of eleven Egyptian bridges were damaged or destroyed.

●

Major-General (res.) Chaim Herzog, former OC Intelligence, tells members of the foreign press that IAF armor and infantry had fought a successful holding battle against a Syrian force of over 800 tanks that had made only "very limited" advances.

Fierce Defensive Battles

Israeli tanks failed to halt tens of thousands of Egyptian soldiers who had crossed the canal.

The second day of the war was the most intense. Exhausted troops faced hundreds of tanks in Sinai and the Golan Heights, and managed to contain the invading armies with the last vestige of their strength. Reservists, mobilized on Saturday, began to arrive in the afternoon. Rumors of thousands of casualties on the first day of battle reached the home front.

Fresh armored troops poured into the north from Syria, waging bitter battles with the remnants of the IDF tank units. Syria continued to bombard northern settlements. Shells fell on Kiryat Shmona and Kibbutz Shamir, causing extensive damage to property.

Syrian armored lines advanced in a three-pronged attack, reaching Quneitra in the north. Nefah Camp was evacuated. Positions along the border, cut off from the rear, were being heavily shelled. Syrian forces reached the B'not Ya'acov bridge, meeting with little resistance before reaching the Hula Valley. Syrian forces of the southern sector penetrated the settlements of Eli Ad and Ramat Magshimim and reached the Gamla axis, seven kilometers (five miles) from the Sea of Galilee.

On the southern front, the Egyptian army continued to cross the Suez Canal. By evening, 11 bridges had been built over the canal and over 400 tanks had invaded the Sinai. The Egyptians controlled a three km (two mile) strip east of the canal. The IDF retreated a number of kilometers east, to its second defense position. Strongholds along the canal were isolated, and some surrendered.

The Egyptians concentrated their efforts on a three-pronged attack: in the area north of Kantara, in the central region on the main road to Refidim, and in the southern region, where the assault concentrated on roads leading to the Mitla Pass and Gidi Pass.

Reserve units began arriving at the front to reinforce the regular Israel Defense Forces troops.

Home-front Hoards Food

Long lines formed outside food stores in most towns. Despite declarations by the Ministry of Trade & Industry that warehouses contained sufficient food supplies to last for over six months, masses continued to hoard huge quantities of food, mostly bread and dairy products.

A wave of volunteers from Israel and abroad offered all possible assistance to the war effort. Hundreds of applications were received from Gentiles who offered to help Israel in its time of need.

The Defense Ministry received telegrams of support and encouragement from Galilee Arabs who of-

Artillery battles. The Egyptians and Syrians have a clear advantage.

fered to contribute to the war effort.

During the second day of the war, 90% of all workers in essential factories were called up to work, in accordance with the emergency regulations approved by the Cabinet on *Yom Kippur.*

Lack of information was the main problem on the home-front. The situation at the front was very hazy, and the home-front was anxious. There was a feeling that at this time Israel was facing its supreme challenge.

Failed Sinai Counter-offensive

Once Israeli reservists had reached Sinai, the IDF launched a massive counter-offensive against Egyptian forces who had crossed the canal. The efforts were concentrated on the three Egyptian beachheads and bridgeheads. Maj.-Gen. Avraham ('Bren') Eden's division operat-

Southern Command Headquarters.

ed in the northern region, Maj.-Gen. Ariel Sharon's division operated in the central region, and Maj.-Gen. Albert Mendler's division was responsible for the southern region.

The counter-offensive, which appeared at the outset to be successful, ended in painful failure. Maj.-Gen. Eden's armored troops, attacking the Egyptians from north to south in an attempt to sweep them from the canal region and establish a bridgehead on the western bank, were repelled and suffered heavy losses.

During the entire day, the IAF continued to bomb missile batteries in the Suez Canal zone. Many fighter jets were shot down by anti-aircraft missiles.

Attempts to attack the Egyptian bridgeheads failed. The enemy continued to establish its position by pouring hundreds of tanks and tens of thousands of troops into the eastern bank of the canal.

There was continued pursuit after Egyptian commandos who had been flown into southern Sinai by helicopter. Dozens of those commandos were killed or captured.

'Arik' Sharon (r), commander of the division, with Chaim Bar-Lev (l), who was appointed OC Southern Front.

Syrians Pushed Back to the Border

The IDF launched its counter-offensive on the Syrian front at dawn. The IDF attacked on three fronts on the northern, central and southern Golan Heights. Most of the Syrian forces were removed from the Golan area. Hundreds of Syrian tanks were destroyed in the battles. At one point, Israeli armored forces crossed the '67 cease-fire lines.

Bitter tank battles raged in the central region, where the Syrians had reached Nefah, the IDF's main base on the Golan Heights, resulting in the retreat of the Syrian armored division which had taken control of Nefah during the night of Oct. 7.

In the evening, after most of the Golan was again under Israeli control, the Syrians launched a counter-offensive, pouring armored reinforcements into the northern Golan

Armored battles north of the Heights.

region. The attack was repelled, and Israeli armored forces reached IDF positions which soldiers had bravely held for the first two days of the war.

The Syrians continued to shell the Hula and Yizrael Valley settlements with 'Frog' missiles, which have a range of up to 70 km (44 miles). Ci-

vilians were wounded and buildings damaged in a number of settlements, including Migdal Ha'emek, Nahalal, Kfar Baruch and Gvat.

The Golani brigade soldiers tried to recapture the Hermon position, but they were repelled after absorbing heavy casualties.

Major-General (res.) Aharon Yariv, special aide to the chief of staff, said in a televised news conference that "This is not going to be a short war." Reviewing the positions on the battlefield, Yariv said that on the Syrian front the cease-fire line had almost been restored and the Syrians had suffered heavy losses. (October 9)

•

Seven IAF *Phantom -F-4's* raid general headquarters in Damascus, bombing it and the Syrian air force headquarters. A *Phantom* was shot down. (October 9)

•

Vice President Spiro T. Agnew resigns in the best interests of the nation and pleads no contest to tax evasion charges. (October 10)

•

Israeli navy bombards the Syrian coast, setting fire to fuel installations and tank depots in Latakia, Banias and Tartus. (October 10)

•

Jordan declares a full mobilization of reservists. King Hussein refrains from attacking Israel from Jordan's border, but sends forces to Syria, participating in the war on the Golan Heights. (October 10)

•

The IAF destroy a power station and a refinery in Homs, Syria. The power station produced 20% of Syria's electricity. The refinery was estimated to have an output of 1 million tons yearly production. (October 10).

•

Arab ambassadors at UN issue a statement, with an implied warning, that oil supplies might be cut to countries that do not support the Arab stand. (October 11)

•

Kissinger said Israel had told the US there was no chance of hostilities breaking out in the Middle East. He said the US had been aware of Syrian and Egyptian troop concentrations but interpreted them as regular maneuvers. (October 12)

•

Tens of thousands of Israeli citizens who wanted to join their army units applied to Israeli consulates in the US. Some were flown to Israel at government expense and others traveled at their own expense. (October 12)

IDF Approaches Damascus

Attack on the Golan Heights. The Syrians were repulsed over the border.

On the fifth day of war on the northern front, the IDF succeeded in moving the battle to Syrian soil. Once Syrian forces had been ousted from the Golan Heights, the IDF took two days to prepare for its thrust into Syria.

On Oct. 9, the IAF bombed strategic targets in the Damascus and Homs region, deep into Syrian territory. Many houses were destroyed in the bombings, and a hospital and Soviet institutions were damaged. The air force also bombed four Syrian airports, including Damascus Airport, having learned that the Soviet Union was airlifting equipment and supplies to Syria.

Meanwhile, the IDF prepared for a massive assault on Syria. Supply lines and ammunition poured into the Golan, and reconnaissance units scouted Syrian territory. On the morning of Oct. 11, fortified Syrian anti-tank formations near Quneitra were penetrated. By nightfall, armored forces had reached 10 km (6 miles) inside Syrian territory, less than 50 km (31 miles) from the capital, Damascus.

Forces Massing in South

Paratroopers on their way to their mission, shortly before crossing the canal.

Shelling from both sides continued on the Egyptian front, but the forces remained more-or-less in their positions.

The Egyptian army took advantage of the respite to dig into the positions captured on the eastern bank of the Suez Canal. Egyptian equipment and reinforcements continued to flow over Suez bridgeheads. The Egyptians succeeded in deploying two armored armies east of the canal, the Third Army in the southern sector, and the Second Army in north Sinai.

Occasional unsuccessful attempts were made to break through IDF defense lines. Egyptian and Israeli fighter jets continued bombing ground forces. The IDF hit a number of airbases, and the Egyptians bombed Israelis at Abu Rudeis working at the offshore oilwell in western Sinai.

In the northern zone, armored forces and infantry succeeded in making contact with the 'Budapest' fortress, the only fortress to hold fast and neither be captured nor abandoned during the war. The remaining Israeli fortresses along the canal were captured, and soldiers were either killed or taken prisoner. The prisoners were brutally interrogated and humiliated in Cairo prisons.

Iraqi Tank Division in the Southern Golan Destroyed

An Iraqi tank division which fought against an Israeli division on the Golan Heights on Oct. 13 was almost totally destroyed. The battle against the Iraqis took place in the area of Kafr Shams, 30 km (19 miles) east of Quneitra, which was almost completely abandoned at the outbreak of the battles. IDF tanks continued to batter Syrian tanks which had attempted a counter-offensive. Scores of Syrian tanks were destroyed. A large Jordanian force which had arrived refrained at this point from entering the battle.

The majority of the Syrian army retreated from the positions held at the beginning of the battles, and re-deployed in a defensive position, some 15 km (nine miles) from Da-mascus. IDF artillery shelled areas south of Damascus, and the IAF bombed Syrian fuel depots and roads used for transporting military equipment to the front.

The Soviet Union and United States started airlifting massive quantities of weapons, ammunition, fighter planes and tanks to Syria and Israel, respectively.

1973
OCTOBER 13 – 16

Egyptian forces lose 200 tanks in an eight-hour battle in an attempt to breach Israeli defenses along a wide sector of the Suez Canal front. (October 13)

•

Israeli tanks advance about 40 kms (25 miles) south-west of Da-mascus. (October 13)

•

Israel protests to France over the appearance of *Mirage* aircraft in Egyptian attacks over the Sinai. The French embargo on the Mid-dle East covers only front-line na-tions and Libya is not considered such a state. France ignores evi-dence that Libyan *Mirages* found their way to Egypt. (October 13)

•

The US begins an airlift to Israel to prevent the Soviet airlift to Syr-ia and Egypt from unsettling the military balance in the region. (October 15)

•

An Ashkelon merchant who re-fused to accept his call-up papers and attacked the person delivering the order, is sentenced to 50 days in jail or a fine of 250 Israeli pounds. (October 15)

•

In a special session of the *Knesset* on the conduct of the war, Prime Minister Meir, speaking on behalf of Israel, said she wished to thank the president and people of the United States for acting in the American tradition of helping a country struggling to withstand aggression. (October 16)

•

Movie star Elizabeth Taylor set out on a fund-raising trail for wounded IDF soldiers. Taylor opened the tour in Rome, contin-uing to Hamburg, Amsterdam, Los Angeles and New York. She also promised to make a substan-tial personal donation to Israel. (October 16)

•

Henry Kissinger and N. Vietnam-ese chief negotiator Le Duc Tho win the 1973 Nobel Peace Prize. The decision was a complete sur-prise to the two men, who had never been named as candidates. (October 16)

•

A Belgian 'Committee of Soli-darity with Israel' is set up in Brussels under the presidency of former premier Gaston Eyskens. (October 16)

IDF Crosses Suez Canal

On Oct. 16, IDF paratroopers and armored corps crossed the Suez Ca-nal at Deir Suwar in the central sec-tor, north of the Bitter Lake, operat-ing behind enemy lines. 'Arik' Sharon's paratroopers, who crossed the canal at night in rubber dinghies, constructed a small bridgehead on the west bank of the canal, and start-ed to destroy anti-aircraft missile sites and to attack Egyptian vehicles and soldiers.

Two days previously, on Oct. 14, the Egyptian armored corps had launched a heavy attack targeted at breaking through the IDF's second-ary defense line, to reach the Mitla Pass. Hundreds of tanks took part in one of the war's fiercest battles, and fighter jets from both sides attacked

The first Israeli tanks cross the canal to the west.

extensively. The Egyptian attack was repelled in the afternoon. Some 300 Egyptian tanks were destroyed that day and the IDF lost 20 tanks.

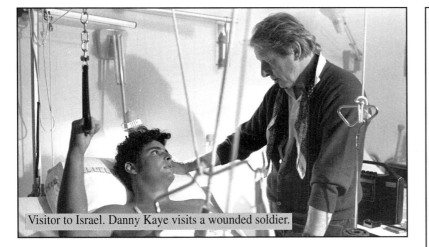

Visitor to Israel. Danny Kaye visits a wounded soldier.

The 'Mezach' Fortress Falls

On Oct. 13, after seven days of intense fighting, soldiers of the 'Mezach' ('pier') fortress surren-dered and were taken prisoner. The southernmost fortress on the Bar-Lev line was surrounded on the sec-ond day of the war, and all efforts to reach it failed. The Egyptians inces-santly bombarded and attacked the stronghold. After three days of bat-tle, the fortress had exhausted its supply of tank missiles, and food and water was rationed. On Oct. 11, res-cue attempts made from the sea by marine commandos failed. The chief of staff ordered the stronghold to surrender, because of increasing fear for the lives of 21 wounded soldiers.

Initial Reports - 656 Killed

On Oct. 14, with battles still raging, the IDF deviated from its custom and started to inform 656 bereaved families that their loved ones had fallen in battle. In previ-ous wars, the IDF had waited un-til the end of fighting, but rumors of the number of casualties on both fronts resulted in a decision to publish details.

The families were informed after bodies had been buried in provisional cemeteries and details of the burial sites were only given after the cease-fire agreement had been signed, and then memorial services took place.

Maj.-Gen. Avraham (Albert) Mendler, a regiment commander in the Sinai, was among the dead. He was killed on Oct. 13 in a di-rect hit on his vehicle.

The main Arab oil producing countries as well as other OPEC members decide to raise oil prices by 70%. (October 17)

•

Seven different Arab states: Saudi Arabia, Libya, Abu Dhabi, Algeria, Kuwait, Qatar and Bahrain, impose an oil embargo on the US in reprisal for its support of Israel. The US imports 1.9 million barrels of oil daily from the Middle East, which comprises six percent of American consumption. According to calculations of American economists, America will be forced to implement fuel rationing within a year. (October 19)

•

Spain suffers extremely severe floods. Five hundred people drown. (October 19)

•

Secretary of State Kissinger began talks in Moscow with Soviet Foreign Minister Kobrynin after a surprise flight. The talks were aimed at ending the Middle East war. (October 21)

•

White House spokesman says that Nixon is "quite confident' that he cannot be impeached. (October 22)

•

The nationwide blackout is still in force. Nevertheless, all citizens were asked to remain tuned to the radio for further instructions, because of the cease-fire. (October 22)

•

Pentagon spokesman, Jerry Friedman, says at a press conference: "We're doing what we were doing before," implying that the US airlift to Israel will continue despite the cease-fire. (October 22)

•

President Nixon capitulates in the face of a constitutional crisis and agrees to hand over the Watergate tape recordings to the court. The House of Representatives begins preliminary investigation into whether the President should be impeached. (October 22)

•

Soviet premier Alexei Kosygin was expected to arrive in Damascus late tonight, apparently to persuade the Syrians to accept the cease-fire. (October 22)

Mt. Hermon Recaptured

Golani soldiers in the Hermon. A valiant struggle for the "eyes of the nation."

On Oct. 22, paratroopers and Golani troops succeeded in recapturing the Mount Hermon outpost and seized two nearby Syrian outposts in a bloody battle. The Israeli position had fallen to the Syrians during the first hours of the war.

The battle, one of the most bitter of the war, continued for 12 hours, from 9.00 p.m. on Oct. 21 until 9.00 a.m. the following morning. Syrian commando units, entrenched in the outpost and its surroundings, repeatedly attacked the Israeli forces, who struggled to reach the mountaintop. Seven Syrian fighter jets which came to aid the land forces were downed in cogfights.

In a television interview at the end of the fierce confrontation, with dozens of bodies strewn over the area, a *Golani* soldier called Mt. Hermon "the eyes of the nation," a term which became a symbol of the war.

Apart from the bitter Mt. Hermon battle, there was a relative lull in the northern sector, occasionally broken by skirmishes between Syrian armored corps and the IDF. The Iraqis announced that they were sending reinforcements to Syria.

IDF Advances to Ismailiya and Suez

Three brigades crossed the wide breach which had been created by the bridgehead that paratroopers constructed on the western bank of the Suez Canal. Hundreds of tanks and tens of thousands of soldiers began to move northwards, towards Ismailiya, and southwards towards the city of Suez. At the same time, armored units advanced westwards and took positions on the Suez-Cairo road. The IDF was then 101 km (63 miles) from Cairo.

On Oct. 17 one of the hardest battles of the war was waged, when paratroopers under the command of Lt.-Col. Yitzhak Mordechai fell into a death trap at the 'Chinese Farm.' The force lost scores of soldiers when ambushed by an Egyptian division entrenched in the sands. The battered soldiers were rescued after a day-long fight.

Paratroopers entering the town of Suez.

Meanwhile, attempting to cut off IDF forces, the Egyptians tried to attack the IDF bridgehead on the western bank of the canal, but the IDF continued to expand it and to ferry additional troops over the canal.

On Oct. 19, after the Egyptians discovered the extent of the bridgehead on the west bank, President Sadat dismissed Chief of Staff Shazli.

UN Accepts Resolution 338

Diplomatic efforts continued alongside military operations. The two superpowers, the US and the USSR, applied pressure on Israel and Egypt to lay down their arms. On Oct. 21, Henry Kissinger arrived in Moscow to coordinate the ceasefire with the Soviets. On Oct. 22, the UN passed Resolution 338 demanding a cessation of war and a start to negotiations to implement a just and permanent peace in the Middle East.

The Third Army Encircled

Soldiers of the Third Army receive food and water supplies. The IDF's trump card.

1973
OCTOBER 23–31

The IDF strengthened its position in battles which developed on both sides of the Suez Canal on Oct. 22 and 23. The Egyptians tried to attack a number of IDF bases near Ismailiya and near the Little Bitter Lake, west of the canal.

Egyptian forces attacked supply convoys and tank positions. The IDF repulsed the assaults and completely encircled Egypt's Third Army on the canal's eastern bank, capturing the Cairo-Suez axis and blocking supply and ammunition lines. The surrounded Egyptians comprised a force of 20,000 soldiers and 200 tanks.

During the following days, despite the cease-fire implemented at 7.00 p.m. on Oct. 23, the Egyptians continued haphazard fighting in an attempt to break out of the Israeli siege of the canal. All their attempts were repelled and the Egyptian Air Force which came to the aid of the ground forces lost 15 fighter jets.

The IDF scattered leaflets over the encircled Third Army, calling on the troops to surrender their weapons in exchange for their safe return to Egypt. Many Egyptian officers and soldiers surrendered at this point.

On Oct. 29, one week after the siege, water and supplies were sent to the Egyptian soldiers under the aegis of the IDF and the United Nations. At the same time, troops of the surrounded Third Army sporadically opened fire on the IDF.

Although a cease-fire was not officially declared on the northern front, the Syrians maintained relative quiet. On Oct. 23 the Israel Air Force bombed a large underground fuel depot near Damascus, and brought down ten Syrian fighter 'planes.

400 Soldiers Missing in Action

A center for the identification of Israeli POW's was set up on Ibn Gvirol Street in Tel Aviv on Oct. 23. Displayed there were scores of pictures, newspaper items, photographs of Egyptian, Syrian and Jordanian television broadcasts, and film shot by various film crews in which Israeli soldiers were seen imprisoned by the enemy.

Mothers, fathers, wives, fellow soldiers, relatives and friends who had received notification of a loved one missing in action repeatedly combed through pictures.

In the first three days since the opening of the center, 50 soldiers who had been captured were positively identified.

The necessity to identify the prisoners from pictures stemmed from the refusal of Syria and Egypt to pass on names of prisoners to the Red Cross.

First wounded soldiers back home from Egypt.

According to the IDF, 440 soldiers had been taken captive, 320 in Egypt and the remainder in Syria. The Egyptians handed over only 47 names to the Red Cross, 42 of whom were soldiers of the 'Mezach' fortress, who had taken a *Torah* scroll with them into captivity.

Chief of Staff David Elazar issued an order of the day to the troops. "We are facing Israel's fiercest battle. It was forced upon us without warning, while the Egyptians and Syrians were assisted by Soviet advisors, instructors and massive supplies of equipment... The Syrian army has received a bitter blow, and the Egyptian army is facing defeat..." (October 23)

•

After 18 nights of darkness, at 6.00 p.m. the blackout in Tel Aviv was lifted. Restaurants lit up, drivers removed the camouflage from their headlights and lights shone through the windows of residences. Dizengoff Center teemed with crowds and the city's cafes were packed. (October 24)

•

The first meeting between senior officers from Egypt and Israel was held in the army tent erected at 'Km. 101' on the Cairo-Suez road. The parties met to discuss the cease-fire and to arrange for supplies to reach the beleaguered Third Army. Maj-Gen Yariv and General Gamasy represent Israeli and Egyptian teams. (October 26)

•

US criticizes its NATO allies for disassociating themselves from the American backing of Israel. The State Department says protection of US interests in the Middle East is also their responsibility. Only Portugal cooperated with US airlift to Israel, other NATO countries refused to allow refueling or shipment of supplies, and claimed neutrality. (October 26)

•

Oil prices in Israel go up in the wake of 70% increase in the world price of crude oil. (October 27)

•

US Defense Department cancels global alert ordered on Oct. 24, when it had appeared the Soviets were going to send a large force to the Middle East. (October 27)

•

The Egyptian Third Army on the east bank of Suez opens fire at a UN convoy bringing it food supplies from Cairo. Israel agreed to the convoy, at a meeting between Maj.-Gen. Yariv and senior Egyptian officer. At a later meeting Egypt is told it could not evacuate the Third Army's wounded until Egypt and Syria provide lists of Israeli POW's. (October 28)

Prime Minister Golda Meir met US President Richard Nixon in Washington and asked him to refrain from pressing Israel to speed up the negotiations with Egypt and Syria. (November 1)

•

The complex question of the encircled Third Army was at the center of the dialog between Israel and the US and was the main reason for Prime Minister Meir's visit to the US. (November 1)

•

Eilat was hit by the Egyptian blockade of Bab el-Mandeb at the entrance to the Red Sea. Since the outbreak of the war, no shipping reached Eilat and 13 vessels were caught in the port. (November 1)

•

A once-a-week ban on driving was imposed to save gas. The law was enforced by stickers indicating the day the driver chose not to drive. (November 6)

•

Israel accepted a US proposal whereby it would continue to permit supplies to the Third Army in return for a prisoner exchange and ending the blockade of the Bab el-Mandeb straits, to be followed by troop withdrawals and peace talks. (November 8)

•

In a *Knesset* speech, *Likud* chairman Menachem Begin demanded the resignation of the government. The *Likud* leader accused the government of incompetence in their assessment preceding the war, and of concealing the truth from the nation. (November 13)

•

Greece declares martial law after student revolt. (November 17)

•

Britain and France sign an agreement giving a formal go-ahead to the digging of a tunnel under the English Channel connecting the two nations. (November 17)

•

Greek army coup ousts President Papadopolous. (November 17)

•

President Nixon's chief economic adviser warns the US faces severe economic slowdown and unemployment rate of 6% if Arab oil cut-off continues. Chancellor Willy Brandt sounds an equally serious warning to West Germany. (November 29)

Cease-fire Agreement in South

First meeting between Israeli and Egyptian officers. The Sinai cease-fire accord was signed in this tent.

The cease-fire accord between Israel and Egypt was signed on Nov. 11 in an army tent west of the Suez Canal, at 'Km. 101' on the Suez-Cairo road.

The accord contained six points: Israel and Egypt would maintain the cease-fire; negotiations would commence on withdrawal to the Oct. 22 lines; daily food and medical supplies would be allowed to the town of Suez; equipment and non-military supplies would be allowed to reach the beleaguered Third Army; UN personnel would be stationed on the Suez-Cairo road; and the POW exchange between the two countries would commence immediately.

Agranat Commission Established

The Agranat Commission. The government fell after its findings were published.

On Nov. 21, the government authorized the setting up of a commission of inquiry to examine the events of the *Yom Kippur* War. The commission was named the Agranat Commission, after the head of the commission Supreme Court President, Dr. Shimon Agranat. Members of the commission were Judge Moshe Landau, Dr. Yizhak Nebentzal, State Comptroller, Lt.-Gen. (res.) Chaim Laskov, Ombudsman of Soldiers' Complaints, and Lt.-Gen. (res.) Yigael Yadin, a Hebrew University professor.

The commission's proceedings were to be held behind closed doors, and would take place in the presence of Attorney General, Meir Shamgar.

Prisoner Exchange with Egypt

On Nov. 15, four days after the cease-fire accord was signed, Israel and Egypt started the POW exchange. Twenty-six wounded Israelis were in the first group to return from Cairo. In exchange, Israel released 415 Egyptian prisoners.

Within one week, all 241 prisoners, together with nine prisoners captured in the War of Attrition who had spent nearly four years in captivity, were returned from Egypt. The Egyptians received in exchange 8,301 prisoners, including three Iraqi pilots who had been shot down in dogfights over the Golan Heights.

The Defense Minister said that he had received information of prisoners who had been captured and not returned, and he feared that they had been murdered in captivity.

All POW's who returned from Egypt, apart from the wounded, were sent to Zichron Ya'acov for a five-day recuperation period. Red Cross units were searching for additional 'MIA' soldiers in the demilitarized area between the Israeli and Egyptian forces.

Families of soldiers killed in action received details on Nov. 4 of the burial place of the soldiers. Hundreds of volunteer teams and IDF officers informed the families of the burial sites, which were determined by the Army Rabbinate according to the battle area. The dead were buried in provisional military cemeteries in settlements in the north and south.

Ben-Gurion Dies at 87

David Ben-Gurion, Israel's first prime minister, died on Dec. 1 at the age of 87, after suffering a stroke. At his bedside were his son Amos, daughters Geula and Renana, and the medical team of Sheba Hospital, who spared no efforts to save him.

Ben-Gurion's coffin was flown to Jerusalem the following day, and lay in state at the *Knesset*. More than 250,000 citizens came in stormy weather to pay their last respects to 'The Old Man,' and long lines of mourners filed past the bier until the small hours of the night, and from dawn the next day.

5,000 people attended the funeral service in Jerusalem. The coffin was then flown by helicopter to Sde Boker for the final ceremony which was attended by 100 people. In accordance with Ben-Gurion's request, there were no eulogies and no volleys fired over his grave.

Ben-Gurion led the Jewish settlement of Israel since the middle of the 1930's. He fought the 'White Book' and strove for the establishment of a Jewish state, which he regarded as the Zionists' major goal.

On May. 14, 1948 he declared the establishment of the State of Israel, and became its first prime minister.

He established the IDF as a united national army, and proclaimed Jerusalem as Israel's capital.

He remained in office until 1963, with a break during 1953-1955, when he went to live on Kibbutz Sde Boker in the Negev. Ben-Gurion held the defense portfolio together with the premiership.

Geneva Peace Conference

Abba Eban and the negotiating team board an airliner on their way to the Geneva peace summit.

After four wars, leaders of Israel, Egypt, Syria and Jordan met for the first time at a peace conference in Geneva, Switzerland. The foreign ministers of the countries participated in the conference, which opened on Dec. 12, and was held under the auspices of UN Secretary-General Kurt Waldheim, the Soviet foreign minister and the American secretary of state. Foreign Minister Abba Eban led the Israeli delegation.

Golda Meir announced that Israel would not meet with Palestinian leaders. According to Meir, the essential discussions on clauses pertaining to peace would take place at a later date, after the elections to the eighth *Knesset*, and they would be carried out by the next government.

'73 - Labor Win Elections, *Likud* is Strengthened

Elections to the eighth *Knesset* took place on the last day of 1973. 4,000 polling stations were open throughout the country, many of which were set up in army units on the western bank of the Suez Canal and the Syrian enclaves conquered by the IDF, east of Quneitra in the Golan Heights.

Labor lost five seats, decreasing to 51. The *Likud* increased its seats to 39. *Likud's* candidate Maj.-Gen. Shlomo ('Chich') Lahat was elected mayor of Tel Aviv, defeating Yehoshua Rabinowitz.

1973

DECEMBER

Two weeks before the EEC summit in Copenhagen, tension inside the Common Market increases due to differences of opinion relating to the oil crisis. (December 1)

•

Colonel Muammar Gaddafi, the Libyan leader, closes the Libyan Embassy in Cairo because of the argument with Egypt over Middle East policies. (December 1)

•

'Pioneer-10' reaches Jupiter after a 900 million kilometer (563 million miles), 21-month voyage, surveys its radiation belt, and continues its voyage to more remote planets. (December 3)

•

Israel's *Yom Kippur* War casualties to date: 2,412 soldiers killed and 508 officially reported missing. (December 8)

•

Defense Minister Dayan meets with US Secretary of Defense Schlesinger to discuss Israel's arms shopping list. The United States agrees to provide Israel with about $1,000 million worth of aircraft, tanks and other weapons to replace Israel's losses in the *Yom Kippur* War and to further strengthen Israel's fighting forces. (December 9)

•

Chief of Staff David Elazar announces that reservists would not be released in the near future. Reservists serving continuously since the beginning of the war would receive extended breaks. (December 15)

•

Spanish premier Admiral Louis Carrero Blanco is killed in Madrid when a bomb planted by the Basque Separatist organisation 'ETA' blew up in his car. (December 20)

•

The six Persian Gulf states announced doubling the price of oil from $5.11 to $11.65 a barrel, effective January 1, 1974. (December 23)

•

Maj.-Gen. 'Motta' Gur, Israel's military attache in Washington, heads Israel's team at disengagement talks with Egypt in Geneva. The parties agreed on five out of eight points. (December 24)

A *Hawk* missile fired at a suspected enemy helicopter caused a fire at the Abu Rudeis offshore oil field in Sinai. The fire cut production by 15%, at a loss of a million lira a day. (January 1)

•

Abba Eban, Yigal Allon and Moshe Dayan drove in a police jeep to their talks with Dr. Henry Kissinger. Most Jerusalemites remained at home, due to the heavy snow that had paralyzed life in the capital. (January 17)

•

In a statement released by the Defense Ministry, Moshe Dayan reiterated his complete confidence in the Israel Defense Forces, emphasizing his faith in the high caliber of the Israeli army's commanders. (January 26)

•

A Norwegian court sentenced five of the six accused in the murder of Ahmed Boushiki on July 21, 1973. The prosecution blamed the *Mossad. Boushiki was mistaken for Ali Hassan Salameh, one of the masterminds of the 1972 Munich Olympics massacre.* (February 1)

•

A new religious Zionist movement has been formed, called *Gush Emunim.* It advocates Jewish settlement in all territories in Israel. (February 6)

•

The tent in which Israel-Egypt negotiations were held at 'Km. 101' on the Cairo-Suez road has been sold by the UN to an Italian industrialist. He presented it to Jackie Kennedy Onassis in appreciation of John F. Kennedy's achievements. (February 6)

•

A book listing the names of 2,521 soldiers, including 609 officers, who fell in the war has been published. All 200,000 books printed were sold-out within hours. 32 bereaved families and 18 families of MIA's asked that the names of their loved ones not be included in the book. (February 27)

•

Israel's *Yom Kippur* War casualties from Oct. 6 - Feb. 12: 2,569 killed. 68 more died during the War of Attrition with Syria until the disengagement agreement was signed in May. (February 28)

Disengagement Accord in Sinai

Israeli and Egyptian chiefs of staff signed a disengagement pact on Jan. 18. The agreement was signed in the negotiation tent at 'Km. 101' on the Suez-Cairo road. Israeli Prime Minister Golda Meir and Egyptian President Anwar Sadat separately signed the arms control appendices to the agreement, which related in principle to the range of weapons permitted along the border area. US Secretary of State Henry Kissinger mediated the agreement.

The accord determined that the IDF would retreat to a point 20 km *(13 miles)* east of the Suez Canal, and 8,000 UN soldiers would separate the two armies.

Officers Against Failed Government

Motti Ashkenazi and thousands of demonstrators demand the resignation of the failed government.

Captain Motti Ashkenazi, commander of the 'Budapest' fortress north of Suez, started a 48-hour hunger strike opposite the Prime Minister's Office on Feb. 10, to demand the removal of Defense Minister Moshe Dayan from his post. Thousands of released soldiers streamed into Jerusalem to support Ashkenazi, who blamed the government for serious failures on the eve of the war.

He reported that as commander of the fortress he had received the first alert of impending war only 20 minutes before its outbreak.

Following the intervention of a number of MK's, Ashkenazi was asked to testify to the Agranat Commission. He was invited to lecture at university congresses and mass rallies, where he repeatedly demanded Moshe Dayan's resignation.

On Mar. 23, five months after the end of the war, Motti Ashkenazi organized a mass rally, bearing the slogan 'Public Responsibility Day,' opposite the Prime Minister's Office in Jerusalem. Thousands of people, mostly released soldiers, participated in the demonstration.

Public pressure continued until the resignation of Golda Meir's government at the beginning of April.

Golda Forms Government

After the elections on the final day of 1973, Golda Meir was forced to request three extensions from President Ephraim Katzir, before succeeding on Mar. 10 to form a coalition with the Labor Party, National Religious Party and Independent Liberal Party. Shimon Peres and Moshe Dayan refused to join the government, but were eventually

Golda and Dayan with soldiers.

persuaded by Golda's fervent pleas.

The new government was almost identical to the outgoing one. Senior ministers remaining in office were Moshe Dayan: defense minister, Pinchas Sapir: finance minister and Abba Eban: minister of foreign affairs. Yitzhak Rabin, a newcomer to the government, concluding his overseas duty, was appointed labor minister.

Agranat Commission Blames Army for *Yom Kippur* Failure

Defense Minister Moshe Dayan studying the Agranat Commission's interim report.

The Agranat Commission, headed by Justice Agranat and appointed to investigate the events of the *Yom Kippur* War, submitted an interim report on Apr. 1 which concluded that Chief of Staff David Elazar and senior military commanders were responsible for serious errors committed on the eve of the war. However, the commission exonerated the political echelon.

After holding 140 sessions and hearing 58 testimonies, the commission recommended that Chief of Staff David Elazar terminate his duties. The commission found that the IDF failed to prepare a detailed defense plan, clear instructions were

not given to OC Southern Command, and Chief of Staff David Elazar did not do enough to make his own evaluation and did not recommend the sufficiently timely mobilization of reserves.

That evening, the chief of staff tendered his resignation, bitterly criticizing the findings of the commission which ignored his achievements during the war itself and the victory of the army which he had headed.

The commission also accused the intelligence system of failure to anticipate the war, and determined that OC Military Intelligence, Maj.-Gen. Eliyahu Zeira, failed in his duty. Zeira and his officers were removed

from their posts. The commission blamed OC Southern Command, Shmuel ('Gorodish') Gonen, for inadequate deployment of the armored corps on the southern front.

On the other hand, the commission commended Prime Minister Golda Meir and said that the defense minister did not have to take additional precautions beyond those taken by the army.

The interim report caused an uproar in Israel, in particular because no steps were taken against the ministerial level. 'Dado' died of heart trouble two years later, aged 51. He never recovered from the anguish of the criticism leveled at him.

Golda Resigns, Rabin Elected

On Apr. 11, 31 days after forming her government, Golda Meir announced her decision to resign, following the interim report submitted by the Agranat Commission. Mass rallies opposite the *Knesset* and public pressure served as the catalyst for her decision.

After Finance Minister Pinchas Sapir refused to head the government, a struggle began between Yitzhak Rabin and Shimon Peres. On Apr. 22, the party voted for the former chief of staff. Rabin received 298 votes, to Peres' 254.

Four days later, President Katzir

asked Yitzhak Rabin to form a government. On June 3, the 52-year old Rabin became Israel's youngest prime minister. Yigal Allon was elected foreign minister, Shimon Peres was made defense minister and Yehoshua Rabinowitz was made finance minister.

Massacre in Kiryat Shmona - 18 Murdered

Sixteen citizens and two soldiers were killed and 15 people wounded on Apr. 11, in a terrorist attack on a Kiryat Shmona apartment block.

Three terrorists affiliated with Ahmed Jibril's organization infiltrated into Israel from Lebanon, reach-

ing the town at 7.00 a.m. They stormed an apartment block, killing residents on the ground floor. They then entered an adjacent four-story apartment building, systematically entering each apartment and slaughtering anyone they encountered.

Most of the casualties were women and children who were at home.

Two soldiers were killed in the confrontation. The terrorists were killed two hours later, when explosives in their bags went off during the exchange of fire.

Israeli envoy Yosef Tekoah raised the issue of Syrian Jewry with Secretary-General Kurt Waldheim. Tekoah claimes that the only solution was to permit the entire Jewish community in Syria to emigrate. (April 2)

•

After the resignation of Chief of Staff Elazar, the National Religious Party demanded the appointment of Ezer Weizman or Ariel Sharon, the only majorsgenerals acceptable to the entire public. (April 6)

•

The Japanese Foreign Ministry denies an Israeli newspaper report that Egypt has asked Japan for aid in setting up a sophisticated military industry to produce television-guided bombs. (April 10)

•

Syrian President Hafez el-Assad is scheduled to fly today to Moscow. Assad will conduct talks with Kremlin leaders, in order to urge the Soviets to take part in current Middle East diplomacy, alongside the US. (April 11)

•

The State Department condemns "brutal and senseless slaughter" in Kiryat Shmona. "[It is] practically the murder of women and children, as we deplore all terrorist activities. In this instance it is particularly regrettable... when the process of peace is already in motion." (April 12)

•

The defense minister appoints Maj.-Gen. Mordechai ('Motta') Gur the tenth chief of staff, replacing David Elazar. During the war Gur served as a military attache in the US. (April 14)

•

At least 12 Syrian soldiers were killed and 16 Israelis wounded in a battle for the summit of Mount Hermon captured by Israel during the war, but abandoned during the winter due to sub-zero temperatures. The Syrians failed to take the peak. (April 14)

•

Six weeks of artillery clashes between Syria and Israel escalated to a virtual full-scale war over the weekend. Both sides were put on full alert following eight hours of aerial activity in which losses were sustained by both sides. (April 21)

Secretary of State Kissinger in Jerusalem for shuttle diplomacy talks, seeking a disengagement agreement between Israel and Syria as the War of Attrition between them enters its 52nd consecutive day. (May 1)

•

Sixteen families settle in Ofira, formerly Sharm el-Sheikh. The settlers complain that fresh agricultural and dairy produce are not available. (May 19)

•

Yitzhak Rabin informs President Katzir that he has formed a new Cabinet. (May 28)

•

Israel and Syria sign a disengagement agreement and will exchange prisoners of war. (May 31)

•

Over two million cheering Egyptians, led by President Sadat, give President Nixon an ecstatic welcome, calling him a man of peace. The US and Egypt sign a nuclear assistance agreement. After President Nixon's visit, US and Syria renew diplomatic relations. (June 12)

•

After a two-year struggle to emigrate, Kirov Ballet dancers Galina and Valery Panov arrive in Israel. (June 15)

•

Foreign Minister Ismail Fahmy says nuclear cooperation between Egypt and USSR will only serve peaceful purposes. (June 16)

•

US President Richard Nixon arrives in Israel for a visit under the dark cloud of Watergate. This is the first visit of an American president to Israel. Less than two months later Nixon announced his resignation. (June 24)

•

A mother and her two children were murdered after three terrorists reached Nahariya from the sea. The terrorists were killed in an assault by the IDF. One soldier was killed and five wounded. (June 24)

•

After members of the orchestra received threats, the Philharmonic Orchestra management decided to reverse its decision to play the works of Richard Wagner, a darling of the Nazi Party in Germany. (June 25)

Twenty-one Schoolchildren are Massacred at Ma'alot

Hostages are rescued from the school building. Most of the teachers left the children with the terrorists.

Twenty-one Safed schoolchildren and four adults were murdered on May 15 in a vicious terrorist attack on Ma'alot in the Galilee. Seventy-four people, mostly children from a Safed school, were wounded.

Three terrorists infiltrated from Lebanon, reached the settlement before dawn, broke into apartments, and murdered three members of a family. The terrorists continued to the Netiv Meir School, where 105 ninth, tenth and eleventh graders from the Safed state religious school were sleeping. The youngsters, accompanied by ten adults, were on a *Gadna (cadet corps)* trip.

The terrorists herded everyone to the end of the second floor passage. Ten children and seven adults managed to escape after a teacher ordered the children to jump out of the window. Ninety-five children and three adults remained captive.

The terrorists demanded the release of 20 of their comrades imprisoned in Israel, threatening to blow up the building if their demands were not met by 6.00 p.m.

At 5.15 p.m., the chief of staff directed the commander of Northern Command to implement a military action to rescue the hostages. Two sharpshooters wounded two of the three terrorists, and soldiers stormed the building.

At this stage, the terrorists opened fire on the children and threw hand grenades into the room where the children were being held and shot those who were trying to jump out of the windows. Twenty-one pupils were killed in the battle which lasted for six minutes.

After the tragic event, bereaved parents demanded that teachers and escorts who escaped from the building, abandoning their children, be put on trial.

Education Minister Aharon Yadlin condemned the teachers. The school principal was accused of forcing the children to go on the trip, and was made to leave Safed.

65 Soldiers Returned from Syria

On May. 31, Israel and Syria finally signed a disengagement pact in Geneva.

The agreement resolved that Israel would withdraw from the Syrian enclave captured during the war, and pull out of Quneitra and four other towns. A United Nations buffer zone would separate the two countries.

The following day, a POW exchange commenced and 12 wounded Israeli prisoners were exchanged for 26 wounded Syrian prisoners. During the first week of June, all 65 prisoners held in Syria were returned to Israel. Most of the prisoners had been brutally tortured.

Israeli prisoners return home from Syria to a hero's welcome.

Israel released a total of 408, mostly Syrian, POW's, including some Iraqis and Moroccans who had been captured.

US President Resigns

US President Richard Nixon resigned on Aug. 7 following the Watergate Affair, one week after the House Judiciary Committee accused him of serious crimes and conduct unbecoming a president.

In his resignation speech, Nixon stated that he was not resigning because of feelings of guilt, but because of decreased congressional support. The Watergate scandal broke after the *'Washington Post'* had investigated espionage and sabotage activities against the Democratic Party in the '72 presidential elections. The affair was revealed following a break-in to plant wire-

Nixon.

tapping equipment at Democratic Party headquarters, located in the Watergate building in Washington. Nixon, who was not involved in the

planning of the break-in, admitted he had tried to hide his assistants' involvement in the affair.

Nixon served as president for five-and-a-half years, accumulating significant state and foreign achievements, particularly the Soviet nuclear weapons' restriction accord, the foundation of relations with China and the termination of the bitter war in Vietnam.

The day after Nixon's resignation, Vice-President Gerald Ford was sworn in as the 38th president of the United States. *One month after Nixon resigned, he received a full pardon from Ford.*

Gush Emunim Settle in Sebastiya

Soldiers evict settlers from Sebastiya. The settlers decided not to resist.

Thousands of *Gush Emunim* members, together with 18 right-wing members of *Knesset*, formed a new settlement near Sebastiya in Samaria. The settlement was evacuated after four days.

The settlers, headed by Benny Katzover, chained themselves together in order to make their evic-

tion difficult for soldiers. Hundreds of soldiers encircled the region, which was declared a closed military area.

In a special Cabinet session held the next day, it was asserted that the settlement posed serious danger to the law and order of the state. Defense Minister Shimon Peres de-

manded that the settlers evacuate themselves from the settlement. The IDF was called in after his demands had been turned down.

The evacuation itself was carried out three days later, and settlers decided not to resist it actively. Soldiers were forced to drag settlers to the waiting 'buses.

Terrorists Kill Four in Beit She'an

Three terrorists infiltrated a Beit She'an apartment building on Nov. 11 and murdered four residents.

The terrorists, members of Naif Hawatmeh's Democratic National Front, broke into the apartment with axes and shot to death the parents of

the family. Their three children managed to jump out of the third floor window into the yard.

The terrorists killed a neighbor who tried to help them and another resident who ran into the stairwell. Twenty residents from two buildings

were wounded, after having jumped out of windows.

The terrorists were killed by IDF soldiers who stormed the building.

Thousands of furious Beit She'an residents demonstrated, demanding the bodies of the terrorists.

1974

JULY - DECEMBER

The Agranat Commission findings submitted to the government decided that former Chief of Staff David Elazar would not be permitted to see the report. (July 10)

Defense Minister Shimon Peres said that support for Israel was so deeply rooted in America that he did not think any new US Administration changes caused by Nixon's resignation would affect it. (August 9)

The head of the Greek Orthodox Church in Jerusalem, Judea and Samaria, Archbishop Hilarion Capucci, was arrested for smuggling arms for the *Fatah* terrorist organization. (August 18)

Sylvia Zalmanson, involved in the hijacking attempt of an airliner in Leningrad and sentenced to ten years' imprisonment in 1970, arrives in Israel two weeks after release from the USSR. (August 22)

The defense minister awarded *Yom Kippur* War medals to three lieutenants-general: the incumbent chief of staff, Mordechai Gur; the chief of staff during the *Yom Kippur* war, David Elazar, and former chief of staff, Chaim Bar-Lev. (September 22)

Former defense minister Moshe Dayan signed a petition organized by the *Likud* protesting the handing over of Judea and Samaria to a foreign government. (October 13)

Prisoners of Zion and Soviet immigrants begin a three-day hunger strike in support of Ida Nudel. Nudel, a 44 year-old Moscow economist, was a *Prisoner of Zion* for over four years. (October 20)

PLO leader Yasser Arafat addresses the UN General Assembly, bitterly denouncing Israel as imperialist, colonialist, reactionary and anti-Semitic. (November 13)

The UN grants the PLO observer status at the UN General Assembly and various other UN bodies. (November 23)

Bishop Capucci is sentenced to 12 years imprisonment for smuggling arms and explosives into Israel on behalf of the Fatah. (December 9)

Over 33% of all Jews leaving the USSR for Israel drop out in Vienna and emigrate to the US. The hundred thousandth Soviet immigrant arrives in Israel. (January 7)

•

Four *Bazooka* missiles are fired at an El Al airliner at Orly Airport in Paris. The missiles miss their target, hit a nearby Yugoslavian airliner and wound two bystanders. A second El Al airliner was attacked at Orly one week later. (January 13)

•

Egyptian President Anwar Sadat said in an interview to a French newspaper that within ten years the Arab world would sign a peace treaty with Israel if Israel did not do anything stupid. (January 26)

•

The Agranat Commission submits its final report to the *Knesset*. It noted lax discipline and a weakening of military order, inefficiency of military intelligence and the inadequacy of the OC Southern Command. All these, combined with the shock of the attack on *Yom Kippur*, contributed to early failures in the war. (January 30)

•

Ethiopian *Falashas*, recognized as Jews under the Law of Return, are entitled to automatic Israeli citizenship. (April 10)

•

Sixty die (including innocent bystanders) in violent clashes between terrorists and *Phalangists* across Beirut. (April 14)

•

The *'Kfir'* (lion cub) is unveiled, as part of Independence Day celebrations. Developed and manufactured in Israel, it is considered one of the best aircraft produced in the world. (April 14)

•

Nearly 15 years after American intervention in Vietnam, Saigon, the capital of South Vietnam, falls into the hands of the North and Vietcong armies. US forces are evacuated. (April 29)

•

Soviet surveillance ship anchored on the edge of Israel's territorial waters, off Atlit. (May 7)

•

PM Rabin offers 'Arik' Sharon the position of advisor on military and security affairs. Ariel Sharon, a *Likud* member, accepts the appointment. (May 29)

Terror at Savoy Hotel

Eight terrorists infiltrated from the sea on Mar. 5, taking over the Savoy Hotel in Tel Aviv and seizing dozens of hostages. Three soldiers were killed and eight hostages wounded during the rescue mission. Among the dead was Col. Uzi Ya'iri, commander of the paratroopers brigade which fought at the 'Chinese Farm' in the *Yom Kippur* War. Seven terrorists were killed and one terrorist was captured.

The terrorists landed in two rubber dinghies on the beach near Geula and Yona Hanavi Streets, and after opening fire on Geula Street, entered the Savoy Hotel, taking hostages and barricading themselves on the top floor. In the negotiations, mediated by a female hotel guest, the terrorists demanded the release of terrorist Archbishop Hilarian Capucci and ten other Palestinians.

Israel Defense Forces' soldiers encircled the hotel and at 4.00 a.m. elite commandos led by Col. Ya'iri succeeded in neutralizing the explo-

The horror took place here.

sives which the terrorists had set.

At 5.00 a.m., the terrorists discovered that soldiers were approaching the hotel, and threatened to blow up the top floor. Within a few mo-

ments, commandos had rescued the hostages. Three soldiers were killed in the battle. Terrorists entrenched in one of the rooms blew themselves up when the commandos broke in.

Citation for Beka'a Valley Hero

Lt.-Col. Avigdor Kahalani receives the Medal of Bravery.

Lt.-Col. Avigdor Kahalani was one of eight soldiers of the *Yom Kippur* War who received the Medal of Bravery - the highest citation in the IDF. Kahalani, regiment commander of the armored Seventh Battalion, under the command of Ya-

nush Ben-Gal, led the small force which destroyed and pushed back hundreds of Syrian tanks which had threatened to break through the last defense line and pour over the Golan Heights towards the Hula Valley. OC Northern Command said

that Kahalani and his small force saved the country from a grave disaster. Kahalani's younger brother, Emanuel, who fell in the *Yom Kippur* War on the Sinai front, received a posthumous decoration for bravery and a citation for valor.

Suez Canal Reopened

On June 5, exactly eight years after shipping lanes had been closed following the Six-Day War, the Suez Canal reopened. At the opening ceremony, President Sadat said that this was a gesture of gratitude to the western world, led by the United

States, for their efforts to achieve peace in the Middle East.

Before the canal reopened, thousands of hours had been invested in retrieving skeletons of ships which had been sunk to prevent free passage, and in dismantling thousands

of naval mines.

After the opening of the Suez Canal, Egypt stated that it would permit free passage through the waterway to Israeli cargo ships, but only on condition that the ships did not fly the Israeli flag.

13 Killed in Refrigerator Bomb Blast in Jerusalem

Evacuation of victims in Zion Square. The booby-trapped refrigerator exploded in the crowded street on Friday.

Thirteen people were killed and 60 wounded after a booby-trapped refrigerator exploded in Jerusalem's teeming Zion Square on Friday afternoon, July 4. The PLO claimed responsibility for the attack.

This was the most vicious attack ever carried out inside Israel. The majority of casualties were seriously wounded by the explosive device - two stolen IDF mortar bombs - which had been hidden inside the old refrigerator.

Hundreds of youngsters from the Musrara neighborhood, near the Old City Walls, attacked Arabs passing through the Nablus Gate. They burned watermelon stands and hit passersby at the East Jerusalem Central Bus Station. Massive police forces dispersed the rioters.

Pinchas Sapir Dies

Pinchas Sapir, Chairman of the Zionist Agency, died of a heart attack on Aug. 12. Sapir was one of the most influential personalities in Israeli politics in the Sixties and Seventies, and since 1965 had been the driving force behind Levy Eshkol's and Golda Meir's victories. He was finance minister, industry & trade minister and the most powerful member of *Mapai*, which had done nothing without his authorization.

He 'inherited' Golda Meir in his capacity as secretary-general of the party, and after Levy Eshkol's death, effected Golda Meir's nomination as prime minister. When Golda resigned in 1974, Sapir was a popular candidate for the premiership, but he refused the position.

An Israel - Egypt Interim Agreement

Signing the Abu Rudeis oil field withdrawal agreement.

Israel and Egypt signed an interim military agreement on Sept. 4 with the mediation of US Secretary of State Henry Kissinger. The accord was signed in Geneva after Kissinger's two-and-a-half month shuttle between Jerusalem, Cairo, Geneva and Washington.

The agreement was based on Israeli withdrawal to the lines of the Gidi and Mitla passes, in exchange for an Egyptian commitment not to attack. Israel also promised to evacuate the Abu Rudeis offshore oil fields.

The pact caused vehement protests and stormy demonstrations in Israel.

Americans and Soviets launch into space for a joint mission. This was the first live broadcast of a *Soyuz* space launch. *Apollo* astronauts link with *Soyuz* cosmonauts for 44 hours of joint experiments. (July 15-24)

●

President Sadat announces his agreement to extend the mandate of the United Nations force in Sinai for three more months, as talks on an interim agreement in Sinai between Israel and Egypt continue. (July 23)

●

Israel Aircraft Industries' improved version of the *Westwind* 8-seater executive jet made its maiden flight. The new *Westwind* costs $1,750,000. (July 24)

●

A fight broke out between Jewish and Arab worshippers in the Cave of the Patriarchs following a dispute over prayer times. Numerous casualties were suffered on both sides. (July 29)

●

The Israeli wheelchair basketball team won the international wheelchair championship after defeating the US team. Many athletes who were disabled in the *Yom Kippur* War participated in the championships. (August 3)

●

Former Emperor Haile Selassie of Ethiopia dies in his sleep aged 83. Dethroned in a military coup on Sept. 12, 1974, with his death a dynasty of 3,000 years comes to an end. (August 27)

●

The PLO seizes Egypt's embassy in Madrid, demands Egypt withdraw from the Geneva peace talks and repudiate its agreement with Israel. The terrorists were later flown to Algiers. (September 15)

●

Savage fighting in Beirut. A Christian militiaman told a French radio reporter that it was difficult to tell who was fighting whom in Beirut. (September 18)

●

An Israeli woman soldier was court martialed after crossing the Syrian border to join an Austrian United Nations officer with whom she was romantically involved. The Austrian officer was dismissed from the UN after the affair was revealed. (September 21)

Guy Mollet, former French premier and leader of the Socialist Party, who brought France into an unwritten alliance with Israel which culminated in the Suez War of 1956, dies aged 69. (October 3)

•

The Soviet physicist Andrei Sakharov is awarded the Nobel Peace Prize for his human rights activities in the Soviet Union. (October 9)

•

Hadassah Hospital on Mt. Scopus is finally re-opened. The hospital had closed when Mt. Scopus became an Israeli enclave as a result of the War of Independence. (October 21)

•

For the first time since 1967, municipal elections are held in the West Bank. 80% of those entitled to vote exercise that right. A landslide victory is scored by the moderate parties. (October 30)

•

The Greek ship 'Olympus,' carrying 8,000 tons of cement, was the first cargo vessel bound for Israel to pass through the Suez Canal under the interim agreement signed between Israel and Egypt. (November 2)

•

El Al back in the air after a 20-day strike. (November 3)

•

As part of the interim agreement with Egypt, Israel quits the Abu Rudeis oil field. (November 3)

•

Israel buys important items at the Sassoon manuscript auction. The National Library buys a 12th century manuscript of the second and third orders of the *Mishna* with commentaries by Maimonides in his own hand, for $470,000. The library also purchased the world's oldest Bible, 9th century 'Damascus Crown,' for $425,000. (November 5)

•

Six Palestinian terrorists, led by the notorious Spanish terrorist 'Carlos,' commandeer the OPEC building in Vienna, taking 11 Arab oil ministers hostage. Their demands include no peace and no recognition of Israel. The Austrian Government allows the terrorists to leave with their hostages for Algiers. (December 21)

UN: Zionism is a Racist and Discriminatory Organization

Thousands wearing yellow patches protest in Jerusalem against the UN resolution equating Zionism with racism.

On Nov. 10, the United Nations General Assembly sank to one of the lowest points in its history, after passing the resolution defining Zionism as a form of racism and ethnic discrimination. The US and all western nations voted against the resolution, but an unprecedented recruitment of all Arab countries, Soviet bloc and African and Asian nations caused the acceptance of the resolution. Seventy-two countries supported the resolution, 35 voted against, 32 abstained and the delegates of three countries were absent.

"Adolf Hitler would feel at home here," said Israel's ambassador to the UN, Chaim Herzog, summing up the disgraceful vote.

One month later, the UN passed another anti-Israel resolution, calling Israel to return the territories conquered in the Six-Day War to the Arab countries.

Seven Killed, Dozens Wounded in Second Zion Square Explosion

Seven people were killed and 46 wounded on Nov. 13, after an explosive device had been hidden in a removal cart on Jaffa Road, opposite Zion Square. The device exploded in the early evening, one of the busiest hours in central Jerusalem. All the dead were youngsters, aged 15 to 17. Most of the wounded were returning from a mass rally against the UN resolution condemning Zionism. The Palestinian Liberation Organization (PLO) claimed responsibility for the attack. The terrorists were arrested shortly after the attack.

Security measures were tightened following the attack; barriers were set up so pedestrians and vehicles entering Jerusalem from the east of the city and from Bethlehem and Ramallah could be meticulously searched.

Hercules Crashes in Sinai, 20 Killed

A *Hercules* cargo aircraft, carrying 20 crew and soldiers, crashed on Mt. Hillel during a storm on Nov. 25. All passengers were killed.

An inquiry showed that the pilot had been thrown off course by the fierce storm, and by the time he had discovered the error, the aircraft was too close to the mountainside. The pilot, Captain Bustan, one of the most experienced *Hercules* pilots, tried to pull the aircraft up, but was unable to clear the mountain peak.

Stormy weather and harsh topographical conditions delayed the rescue mission. Infantry from the dead soldiers' unit reached the mountain peak on foot in the morning and started gathering the bodies.

It was later found that pilot error had caused the fatal accident.

'Land Day.' Six Killed in Galilee Arab Villages

Demonstrating in the Galilee against expropriation of lands. A day of mourning for Israeli Arabs.

'Land Day' was commemorated for the first time on Mar. 30. Riots in Arab villages and settlements ended with six dead, 69 wounded and over 250 arrested.

The events followed the decision of Arab organizations to demonstrate that day against the government's adoption of Israel Koenig's plan. Koenig was the Interior Ministry's northern coordinator.

The main point of the plan was the expropriation of over 400 acres in the Galilee, one third of which

was land owned by Arab villagers. *Rakah*, the biggest Israeli Arab political bloc, was the driving force behind the demonstrations.

The Israel Defense Forces reinforced its troops and concentrated a large presence at the entrance of Arab villages in the Galilee. The army was surprised, however, by the strong opposition in the area. Fierce riots, unprecedented since the establishment of the state, took place in the Galilee villages of Arraba, Deir Hanna and Sakhnin. Crowds at-

tacked soldiers and threw stones, wounding many. A number of soldiers also suffered stab wounds.

In an attempt to curb the rioters, the police placed the three villages under curfew. The curfew was violated, and IDF troops were sent to enforce it.

In many incidents, IDF soldiers opened fire on rioters. An inquiry established to investigate the bloody event justified the shootings.

Since that day, Mar. 3 has been a day of mourning for Israeli Arabs.

'Dado' Dies of Heart Attack

David 'Dado' Elazar, the chief of staff during the *Yom Kippur* War whose resignation was recommended by the Agranat Commission of Inquiry, died of a heart attack on Apr. 15 at a swimming pool near his home, at the age of only 51.

Following his dismissal as chief of staff, Elazar suffered a deep personal crisis from which he never recovered. After leaving the army, he composed an anguished reply to the commission. However, Prime Minister Yitzhak Rabin, a close friend, persuaded him that it would be pointless to reopen the discussions.

Elazar began his military career in the *Palmach*. In the early Fifties, he was OC Central Command, both

Elazar with Golda Meir.

planning and leading numerous missions. He was appointed OC Northern Command in 1964, and during the Six-Day War led the capture of

the Golan and the breakthrough of northern command divisions into the Shomron and Jordan Valley.

At the beginning of 1972 he was appointed ninth IDF chief of staff. In 1973 he realized that war with Syria and Egypt was imminent and in May of that year he had indeed taken preemptive steps.

Despite this, the Agranat Commission found him directly responsible for errors committed on the eve of the war, both in wrongly assessing the situation and in inadequately mobilizing the IDF.

Elazar was one of Rabin's closest friends. His untimely death thwarted Rabin's plan to appoint him as Israel's ambassador to Washington.

Value Added Tax of 8% is imposed on all goods and services sold in Israel. (July 1)

•

The missile ships *'Jaffa'* and *'Tarshish'* will represent the Israeli Navy in a regatta sailing down the Hudson River in celebration of America's bicentennial. (July 4)

•

Rina Mor, Israel's beauty queen, won the Miss Universe title in a Hong Kong ceremony. Five hundred million spectators watched the Israeli queen in a live television broadcast. Israeli newspapers devoted their front pages to the new queen. (July 11)

•

Jimmy Carter chooses Senator Walter Mondale as his running partner in the November US presidential elections. (July 15)

•

The 21st Olympic Games open in Montreal. Israel's Esther Rot Shachamorov comes sixth in the 100 meter hurdles with a time of 13.04 seconds. (July 17)

•

The Russian aircraft carrier *'Kiev'* passed through the Bosphorus Straits from the Black Sea into the Mediterranean. (July 18)

•

Soviet chess master Viktor Korchnoi defects and applies for political asylum in The Netherlands after participating in the annual IBM chess championship there. (July 27)

•

Britain severs its diplomatic relations with Uganda after Idi Amin fails to provide information on the fate of the British-Israeli dual national dragged from a Kampala hospital after her fellow hostages were rescued by Israeli commandos. Idi Amin had Dora Bloch killed after the raid. (July 28)

Rina Mor.

IDF Rescues Entebbe Hostages

Welcoming the released hostages at Ben-Gurion airport. The world was astounded by the spectacular rescue mission.

In a spectacular military operation, the Israel Defense Forces landed at Uganda's Entebbe airport, 4,000 km (2,500 miles) from Israel, and rescued Israeli hostages held there.

Hercules airplanes flew elite commandos, paratroopers and *Golani* troops to Entebbe Airport on Lake Victoria, where the crew and Israeli passengers of the Air France airliner were being held captive.

The airliner had been hijacked en route from Israel to Paris on June 27. The hijackers boarded the airliner at Athens airport and forced the captain to fly to Uganda. Ugandan leader Idi Amin fully cooperated with the terrorists, who demanded the release of 46 terrorists imprisoned in Israel, West Germany and Kenya, in exchange for the release of the hostages.

The hostages included 104 Israeli passengers and 12 Air France crew members. The Israeli soldiers took control of the airport, stormed the terminal and killed all seven terrorists at close range.

Twenty Ugandan soldiers were killed in the battle. One soldier of the Israeli raiding party died and one was wounded. The hostages boarded *Hercules* aircraft waiting on the runway for them and were flown to Israel via Nairobi Airport, where the airplanes were refueled.

In reprisal for the operation, Amin's soldiers killed Dora Bloch, 80, a hostage who had been admitted to a hospital near the airport.

'Operation Entebbe,' commanded by Brig.-Gen. Dan Shomron, became the symbol of daring military operations supported by governments imbued with the belief that they must never surrender to terrorism.

Commander of Elite Commando Unit Killed in Attack on Entebbe

Lt. Col. Yonatan ('Yoni') Netanyahu, commander of the elite commando unit that invaded Entebbe, was killed in the bold operation. Netanyahu, who led the force in the direction of the terminal where the hostages were being held, was killed by a bullet fired by a Ugandan soldier in the air traffic control tower.

Netanyahu was the commander of the main raiding party, comprised of elite commandos and paratroopers. He was killed as he was about to break into the terminal where the hostages were held.

Netanyahu became the symbol of the Israeli fighter. His letters, which

Yoni Netanyahu, the hero of Entebbe, returns home in a coffin.

were published worldwide, portrayed him not only as a daring fighter and commander of one of the IDF elite units, but also as an intellectual, a poet and a philosopher.

The operation's name was changed from 'Operation Entebbe' to 'Operation Yonatan,' in honor of the young commander.

Twenty years later, Yoni's brother Binyamin was elected Israel's ninth prime minister. He defeated Shimon Peres, defense minister responsible for the Entebbe operation. Peres had taken office in 1995 after the assassination of Yitzhak Rabin, who was prime minister in '76 and '95.

Rabin Government Resigns

The prime minister inspects the fighter jets, which flew directly to Israel. Three *F-15's* brought down the government.

Prime Minister Yitzhak Rabin submitted a letter of resignation to the president on Dec. 20, a step which led to the resignation of the entire government and a decision to go to the polls.

The aim of the resignation, which was seen as a brilliant move, was to form a transitional government and thus preempt a vote of no-confidence in the *Knesset*.

The episode began on Dec. 12, during a ceremony at the Hazerim air base celebrating the arrival of the first *F-15*'s in Israel. The event end-

ed near the onset of the Sabbath, and Cabinet ministers arrived home after the Sabbath had begun.

Agudat Israel's Kalman Kahana submitted a no-confidence motion on behalf of the religious parties. In the *Knesset* vote, National Religious Party (NRP) representatives abstained, and during the Cabinet session the following week, all other ministers called on the NRP ministers to draw their own conclusions and resign. All ministers except for the NRP representatives voted in favor of the resolution.

After the NRP ministers refused to resign, Rabin submitted his resignation. The government became a transitional government, which according to the law could not be ousted in a vote of no-confidence.

The climax came months later, when Rabin's wife, Leah, was found to have a foreign currency account in the US, dating back to their time in Washington. The discovery led to Rabin's resignation and the appointment of Shimon Peres as prime minister, until the impending Knesset elections in May 1977.

Arab Horde Takes Over Cave of the Patriarchs

Hundreds of Arab school students broke into the Cave of the Patriarchs in Hebron, *Yom Kippur* eve, Oct. 3. The rioters entered the cave by way

Hebron settler, Rabbi Levinger.

of its southern gate, which was open to Moslems only, desecrating *Torah* books and other religious artefacts. After a violent confrontation, 65 students were arrested by the IDF.

Following the incident, Defense Minister Shimon Peres announced that there would be a permanent guard at the entrance to the cave.

A series of confrontations between the Jewish Kiryat Arba residents and the Arab Hebron residents preceded the riots.

Against the backdrop of the riots, the government decided to permit a small group of Jews to occupy two buildings in the Jewish section of Hebron.

In 1994, an extremist Israeli settler murdered 29 Moslems while they were at prayer in the cave. In 1997, Binyamin Netanyahu returned Hebron to the Palestinians, under the terms of the Oslo Accords.

El Al Airliner Attacked in Turkey

Palestinian terrorists attacked passengers about to board an El Al airliner on Aug. 11, killing four and wounding 21. The El Al airliner was set to take off from Istanbul airport. In their interrogation, the terrorists said that they had trained in Libya and arrived in Turkey aboard a Pakistani airliner the day before the attack.

The four terrorists threw hand grenades at El Al passengers who had passed through passport control and were waiting for a 'bus to ferry them to the airliner. Turkish police killed two terrorists, and one police officer was killed. The terrorists, members of George Habash's NFLP, had planned to join the flight and take hostages in order to initiate negotiations. They decided to attack after failing to obtain flight tickets.

1976

AUGUST - DECEMBER

East Jerusalem Arab merchant who rented his Mercedes to a ministerial figure in July is surprised to discover his car had participated in 'Operation Entebbe.' The white Mercedes was returned to its owner resprayed black. He received $5,000 in compensation. (August 10)

•

Two sailors, Shimshon Brookman and Eitan Friedlander won first place in Europe's championship for sailing boats type 420. This is the first time Israelis have won this sport. (August 14)

•

Mao Tse Tung, Chinese leader since 1949 died aged 82. Mao led the People's Revolution in China, converting it into the largest Communist country in the world. (September 10)

•

Dozens of *Prisoners of Zion* wearing yellow patches march down Moscow's streets in protest against the refusal of Soviet authorities to issue exit visas to Israel for them. The extraordinary march receives extensive media coverage worldwide. (October 21)

•

Jimmy Carter wins the United States presidential election. Carter, a friend of Israel, pushed Israel and Egypt into signing the peace accords. (November 3)

•

Prime Minister Yitzhak Rabin issues a strong warning that Israel will not tolerate a Syrian army move into Southern Lebanon or the region's use as a terrorist base against Israel. (November 8)

•

Yitzhak Rabin refuses to allow a delegation of US senators to visit the atomic reactor in Dimona. (November 8)

•

UN General Assembly calls for the establishment of a Palestinian State led by the PLO in Gaza and the West Bank. (November 24)

•

The French businessman, Shmuel Flatto-Sharon, was detained in Israel after France formally requested his extradition. Flatto-Sharon is suspected of tax evasion and forging of documents. *He later formed an independent party and was elected to the Knesset in May 1977. His activities attracted further investigation.* (November 31)

Abie Nathan's peace ship, *'Voice of Peace'* passed through the Suez Canal after four previous rebuffs and one arrest. An Egyptian official said: "Frankly, Nathan is a special case. He is a real pain in the neck." (January 2)

•

Terrorist Abu Daoud, believed to have organized the 1972 massacre of Israeli athletes and the Entebbe hijacking, was arrested during a visit for the funeral of another Palestinian leader. France freed him, fearing a crisis with Arab States and the PLO. (January 7)

•

A fire broke out in a South African movie theater where the film 'Victory in Entebbe' was running. Throughout Europe there were fires and explosions in theaters screening the film. (January 24)

•

Queen Alia of Jordan is killed in a helicopter crash in south Jordan. (February 9)

•

Prime Minister Yitzhak Rabin retained the leadership of the Labor Party in contest with Shimon Peres. (February 23)

•

Jewish dissident Anatoly Sharansky was arrested by security police in Moscow. Earlier this month the government paper *'Izvestia'* accused him and three other Jews of working for the CIA. (March 15)

•

Herut voted overwhelmingly to place Menachem Begin at the head of the party's list for the *Knesset.* (March 23)

•

An angry crowd used sledgehammers to destroy a Nazi book store in a Jewish area in San Francisco. The shop had been rented out by a Jewish survivor of the Auschwitz death camp, who did not know the kind of establishment his tenants had been planning. (April 1)

•

A demonstration for Soviet Jewry took place in Hyde Park, London with more than 6,000 participants. They marched with banners urging: "Human rights for Soviet Jewry!!" and "Helsinki: Empty Promises, Full Jails!!" (April 17)

•

US newspapers blame Israel for the disappearance in 1976 of 220 tons of uranium aboard freighters en route from Belgium to Italy. (April 28)

Rabin Resigns from Labor Leadership. Peres Steps In.

In a dramatic speech which was broadcast live on television and radio on Apr. 7, Prime Minister Yitzhak Rabin announced that he was taking a leave of absence and would not lead the Labor Party in the May

Rabin. Shortly before his resignation.

elections. He also responded for the first time to correspondent Dan Margalit's reports concerning the $1,000 in a bank account held by his wife, Leah, in Washington, dating back to his days as Israeli ambassador there.

The prime minister said that he would have his parliamentary immunity lifted if a decision was made to prosecute his wife.

The US media compared the revelations with those of Nixon's involvement in the Watergate Affair. Leah Rabin was tried in the Tel Aviv District Court on Apr. 17 and fined IL 250,000.

Following Rabin's surprise resignation, Shimon Peres and Yigal Allon agreed to avoid a renewed struggle over the Labor Party leadership. According to the agreement, Peres would lead the party, and Allon would have a choice of portfolios.

Maccabi Tel Aviv's Great Victory

Israel basketball team 'Maccabi Tel Aviv' defeats Soviet champions 'CSKA.'

Housing Minister Commits Suicide

Housing Minister Avraham Ofer has been found dead in his car on Tel Baruch beach near Tel Aviv. Ofer, whose name had been tied to a financial scandal, shot himself in the head. A suicide note and revolver were found near his body.

In the note, the minister explained the reasons for his suicide: "For weeks and months I've been tortured, my blood has been spilled, I've been libeled and tormented. I have no doubt that the truth will emerge that I haven't embezzled and

I haven't stolen and it is all slander and false accusations, but I don't have the strength to take any more."

The Israeli public and politicians were shocked by the minister's suicide. He had shown no signs of depression in the days preceding his suicide. Three days earlier, he had taken part in a Cabinet meeting and later met privately with Prime Minister Yitzhak Rabin. Ofer had asked Rabin for information on the suspicions against him, which allegedly involved accepting bribes to author-

ize real estate deals.

A confidential meeting had taken place between the prime minister and the ministers of justice, police and finance, the day before the Cabinet session at which the suspicions which had arisen about Ofer and Asher Yadlin were discussed.

Ofer had demanded that the Cabinet make an official announcement that would clear him of all suspicion, but the announcement was not forthcoming. He was given an official state funeral.

Likud Wins Elections. Begin is Prime Minister

Political revolution in Israel. After 29 years of Labor Party leadership in its various forms (*Mapai*, Alignment), the right-wing has won the May 17 elections.

For the first time, there was a television projection based on sample returns. The projection was surprisingly accurate in its forecast: *Likud* - 43 seats, Labor - 32 seats, DMC (*Democratic Movement for Change*) - 15 seats, National Religious Party - 12 seats. The eternal leader of the Opposition, Menachem Begin, who had been defeated in all elections to date, was requested by President Ephraim Katzir to form a coalition government within three weeks.

Begin, who had suffered a serious heart attack shortly before the elections, suffered from heart pains two days after the elections and was hospitalized in Ichilov Hospital. After a short stay, he was discharged and began forming his Cabinet.

In a surprise move, Begin offered the Foreign Ministry to Moshe Dayan, one of Labor's leaders. Despite outrage both in and out of the *Likud*, Begin stood by the appointment offer, and Dayan accepted it.

Begin formed his coalition with the religious NRP and *Agudat Israel*. The DMC joined four months later, and Yigael Yadin was appointed deputy prime minister.

Dayan and Defense Minister Ezer Weizman became the architects of the peace process with Egypt. Eventually, they both left the Begin government in protest at delays in the execution of the peace treaty.

The Arab world was dismayed at the results of the elections, and Egyptian President Anwar Sadat, Syrian President Hafez el-Assad and Saudi King Haled met in a summit to

Newly elected Prime Minister Menachem Begin prays at the Western Wall after his victory.

discuss the issue. US President Jimmy Carter announced that his government was examining the implications on the Middle East situation of Israel's political revolution.

Six months later, Sadat visited Is- *rael, and a new era commenced in the Middle East.*

The Likud Party has remained in government in Israel for most of the 20 years which have passed since May 1977.

54 Killed in Helicopter Crash in Judean Desert

A *Yasur* helicopter crashed during a military exercise in the Judean Desert on May 10. All 44 paratroopers and 10 crew members were killed instantly. The Israel Defense Forces' spokesman delayed the announcement for 48 hours, and the chief of staff ordered the continuation of the exercise.

An investigation found that the crash was caused by human error. The investigation concluded that the helicopter was overloaded with soldiers which affected its operation. As a result of the commission of inquiry's findings, the head of the air force and the chief of staff limited the number of troops permitted on the Yasur to 33 passengers and three crew members.

This was the worst aviation accident in the history of the IDF until then. Some 20 years later, two Yasur helicopters collided over She'ar Yashuv in the north, killing 73 soldiers and crew. There were no survivors of that accident.

Results of a survey show that the majority of the public opposes an Israeli withdrawal to July 4, 1967 borders. 61.6% of those asked claim that territory is preferable to peace, against 23.7% who support a gradual pullback to the 1967 borders. (May 3)

●

Intelligence information led to the arrest of a soldier who was dealing in drugs at the gate of the military headquarters in Tel Aviv. (May 4)

●

The US Senate accepted a compromise worked out by leading business and Jewish groups and resolved to forbid the cooperation of US corporations with the Arab Boycott against Israel. (May 5)

●

The Israeli president inaugurates the first tennis center ever built in Israel, at Ramat Hasharon. American and Canadian Jews donated the funds. (May 6)

●

Forty-four paratroopers and ten airmen were killed when a *Sikorsky* helicopter crashed three kilometers (two miles) north of Jericho during maneuvers. (May 10)

●

Acknowledgment of the development of an original Israeli tank is authorized. The *Merkava* was conceived and designed by Maj.-Gen. Yisrael Tal, with top priority being given to the safety of the tank's crew: a lesson learned in the *Yom Kippur* War. (May 13)

●

Speaking at a ceremony installing a Torah Scroll at Kadum Synagogue, Menachem Begin referred to the fact that the Elon Moreh group moved to the military camp on a "temporary basis" and said: "In a few weeks or months there will be many Elon Morehs and there will be no need for a Kadum." He declared "A Jew has every right to settle in these liberated territories." (May 19)

●

The US nuclear-powered submarine *'Bluefish'* is the first nuclear powered sub ever to call on an Israeli port, Haifa, for a five-day shore leave. (May 27)

●

The Israeli *Kfir* (*'lion cub'*) makes its first international appearance, to take part in the French Air Show outside Paris. (May 31)

An Israeli freighter rescued 66 Vietnam refugees from the sea after neighboring countries had refused to accept them. Prime Minister Menachem Begin said in an emotional speech that Israel would offer them asylum and citizenship. (June 12)

•

The US says that Israel has used US-supplied military equipment to aid the Christians in Southern Lebanon, but that this was not a violation of the US-Israeli agreement. (August 22)

•

After a four-hour foreign policy debate in the *Knesset*, the House rejected talks with the PLO by a 92-4 majority. (September 1)

•

Minister of Agriculture Ariel Sharon presented his blueprint for settlements in Judea and Samaria, which, according to his plan, will be populated by two million Israelis by the year 2,000. (September 2)

•

Djibouti's agreement to bar Israeli shipping from its port was one of the conditions demanded by the Arab League before it could become its 22nd member. (September 4)

•

Israel formally submitted its economic and military aid request to the US government for the next fiscal year. The request totaled $2.3 billion - $1.5 billion in military credits and $800 million for economic assistance. (September 18)

•

The Soviet Union and the US signed a statement which recognized the legitimate rights of the Palestinian people. The American President was stung by a tremendous outcry from Israel's supporters throughout the US, who feared that this represented a weakening of support for Israel. (October 7)

•

Eighty seven passengers aboard a Lufthansa Boeing 737 were hijacked. The pilot was killed by the terrorists at Mogadishu Airport in Somalia. W. German commandos freed the passengers. (October 14)

•

UN General Assembly condemns establishment of Israeli settlements in the administered territories. Israel's Ambassador to the UN, Chaim Herzog, compares the resolution to the Nuremberg Laws. (October 30)

Economic Turnaround

Finance Minister Simcha Ehrlich examining lottery tickets. Annual inflation increased by hundreds of percentage points.

On Oct. 28, less than six months after *Likud's* election victory, Finance Minister Simcha Ehrlich presented his economic reforms, called the 'economic turnaround.'

At a press conference, the finance minister presented a list of economic steps, including the lifting of foreign currency controls, fixing of the dollar exchange rate according to supply and demand, permission to purchase and hold up to $3,000, the raising of VAT from 8% to 12%, cancellation of subsidies and increasing prices of basic commodities by 15%.

The dollar jumped from IL 10.78 to nearly IL 16. Prices of imported products increased drastically, due to the devaluation of the Israeli lira.

In the first two days, the public invested 2.5 billion lira in bonds, savings accounts and shares.

The economic reform brought about a rush of consumer buying. The main fear was of drastic price increases and decreased buying power. Merchants protested the levy on inventory which was imposed by the new reforms.

Ehud Olmert: Organized Crime Exists in Israel

At a dramatic press conference, the young *Likud Knesset* member, Ehud Olmert, presented proof of the existence of organized crime in Israel. Olmert displayed documents detailing the scope of organized crime in Israel and naming leading figures.

He played a tape recording of a meeting he had attended with Maj.-Gen. Rehavam Ze'evi and building contractor Bezalel Mizrahi. Olmert claimed that the two threatened to harm him if he continued his investigation of the Israeli underworld.

Olmert uncovered details of executions, protection money, arson, break-ins, trading in stolen goods, gambling, currency forging and diamond smuggling, and presented data on the scope of drug possession and trafficking.

12,000 Protesters in Bnei Brak Sabbath Demonstrations

On July 14 a crowd of 12,000 ultra-Orthodox Jews gathered in the biggest demonstration in the history of Bnei Brak, protesting against Sabbath travel. Thousands of demonstrators prayed and blew the *shofar*. Two days later, crowds of ultra-Orthodox Jews rioted in the streets and demanded that streets should be closed to Sabbath travel.

Thirty minutes before the Sabbath end, a glass bottle was thrown at police from a balcony on Ha'Shomer Street. The police, wearing helmets and armed with batons, dispersed the protesters who attacked them with bottles and stones. The police commander of the Dan region and his assistant were encircled by a group of ultra-Orthodox Jews who prevented them from leaving the area. A police officer was knocked down by the rioters and dragged along the whole length of the street.

Sadat Comes to Jerusalem

Begin and Sadat.

The State of Israel, together with the entire world, held its breath at 9.00 p.m. on Nov. 19, when Egyptian State President Anwar Sadat emerged from his aircraft at Ben-Gurion Airport. It was hard to imagine that an Egyptian airliner would ever land at an Israeli airport and receive such a welcome. An idea born ten days earlier - when Sadat, addressing the Egyptian People's Council proclaimed his willingness to visit Jerusalem to advance the peace process - became a reality.

Prime Minister Menachem Begin met Sadat's challenge and invited him to Jerusalem. Sadat had declared his unconditional willingness to make the visit in order to initiate peace talks between Israel and the surrounding Arab nations.

His statement caused stormy reaction in the Arab world, especially in Syria, Libya, Iraq and Algeria. Sadat met opposition in Egypt as well, which was expressed by the resignation of his foreign minister. Sadat, in his daring move, gambled not only his position but also his life.

In Israeli security circles, there were those who doubted the sincerity of Sadat's intentions. Chief of Staff 'Motta' Gur was among those who suspected a trick. Two days before Sadat's arrival in Israel, Gur warned about Sadat's aggressive intentions and received a resounding public reprimand from Defense Minister Ezer Weizman.

Shortly after the visit, Weizman announced that he would not extend Gur's appointment. As a result, Ma-

Egyptian President Anwar Sadat emerges from his aircraft. A new era begins in the Middle East.

jor-General Raphael 'Raful' Eitan was appointed in his place.

The entire country prepared for the visit, which was given the code name 'Operation Gate.' Tens of thousands of police and military forces protected Sadat during his three-day stay. He gained the trust and admiration of ordinary citizens and Israeli politicians alike. He made a somewhat radical speech before the packed *Knesset*, visited the Yad Vashem Memorial, participated in a meeting of political factions, prayed at al-Aqsa Mosque and met with Be-

gin a number of times.

Following the historical visit, the Camp David Accords between Israel and Egypt were signed in Washington in September 1978. Israel withdrew from the Sinai Peninsula, which had been conquered in the Six-Day War, and returned all captured territory to Egypt.

Egypt and Israel established diplomatic relations. The slogan that Sadat introduced: "No more war, no more bloodshed" is heard to this day. Begin and Sadat received the Nobel Peace Prize one year later.

1977
NOVEMBER

Sadat states at the opening of the winter session of parliament that he is ready to go to the *Knesset* to negotiate a settlement rather than have one of his soldiers wounded in a new confrontation with Israel, but cautions "Once I am there, there is no power on earth that can stop me from demanding the total Israeli withdrawal from Arab territories and the recovery of Palestinian rights, including their right to set up an independent state." (November 9)

•

Egypt's Foreign Minister Ismail Fahmy resigns. (November 17)

•

The Syrian government condemns Sadat's intention to visit Jerusalem and says: "We will hold him responsible for the repercussions of his decision." (November 17)

•

President Sadat visits Yad Vashem's Hall of Remembrance, paying his respects to the six million Jewish victims of the Holocaust. He signed the Yad Vashem guest book in Arabic and English: "May God guide our steps towards peace. Let us end suffering for all mankind." (November 20)

•

Former prime minister Golda Meir says that the peace process must continue so that "even an old lady like me will live to see the day." President Sadat interrupted, smiling: "I have always said this," and Golda Meir riposted with mock resentment: "Yes, you always called me an old lady, Mr. Sadat," and he and everyone else in the room roared. (November 21)

•

South Africa's Minister of Justice and Police, Jimmy Kruger, accused the country's Jews of sending money to Israel and running away. Foreign Minister R.F. 'Pik' Botha apologized for his colleague's remarks, saying no offense was meant to the Jewish community in South Africa or Israel. (November 23)

•

President Sadat announces in the Egyptian parliament that he is inviting an Israeli representative to Cairo to take part in a preparatory Middle East peace conference. (November 26)

Katyushas on Nahariya

Dozens of *Katyusha* rockets landed on Nahariya on Nov. 11, killing two citizens. In three further salvoes, one woman was killed and five people were injured, including two children. In retaliation, IDF artillery

shelled the port city of Tyre in southern Lebanon, as well as two adjacent refugee camps and six villages. Ten terrorists were killed and 30 injured in the shelling.

The following day, the air force

bombed targets in southern Lebanon, while IDF artillery shelling continued. Foreign correspondents reported one hundred dead. The large number of deaths brought about a wave of severe protests against Israel.

A week of solidarity with Soviet Jewry opens with a special prayer at the Western Wall on the eve of *Hanukkah*. Youth movements and other public organizations held demonstrations throughout the week. (December 4)

•

Egypt severed its diplomatic relations with Syria, Iraq, Libya, Algeria and South Yemen. The decision was made after the five countries decided to 'freeze' their relations with Egypt in protest against Sadat's peace efforts with Israel. (December 5)

•

The Cairo conference opens with both Egypt and Israel pledging their efforts to attain a genuine comprehensive peace for the strife-ridden Middle East. (December 14)

•

Prime Minister Begin arrives in the US for a meeting with President Carter to probe the measure of American support Israel may expect as possible agreements with Egypt and other Arab nations come into focus. (December 14)

•

Following a telephone call from President Carter, President Sadat announces during a press conference in Cairo that he has invited Prime Minister Begin to visit Egypt. Israel's proposals included a substantial withdrawal from the Sinai Peninsula and administrative autonomy in the West Bank. (December 17)

•

Defense Minister Ezer Weizman arrives in Cairo on a spontaneous visit and meets with the Egyptian Minister of War, Gen. Gamasy, and with President Sadat. Weizman gave Sadat a watch engraved with the words "A gift to the president who moved the hands of time forward." (December 20)

•

After meeting President Sadat in Ismailiya, Prime Minister Begin said he believed Israel would have peace "as early as in a few months' time." Begin said the talks had been conducted in sincerity and candor. (December 25)

•

The El Al 'plane bringing Menachem Begin to Egypt is flown by three Israeli pilots who had been prisoners of war. (December 25)

Menachem Begin Makes Historical Visit to Egypt

The Israeli prime minister arrived on Dec. 25 at Egyptian President Anwar Sadat's holiday palace in Ismailiya for summit talks. The Israeli delegation, which included Defense Minister Ezer Weizman and Foreign Minister Moshe Dayan, was met at Cairo airport by Egyptian Vice-President Hosni Mubarak and Prime Minister Mamduch Salam.

In the first round of talks, the two leaders attempted to arrive at an agreement of principles. There was a clear dispute concerning Sadat's demand for Palestinian autonomy on the West Bank.

At a press conference concluding the summit, Sadat said that he had been disappointed by Begin's rigidity but would not give up on his goal of peace. On his return to Israel, Begin expressed the hope that a military and political agreement to serve as a basis for peace between the two nations would be reached within the next three months.

Radical Arab countries condemned the talks, which were called the 'Treason Summit' in their official newspapers. Syrian Defense Minister Mustafa Talas called Sadat a "traitor and beggar of peace."

There were similar reactions in

Begin admires the pyramids.

Israel. The combined headquarters of *Gush Emunim* and the Movement for a Greater Israel went on a public campaign against Begin's peace plan, saying that it "endangers the existence of Israel."

Impressed by the treasures.

Peace Plan Passed in *Knesset*

A majority of 64 *Knesset* members supported the peace plan in a vote on Dec. 28. Eight members voted against the plan, and 40 members of the Alignment and left-wing parties were absent during the vote.

Two *Likud* leaders, Geula Cohen and Speaker of the *Knesset* Yitzhak Shamir opposed the plan.

Those objecting delivered harsh speeches, personally attacking Prime Minister Menachem Begin and accusing him of breaking the commitments he had made on the run-up to the elections.

Massacre on Coastal Road

Eleven terrorists took control of a 'bus on the coastal road on Mar. 11. The bloodshed ended in the evening with a total of 35 dead and 100 injured. Nine terrorists were killed and two captured.

A squad of 13 terrorists had sailed from Lebanon in two *Zodiac* rubber commando dinghies, landing at Kibbutz Ma'agan Michael. Two terrorists had drowned on the way. After murdering an American photographer on the beach, some of the group seized a Mercedes taxi and killed the driver. The rest of the team hijacked an Egged 'bus, whose passengers included many children who were on their way for a day-trip in the north of the country. The hijackers forced the driver to return to Tel Aviv, as they shot at passing vehicles and threw hand grenades.

Police troops and ambulances formed a blockade at the coastal road's 'Country Club junction,' to prevent the 'bus from entering Tel Aviv. A shoot-out took place when

The hijacked 'bus burst into flames at the Country Club junction.

the 'bus came to the junction.

The terrorists fled from the 'bus and hid in the undergrowth and in a nearby building from which they fired missiles at the police. The 'bus burst into flames in a sudden violent explosion. All passengers on the bus were either burned alive or killed by

terrorist gunfire.

Fearing that some terrorists were still loose, an unprecedented curfew was imposed on Tel Aviv. The terrorists belonged to the *Fatah* organization and 'Abu Jihad,' head of the military faction, was responsible for the attack.

'Operation Litani' has Begun

The IDF staged the largest attack it has ever carried out in Lebanon, in retaliation for the coastal road massacre. Shortly after midnight on Mar. 15, the Israel Air Force made an aerial attack together with a coordinated invasion of infantry, armored, artillery and naval forces. Shortly before the battle, the Chief of Military Operations, Major-General Raphael 'Raful' Eitan addressed senior officers with the words, "Revenge for the killing of a small child was not invented by Satan."

IDF forces made a four-pronged attack along the Lebanese border, from the Mediterranean to the area northeast of Metullah on the outskirts of *'Fatahland,'* with the aim of creating a continuous force between the three Christian enclaves in South Lebanon, thereby forming a security belt in conjunction with Major Haddad's Christian militia.

IDF forces reached the Litani River. The IDF spokesman announced that the aim of the operation was to uproot terrorist strong-

holds near the border. In response to the attack, terrorists shelled border settlements. Two members of Kibbutz Manarah were killed.

During the operation, the IDF continued to forge into Lebanese villages and to seize territory. Infantry and armored forces captured Bint Jabel, capturing terrorists in house-to-house raids. A number of Lebanese villages, including Tibnin, voluntarily surrendered to the IDF. Many terrorists escaped during the IDF advance.

Peace Talks Hit Difficulties

The joint Israeli-Egyptian military dialog began in Cairo on Jan. 11. Minister of Defense Ezer Weizman led the Israeli delegation in talks with his opposite number, the Egyptian defense minister. The Israeli delegation included Chief of Staff Mordechai 'Motta' Gur, Chief of Military Intelligence Shlomo Gazit, Deputy Defense Minister Mordechai Zippori, and Major-General Abrasha Tamir.

The joint Israel-Egypt political committee convened in Jerusalem six days later. This was the first time that Israeli and Egyptian representatives had met for direct talks on the peace

Efrat, near Bethlehem, was one of the settlements established during this period.

treaty, mediated by the United States.

At the same time, the Israeli government decided to continue to strengthen Jewish settlements in Ju-

dea and Samaria and the Sinai. According to the plan, another 20 settlements were to be established in the Gaza Strip and Rafiah area.

1978
JANUARY - MARCH

The US re-enters the Middle East peace process as an active participant after President Carter and President Sadat meet in Aswan. (January 4)

•

The Israeli COL index increased by 42.5% in 1977. (January 15)

•

President Anwar Sadat suspends the political committee talks in Jerusalem because of his disappointment with Israel's alleged attempts to stall a comprehensive settlement. (January 18)

•

The US checks for radiation after a malfunctioning Soviet military satelite carrying a nuclear generator disintegrates over Northwest Canada. (January 24)

•

Prime Minister Ian Smith and three moderate black leaders reach a settlement to Rhodesia's 12-year constitutional dispute, and plan to set up a black government in Salisbury by the end of the year. (January 26)

•

Wreckage of *'Cosmos 954'* is found, the nuclear payload missing. No traces found of radiation. (January 30)

•

A Jerusalem 'bus blast kills two and wounds 46. The PLO claims responsibility for the bomb blast. (February 14)

•

The Carter Administration threatens to withdraw its request for advanced *F-15's* and *F-16's* for Israel if Congress blocks proposed sale of *F-15's* to Saudi Arabia and *F-5E's* to Egypt. (February 15)

•

Poisoned 'Jaffa' oranges from Israel are discovered in a number of European cities. It is unclear whether the poison was injected into the oranges in Israel or in Europe. Extensive damage was caused to citrus exports from Israel. (February 17)

•

President Sadat visits the United States and Europe for peace talks. (March 9)

•

Italian Prime Minister Aldo Moro is kidnapped by the terrorist 'Red Brigade.' Italian Mafia threatens to execute members of the Brigade if Moro is not released. (March 16)

1978

APRIL - JUNE

Israel's merchant marine navy set sail again, after a 79-day strike: Israel's longest strike. (April 9)

•

The second agreement of the Panama Canal has been approved by the US Senate. (April 18)

•

On Israel's 30th Independence Day, the census of its population reached 3,677,000. Faiths other than Jewish numbered 581,000. (May 10)

•

Riots and uproar in Teheran. The Moslems demand the overthrow of the Shah. (May 11)

•

Major-General Abrasha Tamir presents the Ministry of Defense plan to extend settlements. Six urban centers will be built with a population of 38,000 families of all social classes, not necessarily having a religious or ideological background. (May 17)

•

Israeli security agents foiled an attack at Orly Airport in Paris by three Palestinians who were spotted trying to mingle with Tel Aviv bound El Al passengers. Two of the three were killed, after they had killed a French police officer. (May 20)

•

Tadiran unveils its new miniature pilotless reconnaissance aircraft, the *Mastiff*, which carries a video camera that transmits data directly to viewers on the ground. (May 29)

•

Six people were killed and 21 injured in an explosion on a number 12 'bus in Jerusalem. The 'bus was half empty, thus averting a heavier toll. (June 2)

•

Vladimir Slepak, who acted as a leader of Moscow Jews campaigning for the right to emigrate to Israel and a member of the Helsinki group, was sentenced to five years of exile in Siberia. Another activist, Ida Nudel, was sentenced to four years in Siberia. Jewish activist Yosef Begun was sentenced to three years of exile. The Soviets contended he violated passport laws, not being allowed in Moscow after a one-year exile in Siberia for "parasitism." (June 21)

IDF Withdraws from Lebanon

The Israel Defense Force withdrawal from Lebanon was completed on June 13, three months after the Litani Operation.

OC Northern Command Major-General 'Yanush' Ben-Gal handed over control of south Lebanese strongholds to the Christian militia at a military ceremony in the town of Mis el-Jabel. Ben-Gal stressed that Israel was committed to protecting the Christians in the south, and stated that ties with strongholds along the border which were equipped and armed before the pull-back would continue via the 'Good Fence.'

The evacuation of south Lebanon was completed smoothly, and the IDF forces reached the Israeli side of the border by the afternoon. Irish, Norwegian and Nepalese units of the United Nations set up bases in a number of evacuated positions and at other points

Israel Wins Eurovision

First place was awarded to 'Abanibi,' the song which represented Israel in the Eurovision Song Contest held in Paris on Apr. 22. The song, performed by singer Izhar Cohen and the 'Aleph Bet' group, was written by Ehud Manor and composed by Nurit Hirsch. The achievement became a national event, capturing headlines in all the Israeli newspapers. Hundreds of Givatayim residents rushed late at night to the home of the singer's family.

Izhar Cohen. Israel's first Eurovision victory.

'Raful' - Chief of Staff

Lieutenant-General Raphael 'Raful' Eitan was appointed the Israel Defense Forces' new chief of staff on Apr. 1, replacing former Chief of Staff Mordechai 'Motta' Gur.

'Raful,' who held the position for five years, was a controversial officer, and many of his decisions were widely criticized by the public. 'Raful' stood at the head of the IDF four years later, in 'Operation Peace for Galilee.'

Yitzhak Navon - Israel's Fifth President

Yitzhak Navon, David Ben-Gurion's former personal secretary, was elected Israel's fifth president on Apr. 15. Navon, a Labor Party candidate, ran opposite Prof. Yitzhak Shaveh, an unknown scientist supported by Prime Minister Menachem Begin. Navon beat Shaveh when a number of coalition *Knesset* members voted for him.

The presidential family. Yitzhak, Ofira, Erez and Na'ama Navon.

Israel and Egypt Sign Camp David Accords

Dialog at Camp David. Begin, Sadat and Carter search for the formula.

On Sept. 9, after 13 days of intense negotiations, Menachem Begin and Anwar Sadat, together with United States President Jimmy Carter, signed the first, historical peace treaty to be entered into by Israel and an Arab country.

The US president initiated the summit at Camp David, the presidential holiday retreat near Washington. The Israeli delegation included Foreign Minister Moshe Dayan, Defense Minister Ezer Weizman, and Attorney General Aharon Barak. Hundreds of journalists who arrived in Washington to cover the summit had to be content with briefings from the White House spokesperson when the retreat was closed to the media.

The talks were on the verge of breaking down on at least four occasions. Some clauses were disputed right up to the signing of the agree-

Friendship at Camp David.

ment. Apart from one short meeting, Begin and Sadat did not meet alone.

The Camp David Accords resolved that both countries would start peace negotiations under the auspices of the UN, and conclude them within three months. The peace agreement was based on UN Security Council Resolutions 242 and 338. Israel was to withdraw all its forces from Sinai and evacuate all settlements there. The Gaza Strip was to remain under Israeli control.

Both parties agreed on full Palestinian autonomy in the Gaza Strip and West Bank within five years. Israel agreed not to establish new settlements during that period. The signed agreement was approved by the *Knesset* ten days later.

Sharansky Sentenced to 13 Years Imprisonment in USSR

Anatoly Sharansky, a Soviet human rights' activist, was sentenced on July 10 to 13 years imprisonment in a labor camp. Sharansky, 29, had been arrested 16 months earlier and charged with treason. During the entire period he was prohibited from meeting with his family, and he was not even allowed to choose his own defense counsel. He was indicted after admitting to passing information to journalist Robert Tott, who was accused of being a western agent.

Mass demonstrations were held worldwide in support of Sharansky, protesting the harsh punishment. His wife, Avital, set out on a world tour to gain his release. She met heads-of-state and ministers, made speeches at rallies and marched at the head of mass demonstrations in many capitals. Sharansky was released in 1986 and is currently Israel's minister of trade and industry.

The Yiddish writer Isaac Bashevis Singer is awarded the 1978 Nobel Prize for Literature. (October 6)

•

The Blair House peace treaty conference opened in Washington. Israel and Egypt draft a peace treaty. After three Cabinet meetings on three consecutive days the Cabinet approved in principle the draft of the peace agreement. (October 12)

•

Polish Cardinal Karol Wojtyla is the first non-Italian Pope elected in 455 years. He chooses the name John Paul II. (October 16)

•

Soviet grand master Anatoly Karpov retains his title after his challenger, Soviet defector Victor Korchnoi, resigned in their 32nd game giving Karpov his sixth victory. (October 20)

•

The Asian Games Federation led by a strong Arab contingent rejected even a token Israeli participation in the eighth Asian Games in Bangkok. (November 15)

•

Three people are killed and 42 injured in a bomb explosion, targeting a 'bus, near Mitzpe Jericho. (November 19)

•

Over 900 members of a religious sect formed in California 15 years earlier commit mass suicide in a jungle camp in Georgetown Guyana. (November 20)

•

The nation mourns former Prime Minister Golda Meir. Prime Minister Begin said: "All her life she fought for the Jewish people, its redemption and its future." President Sadat described Golda Meir as "a political leader of the finest category and an honest adversary in the course of a confrontation we all hope has ended forever." (December 8)

•

Some 1.5 million people marched the streets of Teheran, chanting their determination to topple the Shah, and their hatred for America. (December 10)

•

Soviets issued 30,000 emigration visas this year, the change coming in the wake of the SALT talks, the passage of the Jackson Amendment in Congress (tying trade to emigration), and China's opening to the West. (December 31)

Golda Meir Passes Away

On Dec. 18, four years and eight months after her resignation as prime minister, Golda Meir died at the age of 80 from a malignant disease which had been diagnosed 15 years earlier. Her family was at her bedside when she passed away.

Meir was the first, and so far the only, woman prime minister in Israel. She was born in Kiev, Ukraine in 1898, and emigrated with her family to Milwaukee, in the United States, in 1906. She married Morris Myerson in 1917 and, after joining Zionist activists, emigrated with her husband to Israel in 1921. The couple settled on Kibbutz Merhavya.

Three years later the couple moved to Tel Aviv and Meir took on various positions in the *Histadrut*. After the establishment of the State of Israel, Meir was Israel's emissary to Moscow. A year later she returned home and was elected to the first *Knesset*. She served as minister of labor until 1956, when she was appointed foreign minister in David Ben-Gurion's Cabinet when Moshe Sharett resigned. She held this position until January 1966. After Levi Eshkol's death in 1969, Meir was elected prime minister. The *Yom Kippur* War took Meir and her Cabinet by surprise. She recovered quickly and was decisive in ordering the mobilization of reserve forces minutes after she was informed that war was

Golda Meir is remembered as one of Israel's toughest prime ministers.

about to break out. In April 1974, shortly after forming a new government, she resigned in the wake of public unrest after publication of the Agranat Commission's findings as to the *Yom Kippur* War debacle.

Begin and Sadat Receive Nobel Prize

Sadat did not attend. Begin accepted his own award.

The Nobel Peace Prize has been awarded to Prime Minister Menachem Begin and Egyptian President Anwar Sadat. In its Dec. 10 official announcement, the Norwegian jury stated that the historical November 1977 visit made by Sadat to Jerusalem broke the psychological barrier which had prevented an entire generation from reaching understanding and human contact between Egypt and Israel. The announcement also mentioned the positive initiative and important role played by US President Jimmy Carter.

Sadat refused to attend the ceremony, claiming that the peace accords had not been concluded. His aide, Said Mar'i, represented him. Begin, in his acceptance speech, promised to continue his efforts to achieve peace in the Middle East.

Begin opened his speech with a tribute to Golda Meir, who had died two days earlier. He stressed the Jewish nation's contribution to humanity and his vision of peace and world disarmament.

Khomeini Takes Control of Iran

Mass demonstrations in Teheran. Thousands of Moslem fundamentalists demand the return of Ayatollah Khomeini from exile in France.

1979
JANUARY - FEBRUARY

The last 33 Israelis in Iran, including employees of El Al Israel Airlines, representatives of the Jewish Agency, and former *Knesset* member Mordechai Ben-Porat, were evacuated on Feb. 18 in an airlift to Europe. The Israelis had been in hiding from Khomeini's cohorts who were searching for Israeli hostages.

The Islamic Revolution reached its peak after the Shah left Iran to take asylum in the United States, and the Shi'ite leader, the Ayatollah Khomeini, returned to Iran and formed the Islamic Republic.

After the Shah left on Jan. 1, supporters of the exiled Shi'ite leader took control of powerful positions in the country. The Shah's supporters were arrested and hanged after a brief trial. The army, which tried to fight the Moslem fundamentalists, yielded to the millions who crowded the streets. The masses set fire to the entertainment quarter in Teheran, burned down buildings and raided brothels and casinos, where they dragged out prostitutes, stripped and beat them.

On Feb. 2, Khomeini, 78, returned to Iran. He ordered the closing of all cinemas as well as all radio and television stations. People's courts were set up to try criminals according to Koranic law. The Shah's supporters, including army officers and security officials, were swiftly tried and hanged.

Anti-Israel propaganda increased. The Israeli Embassy was looted and handed over to supporters of Yasser Arafat; they established PLO offices there. Jewish houses were marked with black crosses and the slogan "Jews Out!"

The Great Escape from Ramla Jail

Eight dangerous prisoners, including Solomon Abu, the Jewish gangster considered one of the most dangerous criminals in Israel, escaped from Ramla Prison on Jan. 8.

Immediately after the escape had been discovered, the police initiated the most widespread dragnet ever made. Police forces were stationed at all air and sea ports and barriers were erected throughout the country. Hundreds of police were stationed by the houses of dozens of people, including judges and lawyers, fearing revenge attacks by the escapees. Guards were also placed outside the residences of prosecution witnesses and police officers who had been involved in the criminals' arrests and trials.

The prisoners escaped through the prison's dining room and kitchen, ran over the roof and after reaching the yard, broke through the prison gate. They commandeered a taxi cab outside the prison and escaped.

Two Arab prisoners were recaptured the following day; the other six were captured within two months.

Economic Restraints

The Cabinet on Feb. 8 approved Finance Minister Simcha Ehrlich's economic program. All *Knesset* members, except for Yitzhak Moda'i, supported the plan. The program included a number of economic decrees, among them a revision of the subsidy system on basic food products, and a price hike of 50% to 100% on these products.

Phnom Penh, capital of Cambodia, falls to Vietnamese rebels. (January 7)

•

Biggest annual price rise in Israel since 1951: prices in 1978 went up 50.6% (in 1951 prices rose 57.7%). (January 15)

•

Iran is joyful as the Shah leaves; his departure brings thousands to the streets, singing and dancing and making the 'V for victory' sign. The Shah receives a somber welcome in Aswan. (January 16)

•

The *Knesset* Finance Committee approves 390 houses out of 790 to be built beyond the Green Line and allocates IL 740 million for increasing the population there, building a road in Samaria and installing power, water and sewage systems. (January 17)

•

Former US President, Gerald Ford, who was on a visit to Israel, asked to be allowed to watch the final football game currently being played. He was brought at a latenight hour to the Israel Television building in Jerusalem, where he watched the live broadcast of the game. (January 21)

•

Ali Hassan Salameh, who masterminded the massacre of the Israeli athletes at Munich and was one of the leaders of 'Black September,' is killed by a car bomb in central Beirut. (January 22)

•

Prime Minister Begin called on world Jewry to participate in 'Project Renewal,' the rehabilitation of poor areas and neighborhoods in Israel. Begin spoke to the board of governors of the Jewish Agency. (January 25)

•

White Rhodesians vote for black rule and the proposed constitution of Prime Minister Ian Smith and his black colleagues in government. (January 30)

•

General Zia introduces Islamic law in Pakistan. (February 10)

•

Hanoi requests Soviet help as an estimated 200,000 Chinese invade Vietnam along a 1,200 km (750 miles) front. China says it was a counter-attack designed to defend its borders. (February 16)

President Carter arrives in Cairo in an attempt to win final agreement on the unresolved issues of the elusive Egyptian-Israeli peace treaty. (March 8)

Gush Emunim demonstrators fling stones and eggs at President Jimmy Carter's car. Sixty-six were arrested, including Hanan Porat, *Gush Emunim* leader. (March 11)

Five billion dollars in US aid to Egypt and Israel. The Cabinet in Cairo approved the peace pact unanimously; Israel's cabinet approved it 15:2. (March 15)

A radioactive leak occurs at the Three Mile Island nuclear power plant near Harrisburg, Pennsylvania. (March 30)

Israel's 'Milk & Honey' group wins the Eurovision Song Contest with the song 'Hallelujah' sung by Gali Atari. This was Israel's second consecutive Eurovision win. (March 31)

Ayatollah Khomeini proclaims Iran an Islamic republic. (April 1)

Prime Minister Menachem Begin begins a historic visit to Cairo. Begin says that the Middle East, the ancient cradle of civilization, could once again become a flourishing world center. (April 2)

Seven *Prisoners of Zion*, including Mark Dymshitz and Eduard Kuznetsov, sentenced in Leningrad, arrive in Israel after their surprise release by the Soviet Union. In exchange, the Americans freed two Russian spies who had been sentenced to 50 years' imprisonment. (April 29)

Conservative leader Margaret Thatcher wins the parliamentary elections and is elected British prime minister. (May 3)

The Cabinet votes to build a Jewish settlement on the outskirts of Nablus. (June 3)

F-15's engage in battle for the first time. Five *MiG-21's* are downed over Lebanon after a Syrian attempt to attack IAF bombing of terrorist targets in Damur, Sidon and Tyre. (June 27)

Israel and Egypt Have Signed Peace Treaty

After 30 years of hostility, Israeli Prime Minister Menachem Begin and Egyptian President Anwar Sadat signed a peace treaty between the two countries in a ceremony at the White House in Washington, DC. US President Jimmy Carter signed as a witness.

The American president, who had paid a surprise visit to Jerusalem and Cairo at the beginning of the month, was largely responsible for the treaty, having mediated between the two sides when they reached a deadlock on the Camp David agreements.

Following President Carter's intervention, Egypt relinquished its demand first to have autonomy implemented in the Gaza Strip. Israel received priority in oil supplies from the Sinai, and an American guarantee of fuel supply for a period of 15 years. The pact, serving as the basis for comprehensive peace in the Middle East, was based on United Nations Security Council Resolutions 242 and 338. It determined that Israel would withdraw from the entire Sinai Peninsula within three years, and that the recognized border between the two countries would be the Mandate border. The treaty determined that normal peace relations would prevail between the countries, and Egypt continue to allow free passage of Israeli vessels in the Suez

The handshake of peace. The President of Egypt and Prime Minister of Israel. Center: The 'Best Man,' Jimmy Carter.

Canal. It was also agreed that the parties would start immediate negotiations on Palestinian autonomy in the territories.

The response of the Arab League countries was violent and vehement. Mass demonstrations, confrontations

and attacks on Egyptian embassies were held in Arab capitals. Threats were made to assassinate Sadat and to attack American installations. The Palestine Liberation Organization demanded immediate liberation of Jaffa, Acre and Haifa.

El-Arish Returned to Egypt

After 12 years under Israeli control, El-Arish was returned to Egypt on May 25. The town was handed over during a military ceremony at the Shekem Plaza, on the outskirts of the town. This was the first step in the implementation of the Israel-Egypt peace treaty, in which Israel returned the town along with the coastal strip connecting it to Egyptian territory. The vegetable field of the Ne'ot Sinai settlement was included in the territory returned.

During the ceremony, Menachem Begin and Anwar Sadat announced the opening of borders between the two countries. Egyptians and Israelis would now be able to cross the border to visit. From El-Arish, Begin and Sadat flew to Beersheba.

The day before the El-Arish withdrawal, hundreds of Sinai residents and *Gush Emunim* members had entrenched themselves in Ne'ot Sinai's vegetable field. Soldiers began evicting the protesters 24 hours before the withdrawal.

This turned out to be a general rehearsal for Israel's evacuation of Yamit three years later. Soldiers at Yamit used water cannon, in response to which settlers threw burning torches, vegetables and rocks at them, sprayed the soldiers with poisonous insecticide, and rolled barrels off the roof of a building.

El-Arish is handed over to Egypt in a military ceremony. Twelve years of occupation come to an end.

Moshe Dayan Resigns

Moshe Dayan (c), Menachem Begin (l) and Aharon Barak (r) at Camp David.

On Oct. 21, Foreign Minister Moshe Dayan announced his resignation following the deadlock in the autonomy negotiations and the minor role he believed he had been given in the negotiations.

Dayan claimed that he could not accept the government's stand on the negotiations. However, he stated that he was pleased to have served in Menachem Begin's government because "if Peres, Alon and Eban had been in government, Judea and Samaria would have been returned to the Arabs."

Begin offered the foreign portfolio to Yigael Yadin, expecting Simcha Ehrlich to fill his place as deputy prime minister, taking the finance portfolio from Ehrlich. Yadin refused the offer, and Yitzhak Shamir was appointed foreign minister.

High Court's Decision: Dismantle Elon Moreh

In an unprecedented decision, on Oct. 22 the High Court of Justice instructed Elon Moreh settlement, near Nablus, to be dismantled within 30 days. The court said that settlers and their homes which had been settled on land mainly belonging to residents of the Arab village Rujib, should be taken down and the land returned. The judges unanimously ruled that the settlement had not been built as a result of military expediency, and therefore its establishment on private land was illegal.

In spite of the explicit court ruling, a month later the government decided not to evacuate Elon Moreh, but only three acres.

Begin in Hospital

Begin. Slight dizziness.

Menachem Begin was admitted to hospital on July 22 after suffering a minor stroke. The director of Hadassah Hospital said that the blocked artery in his brain caused dizziness and impaired vision, but that the damaged area was small and Begin's intellectual faculties were intact.

Sadat Visits Haifa

Sadat with Menachem and Aliza Begin (r) and Yitzhak and Ofira Navon (l).

Egyptian President Anwar Sadat visited Haifa during his third trip to Israel. He arrived for a three-day visit on Sept. 4 with his wife, Jehane, who, like her husband, captured the hearts of her hosts.

The Egyptian president was received at a state ceremony at the port of Haifa. During his visit he met with Prime Minister Menachem Begin and President Yitzhak Navon.

Sadat expressed optimism concerning the enlisting of additional Arab states to the peace process. He stressed the rift between Syria and Iraq and the instability of the Syrian government.

Sadat's daughter went on a shopping spree on Dizengoff Street and in Jaffa.

1979 JULY - DECEMBER

Egyptian President Sadat and Prime Minister Begin met for another summit in Alexandria to discuss the peace process and assess the situation in the Middle East. (July 10)

•

Iraq's strongman, General Saddam Hussein took over the presidency, ending President Ahmed Hassan al-Bakr's 11 years in office. (July 16)

•

The fifth round of autonomy talks began in Haifa, with the Egyptian and Israeli delegations locked in differences, both substantive and procedural. (August 5)

•

In his book published this week, Yitzhak Rabin called Labor Chairman Shimon Peres an "untiring subverter" who would spare no pains to conquer the premiership. Rabin said that Peres was unfit to serve as prime minister. (August 10)

•

Israel requested $3.4 billion in US aid for the redeployment in the south, as a result of the peace with Egypt. (September 11)

•

The Cabinet votes unanimously to lift a 12-year military governor's ban on Jews from purchasing land in the occupied territories. (September 16)

•

Argentinean newspaper publisher Jacobo Timmerman, held as a political prisoner in Argentina for over two years, arrives in Israel after being expelled from Argentina. (September 28)

•

Iranian students, followers of Khomeini, seize the US Embassy in Teheran and hold 80 Americans hostage. They demand the extradition of the Shah who was undergoing medical treatment in the US at the time. Women and blacks were released a week later. The Iranian fundamentalists held the remaining 52 hostages for 444 days. (November 4)

•

The Shah is granted political asylum in Panama. The International Court at The Hague orders Iran to free the hostages immediately. (December 15)

•

Five thousand Soviet troops invade Afghanistan after a military coup. (December 27)

Little progress was achieved in the three-day Aswan Summit between Prime Minister Begin and President Sadat on the substantive issues of autonomy. (January 10)

•

Israel's interim pullback in the Sinai to the El-Arish - Ras Muhammad line has been completed. (January 23)

•

Elon Moreh is relocated to Jabel Kabir following a court order, since the site near Nablus belongs to Arabs. (January 29)

•

Israel replaces the Israeli Pound with the Shekel. (February 24)

•

Ahmed Shukeiry, who founded the PLO in 1964, died in Amman at 72. (February 26)

•

Yigal Allon dies aged 62. He served as deputy prime minister and foreign minister between 1974-1977. (March 1)

•

The Italian Jewish Agency director reports that during February, 2,568 Soviet Jewish emigrants left Italy, the majority going to the US. (March 6)

•

Yitzhak Shamir resigns as speaker of the *Knesset* and takes office as Israel's foreign minister, replacing Moshe Dayan. (March 10)

•

Several Western governments are concerned over the growing opposition to Sadat. The opposition objects to Sadat's peace drive and the granting of asylum to the former Shah. (April 3)

•

Eight American soldiers were killed in an unsuccessful attempt to rescue hostages held in the US Embassy in Teheran since November 1979. During takeoff, a helicopter collided with a transport 'plane. (April 24)

•

The prime minister orders an all-out search for the attackers of West Bank Arab mayors, Karim Khalaf of Ramallah and Bassam Shak'a of Nablus who had been wounded. A bomb disposal expert was also wounded trying to defuse another bomb. (June 3)

•

Menachem Begin suffers heart arrest in Jerusalem. (June 30)

Israeli Embassy in Cairo

The first *mezzuzah* at the Israeli Embassy in Cairo.

On Feb. 18, for the first time in both peoples' history, an Israeli embassy has been established in Cairo and the Israeli flag flown over it. The embassy was located in a modest duplex building, at 23, Mohi el-Az Street in Cairo.

After a few days, the first Israeli ambassador to Egypt, Dr. Eliahu Ben-Elissar, submitted his letter of accreditation to President Anwar Sadat in Cairo. At the same time, the Egyptian Ambassador, Sa'ad Mortada, submitted his accreditation to President Yitzhak Navon in Jerusalem, Israel's capital.

Establishing the embassies was yet another stage of normalization of relations between Jerusalem and Cairo, after Israel had returned additional territory in Sinai to Egypt.

Ezer Weizman has Resigned

Minister of Defense Ezer Weizman announced his resignation at the Cabinet meeting of May 25, because of cutbacks demanded in the defense budget. Before resigning, Weizman generally criticized the way negotiations with Egypt had been handled. Prime Minister Menachem Begin responded harshly to Weizman's criticism and declared that he would never forgive the former minister of defense.

A few weeks before resigning, Ezer Weizman shocked *Likud* leaders when he called on national television for elections to be advanced, so that the people could choose their future via the ballot box.

Yeshiva Student Murdered in Hebron

Yehoshua Salome, a *yeshiva* student from Kiryat Arba, was murdered on Jan. 31 in Hebron's *casbah*. An unknown man managed to approach him while he was walking through the crowded market and at close range shot him twice in the back of the head.

As a result of the murder, settlers increased their demands for better security arrangements around the Jewish part of Hebron. The Knesset approved the suggestion of the Minister of Defense, Ezer Weizman, to extend the Jewish part of Hebron. Meanwhile, the Ministry of Housing began to set up projects to preserve important landmarks around the Avraham Avinu Synagogue, as well as new housing projects nearby.

Hebron's *casbah*. Two shots at a *yeshiva* student.

Anwar Sadat - critical.

Geula Cohen - tabled the law.

The *Knesset* has Passed the Law of Jerusalem

On July 30 the *Knesset* passed the Law of Jerusalem in its second and third reading, as tabled by Geula Cohen of the *Tehiya* party. The law stated that "united Jerusalem in its entirety is Israel's capital. It is the place of residence of the State President, the *Knesset*, the Government and the Supreme Court." President of Egypt Anwar Sadat bitterly criticized the *Knesset* decision, saying that it contradicted the terms of the Camp David accords. In a letter he sent to Israel, Sadat accused the government of impeding the negotia-

tions over autonomy. As a result of the crisis, autonomy negotiations between Israel and Egypt were frozen for a few months.

In addition, Sadat charged Israel with a violation of its commitment to freeze settlements on the West Bank. In reply, Begin sent him a letter in which he said that Sadat's accusations were without foundation. On the following day, Aug. 19, a ceremony of settlement took place at the town of Efrat in Gush Etzion and the local *hesder yeshiva*, Shevut Israel, was officially opened.

1980

JULY - SEPTEMBER

Lebanon's powerful *Phalangist* militia secures control over that country's Christian enclaves after former President Camille Chamoun orders his National Liberal Party militias to surrender, ending the bloodiest internecine fighting since 1975. (July 8)

•

France turns down a request from the US and other countries to delay the shipment of weapons-grade uranium to Iraq. (July 12)

•

The Republicans choose Ronald Reagan as their presidential candidate in the upcoming US elections. Reagan chooses George Bush as running mate. (July 17)

•

An Arab is arrested after hurling two hand-grenades into a group of Jewish teenagers on an Antwerp street, killing one and injuring 17. (July 27)

•

Ephraim Borokim, a prominent Teheran Jew, is executed in Iran after being found guilty of spying for Israel. (July 31)

•

A strike by 16,000 workers at Poland's biggest shipyard continues after they reject a new wage offer. Polish leader Edward Gierek admits errors but tells strikers he will not tolerate a challenge to socialism. (August 16)

•

Otto Frank, father of Anne Frank whose diary touched and shocked many, passed away aged 91. Anne and her sister died in Bergen-Belsen and their mother died in Auschwitz. Otto was liberated from Auschwitz by the Soviets in 1945. (August 20)

•

The Polish government and Lech Walesa, leader of the Gdansk shipyard strike, sign an agreement allowing free unions in Poland. (August 24)

•

President Carter pledges to American Jewish leaders that the US would not allow Israel's expulsion from the UN and also said that the US would provide emergency oil supplies if prices go to an inordinate level. (September 8)

•

Iraqi 'planes bomb nine Iranian bases and airports. Iran severs ties with the entire world, declares a war situation and closes Iraqi sea approaches. (September 22)

The West Boycotts the Olympic Games in Moscow

Jimmy Carter - boycotted.

On July 19, the 22nd Olympic Games opened in Moscow, and were boycotted by 60 western countries, including Israel. Most of the western countries responded to the American president, who called on the Olympics to be boycotted in protest at the Soviet invasion of Afghanistan.

Only 80 countries participated in the games. Despite the boycott, Israeli television broadcast the opening ceremony.

On Aug. 3, the games ended. The Soviet Union won 195 medals, 80 of which were gold. East Germany won 125 medals.

Tennis General

And the champion (*aluf*) is General (*rav aluf*) Rabin.

Member of *Knesset* Yitzhak Rabin won the *Knesset's* tennis championship on July 29, after beating Yitzhak Yitzhaki and Shlomo Hillel. MK Shmuel Toledano won the *Knesset's* ping-pong championship.

The Soviets take a major step in reasserting their influence in the Middle East by signing a treaty of friendship and cooperation with Syria. (October 8)

•

Iran rejects President Carter's offer to lift the trade embargo for the release of the 52 American hostages. (October 23)

•

Ezer Weizman's apparent endorsement of President Carter's reelection is sharply condemned by Jewish leaders, pro-Israel Republicans, and even by Democrats. (October 27)

•

Republican Ronald Reagan, a former movie star, is elected as America's 40th president. The Republicans gain control of the Senate for the first time in a quarter of a century. (November 4)

•

17,400 Jews are living in 68 settlements in the territories compared with 3,200 in 24 settlements in 1977 when the *Likud* took office. (November 10)

•

Soviet Jewish activists to address a 75-signature appeal to the Security Council of Europe scheduled to open in Madrid tomorrow. They accuse USSR of failing to live up to its pledges in the 1975 Helsinki agreements. Part of the conference will be devoted to reviewing the human rights provisions of the Helsinki document. (November 10)

•

Israel tells the European Security Conference in Madrid it is concerned that the number of immigrants has decreased rapidly this year after a significant rise in 1979. Israel's Ambassador to France Meir Rosenne also expresses concern over the intensification of anti-Semitic acts in Europe. (November 27)

•

Former Grand-Admiral Karl Doenitz, who succeeded Hitler in 1945 at the end of the war, and then agreed to Nazi Germany's unconditional surrender, dies aged 89. (December 24)

•

The Algerian ambassador to Iran visits the American hostages held by Iranian fundamentalists at the American Embassy in Teheran. (December 26)

Minister Of Religious Affairs Aharon Abuhatzeira Indicted

The Attorney General, Professor Yitzhak Zamir, decided on Dec. 1 to press charges against the Minister of Religious Affairs, Aharon Abuhatzeira, on grounds of receiving bribes. Zamir asked the *Knesset* to lift the minister's immunity.

The attorney general also declared his intention to press charges against three more people involved in the affair: former aide to Abuhatzeira, Moshe Gabai; a diamond merchant and member of the Bnei Brak City Council, Shmuel Dascal; and Bnei Brak Sephardi Rabbi, Amram Korach.

For the first time ever, the *Knesset* was asked to lift the immunity of a member of Cabinet.

After much consideration, Abuhatzeira announced that he was prepared to waive his immunity.

Cabinet Minister Abuhatzeira was exonerated of corruption in that trial, but was convicted in another lawsuit subsequently brought against him.

Aharon Abuhatzeira with the leader of the Opposition. He waived his immunity.

Peres Defeats Rabin

At the Labor Party Assembly on Dec. 17, Shimon Peres won an impressive victory over Yitzhak Rabin, who had declared his candidacy for the party premiership two months earlier.

Peres won 70% of the votes, as against 30% of the vote which went to Yitzhak Rabin.

As soon as the results were published, Rabin announced his acceptance of the voters' choice. The winner, Peres, asked Rabin to overcome personal differences and join forces in order to win the next *Knesset* elections. Rabin shook Peres' hand but did not hide his disappointment.

This was the party's first assembly to take place since being in opposition. The handshake was not broadcast on television, as news reporters decided not to broadcast details of the Labor Party Assembly, after Yosef Lapid, director of the National Broadcasting Authority, had not allowed them to broadcast the election results live.

Close but rivals. Peres won. Rabin accepted the voters' decision.

Car Bomb Explodes Next to Paris Synagogue

Four people were killed on Oct. 3, when a car bomb exploded next to the Reform synagogue in the Latin Quarter of Paris. Twenty people were wounded in the terror attack, most of whom were people praying at the synagogue.

The car bomb had been prepared by a neo-Nazi terrorist group. In the days after the attack, there were huge demonstrations in Paris against anti-Semitic groups, which had gradually been gaining power in France.

Two days later, on Oct. 5, a parcel bomb exploded in a post office branch in Giv'atayim (a suburb of Tel Aviv). Three were killed, and another seven wounded, two of whom were in critical condition. The explosion had occurred after a local resident returned a suspicious-looking parcel to the post office. The assistant manager of the branch opened the parcel, which then exploded. The two were killed on the spot. Another postal worker was seriously injured and later died of his wounds.

Abuhatzeira Exonerated

On the shoulders. Minister of Religious Affairs Abuhatzeira celebrates his acquittal by the Western Wall

On May 24, Minister of Religious Affairs Aharon Abuhatzeira was found not guilty of taking bribes. The judges of the Jerusalem district court exonerated Abuhatzeira and the other three defendants in the case. However, they condemned the system of funding religious institutions as well as the level of public conscience revealed in the trial. Despite the harsh criticism, the judges stated that the testimony of state witness Israel Gottlieb was not sufficient to convict Abuhatzeira.

After the acquittal, Abuhatzeira received a hero's welcome. Hundreds of supporters came to the court, greeted him with a blow of the *shofar*, and bore him on their shoulders. In both Ramla and Bnei Brak, a great round of festivities was announced.

A week before the acquittal, Abuhatzeira's immunity was lifted once again, and he was further charged with theft, fraud, breach of trust and conspiracy to commit a crime. The trial was set for hearing after the forthcoming elections.

Immediately after his acquittal, Abuhatzeira announced that he would not run for election with Minister Yosef Burg, whom he said had tried to destroy him. The minister of religious affairs said that he would run for the Knesset in an independent party, under the name Tami (Tnuat Masoret Israel - The Movement for Israeli Tradition).

Israel Downs Two Syrian Helicopters in Lebanon

On Apr. 28, Israeli Air Force aircraft intercepted two Syrian helicopters which were bombing Christian *Phalangist* forces in Lebanon. This was Israel's first interference in the combat between the Syrians and Christian *Phalangist* forces in Lebanon. Prime Minister Menachem Begin said afterwards that the IDF interference had prevented the complete collapse of the Christians in Lebanon. The Syrians had shelled Beirut. Dozens of Lebanese had been killed and hundreds injured.

As a reaction to the air force operation, the Syrians stationed antiaircraft missiles close to the Israel - Lebanon border. Tension increased in the border area. A special American envoy, Philip Habib, arrived in the Middle East in a final attempt to find a diplomatic solution to the problem, before military steps were taken.

Menachem Begin warned Assad that Israel would not allow the missile presence and the Syrian takeover of Mount Senir in Lebanon.

'Masada' Sunk in Bermuda Triangle

The Israeli cargo ship 'Masada' sank on Aug. 3 off the coast of Bermuda, near the area known as the 'Bermuda Triangle.' Of the ship's 35 crew, 11 survived, amongst whom was the wife of the ship's radio operator, who accompanied him on all trips. After search operations, 12 bodies of crewmen were found, and another 12 were declared missing.

The ship began to sink as a result of an enormous wave which entered the ship's cargo holds. For an entire day, the crew tried to pump out the water, and only after it was clear that this was impossible did the captain order the ship to be abandoned. Fourteen hours before the ship capsized, the captain had turned down an offer of help from the local coastguard station in Bermuda.

1981
JANUARY - MAY

Prisoner of Zion Lev Roitbard arrives in Israel with his wife and son after an eight-year struggle to secure Soviet exit visa. (January 5)

●

The 52 Americans held hostage in Iran are released 90 minutes after President Carter, who secured their release, leaves office and Ronald Reagan is sworn in as the 40th President of the United States. (January 20)

●

Monsignor Jean-Marie Lustiger, a Jew who became a Roman Catholic just before his mother perished in the Holocaust, is appointed Archbishop of Paris. (February 2)

●

About 65,000 people visited the Israeli stand at the Cairo International Book Fair. (February 9)

●

The last of the '1970 Leningrad hijack Jewish defendants' arrives in Israel. Yosef Mendelevich lands in Israel and goes to pray at the Western Wall. (February 18)

●

Prisoner of Zion Anatoly Sharansky is sentenced to six months solitary confinement. His wife Avital appeals to world leaders to save her husband. (March 2)

●

Despite protests of Jewish leaders in the US, President Reagan decides to sell five AWACS 'planes to Saudi Arabia. (March 14)

●

President Reagan escapes an assassination attempt, but is shot in the chest. White House Press Secretary James Brady is wounded in the head. (March 30)

●

'Columbia,' the first space shuttle, is launched from Cape Canaveral for its first flight. This is America's first manned space flight since 1975. 'Columbia' lands at Edwards Air Force base after 54 hours in space. (April 12)

●

Socialist challenger Francois Mitterand defeats President Valery Giscard d'Estaing and becomes France's 21st President. (May 10)

●

Amnesty marks its 20th anniversary with a sweeping condemnation of torture, murder, abduction and imprisonment. It reports nearly half the UN's 154 members are believed to be holding prisoners of conscience. (May 27)

Actress Jane Fonda addresses a mass rally for Soviet Jewry at the UN Plaza in New York. The crowd of 100,000 was the largest attending the annual rally in the past ten years. (June 1)

•

Patricia Derian, Assistant Secretary of State for Human Rights in the Carter Administration, said that Israel had succumbed to threats from the junta in Argentina. The junta had said that unless Israel exercised restraint, Argentina would pursue an anti-Semitic policy against its Jews. (June 6)

•

The first ever test-tube twins, a boy and a girl, are delivered prematurely by cesarean section in Melbourne, Australia. The mother had been implanted with two embryos to ensure successful development. (June 6)

•

Cairo joined the other Arab capitals condemning Israel's destruction of Iraq's nuclear reactor, saying it contradicted the spirit of peace that prevailed at the Sharm el-Sheikh summit. (June 7)

•

French premier Pierre Mauroy condemns Israel for destroying the French-built Osirak nuclear reactor, calling it a "grave and unacceptable act." (June 8)

•

Over 5,000 Holocaust survivors from 23 countries and an equal number from Israel took part in a four-day Celebration of Life in Jerusalem. "Don't tell us it never happened, we were there," asserted Ernest Michel, a New Yorker with the number 1041995 tattooed on his arm. (June 15)

•

Khomeini dismisses the more secular-minded President Bani Sadr, leaving the clergy and their secular supporters in complete control of Iran's post-revolutionary establishment. (June 22)

•

A former Nazi concentration camp guard is sentenced to life imprisonment and eight others are given lesser sentences of up to 12 years for taking part in the murder of some 250,000 at the Maidanek death camp during World War II. The sentencing ends West Germany's longest ever war crimes' trial, which began in 1975. (June 30)

The Air Force has Destroyed the Atomic Reactor in Iraq

The prime minister at an air force base after the bombing of the reactor in Iraq.

On June 7, aircraft of the air force destroyed the Iraqi atomic reactor in what turned out to be one of the most courageous operations ever carried out by Israel. A formation of eight jets flew over Saudi Arabia and caught the Iraqi aerial defense system by surprise. Not one Iraqi missile was fired at the 'planes, which dropped 16 tons of bombs over the reactor. The bombing took two minutes. One Iraqi nuclear scientist was killed. The reactor was destroyed.

The Iraqi ruler, Saddam Hussein, ordered that charges be brought against the commanders of the missile batteries stationed around the reactor, for not firing at the attacking Israeli aircraft.

For some time before the operation, the ministerial defense committee had held confidential deliberations about bombing the reactor to eliminate Iraq's developing nuclear capability. The decision to bomb the reactor was made as a result of an intelligence report, establishing that Iraq would operate the reactor within a month and that after that month, bombing the reactor would lead to a radioactive cloud which would harm residents living in the Baghdad area.

After much hesitation, the government sanctioned bombing the reactor. Prime Minister Menachem Begin and ministers Yitzhak Shamir and 'Arik' Sharon were the main proponents of the action.

The United States condemned the bombing and claimed it was a "major set-back to achieving peace in the Middle East." President Reagan also backed the United Nations resolution condemning Israel, which was passed two weeks later.

The reactor's destruction set back Iraq's capability to develop nuclear weapons by many years.

Only nine years later, when Saddam Hussein invaded Kuwait, did the world, led by America, understand how right Israel had been to bomb the reactor.

Begin Wins the Elections

The June 30 *Knesset* election campaign has been defined as the most violent campaign ever. Thirty-one parties ran for the *Knesset*, while in the previous elections only 22 parties had taken part.

Peres' victory had seemed almost certain, three months before the election. The Labor party's lead in the polls was nearly 25%. Prime Minister Menachem Begin had no control over his party and seemed out of touch with reality. The economy was in a bad state.

Shortly before the elections, Begin decided to change direction, and personally headed one of the most exciting campaigns ever. The new Minister of Finance, Yoram Aridor, began to give away gifts to the public. The gap between the two large

The prime minister hears the news: "We won the elections."

parties lessened daily. The police was informed of disturbances at Labor demonstrations.

The bombing of the Iraqi reactor, three weeks before the elections, was the turning point for the *Likud* party.

On election day, the police force was prepared for demonstrations. 16,000 policemen took part in 'Operation '81.' Contrary to predictions, the elections were organized and quiet.

The results gave a slight advantage to the *Likud*: 48 seats in the *Knesset* in comparison to 47 for the Labor party

Katyushas on Nahariya. Three Killed, Dozens Injured

On July 15, three weeks of intense combat began in the north. The catalyst was terrorist fire on Nahariya, coming from a cannon south of Tyre. Three were killed and nine injured. In response, Israeli aircraft bombed two terrorist headquarters in Lebanon and bridges over the Zaharani and Litani rivers. Dozens of terrorists were killed and many were injured.

The terrorists reacted with heavy fire. In Kiryat Shmona, 14 civilians were injured by *Katyusha* rockets. Occasional firing of *Katyushas* and shells continued in the north until the end of July. Residents of Kiryat Shmona, Nahariya, Metulla and the *kibbutzim* in the Galilee panhandle spent most of their days and nights in bomb shelters. In addition to casualties, major damage was caused to property.

During the entire period, the IDF attacked terrorists in southern Lebanon with artillery fire, and the air force also operated against the terrorists' operational centers in Beirut. In one operation, the IDF attacked a command post of the *Fatah* movement, killing the terrorists. Seven IDF soldiers were injured in the action.

On July 19, in Kiryat Shmona, a 16-year-old was killed and his mother severely wounded when a *Katyusha* hit the family car, as they were on their way south to escape from the *Katyushas*. On July 20, a female member of Kibbutz Misgav Am was killed in a *Katyusha* attack.

Many towns around the country organized help for residents of Kiryat Shmona and Nahariya. Children were invited to summer camps in the center of the country. Many families left their homes and temporarily moved south.

Only at the end of July did the situation calm down, and peace again came over Kiryat Shmona.

'Arik' Sharon - Minister of Defense

Full of confidence. The new minister with his aide Eli Landau.

On July 15, President Navon nominated Menachem Begin to form the new government. Begin undertook to step down as leader if he could not form a government within 21 days. On Aug. 4 agreements between the *Likud* and the religious parties were signed. The coalition agreement between the *Likud* and *Agudat Israel* contained exemptions from military service for *yeshiva* students and *hozrim b'tshuva (religious penitents)*.

'Arik' Sharon received the defense portfolio. Yitzhak Shamir remained minister of foreign affairs and Yoram Aridor, minister of finance. Minister of Housing and Development David Levy at first refused to join the government after the Ministry of Absorption had been taken from him and given to Aharon Abuhatzeira. A day later, he was appeased and joined the government, within two weeks being appointed deputy prime minister.

Herzl Avitan Escapes Arrest

On Sept. 23 Herzl Avitan escaped from prison while on home leave, visiting his sick father. Avitan had served two of 15 years of his sentence in prison, awarded to him for planning and executing a large heist of Bank Leumi in 1979. Avitan was caught two years later in Paris and was extradited to Israel.

1981

JULY - SEPTEMBER

Serious riots take place in Brixton, South London. Police are attacked by black and white youngsters following an incident. Many buildings and cars are set on fire. (July 10)

•

Britain's Prince Charles marries Lady Diana Spencer. An estimated one billion people worldwide saw the ceremony on television. The wedding was of such splendor that the Archbishop of Canterbury, who conducted it, described it as "the stuff fairy tales are made of." *Fifteen years later the wedding of the century became the divorce of the century.* (July 29)

The US shoots down two Libyan *SU-22's* over the Mediterranean, and protests to Libya on its unprovoked attack. Libya claims a 200-mile territorial limit in the Gulf of Sirte. Oil firms employing many of the 2,500 Americans in Libya were advised to require their American employees to leave Libya because of deteriorating relations between Tripoli and Washington. (August 19)

•

The Soviet Union told its East Bloc allies that strict adherence to Moscow-style Marxism and tight internal control would be required to prevent troubles such as those of Poland from affecting their countries. (August 23)

PLO terrorists attack Vienna's oldest and largest synagogue during Sabbath services. Two are killed, 19 wounded. The two terrorists are captured. (August 29)

•

The Iraq-Iran war enters its second year. (September 4)

•

A team of US officials tells NATO representatives in Brussels that the Soviets have lost 10,000 men since their intervention in Afghanistan in late 1979. (September 21)

The Senate ends an almost two century all-male tradition and confirms Sandra Day O'Connor as an associate justice of the Supreme Court. (September 21)

•

France's new, high speed TGV Paris to Lyon train takes two hours 40 minutes, at an average speed of 260 kph *(163 mph)*, compared to almost four hours on a conventional train. (September 22)

Sadat is Assassinated

President of Egypt Anwar Sadat was assassinated on Oct. 6 during a military parade which took place on the eighth national memorial day for the *Yom Kippur* War. Sadat was shot by Moslem extremists who opposed his pro-peace policy.

Sadat (r) with his vice-president, Hosni Mubarak (l).

During the parade, a truck pulled up in front of the grandstand and the assassins jumped out of it while shooting at the president. Sadat was fatally injured and died after two hours on the operating table. Another 11 people were killed and 27 injured, among them Ireland's minister of defense and the Belgian ambassador to Egypt. Three of the attackers were killed on the spot, and another three were caught.

Hosni Mubarak, Sadat's deputy, took his place. At 8.00 p.m., Mubarak broadcast an announcement of the president's death, stating that Egypt would continue to fulfil all obligations and accords regarding the peace talks entered into by Sadat.

Immediately after the official announcement had been made, Prime Minister Menachem Begin sent his condolences to Sadat's widow, Jehane. "President Sadat was murdered by the enemies of peace," he said. Begin expressed the grief of the entire Israeli people, and Israel's participation in the Egyptian period of mourning. Begin led the Israeli delegation to the funeral in Cairo. He was accompanied by ministers Sharon, Shamir and Burg.

Moshe Dayan has Died

Moshe Dayan, the fourth chief of staff of Israel, died of a heart attack on Oct. 16, at the age of 66. Dayan was born on Kibbutz Deganya, and was chief of staff during the 1956 War, minister of agriculture in Ben-Gurion's government, and minister of defense during the Six-Day War, the War of Attrition and the *Yom Kippur* War. He was also minister of foreign affairs in the *Likud* government which signed the Camp David peace accords with Egypt.

Moshe Dayan left his mark on some of the most significant events shaping the first 40 years of the

How we shall remember him.

State. Even though he was a legend in his lifetime, and very popular internationally his status was questioned following the Yom Kippur War. Many criticized him for his partial responsibility for the 'Mehdal' (the 'Omission'), when Israel's intelligence services failed to warn of impending war. Yitzhak Rabin did not include him in his 1974 government, but Menachem Begin returned him to power when he appointed him minister of foreign affairs in his 1977 government.

The Golan Heights Annexed To Israel

The Golan Heights Law, which annexed the area to Israel, was ratified by the *Knesset* on Dec. 14, only 24 hours after it was tabled. Sixty-three *Knesset* members voted in favor of the law, among them eight members of the Labor party who rebelled against the official party line which rejected the proposal.

The draft law, which indicated a dramatic turn in Israel's policy, was submitted by Prime Minister Begin. Begin, in a wheelchair, sneaked out of hospital a few hours earlier, in order to take advantage of the most favorable timing for the bill.

Syria registered its sharp disapproval of the new Israeli law. The Syrian minister of defense said: "The best reaction to Israel's decision is a show of force." The IDF prepared for all possible Syrian reactions. The United States was also furious with Israel for not having been consulted. The Reagan government declared that the law contradicted international law, and was thus unacceptable. The UN also followed this opposition, in a resolution demanding an immediate repeal of the law.

Battles with Settlers who Resist Evacuation at Yamit

Thousands of male and female soldiers started evacuating the last opponents of the Yamit pull-out on Apr. 24. The evacuation was very violent, and included the burning of tires and torches, shootings and the stoning of soldiers by protesters, many of whom fortified themselves on the rooftops, threatening to attack soldiers who therefore had to use force. Among the settlers were Members of *Knesset* Geula Cohen, Yuval Ne'eman and Hanan Porat. Dramatic pictures were published worldwide of civilians, including women, pouring water on soldiers and stoning them. The evacuation took many hours.

Another focus of resistance was a house in which Rabbi Meir Kahane's supporters and some new American immigrants fortified themselves and threatened suicide. Some of them locked themselves into a bomb shelter and threatened to blow it up. Rabbi Kahane was hurried to Israel from New York, and only when he had arrived did he convince his followers to obey the authorities and evacuate the buildings.

The monument at the entrance to the town was another center of resistance, when soldiers tried to bring down Tzahi Hanegbi and another 20 students who had climbed on top of it. Only after the media covered the negotiations did Hanegbi agree to be evacuated.

The evacuation of residents from Yamit was only completed four days later, and then at the order of Minister of Defense Ariel Sharon the town was bulldozed. Egypt received 'scorched earth.'

The government compensated Yamit's evacuated citizens.

On the roofs of Yamit.

The Worst Riots in the Territories Since 1967

The closure of Bir Zeit University on Mar. 20 sparked riots in the West Bank. The IDF was forced to take over the municipalities of El-Bira, Ramallah and Nablus, an action which aggravated the riots.

After the closure, there was a three-day strike in the territories. One resident was killed, and two girls and three soldiers were injured. The IDF imposed a curfew on some of the towns in the territories because of the riots, and the forthcoming 'Land Day.' In one incident, two settlers in Ramallah shot at Arab citizens. This was filmed and broadcast on television, leading to a wave of international outrage. The following day, the riots spread to all towns on the West Bank, and another youth was killed in Ramallah.

The opposition tabled a vote of no confidence in the *Knesset*. The result was a tie (58:58). As a result of the vote, the prime minister announced his intention to resign, but withdrew it as a result of pressure from the religious parties.

On the day of voting, the riots spread to the Gaza Strip. Hundreds of youths burned tires and blocked main roads in the strip. Soldiers were forced to shoot at the large crowds, and shocking pictures were broadcast by international television channels. After five days, the riots had claimed seven fatalities.

These were the most violent riots in the territories since 1967, when those territories had been occupied as a result of the Israeli victory in the Six-Day War

Evidence has reached Israel of a growing campaign in Poland blaming the Jewish population for all shortages Poland has suffered since the imposition of martial law. The Polish government has so far failed to repudiate the campaign. (January 1)

●

Foreign Minister Yitzhak Shamir meets Pope John Paul II in the Vatican, who calls on Israel to make a firm commitment towards a "just and lasting solution" to the Palestinian problem. (January 7)

●

Ida Milgrom saw her son Anatoly Sharansky for the first time in 18 months. She said he was kept on a starvation regime for 185 days in 1981 and was only fed every other day. (January 8)

●

After 16 days of fighting between the Moslem Brotherhood (who are opposed to the minority Alawi rule in Syria), and the army, parts of the city Hama have been reduced to rubble. Reports are received that over 40,000 residents were purged by President Assad who wished to underline his attitude to resistance. (February 17)

●

French President Francois Mitterand visits Israel. He declined to make a joint statement with Prime Minister Begin. (March 3)

●

The French newspaper *'Le Matin'* quoted an Israeli returning from Teheran who said Khomeini approved arms deals with Israel, ruling that "Israel is Satan but in our country's situation we have to deal with Satan himself." (March 17)

●

After 15 years under Israeli control, the Sinai Peninsula is returned to Egypt. President Mubarak congratulates Prime Minister Begin on fulfilling the accords. (April 25)

●

The US sides with Britain after the Falklands negotiations with Argentina have failed. (April 30)

●

The government decides that El Al will no longer fly on Saturdays. (May 2)

●

5,000 British troops secure a 26 sq. km bridgehead on the Falklands after an invasion that cost 46 lives and one frigate. (May 22)

The British tighten the net around Port Stanley after capturing strategic hills around the Falklands capital. (June 1)

•

Soviet tugs push the *Greenpeace* yacht *'Sirus'* out of Leningrad harbor. *Greenpeace* demands an answer to a telegram sent to President Brezhnev, demanding that he declare a unilateral freeze on nuclear testing. Daniel Ellsberg met with a Soviet government-backed peace committee. He described the meeting as useful but they refused to pass the *Greenpeace* letter to Brezhnev. (June 2)

•

Iraq says its air force jets have broken the sound barrier over Teheran and the holy city of Qum in warning flights to demonstrate that Iraq can reach any target in Iran, and to deter Iran from shelling anew any city or civil installation. (June 2)

•

Military sources in Pakistan state that Soviet and Afghan troops fought one of the major battles of the war against the *Mujahadeen* rebels. Both sides claimed victory in the three week battle in the Panjsher Valley, about 65 kms *(40 miles)* from Kabul. (June 3)

•

British *Harrier* jets dropped thousands of leaflets calling on the besieged Argentine troops in Port Stanley to surrender, while the British marines continued to bombard positions around the city for the third day. (June 3)

•

London police have thrown a security net over prominent Jews who are on an international hit list uncovered in raids, after the assassination attempt on Israel's Ambassador to Britain, Shlomo Argov. (June 5)

•

The US is appealing strongly for restraint in response to Thursday's assassination attempt on the Israeli ambassador in London. The Americans are worried that Israel might undertake a massive ground attack against the PLO in Lebanon, beyond Friday's and today's air strikes. The State Department called the ambassador's shooting "despicable." (June 5)

•

Several US Sixth Fleet ships patrol the Lebanese coast. The Secretary of Defense says their mission is to assist refugees. (June 5)

Israel's Ambassador to Britain Shot and Severely Injured

On June 6, Shlomo Argov, Israel's Ambassador to Britain, was shot while leaving a private dinner party at a hotel in London. Argov's bodyguards shot the assassin and wounded him. Argov was severely wounded. In a long surgical operation, pieces of bullet were extracted from his skull. Abu Nidal's organization took responsibility for the assassination attempt.

The next morning, the Israeli government held an urgent meeting, and it was decided that there had to be a firm reaction to terror attacks in Israel and around the world: "Israel cannot continue with its one-sided policy of restraint. The period of terror attacks occurring without Israeli reaction is a thing of the past."

The IDF Prepares for War

The IDF returns fire after the *Katyusha* rockets. The fire spread from Nahariya to Kiryat Shmona.

On Friday, June 4, immediately after the Argov assassination attempt had been reported, air force jets started to attack terrorist targets in Lebanon.

The main target was Beirut's soccer stadium, which was used by the PLO as a large ammunition depot. Many targets were also hit in southern Lebanon. The terrorists' reaction was harsh: from noon that day, 500 *Katyusha* rockets were launched at northern Israel and mortars and old *T-34* Russian tanks were also used by them.

The fire fell on the entire northern part of Israel, from Nahariya in the west to Kiryat Shmona in the east. It appeared that the fire was being coordinated by the Supreme Military Council of Lebanon. In spite of the heavy fire, the number of Israeli casualties was small. One soldier was killed and 11 civilians were injured. Two hundred and twenty Lebanese were killed and hundreds injured in the Israeli Air Force attacks on targets in Lebanon.

In response to the shells falling on Israel, on June 5 Israeli armored forces crossed the border into south Lebanon. The firing continued and Israel went into a state of war: the IDF called up large reserve forces, and roads were choked with tank convoys and artillery pieces on their way to the northern border. Northern residents who had been in their bomb shelters since Friday prepared for a long stay there.

There was strong international condemnation of events. The US demanded both sides cease fire and return to the *status quo* existing before June 4. The American defense secretary stated he had asked the president to cancel the special defense arrangements existing between the US and Israel. The UN Security Council also condemned the two sides.

Large armored forces enter South Lebanon.

War to Bring 'Peace for Galilee'

The minister of defense parts from soldiers who cross the border into Lebanon in an armored vehicle.

IDF forces took over the Lebanese town Nabatiyeh and main locations in Tyre and Sidon and prepared to head towards Beirut. Missile ships off the coast shot at major highways leading north from the coastal cities, and at the refineries south of Sidon. They also prevented terrorists and residents from escaping to the Beirut area.

At the end of the first day of the war, all Lebanese coastal cities had been laid siege. The Israeli Navy landed large numbers of paratrooper units south of Beirut, who captured the hills surrounding the city and awaited further instructions. At this point the Syrian army did not become involved, and its forces retreated northwards. An Israeli *Skyhawk* aircraft and a helicopter were brought down by terrorist fire.

The operation was approved by all ministers at the Cabinet meeting that morning. The operation's goal, outlined at the meeting, was to create a 40 km *(25 mile)* security zone as a buffer to the northern border. The operation's name changed from 'The Plan of the Pine Trees' to 'Operation Peace for Galilee.'

IDF Conquers the Beaufort

In a joint operation, soldiers of the *Golani* unit took over the Beaufort fortress, located 717 meters *(2,150 feet)* above sea level, overlooking both the Christian enclave in S. Lebanon and the Galilee. The Beaufort had become the terrorists' base in S. Lebanon from where they launched hundreds of *Katyusha* rockets on the northern settlements.

The battle began on the night of June 6, after serious artillery shelling of the area by the air force. Despite the heavy fire, the terrorists did not give in, fortifying themselves in the deep underground dungeons built by Crusaders.

Two *Golani* teams, commanded by Major Goni Harnik, penetrated the fort from the mountain's steepest side, under cover of dark. At dawn they entered the two wings of the fort itself, in two lines, and opened fire. All terrorists were killed in the battle. Six soldiers of the *Golani* unit, including Harnik, were killed.

Taking over the Beaufort enabled large numbers of Israeli forces to head north safely. The capture of the

Soldiers being briefed before one of the battles.

castle played a large part in boosting morale. On the morning of June 7, shortly after the mountain had been captured, Begin and Minister of Defense Sharon arrived to express their appreciation to the soldiers.

Raya Harnik, Goni's mother, became a leading figure in the battle for Israel's withdrawal from Lebanon and an end to the Lebanon War.

1982
JUNE 6

Leaders of the seven major industrial powers ('G-7') reached a broad agreement on monetary stability and credit to the Eastern Bloc. The G-7 called on Israel and the Palestinians to "cease immediately and simultaneously all military activities." Prime Minister Margaret Thatcher said that all governments at the Versailles G-7 summit meeting backed Britain's efforts to retake the Falkland Islands from Argentina.

•

British patrols clashed with Argentinian outposts around Port Stanley and moved closer to the city. The main Argentine defense line is believed to be 1.6 kilometers (one mile) from the town.

•

A spokesman for the rebels in Chad says that the rebel forces have broken through the government defense lines, killing hundreds of government troops, and that the rebels led by former Prime Minister Habre are within only an hour of Chad's capital, the city N'djamena.

•

The 94 members of the non-aligned countries request an emergency meeting on Namibia of the UN Security Council to enforce a withdrawal of South African troops from South West Africa.

•

Egypt calls for immediate ceasefire between Israel and the Palestinians and for the withdrawal of all Israeli forces from Lebanon. Mubarak's political adviser, Osama el-Baz, says "this Israeli attack will block the comprehensive peace process and increase tension and instability" in the region.

•

The Soviets condemn Israel. The Tass news agency charges that Israel has unleashed a "fifth war against the Arabs" by sending troops into South Lebanon and that Jerusalem is bent on the physical extermination of the Palestinians. Tass also said that the Israeli attacks were made with the foreknowledge of the US.

•

US special Middle East envoy Philip Habib may move forward his planned trip to the area and arrive in Lebanon today in an attempt to salvage the broken ceasefire between Israel and the PLO.

The economic summit of the seven industrial powers ended at Versailles. President Reagan came out of the summit with a vaguely worded agreement with the other six to limit trade credits to the Eastern Bloc. The US had claimed the credits would enable the USSR to use its limited resources for a military buildup; the other six agreed because of the USSR's low credit rating, rather than the Soviet military buildup potential. USSR and their allies have an estimated $80 billion debt. (June 7)

•

President Reagan met with the Pope and discussed the issues of the South Atlantic, Iran, Iraq and Lebanon. (June 7)

•

In London President Reagan tells the assembled members of the House of Lords and the House of Commons that it is time for the West to begin a worldwide crusade for democracy "that would leave Marxism and Leninism on the ash-heap of history." (June 8)

•

Jewish communities around the world are organizing to raise emergency funds for Israel. The United Jewish Appeal and Keren Hayesod (*Jewish Foundation*) established telephone hookups with headquarters abroad to counter distorted reports about the fighting, and to increase communities' involvement with Israel. (June 9)

•

Four British ships are hit in three bombings and rocket attacks by Argentine war 'planes in the area of the Falkland Islands. The British shot down seven *Skyhawks* and *Mirages*. (June 9)

•

According to news agencies quoting Egyptian foreign ministry sources in Cairo, Egypt will not sever its diplomatic relations with Israel or recall its ambassador in the wake of Israel's invasion of Lebanon. (June 10)

•

The US government is pointedly refusing to join most of its Western allies in publicly condemning Israel's invasion of Lebanon. The most that Secretary of State Haig would say under intense press questioning was that Israel had "not evidenced sufficient flexibility" to make a visit by him to Jerusalem "worthwhile at this time." (June 10)

Dozens of Syrian Aircraft Downed in Combat in Lebanon

The IDF takes over Damur.

A convoy crosses the bridge over the Awali River.

On June 9, the Israeli Air Force, commanded by David Ivry, destroyed dozens of Syrian missile batteries and downed dozens of Syrian aircraft in what has been defined by foreign military commentators as "one of the most impressive aerial combats in history."

Twenty four hours earlier, Syria entered the war by firing missiles at Israeli aircraft. The prime minister and minister of defense ordered the air force to attack missile batteries in response. Over a hundred Israeli aircraft took part in the battle.

Special 'smart' missiles were used and batteries were destroyed before the Syrians managed to react. The batteries were destroyed at the outset, following the lesson learned during the *Yom Kippur* War, in which Israeli aircraft had been downed by enemy missiles. Within two hours, all Syrian missile battery ranges had been destroyed.

Dozens of Syrian *MiG-21* and *MiG-23* aircraft were downed. According to foreign estimates, over a hundred aircraft were destroyed; that day the IDF neutralized a third of the Syrian air force and half of its missile power. The IDF, for its part, bore no casualties.

At the same time, ground combat continued. The IDF conquered the town Damur and drove out the Syrian forces eastward.

The Deputy Chief of Staff Killed

The Deputy Chief of Staff, General Yekutiel ('Kuti') Adam, was killed on June 10 in combat against a terrorist cell, while on his way to one of the IDF headquarters set up on the battlefield.

General Adam was deputy chief of staff until January 1982, and then left for military studies in America. As the war commenced, he was called back. 'Kuti' was about to be nominated to head the *Mossad*.

Killed with General Adam was his assistant, Colonel Chaim Sela.

Both officers were on their way to IDF headquarters in Damur, when they were caught in the middle of terrorist bombing and tried to find shelter in local buildings. A terrorist cell was hiding in the same shelter and killed them. The terrorists in turn were killed by IDF forces.

General Adam, an outstanding of-

General 'Kuti' Adam in his last photo, a few moments before he was killed.

ficer and fighter, was considered to be an appropriate choice to replace

'Raful' as chief of staff. However, he had decided to decline.

The Ceasefire has Collapsed

Thanks to the major diplomatic efforts of American envoy Philip Habib, a cease-fire was declared between the Israeli and Syrian armies, on June 11. Israel's condition was that a *status quo* be maintained and that neither side would use the break in fighting to bring more forces or ammunition to the battlefield.

To persuade Israel to cooperate in the cease-fire, the American government threatened to change its policy of restraint.

The cease-fire gave IDF soldiers their first vacation since the operation began. Soldiers used the break to improve conditions in the field and to call home.

The first cease-fire lasted nine days and was violated by the Syrians, who shot at the IDF in the central sector. At the same time, there was combat against PLO terrorists in West Beirut.

Fierce Armored Combat on the Beirut-Damascus Highway

Resting before moving on.

Destination: Beirut - Damascus highway.

The cease-fire collapsed, and on June 24 Syrian and Israeli units battled on the Beirut-Damascus road.

The battle took place mainly in Hamdoun. IDF forces had to deal with extremely heavy fire. On the first day of renewed battle, 16 Israeli soldiers were killed and 47 injured. One of the problems the IDF had to overcome was the extremely difficult road surface.

IDF forces bombarded Syrian headquarters and injured dozens of Iranian volunteers who had come to assist the enemy. Syrian *MiG* war 'planes that had attempted to hit the land forces were downed.

The IDF also fought terrorists in the Beirut area, attacking their centers, and besieging the city.

The following two days were difficult. The Syrian army recruited additional forces to block IDF control of the Beirut-Damascus highway. During the combat, an IDF unit was ambushed near the town of Sultan Ya'acoub. The unit suffered heavy losses, and seven soldiers were declared missing in action.

Three of them are still considered MIA, and despite great efforts to discover what has happened to them, the matter still remains unresolved.

Fighting from house to house.

John Demjanjuk, 62, stripped of his US citizenship for concealing his past as a Nazi collaborator, is arrested after eluding the immigration authorities for more than a week. (July 19)

●

A bomb hidden in a suitcase explodes near the El Al counter at Munich airport. No one is hurt. (July 30)

●

The 38th anniversary of the Polish uprising in Warsaw is marked with official ceremonies, but hundreds use the opportunity to demonstrate their support for 'Solidarity' movement. (August 1)

●

Two gunmen went on the rampage at the Goldberg restaurant in Paris, killing six and wounding 21, in the worst anti-Jewish attack in recent years. The two gunmen drove away as the police arrived. A group called *'Action Directe'* claimed responsibility for the act. (August 9)

●

The American movie star Henry Fonda, who won an Oscar for his final film 'On Golden Pond,' dies at the age of 77. (August 12)

●

Nahum Goldmann, founder-President of the World Jewish Congress and former President of the World Zionist Organization, dies aged 87. (August 30)

●

The dissident 'Helsinki Group' set up to monitor Soviet compliance with the Helsinki Human Rights Accords, said it was folding after one of the last three members, Sofia Kallistratova was told she may face trial. Yelena Bonner, Andrei Sakharov's wife, said that under such pressure from the authorities the group could no longer function. (September 8)

●

Amin Jemayel (the brother of Bashir Jemayel), seen as Syrian-orientated, is elected as Lebanon's president. (September 14)

●

Princess Grace of Monaco, who abandoned Hollywood stardom to marry a prince, dies of injuries sustained in a car crash on Monday. (September 14)

●

US Marines enter Beirut, together with Italy and France, as Israel withdraws its forces from Beirut. (September 29)

The Sabra and Shatilla Massacre

In response to the murder of Lebanon's President Bashir Jemayel three weeks after his election, on Sept. 16 a Christian *Phalangist* force entered Sabra and Shatilla refugee camps in West Beirut. The *Phalangists* murdered hundreds of Palestinians in cold blood, including women and children. Although the IDF did not take part in the massacre, world opinion held Israel responsible, because the area was controlled by the IDF and because of the cooperation between Israel and the *Phalange*.

News of the massacre was delayed in reaching Israel because of the Jewish New Year holiday. When details of the massacre had been made public, there was an outrage. The Labor party demanded the resignation of the prime minister and minister of defense, and the establishment of a commission of inquiry, similar to the Agranat Commission. Horrifying photographs of murdered women and old people were published internationally. The world pointed the finger of blame at Israel for closing its eyes to the murderous activities of the Christian *Phalange*.

A week after the massacre, 400,000 people (10% of the Israeli population gathered in Tel Aviv in the biggest demonstration ever to have taken place in the history of Israel, to demand Israeli withdrawal from Lebanon and the establishment of a commission of inquiry.

President Jemayel of Lebanon Killed in Bombing

Bashir Jemayel with 'Raful.' A Syrian plan.

On Sept. 14, three weeks after his election as Lebanon's president, Bashir Jemayel was killed when his headquarters were destroyed by a car bomb explosion. Jemayel commanded the Christian *Phalange* and was a loyal ally of Israel. He was to a large extent responsible for Israel's decision to go to war in Lebanon. Israel had arranged for Jemayel to be elected president, in order to ensure its influence in Lebanon. Prime Minister Menachem Begin had sent his personal greetings, congratulating him on his election, and had referred to him as Israel's friend.

Syria took responsibility for the blast at *Phalange* headquarters in East Beirut which caused Bashir Jemayel's death.

Armored Brigade CO Resigns for Conscientious Objections

Colonel Eli Geva. Conscientious objector.

In his letter to the chief of staff and minister of defense, dated July 22, Brigade-Commander Colonel Eli Geva requested that he be relieved of his duties due to conscientious objections.

Geva, considered to be one of the best officers in the army, explained that his conscience did not allow him to take part in the attack on Beirut and the harming of innocent civilians. After Geva had refused to retract his letter, the chief of staff canceled his appointment as an armored brigade commander.

The story stunned the army. It was initially kept secret and only after it had been leaked to the press did the IDF spokesman issue an official statement, without disclosing Geva's name.

The IDF Attacks West Beirut

On Aug. 1, the IDF started an offensive against terrorists besieged in West Beirut. Aircraft, ships, long-range cannon and tanks took part in the battle. Paratroopers took over Beirut airport. The IDF spokesman reported that the attack came in response to the terrorists' violation of the cease-fire.

The next day, paratroopers and armored corps occupied Hay es-Salaam in south-east Beirut and were stationed in posts overlooking Burj el-Burajna refugee camp, one of the terrorists' main strongholds. Infantry forces positioned themselves in the National Museum area, and prepared to attack.

At night, IDF forces penetrated the el-Uza'i refugee camp, another major terrorist stronghold. Eighteen IDF soldiers were killed in combat. Tens of thousands of civilians left Beirut for the north, as did hundreds of terrorists. *Ten days later an agreement was reached allowing the terrorists to leave Lebanon.*

The Military Governor's Building in Tyre Collapses, with 75 Dead

1982
OCTOBER - DECEMBER

Searching for survivors in Tyre. There was no sign of a terrorist bombing.

The military governor's building in Tyre collapsed on Nov. 11 as a result of a huge explosion. The seven-story building was completely destroyed, and dozens of soldiers were buried alive. Large teams of engineer and medical corps worked for three days to save survivors. The explosion also killed arrested terrorists who were being held in the basement of the building.

Bad weather and constant rain made it difficult for rescue teams to work. After three days, the search ended and the tragic outcome was made known: 75 soldiers and security forces had been killed and 24 injured.

A commission of inquiry set up by the chief of staff revealed many security lapses, but there was no sign of a terrorist bombing. It ap-peared that the explosion had been caused by a gas leak. Israel declared Nov. 15 a day of national mourning.

Soldiers of the rescue teams received awards. Similar rescue teams throughout the world studied the Israeli rescue methods. IDF rescue teams have since assisted in international earthquake rescue missions in Armenia and Mexico.

Terrorists Carry Out Attack on a Synagogue in Rome

In a terrorist attack on a synagogue in the old quarter of Rome, a two-year-old was killed and 34 Jews injured on Oct. 19. The attack was defined as "the most severe anti-Semitic action in Italy since World War II."

Five youths waited at the rear entrance to the synagogue for the end of the *Simhat Tora* celebrations. When the ceremony was over, the attackers threw three hand-grenades and opened fire on the worshippers. After the two-minute attack, the terrorists fled the site.

Large police forces closed the old Jewish quarter and began searching for the terrorists, whose portraits were distributed all over Europe.

The heads of the Jewish community in Rome decided to close all stores in Rome owned by Jews for two days. They accused Italy's government of the murder. Ten hours after the attack, two small bombs exploded in the city, one near the Syrian Embassy and another near a Moslem center.

Chancellor Helmut Kohl's central right government takes office pledging economic revival. Kohl takes over from Social Democrat Helmut Schmidt in an unprecedented parliamentary vote Friday. (October 4)

•

The Polish parliament votes to outlaw all unions including 'Solidarity,' and form new unions along strictly defined lines, formally ending an unprecedented two-year experiment in worker democracy. (October 8)

•

Police used tear gas this afternoon to disperse some 100 angry demonstrators protesting the attack on Rome's main synagogue which killed a two-year-old boy and wounded 34. (October 9)

•

Colombian-born novelist Gabriel Garcia Marquez won the 1982 Nobel Prize for Literature. His best known novel, 'One Hundred Years of Solitude,' has been translated into many languages, including Hebrew. (October 21)

•

Leonid Brezhnev dies aged 75, after 18 years in power. Yuri Andropov is elected as General Secretary of the Communist Party to succeed Brezhnev. (November 10)

•

Leader of the banned 'Solidarity' movement, Lech Walesa, returns to the roar of the crowds after eleven months of martial law internment. (November 14)

•

Prisoner of Zion Vladimir Slepak returns to Moscow after five years internal exile in Siberia. He had been exiled on charges of "hooliganism." (December 6)

•

Foreign Minister Yitzhak Shamir says he has received assurances from top Argentine officials to investigate the fate of Jews who disappeared during the military crackdown on leftist guerrillas. Humanitarian groups estimate that 6,000 disappeared in the late Seventies, among them about 1,000 Jews. (December 15)

•

Arthur Rubinstein, one of the 20th century's greatest pianists, and a fierce supporter of Israel, dies at 95. Rubinstein gave his name to the first piano competition held in Jerusalem. (December 20)

Jewish emigration from the Soviet union slumped to a 10-year low of 2,700 last year. The number of Soviet Jews denied emigration visas hovered at around 2,000 for years, but now is up to 8,000. Last year only 18.9% of the emigrants continued to Israel, most of the rest went to the US. (January 8)

●

Meyer Lansky, the reputed financial genius of the US underworld, died aged 82. The king of gambling will be remembered in Israel for his long and unsuccessful struggle to become an Israeli citizen. (January 15)

●

OPEC oil ministers end an emergency meeting in Geneva and fail to agree on critical issues such as production quotas, that threaten to send oil prices lower and prolong the oil glut that has undermined the cartel's power to fix prices. (January 24)

●

Former Gestapo official Klaus Barbie was extradited from Bolivia to France to face charges of ordering the killing of thousands of Jews and anti-Nazis during World War II. His presence in Bolivia was made public in 1972 by French Nazi hunters Serge and Beate Klarsfeld. (February 5)

●

The oil ministers of OPEC agree to cut $5 off their base price to $29 a barrel and a combined production ceiling of 17.5 million barrels a day. This was the first cut in crude oil prices in a decade. (March 15)

●

Chaim Herzog was elected Israel's sixth president, beating the right-wing candidate, Judge Menachem Elon. (March 22)

●

Barney Clark, the world's only recipient of a permanent artificial heart, the *Jarvik-7*, died after 112 days with the device. (March 23)

●

West German Christian Democratic leader Helmut Kohl, whose center-right coalition won a resounding victory in this month's general elections, is formally elected chancellor by the Bundestag. The environmentalist anti-NATO Greens entered the parliament for the first time with 29 seats. (March 29)

Grenade Thrown at *Peace Now* Demonstrators. Grunzweig Dead

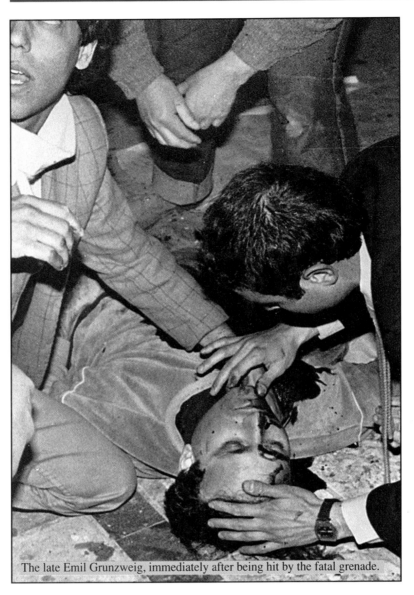

The late Emil Grunzweig, immediately after being hit by the fatal grenade.

On Feb. 10, minutes after the end of a *Peace Now* demonstration in front of the Prime Minister's Office in Jerusalem, a hand grenade was thrown at demonstrators and Emil Grunzweig, one of the organizers of the demonstration, was killed. Ten people were injured, including Avraham Burg, son of Yosef Burg, the minister of the interior.

The IDF-manufactured grenade was thrown from a copse of pine trees. Demonstrators later reported hearing the word "Now!" shouted, seconds before it was thrown.

The *Peace Now* demonstration had started in the center of Jerusalem, and protesters then slowly made their way towards the government buildings, continuously harassed by right-wing opponents. The final provocation was the throwing of the fatal grenade.

More than 10,000 people came to Grunzweig's funeral in Haifa. Grunzweig, aged 35 at the time of his death, had immigrated to Israel from Romania as a child and was an officer in the army. He had decided during his last period of military service in Lebanon to protest the government's policy.

After some months of inquiry, intelligence services located the man who had thrown the grenade. Yona Avrushmi, a young Jerusalem man, admitted he had been influenced by right-wing propaganda. He was sentenced to life in prison.

The Conclusions of the Kahan Commission: Dismiss 'Arik' Sharon

The Kahan Commission, assigned to investigate the Sabra and Shatilla massacre, submitted its findings to Prime Minister Menachem Begin on Feb. 7. Those most severely hurt: Minister of Defense 'Arik' Sharon, Chief of Staff Raphael Eitan, and Head of Intelligence, General Yehoshua Saguy. Also criticised were the Northern Region Commander, Amir Drori, and IDF Commander of the Beirut Sector, General Amos Yaron.

The commission interrogated 48 witnesses, including the prime minister, the minister of defense, government ministers, high-ranking IDF officers and *Phalange* officers. It determined that Israel had been only indirectly responsible for the massacre, but could have prevented it; the *Phalange* who had entered the refugee camps had done so with the knowledge of the government, and with IDF encouragement. The commission also concluded that the military and the minister of defense did not thoroughly report all relevant information to the prime minister and other Cabinet ministers. The commission recommended that the minister of defense should draw his own personal conclusions and that the prime minister should exercise his right to sack the minister of defense.

Immediately after the conclusions had been published, the minister of defense announced he would not resign. Ministers and coalition members of the Knesset announced that if Sharon did not resign, they would demand Begin's resignation.

The Israeli public was split into two camps: those who thought that Sharon should resign, and those who opposed that view. Many demonstrations took place in Tel Aviv and centers throughout Israel.

On Feb. 14, a week after the report had been published, the Cabinet, by a 16 to one majority, decided to remove Sharon from the Ministry of Defense. Only Ariel Sharon voted against his removal. He remained in the Cabinet as a minister without portfolio.

The commission decided not to take action against the chief of staff, Raphael Eitan, despite its harsh criticism, since his term was almost over. Two months later, 'Raful' was replaced by his second-in-command, General Moshe Levy.

Begin: "I Cannot Continue"

The mystery of Prime Minister Menachem Begin's resignation and reclusive behavior remains unsolved.

At the cabinet meeting of Aug. 28, Prime Minister Begin announced his retirement from his position and from political life altogether. The announcement stunned the Israeli public, although it had been preceded by rumors of his failing health and refusal to leave home. Begin's aides had tried to hide his deteriorating condition from the public for a long time. In his resignation announcement, Begin did not explain his decision. He simply said that he could not continue.

To this day no clear reason has been given for Begin's resignation. It is assumed that several issues had broken his spirit: the death of his wife Aliza, the Lebanon War, and the permanent protest demonstrations outside his house against the continuous deaths of soldiers. Begin declined pleas from his Cabinet that he withdraw his resignation. That day, there was a demonstration outside his house. Right-wing supporters urged Begin to return to his job, while 'Peace Now' supporters congratulated him on his decision.

Begin's resignation caused a constitutional problem since Begin had not submitted a formal letter of resignation to President Herzog. Three weeks later, the president asked Yitzhak Shamir, minister of foreign affairs in Begin's government, to form a new government.

Peace Agreement with Lebanon

After extensive discussions and numerous visits by American Secretary of State for Foreign Affairs, George Shultz, and envoy Philip Habib, an accord ending the war between Israel and Lebanon was finally signed on May 6.

According to the accord, Israel would maintain a military presence up to 45km *(28 miles)* north of the border, in an area defined as a security zone. UN forces would be stationed north of that zone. It was also agreed that only two Lebanese brigades would be stationed in the security zone, which would be demilitarized and missile-free. The status of the SLA (South Lebanon Army) was defined as the official force in the declared zone, to be commanded by Major Sa'ad Haddad.

The Cabinet meeting at which the accord was approved was the longest meeting in the State's history. Seventeen voted in favor of the peace accord, and only two opposed: 'Arik' Sharon and Yuval Ne'eman.

Israeli and Lebanese representatives sign the peace accord.

As a result of the agreement, President Ronald Reagan canceled the embargo on Israel and permitted it to receive F-16 jet fighters. Prime Minister Begin was invited to the United States for a visit.

Western countries were pleased with the accord, but the USSR and Syria refused to accept it. In any event it was never applied since one of its conditions stipulated full Syrian withdrawal from Lebanon.

1983
APRIL - AUGUST

Vladimir Slepak, known among Soviet Jews as the "father of *Aliya*" marked the 13th anniversary of the submission of his application to leave the USSR. There is no sign his application will be approved. Slepak has been refused emigration for longer than any other Soviet Jew. (April 12)

•

An entire section of the American embassy in Beirut collapsed in a major explosion. Seventy people were killed. The blast was said to be intended for US negotiator Philip Habib. He was unhurt. (April 19)

•

Bruno Kreisky announced his resignation after 13 years as Austrian chancellor. (April 24).

•

The military in Argentina admitted mistakes were made and innocent people were killed during the suppression of leftist guerrillas, but insisted they acted to save the nation. Local and international human rights groups say that between 6,000-15,000 'disappeared' between 1975-1979. (April 28)

•

One of the greatest journalistic hoaxes in recent times ended when German Interior Minister Friedrich Zimmerman announced that Hitler's alleged diaries were crude forgeries. The London *'Sunday Times'* bought the publication rights for £26,000. A Nazi regalia dealer admitted to forging the diaries with the assistance of a *'Stern'* reporter. (May 6)

•

AIDS, the disease that has claimed hundreds of lives in the US, has arrived in Europe from Central Africa. So far 40 cases have been detected in Europe, 30 of them in Belgium. (July 12)

•

The 105-family Conservative congregation of Clifton Park, New York elected a woman, Beverly Madgison, to be their first full-time rabbi. (July 17)

•

The first World Congress of North African Jewry opened with an evening of music and dance at the Bloomfield Stadium in Jaffa with 15,000 spectators. The congress consisted of artistic and cultural events that lasted until August 4. The president called on the participants from abroad to immigrate to Israel. (July 25)

Israel and US Jewry mourn Senator Henry Jackson who died at 71. For over 40 years Jackson was Israel's most powerful and consistent US friend. (September 1)

•

Jewish activist Yosef Begun was sentenced to seven years and another five years in internal exile for disseminating anti-Soviet propaganda. Begun had applied for a visa to emigrate to Israel in 1971. (October 14)

•

French political commentator Raymond Aron died at 78. Aron was a supporter of Israel although in recent years he was highly critical of Israel's policies in Lebanon and the territories. (October 17)

•

Teddy Kollek, Shlomo Lahat and Arieh Gurel won by landslides in the municipal elections in Jerusalem, Tel Aviv and Haifa. All three remained in power until 1992. (October 25)

•

Israel's monthly inflation record shattered. The 21.5% rise in the Consumer Price Index was the highest ever. (November 15)

•

Ariel Sharon's libel suit against *'Time'* magazine began in New York. Sharon sued the magazine and a reporter for $50 million for accusing him of responsibility for the Sabra and Shatilla massacres. *He won the suit but not the damages.* (November 24)

•

An agreement to build the largest solar pond power plant was signed between the Southern California Edison company and Ormat Turbines of Yavne in Israel. Ormat is the world's leading developer of solar ponds and low temperature generators. (December 20)

•

Excerpts from a film made by Alfred Hitchcock on Nazi concentration camps, previously unseen by the public, were shown on British television. The documentary was discovered in the British War Museum's archives, and was not released at the time for fear of undermining reconstruction efforts in post-war Germany. Hitchcock had been commissioned by the British Information Ministry to make the film at the end of the war. (December 21)

150 American Marines Killed in Beirut Explosion

A truck packed with 900kg *(1,980 lbs)* of explosives exploded on Oct. 23 in the grounds of the headquarters of the American and French marines stationed in Beirut. The truck, driven by an Arab suicide-bomber, sped into the yard after crashing through all security roadblocks. Two buildings, housing 160 American and 73 French soldiers, collapsed in the explosion. An organization identified with Syria took responsibility for the action.

Rescue operations continued for several days; 150 bodies were recovered, most of them American. Most of the 75 injured were French. Some of the injured soldiers received medical treatment in Israel. In addition, Israel offered to send rescue teams and assist in the rescue operations.

After the event, it was discovered that two weeks earlier the Lebanese army had warned American forces of an anticipated terrorist bombing. The Lebanese had warned the Americans of the possibility of a car bomb which would be brought in from the Lebanon Valley. US President Ronald Reagan announced immediately after the bombing that he would not reduce the marine force presence stationed in Lebanon.

Captive Exchange: 6 Israeli Soldiers for 4,765 Terrorists

On Nov. 23, six *Nahal (pioneering youth brigade)* soldiers who had been captured in combat in 1982 were returned in exchange for 4,700 terrorists who had been imprisoned in the Antzar facility in Lebanon, and 65 prisoners who had been imprisoned in Israel.

The six: Avi Kornfeld, Reuven Cohen, Rafi Hazan, Benny Gilboa, Avi Montbeliski and Eli Aboutbul had been held hostage by Arafat's forces and were released after negotiations lasting almost a year. The operation was named 'Raisin Pie.'

During negotiations, the PLO demanded that Israel also release the Japanese terrorist, Kozo Okamoto, and return Udi Adiv, a member of the Syrian espionage and terror unit. These demands were declined by Israel but Okamoto was released in a later prisoner exchange. Meanwhile, 3,600 of the released terrorists chose to stay in Lebanon and the other 1,100 asked to be flown to Algiers.

Freed terrorists board a 'plane on the way to freedom.

The Second Tyre Disaster. Lethal Suicide Bombing in Lebanon

On Nov. 11, two weeks after the bombing of the American marine headquarters, a car bomb entered the Israeli headquarters in Tyre. Sixty were killed in the blast, including 28 soldiers, border patrol policemen and GSS agents. Twenty nine were injured. The *Islamic Jihad* took responsibility for the attack.

The car bomb, loaded with 500 kg *(1,100 lbs)* of explosives, broke in at 6.00 a.m. Despite the guards' shooting, the driver managed to enter the compound and activate the bomb, destroying the GSS and Border Police headquarters. Fortunately, most soldiers were sleeping in their tents and so were saved.

Rescue teams that rushed to the scene also had to deal with the explosions of ammunition caused by the bombing. The rescuers used lessons learned after the previous bombing in Tyre, in November 1982, and applied new techniques for the first time being assisted by dogs.

Preliminary investigations indicated that the terrorist, who had been under the influence of drugs, drove the car from Ba'albek, in the Lebanon Valley. The guards' shooting had slowed him down, and prevented a greater disaster.

A 300 Line 'Bus is Hijacked

On Apr. 13, soldiers of a special IDF unit rescued passengers of an Egged 'bus, that had been hijacked by four terrorists on its way from Tel Aviv to Ashkelon. The 'bus, carrying 25 passengers, stopped at the entrance to the refugee camp Dir el-Balah in the Gaza Strip.

The soldiers killed two of the terrorists in the first round of fire. A female soldier who had been travelling on the 'bus was killed during the rescue operation.

The hijack took place the previous evening, when the 300 line 'bus left Tel Aviv on its way to Ashkelon. The four young terrorists, armed with knives, forced the 'bus driver to drive to Gaza. Soldiers chasing the 'bus shot at its wheels and stopped it by Dir el-Balah. Seven hostages escaped as soon as the 'bus stopped.

Two of the terrorists were caught during the operation. After a short investigation, the terrorists were handed over to the GSS, who shot them on the spot. Media cameramen on the scene managed to take pictures of the terrorists being taken away, while they were still alive.

When the killing was exposed, the army and the General Security Serv-

The hijacked 'bus.

ices blamed each other.

The commission of inquiry established by Minister of Defense Moshe Arens determined Colonel Yitzhak Mordechai was responsible, since he had admitted using force against them. However, it was later discovered that GSS men who had been interrogated by the commission had

given false testimony, by changing facts and coordinating their stories. The head of the GSS, Avraham Shalom, who was eventually forced to retire, claimed that the terrorists had been killed on the instructions of Prime Minister Shamir. Shamir denied giving such an order or even knowing of the killing.

The 'Baba Sali' Dies

The 'Baba Sali' died on Jan. 8, at the age of 94 and was buried at Netivot. Fifty thousand of his followers attended his funeral.

Since then, his memorial day has been commemorated with great festivity by members of the North African community, with hundreds of thousands taking part. His son, Baruch Abuhatzeira, took his place.

Festivities in Netivot on 'Baba Sali's' memorial day.

Jewish Underground Arrests

Dozens of young Jewish settlers, including senior reserve officers in the IDF, were arrested on Apr. 27 when a Jewish underground movement was uncovered in the occupied territories.

The GSS exposed a well organized movement, whose members were highly trained in weaponry and explosives. After the arrests, it was discovered that some of the members had been under surveillance for three years, since the assassination of mayors in Judea and Samaria in 1981. The leaders of the movement, Men-

achem Livne and Yehuda Etzion, enjoyed the support and encouragement of several rabbis in Judea, Samaria and the Gaza Strip.

Most of the arrested were from Kiryat Arba and religious villages on the Golan Heights. Leaders in Kiryat Arba were accused of having served as GSS agents.

Under interrogation, most suspects admitted taking part in anti-Arab operations: the assassination of mayors, murders at the Islamic College of Hebron, the severe wounding of a policeman who tried to neutral-

ize a bomb they had planted, an attempt to bomb the Temple Mount, grenades thrown in Hebron, etc.

The arrests shocked the Israeli public. It was hard to believe that these young, educated men would engage in such violent action.

The trial of 27 members began on June 16. They were convicted and sentenced to various terms of imprisonment, ranging from eight years to life. Over the years, many received improved prison conditions. After some years, President Herzog even pardoned some of them.

1984
JANUARY - APRIL

Major Sa'ad Haddad, commander of the South Lebanon militias, died at 47. Lebanon's government sent Major-General Antoine Lahad to replace Haddad. (January 14)

●

Malcom Kerr, president of the American University in Beirut, is killed by the *Islamic Jihad.* They said he was a victim of the American military presence in Lebanon. (January 18)

●

President Reagan unveils plans to spend up to $5.6 billion in the next two years to develop the Strategic Defense Initiative (SDI) known as 'Star Wars.' Reagan's budget proposal carries a $180.4 billion deficit. (February 1)

●

Astronauts Bruce McCandless and Robert Stewart were the first humans to fly free in space, using a gas powered jet pack, to propel themselves as far as 97 meters *(320 feet)* from the *'Challenger.'* They remained outside for 90 minutes. (February 7)

●

Yuri Andropov, who ruled the USSR in ill health for 15 months, died at 69. Konstantin Chernenko, 72, became the oldest man to rule the Soviet Union. His election was seen as a victory of the conservative old guard of the Communist Party opposed to reforms. (February 9)

●

Jewish refugees from Ethiopia arrive in Israel via Sudan. Both Sudan's vice-president and its ambassador to Washington said in a documentary 18 months ago that Sudan had no objection to Ethiopian Jews leaving for a "third country." A documentary called 'Falasha - The Exile of the Black Jews' was made by Israeli-born Simcha Jacobovici working for the Canadian Broadcasting Company. (March 6)

●

Western experts sent to Iran to investigate charges that Iraq used chemical warfare against Iranian troops determine the charges are true. (March 25)

●

A policewoman was killed and ten were wounded as shots were fired from the Libyan Embassy in London into a crowd of Libyan exiles who were demonstrating there against Libyan leader Colonel Muammar Gaddafi. (April 17)

The Wiesenthal Center released documents indicating that Archbishop of Milan Schuster helped Walter Rauff, the man who invented the gas van that exterminated Jews as part of the Final Solution, to escape from Europe after World War II. Rauff has been in Chile since the end of the war. Other documents released indicate the Vatican may have provided escape routes for at least another 20 Nazis. (May 10)

●

The US arms control and disarmament agency reports that arms sales, which in 1972 were less than $300 billion, will reach $970 billion this year. (May 14)

●

Arab concern mounts over attacks on tankers in the Gulf. A Panamanian freighter was sunk by an Iraqi missile. Iran crippled two Kuwaiti tankers and rocketed a Saudi tanker. (May 18)

●

Martina Navratilova wins the women's Wimbledon singles title for the third consecutive year, defeating Chris Evert Lloyd by 7-6, 6-2. (July 7)

●

John McEnroe defeats Jimmy Connors for the men's singles title 6-1, 6-1, 6-2. He was the first American since Don Budge in 1938 to win three consecutive titles. (July 8)

●

Geraldine Ferraro is the first woman to be a candidate for US vice presidency. (July 12)

●

The 32nd Olympic Games opened in Los Angeles. (July 28)

●

Judith Resnik is the first Jewish American female scientist in space, traveling on board the 'Discovery.' (August 30)

●

US Navy Secretary John Lehman announces the navy is leasing 12 Israeli made 'Kfirs' from the IAF. (August 31)

●

France and Libya agree to pull their forces out of Chad, thus ending a 13-month military standoff in that country. (September 17)

●

Binyamin Netanyahu is appointed Israel's ambassador to the UN. (September 19)

Tie Between the Right and Left

Labor shock. Hopes of victory were shattered.

Celebrations in the *Likud*. Despite predictions, they were not defeated.

The Labor Party's hopes for a victory in the 11th *Knesset* elections were shattered on the night of July 23, after votes had been counted. Labor received 41 mandates, in comparison to its 47 in the 10th *Knesset*. The *Likud*, despite a record of 400% inflation and the serious implications of the Lebanon War, won 41 mandates, in comparison to its 48 in the 10th *Knesset*.

Labor's three leaders were Shimon Peres, Yitzhak Navon who had declined a second term as president, and Yitzhak Rabin who had replaced Chaim Bar-Lev as potential minister of defense at the last minute.

After the smaller parties had been included, two equal blocs were formed: the Left and the Right, each blocking the other.

Negotiations to form a national unity government were already under way on election night. Each of the two main parties was interested in leading the coalition.

Two small parties tipped the balance of power: the *Yachad* party, headed by Ezer Weizman, which had won three seats, and the National Religious Party, which had won four seats in the *Knesset*.

Exchange of POW Captives: Six Israeli Prisoners for 291 Syrians

On June 28, six Israeli captives were returned in exchange for 291 Syrians captured during the Lebanon War. In addition to the soldiers, Israel released 13 Druze residents of Golan Heights villages and eight Syrian citizens. The Syrians returned five bodies of soldiers killed in the Lebanon War. Three soldiers captured by Ahmed Jibril's movement were not included in the deal.

The negotiations took several months and were conducted by the Red Cross. Israel demanded the return of Eli Cohen's body, but Syria refused. The captives returned were:

pilot Gil Fogel, whose 'plane had been shot down in July '82, Ariel Lieberman, who had been taken prisoner in the Sultan Ya'acoub battle and Yohanan Alon, who accidentally crossed the border in August 1982. The other three were guards from the Israeli delegation office in Beirut.

Govt. Leadership Rotation: 2 Years Peres, 2 Years Shamir

Shimon Peres presented his unity government on Sept. 13. There were 25 ministers in the Cabinet from the following parties: Labor, *Likud*, NRP, *Yachad*, *Shas* and *Shinui*. The coalition represented 97 members of *Knesset*.

The coalition agreement included an attempt to strengthen peace with Egypt, efforts to involve additional Arab states in peace negotiations, concensus on the importance of a united Jerusalem, objections to any negotiation with the PLO and the attempt to build more settlements.

The legal document was drafted by members Moshe Shahal and Dan Meridor. A few moments after the agreement had been drafted, Peres and Shamir praised the agreement, which had made history. The most important point in the accord was the rotation between Peres and Shamir. Shamir was supposed to be minister of foreign affairs for two years in Peres' government, and vice versa. Yitzhak Rabin was minister of defense and Yitzhak Moda'i was minister of finance. The agreement also determined that the dismissal of a minister would have to be approved by that minister's party.

The two top priorities of the government were that the IDF leave Lebanon and that a new economic policy be formulated to halt inflation.

Prohibited Import of New Cars, Television Sets and Refrigerators

On Oct. 2 the new economic program was made public. It forbade the import of many products, amongst them cars, colored TV sets, refrigerators, VCR's and another 50 products considered to be luxuries. The Cabinet also decided that only $1,000 in cash would be permitted to be taken out of the country. All these measures were intended to save foreign currency.

In addition, many new taxes were announced, such as education tax, social security tax, etc. The government, employers and unions agreed to freeze prices and wages.

Within two years Peres reduced the 400% inflation to only 40%.

Anti-tank Missile Shot at Arab 'Bus in Jerusalem

Ben-Shimol being taken to prison. He stole the missile from the army.

David Ben-Shimol, a young man from Jerusalem, shot a *Lau* anti-tank missile at an Arab 'bus on Oct. 28, while the bus was traveling to Hebron. One passenger was killed and another 10 were injured.

Next to the missile's launcher was a letter stating that the action had been carried out by a group named 'The Revengers.' The group called on the government to pass a death sentence on an Arab terrorist from Dehaishe who had killed a couple of students. Ben-Shimol had stolen the missile during his military service. *Ben Shimol was sentenced to life imprisonment. He has been trying to obtain a pardon.*

Soldier Hadas Kedmy Murdered

The body of 20-year-old soldier, Hadas Kedmy of Kibbutz Kfar Masaryk, who had been missing since Nov. 29, was found after a two week search, in a pine forest near Damon Prison, in the Carmel hills.

As soon as she had been declared missing, the police suspected she had been taken hostage by a terrorist group and would be used as a bargaining chip.

Initial findings showed that Kedmy had been viciously murdered for

Hadas Kedmy. Unsolved murder.

nationalist motives. As a result of the murder, the chief of staff forbade soldiers to hitchhike at night.

Another equally horrifying murder had occurred on Oct. 22 near Carmizan convent, between Jerusalem and Beit Jallah. Two students who were out strolling were viciously murdered by an Arab resident of Dehaishe refugee camp. The murder was extremely shocking and once again many demanded that the death penalty be handed down to terrorists.

An IRA bomb misses Prime Minister Margaret Thatcher during the Conservative Party conference at the Grand Hotel in Brighton. Three were killed and 32 injured. (October 2)

●

The 1984 Nobel Peace Prize was awarded to South Africa's leading black clergyman, Bishop Desmond Tutu. (October 16)

●

Secretary of State George Shultz said that Soviet persecution of its Jewish population "seems to be getting worse." He cited an increase in official propaganda that goes as far as to compare the State of Israel to Nazi Germany. He also cited the arrest of four well-known Hebrew teachers in what appeared as an intensifying campaign of repression aimed at Jewish cultural activities. (October 22)

●

Indira Gandhi was assassinated by three Sikh bodyguards in apparent revenge for the storming of the Sikh Golden Temple by the Indian army in June. (October 31)

●

RAF and Soviet 'planes begin arriving in Addis Ababa to airlift food to the famine victims in Ethiopia. (November 3)

●

Svetlana Alliluyeva, who portrayed her father Joseph Stalin as a monster in her memoirs, returned to Moscow seventeen years after defecting to the West. The government returned her Soviet citizenship to her and granted citizenship to her 13-year-old daughter. (November 3)

●

President Reagan wins a landslide victory in the presidential elections over Democrat Walter Mondale. (November 6)

●

A cyanide leak from Union Carbide's pesticide plant kills at least 2,500 people and hospitals treated some 125,000 injured in Bhopal, India, in one of the worst industrial accidents on record. (December 3)

●

China and Britain sign the agreement that returns Hong Kong to China in 1997 and guarantees its capitalist system for fifty years thereafter. The agreement was signed in Peking by Prime Ministers Zhao Ziyang and Margaret Thatcher. (December 19)

The government will decide on Sunday that a commission of inquiry investigate the inner workings of Israel's leading banks, with respect to the 'bank shares affair.' (January 4)

•

Sempo Sugihara, a Japanese diplomat posted in Lithuania who had defied his government's orders in 1940 and issued transit visas that saved nearly 6,000 Jews in World War II, was decorated in Tokyo with the Yad Vashem medal. (January 18)

•

Eight Jewish twins returned to Auschwitz for the first time in 40 years to re-enact the forced 'death march,' which took place before the camp was liberated by the Russians. Out of 750 pairs of twins used by Dr. Josef Mengele (the 'angel of death') in pseudo-medical experiments, only 180 children survived; 2,500,000 Jews perished in Auschwitz during the war. (January 27)

•

Israel's first HIV positive diagnosis. The woman was infected by a blood transfusion at Hadassah Hospital, Jerusalem. (January 29)

•

Gibraltar's frontier is opened, after a 16-year siege initiated by Franco in 1969 in an attempt to force Britain to surrender the colony. Spain's imminent entry to the EEC prompted the opening of the border. (February 3)

•

An 'Ariane-3' rocket launched a communications satellite called 'Arabsat' for the Arab League, that is intended to provide telecommunications services to its 22 countries in the Middle East and North Africa. (February 8)

•

Nelson Mandela rejects the South African authorities' proposal to set him free. (February 10)

•

Prime Minister Shimon Peres will have an audience with Pope John Paul II. (February 17)

•

Researchers estimate that 400,000 Americans have been infected with HIV. (February 21)

•

Ariel Sharon's libel suit against 'Time' magazine ends. The jury decides that the magazine published inaccurate facts unintentionally. (February 22)

Ethiopian Jews Arrive in Israel

The first minutes in Israel. 6,000 Jews were brought from Ethiopia.

On Jan. 4, the dramatic operation to airlift thousands of Ethiopian Jews was made public. During 'Operation Moses,' which continued for some months, more than 6,000 Jews were brought to Israel.

The secret operation began at the end of 1984, after years of drought and Ethiopian army persecution had convinced Israeli leaders that the Jewish Ethiopian community must be brought to Israel.

Once the decision had been taken, the *Mossad* started to organize a base of helpers in Sudan, who assisted in bringing the Ethiopian Jews to Sudan.

The Jews, most of whom had lived in deserted villages, made the long journey - up to hundreds of kilometers - on foot. They were placed in special camps in Sudan and at the end of 1984 were flown to Israel on European charter flights. The government of Sudan also assisted, in response to the intervention of the US Administration.

The operation was made public prior to its completion. The authorities in Ethiopia were caught by surprise and immediately tried to snipe at convoys. Sudan stopped allowing flights to take off from its territory.

The Arab world raged against Sudanese cooperation with Israel, and threatened to boycott Sudan.

The US quickly provided help, and American aircraft brought the final immigrants to Israel.

Most of the Jews arrived in Israel in bad health, suffering from severe cases of malnutrition. Some were hospitalized and the rest were dispersed into absorption centers throughout the country.

Israel Withdraws from the Lebanon

Following a government decision made on Jan. 14, the IDF began pulling back from Lebanon. The evacuation was made in three stages. The first stage, taking five weeks, included the evacuation of Sidon and Nabatiyeh. After four weeks, the IDF left the eastern sector and settled in the Hatzbiyeh village area. The third stage was planned for June, and included establishing an international border and a security zone jointly with the South Lebanon Army.

The decision to leave Lebanon was extremely controversial. Almost all *Likud* ministers, headed by Yitzhak Shamir, opposed the decision, which was passed thanks to the vote of Labor ministers and other supporters of Peres.

However, a poll revealed that over 90% of the population supported the decision.

Parting from Beirut.

Residents of the north claimed that the IDF was neglecting the Galilee and that pulling back from Lebanon would encourage terrorism and give the terrorists a sense of victory. Left-wingers, on the other hand, demanded the IDF's immediate evacuation from Lebanon to the international border, without any interim stages being implemented.

The evacuation was completed in June. Throughout, the IDF dealt with dozens of heavy terror attacks, costing the lives of many soldiers.

Jibril Deal: Three Soldiers in Exchange for 1,150 Terrorists

After three years of captivity, Hezi Shai, Nissim Salem, and Yosef Groff were swapped on May 20 for 1,150 terrorists imprisoned in Israel. Groff and Salem were captured with six other *Nahal* soldiers who had meanwhile been released. Hezi Shai was captured in the battle of Sultan Ya'acoub in the Lebanon War. All three were held by Ahmed Jibril's organization.

Among the terrorists also released by Israel was Kozo Okamoto, the Japanese who had taken part in the slaughter at Lod airport in 1972. Similarly freed were the terrorists responsible for the 1969 murder of 11 people in the explosion at Jerusalem's Mahane Yehuda market, those who hijacked the 'bus on the coastal highway in 1978 in which 35 were killed, and many others.

In Israel, harsh criticism was lev-

Defense Minister Yitzhak Rabin, welcoming Nissim Salem, one of the returned captives.

eled at the government because of the high price paid for the return of the three captives. Hundreds of settlers demonstrated opposite the home of Prime Minister Shimon Peres. Deputy Prime Minister Yitz-

hak Shamir and other Likud ministers demanded that members of the Jewish underground also be released. Many Knesset members from the Alignment and left-wing factions also criticized the decision.

Habonim Tragedy. 19 Children Killed in Collision with Train

Nineteen seventh-grade schoolchildren from Brenner School in Petah Tikva were killed on June 11 when a 'bus collided with a train close to Moshav Habonim. The 'bus driver, one teacher and one armed escort were also killed; sixteen were wounded, most of them seriously.

The Brenner schoolchildren had left in four 'buses for a trip to Habonim beach in the north. As required, the 'bus driver had stopped before the crossing, then began to move slowly, but did not manage to cross in time. The train, on its way from Haifa, crashed into the 'bus.

A commission of inquiry appointed to investigate the affair found

Police at the site of the tragedy immediately after the collision.

many deficiencies in safety procedures for school journeys and in the

marking of dangerous junctions and railway crossings.

Boat Sunk en Route to Attack

A terrorist boat, on its way to carry out an attack in Tel Aviv, was sunk by a naval missile ship, 100 km *(63 miles)* from shore, on Apr. 20. The boat had left Algeria the previous day, bearing no identification marks.

Aboard the *'Atavirus'* were 28 terrorists, who had planned to disturb the Independence Day celebrations about to take place in Israel

that week. Eight terrorists were retrieved from the sea.

Under investigation, the eight captured men said that they had been sent to bomb three population centers and to negotiate the release of terrorists held in Israel.

The investigation revealed that the unit had been sent by Abu Jihad, the head of the military section of the PLO, who had told them to kill

as many Jews as possible. They had been trained at the PLO headquarters of 'Force 17' in Tunis, and were considered to be elite members of that organization.

The commander, one of the survivors, told a press conference that their ultimate goal had been to take over army staff headquarters in Tel Aviv and to try to release 150 terrorists held captive in Israel.

Marc Chagall died at his home aged 97. He was one of the greatest Jewish artists of all times. Amongst his artworks, he designed the mosaics and Gobelins for the *Knesset's* reception hall that depict the entire panorama of Jewish history. (March 28)

●

The first Jewish history book in Serbo-Croat was published recently in Yugoslavia. The 490 pages follow the history of the Jews from biblical times to the present day. (April 11)

●

The US and Israel signed a free trade agreement that is to eliminate all trade barriers between the two within the next ten years. (April 22)

●

President Reagan arrived in Germany on a tour that included a visit to the Bitburg cemetery where 49 SS soldiers are buried. Some 300 demonstrators protested the visit. A banner read: "No rehabilitation for the SS - they are murderers not victims." (May 1)

●

Forty-two people were killed in disturbances that broke out in Belgium between Liverpool and Juventus supporters before the European Cup soccer final. Most of the injured were Italians crushed in fights between the supporters. (May 29)

●

A body said to be that of Dr. Josef Mengele of Auschwitz was exhumed in Embu, Brazil. International experts agreed the body was that of Mengele's, although some people still doubt the findings. (June 6)

●

The final stage of the evacuation from Lebanon has been concluded. As the last soldiers arrived in Kiryat Shmona, two *Katyusha* rockets fired from Lebanon landed on the town. (June 10)

●

A TWA flight was hijacked en route from Athens to Rome. The Shi'ite hijackers demanded that Israel release 700 Shi'ites held in Israel in exchange for the 39 passengers. Israel released 31 Shi'ites as a gesture to help negotiations. After 17 days the hostages flew out of Damascus. Shortly afterwards Israel released 300 Shi'ites in what was claimed to be unrelated to the hijacking. (June 14)

IAF Bombs PLO in Tunis

On Oct. 1, the Israel Air Force attacked three PLO headquarters buildings in Tunis, wounding 156 PLO employees, in retaliation for the murder of the Israelis in the Cypriot port of Larnaca. PLO leaders, among them Yasser Arafat, were saved. Abu-Tayeb, the 'Force 17' commander responsible for Yasser Arafat's own security, was killed in the bombing.

The Tunis attack took place further away than any operation ever executed by the IAF: 2,460 kilometers (1540 miles) from Israel. The 'planes refueled in mid-air, during the five-hour flight.

The entire Cabinet, headed by Prime Minister Shimon Peres, had been in favor of the operation, with one exception, Ezer Weizman, who was worried about repercussions on Israeli-Egyptian relations.

Most countries in the world, except the United States, condemned the operation. President Ronald Reagan sent Peres a cable expressing satisfaction.

Egyptian Soldier Kills Seven Israelis on Ras Burka Beach

Seven tourists, including four children, were killed, and three children were wounded on Oct. 5 when an Egyptian soldier sitting in a guard post opened fire on a group of Israelis strolling on Ras Burka beach in the Sinai.

The Israeli tourists, most of them from Jerusalem, were vacationing in Sinai. They were staying on the beach, and from there walked in the direction of the Shaham panoramic viewpoint, a sandy hill overlooking the beach. The Egyptian soldier, who was sitting at the Shaham look-out post, opened fire at close range. The evacuation of the dead and wounded took a considerable time.

The Egyptian gunman had been involved in the past in a number of shooting incidents, firing at Israeli boats near the Coral Reef. An orthodox Moslem, the soldier began to fire immediately after finishing his prayers. He accompanied the shooting with shouts of "Allah u-Akbar" (Allah is Great). The official Egyptian version stated he was deranged.

The body of one of the tourists is returned to Israel.

Terrorists Capture 'Achille Lauro.' Three Israeli Yachtsmen Murdered

On Oct. 7, 12 terrorists from the National Front for the Liberation of Palestine captured the Italian liner, 'Achille Lauro,' which had been sailing on the high seas, some 50 kilometers (31 miles) from Port Said. The terrorists demanded that Israel release 50 'Force 17' terrorists from Israeli jails. They announced that they had booby-trapped the vessel and any attempt to take control would cause the devices to be activated. The boat was carrying 800 passengers at the time.

When the Syrian authorities refused to grant the terrorists permission to enter their territorial waters, they headed for Cyprus and announced by radio wireless that they had started to kill the passengers. On the instructions of PLO headquarters to end the hijacking, the terrorists ordered the boat to Port Said, where they surrendered.

An hour after the hijacking ended, it emerged that the terrorists had murdered a Jewish-American invalid passenger, Leon Klinghoffer, in cold blood. When the Syrians had refused to permit the vessel to enter their territorial waters, the terrorists had pushed Klinghoffer, in his wheelchair, over the deck into the sea.

Two weeks earlier, on Sept. 25, three terrorists had commandeered a yacht moored in Larnaca, Cyprus and murdered the three Israelis on it.

The murder, which took place on Yom Kippur, shocked Israel. A week later, many yacht owners took part in a sail from Haifa to Larnaca in memory of the victims.

Three Israelis were murdered on this yacht in Cyprus.

Pollard Arrested in United States

Pollard. Sent away from the embassy.

Jonathan Pollard, an American Jew who worked for Naval Intelligence and spied for Israel, was arrested on Nov. 21. Pollard tried to request political asylum at the Israeli Embassy in Washington, but was expelled by security staff there. FBI agents were waiting for him outside the embassy's doors.

Pollard worked in a counter-terror intelligence unit, and was exposed after colleagues noticed that he was taking an interest in information unconnected to his field of work. A colleague turned to the FBI, whose agents began to trail Pollard. After a short time, he was summoned to an internal intelligence investigation, admitted passing on classified information to Israel, but said he had not received financial reward A search of his home revealed classified documents. Pollard promised to lead his investigators to his Israeli accomplices and on the basis of that promise he was not arrested at that stage.

Pollard's imprisonment caused one of the most severe crises in Israeli-American relations. The Americans decided to cancel the planned official visit to Washington of a senior Israeli public figure which had been scheduled for that time.

The affair caused great embarrassment in Israel, especially when it emerged that the security services' chiefs knew nothing of the Israeli spy's Washington operations. Pollard had been recruited and handled by a secret office set up by Rafi Eitan, a senior Mossad operative.

Israel recalled a number of senior diplomats involved in the affair, as a result of the disclosure, among them Aviam Sela, a senior IAF officer who had been Pollard's handler. Sela had been one of the IAF's outstanding pilots, commanding the IAF squadron which had destroyed the atomic reactor in Iraq five years earlier. He was now depicted in the United States as America's 'Public Enemy No. 1,' after Jonathan Pollard.

Pollard was sentenced in the US to life imprisonment. Despite countless requests from Israel, all American presidents have refused to pardon the spy, or allow a prisoner exchange.

Sela. The handler.

Eitan. The recruiter.

Reagan. No pardon.

Terror Against Israelis in Europe

Seventeen El Al passengers traveling to Israel were killed in two terror attacks carried out on Dec. 27 at Rome and Vienna airports.

At nine o'clock in the morning three terrorists entered the cafeteria at Rome airport, opened fire and hurled hand grenades in all directions. Fifteen were killed and 70 wounded in the attack. Israeli security staff killed two of the attackers, and the Italians eliminated the other.

At 11:30 a.m., three terrorists broke into the departure lounge at Vienna airport, throwing grenades and firing from automatic weapons on travelers waiting by the El Al counter. Israeli security agents returned fire. Two passengers were killed, among them an Israeli citizen, and 39 wounded, 20 seriously. The terrorists escaped by car and were arrested after a chase in which there was an exchange of fire.

1985
NOVEMBER - DECEMBER

At least 25,000 people die in a volcanic eruption in Colombia. The city Amero and its vicinity were completely destroyed by the eruption of the volcano Nevado del Ruiz, which lasted several days. (November 13)

•

President Reagan and Soviet leader Gorbachev met in Geneva for the first summit in six years. The two established a good personal rapport. Both seemed keen to overcome the deep mistrust which marked relations since the Soviet invasion of Afghanistan in 1979. The Soviets indicated they no longer demanded concessions on Star Wars. The two leaders agreed to one summit a year. (November 19)

•

An Egypt Air flight was hijacked from Athens to Malta Saturday. Maltese officials reported 59 people were killed during an Egyptian commando rescue attempt, 30 others were wounded. An American and an Israeli were shot by the terrorists and died from their wounds. (November 24)

•

President Reagan has signed legislation that formally postpones a $1.98 billion arms sale to Jordan. Reagan said that the arms would not be sold to Jordan unless it commenced serious peace talks with Israel. (November 27)

•

American Motors announce that the World War II work horse, the *Jeep*, is going out of production in January. *'Jeep'* is a nickname for GP, general purpose vehicles. The *Jeep* started coming off the production line in November 1940. (November 28)

•

The widow of opposition leader Benino Aquino, Corazon Aquino 52, declares her candidacy in the Filipino elections set for February 7 by incumbent President Ferdinand Marcos. (December 3)

•

Court in Argentina convicts five former military leaders (including former president Jorge Vidales who receives a sentence of life imprisonment), of using criminal methods against leftist guerrillas during the military junta from 1976-1983 when at least 6,000 disappeared after being kidnapped by security forces. (December 10)

1985 sees fewest immigrants since Israel's establishment. There were 11,298 new immigrants with the previous low at 11,326 in 1953. (January 5)

•

Israel awarded honorary citizenship to Raoul Wallenberg. Wallenberg was first secretary of the Swedish Embassy in Budapest from July 1944 and helped save thousands of Jews from deportation by giving them Swedish documents. The Soviets arrested him in 1945 and he has not been seen since. (January 16)

•

US space program suffers a severe blow when the 'Challenger' space shuttle explodes a few seconds after blast-off. All seven astronauts perished, among them the first Jewish astronaut, Judith Resnik, 36, who was on her second flight. (January 28)

•

South Africa aborted the release of imprisoned black nationalist leader Nelson Mandela as part of an East-West prisoner swap, claiming that Pretoria's conditions for the release had not been met. (February 11)

•

The Soviets send into orbit a large new space station called 'Mir' (peace). (February 20)

•

Prime Minister of Sweden Olof Palme is assassinated in a street in Stockholm. An urban guerrilla group claimed responsibility for the deed. (February 28)

•

John Demjanjuk was extradited from the US and escorted to Israel by two American policemen. He was immediately driven away in an armed convoy from Ben-Gurion Airport to the Jerusalem prison. (February 28)

•

The World Jewish Congress produced documents proving Kurt Waldheim was a member of General Alexander Loehr's staff in Salonika. The general was responsible for the deportation of 42,000 Greek Jews to the camps in World War II and the massacre of thousands of Yugoslav civilians. WJC President Edgar Bronfman said that Waldheim, former UN Secretary General and Austrian presidential candidate, had engaged in "one of the most elaborate deceptions of our times." (March 5).

Released Sharansky Arrives in Israel

Received a hero's welcome.

The battle for the release of *Prisoner of Zion*, Anatoly Sharansky, ended on Feb. 11 in a prisoner exchange. Soviet agents were released from prisons in the US and Europe, in exchange for Sharansky and three agents from the West.

Sharansky, a brilliant mathematician, became for many a symbol of Soviet oppression of Jews. He had been spokesman for the *Prisoners of Zion* group of *refuseniks*, and as such had many contacts with foreign correspondents. He was refused permission by the authorities to emigrate to Israel as early as 1974. He was tried and convicted of spying for the US and sent to labor camps for many years, under extremely harsh conditions. His wife, Avital, was able to emigrate to Israel years before her husband was released and campaigned tirelessly for his release.

After spending some years putting his private affairs in order, Sharansky, disappointed with government handling of Soviet immigrants, decided to enter the political arena. In the 1996 elections, his party, Yisrael be Aliya, won seven Knesset seats, and he was appointed minister of trade and industry in the Netanyahu government.

Lebanon: 2 Israeli Soldiers Kidnapped

Rahamim Elsheikh.

Yosef Fink.

Two soldiers were kidnapped on Feb. 17 by a *Hizbullah* unit which ambushed an Israeli civilian convoy in South Lebanon. Rahamim Elsheikh and Yosef Fink, two soldiers from *yeshivot hesder (religious students who, by special arrangement, serve in the IDF)*, were attached to the convoy as security officers. The *Hizbullah* team activated an explosive device as the second vehicle in the convoy passed. Two SLA *(South Lebanese Army)* soldiers were killed in the explosion and one IDF officer was seriously wounded.

Having activated the device, the terrorists succeeded in kidnapping the two soldiers who were lying wounded among the destroyed remains of the vehicle.

The IDF reacted swiftly but did not manage, to trace the kidnappers and their prisoners. Large forces immediately entered South Lebanon where they combed all villages in the area. After the first day's search, Hizbullah announced that it would kill the prisoners if the IDF remained in Lebanon. After the third day Hizbullah announced that its fighters had killed one of the soldiers. During the searches, scores of Hizbullah terrorists and two IDF soldiers were killed.

Hava Ya'ari Arrested

Hava Ya'ari.

Hava Ya'ari and Aviva Granot were arrested on Jan. 12 on suspicion of having murdered the tourist Mella Malevsky a few days previously on Tel Aviv's Tel Baruch beach. Chief Inspector Michel Haddad was put in charge of the investigation.

Granot and Ya'ari were tried and convicted of murder. During the trial it became clear that the motive for the murder was Malevsky's money ($50,000). They had taken Malevsky to the beach in their car, where they beat her and reversed a car over her, causing her death. The two women received life sentences.

The GSS Affair: The Attorney General and GSS Chief Resign

The 'Bus No. 300 Affair' began with the GSS killing of two terrorists whom the GSS had captured alive after the terrorists had attacked a hijacked 'bus No. 300, in April 1984. This scandal led to the GSS Affair, which caused the resignation of the Attorney General, Yitzhak Zamir, and the replacement of the GSS chief, Avraham Shalom.

On May 25, the attorney general suggested that Shalom and other senior officers in the organization be tried for having concealed evidence from the commission of inquiry investigating the terrorists' death.

The attorney general launched an investigation, following information that reached him from senior GSS operatives, during which it emerged that the service chiefs had covered up evidence and blamed the killing on Brig.-Gen. Yitzhak Mordechai, Commanding Officer of the Paratroopers Brigade. Mordechai had been tried and had admitted to beating them during the investigation. He had been acquitted of responsibility for their deaths and had been promoted to major-general.

At the beginning of 1986, following internal struggles within the organization, three of its top agents (Reuven Hazak, Peleg Radai and Rafi Malka) exposed the true story

Yitzhak Zamir after announcing his resignation.

and the fabrication of evidence by high-ranking GSS operatives. The trio claimed that the GSS chief had ordered one of the service's senior officers to kill the terrorists, and that another senior officer, Yossi Ginossar, had been party to the fabrication of evidence submitted to the Zorea Commission.

Avraham Shalom responded by suspending them. The three applied to Attorney General Yitzhak Zamir, demanding an investigation. Prime Minister Shimon Peres and Foreign Minister Yitzhak Shamir tried to prevent Zamir from conducting an investigation, and the affair was turned

over to the police. A panel headed by Commissioner David Kraus questioned the prime minister and foreign minister, senior GSS operatives and others. During the investigation, the GSS chief claimed that he had received clear instructions from Yitzhak Shamir (prime minister at the time). At that stage, having been prevented from continuing to investigate the affair, the attorney general resigned from his post.

Eventually, following the intervention of Adv. Ram Caspi, it was decided to accept the resignation of the GSS chief, in return for which he and his officers were pardoned.

Historic Meeting in Morocco

Prime Minister Shimon Peres arrived on July 22 for a surprise visit to the palace of King Hassan of Morocco. The 48-hour visit took place after secret contacts over a number of weeks, and was part of the king's initiative to obtain a declaration from Israel that it would make concessions in the region.

The pair conducted three rounds of talks during the visit, but did not reach any significant agreement. The visit's primary importance lay in its lack of secrecy and King Hassan's declaration of intent.

The king and prime minister at the palace. In the center, Rafi Edri.

Chernobyl Reactor Tragedy

More than 10,000 people perished on May 1 in a radioactive disaster which was the worst disaster of its kind ever to take place. The atomic reactor in Chernobyl, near Kiev in

the Soviet Union, began to leak, and the reactor's core exploded.

In addition to those killed by the explosion, hundreds of thousands were injured by radioactive fall-out.

The entire continent of Europe panicked at the prospect of radioactive rain. All cities close to the reactor were evacuated. To this day, many people still develop various cancers.

The United States bombed terrorist bases in Libya following the downing of an American TWA passenger jet. The US action damaged facilities in Libya such as command installations, logistical bases and training camps. Libyan backing of the terrorist bombing of a Berlin discotheque frequented by American soldiers, in which two were killed and 191 wounded, also came to light. (April 14)

●

A suitcase containing explosives prepared by a Syrian agent was discovered in the cargo hold of an El Al jet in London. The suitcase belonged to an Irish tourist who did not know that the suitcase given her by her Syrian boyfriend was packed with explosives. (April 17)

●

Marcel Dassault, father of France's modern air industry and designer of the *Mirage,* died in Paris at 94. (April 18)

●

At least four men attacked Interpol's headquarters in Paris. Pamphlets of the left-wing terrorist organization *'Action Directe'* were found at the scene. (May 16)

●

After many years of controversy, the Berlin municipality decided to turn the villa in Wannsee into a memorial site. It was there that the Nazis took the decision on the final solution of the Jewish problem 44 years ago. (June 5)

●

Kurt Waldheim won Austria's presidential elections despite revelations about his military activities in World War II. (June 8)

●

A flotilla of ships paid their respects to the renovated *Statue of Liberty,* as the presidents of the United States and France rekindled the monument's torch. The statue, a gift from France, had been originally unveiled on October 28, 1886. (July 3)

●

The father of the nuclear submarine, Admiral Hyman Rickover, died at 86. The first nuclear submarine, *'Nautilus,'* was launched in 1954. (July 7)

●

Twenty two are slain in Istanbul's central synagogue. The two terrorists' bodies are found dead among the carnage and destruction. (September 6)

The House of Congress overturns President Reagan's veto of a bill imposing sanctions on South Africa due to South Africa's apartheid policy. (October 2)

•

President Reagan and Secretary Gorbachev begin their summit at Reykjavik, Iceland. The Soviets insist that anti-missile research be confined to the laboratory. Reagan declares: "This we could not and will not do." (October 11)

•

Elie Wiesel wins the 1986 Nobel Peace Prize. The prize committee said that his message is one of peace, atonement and human dignity and is based on personal experience in Hitler's camps. Wiesel's commitment, originating in the suffering of the Jewish people, has widened to embrace all repressed peoples and races in the world. (October 14)

•

Britain severed its diplomatic relations with Syria over its involvement in an attempt to blow up an El Al jumbo with 380 passengers last April. Nizar Hindawi, who hid the bomb in Ann Murphy's belongings, was sentenced to 45 years imprisonment. (October 25)

•

President Reagan confirms that he authorized the shipment of US arms to Iran, but insists it was to influence a post-Khomeini power struggle rather than 'ransom' for the release of American hostages in Lebanon. (November 13)

•

President Reagan announced the resignation of National Security Adviser John Poindexter and Lieutenant-Colonel Oliver North over the disclosure that $30 million from the proceeds of authorized arms sales to Iran were diverted secretly, with Israel's aid, to finance the 'Contras' in Nicaragua. (November 25)

•

The dissident physicist Andrei Sakharov is freed from internal exile in Gorky in the Soviet Union. (December 19)

•

Following a High Court of Justice decision that the minister of interior has no authority to add the word 'convert' to the religion box on an identity card, the minister, Rabbi Yitzhak Peretz, resigned. (December 31)

Vanunu Hijacked to Israel

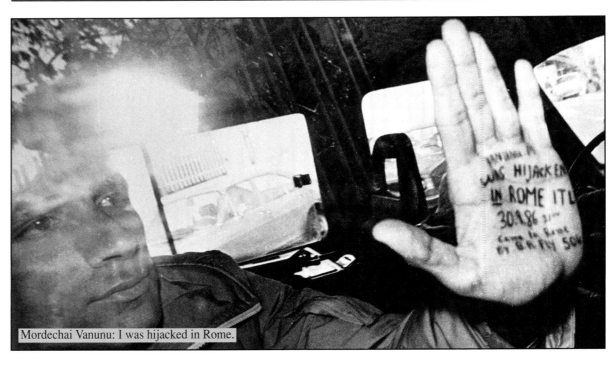

Mordechai Vanunu: I was hijacked in Rome.

Mordechai Vanunu, the young man working at the Dimona nuclear reactor who exposed Israel's nuclear secrets, was hijacked in Rome on Oct. 26, and sent by boat to Israel, according to overseas publications.

Vanunu smuggled abroad photographs and information about Israel's nuclear capability, details of which were carried by the British 'Sunday Times' newspaper.

Some months previously, a Co-lombian journalist had revealed photographs of the Israeli nuclear reactor which he had been given by Vanunu, whom he said was in hiding.

A journalist from the newspaper was sent to Australia, where he received corroborative documents. Vanunu was flown to London, where he met with British nuclear scientists, who became convinced that his information was authentic.

Shortly after, the article was pub-lished and Vanunu disappeared. Later, Shimon Peres admitted he was in Israel, but refused to disclose details.

It emerged that Vanunu had been tempted by a female Mossad agent to fly for a lover's meeting from London to Rome, where he was drugged, kidnapped and taken to Israel. He was tried and convicted of espionage and passing on classified information, and was sentenced to 18 years' imprisonment.

Ron Arad is Captured

During an attack on terrorist targets south of Sidon, a *Phantom* jet participating in the operation was hit. The two crew members bailed out. The pilot was swiftly rescued by military helicopters. The navigator, Ron Arad, was captured.

Immediately after his capture, Arad was taken to one of the *Shi'ite* organization's factions, whose leader Nabih Berri announced that he was holding the navigator. Contact with Arad was maintained for the first two years; letters and video cassettes arrived in Israel, and with the help of European mediators, negotiations

were conducted for his release.

This was to be the beginning of

Ron Arad: 11 years in captivity.

one of Israel's most painful affairs. Eleven years after he was captured there is still no information about the fate of the captured navigator.

Ron Arad was held for two and a half years by Amal, was later transferred to the Hizbullah, and subsequently disappeared.

Over the years, Israel has kidnapped a number of senior Hizbullah operatives in order to find out what happened to Arad, and to try to use them as hostages, but in vain. Israel continues to hold Iran responsible for his fate, as sponsor of Hizbullah's operations.

Premiership Rotation

The national unity government reached the middle of its term of office. Despite many prior doubts as to whether the rotation agreement would be kept, on Oct. 20, Prime Minister Shimon Peres gave up his place to Foreign Minister Yitzhak

Shamir. Yitzhak Rabin continued to serve as minister of defense in the Shamir government.

The coalition agreement was postponed for ten days following a series of coalition crises and mutual recrimination between the *Likud* and

the Alignment. Nevertheless, Peres fulfilled the agreement signed two years previously.

Peres achieved two of his main objectives: the IDF left Lebanon, and inflation, which had reached 400% in 1984, was reduced to 48%.

Demjanjuk Trial Opens

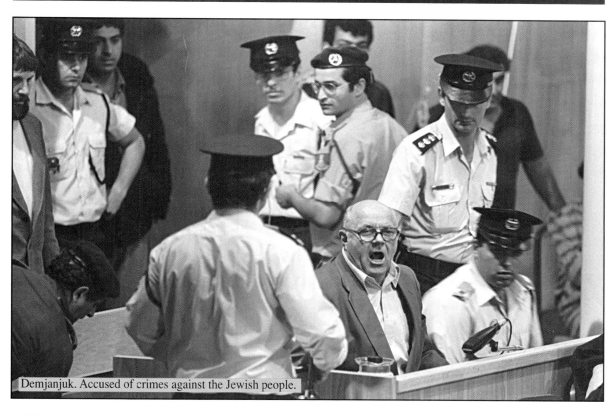

Demjanjuk. Accused of crimes against the Jewish people.

For the second time in the history of the State, someone accused of crimes against the Jewish people during the Second World War has been indicted in Israel.

John Demjanjuk has been accused of having operated the gas chamber in the Treblinka death camp in Poland, and having caused the death of some 900,000 Jews. He has also been accused of having sadistically abused hundreds of Jews and

of having killed them with his bare hands. His trial opened on Feb. 15, presided over by Supreme Court Judge Dov Levin. State Prosecutor Yona Blatman demanded a sentence identical to that imposed on Adolf Eichmann: death by hanging. The American defense attorney, Mark O'Connor, claimed that Demjanjuk was not 'Ivan the Terrible.' He based his claim on documents which showed that Demjanjuk had been

imprisoned in a Ukrainian POW camp, and could not therefore have carried out the alleged deeds.

The trial had been intended to last six months, but continued for more than three years. Demjanjuk was convicted and sentenced to death; only after four more years did the Supreme Court decide to acquit him because of grounds of reasonable doubt and deport him back to the United States.

Ernst Japhet Pension Scandal

Israel was in a state of shock on Jan. 2, following the disclosure of details of Ernst Japhet's conditions of retirement. Japhet, who had been chairman of the board of directors of Bank Leumi and one of the most powerful people in the Israeli economy, was forced to retire after publication of the Beijski report. He received retirement compensation of millions of shekels, and an enormous pension of $30,000 per month.

Japhet.

Additional details of the bank's all-powerful chairman's financial compensation slowly emerged, as well as the fact that he himself had sanctioned these exceptional terms.

Following these revelations, the bank's employees went on strike, and senior bank executives resigned. Ten days later, Japhet left Israel for New York, where he remained until returning in 1993 to stand trial. Ernst Japhet died in 1997.

'Molotov Cocktail' Hurled at Car. Alfei Menashe Mother Dies

On Apr. 11, terrorists hurled a *'Molotov cocktail'* at the car of the Moses family, traveling on the road from Kalkilya to their home in Alfei Menashe. The fire killed Ofra and

Tal Moses, and wounded Ofra's husband Avraham, her children Nir and Adi, and another child who had been in the car. Ofra Moses, 34, had been four months' pregnant.

Avraham Moses escaped from the car while he himself was completely alight. Ofra did not succeed in undoing her safety belt and was trapped in the car. She burned to death.

Speaking at a Dead Sea hotel, the prime minister invited King Hussein to cross the water and conduct direct peace negotiations with him. (January 8)

Beirut's hostage crisis deepened yesterday as Britain launched a search for Anglican envoy Terry Waite. According to a Moslem religious source, Waite was abducted because he failed to secure more arms for Iran. (January 28)

Prisoner of Zion Yosef Begun was freed from prison. He was sentenced in 1983 to seven years imprisonment and five years exile for anti-Soviet activity. (February 15)

Prime Minister Yitzhak Shamir announced that despite American opposition, Israel intends to continue with the *Lavi* project. The United States subsequently stated that it would grant Israel some $400,000 million as compensation for its expenses in connection with the 'plane. (February 18)

Jewish and Catholic leaders finally reached an agreement to move the Carmelite nuns' convent from Auschwitz. Jewish leaders and communities had felt it inappropriate at the memorial site for the Jewish dead. (February 22)

Mikhail Gorbachev made a fresh attack on opponents of *Glasnost* saying that more democracy was essential to stop the Soviet Union from lapsing into stagnation. (February 25)

Comedian Danny Kaye died aged 74. Kaye was a man of true Jewish spirit and a true friend of Israel. He was also a roving ambassador for UNICEF. (March 2)

Soviet policy shows signs of softening as 1,000 Jews a month are now leaving the Soviet Union. (April 1)

Primo Levi, best-selling novelist and survivor of Auschwitz, committed suicide at 67. His book 'Survival in Auschwitz' was an international bestseller. (April 11)

US puts Austrian President Kurt Waldheim on 'watch list,' barring entry to US pending investigation into World War II activities, and service as a *gauleiter*. (April 27)

The trial of Klaus Barbie opens. Barbie, head of the Gestapo in Lyon and known as the 'Butcher of Lyon,' was extradited from Bolivia to France in 1983. Barbie was found guilty of crimes against humanity and sentenced to life imprisonment. (May 11)

●

The USS 'Stark' is attacked by an Iraqi Exocet missile while on routine patrol in the Persian Gulf. Thirty-seven crew are killed. Iraq expresses profound regret for the attack. (May 17)

●

Mathias Rust, 19, flew a Cessna from Finland and landed in Moscow's Red Square. Soviet Defense Minister Sergei Sokolov and head of the air force Alexander Kuldonov were dismissed. (May 28)

●

Israel's Ambassador to the UN, Binyamin Netanyahu, succeeded in obtaining from UN archives the files of 489 war criminals, among them senior Gestapo officers, concentration camp commanders and senior Nazi government officials who were responsible for the implementation of the 'Final Solution.' (June 8)

●

Margaret Thatcher and the Conservatives won the British elections for the third time. (June 11)

●

Yuli Edelstein, former Prisoner of Zion, arrives in Israel with his family after nine years of being a 'refusenik.' In 1996 he became Israel's Minister of Absorption (in Yisrael be' Aliya party). (July 12)

●

The US Navy begins escorts of oil tankers in the Persian Gulf where they are threatened by Iranian attacks. (July 21)

●

As many as 300 Iranian pilgrims were killed during the Hajj to Mecca, as thousands of pilgrims blocked others from reaching the Ka'aba. They switched from religious hymns to political slogans and refused to disperse as the Saudi riot police ordered. (August 1)

●

Rudolf Hess, Hitler's deputy until his peace flight to Britain in May 1941, commits suicide in Spandau prison. He was sentenced to life imprisonment by the Nuremberg tribunal in 1946. (August 17)

20 Years after the Six-Day War: Serious Riots in the Territories

A weekend of particularly severe violence took place in Judea and Samaria, marking 20 years since the end of the Six-Day War and five years since the Lebanon War. One youth was killed in Nablus and five residents were wounded in the disturbances of June 5 and 6.

A large group of settlers from Kiryat Arba burst into the Dehaisheh refugee camp near Bethlehem and damaged much property belonging to local residents. The settlers also beat soldiers who were summoned to the camp.

There were partial strikes on commerce. PLO flags were unfurled and Israeli flags burnt in Ramallah, Nablus, Hebron and East Jerusalem. A 15-year-old youth was killed in the refugee camp Eskar near Nablus. People were also wounded in Nablus, Abu Dis and Kabatiyeh.

In Kabatiyeh, a petrol bomb was thrown at an Israeli car, shattering its windscreen, but not wounding anyone. Those responsible were arrested shortly afterwards.

It seemed, with hindsight, that these disturbances were some sort of preparation for the 'Intifada' (the 'Uprising') that was to break out six months later.

The *Lavi* Project Halted

Would no longer take off. The *Lavi*.

The government decided on Aug. 30, by a majority of 12 to 11, to halt the Lavi project. Minister of Health Shoshana Arbeli-Almoslino abstained. Immediately after the decision, Israel Aircraft Industries employees began to demonstrate throughout the country. Thousands blocked roads and junctions, and clashed with hundreds of policemen who tried unsuccessfully to disperse them.

Only after two stormy days did the demonstrators leave, once Prime Minister Yitzhak Shamir had promised them, inaccurately, that they would not be affected by the cancellation of the project.

The Lavi project had begun five years earlier, when it had been decided to develop an Israeli-made fighter aircraft to be the main combat aircraft for the year 2000. However, an American study revealed the project would cost hundreds of percent more than planned, sales would be limited, and that from an economic viewpoint there was no point in developing the Lavi.

The cancellation of the project took place amid a confrontation between Likud ministers, headed by Defense Minister Moshe Arens, who demanded the continuation of the project, and Alignment ministers, among them Yitzhak Rabin, who opposed the continuation of its development. As a result of the cancellation, 4,000 employees were dismissed from Israel Aircraft Industries.

After the government decision to halt the Lavi project, the United States undertook to increase defense assistance, pay external debts linked to the project and supply Israel with 150 advanced F-16's.

Three *Givati* Soldiers Killed in South Lebanon

On Sept. 15, three soldiers, including an operations commander and his deputy, were killed in a clash between Givati soldiers and a terrorist cell. Four soldiers were wounded.

The 15-man cell was on its way from its base in Syrian-controlled territory to carry out an attack at an IDF post along the northern border.

The 'Intifada' Breaks Out

Six years of rebellion. Children of rocks confront IDF soldiers.

The people's rebellion in the territories, known as the 'Intifada' (the 'Uprising') began on Dec. 9 with serious disturbances in the Gaza Strip, following a road accident in which four residents of the Jebalya refugee camp were killed. The camp's residents claimed that a Jewish truck driver deliberately hit them, in revenge for the murder of a soldier in the Gaza Strip two days earlier.

The disturbances spread from the Gaza Strip to Judea and Samaria. A patrol unit was attacked with stones in the Nablus casbah and was forced to open fire and kill one of the demonstrators. In the Gaza Strip, a child was killed and 15 demonstrators were wounded by gunfire from Israeli soldiers. Six policemen were wounded during the dispersal of schoolchildren who were demonstrating in Kalandiya to the north of Jerusalem.

The 'Intifada' brought tens of thousands of Palestinians out onto the streets. The army facing them tried to adapt itself to a new situation. In response to the stones and petrol bombs, the soldiers fired rubber and plastic bullets and live ammunition, and used truncheons and gravel cannon. Groups of rioters - soldiers disguised as Arabs - operated among the demonstrators trying to trace the leaders of the revolt.

Within weeks the riots and confrontations between demonstrators and the army had intensified. Thousands of Palestinians were arrested on suspicion of disturbing the peace, and incitement. Detention camps were set up at a number of central locations in the territories and thousands of prisoners streamed into them. The IDF established a special detention camp in order to absorb them all.

By the end of December, there were 21 Palestinians dead, and 179 wounded; 41 Israeli soldiers and 27 civilians were wounded.

The Palestinian struggle was led by women and children who attended mass demonstrations every day. All commercial trade in the territories was suspended and severe punishment was imposed on those refusing to close their businesses.

Night of the Hang-gliders: Terrorist Kills 6 Soldiers

A terrorist who arrived on Nov. 25 from Lebanon on a hang-glider succeeded in penetrating a military Nahal base close to Kiryat Shmona, where he killed six soldiers. The terrorist was killed by a soldier after a gunfire battle. Another terrorist landed in the security strip and was killed in a clash.

The incident shocked the public *and military. The brigade commander was dismissed. The camp watchman, who had run away from his post when he saw the terrorist approaching, was put on trial.*

The dead terrorist became a national hero in the territories. Two weeks later the 'Intifada' broke out and fed on the Nahal incident, which exploded the myth of Israeli soldiers.

'Refusenik' Ida Nudel Arrives

Ida Nudel.

Following 16 years of determined struggle, *Prisoner of Zion* Ida Nudel received permission to emigrate to Israel, and on Oct. 15 arrived at Ben Gurion Airport.

Nudel, a small and obstinate woman, one of the best known 'refuseniks' and the mother figure to others in Russia, received her long-awaited exit permit 48 hours before landing in Israel. Actress Jane Fonda, who was at the crowded airport to welcome her, had championed her cause.

Israeli tennis player Amos Mansdorf defeats Ramesh Krishnan, to be rated 20th in world tennis. (January 10)

•

Isador Isaac Rabbi, who won the 1944 Nobel Physics Prize, died at 89. His work made possible the measurements needed to develop the laser, the atomic clock and guidance systems for missiles. During World War II he helped develop radar and was a senior adviser to the 'Manhattan Project.' Rabbi was a Jew who came to the US as an infant from Austro-Hungary. (January 12)

•

Prisoner of Zion Yosef Begun arrived in Israel, ending 16 years of KGB harassment, imprisonment and refusal of an exit visa from the Soviet Union (January 19)

•

The first global AIDS conference opens in UK, with experts from the World Health Organization and experts from 150 countries, to plan a global strategy against the AIDS epidemic. (January 26)

•

George Orwell's book '1984,' with its vision of totalitarianism, is to be published in Russia for the first time. The book was banned in the USSR when it appeared 40 years ago. (February 25)

•

The Iranians fired two missiles on Baghdad. This brought the number of missiles fired to four since the 'war of cities' resumed Sunday. Iraq announced it had fired 17 missiles since Monday. (March 1)

•

Three IRA guerrillas were shot dead by the SAS on Gibraltar. They were suspected of planning to bomb the weekly changing of the guard outside the governor's residence. They were unarmed as they walked to the Spanish border. (March 6)

•

'Sy' Keinen died, at 83. Keinen founded the American Israel Public Committee in 1954. AIPAC is the major pro-Israel lobby in Congress. (March 23)

•

The leftist Sandinista government and the *Contras* in Nicaragua agreed on a 60-day cease fire as a first step to end the six-year war there. The sides are scheduled to begin talks on a permanent truce April 6. (March 24)

Russian Spy Kalmanovitch

Shabtai Kalmanovitch, who had arrived in Israel from the Soviet Union in 1973, and over the years had become a prominent businessman, well-respected in the diamond trade, was arrested at the end of Dec. 1987, but his arrest was only made public on Jan. 10.

Kalmanovitch used to make frequent visits to Africa and eastern Europe as part of his many business dealings, and he had even been appointed consul of Sierra Leone in Israel. This enabled him to travel without security checks.

In 1975, the General Security Services (GSS) already suspected that Kalmanovitch was passing on secret information about Israel to foreign nations. However, for various reasons, no official inquiry was then initiated against him. As time passed, Kalmanovitch managed to get close to Israel's political elite and contributed large sums of money to finance various political parties. His good political connections gave

Shabtai Kalmanovitch. Nine years in jail.

him free access to sources of confidential information.

At the end of 1986, new information was received about his involvement in activities against the state and his meetings in the Soviet Union with high-ranking Soviet officials working in the espionage services.

The investigation file was reopened, and he was arrested on one of the rare occasions when he arrived in Israel for medical treatment. Publication of his arrest shocked Israel's political elite. *After a ten-month trial, Kalmanovitch was sentenced to nine years in jail*

The Uprising Continues

The *'Intifada'* that erupted at the end of December gathered momentum. Each evening, television News programs in Israel and throughout the world screened pictures of children throwing rocks and stones and Israeli soldiers chasing them through alleys. A war of child and stone.

On Feb. 26, CBS broadcast a film in which soldiers armed with truncheons and rocks were shown beating two arrested youths. The report aroused international anger and shock. In a number of cities throughout the world demonstrators shouted: "Murderers of children go home!"

After the screening of the film, the four soldiers photographed in the news report were arrested. One was arrested that same day in the dining-room of his *kibbutz*.

The disturbing photographs were published worldwide every evening.

Terrorists Seize 'Bus Full of Workers from Dimona Center

Three terrorists, who infiltrated from Egypt on Mar. 3, seized a military car carrying four unarmed officers in civilian clothes, who escaped from the vehicle.

The terrorists reached Dimona's nuclear center, where they seized a 'bus carrying employees, most of

whom were women.

The terrorists, members of *Fatah*, demanded the release of all Palestinian prisoners in Israeli jails.

Two hours later, when shots were heard from the 'bus, the chief of staff, who was on the spot, decided to order the police special anti-

terrorist unit to storm the 'bus.

The operation lasted only a few seconds. The three terrorists were shot dead. Three of the 'bus passengers were also killed.

The 'bus attack was known afterwards as 'The Mothers Bus' because so many mothers were on the 'bus.

'Abu Jihad' Assassinated in Tunis

Khalil el-Wazir, nicknamed 'Abu Jihad' *(Father of the Holy War)*, Yasser Arafat's military deputy, was killed at his suburban Tunis home in a daring liquidation operation carried out by a commando force.

It was almost 2.00 a.m. when a group of fighters, 30 in number according to the testimony of neighbors, assassinated 'Abu Jihad' at close range. His bodyguards were also killed. His wife and children who were in the house were not wounded. Three vehicles used by the assas-

'Abu Jihad.' At close range.

sins were found abandoned on a beach a short while later.

The PLO blamed Israel, but Israel has never admitted responsibility, even though the modus operandi was typical of the IDF's elite unit.

Military analysts explained that this operation bore all the hallmarks of Israel's elite commando unit, Sayeret Matkal, and that this operation had been carried out in retaliation for the attack on the Dimona 'bus. Israel has continued to deny any connection with the operation.

Group of Hikers from Alon Moreh Settlement Attacked near Kfar Bita

One young girl was killed and 15 wounded on Apr. 6 when a group of young people from the Alon Moreh settlement went out walking.

While they were hiking through one of the *wadis* close to Kfar Bita in Samaria, they were attacked by scores of Arabs who surrounded

them, stoned them and demanded that they accompany them back to their village. One of the group's security guards began to shoot in the air. Two village residents were killed in the shooting.

In retaliation, the Arabs threw stones and building blocks and hit

the guard; one of the hikers, Tirza Porat, aged 15 was killed. Two Red Crescent ambulances evacuated the wounded to a nearby IDF base.

As a result of the serious incident, the IDF blew up 13 houses in Kfar Bita and dozens of residents were arrested for questioning.

Court Returns Adopted Girl to her Mother in Brazil

Bruna: Abducted from her biological mother in Brazil and brought to Israel.

On Apr. 22 an affair hit the headlines which moved many hearts. The high court of justice prohibited a Ramla couple, who had adopted a baby girl from Brazil, from leaving the country until a petition had been heard from the biological mother, who had arrived from Brazil. The mother claimed that her baby, Bruna, had been seized from her in Brazil, and handed over for adoption without her knowledge. The Israeli couple, like other childless couples, had received the child from an adoption agency in Brazil, without knowing that the baby had been abducted from her mother.

The heartbreaking case continued for some months. On June 29, the court decided that the child should be taken from her adoptive parents and returned to her mother.

Bruna returned to her poor neighborhood in Brazil, and an entire nation tearfully followed the separation from her adoptive parents, who had given her the best they could for two long years.

The intermediary who was found guilty of the abduction was given a jail sentence in Brazil.

1988
APRIL - JUNE

The London *'Sunday Times'* reported a huge weapons deal between Israel and China. Israel will sell missile warheads to China and develop a combat warplane similar to the *Lavi*. The deal is worth close to one billion dollars. (April 3)

Mikhail Gorbachev confirms that Soviet troops will begin their withdrawal from Afghanistan on May 15. (April 8)

Deputy Chief of Staff Ehud Barak announces that in 1989 reserve soldiers will serve 62 days (twice the usual time). (April 11)

Hundreds of young Israelis took part in the 'March for Life' from Auschwitz to Birkenau in Poland. The march was held to mark the 45th anniversary of the Warsaw Ghetto Uprising. (April 14)

In retaliation to renewed Iranian mining of Gulf waters, the US destroyed two Iranian drilling platforms and a gunboat in the Gulf. (April 18)

A Jerusalem court convicts John Demjanjuk of the murder of Jews and has sentenced him to death. (April 25)

Francois Mitterand was elected for a second seven-year term as president of France. (May 8)

The Soviets began pulling out their 115,000 soldiers from Afghanistan, after more than eight years of war. (May 15)

President Gorbachev and President Reagan opened their five-day summit in Moscow. At the end of the summit the leaders confirm progress towards reaching a Strategic Arms Reduction Treaty to substantially cut strategic weapons arsenals. (May 29)

Jean Marie le Pen lost his seat in parliament. His anti-immigration National Front party lost 31 seats. (June 12)

Gorbachev proposes radical reforms: A full time legislature, the leasing of farm land by farmers to increase production and to end chronic food shortages, an overhaul of state pricing system, and guarantees of privacy. (June 28)

1988

JULY - DECEMBER

The US guided missile destroyer *'Vincennes'* mistakenly shot down Iranian airliner with 298 aboard in the Straits of Hormuz. The destroyer was engaged with Iranian gunboats as the 'plane closed in on it outside civilian flight routes. (July 3)

Robert Maxwell buys the Israeli newspaper 'Ma'ariv'. (July 26)

Iran and Iraq implemented UN Security Council Resolution 598 establishing a cease-fire in the eight-year war between them. It is estimated that one million people died in the war. (August 20)

Israel launches the *'Ofek 1'* satellite to circle the globe every 90 minutes. The successful launch places Israel in the group of nations with satellite-launch capability. (September 19)

The space shuttle *'Discovery'* is launched into orbit for America's first manned space mission since the *'Challenger'* disaster of January 1986. (September 29)

Four hundred dead in a week of rioting in Algiers over food prices and food shortages. (October 11)

Egyptian writer Naguib Mahfouz wins the 1988 Nobel Prize for Literature, for creating an Arabian narrative that applies to all mankind. He is the first Arabic language writer to win the prize. (October 13)

George Bush becomes the 41st President of the United States after defeating Democrat Michael Dukakis. (November 9)

Earthquake in Armenia kills an estimated 55,000, leaves 500,000 homeless. Israel sends a rescue team and equipment on a IAF Boeing. (December 7)

A terrorist bomb destroys Pan Am flight over Lockerbie Scotland, killing 258 passengers and crew and another 17 on the ground. (December 21)

'Time' magazine departs from tradition of naming a Man of the Year in 1988, and designates endangered Earth as Planet of the Year. (December 26)

Two *F-16* Jets Collide in Mid-air: Both Pilots Killed

F-16. First ever training collision.

Two air force pilots, Lieutenant-Colonel Ram Koller and Major Ehud Falk, were killed on Aug. 15 when their two *F-16* fighter aircraft collided during training exercises over the Dead Sea area.

The two pilots had each accumulated much experience during their many years in the Israel Air Force. Koller, leader of the aerial exercise, had not noticed the approach of Falk's aircraft.

This was the first training collision involving F-16's.

A commission of inquiry appointed by the air force determined that the cause of the collision was human error and technical failure.

Likud Wins Elections. Alignment Joins the Shamir Government

The red carpet awaits Shamir in an African country. Voters preferred him to Peres.

President of Israel Chaim Herzog instructed Yitzhak Shamir to form a government following the elections held on Nov. 11, recommending a national unity government in partnership with the Alignment.

Shamir tried in vain to form a narrow-based coalition with the religious parties, and six weeks after the elections the heads of the *Likud*, Alignment and the religious parties finalized agreement on coalition negotiations for the formation of a unity government. Three days later, Shamir and Peres announced that they were forming a national unity government led by Shamir, with no rotation. The new government was presented to the *Knesset* on Dec. 22.

The 12th Knesset elections indicated the beginning of a trend which was to intensify in the following elections: Shas won six seats and became a dominant force among the haredim. At the same time, the power of the large parties declined: the number of Likud seats decreased from 41 to 40, the Alignment from 44 to 39, and the religious parties together grew in strength to 18 seats.

The President Remits Underground Sentences

President Herzog on June 5 commuted the sentences of Menachem Livne, Shaul Nir, and Uzi Sharbf. The three 'Jewish underground' prisoners had originally been sentenced to life imprisonment; their sentences were commuted to ten years in jail. The three had also been convicted of terrorism in aggravated circumstances, establishing a terrorist organization, and using weapons for purposes of terror. After the sentences had been commuted, 14 months of imprisonment remained until their release; those 14 months were spent in a *yeshiva* in Afula.

President Herzog explained his decision by citing the fact that the trio had expressed profound, sincere

Underground prisoners.

and full remorse.

Later it became clear that extremely heavy pressure from Prime Minister Yitzhak Shamir and Minister of Justice Dan Meridor had pre-

ceded the pardon.

The remission aroused public controversy. *Knesset* members from the NRP and right-wing parties supported the president and congratulated him on his decision, but were ranged against left-wing *Knesset* members, the State Comptroller, Miriam Ben-Porat, and public organizations for integrity in government. They all protested vigorously, claiming that the president had used his right to grant pardons for political ends, and had thus acted unconstitutionally.

Livne, Nir and Sharbf were released a year later and returned to their homes. None of them has since entered public life.

Once venerated as a living god, Japanese Emperor Hirohito dies of cancer at the age of 87 after a 62-year reign. (January 7)

●

George Bush takes an oath as 41st president of the United States of America. (January 20)

●

Hundreds of Afghan civilians are killed in Soviet reprisal bombings. (January 26)

●

South African President P.W. Botha resigns the leadership of South Africa's ruling white National Party but says he will continue as head of the government. (February 3)

●

The author Salman Rushdie is condemned to death by a *'fatwa'* of the Iranian leader Ayatollah Khomeini for blaspheming Islam in his novel 'The Satanic Verses.' (February 14)

●

The director general of the Ministry of Religious Affairs announces his opposition to translation of Salman Rushdie's book, to prevent Israeli Arab enragement. (February 23)

●

1,100 Jewish leaders and intellectuals from around the world attend the Israeli Prime Minister's Conference on Jewish Solidarity with Israel. (March 20)

●

Nearly 100 people are killed in a British soccer disaster in Sheffield when a stadium safety barrier gives way. (April 15)

●

Forty seven sailors die in the worst explosion ever to occur in the US Navy, on the battleship USS *'Iowa.'* (April 19)

●

Over 500 demonstrators die in Tiananmen Square, Beijing, during the People's Liberation Army attack on hundreds of thousands of pro-Democracy students holding out for seven weeks there. (June 4)

●

A year and a half after the release of "The Final Temptation of Jesus Christ" the Supreme Court ruled that the Censor's ban on the film be overturned. The original reason for censorship had been to avoid "hurting the religious community's feelings." (June 15)

Rafi Nelson's Village Closes

Rafi Nelson's village. The symbol of Israeli bohemian life was closed by the Egyptians.

Taba was returned to Egypt on Feb. 26. Shortly afterwards, Egypt announced that it would close Rafi Nelson's holiday village, since its style ran counter to Islamic values. *Nelson's village had been the favorite fun spot for Israeli bohemian society since the Six-Day War and has since been re-opened.*

Rich Contribute to Political Parties

On June 6, the State Comptroller revealed the names of 20 people, each of whom had contributed hundreds of thousands of shekels to the large political parties, which had opposed publication of those names.

Heading the contributors to the *Likud* were many arms dealers and investors in Israel's defense industry.

Prominent among contributors to the Alignment were Charles Bronfman, Jean Friedman and Leon Tamman. *Despite the report, regulations concerning political fund-raising were not changed.*

The World Jewish Congress and the Jewish Agency open their first office in an Eastern Bloc community, in Budapest. (July 10)

US President Bush sets a final date for building a manned moon station and sending astronauts to Mars: the year 2000. (July 19)

South African doctors and medical staff ignore the 'whites only' law and treat thousands of black patients descending on 'whites only' hospitals. (August 2)

In Poland, Lech Walesa forms eastern Europe's first government to be dominated by non-communists. (August 17)

Hizbullah publishes a photograph of a hanged man, and say it is the American hostage, Colonel Higgins. *Hizbullah* claims its hanging of Higgins is in retaliation for Israel's kidnap of Sheikh Obeid. The US expresses dissatisfaction that it had not been forewarned of the hanging. (August 20)

"Trade your car for freedom" becomes a byword in East German - Hungarian deals as thousands of East Germans attempt to cross the border. (August 22)

Demonstrators link hands on the 50th anniversary of the Stalin-Hitler pact: a 600 km (375 miles) human chain across the Baltic States in a call for independence. (August 23)

The first pictures from Neptune and its moon Triton are transmitted back to Earth by the spaceship *'Voyager 2.'* (August 26)

The Chinese people are ordered to learn 40 slogans to mark the 40th anniversary of the Communist state. (September 10)

UN Secretary-General Javier Perez de Cuellar says he believes the PLO has asked the Bush Administration for a visa so Yasser Arafat may address UN. (September 19)

Pope John Paul II declares that the church had been wrong to oppose Galileo. (September 24)

Abie Nathan is convicted under the terms of a new law forbidding contact with PLO members and is sentenced to six months imprisonment. *The law was rescinded in 1992.* (September 28)

Sixteen Passengers Killed when Terrorist Rolls 'Bus into Abyss

It was only possible to reach the 'bus with ropes to try to rescue the dead, and the wounded who were crying for assistance.

Sixteen passengers were killed and 27 wounded on July 6 when a terrorist caused a No. 405 'bus on its way from Tel Aviv to Jerusalem to roll down a hillside. During the journey, when the 'bus reached the Abu Ghosh area, the terrorist, an *Islamic Jihad* operative who worked in Tel Aviv's Carmel Market, approached the 'bus driver, grabbed the steering wheel and forced the 'bus to the side of the highway; it broke the safety barrier and hurtled into an abyss.

The difficult terrain made the rescue operation very difficult, and it took a long time before the wounded could be brought up. Ropes had to be used to reach the 'bus and raise the wounded to the roadside.

The terrorist received a prison term of 16 life sentences.

Sheikh Obeid Kidnapped in Lebanon

On July 27, *Sayeret Matkal* fighters infiltrated the village of Jibchit in South Lebanon in order to kidnap Sheikh Obeid, a leader of *Hizbullah* in South Lebanon.

Obeid was seized in order to put pressure on *Hizbullah* to agree to a prisoner-swap or to pass on information to Israel concerning the fate of its kidnapped soldiers, Rahamim Elsheikh and Yossi Fink, and the captured navigator Ron Arad.

Obeid. Pressure on the *Hizbullah*.

The elite unit (which according to overseas publications was comprised of 12 commandos) made a helicopter landing close to the village, and after the commandos had surrounded the sheikh's house and killed his bodyguard, they tied him and took him to the helicopter.

Obeid was transferred to an Israeli prison, but the Hizbullah's leadership refused to negotiate. The Sheikh is still imprisoned in Israel.

Israeli Reserve Army Officers Trained Members of the Colombian Drug Cartel

On Aug. 31, the police started to investigate members of the Hod Hahanit *(Spearhead)* Company in Colombia. The company, owned by Yair Klein and Amatzia Shuali (two reserve army officers and former security service operatives), had trained mercenaries in Colombia to protect the farmers. Suspicions that the company was aiding the Colombian drug cartel were investigated.

As a result of the findings, the Ministry of Defense ordered the families of Israelis working in Colombia to leave the country.

IAF's Brig.-General Rami Dotan Suspected of Receiving Bribes

Brig.-Gen. Rami Dotan, in charge of equipment supply in the air force, was questioned on Nov. 16 following information that he had accepted bribes from American companies which supplied equipment and arms to the Israeli Air Force.

The affair was first investigated some months previously. Ofer Pa'il, a buyer for the Ministry of Defense procurement delegation in the United States, and the son of former *Knesset* member Meir Pa'il, reported to then Director-General of the Ministry of Defense, David Ivry, that Dotan had received a bribe of tens of millions of dollars. Dotan was questioned, but since the investigators did not have sufficient evidence against him, it was recommended that he be released and the file closed.

A committee set up by Avihu Bin-Nun, the officer commanding the air force, cleared Dotan. The committee's conclusions were not accepted by David Ivry, who decided to pass the matter on to another committee, which recommended that the military police be brought in.

At the outset Dotan denied the accusations against him, subsequently admitting his guilt. Eleven months later he was indicted. He admitted the crimes and, in a plea-bargain agreement, was sentenced to 13 years imprisonment, demotion to the rank of private and a heavy fine.

The bribery affair caused severe damage to relations between the US and Israel. One of the objectives of the plea-bargain agreement with Dotan was to avoid a trial which would have revealed many details embarrassing to Israel.

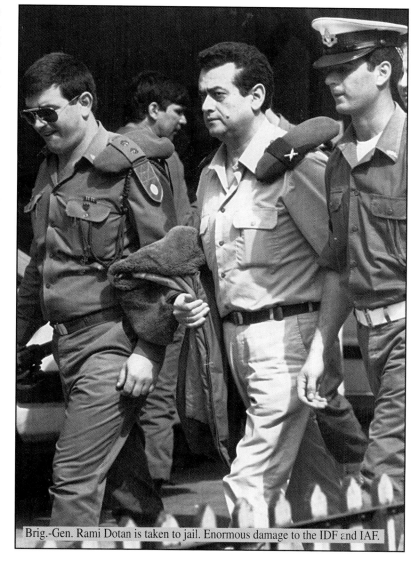

Brig.-Gen. Rami Dotan is taken to jail. Enormous damage to the IDF and IAF.

During the investigation, it was disclosed that Dotan had hired people to eliminate Ofer Pa'il after he had complained about him. Only a miracle had saved Ofer Pa'il from being killed.

Givati Trials; Officers and Soldiers Abused Arabs

On Oct. 3, the second trial commenced of *Givati* soldiers who had been involved in abusing residents of the territories during the 'Intifada.' Some four months earlier, three soldiers had been convicted of abusing a refugee camp resident and carrying out an illegal order.

At the end of the prolonged trial, a military court determined that their behavior had been "shameful and ugly," and sentenced them to jail.

The two Givati trials publicized the norms of behavior of IDF soldiers during the 'Intifada.' At the same time, two senior officers were questioned about issuing illegal commands: Col. Yehuda Meir, commander of the Nablus region, who ordered his soldiers to break the hands and legs of 12 stone-throwers, and the commander of the Givati brigade, Col. Effi Fein, who ordered his soldiers to respond with violence to any breach of the peace.

Meir was demoted to the rank of private, and left the army without a jail sentence. Fein, a hozer b'tshuva (newly repentant Jew), was sent to study abroad and later returned to the army where he was promoted to brigadier-general.

Syrian *MiG* Lands in Megiddo

On Oct. 11, a Syrian *MiG-23* landed at an airport close to Kibbutz Megiddo. The pilot, who had been on a training mission in Syria, crossed the border and flew undisturbed for seven minutes through Israeli airspace.

The pilot disembarked from the 'plane, raised his hands and said: "I want to defect."

The aircraft, equipped with advanced avionic technology, had been visible on radar screens before it crossed the border. Due to an error, fighter aircraft were not scrambled, and two brigadiers-general were reprimanded.

Syria claimed the 'plane had landed because of a technical fault, and the pilot taken prisoner.

1989

OCTOBER - DECEMBER

The Dalai Lama, Tibet's exiled spiritual and political leader, is awarded the Nobel Peace Prize. (October 5)

●

Two hundred and seventy five dead in earthquake in San Francisco. President Bush signs a disaster order. (October 17)

●

Prague police attack a crowd of 10,000 who are demonstrating for a new government. (October 28)

●

East Germany demolishes the 28-year old Berlin Wall as Berlin is reunited. East Germans travel west. (November 9)

●

Millions strike in Czechoslovakia, paralyzing the entire country, in attempt to bring down communist rule. (November 28)

●

Fighters of the *Duvdevan* unit eliminated four terrorists from the 'Black September' group in the Nablus *casbah*. The terrorists had been responsible for killing over 15 collaborators. (December 1)

●

United States President George Bush urges the Soviet President Mikhail Gorbachev to end the Cold War. (December 3)

●

The imprisoned leader of the African National Congress, Nelson Mandela, has his first meeting with S. African President F.W. de Klerk. (December 13)

●

Twenty-two thousand United States soldiers storm Panamanian military bases in a bid to oust strongman Manuel Antonio Noriega, wanted in the US for drug offenses. (December 20)

●

Sixty thousand people were killed during Romanian anti-Communist revolt. Romanian President Nicolae Ceausescu was executed after a secret trial. (December 25)

●

Prime Minister Shamir dismisses minister Ezer Weizman after learning of his contacts with PLO members. During the affair, it became clear that the GSS had been tapping the minister's telephone. Following threats of the Labor Party to quit the unity government, Weizman was reinstated. (December 31)

An oil slick from Iranian super-tanker moves towards Morocco's shores and threatens to become the world's worst ecological disaster. (January 2)

•

Communist Meir Vilner resigns from the *Knesset* after 42 years. Vilner was the last member of the *Knesset* to sign the Declaration of Independence. (January 8)

•

China's Premier Li Peng ends seven months of martial law which started following June 1989's massacre in Tiananmen Square. (January 10)

•

Six thousand hunger strikers gather in front of the government palace in Tbilisi demanding Georgian independence. (January 17)

•

Clashes between Soviet troops and Azeri nationalists in capital Baku as vast crowds defy Moscow-imposed state of emergency. Sixty-two dead. (January 21)

•

Pieces of the Berlin Wall are selling in the United States for $30,000. (January 26)

•

South African black leader Nelson Mandela, the last leading ANC activist captured in the Sixties to remain in prison, is freed after 27 years in prison. *Mandela went on to become President of South Africa.* (February 11)

•

Minister of Trade & Industry Ariel Sharon suddenly announces his resignation from the government. (February 12)

•

Despite American demands, *Likud* ministers decide that East Jerusalem Arabs will not be allowed to participate in elections in the territories and in the political process. American Secretary of State Baker also demanded that settlements be frozen as a condition for further assistance by US. (March 5)

•

Vienna opened a collection of rare Jewish ritual objects as the first part of a planned Jewish Museum. (March 7)

•

More than 1,600 candidates and 27 parties compete for 386 seats in Hungary's national assembly in the first free national elections held in Hungary since 1945. (March 25)

The 'Stinking Manipulation.' Peres Topples the Shamir Government

Mar. 15 marked the first time an Israeli government had been toppled by a no-confidence vote. Sixty *Knesset* members from the Left together with three from *Agudat Israel* voted in favor, while 55 *Knesset* members from the *Likud* and right-wing parties voted against. *Shas* members abstained, with the exception of Minister Yitzhak Peretz who left *Shas* and voted with the *Likud*.

The events, referred to as the 'stinking manipulation,' had been planned in advance by opposition leader Shimon Peres and Aryeh Deri of *Shas*. The vote was preceded by Prime Minister Shamir's decision to dismiss Minister of Finance Shimon Peres, because of Peres' views and actions in conducting negotiations with the Palestinians.

The day after the vote, all members of the Alignment announced their resignation from the government. Once the Council of Sages instructed *Agudat Israel* to support a

Peres and Shamir. The manipulation did not succeed.

government led by Shimon Peres, President Herzog empowered him to form a government.

In April, Peres formed a government and requested permission from the president to convene the *Knesset*. In a surprise move, two *Knesset* members, Avraham Verdiger and Israel Mizrachi of *Agudat Israel*, announced that they would not support this government. *Shas* announced that it would support a government headed by the *Likud*.

On June 8, the Shamir government managed to form a government supported by the Likud, the religious parties, Tehiya, Tsomet, Moledet and lone members of Knesset.

Nine Israeli Tourists Murdered in 'Bus on their Way to Cairo

The bodies of the tourists are returned to Israel.

Nine Israeli tourists were killed and 17 wounded on Feb. 4 in an attack carried out by Moslem fundamentalists on an Israeli tourist 'bus which was carrying 31 Israelis, traveling on the highway from Ismailiya to Cairo. Two masked terrorists blocked the path of the 'bus with their car, and immediately opened fire with submachine guns and threw hand grenades.

Egyptians traveling along the highway transferred the wounded to Heliopolis Hospital in Cairo, from where they were later flown to Israel.

An anonymous 'phone call to an Egyptian news agency shortly afterwards announced that the attack had been in retaliation for the policy of the Mubarak government with regard to Egyptian Moslem organizations.

Following the murderous attack,

security at Israeli offices in Egypt was stepped up. President Hosni Mubarak sent condolences to the families of the victims.

The following day the Egyptians arrested scores of suspects in connection with the attack. It turned out that the driver of the terrorist car was the 'bus driver's brother. The three terrorists were sentenced to life imprisonment.

Soviet Immigration Begins

Just arrived. Half a million new immigrants in four years.

On May 1, the Jewish Agency announced that a record number of Soviet immigrants had arrived in Israel during the course of April.

The wave of immigration from the Soviet Union which began at the end of 1989 brought 200,000 new immigrants to Israel by the end of 1990, and was a surprising turnaround after long years of meager immigration. The change occurred when Soviet leader Mikhail Gorbachev adopted a liberal policy and mutual representative offices in Israel and the Soviet Union were opened. An amendment to the American immigration laws also led to a smaller number of Jews leaving Russia who did not immigrate to Israel.

The Jewish Agency and the Ministry of Absorption prepared for the arrival of the immigrants, rapidly arranging absorption centers and caravan sites to house them. Many *ulpans (schools for intensive Hebrew study)* and special professional training centers were established.

The Soviet immigration, the largest wave of immigration in the history of Israel, continued steadily until 1994. More than 500,000 Soviet Jews reached Israel during the course of four years.

Ami Popper Murdered Seven Workers from Gaza

Ami Popper, a young man from Rishon Le'Zion, opened fire at close-range at a group of workers from the territories who were waiting next to a gas station in Rishon Le'Zion on May 20. Seven workers were killed and 21 were injured.

Popper, armed with a *Galil* gun, came from a nearby orchard and ordered the workers, waiting for Israeli employment, to line up and present their identity cards. Suddenly, Popper began shooting at the men.

After the shooting, Popper fled the site and later turned himself in. He claimed in the investigation that he was provoked by a deep sense of depression after his girlfriend had left him. Popper said that he had worked alone and that he had taken the gun from his brother who was a serving soldier.

Years after he had received a sentence of life imprisonment, Popper changed his story and claimed that

Ami Popper.

one of the murdered Arabs had sexually abused him years before, when he was a child.

Popper, who was found to be sane, was sentenced to seven life sentences. While in prison, he became Orthodox, married, and became a father. In recent years, he has been making efforts to receive a pardon and an early release.

Investigation Against Minister of the Interior

On June 1, complaints were filed against Shas Minister of the Interior, Aryeh Deri, after investigative reports in *'Yedioth Aharonot'* had uncovered suspicions that he had received bribes and unlawfully transferred money.

So began the Deri Affair, one of the most significant scandals of the Nineties. For a long time Deri refused to cooperate with police investigators and did not answer questions. Three years later, he was indicted for personal violation of the law. He was forced to resign from the Cabinet after being indicted. He continues to serve as leader of Shas, and is still an influential figure.

Israel's ambassador to Egypt, Professor Shimon Shamir, resigns because of his disagreement with Israeli government official policy. *(In 1994, Shamir was appointed Israel's first ambassador to Jordan.)* (July 3)

Dow Jones' average hits all-time high at 2,969.80 points. (July 12)

Fifty million abortions a year kill over 200,000 women annually around the world. (July14)

Soviet President Mikhail Gorbachev ends the Communist Party's media monopoly. (July 15)

The Soviet premier warns of increasing social tension as the Soviet Union faces bread shortage. (July 15)

An explosive device exploded at Tel Aviv's 'Jerusalem Beach,' while the area was packed with hundreds of bathers. A Canadian tourist was killed and 18 were lightly wounded. (July 28)

Troops loyal to Liberian President Samuel Doe massacre over 600 refugees sheltering in a church in the Liberian capital Monorovia. (July 30)

Iraqi tanks invade Kuwait heading a *Blitzkrieg* invasion that overwhelms the tiny emirate and ousts the most stable royal family in the Gulf. (August 2)

Two youngsters from Jerusalem, Ronen Carmani and Lior Tubol, were kidnapped and murdered by terrorists. The two were kidnapped while waiting for a ride in the Ramot neighborhood, in the northern part of the city. Two days later, Jews attacked Arabs in Jerusalem following the discovery of the two bodies. (August 4)

Observing the 45th anniversary of the atomic bombing, the people of Hiroshima renew a call for a ban on nuclear weapons. (August 7)

US troops land in Saudi Arabia. (August 9)

More than 50,000 supporters of the fundamentalist *Moslem Brotherhood* march in Amman demanding holy war (*'Jihad'*) against Israel and the United States. (August 31)

Saddam Hussein Invades Kuwait

Oil fields aflame in Kuwait.

Iraq's army invaded Kuwait on Aug. 2, and took over the country within hours. Iraq's President Saddam Hussein announced that Kuwait was part of Iraq and that he had no intention of withdrawing his forces, despite protests by Arab countries, the US and European countries.

Saddam Hussein annexed Kuwait to Iraq on Aug. 8, announcing that his country would discuss the crisis only if Israel retreated from the territories it had conquered in the Six-Day War. The US recruited an international task force and began deploying in the Persian Gulf.

The Israeli government distributed gas masks to its citizens, in light of information received about Hussein's intention to incinerate Israel with chemical weapons.

Five Soldiers Killed at Tze'elim

Five reserve duty soldiers were killed and ten were injured on July 17, during a training accident at Tze'elim base in the south.

The accident was caused by the mistake of an officer in charge of the range, which led to the shooting of an artillery shell at the soldiers.

The accident, known as 'Tze'elim 1,' exposed a long series of defective regulations at the IDF's central training base.

First Experiment of *Hetz* Missile

The '*Hetz*.' The first experiment was successful.

The *Hetz,* an anti-missile missile manufactured by Israel's Aircraft Industries, was first launched from the experiment's base on Aug. 9. Most of the experiment's goals were achieved by the test launch. The *Hetz* was intended to provide Israel with the capability to intercept ballistic missiles from a high altitude in the outer atmosphere.

The Iraqi invasion of Kuwait and the threat of missiles launched at Israel had emphasized the importance of developing such a missile. The limited *Patriot* missiles had been the West's only defense against long-range Soviet missiles.

The development of the Hetz began in 1987, in collaboration with a group of experts from the American defense ministry; most of its budget came from the United States.

21 Arabs Killed in Riots

Thousands of Arabs stormed the police station on the Temple Mount on Sept. 8, set it afire, and stoned worshippers praying at the Western Wall in the middle of *Succoth*. Dozens of policemen and Jews were injured by the stones. The few policemen who were guarding the Wall were in danger, and began shooting at the crowd from close range. Reinforcements arriving from police headquarters were also forced to make their way through the fire. Twenty one Arabs were killed and more than 140 were injured. Twenty six Jews were also injured.

The riots were triggered by the Moslem fear that *Ne'maney Har Ha'Bayit (Temple Mount loyalists)* were about to attempt to lay the corner stone for the Third Temple. Hundreds of young Moslems had gathered on the Temple Mount in the early morning; the police had taken note of the gathering but had not requested reinforcements.

Later, at the commission of inquiry established to investigate the incident, Chief of Police Ya'acov Turner claimed that an increase of police force would only have led to an escalation in the riots.

The UN Security Council condemned Israeli police handling of the riots; all European countries concurred with that condemnation.

Gas Masks are Distributed

The gas mask kit became an integral part of life. "Never leave home without it."

The Israeli government decided on Oct. 1 to distribute defense kits against chemical weapons, in light of Saddam Hussein's war threats.

Two weeks later, distribution points were set up for distributing the kits, which had previously been stored in the IDF's emergency warehouses.

The *'Motorbank'* Caught

Roni Leibovitz; 22 bank branches.

Roni Leibovitz robbed 22 bank branches in seven months, until he was caught on Sept. 18, after robbing a bank in Givatayim. Leibovitz entered numerous bank branches, wearing a helmet and armed with a gun, emptied the cashiers' tills and escaped on his motorcycle. As a result of his method, Leibovitz became known as the 'Motorbank.'

The public felt a certain admiration for the 'Motorbank,' who successfully robbed so many banks and made the police seem quite helpless. Every robbery made lead headlines in the newspapers.

Leibovitz' father was a businessman with capital estimated at millions of *shekels*. When Leibovitz was caught, he told one of the investigators that he had huge debts because of unsuccessful business ventures and the villa he was building. Found in his possession were two motorcycles, a van on which Leibovitz loaded his motorcycle, and a gun. Leibovitz confessed to having committed all the robberies.

Leibovitz received 20 years' imprisonment.

1990
SEPTEMBER - OCTOBER

Saddam Hussein frees hundreds of Western hostages, most of whom are women and children. (September 1)

A day before the 50th anniversary of the war that had ended with their separation, East and West Germany sign a treaty meant as a final blueprint for uniting them. (September 2)

The mainly Russian-speaking region in Soviet Moldova declares its independence. (September 5)

Victor Ostrovsky, a former *Mossad* agent, publishes a book about the *Mossad*. Israel tried to prevent its publication, but to no avail. The book caused Israel extensive damage. (September 5)

US President George Bush and Soviet President Mikhail Gorbachev end an emergency summit with a joint demand that Iraq pull out of Kuwait. (September 9)

Bill Cosby and Michael Jackson are at the top of the money-making list in the world of entertainment. (September 16)

World fear of war in the Gulf propels oil price up to $40 per barrel. (September 24)

Head of Hungary's Jewish Community issues call for Israeli help in combating rising anti-semitism in Hungary. (September 29)

Bush administration and Israel's Ministry of Foreign Affairs finally agree on the terms for $400 million US-backed government guarantees, to underwrite Soviet Jewish absorption. (October 2)

Germany's neo-Nazi National Democratic Party convenes for the first time in former East Germany amid protests by some 250 demonstrators and heavy police surveillance. (October 7)

A senior aide to Chancellor Helmut Kohl appeals to Soviet President Gorbachev to stop the recruiting of former East German agents to spy for Moscow in united Germany. (October 7)

Soviet President Mikhail Gorbachev wins Nobel Peace Prize. (October 15)

Kahane Murdered in New York

Rabbi Meir Kahane, leader of the extreme right-wing party *Kach*, was assassinated on Nov. 6, after a meeting in a hotel in New York. The killer, an American citizen born in Egypt, shot at Kahane from close range and fled the site.

While he was being chased by the police, the assassin also shot an American policeman.

The killer was not convicted of having murdered Kahane, due to technical faults in the indictment, but was convicted of possessing a gun and shooting a local policeman. Later, he was sentenced to life imprisonment for his part in preparing the car bomb which exploded at the Twin Towers building in New York.

Thousands of followers participated in Kahane's funeral in Jerusalem. Mourners attacked Arabs whom they encountered on their way to the burial.

After their leader's death, Kahane's followers split into two movements - Kahane Chai (Kahane Lives) headed by Kahane's son, and Kach headed by Baruch Marzel. The two organizations were outlawed in 1994, after Baruch Goldstein's massacre at the Machpela Cave (Tomb of the Patriarchs) in Hebron.

Meir Kahane. Shots at close range.

Soviet President Mikhail Gorbachev asks Germany for financial aid in his first visit to Germany since German unification on October 3. (November 10)

Poland and Germany have signed a treaty confirming their border along the Oder and Neisse rivers. (November 14)

European leaders sign an East - West arms pact, formally ending the Cold War. (November 20)

British Prime Minister Margaret Thatcher resigns after the Conservative Party revolted against her, closing an era in which she reshaped Britain and helped end the Cold War. (November 22)

Minister of Absorption Yitzhak Peretz causes a public storm, saying that at least one third of the immigrants from Eastern Europe are not Jewish. (November 26)

The UN Security Council sets a final date for Iraq to withdraw its forces from Kuwait: January 15. (November 27)

At a press conference, president of the 'Zionist Forum' Natan Sharansky warns that unless employment and housing are found for the 500,000 new Soviet immigrants, a civil war between veteran Israelis and newcomers will erupt. (November 30)

Chad's President Hissene Habre flees the capital as Libyan-backed rebels encounter no resistance from Habre's demoralized soldiers. (December 1)

Construction of the Channel Tunnel, a 33 km (21 mile) tunnel connecting France and Britain, is completed. (December 1)

A ferry sinks while transporting American sailors from Haifa Port to their aircraft carrier. Twenty-one men were drowned and 47 injured. The drunken sailors had gathered on one side of the ferry, causing it to sink. (December 21)

The author Salman Rushdie embraces Islam and disavows parts of his book 'The Satanic Verses' for which Iranian leader Khomeini had condemned him to death. (December 24)

Leading Bank Managers Indicted

Twenty two top bank managers and accountants were indicted on Dec. 31, for violations relating to manipulation of bank shares. The violations were: fraud connected with securities, deception of clients, influencing the price of securities and false registration of documents of incorporation.

Indictments were submitted against the managers of Bank Leumi, Discount Bank, Bank Mizrahi and Bank Hapoalim. Despite the judges' ruling that the indictments should not be made public, it was apparent that the bankers were accused of having influenced their clients to purchase securities without requiring the necessary guarantees, and had conditioned the granting of credit on the purchase of the bank's own shares. The bankers were also accused of forging documents for the purpose of covering up transactions to raise money from foreign banks.

The bankers' trial lasted more than five years.

The bank heads were found guilty and fined heavily.

Diplomatic Relations with USSR Restored

The first Soviet ambassador is received by President Herzog.

Prime Minister Yitzhak Shamir and the Soviet Minister of Foreign Affairs Edouard Shevardnaze met in Washington on Dec. 12, 23 years after Israel and the Soviet Union had severed their ties, and agreed to restore diplomatic relations between the two countries. Two weeks later, on Dec. 26, the two countries announced the re-establishment of full diplomatic relations between the USSR and Israel.

This was the first meeting between senior government representatives since Israel had severed its ties with the USSR after the Six-Day War. They also discussed strategic cooperation should Iraq attack Israel.

Scuds Land on Israel

The remains of a home in Ramat Gan. Luckily, no one was at home.

Eight *Scud* missiles landed on Tel Aviv and Haifa on the night of Jan. 17, 24 hours after the United States and its allies first attacked Iraq. The missiles caused much damage but fortunately no fatalities.

Israel's citizens were instructed to wear gas masks and to take shelter in pre-prepared sealed rooms because of the fear that chemical missiles would be launched. Israel was divided into six areas which received specific instructions from Israeli radio and television. Sirens were accompanied by the broadcast code words: "Viper! Snake!"

Many Tel Aviv residents left the city after the first missiles had landed. Families went to Eilat or Jerusalem, and to relatives in other parts of the country that had not been hit by missiles. Palestinians in the occupied territories danced on their roofs and accompanied the *Scuds* on their way to the Tel Aviv area with dancing and clapping and ululating.

The missiles had a paralyzing effect on Israel's financial markets for several days. The education system was suspended for a longer period.

Thirty-nine *Scud* missiles had landed in Israel by Feb. 25; none

carried a chemical warhead. Most *Scuds* were aimed at the center of the country and some at Haifa. Much property was damaged. One man died when his house was hit by a missile; three people died of heart attacks. Approximately 300 people were lightly injured.

The damage caused by the *Scuds*, and to some extent by the *Patriots*, was estimated at tens of millions of dollars. More than 9,000 apartments and hundreds of businesses were damaged. Hundreds of buildings were severely hit, some of which had to be completely rebuilt.

'Desert Storm' Against Iraq

On the night of Jan. 16, 24 hours after the expiry of the UN's ultimatum to Iraq demanding that Iraq remove its forces from Kuwait, the US commenced its aerial attack against Iraq. The operation was headed by General Norman ('Stormin' Norman') Schwartzkopf, commander of American forces in the Gulf. American Air Force aircraft began their attack by shelling the center of Baghdad, Saddam Hussein's palace, and missile bases in West Iraq.

Twenty-four hours later, Iraqi *Scud* missiles struck Israel and Saudi

Arabia. American and British pilots did not manage to locate the mobile *Scud* launchers, and the missiles continued to fall, despite the heavy air bombardment of Iraq.

After three weeks of heavy assault, including the use of sophisticated *Cruise* missiles and *Stealth* bombers, preparations for the ground attack begun. By this time, Iraq's economic structure had been badly damaged, including the electricity system, transportation and public buildings. Many of Baghdad's citizens fled the city, which suffered

both casualties and severe damage to property. All attempts to harm Saddam Hussein failed.

The ground attack was launched in the third week of February. Kuwait was conquered within days and the Iraqi forces retreated. Armored lines of allied forces penetrated Iraq and moved northwards, destroying hundreds of tanks. On Feb. 28, the American president announced that the war had ended. The main target, to oust Saddam Hussein, had not been achieved. Israel was not involved in the combat.

1991
JANUARY - FEBRUARY

Two batteries of *Patriot* missiles arrive in Israel with US operators, and are stationed in the center of the country. (January 3)

•

Five foreign airlines announce the cessation of their flights to Israel due to the war threat; other foreign airlines raised their airfares due to the increase of insurance rates. (January 3)

•

UN Secretary-General Javier Perez de Cuellar arrives in Iraq in an attempt to be a 'last messenger of peace.' (January 12)

•

Two thousand gas masks are also distributed for the benefit of medical crews and chronic patients in the territories. (January 13)

•

Hundreds of thousands protest against Soviet President Gorbachev outside the Kremlin, shouting: "Out! Out!" (January 20)

•

Since the Gulf War broke out, the US authorities have detected more than 700 attempts to evade the UN embargo on Iraq. (January 30)

•

South African President F.W. de Klerk pledges to wipe *apartheid* off the statute book by June this year. (February 1)

•

US polls show that 45% of all Americans would support the use of nuclear weapons against Iraq. (February 3)

•

Irish Republican Army's bomb, aimed to kill the British prime minister and his War Cabinet, explodes at the official residence at 10 Downing Street, where the Cabinet was conducting an emergency meeting. (February 7)

•

Minister of Defense Moshe Arens meets with American President George Bush at the White House, in order to emphasize that Israel's patience with respect to the *Scud* missiles is limited, and the Israeli Air Force is standing on full alert to strike at missile bases. During their meeting, Arens received a report from Israel that a *Scud* had fallen near his home in Savyon. (February 11)

•

Iraqi military chiefs meet to discuss a truce, after a 100-hour *'blitzkrieg'* by the allied forces. (February 28)

Germany's Lufthansa airline is to fly here today in a pointed attempt to be the first foreign airline to return, among those which halted their flights during the Gulf War. (March 1)

The first 14,000 American soldiers fly out of Saudi Arabia, heading home. (March 8)

In a poll held in Soviet Georgia, 99% of all Georgians voted to secede from the Soviet Union. (April 1)

A new commander for the northern region is appointed. Yitzhak Mordechai replaces Yossi Peled, who has resigned from military service. Mordechai has already served as OC Central and Northern regions and is now known as the 'general of the three regions.' (April 8)

Berlin cable television broadcasts calls for a fascist revival and celebration of Hitler's birthday from a station sponsored by the government. (April 8)

Former Indian prime minister Rajiv Gandhi is killed in a bomb explosion at an election rally in the south of India. (May 12)

Boris Yeltsin is elected president in the first democratic elections in the Soviet Union. (June 12)

Earthquake in northern Iran demolishes scores of villages and towns, killing over 50,000 people. (June 21)

Seven Israeli hikers, traveling in Kashmir, escaped from Moslem terrorists who were about to murder them. One of the hikers was killed in an exchange of fire. Three were injured and one remained captive. (June 23)

Croatia and Slovenia declare their independence from Yugoslavia. (June 25)

US and USSR sign a 700-page agreement ('START') for the 30% reduction of their arsenals of strategic nuclear weapons. (July 31)

John McCarthy, the British journalist held hostage in Lebanon, is released. (August 8)

'Operation Solomon' Airlifts 14,000 Ethiopian Jews

On May 25, 'Operation Solomon' was completed, bringing more than 14,000 Ethiopian Jews to Israel in an airlift of 36 El Al and air force aircraft: the largest number of immigrants ever brought together to Israel in only one day.

'Operation Solomon' was made possible thanks to an agreement between the Israeli government and Ethiopian rebels. The international press reported that Israel paid the Ethiopian government $35 million to allow the Jews to fly to Israel.

The decision to rescue the Jews who had remained in Ethiopia was made after the Cabinet received news of bitter battles between rebels and the Ethiopian government. Upon receiving the news, American and Israeli agents began setting up a network of collaborators within the Ethiopian government to serve as an emergency tool in case of need. The agents also began to concentrate the Ethiopian Jews in Addis Ababa, in preparation for the flight.

On the 'plane on the way to Israel.

Once final approval had been received, the aircraft left Israel and carried out more than 40 airlifts within 35 hours. The security aspects of the operation were undertaken by Israeli soldiers from elite units, who flew on the 'planes from Israel to Ethiopia. Doctors and medical crews were also flown, to provide first aid. Five babies were born during the rescue flights.

The immigrants were dispersed in various absorption centers throughout the country. Many families were reunited after years of separation in the Eighties after 'Operation Moses.'

Ehud Barak - Chief of Staff

Ehud Barak.

Ehud Barak, former deputy chief of staff, was appointed chief of staff on Apr. 1, to replace Dan Shomron. Barak, who had been commander of *Sayeret Matkal*, is considered to be one of the IDF's most brilliant officers. He announced plans to transform the IDF into a small but sophisticated, modern army.

After four years of service as chief of staff, Barak joined the Labor party, which he now leads.

Severe Sanctions Imposed on Iraq

Saddam Hussein. Restoring military capability.

After the liberation of Kuwait, the UN imposed sanctions on Iraq's army. Iraqi Air Force flights were banned in large areas of the country, mainly near areas inhabited by the Kurds. American aircraft patrolled the area to ensure that the sanctions were maintained. In addition, Saddam Hussein was forced to guarantee that UN teams could identify and destroy Iraq's missiles, chemical weapons and nuclear infrastructure.

Peace Talks in Madrid

Israel, Egypt, Jordan, Syria and the Palestinians around one table.

1991
SEPTEMBER - DECEMBER

After much diplomatic effort, on Oct. 30, the International Middle East Peace Committee took place in Madrid, Spain. American, Soviet, Israeli, Egyptian, Jordanian (participating as part of the Palestinian delegation), Syrian and Lebanese heads of state and foreign ministers attended the talks. Representatives of the European Community also took part.

At first, Israel refused to participate in the talks. Only in response to American pressure did Prime Minister Yitzhak Shamir agree to attend.

Shamir, who opposed the talks, brought an exceptionally 'hawkish' delegation to Madrid. Arab leaders attending the talks would not shake Shamir's hand and even refused to sit next to him.

The conference began with speeches in which each country presented its position. The American and Soviet presidents spoke in favor of territorial compromise. The Syrian and Jordanian representatives' speeches were extreme, and Shamir spoke of Israel's willingness to talk

to Jordan and Syria directly, without the intervention of the super-powers. The head of the Palestinian delegation, Haidar Abd al-Shafi, demanded that the Palestinian refugees' right of return be recognized.

'Madrid' did not achieve any of its goals. Shamir referred to the speech of the Syrian minister of foreign affairs as a "Goebbels' speech," and the Syrians called Shamir a "terrorist." Nevertheless, the first steps were taken towards an international process to achieve peace.

Mysteriously Drowned at Sea: Media Tycoon Robert Maxwell

Media tycoon, publisher and chairman of the board of directors of the daily newspaper 'Ma'ariv,' Robert Maxwell drowned at sea on Nov. 5, under mysterious circumstances. Maxwell was vacationing on his yacht in the Canary Islands, fell off the deck and drowned. Several hours later, his body was found and the press was notified of his death.

Maxwell, a former member of the British Parliament, was an avid supporter of Israel. In 1988, he began conducting business in Israel, became the controlling shareholder of 'Ma'ariv' and purchased shares in the leading Israeli companies Teva and Scitex.

President Chaim Herzog, Shimon Peres and Ehud Olmert, the minister

On the famous yacht from which he disappeared.

of health, attended his funeral and praised Maxwell's great contribution to the State of Israel.

Maxwell left behind a dying empire and endless debts. After his *death, the police investigated his two sons, only to discover that Maxwell was involved in fraud on a grand scale, and had pledged his employees' pension funds to obtain loans.*

The judge dismisses the case against Oliver North in the Iran-Contra affair. (September 16)

•

Four hundred thousand people gathered at '*Metallica*' concert in Russia, the first big rock concert ever held there. (September 28)

•

The Yugoslav army tightens around Dubrovnik and Vukovay, as fighting rages all over Croatia. (October 2)

•

The Democrat Arkansas governor, Bill Clinton, announces his campaign for the United States presidency. (October 3)

•

Sheikh Ahmed Yassin, the spiritual leader of the *Hamas*, is convicted of incitement to the murder of Jews and is sentenced to life imprisonment plus another 15 years. (October 16)

•

The NBA star Magic Johnson, the most famous of all current basketball stars, announces to a press conference that he is infected with the HIV virus and is therefore retiring from professional basketball. (November 9)

•

Islamic Jihad frees hostage Terry Waite, who was kidnapped in Beirut in January 1987, while he was acting as an envoy of the Archbishop of Canterbury with CIA complicity. (November 18)

•

Hundreds of photographs of the 'Hidden Scrolls,' which had not yet been published in Israel, were published in a book in the US, without having received approval of the Antiquities Authority in Israel. (November 21)

•

The UN General Assembly, in a majority vote of 111 to 25, rescinds the 1975 resolution which had stigmatized Zionism as a "form of racialism and racist discrimination." Six Arab countries did not participate in the vote. (December 16)

•

Heads of 11 former Soviet republics proclaim a new commonwealth and put an end to the Soviet Union. (December 21)

•

Mikhail Gorbachev resigns as the Soviet Union's eighth and final leader. (December 25)

Salvadorean government and rebel officials sign an accord to end their civil war minutes before the term ends of UN Secretary General Javier Perez de Cuellar, who had shepherded efforts to stop the fighting. (January 1)

Algeria's high security council decrees as void the nation's general elections which had given Moslem fundamentalists a landslide lead. (January 12)

The European Community recognizes Croatia and Slovenia as independent nations. (January 15)

Moledet and *Tehiya* resign from the government in Israel following the decision to commence negotiations with the Palestinians. (January 16)

Israel and Communist ('Red') China establish full diplomatic relations. Minister of Foreign Affairs David Levy visits China and signs the agreement. (January 24)

Security Council nations hail the end of the Cold War as a new dawn for a stronger United Nations and agree to work together to dismantle the world's arsenals of nuclear weapons. (February 1)

The lost city of Ubar, celebrated in the Koran, is discovered by a Los Angeles team of archeologists. (February 5)

Former World heavyweight boxing champion Mike Tyson is found guilty of rape. (February 11)

Explosions strike coal mine under Black Sea town of Kozlu, turning the mine into a poisonous inferno. Over 200 die. (March 3)

Head of security at the Israeli embassy in Ankara is killed by a car bomb; *Islamic Jihad* organization claims responsibility. (March 7)

President F.W. de Klerk wins a referendum in South Africa that gives him a mandate to close the book on apartheid. (March 17)

UN imposes trade sanctions and arms embargo on Libya for failing to surrender suspects in terrorist bombing of commercial jetliners in 1988 and 1989. (March 31)

Begin has Died

Respected leader and democrat.

Menachem Begin, leader of *Herut* and Israel's sixth prime minister, died on Mar. 9, at the age of 79.

Before the establishment of Israel, Begin commanded the IZL. Since the first *Knesset*, in 1949, he was a member for *Herut*, first in opposition to *Mapai* and then in opposition to the Labor Party.

In the early Fifties, he opposed negotiations with West Germany and the reparations agreement; for years he was Ben-Gurion's greatest rival.

Begin joined the national unity government before the Six-Day War and resigned after the signing of the cease-fire agreement in the Sinai.

In May 1977, Begin successfully steered the *Likud* to a political revolution, forming a *Likud* government. As prime minister, he signed the peace treaty with Egypt, received the Nobel Peace Prize, ordered the air force to attack the nuclear reactor in Baghdad, and decided to wage war in 'Operation Peace for Galilee.' After 14 months in office, he resigned and became a virtual recluse.

Menachem Begin was a respected leader and great democrat. He was buried on the Mount of Olives in Jerusalem, next to his dear wife, Aliza.

Ayalon Highway Flooded

Israel's main transport route was flooded and closed to traffic.

On Jan. 1, the Ayalon and Yarkon rivers overflowed, flooding Tel Aviv and causing casualties. For the first time since 1950, snow fell on Tel Aviv and Haifa. The Ayalon highway was flooded and closed to traffic.

Next Prime Minister - Direct Election

On Jan. 1, the *Knesset* approved a draft law for the direct election of the prime minister. Fifty seven voted in favor and 56 voted against it, the only coalition member to join the opposition vote being 'Bibi' Netanyahu.

Car Bomb Destroys Israel's Embassy in Argentina

Twenty-two people, including four Israelis, were killed in a car-bombing outside Israel's embassy in Buenos Aires. The 252 injured were embassy workers and passersby.

The car bomb, carrying over 100 kg *(220 lbs)* of explosives, had been parked in front of the embassy a mere five minutes before the explosion shattered the building. Twenty-four hours after the explosion, an Israeli rescue unit arrived to assist in locating survivors and bodies.

The *Islamic Jihad* organization claimed responsibility for the Argentine explosion, intended to revenge the assassination of Sheik Abbas Musawi, secretary of the *Hizbullah* in Lebanon, who had been killed by the IDF a month earlier.

Election Victory for Rabin

The smile of a winner, receiving the results.

The Labor party, led by Yitzhak Rabin, defeated the *Likud*, led by Yitzhak Shamir, on June 23, by a wide margin: 44 seats to 32 for the *Likud*. The Labor Party's campaign slogan was: "Israel awaits Rabin."

Tsomet, Raphael Eitan's party, had an impressive achievement: an increase from two to eight seats. *Shas*, led by Aryeh Deri, maintained its power: six members of *Knesset*.

On election night, immediately after the results were announced, Rabin announced he did not intend to form a national unity government. Yitzhak Shamir, the defeated prime minister, announced he was contemplating resigning from his role as leader of the *Likud*: "I am at the end

Yitzhak Shamir.

of my personal and political path," he said in a television interview, broadcast at 3.30 a.m.

Rabin attempted to form a wide coalition to include *Tsomet* and the religious parties. Eventually, a narrow coalition was formed, with *Shas*, *Meretz*, and the support of five Arab members of *Knesset*. Rabin appointed himself minister of defense and Shimon Peres was made minister of foreign affairs.

Several hours after the extent of the *Likud's* defeat became apparent, member of *Knesset* Binyamin Netanyahu announced that he considered himself a candidate for the *Likud's* leadership and the one to restore the *Likud* to power.

Soldiers Disguised as Arabs Exposed

The evening News of May 1 exposed the IDF *Shimshon* and *Duvdevan* units, which played a major role in combating the '*Intifada*.'

In the report, a former soldier in one of the units described the training which qualified soldiers for capturing wanted Arabs. The soldiers were presented as easily inclined to

fire their guns, causing almost every arrest to develop into a gun fight.

Israel received enraged reactions from countries protesting military 'assassination squads.' Within days, the report was broadcast worldwide.

Chief of Staff Ehud Barak protested against the report saying the IDF had not been given the chance

to respond. Barak claimed that the broadcast endangered soldiers' lives.

Nevertheless, exposure of the units only increased motivation of young men wanting to join them. During the course of the 'Intifada,' the two units were responsible for numerous arrests of terrorists and the prevention of terror attacks.

Angered by the US and European Community's decision to recognize Bosnia Hercegovina, Serbs proclaim their own state as fighting continues. (April 7)

•

The British Prime Minister John Major wins elections, extending the 13 years of right-wing Conservative rule into an historic fourth term. (April 9)

•

An Irish Republican Army bomb explodes in London's financial district, killing three people and injuring 90 others. (April 10)

•

ANC leader Nelson Mandela announces he and his wife Winnie have agreed to part. He confesses an abiding love, marred by pain. (April 13)

•

Over 100 were killed and 600 injured when a series of explosions ripped through the sewage system of the Mexican city of Guadalajara. (April 22)

•

The Koor consortium announces a profit for 1991 of NIS 203 million, its first profit after five years of huge losses. (April 29)

•

Hollywood film star Marlene Dietrich dies in New York. (May 6)

•

President Boris Yeltsin signs decrees creating a Russian army and naming himself as its commander in chief. (May 7)

•

The UN Security Council votes for sanctions to be imposed on Serbia and Montenegro (Serbia's only sister republic in what remains of the Yugoslav federation), accusing the two of sparking Europe's bloodiest fighting and greatest flight of refugees since World War II. (May 29)

•

UN Secretary General Boutros-Boutros Ghali blames both rich and poor countries for a sick planet as he opens the Earth Summit which seeks to promote growth that does not harm the environment. (June 3)

•

Mikhail Gorbachev arrives in Israel for a private visit, and is officially received. Gorbachev no longer fulfills any official function in Russia. (June 14)

A House panel clears US President George Bush of allegations that he took part in the 1980 Paris meeting where a deal was made with Iran to delay the release of American hostages. (July 2)

•

A car bomb explodes near the motorcade of the French first lady, Danielle Mitterrand, visiting Iraqi Kurdistan, leaving her unharmed but killing four others. (July 6)

•

The World Jewish Congress holds a special three-day conference in response to the rise of racism, xenophobia and anti-Semitism worldwide. (July 7)

•

Panamanians celebrate after a US court sentences former strongman Manuel Noriega to 40 years in prison on drugs charges. The government declares it the end of a painful chapter in its national history. (July 10)

•

A Sicilian anti-Mafia judge and five others are killed in a car bombing two months after Mafia gangsters had killed that judge's mentor in a bomb attack. (July 19)

•

At its first Cabinet meeting, the government decided to freeze the building of new settlements in the occupied territories. (July 19)

•

Czechoslovak President Vaclev Havel resigns after Slovakia declares its sovereignty. (July 20)

•

Despite new aid to Somalia, French doctors and UN officials warn of vast areas where people chew filthy rags and goatskin to survive, dying at a rate of 2000 a day . (August 20)

•

Hurricane 'Andrew' batters Florida with howling 275kph *(172 mph)*, winds killing 15 people. (August 24)

•

Troops in South African 'black homeland' shoot dead 28 ANC protesters and wound nearly 200. (September 8)

•

As a result of Prime Minister Yitzhak Rabin's statements about his willingness to talk with Syria about the future of the Golan Heights, thousands demonstrated against him at Ben Gurion Airport as he left on his first official visit to Washington. (September 12)

Soldier Killed While Playing 'Net Roulette' in the Air Force

Amir Malt, a soldier serving on an air force base in the south, was severely injured while playing the game 'net roulette.' Malt died from his wounds a few days later, on July 27. A female soldier, Lilach Bar Natan, was also seriously injured.

The game was played as a test of courage for newly arrived soldiers who were to serve as flight controllers on the base. They were tied in small plastic handcuffs to a security net which was used to brake jets as they landed. One of the soldiers would operate the net, which rose at tremendous speed. Until the current tragedy, no soldier had been harmed. Later, it was discovered that Malt and Bar-Natan had not been tied to the net before it had been strung.

'Net roulette' had been popular in the air force for many years; many officers knew of the game and even took part in it.

After an investigation by military police, three soldiers were indicted; they were reprimanded and given suspended prison sentences.

The victim's parents appealed the light punishment. Several months later, a re-trial was held, and two officers were arrested and demoted. The parents protested to the chief of staff and the minister of defense that more senior air force officers had not been put on trial.

1st Olympic Games Medals: Yael Arad and Oren Smadja

Examining the medal closely. Rabin with Israeli heroine, Yael Arad.

For the first time in Israel's Olympic history, Israeli athletes have been awarded medals. On July 30, 1992, judoist Yael Arad won the silver medal in Barcelona. Two days later, fellow judoist Oren Smadja was awarded the bronze medal.

All Cabinet ministers, including Prime Minister Yitzhak Rabin, sent the winners congratulatory telegrams. The non-profit organization Keren Ha'Zahav, founded to reward medal winners, announced that it would grant Arad and Smadja NIS375,000. Many companies announced that they too would donate money to the medalists.

The historic triumph was given international coverage. Many newspapers emphasized the long way Israel had come from the tragic slaughter of Israeli athletes at the Munich Olympics in 1972 to these medals at Barcelona.

Four Social Workers Murdered

Tragedy in Jerusalem. On Sept. 8, a mentally unstable man took control of a mental clinic in Kiryat Yovel in Jerusalem, and shot four social workers. The young man, a patient at the clinic, was armed with a gun which he had received from the security company which employed him. He had come to the clinic to protest about his treatment.

After the murder, the young man went up to the roof of the building and began shooting at the policemen who had surrounded it. He was fatally shot a short while later.

El Al *Jumbo* Cargo Jet Crashes in Amsterdam

On Oct. 4, an El Al Boeing-747 cargo 'plane crashed into a residential district in Amsterdam, Holland. Three crew members and an Israeli passenger were killed. Two hundred and fifty residents of the neighborhood were killed.

The aircraft lost two of its engines shortly after take-off. The pilot, Yitzhak Fuchs, tried to return to the airport, but lost control of the 'plane and crashed into a tall residential building.

At the beginning of 1997, it was *revealed that many of the area's residents had developed cancer. Investigators claim that the cause was the disintegration of uranium weights balancing the aircraft, in the fire which broke out immediately after the crash.*

450 *Hamas* Activists Deported

450 *Hamas* activists were put on 'buses and taken north.

The Cabinet decided to deport 450 members of *Hamas* and the *Islamic Jihad*. This decision was approved as a response to the murder of border policeman, Nissim Toledano, kidnapped on Dec. 13 and murdered, after Israel had refused to surrender to an ultimatum and release imprisoned terrorists.

The deportees were taken from their homes immediately after the murder. On Dec. 17, the High Court of Justice rejected petitions submitted against the mass deportation, and

truckloads of deportees crossed into Lebanon. All Cabinet ministers, excluding the minister of justice, supported the deportation.

The deportees were transferred to tents set up by the Red Cross in the no-man's-land between the security zone and the area controlled by the armies of Lebanon and Syria.

Israel was harshly criticized by the world. The American president condemned the deportation and announced that unless the deportees were returned to Israel, he would be

forced to reconsider the continuation of his support of Israel.

The deportees received unprecedented coverage by the international media, whose television crews photographed them coping with the snowy, ice-cold winter (omitting to film the generators, etc. sent by Syria). The reports caused severe damage to Israel's international image.

Several months later, following incessant international pressure, Rabin decided to return the deportees to Israeli prisons.

Five Soldiers Killed at Tze'elim

On Nov. 5, during a training exercise for elite commandos of *Sayeret Matkal*, a missile was accidentally shot at soldiers preparing dummy targets for the exercise. Five were killed and six injured.

According to international press reports, the unit was training for the elimination of Iraq's leader, Saddam Hussein, which was planned to take place soon after. The entire senior echelon of the IDF was present:

Chief of Staff Ehud Barak, Chief of Intelligence Uri Saguy, General Amiram Levin, and others.

Investigators determined that the exercise had not been properly prepared, written security instructions had not been issued, and a security officer had not been appointed. It was decided to prosecute two *Sayeret Matkal* officers. The committee also determined that Generals Levin and Saguy, responsible for the exer-

cise, should not be prosecuted.

The incident, known as 'Tze'elim-2,' started a war of the generals in the Israel Defense Forces.

Chief of Staff Ehud Barak was accused of leaving the site shortly after the tragedy, without assisting in the rescue of wounded soldiers. This claim was repudiated by generals present at the time, but political opponents have tried to make use of the allegation on various occasions.

Israel's university lecturers declare a strike in their ongoing battle to have their salaries linked to the average wage of other sectors. (January 1)

●

US President George Bush and Russian President Boris Yeltsin sign 'START 2' - a strategic missile reduction treaty. (January 3)

●

United States issues a 48-hour ultimatum to Iraq to remove missiles threatening US 'planes in the southern safety zone. (January 6)

●

Rudolph Nureyev, the Kirov Ballet's leading star in 1961 when he became the first Soviet star to defect, dies of AIDS. (January 6)

●

A Liberian oiltanker rams rocks in the Shetland Isles; its crude oil cargo of 619,300 barrels causes immense pollution. (January 6)

●

The Allies bomb missile sites in southern Iraq to punish Saddam Hussein for violating the ceasefire terms. (January 13)

●

Bill Clinton is sworn in as America's 42nd president. (January 21)

●

Professor Yeshayahu Liebowitz waives the Israel Prize because of the public storm caused by its award to him. Prime Minister Yitzhak Rabin had announced that he would boycott the ceremony if Leibowitz received the prize. (January 25)

●

Rabbis Israel Lau and Eliyahu Bakshi Doron are elected chief rabbis of Israel. (February 21)

●

Five people are killed and more than 1,000 injured in a bombing at the World Trade Center in Manhattan. (February 26)

●

President Boris Yeltsin assumes special power for five weeks, forces a referendum as to who rules the country and issues a decree placing the Russian media under his control. (March 22)

●

Two mobile police are killed by terrorists who shoot them as they rest by the roadside in the early hours of the morning. (March 30)

"I Cheated on Sara. Criminals are Trying to Blackmail Me"

Mr. and Mrs. Netanyahu. On live television, 'Bibi' admitted having an affair with another woman.

Binyamin Netanyahu raised a storm on Jan. 14. The *Likud's* leading candidate for party leadership appeared on the News to announce to millions that senior party members were threatening him and his wife Sara. He said it had been threatened that if he continued in the race, a videotape documenting his intimate relations with another woman would be publicized. Netanyahu admitted having an affair, and claimed that his wife had received an anonymous threatening call the day before.

Netanyahu did not mention any names. Nonetheless, when he said a senior member of the *Likud* "who is surrounded by criminals" was behind the episode, it was obvious he was referring to David Levy. 'Bibi' claimed people had broken into various homes and offices where he had spent time, and had installed hidden cameras and 'bugged' his telephones and fax machines.

On Jan. 17, Netanyahu filed a complaint with the police. A week later, the second woman was exposed: Ruth Bar, a marketing consultant. The videotape was again publicly discussed when Netanyahu and Levy met on Mar. 17, in a television interview program. Levy demanded that Netanyahu disclose the names of suspects. Netanyahu called Levy 'Napoleon.' On Mar. 26, 'Bibi' Netanyahu was elected leader of the *Likud*. The police investigation of the matter remained unfruitful.

Yair Levy Jailed

On Jan. 21, District Court Judge Aryeh Segalson ignored the plea bargain with former member of *Knesset* Yair Levy, and sentenced him to five years' imprisonment.

Levy, one of the strongest members of *Shas*, had entered into a plea bargain with the prosecution. Levy admitted to having stolen NIS300,000 from El Ha Ma'ayan, the educational organization which he had headed, as well as admitting to an additional 115 charges attributed to him in the indictment. Under the plea bargain, the charges were converted from theft to managerial irregularities, but the judge decided not to accept the plea bargain and sent Levy to prison for five years. Levy's wife was sentenced to community work.

Ezer Weizman Israel's Seventh President

Another Weizman at the presidential residence. Ezer.

On Mar. 24, the *Knesset* elected Ezer Weizman, Labor's candidate, as Israel's seventh president. Sixty-six members of *Knesset* supported him; 53 supported the *Likud* candidate, Dov Shilanski. The seventh president is the nephew of Israel's first president, Chaim Weizmann.

Minister Aryeh Deri Accused of Fraud and Receiving Bribes

On June 20, after three years of police investigation, the prosecution finally submitted an indictment against Minister of the Interior, Aryeh Deri. The Attorney-General, Yosef Harish, read the indictment to Deri. Deri's reaction to the charges: "A weight has been lifted from my heart."

Aryeh Deri was accused of receiving bribes, fraud, breach of trust, fraudulent receipt under aggravating circumstance and the false registration of corporate documents. According to the charges on the indictment, Deri wrongfully took $150,000. One of the prosecution witnesses was Deri's former friend, Ya'acov Shmuelevich, who had turned state witness.

The indictment only dealt with the minister of the interior's private affairs. An additional indictment, concerning violations in Deri's public capacity, had also been prepared and would be submitted when the first trial had finished.

Shulamit Aloni Removed by Rabin from the Ministry of Education

Pressure applied by the Orthodox parties took its toll. Rabin was forced to sacrifice Aloni, to preserve the Cabinet.

Several statements made by Minister of Education and Culture, Shulamit Aloni, enraged *Shas* members of *Knesset*. On May 6, the religious party demanded that the minister be removed from office. After several difficult meetings with the prime minister, Aloni announced that she was prepared to leave the Ministry of Education and Culture in order to prevent the break-up of the government, which would have harmed the peace process.

To everyone's surprise, Aloni's colleagues from *Meretz* did not stand by her during the crisis.

On May 19, the prime minister temporarily assumed the education and culture portfolios. Ten days later, he announced the Cabinet changes: Aloni was made minister of communications, science and culture; Amnon Rubinstein was made minister of education.

Name is Disclosed of Officer Accused of Serious Espionage

Seven years after his arrest on suspicion of espionage, on June 3 the High Court of Justice permitted publication of the incident involving Yosef Amit, who had tried to sell intelligence information.

Amit had served in the elite commando unit *Sayeret Egoz*, had been injured during the Lebanon War and had been transferred to the Intelligence Corps. In 1977, he was arrested on suspicion of involvement in a drugs deal. After his arrest, Amit was discharged from service, and institutionalized in a mental hospital.

On his release from the army, Amit had participated in a course for private investigators.

Amit, who had kept sensitive intelligence information in his house, was put on trial in 1987. He was imprisoned in the psychiatric ward of Ayalon Prison. For a long time he tried to contact journalists and interest them in the wrongs he claimed to have suffered, but censorship prevented any publication of the affair.

1993

APRIL - JUNE

Four members of *'Abu Nidal'* organization indicted in Washington for conspiracy to kill Jews and blow up Israeli embassy. (April 1)

•

A radiation leak in Western Siberia is seen as the worst nuclear accident since Chernobyl. (April 7)

•

An 83-year-old Israeli kidney patient requests the court to instruct the hospital to refrain from extending her life by means of medical equipment. Judge Uri Goren rules that the physicians are entitled to decide not to connect her to medical equipment. (April 7)

•

Three Israeli soldiers are killed in Lebanon by a roadside bomb explosion. (April 13)

•

Mass suicide, designed to fulfil 'biblical prophecy' ends a 51-day siege at the headquarters in Waco, Texas of religious fanatic David Koresh; 85 dead. (April 19)

•

World leaders attend the opening of the Holocaust Memorial Museum in Washington DC. (April 22)

•

According to a poll, 93% of Israelis own telephones, 90% own washing machines and televisions. In Jerusalem only 72% own televisions. 53% of the entire population own private cars, 43% own VCRs and 20% own personal computers. (April 28)

•

A suicide bomber kills Sri Lankan President Ramasinghe Premadasa at a May Day rally in central Colombo. (May 1)

•

Thousands of Turks riot in the German city of Solingen after five Turks die in an arson attack carried out by neo-Nazis. (May 31)

•

The United Nations attacked the Somali warlord Mohammed Farrah Aidid's forces in retaliation for the killing of 23 UN soldiers. (June 12)

•

The World Jewish Congress announces it is forming a special unit to protect the human rights of non-Jews. (June 17)

•

US missiles ripped into Iraq's intelligence headquarters to avenge an alleged plot to kill former US president, George Bush. (June 27)

Terrorists boarded a Jerusalem 'bus and killed a woman passenger, then kidnapped another woman and her car and fled south, where they were stopped and shot at a security barrier. The kidnapped woman driver was also killed. (July 2)

•

Sheikh Omar Abdel Rahman, whose followers were accused of the World Trade Center bombing, surrenders to United States immigration officials. The sheikh was later charged with the World Trade Center bombing. (July 3)

•

After 350 years of white domination in South Africa, a date for the first all-race elections has been set. (July 3)

•

The G-7 Summit opened in Tokyo with a joint demand to end the Arab Boycott. (July 7)

•

Russia's central bank announces the withdrawal of all pre-1993 bank notes and causes chaos in Russia. (July 23).

•

US Secretary of State Warren Christopher abruptly returns from Singapore to Washington, curtailing his visit to the Pacific Rim, because of the Israel-Lebanon crisis. (July 27)

•

One hundred earthquakes occur in Israel; the strongest, centred south of Eilat in Sinai, registering 5.8 on the Richter scale. (August 3)

•

Twenty one critically ill adults and children from Sarajevo arrive in Britain for medical treatment. (August 18)

•

The Egyptian interior minister was badly hurt in an assassination attempt in Cairo. (August 18)

•

A German Second World War U-boat which was thought to have jewels, paintings and Nazi papers on board, was raised 48 years after being sunk off a Danish island. (August 23)

•

The Israeli government convenes to approve the agreement of 'Gaza and Jericho first,' that was consolidated during secret talks with the Palestinians in Oslo. Ministers Aryeh Deri and Shimon Shetreet abstain. Right-wingers call for civil revolt. (August 30)

'Accountability' Against *Hizbullah*

During the summer, security problems in northern Israel escalated. On July 8, two *Givati* soldiers were killed by terrorists. The next day, three paratroopers were killed on the northern border of the security zone; another soldier who had been severely wounded died a few days later. On June 13, America requested that Israel exercise restraint towards Lebanon.

On July 20, terrorists launched *Katyusha* rockets on Kiryat Shmona and other settlements on the northern border. The residents of the north spent their weekend in bomb shelters. Prime Minister Yitzhak Rabin visited the area and promised retaliation. On July 22, a military medic was killed while trying to assist soldiers at the North Lebanon Forces' post. The next day, the IDF reinforced its forces along the border and in the security zone. Television

Ready for shelling *Hizbullah*.

showed convoys of tanks and cannon entering the security zone.

'Operation Accountability' commenced on July 25. The IAF shelled terrorist headquarters, bases, training camps and specific targets - mainly

homes of *Hizbullah* activists. IDF tanks and cannon shelled civilian villages which had served as bases for members of *Hizbullah*. One Israeli soldier was killed and three were injured by a missile launched at their tank. The navy attacked Jibril's headquarters in Tripoli.

The IDF broadcast a warning to the inhabitants of South Lebanon, and gave them the opportunity to leave their homes and move north, intending to turn them against the terrorist organizations. Convoys of refugees moving towards Beirut were also supposed to pressure the Lebanese government.

The Galilee's inhabitants went down to their shelters. As anticipated, the terrorists reacted by launching *Katyushas* on northern settlements. Two were killed and 13 injured. All children were evacuated to the center of the country.

From Yemen to Ashkelon and Rehovot

Yemenite new immigrants. Still wearing traditional Yemenite attire.

A great secret emerged on July 17: since August 1992, 246 Yemenites had immigrated. The immigrants had gone to absorption centers in Rehovot and Ashkelon. Only 1,000 Jews remained in Yemen. *Later, the battle for immigrants' hearts began: Orthodox representatives tried to persuade them to become Orthodox.*

Approved for Publication that Spy Klingberg is Imprisoned in Israel

Ten years after his conviction for espionage, publication of details of 75-year old Professor Marcus Klingberg's imprisonment in Israel was allowed by the Censor. Klingberg immigrated to Israel in 1948, and served as a lieutenant-colonel. Later, he was appointed deputy manager of the biological research center in Nes Ziona, and controlled all Israel's biological weapons secrets. He admitted that since arriving in Israel he had been working for Soviet intelligence and had relayed information about his field of expertise. Members of the security services claimed Klingberg was the most harmful spy in the history of Israel.

Oslo Accord is Signed

1993 SEPTEMBER

Oslo's architects: Peres (l), Rabin (c), Clinton and Arafat (r).

After many years of hatred and war, on Sept. 13 the historic moment arrived: Israel's prime minister and the chairman of the PLO shook hands on the White House lawn. The Oslo Accord, drawn up by Yossi Beilin and his team, had become an agreement between the two peoples.

In Israel, the signing of the agreement received mixed reactions. 40,000 people came to Kikar Malkei Israel on Sept. 4 to express their support. Two days later, 50,000 right-wingers marched in Jerusalem. A violent encounter between the demonstrators and the 2,500 policemen securing the demonstration resulted in the arrest of dozens of demonstra-

tors, who attempted to break into government offices. The demonstrators stood outside the Prime Minister's Office into the late hours, and were dispersed by police who were forced to use water cannon.

On Sept. 9, Prime Minister Rabin signed the accord in Tel Aviv, while Arafat signed it in Tunis. Arafat pledged to work towards the removal of the 26 clauses of the Palestinian Covenant which called for the destruction of Israel, and announced the PLO's recognition of the State of Israel and its desire to solve the dispute in a peaceful manner. Israel pledged to carry out various gestures towards the Palestinians.

On Sept. 11, Rabin and his entourage flew to Washington for the official signing ceremony. Two days later, Rabin and Arafat signed the document.

The ceremony was broadcast on television, and hundreds of millions of viewers throughout the world watched President Bill Clinton, the agreement's 'best man,' lightly push Arafat and Rabin towards each other, until the two former enemies indeed shook hands.

Meanwhile, members of *Hamas* and the *Islamic Jihad* tried to undermine the signing of the agreement by carrying out acts of terror, in the form of horrific suicide bombings.

Deri Has Resigned

On Sept. 8, following a High Court petition submitted by the Movement for Quality Government against Aryeh Deri's membership in the Cabinet, the judges ruled: "The violations attributed to Aryeh Deri are extremely serious and the fact that he has not been removed from office damages the credibility of the government." In response, Minister of the Interior Aryeh Deri announced his immediate resignation from the Cabinet, promising: "The trial will be short. My innocence will be proven."

On Sept. 22, Deri agreed to give up his parliamentary immunity; it was removed on Sept. 26.

Stars in the Park

Michael Jackson.

Madonna.

Two international superstars arrived in Israel to perform in Hayarkon Park. The first was Michael Jackson, who performed on Sept. 19, exciting 70,000 fans. Beforehand, he visited the Old City of Jerusalem, and Masada. Two weeks later, 50,000 came to watch Madonna.

Bosnian President Alija Izetbegovic and Bosnian Serb leader Radovan Karadic agree on a new cease-fire. (September 1)

Scottish hiker Ffyona Campbell arrives in Tangiers after walking from Cape Town. She was the first woman to walk the entire length of Africa. (September 1)

Shimon Levinson, colonel (res.) in IDF Intelligence, was sentenced to 12 years imprisonment, having been found guilty of carrying out espionage for Russia. (September 2)

The European Commission of Human Rights rules that Britain should face a European court over the killing by the SAS of three IRA members on Gibraltar in 1988. (September 6)

The Vatican says that in view of the Oslo Accords with the Palestinians, it is ready to establish full diplomatic relations with Israel. (September 19)

Israel's Chief Rabbi, Israel Lau, met with the Pope in Rome. The Vatican's announcement regarding the establishment of ties with Israel made this meeting possible. (September 20)

President Boris Yeltsin attempts to seize complete control of Russia by ousting congress and announcing new elections in December. (September 21)

The Supreme Court rejected all petitions relating to the acquittal and release of Ukrainian Demjanjuk, who was taken to a 'plane and deported to America. Demjanjuk's trial lasted almost seven years. (September 21)

According to American polls: 90% of US Jews call Israeli-PLO joint recognition a 'positive' act. (September 26)

Red Cross reports say thousands of Somali refugees, sheltering in refugees camps in Kenya, have been raped, robbed or killed by Kenyan police. (September 27)

The worst earthquake in India in 50 years has left more than 300,000 dead. (September 31)

Minister of Foreign Affairs Shimon Peres and Crown Prince Hassan of Jordan meet at the White House in order to advance peace talks between Jordan and Israel. (October 1)

Sheikh Amin el-Tarif, the spiritual leader of the Druze, dies at the age of 95. At his death, the Druze sect was unable to agree on a successor. (October 1)

Russian President Boris Yeltsin crushes hardliners' revolt led by Vice President Alexander Rutskoi in ten hours of bloodshed in Moscow. (October 4)

US and Canadian warships position themselves off the coast of Haiti in order to force Haiti military to allow the ousted president to return to power. (October 17)

ANC leader Nelson Mandela and South African President F.W. de Klerk win the Nobel Peace Prize. (October 17)

The Italian film maestro Federico Fellini dies aged 73. (October 31)

Juan Carlos, King of Spain, arrives in Israel on an official visit of a few days. (November 8)

A Ukrainian cult leader whose 150,000 members intended to commit mass suicide aborts the plan saying "the end of the world is canceled." (November 14)

Fighting continues in Bosnia as peace talks commence in Geneva. (November 30)

The parents of soldier Zecharia Baumel, missing in action since the battle of Sultan Ya'acoub in the Lebanon War, receive his ID dog-tag, as negotiations about the MIA's continue. (December 2)

Princess Diana announces retreat from public life. (December 4)

Europe's largest and oldest cemetery, in Worms, Germany has been vandalized by a group of neo-Nazis. (December 20)

The white South African parliament ends apartheid, adopting a constitution that involves revolutionary changes. (December 22)

Hamas Reacts to Oslo

While Israel and the PLO have been promoting peace, the opposition organizations have escalated terror attacks in an attempt to undermine the agreement.

Two Israelis were killed while swimming in Wadi Kelt. The killers escaped to Jericho. On Oct. 24, two reservists on their way home from Gush Katif were killed. On Oct. 29, an Israeli from Beit El, near Ramallah, was kidnapped and murdered. In reaction, settlers blocked roads and burnt Arab vehicles. Dozens of settlers and right-wing supporters demonstrated outside the prime minister's residence in Ramat Aviv.

On Oct. 30, a property dealer, Ahmed Uda, was murdered in a store in Kalkilya. On Nov. 7, terrorists attacked the car of former member of *Knesset*, Chaim Drukman. Drukman's driver was killed and Drukman himself was injured. On Nov. 17, a reserve duty soldier standing next to a coffee shop at Nahal Oz was killed. The terrorist, armed with a knife, was caught. On Dec. 1, a kindergarten teacher from Beit El was murdered during an attack on a 'bus carrying children, near el-Bira. In retaliation, settlers went out to Hebron and shot at passersby. Nine Palestinians were injured.

On Dec. 6, Mordechai Lapid and his son Shalom were killed near Hebron. The Lapid family, from Givat Haharsina in Hebron, was taking their son, Shalom, to a soldiers' hitch-hiking spot. A Peugeot passed them and opened fire. Father and son died instantly. The children, Bezalel, Yossi and Chaim, were injured. On Dec. 22, two youngsters on their way from Ofra to Bnei Brak were shot by three *Hamas* terrorists.

On Dec 24, Lieutenant-Colonel Meir Mintz was shot while driving his 'Jeep' near Dugit settlement. Mintz, who was responsible for all special operations to capture wanted criminals in the Gaza Strip, was the most senior officer to be killed since the beginning of the '*Intifada.*'

First McDonald's Branch

The first branch at the Ayalon shopping mall. Thousands came to see and taste the American miracle.

On Oct. 14, the first branch of McDonald's in Israel opened in the Ayalon shopping mall in Ramat Gan. Long lines of people queued at the outlet, waiting to see the American miracle. Since that day, dozens of branches have opened in Israel, including *kosher* ones.

The Ayalon shopping mall branch is considered to be one of McDonald's largest branches in the world.

At the beginning of 1997, a dispute took place between McDonald's and the real-estate company, Africa-Israel, following Africa-Israel's announcement that it would not allow the newly built Ramat Aviv branch to open on the Sabbath.

Ehud Olmert Defeats Teddy Kollek

The great surprise of municipal elections took place in Jerusalem. Ehud Olmert defeated 80-year-old Teddy Kollek, who had served as the city's mayor for 27 years. Kollek, who submitted to Labor party pressure to stand as a candidate, lost the elections after Olmert had reached a secret agreement with the Orthodox, who promised him their support. On Nov. 2, more than 95% of the Orthodox came to the ballots and guaranteed Olmert's victory.

Another surprise awaited candidates in Tel Aviv. Contrary to all polls, Roni Milo, who had run as an independent, beat Labor candidate Avigdor Kahalani. In Haifa there were no surprises. Labor candidate Amram Mitzna was elected mayor of the northern city.

Cave of Patriarchs Massacre: 29 Arabs at Prayer Killed

One of the murdered in Hebron. Twenty-nine people were killed.

The 115 bullets fired by Baruch Goldstein in the Cave of the Patriarchs on *Purim*, Feb. 25, resulted in a bloodbath at the Moslem prayer hall. Twenty-nine were slaughtered and more than 100 were injured.

Baruch Goldstein, Kiryat Arba's doctor and an ardent *Kach* activist, arrived at the Cave of the Patriarchs in the early morning. He was dressed in army uniform, and was recognized by the guards, who did not attempt to stop him. Goldstein crossed a room where several Jews were praying, and entered the Moslem prayer site.

While worshippers were kneeling facing Mecca, Goldstein began firing his army-issue automatic rifle at their defenseless backs.

After four minutes of non-stop shooting, Goldstein ran out of bullets. Those Moslems who remained able to defend themselves attacked Goldstein and beat him to death.

The shock both in Israel and around the world was unprecedented. Prime Minister Yitzhak Rabin phoned Yasser Arafat and expressed his sorrow and shame.

Some weeks later, Kach and Kahane Chai were declared to be terrorist organizations and outlawed. Despite public pressure, the incident was not used to vacate the Jewish settlement in Tel Romeida, Hebron.

Commander Dies in 'Copter Accident

General Tamari.

Central Region Commander, General Nehemia Tamari, was killed in a helicopter crash, while it was attempting to land. Tamari had been visiting the Beit She'an area, to follow a terrorist chase taking place in the valley. At approximately 2.00 a.m., Tamari decided to return to base in the *Sayfan (Bell-206)* helicopter. Due to difficult weather conditions, a strong north wind and heavy fog, which severely limited visibility, the helicopter hit one of the military base's high antennae.

Murderer Baruch Goldstein.

Two High-school Students Murder Herzliya Taxi Driver

Derek Roth, a 51 year-old taxi-driver from Netanya, was murdered in Herzliya on Jan. 9. At first it was thought to be a nationalistic murder.

Two days later, the police arrested three teenagers, aged 15 and 16, from Herzliya. Two of the boys admitted their involvement in the murder. Each tried to blame the other. The police arrested the boys after one of them had bragged to his friends, telling them of the murder.

The two boys, who studied in a high-school in Herzliya, planned the mugging and murder of the driver. They entered Roth's taxi and asked to be driven to the beach in Herzliya Pituach. There, they aimed a stolen gun at his neck, took his ring and necklet, and fled from the scene.

The two boys, who belonged to a violent gang in Herzliya which had terrorized the area's youth, were convicted of murdering the taxi-driver and were both sentenced to long prison terms.

The Irish Republican Army announces three days of cease-fire, the first cease-fire in 19 years. (April 5)

A jury awarded more than $3.8 million in damages to Rodney King, whose beating at the hands of white policemen caused the worst race riots in the United States this century. (April 20)

Richard Nixon, former president who had been forced to resign due to the repercussions of the Watergate Affair, died at the age of 81. (April 21)

ANC leader Nelson Mandela wins South Africa's first all-race national elections. (May 2)

Chaim Bar-Lev, a former chief of staff, minister and Israeli ambassador to Moscow, died after a long illness. (May 7)

Yemen sinks into civil war as fighting between north and south Yemen reaches the capital, Aden. (May 8)

Former US first lady Jacqueline Kennedy-Onassis dies aged 64. (May 20)

Flesh-eating bacteria killed nine people in two weeks causing panic in England. (May 25)

The Nobel Prize-winning author Alexander Solzhenitsyn, exiled from the Soviet Union for non-communist ideas, returns to Russia after 20 years in forced exile. (May 28)

Veteran US paratroopers in their seventies jump once more over Normandy during the ceremonies to mark the 50th anniversary of 'D-Day.' (June 5)

The Lubavitch Rabbi Schneerson, leader of Habbad (a Hassidic sect of Jews), dies at the age of 92 in the United States. The rabbi's followers still believe that he will resurrect himself as the messiah. (June 12)

After a five-hour highway manhunt, Los Angeles police catch former football star OJ Simpson, who was charged with murdering his ex-wife, Nicole and friend, Ronald Goldman. (June 18)

Labor Party Loses the *Histadrut* to Haim Ramon

In the May 10 elections, the Labor party lost control of the *Histadrut* for the first time ever. Haim Ramon, former minister of health, who had established the movement *Haim Hadashim (new life)* a month before the elections, won the public over and defeated Haim Haberfeld, the *Histadrut's* incumbent secretary general. Ramon's faction won nearly 50% of the votes, almost double the votes won by the Labor Party. Members of *Knesset* Amir Peretz and Shmuel Avital had left the Labor Party with Ramon.

Ramon had resigned from the Labor Party after the health bill which he had proposed had not been endorsed by the Cabinet, mainly due to pressure applied by the Histadrut. Ramon was elected secretary-general of the Histadrut, and spent 18 months restructuring the organization, stripping it of some of its most powerful bodies.

Surprise of the elections.
Ramon: New Life at the *Histadrut*.

Terrorist Attacks in Afula and Hadera

On Apr. 6, on the evening of 'Holocaust Day,' a car-bomb exploded in Afula, killing seven people and injuring 44.

The bombing was part of *Hamas'* efforts to jeopardize the Oslo agreement signed by Israel and the Palestinians. A suicide bomber from the village of Kebatiyeh, near Jenin, blew himself up in a car loaded with 175 kg *(389 lbs)* of explosives, gas balloons and nails. The explosion occurred opposite the city's central 'bus station, just as 'bus No. 348 stopped on its way to Migdal Ha'emek. Most of the victims were high-school students from nearby Ben-Gurion School.

On Apr. 13, the *Hamas* once again struck: six people were killed and 32 injured by a suicide bombing. A terrorist from Yabed village in Samaria boarded 'bus No. 820 on its way from Afula to Tel Aviv and blew himself up in the center of the 'bus. Most of the victims were soldiers.

After the bombing, Yasser Arafat called Yitzhak Rabin and offered his condolences

On Apr. 16, Jordan outlawed the Hamas organization, in response to Israel's request, in its fight against terrorism.

Uzi Meshulam has been Captured

On May 10, six weeks after barricading himself with his followers in a house in Yehud, Rabbi Uzi Meshulam was captured by the police.

Meshulam was persuaded to meet the chief of police at the nearby Avia Hotel late at night. When he arrived at the hotel, Meshulam was captured by waiting policemen.

The police also arrested many of Meshulam's followers throughout the country. For six weeks, Meshulam and his men had shocked the whole country.

Meshulam demanded that an investigation committee be appointed to examine the disappearance of Yemenite children in the Fifties.

Shots were fired at police and passing cars from inside the house.

The police Commander of the Central Region, Gaby Last, entered Meshulam's house in order to speak to him, but was forced to leave after his life was threatened.

After Meshulam's arrest, the po-

Uzi Meshulam is taken to prison.

lice forcefully broke into the house in Yehud. His followers, who had fortified the house, refused to surrender and shot at the police.

Shlomo Asulin, one of Meshulam's followers, was killed while trying to shoot at a police helicopter.

Rabbi Uzi Meshulam was put on trial, convicted, and sentenced to 11 years' imprisonment.

Arafat Arrives in Gaza

Tens of thousands await the arrival of Arafat at Gaza's central square.

On July 1, six weeks after the IDF had completed its evacuation of Gaza, PLO leader Yasser Arafat arrived in the Gaza Strip, accompanied by a hundred people. His entourage included his adopted orphans, 'Oum Jihad' the wife of 'Abu Jihad' who had been killed in Tunis, Farouk Kadoumi and poet Mahmud Darwish. Arafat flew from Tunis to Cairo, and from Cairo by helicopter to the Egyptian side of the Rafiah terminal.

After he had crossed the border, Arafat kissed the soil.

Hundreds of thousands of people awaited Arafat in Gaza's central square. Two people were killed when a tree on which they had been sitting fell, and 108 people were injured by the crowds.

On July 2, Arafat spoke at the Jebalya refugee camp and met with a delegation of Israeli Arab members of Knesset.

On July 5, Yasser Arafat arrived in Jericho. Settlers blocked roads and burnt tires in an attempt to prevent the hundreds of invitees from attending the ceremony. *Knesset* member Toufik Ziad, an invitee, was killed in a car accident on his way back from Jericho to Jerusalem.

Whilst in Jericho, Arafat conducted the National Palestinian Council's first ever meeting to be held on Palestinian soil.

Alice Miller Wants an Air Force Flight Course

On Aug. 14, Alice Miller, whose request for air force flight course tests had been rejected, filed a petition in the High Court of Justice against the chief of staff and the minister of defense.

The court found in Miller's favor, ruling unanimously against discrimination between men and women on the flight course. Her fight opened the doors of the prestigious course to women.

Rabin and Hussein Meet in Washington

On July 25, Prime Minister Yitzhak Rabin met with King Hussein in Washington. The two declared that the state of war between Israel and Jordan had ended. The Washington ceremony was preceded by a meeting between Minister of Foreign Affairs, Shimon Peres and Jordanian Prime Minister, Abd al-Salaam Majali, on the Jordanian side of the Dead Sea.

PLO leader Yasser Arafat objected, but Jordan assumed responsibility for the Moslem holy sites in East Jerusalem, in the Old City.

On Aug. 3, the Jordanian king made an unprecedented flight over Israel. Hussein himself piloted a royal Jordanian airliner, and was escorted by three Israeli Air Force *F-15* fighter jets.

Hussein spoke on the telephone with Prime Minister Rabin and congratulated him. "It's wonderful to be flying over your country" said the King emotionally, and then continued his flight to Jerusalem over the Temple Mount.

Car Bombs in Buenos Aires and London

On July 18, terrorists activated a car bomb next to the Jewish community center in the heart of Buenos Aires. Thirty-seven were killed and 59 declared missing. The seven-story building collapsed. Israel sent special teams to Argentina to help rescue people trapped in the ruins. A week later, on July 26, a car bomb exploded next to the Israeli Embassy in London. Thirteen people were injured.

Rwandan rebels capture Kigali and the last major government-held town, Butare. (July 6)

Soldier Arieh Frankenthal was kidnapped and murdered. Frankenthal accepted a lift in a car in which disguised *Hamas* members were seated. (July 7)

North Yemen forces conquered the capital Aden thus crushing southern bids to recreate an independent state. (July 7)

North Korean leader Kim Il Sung dies at the age of 82. (July 8)

Eight IAF 'planes land in Zairean provincial town of Goma, in hourly intervals, unloading medical equipment and water. (July 25)

The Israeli 'invasion' of Turkey has begun. There are 99 flights to Turkey every day. According to estimates, 300,000 Israelis have visited Turkey since the beginning of 1994. (August 1)

'Carlos the Jackal,' most wanted terrorist in the world for the past 20 years, was arrested in Sudan and flown to France. (August 15)

Cuban leader Fidel Castro opened Cuba's doors and allowed Cubans to leave the country. (August 25)

Harry Rosenblatt, last survivor of the British army's Jewish Legion, died aged 101. (September 1)

Serb nationalists in northern Bosnia renewed ethnic cleansing: 2,000 Moslems were driven from their homes. (September 18)

After reaching a compromise, 6,000 American Marines land in northern Haiti to begin dismantling the Haitian army's heavy weaponry. (September 20)

A deadly plague spreads over northern India; 400,000 people flee south while hundreds die. (September 28)

The end of a 19-day hunger strike in Gamla against Israel's withdrawal from the Golan Heights, as part of a peace agreement with Syria. MK Avigdor Kahalani persuaded the hunger strikers to end their strike. (September 29)

Prime Minister and Minister of Defense Yitzhak Rabin has decided that Amnon Lipkin-Shahak will be Israel's next chief of staff, to replace Ehud Barak on January 1, 1995. (October 6)

●

Norwegian Nobel Prize Committee announces the names of the Nobel Peace Prize laureates: Yitzhak Rabin, Shimon Peres and Yasser Arafat. (October 14)

Rabbi Avraham Hamra, 51, chief rabbi of Damascus, arrives in Israel together with his wife and six children. It has now been publicized that during the past two years 3,670 Syrian Jews have left for the US, 1,262 of them then secretly emigrated from US to Israel. (October 18)

●

Bill Clinton addresses Jordanian Parliament and says that US has a deep respect for Islam, but "will combat those extremists who cynically exploit religion as a 'cloak' to perpetrate violence in a bid to undermine the Israeli-Arab peace." (October 27)

●

A wild storm kills more than 400 people in Egypt. (November 2)

●

The Republican Party wins most seats in the United States election for Congress. This is the first totally Republican-dominated Congress in 40 years. (November 9)

●

Iraqi President Saddam Hussein announces that Iraq formally recognizes Kuwait and its borders. (November 10)

●

NATO launched a 30-aircraft attack on a rebel Serb-held airfield in Croatia. This was the biggest NATO raid ever. (November 11)

●

Russian troops invade the breakaway republic of Chechnya in a bid to restore Moscow's control over the region. (December 11)

●

Israel and Jordan open reciprocal embassies. (December 11)

●

An elite French commando unit stormed an Air France airplane that had been hijacked in Algiers, killing all four hostage-takers and saving 170 passengers. (December 26)

Peace Treaty with Jordan

Ezer Weizman, King Hussein, Bill Clinton, Yitzhak Rabin, Prince Hassan and Warren Christopher. (r to l)

On Oct. 26, Jordan became the second Arab country to sign a peace treaty with Israel. In an impressive ceremony in the Arava, Prime Minister Yitzhak Rabin and Hussein, King of Jordan, signed the peace treaty in the presence of American President Bill Clinton. Clinton added his signature to the agreement as a witness. Clinton came to Israel after the ceremony and addressed the *Knesset*.

The agreement between Israel and Jordan provided for steps towards normalization of relations in various areas, particularly: tourism, post and communications, culture, science, environment, water, energy, health and agriculture.

Soldier Nahshon Wachsman Kidnapped

On Oct. 9, Nahshon Wachsman, a *Golani* corporal, was kidnapped on his way to visit his girlfriend.

The next day, *Reuters* broadcast a video showing Wachsman tied up and frightened. In a shaky voice, he told his mother not to worry. He also appealed to the government to comply with his captors' demands and release Sheikh Yassin, Sheikh Obeid and Salah Shehada; otherwise he would be killed. His captors presented an ultimatum: if their demands were not met by 9.00 p.m. on Oct. 14, they would kill him.

The entire country responded to his parents' call for a Sabbath vigil, with candles to be lit in all homes.

Futile attempts to negotiate with the captors continued until then. At the same time, Israeli intelligence tried to locate the abducted soldier. Shortly before the deadline, his location was found in an isolated house in Bir Nab'ala, near Ramallah.

At 8.00 p.m., an hour before the time expired, a *Sayeret Matkal* team stormed the house. Explosive devices failed to blow up simultaneously to force entries to the besieged house. Wachsman was held in a small room behind a thick iron door, which was not opened.

Captain Nir Poraz, the commander, was killed during the battle with the kidnappers. Before being shot, the captors executed the bound soldier. One shot in the neck. Six shots in the chest. The rescue had failed.

Hamas Sabotages Peace

As attempts to bring peace to the Middle East progressed, *Hamas* and *Islamic Jihad* continued their acts of terror. On Oct. 9, shortly before midnight, two terrorists opened fire and threw hand grenades at passersby in the Nahlat Shiv'a pedestrian mall in Jerusalem. Two people were killed and 16 injured.

On Oct. 19, a *Hamas* suicide bomber blew himself up on a No. 5 'bus on Dizengoff Street in Tel Aviv. The terrorist was holding a bag containing 20 kg *(44 lbs)* of explosives, and blew himself up when the 'bus

Terror in Tel Aviv.

neared Dizengoff Circle. Another 'bus, in the other lane, was also wrecked. The outcome was tragic: 22 were killed, 46 injured and an entire nation was unable to recover from the shock and return to normal.

On Nov. 11, a suicide bomber from *Islamic Jihad* blew himself up in front of an IDF post at the Netzarim junction in the Gaza Strip. Three officers were killed.

On Nov. 19, another attack took place at exactly the same spot. *Hamas* terrorists shot at an IDF post, killing one soldier.

Two Suicide Bombers Blow Themselves up at Beit Lid

Soon after the terror attack.

On Jan. 22, two suicide bombers blew themselves up at Beit Lid junction. Twenty-one people were killed and 34 injured, most of them soldiers. The fatal attack took place on Sunday morning, when many soldiers were waiting at the junction for transport to their bases.

The first blast was heard at 9.20

a.m. An *Islamic Jihad* member, wearing IDF uniform, blew himself up next to a kiosk at the junction, at a time when it was packed with soldiers. Most of them were injured by the explosion. Soldiers and civilians rushed to help the injured people. At this point another terrorist, also disguised as an IDF soldier, blew him-

self up at the heart of the junction. The second explosion was even more fatal. *Later it was discovered that a third terrorist was supposed to have blown himself up too, but had fled from the site. The third terrorist was only caught 18 months later. After the attack, the government closed off the territories by roadblocks.*

David Levy Resigns from the *Likud*

On June 18, at a meeting with his supporters, David Levy announced his resignation from the *Likud* and his establishment of a new party. Levy also announced his intention to run for prime minister in the upcoming 1996 elections.

The rift between David Levy and Binyamin Netanyahu began with the 'videotape affair.' Netanyahu had claimed that David Levy and his men were trying to blackmail and threaten him about the publicizing of a video cassette which allegedly documented his betrayal of his wife. The distance between the two continually widened. In spite of Netanyahu's attempts to appease Levy, Levy refused even to meet with him.

In December, member of Knesset David Magen joined David Levy and

his camp. Together, they established the Gesher party.

David Levy (r).

Shahak Replaces Barak

On Jan. 1, Amnon Lipkin-Shahak was appointed chief of staff to replace Ehud Barak. Shahak had spent most of his army service in para-

trooper units. *As chief of staff he would have to cope with Hamas' fatal attacks, Hizbullah's massive pressure in the north, the transfer of ter-*

ritories to the Palestinian Authority and (with the promise of peace) the declining motivation of youth to join the army and volunteer to elite units.

The British Prime Minister John Major defeated a right wing challenger and remained head of the Conservative Party. (July 4)

•

For the first time since his trial, Mordechai Vanunu, the nuclear spy, was brought to court, following his demand that his isolation conditions be changed. The judge denied his request, but allowed him two telephone calls a month, a personal computer, and face-to-face meetings with his relatives. (July 11)

•

The UN 'safe area' of Srebrenica fell to the Bosnian Serbs despite a NATO airstrike designed to end a five-day offensive against the eastern enclave. (July 11)

•

United States President Bill Clinton announced the normalization of relations with its former enemy, Vietnam. (July 11)

•

French President Jacques Chirac admits that France shared responsibility for deporting Jews to Nazi death camps during the Second World War. (July 16)

•

The prime minister appointed two new ministers: Ehud Barak as minister of the interior and Yossi Beilin as minister of economic affairs. (July 17)

•

Two hikers were murdered by terrorists in Wadi Kelt. Uri Shahor and Ohad Bahrah were shot to death from close range whilst bathing in one of the pools. The murderer escaped to Palestinian controlled Jericho. (July 18)

•

Four people were killed and 40 injured when a bomb exploded aboard a Metro underground train in central Paris. (July 25)

•

The Walt Disney Company pays $19 billion for Capital Cities ABC Inc., surprising the world with a deal to create the world's largest entertainment company. (July 31)

•

Demonstrators of the right-wing settler movement 'Zo Artzenu' ('This is our country'), block 80 junctions throughout the country to protest against government policy; 130 demonstrators are arrested. (August 8)

Three Teenagers Trampled to Death at Arad Festival

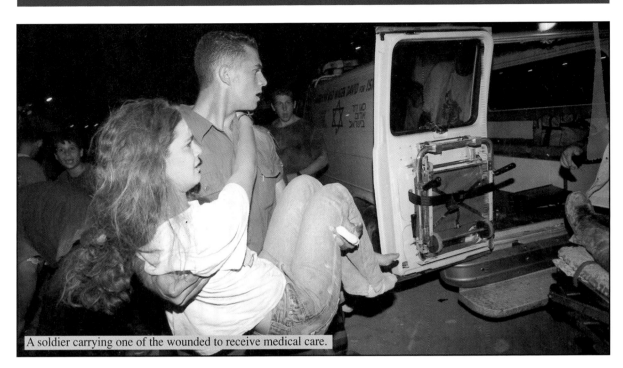

A soldier carrying one of the wounded to receive medical care.

On July 17, a terrible tragedy took place at the Arad Rock Festival. Thousands of teenagers stood at the gate of the stadium, where the rock band 'Machina' was supposed to hold its farewell performance. At the organizers' instructions, the other gates were not opened, and thousands of young people gathered next to one gate. As a result of crowd pressure and density, the gate collapsed on the youngsters standing next to it. Three teenagers were crushed to death in the commotion that followed the collapse of the gate: Na'ama Elkariv, Eitan Peled and Chen Yitzhak. More than 100 people were injured.

A preliminary report was published a week after the tragedy: 25,000 tickets had been sold for the concert, which exceeded the permitted quota, the festival had not been assigned a security officer, and only 54 policemen supervised the tens of thousands of teenagers, without having been trained to do so.

'The Engineer' Activated the Suicide Bombers

On July 24, seven were killed and 32 injured on the No. 20 suicide 'bus, on its way from the Atidim terminal to Tel Aviv's Carmel Market.

'The Engineer.'

When the 'bus stopped next to the Ayalon shopping mall, a terrorist alighted, seating himself in the center of the vehicle. When it reached the diamond exchange area in Ramat Gan, he activated the explosives in his case. The result was lethal.

This was one of the attacks planned and executed by Yihye 'The Engineer' Ayyash's men. Ayyash soon became the most wanted man in the territories.

Less than a month later 'The Engineer' struck again: on Aug. 21, a suicide bomber activated explosives on a Jerusalem No. 26 'bus, opposite a school, in the northern part of the city. Five were killed and 107 injured. The familiar sights were seen once again: the security forces and Hevra Kaddisha (the Burial Society), and hundreds of right-wingers, shouting harsh criticism at the prime minister and demanding he take strong action against Arabs.

'Motta' Gur Commits Suicide

On July 16, Deputy Minister of Defense 'Motta' Gur committed suicide in his backyard. Gur had been a senior commander in the Paratroopers Corps, and one of the liberators of Jerusalem in the Six-Day War. He was appointed chief of staff after the Yom Kippur War, and later served as a member of Knesset, minister of health and deputy minister of defense. Gur had fought cancer courageously for nine years.

Fire in Sha'ar Hagai

A forest fire caused one of the most severe natural disasters in the history of Israel. It raged for many hours, destroying dozens of houses on the entry to Jerusalem.

Right-wing Protests Against Rabin and Oslo Agreement

Right-wing demonstrations.

The signing of the 'Oslo-2 Agreement' on Sept. 28 served as the signal for unprecedented demonstrations and incitement, which focused viciously on Prime Minister Yitzhak Rabin, and Minister of Foreign Affairs Shimon Peres.

The demonstrations were preceded by severe incitement, heard in Israel and abroad. On Sept. 10, American Orthodox rabbis declared Rabin a traitor and a *moser (collaborator)*, whose government had betrayed the interests of the country.

On Sept. 13, right-wingers held a memorial ceremony for the victims of terror who had been killed since the signing of the Oslo Agreement. Two years earlier, opposition leader Binyamin Netanyahu had been photographed leading a demonstration headed by a coffin wrapped in the Israeli flag. Demonstrators shouted at Rabin and his government.

On Oct. 5, the day on which the Cabinet approved 'Oslo 2' by a small majority, 30,000 right-wingers violently demonstrated in Zion Square, in the heart of Jerusalem. On a balcony stood the leaders of the right. The crowds below held posters of Rabin wearing the uniform of an SS soldier.

On Oct. 12, the prime minister was attacked by right-wingers while taking part in a convention at the Wingate Institute. Rabbi Nathan Ofir of the Hebrew University tried to physically hurt the prime minister and was pushed away by bodyguards.

After this, the GSS decided to expand the bodyguard unit, fearing for the life of the prime minister and his senior party members.

Iranian 'Plane is Hijacked to Israel

An Iranian 'plane with 177 passengers and crew members on board was hijacked by an armed flight attendant. The 'plane landed in Israel on Sept. 19. Jordan had refused to allow the 'plane to land on its territory, and only after the pilot had announced that the 'plane was running out of fuel, did Israel permit the pilot to land at Uvda Airport, near Eilat.

The passengers and crew spent the night at the airport. Relatives of Ron Arad, the Israeli navigator who had been taken hostage and was reported to be held in Iran, came to the airport and gave the Iranians written material about their loved one. The family demanded that the prime minister should not release the 'plane and its passengers until Iran had disclosed details about Arad.

Islamic Jihad Leader Killed

On Oct. 25, Fathi Shkaki, one of the leaders of the *Islamic Jihad*, was killed on the island of Malta. Shkaki was executed at the entrance to the hotel where he had been staying under the name Ibrahim Ali Shawishi.

A motorcyclist awaited Shkaki near the entrance to the hotel, and shot him from close range. The motorcycle was later found abandoned near the beach.

Shkaki had been responsible for the financing and execution of the suicide bomb attacks in Beit Lid and Kfar Darom, in which 28 people had been killed and dozens injured.

Maltese investigators said the assassins, who fled from the island by sea, worked for the *Mossad*. Israeli offices abroad declared a state of high alert, fearing revenge attacks.

A Quebec referendum decides against secession from Canada. (November 1)

Jenin is evacuated in line with the redeployment specified in the 'Oslo Accords.' (November 14)

A car bomb explosion outside the Egyptian embassy in Pakistan leaves 16 dead and over 60 injured. (November 19)

Lech Walesa loses Polish election to telegenic ex-Communist Alex Kwasniuwski. (November 20)

The 'Beatles' release their first record in 25 years. The single 'Free as a Bird' was recorded by John Lennon in New York before he died, and now the voices of the other three members of the band have been added to the recording. (November 20)

The presidents of Bosnia, Croatia and Serbia initial a peace agreement to end the Balkan War and provide for a unified democratic Bosnian state. (November 21)

Noa Ben-Artzi, Prime Minister Rabin's granddaughter, signs a $1,000,000 contract for her memoirs. (December 6)

The IDF pulls out of Tulkarm as part of its withdrawal from the main towns in the occupied territories. (December 10)

One day ahead of schedule, the IDF withdraws from Nablus. Palestinian crowds accompanied the withdrawing troops with spitting and cursing. (December 11)

Beilinson and Golda hospitals are united into a medical center, the Rabin Medical Center, named after the late prime minister. This is the first time two hospitals in Israel have become one medical center: it is now the largest hospital in Israel. (December 27)

Rabin Medical Center.

Yitzhak Rabin Assassinated

The square of candles. Here, the prime minister of Israel was assassinated.

"Shalom Haver." Noa Ben-Artzi mourns grandfather Yitzhak.

On Saturday night, Nov. 4, three gun shots fired by assassin Yigal Amir prematurely ended the life of Yitzhak Rabin, Israel's prime minister. Rabin was shot immediately after a peace rally in Tel Aviv, where hundreds of thousands had demonstrated their support for the peace process and their love and affection for Rabin and Peres as their leaders. Rabin was rushed to nearby Ichilov Hospital, where he died an hour later on the operating table.

Yitzhak Rabin, the IDF's chief of staff during the Six-Day War and a Nobel Peace Prize laureate, died at the age of 73.

The entire nation was stunned, and national mourning was declared. More than a million people filed past the coffin which lay in state in the courtyard of the *Knesset*, to pay their last respects to the prime minister. Tens of thousands of teenagers came to Kikar Malkei Israel, lit memorial candles, expressed their intense emotion with graffiti, and sang softly in memory of the prime minister who had been murdered for his peace plan. The mourning children in the square were named the "children of the candles." After the *shiva*, the square was renamed 'Rabin Square.'

Rabin's funeral was attended by world leaders from 80 countries. Among them were Presidents Clinton and Mubarak, King Hussein and the Queen of the Netherlands, German Chancellor Helmut Kohl, Russian Prime Minister Chernomirdin, and British Prime Minister John Major. Speeches and eulogies were heard but most moving of all were the words of Noa Ben-Artzi, Rabin's 19-year old granddaughter, who mourned not only the assassinated prime minister but also her grandfather, Yitzhak. Tens of millions around the world cried together with Noa and the State of Israel.

President Clinton also touched hearts by ending his eulogy with the Hebrew words of farewell: *"Shalom Haver"* (*"Goodbye, friend"*). The words were quickly adopted as an expression of tribute by the whole nation, still seen on bumper stickers.

The heads of the GSS were interrogated by a commission of investigation established immediately after the murder. It concluded that the prime minister had not been properly guarded. The GSS head resigned and departmental heads were suspended and later resigned.

The murder brutally exposed the painful divisions within Israel. Leaders of right-wing parties, including many members of *Knesset*, were accused of wild incitement which had led to the act. Extreme right-wingers were arrested, and certain rabbinical figures from the settlements were interrogated on suspicion that they had given religious legitimacy to the murder on the basis of *Din Rodef* (*law of an assailant*).

Minister of Foreign Affairs Shimon Peres was appointed prime minister and minister of defense, 18 days later. Peres pledged to continue Rabin's way - the way to peace and the realization of the Oslo accords.

Assassin: Yigal Amir, Law Student

Yitzhak Rabin's assassin was Yigal Amir from Herzliya, a 26-year old law student.

Amir was arrested at the site of the murder, immediately after firing the fatal shots. He confessed, stood trial, was convicted and sentenced to life imprisonment. To this day, he has expressed no remorse.

An extreme right-winger, Amir perceived Rabin as a traitor and opposed his peace policies.

It was later discovered that Amir had tried to murder Rabin on previous occasions.

Dozens Killed by Suicide Bombs. The Peace Process Collapses

Twenty seven people were killed and 78 injured on Sunday, Feb. 25, when two suicide bombs exploded. The first blast occurred in the center of Jerusalem, in the early morning. Only the day before, Prime Minister Shimon Peres had decided, against the recommendation of the GSS, to lift the closure of the territories. A terrorist from the territories, a student of Yihye Ayyash, blew himself up on 'bus No. 18, en route to the central 'bus station. Many soldiers on their way to their bases and early-rising workers were on the 'bus.

Several hours later, another terrorist blew himself up at a soldiers' pick-up point in Ashkelon. A woman soldier was killed, and 34 other soldiers were injured.

On Mar. 3, another terrorist blew himself up on the No. 18 'bus in Jerusalem, not far from the site of the previous blast. Eighteen were killed, dozens injured. The Cabinet decided to form a special unit of 800 security guards to protect 'buses.

These precautions did not prevent the next suicide explosion. The following day, the eve of *Purim*, at 4.00

p.m., a suicide bomber blew himself up at the entrance to Dizengoff Center in Tel Aviv. The shopping mall was swarming with people, mainly little children and youth in *Purim* costumes, who had come to enjoy the festival. Fourteen died and 157 were injured.

In a desperate attempt to save the peace process and his government, Shimon Peres convened an international committee against Islamic terror in Sharm el-Sheikh on Mar. 13. President Bill Clinton also paid a short but encouraging visit to Israel.

'The Engineer' Killed in Gaza

On Jan. 5, Yihye ('The Engineer') Ayyash, the most wanted man in the territories, was blown to pieces by a booby-trapped, remote-controlled mobile 'phone. Yihye Ayyash was responsible for preparing explosives used by *Hamas* suicide bombers.

Ayyash, accountable for the deaths of 50 Israelis and the wound-

ing of 340, had fled to the Gaza Strip and hid in Beit Lehaya, a refugee camp near the Erez Checkpoint. In spite of the security forces' efforts, they were unable to locate the terrorist, revered by many Palestinians and known as 'The Engineer' because of his expertise - and experience - in bomb-making.

However, on Jan. 1 his luck ran out. The GSS had apparently located his wife; assisted by a collaborator, the son of Ayyash's landlord, 'The Engineer' was handed a cellular telephone. It rang at 11.00 a.m. Ayyash's father was on the line. The explosives were activated. 'The Engineer' died. Like his victims. Instantly.

MDA Destroys Ethiopian Blood

Thousands of Ethiopians demonstrate in Jerusalem against the 'blood discrimination.'

An investigative report by *Ma'ariv*, an Israeli daily newspaper, revealed that *Magen David Adom* (*Israel's 'Red Cross'*) was destroying blood donated by Ethiopians, from fear that it was contaminated with AIDS. This policy sparked bit-

ter protests by the Ethiopian community, which demonstrated outside the Prime Minister's Office on Jan. 28.

The police, anticipating a quiet demonstration, were not prepared to cope with one of the most violent demonstrations in Israel's history.

Tens of thousands of Ethiopian demonstrators attacked policemen with stones and metal bars. The police used water cannon and tear gas. Forty one policemen were injured. Six hundred cars belonging to government workers were damaged.

France's former Socialist president, Francois Mitterand, who deftly outmaneuvered opponents to lead France from 1981 to 1995, died at 79. (January 8)

●

A Zairean cargo 'plane crashes into a crowded market in the center of Zairean capital Kinshasa killing 250 people. (January 8)

●

Chechen fighters and Russian troops fought fierce street battles after rebels seized about 1,000 hostages in a hospital in southern Russia, demanding a Russian withdrawal from Chechnya and an end to the 13-month war in the breakaway republic. (January 9)

●

The trial of Yigal Amir, assassin of Yitzhak Rabin, opens in Tel Aviv. Amir repeats his version that he had not intended to murder the prime minister but merely to wound him and remove him from office. Two months later, Amir was sentenced to life plus six years imprisonment. (January 23)

●

A fire guts the Venice opera house 'La Fenice,' a 204-year-old jewel that was one of Italy's greatest artistic institutions. (January 30)

●

The world chess champion, Gary Kasparov, defeated *'Deep Blue,'* the IBM computer. Notwithstanding that it has a calculation capacity of 200 million moves per second, Kasparov won the match in 73 moves. (February 12)

●

A man with four guns shot dead 16 children and a woman teacher at a Scottish school in Dunblane before turning the gun on himself. (March 13)

●

Sarajevo, divided into warring communal ghettos four years ago, becomes a reunited city when Moslem-Croat authorities take control of the last district held by Serbs. (March 19)

●

The European Union bans British beef exports to the world, hoping to contain the 'Mad Cow' disease. (March 26)

●

The Shamgar Commission, which investigated the murder of Prime Minister Yitzhak Rabin, determines that the GSS had failed to perform its duty. (March 28)

1996

APRIL - MAY

Historic visit of Israeli prime minister to Qatar and Oman. Peres was criticized in Israel for not canceling the visit despite the rainfall of *Katyusha* rockets falling on Israel's north. (April 1)

•

Britain's Prince Andrew and his wife Sarah filed for divorce after ten years of marriage and a four year separation. (April 16)

•

The G-7 leaders and Russia announce at a summit on nuclear arsenal reduction that Chernobyl will close by the year 2000. (April 20)

•

The National Palestinian Council convenes to annul the sections of the Palestinian Covenant which called for the destruction of Israel and a denial of Israel's right to exist, by a vote of 504 to 54. This annulment is one of the conditions of the 'Oslo Accord,' and entails the return to the area of many Palestinian former terrorists, bombers and hijackers from around the world. *A controversy still remains in Israel as to whether the vote actually annulled the offending sections, or simply voted to set up a committee to review them.* (April 24)

•

A gunman killed 33 people in Australia's worst shooting rampage. (April 28)

•

Thirty four years after the previous failed efforts to satisfy Jewish claims to funds in Swiss banks, Swiss bankers and Jewish leaders sign an agreement setting up an 'independent committee of eminent persons' to review the accounts again. (May 2)

•

In what became the main espionage case since the end of the Cold War, Russian intelligence officials give Britain a list of nine 'career spies' to be expelled. (May 7)

•

A *Valujet DC-9* passenger 'plane with 90 on board crashed in Florida's Everglades near Miami international airport. (May 11)

•

A gunman, angry over Turkish-Israeli military cooperation, tried to assassinate Turkish President Suleyman Demirel. (May 18)

•

Iraq and the UN sign an agreement to allow Saddam Hussein to sell oil to buy food and medicine for his suffering people. (May 20)

Upheaval. Netanyahu Defeats Peres, is Elected Prime Minister

A moment before being informed that he was Israel's next prime minister. Binyamin Netanyahu (r) with David Levy (c) and Yitzhak Mordechai (l) address the party at the Exhibition Grounds.

On May 29, *Likud* leader Binyamin Netanyahu defeated Prime Minister Shimon Peres, and became the first Israeli prime minister to be elected by direct election. Netanyahu's victory was not predicted by the polls, which had indicated a 3-5% margin of victory for Peres.

Despite occasional battles over the location of election hoardings, the election campaign for the 14th *Knesset* was relatively quiet. No general assemblies were held, and both parties decided to cancel the large assembly planned for the eve of elections. The Labor Party was calm and confident of its forthcoming victory, and so made little use of issues surrounding Yitzhak Rabin's assassination, including religious incitement, as ammunition in the fight over the votes.

On May 26, Israeli television broadcast a debate between the two candidates. Netanyahu, who had prepared for the debate carefully, defeated Peres, who came across as old, tired, exhausted, and unfocused.

On the morning of May 29, 7,751 ballot stations opened. Towards the evening, it was reported that about 78% of the four million citizens entitled to vote had indeed exercised their right to do so.

During the long night after the closing of the stations, pollsters prematurely announced a victory for Peres. When the actual results were announced, it became clear Netanyahu had won by 30,000 votes. Labor and *Likud* lost significant numbers of seats to the smaller parties.

'Operation Grapes of Wrath.' 100 Lebanese Civilians Killed

After a long period of unrest in the north, Shimon Peres' Cabinet decided to wage 'Operation Grapes of Wrath' in Lebanon. The operation had been preceded by numerous *Katyusha* rockets fired at Israel's northern communities.

On Apr. 11, the IDF began attacking *Hizbullah* posts in South Lebanon with artillery and jets. Most of northern Israel's inhabitants were evacuated to the center of the country. On the Lebanese side of the border, almost half a million refugees fled north.

Despite the heavy artillery and air force attacks, the *Hizbullah's* operational capability was not destroyed. They continued launching *Katyusha* missiles at the northern settlements.

On Apr. 18, in retaliation for the shelling by terrorists positioned next to Kfar Kana, south of Tyre, the IDF shelled the area and accidentally damaged a UN building. The building served as a shelter for hundreds of Lebanese civilians, including *Hizbullah* families, and the outcome was fatal: 100 were killed and 80 injured. Israel admitted its mistake but the horrifying photos published around the world turned the *Hizbullah* into the real winner of the battle.

Government Without 'Arik' Sharon

Although Netanyahu owed his election victory to him, 'Arik' Sharon made known that he was to remain outside the Cabinet. The prime minister gave in, only after receiving an ultimatum from David Levy.

1996

JUNE - JULY

Despite his seeming optimism, newly elected Prime Minister, Binyamin Netnyahu, encountered difficulties in forming a government. On June 16, Ariel Sharon, Dan Meridor, Benny Begin and Moshe Katzav announced that they would not serve as ministers in Netanyahu's government. At the same time, agreements were signed with the NRP, the *Third Way* and *Shas*.

On June 18, David Levy announced his intention to stay away from the *Knesset* swearing-in ceremony, due to Netanyahu's decision not to include 'Arik' Sharon in his cabinet. That day, journalist Yoav Yitzhak petitioned the High Court against lawyer Ya'acov Ne'eman's appointment as minister of justice.

Minister of Foreign Affairs David Levy threatened to resign from the government unless a position was found for Sharon. *A month after the government was sworn in. a special position was created for him: the Ministry of National Infrastructure.*

Underworld Murders

Aslan. An unsolved murder.

The gangland warfare in Tel Aviv's underworld, which began in Feb. 1993 with the murder of Yechezkel Aslan, was renewed a year later, when an unknown killer murdered his widow, Shoshana Aslan, on June 27.

After the second murder, Ilan Aslan, Yechezkel Aslan's brother, attempted to murder Ze'ev Rosenstein, suspected of murdering Yechezkel Aslan and his wife. Rosenstein's life was miraculously saved. Aslan and two other men were arrested. After his release from prison, Ilan Aslan disappeared; the police believe he was murdered.

Three Reservists Killed on Jordanian Border

On June 26, three IDF soldiers on reserve duty were killed and two soldiers injured, when their patrol was ambushed by terrorists in the Jordan Valley. Three of the soldiers had been on foot patrol along the border fence between Israel and Jordan and the other two had been driving close behind them.

Three terrorists, who had swum across the River Jordan, ambushed the soldiers and opened fire. The first three soldiers were killed instantly. The other two abandoned the vehicle, hid in bushes and did not return fire. The terrorists took the vehicle and machine gun mounted on it.

The force called in as reinforcement was also attacked, before the terrorists fled back to Jordan.

The next day, King Hussein tele-

Hussein. Apologized.

phoned Prime Minister Netanyahu and apologized for the episode.

The IDF and public were critical of the soldiers' failure to fire at the terrorists.

A six year-old boy chosen by China as the highest spiritual leader in Tibet, against the wishes of the Dalai Lama, has been initiated as a monk. (June 2)

•

China carried out a nuclear test in its western desert, arousing a storm of condemnation around the world, since China joined the Comprehensive Test Ban Treaty two days earlier. (June 8)

•

A 15-strong delegation of Sinn Fein from the Irish Republican Party were kept outside the building where British and Irish premiers held peace talks. (June 11)

•

The jazz legend, Ella Fitzgerald, dies at her Beverly Hills home, aged 76. (June 15)

•

Former socialist premier, Andreas Papandreou, who broke the Greek Right's long grip on power and infuriated allies with maverick anti-West stands, dies aged 77, following a heart attack. (June 23)

•

Professor Itamar Rabinovitch, Israel's ambassador in Washington, announces his resignation. Rabinovitch left Washington in September, and was replaced by Eliahu Ben-Elissar. (June 23)

•

The bombing of a US military compound in Saudi Arabia kills 19 and wounds hundreds, making it the deadliest terror strike ever against the US in the Persian Gulf area. (June 25)

•

The former militia chief Paul Touvier, the only Frenchman convicted of crimes against humanity during World War II, died in prison, aged 81. (July 17)

•

A TWA *Boeing-747* exploded over the Atlantic shortly after takeoff from Kennedy Airport, New York. All 228 passengers were killed. (July 19)

•

The largest Olympic Games ever held, with 11,000 athletes from 197 countries competing, was opened in Atlanta, USA. A week after the opening, two people were killed by a bomb at the athletes' Olympic village. (July 21)

•

After its final nuclear test, China declares it will start a moratorium on nuclear testing. (July 29)

American scientists discover evidence of the existence of life on Mars, 3.6 billion years ago. The discovery centers on an organic compound found on a meteorite of the planet. (August 7)

•

A South Korean court sentences former president Chun Doo Hwan to death on charges of masterminding the 1979 coup and a massacre of pro-democracy demonstrators the following year. (August 26)

•

Yasser Arafat and Binyamin Netanyahu meet at the Erez Checkpoint and shake hands. Cabinet ministers expressed fury at the meeting. (September 4)

•

The summit between Netanyahu and Arafat in Washington did not result in an understanding. President Clinton decided to send his advisor Dennis Ross to mediate between the two parties. There is still no agreement regarding deployment from Hebron as called for under the terms of 'Oslo.' (October 2)

•

Argentine Jewish leaders urge security forces to put a stop to the destruction of Jewish cemeteries after 100 tombs were smashed and painted with Nazi symbols. (October 20)

•

French President Jacques Chirac arrives in Israel, refuses to address the *Knesset* and causes an international incident in the Old City with an outburst at his Israeli bodyguards. He then threatens to go back to France. (October 22)

•

President Clinton easily wins his second election, to serve another term as president. (November 6)

•

A Saudi Arabian *Jumbo* jet and a Kazakh airliner collide in midair west of New Delhi, killing 250 people. (November 12)

•

A powerful bomb kills two and wounds 80 at a Metro station in the heart of Paris during the evening rush hour. (December 3)

•

Guerrillas from the 'Tupac Amaru' rebels take hundreds of diplomats, business leaders and other top officials hostage at a glittering reception in the compound of the Japanese ambassador's residence in Lima, Peru. (December 18)

26 Killed in Battles after Western Wall Tunnel Opened

The opening of the Hasmonean Tunnel led to bloody clashes.

On Sept. 24, the prime minister decided to open the tunnel entrance to the Western Wall to tourists. The Hasmonean tunnel was originally built in the 2nd century BCE, and is situated near the Western Wall. Tens of thousands of Palestinians followed Arafat's call and took part in violent demonstrations and riots.

The next day, Sept. 25, riots escalated and exchanges of fire took place between the Israeli army and police and hundreds of Palestinian Authority police. Twelve IDF soldiers were killed in riots which erupted on the whole West Bank and Gaza Strip. Fire was also exchanged at Rachel's Tomb, at Ramallah, Kfar Darom and the Erez Checkpoint.

On Sept. 26, the battles increased. Eleven IDF soldiers and 69 Palestinians were killed during that day, and a state of emergency was declared. The IDF placed numerous tanks near centers of population as warnings. The most difficult battle occurred at Joseph's Tomb in Nablus, where hundreds of armed Palestinians surrounded the IDF stronghold. The IDF sent reinforcements there. Five of the reinforcement soldiers were killed on their way to Joseph's Tomb. The IDF defined the situation as a state of war. Colonel Nabiya Mar'i, deputy commander of the Gaza brigade, and two border patrol officers were killed. The commander of the southern region threatened to take tanks into the center of Gaza if the situation did not cool down.

Bar-Ilan Street will Not Close

Thousands demonstrate on Bar-Ilan Street. The Orthodox did not succeed in closing the street.

The Tzameret Committee, appointed to examine relations between Orthodox and Secular in Jerusalem and specifically the closing of Bar-Ilan Street to traffic on the Sabbath and holidays, submitted its findings on Nov. 4.

It decided that Bar-Ilan Street would be closed on the Sabbath and holidays only during prayer hours, subject to alternative traffic routes being found for the secular public. It recommended cultural institutions be open on the Sabbath, and that all subsidized building be halted, so that Jerusalem should not be transformed into an Orthodox city, which would eventually decline.

The Minister of Justice Resigns

On Aug. 8, the attorney general instructed the police to commence investigations into justice minister Ya'acov Ne'eman. Ne'eman was suspected of interference in trial proceedings. The attorney general's decision caused Ne'eman to resign. He announced his intention to resume his position once he had proved his innocence. Tzahi Hanegbi was then appointed acting minister of justice. Three months later, the appointment was made permanent. *Ne'eman was exonerated in mid-1997, and appointed minister of finance.*

73 Soldiers Killed in Crash Between Two *Yasur* Helicopters

Prime Minister Netanyahu at the site of the crash.

The worst air disaster in the history of Israel occurred on Feb. 4, a few minutes after 7.00 p.m., when two *Yasur (Sikorsky Ch-53)* helicopters, transporting forces to the Security Zone, collided over Moshav She'ar

Yashuv in the Galilee. All 73 soldiers on the helicopters died. Most were combat soldiers from the *Nahal*, *Golani* and armored corps.

One of the helicopters crashed over She'ar Yashuv into a guest

house, which was miraculously vacant. The accident occurred as the helicopters were about to cross the Lebanese border to their destination, with their outer lights turned off.

The helicopters were ablaze for hours. Their full gas tanks increased the flames, as did explosions of large quantities of ammunition they were carrying. The 25 ambulances which rushed to the site could do nothing. No one was saved. IDF forces could only retrieve bodies. The commander of the air force appointed a commission of inquiry, headed by General (res.) David Ivry. Its interim report stated that the accident appeared to have been caused by human error.

The Cabinet announced a day of national mourning. Israeli flags were flown at half mast and all cultural events were canceled.

On Apr. 17, the commission's official findings were published: a base commander holding the rank of brigadier-general was reprimanded, and the commander and deputy of the Yasur squadron were dismissed from any position of command.

Police Investigate Appointment of Attorney General Roni Bar-On

On Jan. 25, five days after the publication of Israel TV Channel One's 'scoop' by reporter, Ayala Hasson, regarding the 'deal' surrounding the appointment of Attorney General, Roni Bar-On, in consideration for *Shas'* vote in favor of the army pull-back in Hebron, the Cabinet decided to pass the issue to the police for investigation. The decision was made on Prime Minister Netanyahu's recommendation.

Reporter Ayala Hasson exposed a deal made between Aryeh Deri and Netanyahu, by which *Shas* would vote in favor of the army pull-back

Bar-On. Police investigation.

in Hebron, in consideration for which the Cabinet would appoint Roni Bar-On as attorney general. Bar-On would then, as attorney general, arrange a plea bargain for Deri.

Bar-On was appointed on Jan. 10, but resigned 48 hours later, following public uproar at the appointment of an unknown lawyer for this important position.

Netanyahu and Minister of Justice Tzahi Hanegbi were interrogated under caution. *Some weeks later, the Cabinet unanimously appointed District Court Judge Elyakim Rubinstein as attorney general.*

Netanyahu Redeploys in Hebron

On Jan. 15, at 2.00 a.m. the *Knesset* ratified the Hebron agreement, calling for the redeployment of the IDF from the Arab part of Hebron, in accordance with the 'Oslo Accord.' On the night before the decision,

Binyamin Netanyahu met with Yasser Arafat at the Erez Checkpoint to finalize the agreement.

The Cabinet meeting, at which the agreement was approved, was tense. Minister of Science Benny

Begin announced his resignation from the government.

Twenty-four hours after the decision, the IDF completed its redeployment in Hebron. The move went smoothly, encountering no protests.

1997
JANUARY - FEBRUARY

Nine Palestinians are injured when a soldier opens fire in Hebron's *casbah*. A *Nahal* officer brought him to the ground and disarmed him. The soldier was found unfit to stand trial. (January 1)

•

Threats were received on the life of Minister of Defense Yitzhak Mordechai, due to his moderate position in negotiations with the Palestinians. The police and GSS reinforced security measures to protect him. (January 4)

•

Fifty thousand Bulgarians raised a huge opposition rally and the Bulgarian president was forced to give in to the public's demand for a general election. (January 12)

•

A massive bomb explodes outside the labor sessions court in Lahore, Pakistan, killing 25 and injuring 100. (January 16)

•

US *Delta* rocket carrying a $40 million US Air Force navigational satellite explodes ten seconds after lift-off. (January 18)

•

President of Israel Ezer Weizman returns his flying equipment, after criticism in the IAF following media reports that 72-year-old Weizman continues to fly helicopters. (January 22)

•

China's paramount leader, Deng Xiaoping dies from an advanced stage of Parkinson's Disease. Deng, a veteran communist revolutionary who guided China from political chaos and economic ruin towards prosperity, was 92 at his death. (February 17)

•

A Palestinian gunman fired into a crowd on the Empire State building's 86th floor observation deck. One tourist was killed and 6 injured before he shot himself in the head and later died. (February 24)

•

Binyamin Netanyahu, back from Washington, denies reports he had promised the Americans to freeze a plan to build 6,500 Jewish housing units on land seized in 1967 between Bethlehem and Jerusalem. "Illegal," said Yasser Arafat. Meanwhile 90 Bedouin were evicted from their West Bank homes to allow expansion of a Jewish settlement. "Racist" said an Israeli peace group. (February 26)

Albania asked the European Union for military assistance to restore order in the country after the economy's collapse, resulting from a failed gambling game. (March 13)

•

Severe crisis between Israel and the Palestinians after the government's decision to build at Har Homa. Two weeks after the decision, bulldozers started work at the site. This led to a wave of demonstrations and riots in the territories. (March 14)

•

Boris Yeltsin announces that Russia wishes to join the European Union. (March 23)

•

Israeli billionaire Shaul Eisenberg dies in China and is brought back to Israel for burial. (March 27)

•

The London 'Sunday Times' exposed the identify of Cindy, an American Mossad agent, who had been involved in the abduction of nuclear spy, Mordechai Vanunu. Cindy's real name was published in the newspaper, thus putting her life at risk. (April 6)

•

Hundreds of thousands of Iranians call for Germany's downfall; Iran says it will recall its envoys over German accusations that it ordered political killings. (April 13)

•

Chaim Herzog, Israel's sixth president between 1983 to 1993, died of heart failure. (April 17).

•

More than 340 Moslem pilgrims, were killed when a fire, caused by their cooking arrangements, broke out at their camp near Mecca. (April 20)

•

After four months of standoff at the Japanese ambassador's residence, Peruvian troops rescued 71 hostages. All 14 terrorists were killed. (April 22)

•

Two young Israeli women, Hagit Zavitzky and Liat Kastiel, were brutally murdered while hiking in Wadi Kelt, near Kfar Adumim. An Arab shepherd confessed to the murder. (April 24)

•

Douglas Peterson, shot down in a bombing raid in the Vietnam War and taken prisoner by the Viet-Cong, returned to Hanoi as the first American ambassador. (April 25)

The Prosecution Rejects Police Recommendation to Indict Netanyahu

On Apr. 20, State Prosecutor Edna Arbel, and Attorney General Elyakim Rubinstein published their decision regarding the appointment of the attorney general, known as the 'Bar-On for Hebron Affair.'

In their report the two decided that there had been a serious attempt to subvert the state prosecutor's office in Israel, and that "people who have been indicted, gathered together for personal interest to determine who would be the attorney general, whilst exploiting connections and political power, and had succeeded in their action."

Nevertheless, the two determined in an elaborate decision that despite severe findings against senior political personalities and despite the police recommendation to indict Prime Minister Binyamin Netanyahu, Minister of Justice Tzahi Hanegbi and member of Knesset Aryeh Deri, leader of Shas, the prima facie evidence was insufficient to support indictments against Netanyahu and Hanegbi. The state prosecutor and attorney general determined there was sufficient evidence to indict Aryeh Deri.

Immediately after the decision had been publicized, Netanyahu addressed the nation on both television channels and admitted that he had made mistakes concerning the affair. He promised to correct those mistakes and improve the procedure of appointing senior civil servants.

The prosecution's decision enraged both the opposition and Shas. Members of Knesset from Meretz and the Labor party immediately filed petitions with the High Court, demanding a review of the prosecution's decision not to indict Netanyahu and Hanegbi.

Shas claimed the decision to single out Deri for prosecution was racial discrimination. On Apr. 23, thousands gathered in a mass rally of support for their party's leader.

The former attorney general demanded a state commission of inquiry to probe the public aspects of the affair, as they related to the culture of government in Israel.

7 Schoolgirls Murdered at Naharayim

Royal condolences. Hussein and Minister of Foreign Affairs David Levy at the home of one of the victims.

On Mar. 13, a Jordanian soldier opened fire from close range at eighth grade schoolgirls from Beit Shemesh, who were visiting the 'Island of Peace' in Naharayim, a small Jordanian enclave near the international border. Seven girls were murdered, and a teacher and five other pupils were injured.

Jordanian soldiers who had been near the site struggled to disarm the soldier, but managed to do so only after he had emptied two magazines of his weapon. A few of the injured girls were taken to a Jordanian hospital near Naharayim.

Three days later, in an exceptional and moving gesture, King Hussein and his daughter arrived in Israel to make condolence calls on each of the seven devastated families.

3 Killed in Bombing at Coffee Shop

In a suicide bombing at the heart of Tel Aviv, three young women were killed on Mar. 21, as they were sitting in the 'Apropos' coffee shop on Ben-Gurion Boulevard. Dozens were injured, including children in Purim costumes, and a baby whose mother was one of the fatalities. The bomber, an Arab from Kfar Tzurif near Hebron, was also killed.

The bombing occurred on Friday afternoon, when the coffee shop was packed with people. The terrorist, carrying a large bag, aroused the suspicions of the coffee shop's shift manager, but the bomb exploded before he managed to do anything.

The security services found the terrorist's identity card at the site, and then discovered a Hamas cell in his home town which had been responsible for 11 murders of Israelis, including the soldier Sharon Edri, missing since Sept. 9, 1996.

Minister of Finance Resigns

On June 18, less than a week after the High Court of Justice had cleared Binyamin Netanyahu of suspicions relating to the appointment of Attorney General Roni Bar-On, the prime minister caused the resignation of Minister of Finance Dan Meridor.

The direct cause for his resignation was a dispute with the Governor of the Bank of Israel. Despite Netanyahu's denials, the maneuver was seen by the public as a closing of account with the minister of finance, one of Netanyahu's chief opponents in the Cabinet.

The Cabinet met shortly before the resignation. During that meeting, Meridor discovered that most ministers supported Netanyahu and the Governor of the Bank of Israel, on the issue of the margins of fluctuation of the rate of exchange.

Minister of Finance Dan Meridor had led the ministers opposing Bar-On's appointment as attorney general, and even spoke in several forums of damage to the rule of law.

After his resignation, Meridor said he was leaving the Cabinet with a clear conscience, after concluding that he did not trust Netanyahu as prime minister.

Netanyahu with Minister of Finance Meridor.

Gregory Lerner's Ties with the Russian Mafia are Investigated

Gregory Lerner, a Russian businessman living in Israel under the name Zvi Ben-Ari since his immigration in 1989, was arrested at the airport on May 12. In the police application for an arrest warrant, Lerner was described as head of the Russian Mafia in Israel.

Police investigators claimed Lerner was involved in the murder of a well-known banker and a television reporter in Moscow. He was also accused of fraud and laundering

Gregory Lerner.

tens of millions of dollars. Police suspect that Lerner had also falsely represented himself as Jewish in order to obtain an Israeli passport.

In Israel, Lerner established a successful financial company. Buying influence with his money, he quickly cultivated associations with political leaders, especially members of *Yisrael be'Aliya* to which he donated significant amounts of money. Several public figures were investigated in this connection by police.

Barak Wins Primaries

Ehud Barak. 50% in the primaries.

On June 3, former chief of staff Ehud Barak won the Labor Party primaries and was elected the new chairman of the party. Barak received 50% of the votes and defeated the other candidates: Yossi Beilin, Shlomo Ben-Ami and Ephraim Sneh.

After his victory, Barak and his wife visited the grave of Yitzhak Rabin, who had appointed him as minister of the interior shortly after Barak had completed a four-year term as chief of staff.

Barak announced his intention to overthrow Netanyahu's government as soon as possible.

3 Paratroopers Killed in Lebanon

On May 26, three soldiers of a paratroop patrol returning from operational activity encountered a *Hizbullah* ambush, north of the security zone in South Lebanon. The three killed included the unit's deputy commander.

During May and June, *Hizbullah* increased its terrorist activity against the IDF. In one action, a *Merkava* tank ran over a land mine; four soldiers were injured and one of them later died of his wounds.

1997

MAY - JUNE

After 18 years in opposition, the Labor Party, led by Tony Blair, wins the British General Election. (May 3)

●

Over 2,400 people die and thousands are forced to leave their homes in an earthquake in northern Iran. (May 12)

●

Space shuttle 'Atlantis,' carrying a crew of seven, sets off in pursuit of Russia's orbiting space station 'Mir,' which is in urgent need of an oxygen generator and other repair equipment being ferried to it. (May 16)

●

Mohammad Khatami, a moderate cleric, wins the elections in Iran. (May 24)

●

NATO and Russia sign a historic treaty dealing with a new security partnership between the two entities. (May 27)

●

Former Minister of Justice, Ya'acov Ne'eman was acquitted of interfering with a witness in the Deri Trial. The court accepted Ne'eman's defense that he had acted in good faith and had not tried to influence a chief witness in the trial. (May 27)

●

Former veteran Timothy McVeigh is sentenced to death for the April '95 Oklahoma City bombing in which 168 people died, including many children who had been at a day care center in the federal building which McVeigh bombed. (June 13)

●

A drug addict who stole a bag on a crowded Tel Aviv beach prevented a tragedy when he discovered a bomb, weighing 5 kg *(11 lbs)*, in the stolen bag. (June 20)

●

After the longest trial in English legal history, two activists are found guilty of libeling hamburger giant, McDonald's. (June 20)

●

Politicians are shocked by media exposure of the meeting between Minister of National Infrastructure 'Arik' Sharon and Abu Mazen, deputy PLO leader. (June 27)

●

Shock amongst top politicians after the meeting between Minister of National Infrastructure Ariel Sharon and Abu Mazen, the No. 2 in the PLO, was exposed by television reporter Amnon Abramovitch. (June 27)

Mike Tyson is suspended and $30 million purse frozen for biting Evander Holyfield's ear off in championship fight. (July 2)

•

Japan mobilizes a fleet of more than 100 ships to contain a huge oil slick in Tokyo Bay in a battle against the country's worst ever oil spill. (July 3)

•

After a seven month journey of 500 million km (313 million miles), NASA's Mars *Pathfinder* rover vehicle lands on the cold surface of the red planet and begins transmitting photographs to Earth. (July 4)

•

A paratrooper major was killed in an encounter with a Hizbullah cell in South Lebanon. Three weeks earlier, three paratroopers were killed in similar circumstances. (July 6)

•

Erick Priebke, former SS captain, is convicted of taking part in the wartime massacre of 335 civilians and ordered to serve five years in prison. (July 22)

•

Claridges investment company decides to buy controlling shares in Koor consortium from the American Shamrock Company, for NIS 1.3 billion ($365 million). This is the largest financial transaction ever to take place on the Israeli market. (July 22)

•

After 156 years of colonial British rule, Hong Kong is returned to China. President Zhang Zemin hails the handover as a triumph for the China. He says Hong Kong will keep its freedoms and the people of Hong Kong were masters of their own piece of China. (July 31)

•

A British tourist was murdered and his girlfriend shot by an Israeli who gave them a lift from Eilat. Two weeks later the murderer, a major (res.), was apprehended. The background to the murder is still unknown. (August 13)

•

A delegation of Arab and Druze members of *Knesset* met in Damascus with the Syrian president. (August 16)

•

Azzam Azzam, a Druze Israeli arrested in Egypt, was sentenced to 15 years' imprisonment with hard labor for spying. (August 31)

Death of Diana, the Princess of Wales

The queen of hearts.

Princess Diana, former wife of Prince Charles, heir to the British throne, died on August 31 in a fatal car accident in Paris. The Mercedes in which the Princess was traveling with her companion, the Egyptian billionaire Dodi el-Fayed, hit a cement bollard in a tunnel in the center of Paris. The investigation conducted by the French police found that the driver, a security official at the 'Ritz Hotel' (owned by el-Fayed's father), was drunk. At the moment of the collision he was driving at a speed of approximately 200 kph *(120 mph)*, while trying to avoid paparazzi photographers on their motorcycles who were trying to obtain exclusive photographs of Princess Diana and her lover.

The death of the princess shocked hundreds of millions around the world. Britain and other countries mourned her death.

In Britain, the pained atmosphere was similar to the mourning atmosphere in Israel after the assassination of Prime Minister Yitzhak Rabin.

Diana's tragic death ignited a public debate, fueled by an eloquent eulogy delivered by her brother, the Earl of Spencer, as to press coverage of her two sons, especially William the future King of England.

Four Australian Sportsmen Killed

Team members escape from the collapsed bridge.

Four members of the Australian delegation to the Maccabia Games were killed as a result of an iron bridge, which had been specially built for the occasion, collapsing into the Yarkon river on July 16.

More than 100 Australians were on the bridge when it gave way, as they were entering the official opening ceremony at Ramat Gan Stadium. Two sportsmen died immediately. A sportswoman and a sportsman both died two weeks later as a result of having swallowed poisonous water from the river. Dozens of Australian sportsmen were injured.

Despite the tragedy, the Maccabia's organizers decided to continue with the opening ceremony. They later explained their decision by saying that at the time they had no information about casualties. Only an hour later, when they were informed of at least one fatality, did the organizers announce that the ceremony was to conclude early. After a day of mourning, the Maccabia events continued.

Jerusalem Suicide Bombs Kill Fifteen

Scenes of horror minutes after the explosion.

Thirteen people died and over 120 were injured when two suicide bombers blew themselves up in the center of the Mahane Yehuda Market in Jerusalem on July 30. The tragedy occurred at 1.10 p.m., when two suicide bombers from the *Hamas* arrived at Hafetz Haim Street in the center of the market. They were both carrying a suitcase containing over ten kilograms *(22 lbs)* of explosives mixed with nails and screws, and stationed themselves 30 meters *(33 yards)* from each other, at the entrance to two packed stores, making sure to remain in eye contact. They activated their explosives almost simultaneously.

The result was horrifying. Within seconds, the swarming market turned into a bloodbath. Dozens of people lay in their own blood. Fruit and vegetables had been blown everywhere. Most of the victims were elderly folk, who had come to the market for their Sabbath shopping. The victims included Arabs who worked at the market.

5 *Golani* Burnt to Death in Lebanon

Five *Golani* soldiers were burnt to death on Aug. 28, during operational activity in South Lebanon.

A force of 15 soldiers, commanded by the head of a division, noticed a cell of terrorists making their way towards Israel's security zone. At least five terrorists were killed in the exchange of fire. The artillery launched during the battle resulted in a huge fire.

The fire, at first distant from the soldiers, changed direction quickly and approached them. Most of the soldiers managed to escape the fire and were rescued. Some were injured. Five soldiers were caught in the flames surrounding them. Four died immediately. A fifth died of his wounds in hospital two days later.

Despite the announcement made by OC of the Northern Region that the force operated well and the fire was caused by a terrible natural catastrophe, soldiers who took part in the operation reported that the force requested permission to retreat because of the fire but the battalion commander had refused to approve their request.

Attack in Jerusalem

On September 4 three terrorists executed suicide attacks in Jerusalem's Ben Yehuda mall, killing a 20-year old man and three 14-year old schoolgirls. On September 8 another victim died of his injuries. Two men and a woman, dressed as tourists, blew themselves up in three different places along the mall.

Despite Arafat's statement that the terrorists had arrived from Europe and not from the autonomous areas, the security services discovered their identities and the village from which they originated, A-Shamaliah near Nablus.

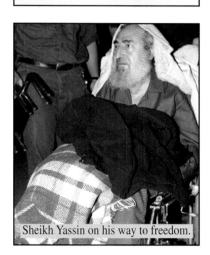
Sheikh Yassin on his way to freedom.

Mossad Agent Accused Of Submitting False Information

Yehuda Gil, a veteran Mossad agent, was arrested on suspicion of having submitted, during a period of years, false information on Syrian military intentions. The case was revealed on December 12 by Ha'aretz military correspondent Ze'ev Schiff.

Gil, aged 63, is accused of having fabricated in the course of the years intelligence reports and slanting them to conform with his own rightist political beliefs.

Senior Mossad functionaries fear that on at least two occasions, in the summer of 1993 and the autumn of 1996, Gil submitted incorrect information from a supposedly senior source within the Syrian government, suggesting that Syria was preparating for war with Israel. The information submitted in 1996 created tension that almost resulted in a military escalation between Syria and Israel.

12 Israeli Commandos Killed in Lebanon

On September 5 twelve members of a naval commando were killed during a mission in Lebanon. The dead included lieutenant-colonel Yossi Korkin, one of the senior officers of the commando. The body of staff-sergeant Itamar Iliya had to be left at the site of the battle.

An IDF force on its way to an assignment in South Lebanon stumbled upon an ambush consisting of a powerful roadside charge placed by the Hizbullah. The detonation activated the explosives carried by one of the soldiers in his backpack.

The two almost simultaneous explosions killed eleven of the sixteen soldiers and alerted other nearby Hizbullah forces. One soldier who had not been injured returned fire and succeeded in calling for assistance. A rescue company arrived by helicopter, whose physician was killed while treating the wounded.

Mossad Failure in Jordan

Two Mossad agents who on September 25 attempted to kill Haled Masha'al, head of the political department of Hamas in Jordan, were caught by Masha'al's bodyguard who handed them over to the Jordanian police. The agents, who carried false Canadian passports, had injected a slow-acting chemical substance into Masha'al's ear intended to kill him within a few hours.

The incident provoked a crisis in Israeli-Jordanian relations and caused considerable anger in Canada. Israel was compelled to rush an antidote to Jordan, which saved Masha'al's life. The two Mossad agents were released on October 6 after Israel had freed Ahmed Yassin, the leader of the Hamas movement, and dozens of other Palestinian terrorists.

The assassination attempt caused considerable damage to Israel, compromising the reputation of Prime Minister Benyamin Netanyahu and the Israeli security services.

Because of severe criticism within Israel the government established an inquiry commission – the Tschehanover Committee, which on October 9 began its investigation of the circumstances of the failed attempt.

Attempt To Depose Benjamin Netanyahu

An attempt of senior Likud officials to depose Benjamin Netanyahu as head of Government and leader of the Likud party was defeated. According to information the instigators of the attempt were Jerusalem mayor M.K. Ehud Olmert, Minister Limor Livnat and Tel-Aviv mayor Ronni Milo.

The initiative was taken on November 11, immediately following the conclusion of the Likud convention which decided to cancel the primaries for the Knesset election roster. Apparently the instigators met with three other Likud Knesset members, Dan Meridor, Ze'ev Begin and David Re'em, with a view to mobilizing 61 Knesset members for a vote of non-confidence in the government followed – at a later stage – by an expression of non-confidence in the prime minister by 80 parliamentarians. This would have enabled them to replace the premier with another candidate.

According to press reports a total of 10 MK's of the ruling coalition agreed to vote against Netanyahu. The plan was prematurely revealed by Ronni Milo, enabling the prime miniser to take remedial measures immediately upon his return from a visit to Great Britain and the United States. The prime minister was able to prevent the conspiracy by promising to conduct a referendum amongst the entire Likud membership and to reassess the decision to cancel the primaries.

Netanyahu at the Likud convention.

Ehud Barak, leader of the Labor Party, made a public apology to the Oriental community of Israel in the name of the Labor establishment for the wrongs that were inflicted on them during several generations of Labor governments. (September 25)

•

Due to lack of evidence, the Supreme Court cleared former Jewish Agency chairman Simcha Dinitz, who had been convicted by the District Court of using his Jewish Agency credit card for personal use. (October 14)

•

The state prosecutor decided there were insufficient reasons to issue an indictment against Egyptian ambassador to Israel Mohammed Bassiouni. Bassiouni was accused by a belly dancer of an attempt to rape her. (October 16)

•

The Tel Aviv District Court rejected the slander suit launched by minister Ariel Sharon against the newspaper Ha'aretz and decided that Sharon deceived the former prime minister Menahem Begin during the Lebanon war in 1982. (November 4)

•

250.000 people attended the rally commemorating the second anniversary of the assassination of the late prime minister Yitzhak Rabin. The rally turned into a protest meeting against premier Netanyahu and his policies. (November 8)

•

The head of the prime minister's office, Yvette Lieberman, announced his resignation. Lieberman explained his decision to resign from his wish to be able to act freely within the Likud party and to help promote the re-election of premier Netanyahu to a second term of office. Three days afterwards the Israel police published a recommendation for the indictment of Lieberman for past breaches of the law. (November 23)

•

The government suffered a series of defeats during the budget vote in the Knesset. The revolt against the Minister of Finance and the Prime Minister was led by Foreign Minister David Levy, in protest about the Prime Minister's refusal to honor his written undertakings aimed at easing the plight of the neediest sections of the population and the development towns. (December 26)

ALPHABETICAL INDEX OF NAMES AND EVENTS

Abdullah, King - Jordanian ruler, grandfather of King Hussein; he was murdered at the al-Aqsa Mosque in 1951 because he intended to make peace with Israel.

Abuhatzeira Aharon - Religious politician and minister in right-wing governments.

'Abu Jihad' - Arafat's deputy, who was eliminated in 1988 at his home in Tunis by *Mossad* agents.

Adam Yekutiel - Major-General in the IDF, killed in 1982 in the Lebanon War during a battle with terrorists.

Adenauer Konrad - Leader of West Germany after World War II; responsible for the introduction of diplomatic relations with Israel.

Adiv Ehud - Jewish member of a Jewish-Arab espionage network exposed in 1972; sentenced to 17 years imprisonment.

Agnon S.Y. - Nobel Prize for Literature laureate in 1966.

Agranat Commission - The commission of inquiry set up in 1974 to examine the events and omissions of the *Yom Kippur* War.

Agranat Shimon - Supreme court judge; member of the Agranat Commission.

al-Aqsa Mosque - A Moslem mosque on the Temple Mount which was set on fire in 1969 by a deranged Australian tourist; one of the most sacred Moslem sites.

Allon Yigal - Commander of the *Palmach*, member of *Knesset* and minister in Israel's Cabinets during the years 1955-1977; he died in 1980.

Aloni Shulamit - Founder of the civil rights movement in Israel; member of *Knesset*, leader of the Meretz Party and minister in left-wing governments.

'Altalena' - A ship containing arms for the IZL, sunk off the Tel Aviv coast during the War of Independence by order of David Ben-Gurion, in order to avoid a possible split of the nation into two armed camps.

Amin Idi - Ugandan leader who collaborated with the Palestinian hijackers of an Air France airliner at Entebbe in 1976.

Amir Yigal - Prime Minister Yitzhak Rabin's assassin, who was sentenced to life imprisonment in 1996. He shot Rabin at point-blank range in the back as Rabin was leaving a peace rally in Tel Aviv.

Amit Yosef - IDF officer convicted of espionage in 1987, details of which were released in 1993.

Arad Ron - IAF navigator whose 'plane was shot down in Lebanon in 1986, when he was captured by *Hizbullah* terrorists; his fate is unknown to this day.

Arad Yael - Israeli judoist who won a silver medal at the 1992 Olympic Games in Barcelona.

Arafat Yasser - Chairman of the PLO's military branch since 1964; he took control of the organization later and became the Palestinians' leader. Arafat was born in Cairo despite claiming to have been born in Jerusalem.

Arbel Edna - State prosecutor in 1997.

Arens Moshe - *Likud* politician and member of *Knesset* who was also Israel's ambassador to the US and senior minister in right-wing Cabinets.

Argov Nehemia - Prime Minister David Ben-Gurion's military secretary, he committed suicide in 1957 after having run over a cyclist.

Argov Shlomo - Israel's ambassador to Britain who was critically injured by a Palestinian terrorist in 1982; this was one of the major catalysts for The Lebanon War.

Aridor Yoram - *Likud* politician who was appointed in 1981 minister of finance in Menachem Begin's Cabinet.

Ashkenazi Motti - IDF officer (res.) who had been commander of the 'Budapest' fortress north of the Suez Canal, and who led the protest movement against Golda Meir's government in 1974, because of *Yom Kippur* War failures.

Austerity - A rationing regime enforced during Israel's first years.

Avi-Isaac Dan - Successful Israeli lawyer who, in recent years, has been involved in numerous major trials, including that of Aryeh Deri as his defending counsel, and whose name was mentioned as the source for exposing the 'Bar-On Affair' in 1997.

'Aviv Neurim' - A daring mission in Beirut in which top PLO officials were eliminated in 1973.

Avneri Uri - Left-wing journalist who was elected to the *Knesset* in 1965 as representative of 'Ha'Olam Hazeh.'

Ayalon Ami - Head of the GSS since early 1996, and formerly head of the navy.

Ayyash Yihye - Known as 'The Engineer,' he was responsible for the death of scores of Israelis in suicide bombings carried out by *Hamas*. He was killed in 1996, when his booby-trapped remote-controlled mobile 'phone blew up in his hand.

Azar Shmuel - Member of the Jewish espionage network exposed in Egypt in 1954, who was later executed in January 1955, together with Dr. Moshe Marzuk; the affair became known as 'The Lavon Affair.'

Bakshi Doron Eliyahu - Israel's Chief *Sephardi* Rabbi.

Bank Shares' Crisis - A serious economic crisis in which a significant segment of the public, investing in bank shares, lost most of their savings.

Bar-Lev Chaim - Chief of staff in 1968. The fortification line along the Suez Canal was named after him. Later appointed member of *Knesset*, he served as a minister and Israel's ambassador to Russia; he died in 1994.

Bar-On Affair - An attempt to appoint Advocate Roni Bar-On as attorney general in 1997. The affair, which involved the prime minister and the minister of justice, was presented as a conspiracy to take over the functions of State prosecution.

Bar-On Roni - Appointed in 1997 as the government's attorney general, he resigned two days later, following a huge public uproar at his lack of qualification. A police investigation of the 'Bar-On Affair' was then instituted.

Barak Aharon - Attorney-General during the drafting of the Camp David accords. Elected the current Chief Justice after Judge Meir Shamgar retired.

Barak Ehud - Commanded 'Sabena Operation' in 1972, commander of *Sayeret Matkal*, chief of staff, minister of interior; made head of Labor party in 1997.

Bashevis-Singer Isaac - Jewish author. Nobel Prize for Literature laureate in 1978.

Be'er Israel - Military correspondent and reserve officer who was caught in 1961 as a Russian spy.

Be'eri Isser - Chief of *Haganah* intelligence, he was behind the decision to execute Meir Tubiansky.

Beaufort - Crusader fortress in south Lebanon which had become a fortified terrorist base and was conquered by *Golani* soldiers in a fierce battle in 1982.

Begin Binyamin ('Benny') - A right-wing politician, the son of Menachem Begin, vehement opponent of Prime Minister Netanyahu, he resigned from government after some months as minister of science.

Begin Menachem - IZL leader, who established *Herut*. He headed the party until 1983, and was elected Israel's sixth prime minister in 1977. He died in 1992.

Beilin Yossi - Labor party politician, holding a doctorate in political science, considered to be the architect of the Oslo accords between Israel and the PLO in 1993. Minister in the Cabinets of Yitzhak Rabin and Shimon Peres. He ran for the premiership of the Labor Party in 1997.

Ben-Aharon Yitzhak - Secretary general of the *Histadrut* in the early Seventies.

Ben-Ami Shlomo - Professor and Labor party diplomat and politician who presented his candidacy to head the Labor party in 1997.

Ben-Artzi Noa - Grand-daughter of Prime Minister Yitzhak Rabin. Her eulogy at her grandfather's funeral in 1995 moved hundreds of millions of hearts worldwide.

Ben-Eliezer Binyamin ('Fuad') - Politician and Labor party. Minister in the Cabinets of Rabin and Peres.

Ben-Elissar Eliahu - *Likud* politician. Member of *Knesset*, Israel's past ambassador to Egypt and current ambassador to the US.

Ben-Gal 'Yanush' - Armored brigadier in *Yom Kippur* War, OC of northern region prior to The Lebanon War in 1982.

Ben-Gal Yosef - IDF intelligence agent who was arrested in Switzerland in 1963 after threatening families of German scientists who were employed by Egypt.

Ben-Gurion David - Israel's first prime minister, he declared the establishment of the State on May 15, 1948. He led the Labor party for many years and died in 1973.

Ben-Gurion Paula - Wife of the prime minister, who influenced him greatly; she died in 1968.

Ben-Menachem Yitzhak (Gulliver') - A paratroopers officer, killed in a Sea of Galilee reprisal in 1955.

Ben-Natan Asher - Israel's first ambassador to West Germany, he presented his credentials in 1965.

Ben-Porat Miriam - State comptroller since 1988; previously a high court judge.

Ben-Yair Michael - Attorney General in Rabin's Cabinet, he resigned from office in 1997, which resignation opened the way for the Bar-On Affair.

Ben-Zvi Itzhak - Israel's second president; he died in 1963.

Bennett Max - An Israeli intelligence officer who was captured in Egypt in 1954. He committed suicide in prison after undergoing cruel interrogations and torture.

Bernadotte Count Folke - A Swedish mediator, murdered in Jerusalem by the *Lehi* underground headed by Yitzhak Shamir (later to be *Likud* prime minister).

Bin-Nun Avihu - Commander of the IAF, who resigned from duty after the 'Rami Dotan Affair.'

Biton Charlie - One of the founders of the '*Black Panther*' movement; former member of *Knesset*.

Black Market - Sales of rationed products and later dollars without license, for exorbitant prices.

'Black Panthers' - A social protest movement of underprivileged neighborhoods in Jerusalem initiated in the early Seventies.

'Black September' - Violent incidents in Jordan in September 1970, during which King Hussein eliminated the PLO's control over the country.

Bloch Dora - An Anglo-Israeli woman, one of the Entebbe hostages in the 1976 hijacking, she was hospitalized in Kampala and murdered at the hospital by Idi Amin's soldiers.

Boushiki Ahmed - Moroccan waiter who was assassinated by *Mossad* agents in Norway in 1973 after being mistakenly identified as a senior PLO member.

Burg Avraham - Son of former minister, Yosef Burg; a Labor party politician and current chairman of the Jewish Agency; his mentor was Professor Yeshayahu Leibowitz, the controversial religious theorist and philosopher.

Burg Yosef - NRP member of *Knesset* and minister in Israeli governments from 1955 to 1988 where he served as minister of health, post, welfare, interior, police and religion.

'Bus No. 300 - A 'bus that was hijacked by four terrorists in 1984. After the re-capturing of the 'bus, two of the hijackers were executed by the GSS. The affair caused a storm in Israel with repercussions lasting for many years.

'Bus No. 405 - A 'bus which was on its way from Tel Aviv to Jerusalem in 1989, and which plunged into an abyss because of the action of terrorists.

Camp David - A resort of the US president, at which the historic peace treaty between Israel and Egypt was signed.

Capucci Hilarion - Archbishop who was head of the Greek Orthodox Church in Jerusalem, Judea and Samaria; he was arrested after smuggling arms for the *Fatah* organization in 1974, and awarded 12 years in prison.

Carlebach Azriel - Founder and first editor of daily paper *'Ma'ariv'*; died in 1956.

Cave of the Patriarchs - Also known as the Machpelah Cave. One of the holiest sites in Israel, it is sited at Hebron. According to Jewish tradition, it is the burial site of the patriarchs. A source of endless confrontation between settlers and Palestinians.

Cherbourg boats - Five missile boats abducted from the French port and secretly brought to Israel.

'Chinese Farm' - A heroic battle of paratroopers in the Sinai during the *Yom Kippur* War. The commander of the paratroopers' battalion was Lieutenant-Colonel Yitzhak Mordechai, today serving as minister of defense.

Cohen Eli - Israeli spy who succeeded in infiltrating the Syrian government, he was publicly hanged in Damascus in 1965.

Cohen Geula - Right-wing politician. One of the strongest opponents to the Camp David Accords. Mother of Tzahi Hanegbi.

Cohen Haim - Attorney general in the early Fifties and supreme court judge.

Cohen Nadia - Eli Cohen's widow, she has been fighting to bring his body to Israel for burial, since 1964.

Cohen Uriel - Pilot of the El Al 'plane that was attacked in Munich in 1970, he was wounded while attacking one of the terrorists who let off a hand grenade.

Cohen Izhar - Israeli singer who won the 1978 Eurovision.

'Dakar' - An Israeli submarine, which disappeared with its crew in 1968. Despite extensive searches which continue to this very day, the mystery has never been solved.

Dassa Robert - Member of the espionage network arrested in Egypt in 1955. Released after the Six-Day War.

Dayan Assaf ('Assi') - Son of Minister of Defense, Moshe Dayan. Flew in the El Al 'plane that was attacked in Athens in 1970. Today, an author, actor and film director.

Dayan Moshe - IDF's fourth chief of staff, he was appointed minister of defense in 1967 and minister of foreign affairs in 1977; Dayan died in 1981.

Dayan Yael - Labor party member of *Knesset*, daughter of Moshe Dayan, and human rights activist.

Demjanjuk John - A Ukranian who was brought to trial in Israel and charged with having executed war crimes at the Treblinka death camp. After a long trial, he was exonerated for lack of sufficient evidence and deported back to the US.

Deri Aryeh - *Haredi* activist, one of the founders of *Shas* and its most powerful political figure. Involved in various affairs: in 1990, suspected of theft and receipt of bribes, an investigation against him was commenced; that trial still continues, having forced him to leave the Ministry of the Interior. A trial pends against him on charges of conspiracy, in the Bar-On Affair.

'Dollar Account Affair' - The exposure of Leah Rabin's bank account in Washington in 1977, which led to Rabin's resignation as leader of the Labor party.

Dori Ya'akov - IDF's first chief of staff, who headed the army during the War of Independence.

Dotan Rami - Brigadier-General in the IAF, who was arrested in 1990 and convicted of bribery under aggravating circumstances.

Drori Amir - OC of the northern region who was reprimanded after the massacre at Sabra and Shatilla refugee camps.

Drukman Chaim - A rabbi and religious politician who was attacked by terrorists in 1993; his driver was killed in the incident.

Dweik Moshe - He threw a hand grenade into the *Knesset* in 1957 and injured Prime Minister Ben-Gurion and several ministers.

Eban Abba - Israel's ambassador to the United Nations and the United States from 1949 to 1950. Served as minister of education and culture and minister of foreign affairs in *Mapai* Cabinets.

Edelstein Yuli - Was a *Prisoner of Zion* in the USSR. Minister of absorption since 1996 in Likud coalition, as an *Yisrael be'Aliya* member.

Eden Avraham ('Bren') - Battalion commander on north Sinai front during *Yom Kippur* War.

Edri Rafi - Labor party politician who was involved in the setting up of the meeting between Shimon Peres and King Hassan of Morocco in 1986.

Edri Sharon - An IDF soldier who was kidnapped and murdered by *Hamas* terrorists in 1996. His body was discovered only several months later.

'Egoz' - An immigrant ship from Morocco, sunk en route to Spain in 1961.

Eichmann Adolf - One of the highest ranked Nazi criminals in the Second World War. He escaped after the war to Argentina, where he was kidnapped in 1960 by the *Mossad*. He stood trial in Israel and was executed in 1962.

'Eilat' - An Israeli destroyer sunk by the Egyptians in 1968.

Einstein Albert - Physicist and Nobel Prize laureate, who was Ben-Gurion's candidate for president of Israel.

Eitan Rafi - An Israeli intelligence agent who recruited Pollard to spy on the US.

Eitan Raphael ('Raful') - Paratrooper officer, commanded the paratroopers' force that parachuted into the Mitla Pass in 1956. Chief of staff from 1978 to 1983. Entered politics as head of *Tsomet* party. Minister in *Likud* governments, currently serving as Minister of Agriculture and the Environment.

Elad Avri - Operated an espionage network in Egypt. Escaped, captured in Israel, convicted for turning in the underground's members and sentenced to imprisonment.

Elazar David ('Dado') - Chief of staff during the *Yom Kippur* War. Discharged at the recommendation of the Agranat Commission in 1974. Died in 1976.

Elbaz Nathan - A soldier of Moroccan origin who heroically saved the lives of his comrade soldiers when he ran with a live hand-grenade out of a tent full of soldiers and died while embracing it to minimize the danger for other soldiers in the vicinity.

Eliav Lova - Secretary general of the Labor Party. Resigned from the Labor Party in favor of a left-wing movement.

Elrom Ephraim - Israeli consul in Turkey who was kidnapped and murdered by Moslem extremists in 1971.

Elsheikh Rahamim - IDF soldier kidnapped by *Hizbullah* in 1986 who died in captivity.

Erlich Simcha - Liberal politician who was appointed minister of finance in Begin's Cabinet. Died in 1983.

Farouk - King of Egypt who was dethroned in 1952.

Fatah - One of the military wings of the PLO.

'Fatahland' - An area in Lebanon, north of Mt. Hermon, which served as a base for terrorist operations against Israel's northern settlements.

Fedayeen - Across border infiltrators from Arab countries who injured many Israelis in the Fifties.

Fine Effi - Brigadier-General in IDF who commanded *Givati* division and mentioned more than once as suspected of having given soldiers and officers orders to physically hit Palestinians during the *Intifada*.

Fink Yosef - IDF soldier, kidnapped by *Hizbullah* in 1986; died in the terrorist organization's captivity.

Gal Uzi - Inventor of the *Uzi* submachine gun.

Galili Israel - A Labor party minister, member of Golda Meir's inner circle.

Gamasy Muhammad - Egypt's representative in *Yom Kippur* cease-fire talks.

Gas masks - Masks against chemical gases, distributed to Israel's citizens in 1990 during the lead-up to The Gulf War.

Gazit Shlomo - IDF Major-General who participated in 1978 military talks in Egypt.

General Security Services (GSS) - The security services responsible for the security of Israel within the State's borders.

Geva Eli - Armored Brigadier who left the IDF in 1982, for conscientious objections to The Lebanon War.

Gillon Carmi - Head of the GSS who resigned in January 1996 due to the failure of the GSS to prevent Yitzhak Rabin's murder.

Ginossar Yossi - A senior GSS officer who was involved in the fabrication of evidence presented to a commission investigating who killed the hijackers of the No. 300 'bus. He was pardoned by Chaim Herzog and resigned from the service.

Golani - Elite infantry brigade, responsible for numerous operations across the Israeli border.

Goldmann Nahum - President of the World Jewish Congress; died in 1982.

Goldstein Baruch - A member of *Kach*, who massacred 29 Moslems in the Cave of the Patriarchs by shooting them in the back as they were praying. He was killed by surviving worshippers. His wife attempted to have those survivors tried for murder.

Goren Shlomo - IDF chief rabbi during the Six Day War. He was later elected chief rabbi of Tel Aviv and chief rabbi of Israel.

Gorodish Shmuel - OC Southern Region in the *Yom Kippur* War. Discharged at the recommendation of the Agranat Commission.

Gottesman Sam - American millionaire who assisted in the purchase of the 'Hidden Scrolls.'

Gottlieb Israel - Orthodox politician. State witness in 1981 at the trial against Minister of Religious Affairs, Aharon Abuhatzeira.

Grunzweig Emil - *Peace Now* activist who was killed in 1983 by a grenade thrown by an Orthodox man at demonstrators against Minister of Defense, Ariel Sharon.

Gulf War - The war initiated by the US and its allies against Iraq in 1991, after Iraq's invasion of Kuwait. Dozens of *Scud* missiles were launched at Israel during the war.

Gur Mordechai ('Motta') - Paratroopers' officer who participated in numerous reprisals in the Fifties. He headed the force that liberated the Old City of Jerusalem in 1967. Chief of staff and Labor minister. Died 1995.

Gush Emunim - Settlement movement of 'Religious Zionists.' Established in the early Seventies to populate Judea, Samaria and the Gaza Strip.

HaGashash HaHiver - Israeli folklore: an entertainment group performing since 1963.

Habash George - Leader of the 'Popular Front for the Liberation of Palestine.'

Haberfeld Haim - Secretary general of the *Histadrut* in 1994. Lost to Haim Ramon in the elections.

Habib Phillip - American diplomat and envoy, who came to the Middle East in 1981 in an attempt to mediate between Israel and Syria and Lebanon.

Habonim tragedy - A horrifying crash between a 'bus full of children and a train in 1985. Nineteen children were killed.

Hacham Amos - Winner of the first international Bible competition.

Haddad Sa'ad - Christian Lebanese officer; the first commander of the South Leban-on Army (SLA).

Halevi Binyamin - The presiding judge at the Kastner trial; he accused Kastner of 'having sold his soul to Satan.' Later elected Supreme Court judge and member of *Knesset*.

Hamas - An extremist Moslem organization responsible for the murder of scores of Israelis as well as for many other bloody terrorist attacks.

Hanegbi Yitzhak ('Tzahi') - *Likud* politician who was active as a student in the battle against withdrawal from Sinai town of Yamit; member of *Knesset* and minister of justice in Netanyahu's government.

Har-Zion Meir - An outstanding member of 'Unit 101' and a paratrooper. Headed the reprisals in the Fifties; seriously wounded in 1956.

Harel Isser - Head of *Mossad* and GSS who was responsible for the capture of Nazi war criminal Adolf Eichmann in 1960.

Harkabi Yehoshafat - Major-general and head of intelligence. Discharged from duty after the mobilization of reserves drill in 1959.

Harnik Goni - *Golani* commander who died in the battle over the Beaufort Castle in the Lebanon War in 1982.

Hasson Ayala - Television reporter who exposed the scandal behind the attempt to appoint Advocate Roni Bar-On as attorney general.

Hausner Gideon - The attorney general and prosecutor in the trial of Adolf Eichmann in 1961.

Hazak Reuven - High ranking officer of the GSS. Demanded the discharge of the head of the GSS in 1986, and was forced to resign from the organization.

Heletz - A *moshav* in the northwestern Negev, near which the first oilfield in Israel was discovered in 1955.

Herut - Right wing party established by Menachem Begin.

Herzl Ze'ev Binyamin - Envisioned the State of Israel; died in 1904. His body was brought to Israel in 1949 and reinterred on what is now called Mt. Herzl in Jerusalem.

Herzog Chaim - Major-General who also served in the British army (and was one of the liberators of Belsen), head of military intelligence, the son of Israel's chief rabbi, one of Israel's top lawyers, Israel's ambassador to the UN and president of Israel from 1983 to 1993. Died in 1997.

'Hetz' - An anti-missile missile. Developed by Israel and financed by the US. Designated for operational use within a few years.

Hilmi Abbas - Egyptian pilot who defected to Israel with his 'plane in 1964.'

Hod Mordechai - IAF commander in the Six-Day War.

Hofi Yitzhak - OC of the northern region in the *Yom Kippur* War.

Horowitz Yigal - Politician and member of *Knesset,* he was appointed minister of finance in 1979.

Hussein King - Son of Prince Talal, he assumed his place in 1952 as King of Jordan. Hussein, a Bedouin of the Hashemite dynasty, made peace with Israel in 1994 after years of quiet diplomacy and secret meetings; he is much respected by Israelis.

Ilan Uri - Israeli soldier who committed suicide in Damascus Prison in 1955 after having being tortured by the Syrians while in captivity.

Imber Naftali Herz - The author of the words of Israel's national anthem '*Hatikva*' (*the Hope*). His body was brought to Israel in 1953.

'Intifada' - An uprising by the Palestinians in the territories, sparked in 1987 and ended in 1993.

Iraqi Reactor - A nuclear reactor at Osirak in Iraq that was bombed and destroyed by the IAF in 1981.

Ivry David - Major-General in the IDF; IAF commander, subsequently director- general of the Ministry of Defense.

Jabotinsky Johanna - Ze'ev Jabotinsky's wife, whose body was brought to Israel from New York in 1964 for re-interment.

Jabotinsky Ze'ev - Leader of the revisionist movement, whose body was brought to Israel from New York in 1964 for re-interment.

Japhet Ernst - A top banker, whose outrageously high, self-awarded pension scheme was exposed in 1987, shortly after which he was forced to retire due to the report of a commission of inquiry. He died in the US in 1997.

Jarring Gunnar - UN mediator between Israel and Egypt in 1970.

Jemayel Amin - Brother of Bashir; after his brother's assassination, he became the elected president of Lebanon, known for his pro-Syrian sympathies.

Jemayel Bashir - Leader of the Christian *Phalangists,* assassinated in Beirut in 1982, shortly after his election as president of Lebanon; known for pro-Israel sympathies.

Jerusalem Law - Passed in 1980, it proclaims united Jerusalem the capital of Israel.

Jewish Underground - An organization of settlers who booby-trapped cars and murdered Arabs in the territories. The Underground was exposed in 1984 and its members were sentenced to imprisonment.

Jibril Deal - An exchange of three Israeli POW's for 1150 terrorists in 1985.

Kafr Kassem - An Arab village in the 'triangle,' 43 of whose inhabitants, including women and children, were erroneously killed by IDF soldiers in 1956, when they broke a curfew without knowing of its existence.

Kahalani Avigdor - Armored division officer, commended for heroism in both the Six-Day and *Yom Kippur* wars. Member of *Knesset* and incumbent minister of internal security.

Kahane Meir - Leader of the Jewish Defense League in New York. An extreme right-winger, who was murdered in New York in 1990.

Kalmanovitch Shabtai - Businessman of Russian origin, who was arrested in 1988 for spying for the Soviet Union.

Kaplan Eliezer - Minister of finance in Ben-Gurion's Cabinets; died in 1952.

Kastner Israel - A *Mapai* activist convicted of collaborating with the Nazis. He was murdered in 1957.

Kastner Trial - A trial that shook the public in the Fifties, and dealt with the fate of Hungarian Jewry during the Second World War.

Katyushas - Rockets fired by terrorists at Israel's northern settlements and towns.

Katzav Moshe - *Likud* politician, minister in right-wing Cabinets. Minister of tourism since 1996.

Katzir Aharon - A world-renowned scientist who was killed in 1972 in a terrorist attack at Lod airport.

Katzir Ephraim - A professor of bio-chemistry, who was elected Israel's fourth president in 1973; the brother of Professor Aharon Katzir.

Katzover Benny - One of *Gush Emunim*'s leaders in 1974.

Khaled Leila - A hijacker of an El Al 'plane at Munich in 1970, captured but released by the Germans. One of the PLO's symbols of struggle, she recently voted against changing the PLO Covenant to recognize Israel's right to exist, as required by 'Oslo.'

'Kilometer 101' - A site on the Cairo-Suez road where the initial talks for the cease-fire agreement between Israel and Egypt were conducted.

Kissinger Henry - American secretary of state in President Nixon's government. He mediated between Israel and the Arab countries in 1973. Winner of Nobel Prize for Peace in 1973 for his efforts to end the Vietnam War.

Klingberg Marcus - Expert in biological warfare, who spied for the USSR in Israel and was arrested in 1983. Considered to be the most harmful spy in Israel's history.

Klinghoffer Leon - An American Jewish wheelchair-bound tourist, cruelly murdered by terrorists aboard the cruise ship '*Achille Lauro*' in 1985.

Kollek Teddy - One of the people most close to Ben-Gurion. Mayor of Jerusalem for 29 years, and internationally identified as such.

Kreiski Bruno - Chancellor of Austria in 1973, he closed the immigrant transit camps after a terrorist attack, in an attempt to appease the Palestinian perpetrators.

Lahat Shlomo ('Chich') - Major-General in the IDF. Mayor of Tel Aviv from 1974 to 1993.

'Land Day' - Stormy demonstrations of Israeli Arabs protesting the expropriation of lands. Since 1976, 'Land Day' has been annually commemorated.

Landau Eli - Aide to Minister of Defense Ariel Sharon. Elected mayor of Herzliya in 1988.

Landau Moshe - Supreme court judge. Chief justice at the Adolf Eichmann trial.

Lapid Mordechai - Hebron settler who was killed together with his son Shalom, in a terrorist attack in 1993.

Lapid Yosef - Famous journalist, appointed executive director of the Broadcasting Authority in 1977.

Laskov Haim - Promoted as the IDF's fifth chief of staff, in 1958.

Lavi - A model of a combat aircraft developed by Israel, whose development was stopped in 1987 due to financial problems and political pressure by the US.

Lavon Affair - Also known as 'The Mishap.' An espionage affair exposed in Egypt in 1954, which embarrassed Israel's top political echelon, including PM Ben-Gurion and Minister of Defense Pinchas Lavon who claimed no knowledge of the network.

Lavon Pinchas - Labor party politician and minister of defense in 1954; the repercussions of the 'Mishap.' Died in 1976.

Law of Return - The law declaring every Jew's right to immigrate to Israel and receive Israeli citizenship.

Leibovitz Roni - A bank robber caught in 1990 after robbing 22 branches in seven months, and known as the 'Motorbank' as he arrived at each bank on a motorcycle and entered wearing a helmet.

Lerner Gregory - Russian new immigrant businessman suspected of having ties with the Russian mafia and of attempting to bribe Israeli politicians. He was arrested in 1997.

Levinger Moshe - A leader of the ultra-right-wing religious settler movement in the territories, who lives in Hebron.

Levy David - *Likud* politician, member of *Knesset* and minister in right-wing governments. The incumbent minister of foreign affairs since 1996.

Levy Maurice - The physician who performed the first heart transplant in Israel, in 1968.

Levy Moshe - Paratroopers officer. Chief of staff after 'Raful' and the Lebanon War.

Levy Victor - Member of the Jewish underground who was arrested in Egypt in 1955, and released after the Six-Day War.

Lieberman 'Yvette' Alexander - Executive director of the Prime Minister's Office. Considered one of the closest people to Binyamin Netanyahu.

Livne Menachem - Settler leader of the Jewish underground which was exposed in 1984; sentenced to life imprisonment and released in 1990.

Lock Mordechai - An Israeli double agent for Egypt, arrested in 1964 at Rome airport after the Egyptians tried to forcibly transfer him to Egypt in a diplomatic bag.

Lotz Wolfgang - An Israeli spy known as 'the spy on horseback,' caught in Egypt in 1963 and released in 1968; an IDF major.

Ma'abarot - Transit camps: tents and tin huts in which hundreds of thousands of new immigrants were housed on arrival in Israel in the Fifties.

Ma'alot Massacre - The murder of 21 schoolchildren from a Safed school who were captured by terrorists in Ma'alot in the Galilee in 1974.

Madrid Conference - An international peace conference in 1992, participated in by Israel and her Arab neighbors.

Magen David - *Likud* politician, member of *Knesset* and minister who formed the *Gesher* party with David Levy in 1995.

Maimon Yehuda Leib - Minister of religious affairs in Ben-Gurion's government who caused the resignation of the government in 1950 by his stand on education in the immigrant camps.

'Magic Carpet' - an operation which achieved the transfer of Yemen's Jews to Israel in 1949.

Malka Rafi - High ranking officer in the GSS who demanded the resignation of the head of the GSS in 1986, but was himself forced to resign from the organization.

Mapai - The workers party, which dominated Israeli politics in various incarnations.

Margalit Dan - Journalist and television host who exposed the Rabin family's bank account in the US in 1977, as a result of which Rabin resigned from the premiership.

Marzuk Moshe - A member of the Jewish espionage network exposed in Egypt in 1954, he was arrested and executed in 1955.

Maxwell Robert - A British media tycoon, who purchased the Israeli daily newspaper *'Ma'ariv.'* Maxwell drowned in 1991 under mysterious circumstances, and was buried in Jerusalem.

Meir Golda - Labor party leader, minister of foreign affairs and Israel's fourth prime minister, Golda served as the latter during the *Yom Kippur* War and died in 1978.

Meir Yehuda - Colonel demoted to the rank of private and discharged from the army in 1990, after commanding soldiers to hit Palestinians during the *'Intifada.'*

Mendler Albert - Division commander on the southern Sinai front in the *Yom Kippur* War; killed during the war.

Mengele Josef - A Nazi physician responsible for physical experiments on Auschwitz Camp's Jews. Despite extensive searches, Mengele was never captured.

Meridor Dan - *Likud* politician; secretary of Begin's Cabinet, and minister of justice in the Shamir government. Binyamin Netanyahu's biggest rival in the *Likud*, he was forced to resign from the Ministry of Finance in 1997 by Netanyahu's manipulation.

Meron Hanna - A theater and television actress who was seriously wounded during the attack on El Al passengers at Munich Airport in 1970.

Meshulam Uzi - Headed an extremist group that confronted the police in 1994, to highlight their demand to investigate the fate of Yemeni children who went missing on arrival in Israel. Sentenced to 11 years imprisonment.

Military Government - Strict restrictions imposed on Israeli Arabs in the Fifties and Sixties.

Miller Alice - A female soldier who petitioned the High Court of Justice against the IDF's decision not to allow female soldiers to enlist on flight courses. The court accepted the petition in 1994 and opened the doors of the course to female soldiers.

Milo Roni - Mayor of Tel Aviv from 1993, formerly minister of police in *Likud* government.

Mirage - French-made warplane bought by Israel which dominated the skies in the Sixties.

Mista'arvim - IDF units operating in the territories, whose soldiers are disguised as Arabs.

Mitla Pass Battle - A heroic battle of paratroopers in Sinai in 1956.

Mizrachi Bezalel - A famous contractor who won a libel suit against the newspaper *'Ha'Aretz,'* after an investigative report placed him at the top of Israel's organized crime.

Mizrachi Israel - *Agudat Israel* member of *Knesset,* who refused to comply with the instruction of the Council of Sages in 1990 to support Peres' government.

Moda'i Yitzhak - *Likud* politician, member of *Knesset* and minister in right wing governments.

Mordechai Yitzhak - Paratroopers' officer and commander of the paratroopers force at the 'Chinese Farm' during the *Yom Kippur* War. Major-general in the IDF and as of 1996, minister of defense.

Mortada Sa'ad - The first Egyptian Ambassador to Israel, appointed in 1980.

Mossad - The intelligence services' branch responsible for special, covert operations.

Mubarak Hosni - Vice president of Egypt until 1981; he was appointed president after Sadat's assassination. He himself has escaped assassination attempts.

Munich Massacre - The murder of Israeli athletes at the 1972 Munich Olympic Games.

Nahal - Pioneering combat unit whose soldiers combined operational military service with settlement activities.

Narkiss Uzi - OC of the central region during the Six-Day War.

Nasser Gamal Abdel - Egypt's leader from 1954 to 1970.

Nasser Kamal - PLO's spokesperson. Killed in operation *'Aviv Neurim'* in Beirut in 1973.

Nathan Abie - Peace pilot, who flew in a light 'plane to meet Egyptian President Nasser in 1966.

Nathanzon Phillip - Member of the espionage network exposed in Egypt in 1954. Arrested and later released after the Six-Day War.

National Unity Government - A Cabinet comprised of both right-wing and left-wing parties, formed before the Six-Day War and again in 1984 when the leadership was rotated between Shimon Peres and Yitzhak Shamir.

National Water Carrier - An enterprise for the transfer of water from the Sea of Galilee to the Negev.

Navon Ofira - Wife of Yitzhak Navon, who died in 1993.

Navon Yitzhak - Israel's fifth president, from 1978 to 1983. Formerly, David Ben-Gurion's secretary; he was appointed minister of education in 1984 for Labor in the National Unity Government.

Ne'eman Ya'acov - A prominent lawyer, originally minister of justice in the current government who resigned on his indictment; he was exonerated in 1997 and appointed minister of finance in July 1997.

Ne'eman Yuval - World renowned professor in the field of nuclear physics. Formed the party *Tehiya* in 1981, elected to the *Knesset* and appointed minister of science and technology, and minister of energy and infrastructure.

Nebentzal Yitzhak - A member of the Agranat Commission set up to investigate the omissions of the *Yom Kippur* War.

Netanyahu Binyamin - Leader of the *Likud* and Israel's prime minister since 1996.

Netanyahu Sara - Wife of Prime Minister Binyamin Netanyahu.

Netanyahu Yonatan ('Yoni') - *Sayeret Matkal's* commander; killed at Entebbe airport in 1976 in the operation to rescue hostages. The brother of Prime Minister Binyamin Netanyahu.

Night of the Hang-gliders - An omission in 1987, as a result of which a terrorist reached Israel by hang-glider, landed at a military base in northern Israel and killed six soldiers.

Ninio Marcelle - Member of the espionage network exposed in Egypt in 1954. Arrested in 1954 and released after the Six-Day War.

Nissim Moshe - Son of the chief rabbi of the Fifties, he served as minister of finance and minister of justice in right-wing governments.

Nudel Ida - Immigration activist and *Prisoner of Zion*. Released and arrived in Israel in 1987.

Obeid Sheikh - Lebanese sheikh and leader of the *Hizbullah* in south Lebanon, kidnapped by the IDF in 1989, in an attempt to pressure *Hizbullah* leaders into releasing Ron Arad.

Ofer Avraham - Minister of housing, who committed suicide in 1976 after his name was linked to scandals.

Ofer Shalom - Border patrol policeman, accused of taking part in the Kafr Kassem massacre.

Okamoto Kozo - Japanese terrorist caught after committing a cruel massacre at Lod airport in 1972, together with two other terrorists; sentenced to life imprisonment and released in the Jibril Deal in 1985.

Olmert Ehud - Mayor of Jerusalem since 1993, formerly minister of health in a *Likud* government.

'Operation Grapes of Wrath' - A military operation against *Hizbullah* in Lebanon in April 1996, as Shimon Peres' government's response to continuous losses of soldiers in the security zone and *Katyushas* on Kiryat Shmona.

'Operation Litani' - A military operation in 1978; in retaliation to the terrorist attack on the No. 300 'bus, the IDF conquered areas in south Lebanon.

'Operation Moses' - The dramatic operation in 1984 to bring Ethiopian Jewry to Israel.

'Operation Peace for Galilee' - A war in Lebanon in 1982, during which the IDF conquered extensive areas in Lebanon and forced the PLO out of Beirut, before becoming bogged down in what became known as Israel's 'Vietnam.'

'Operation Sinai' - A military operation to conquest the Sinai Peninsula in 1956.

'Operation Solomon' - The operation in 1991 in which 14,000 Ethiopian Jews were airlifted to Israel in the course of a single day.

'Operation Yonatan' - The rescue of hijacked hostages at Entebbe, Uganda, in 1976.

Oslo Agreement - An agreement between Israel and the Palestinians which was signed in 1993.

Palmach - The striking force of the *Haganah* before the War of Independence, originally created to ward off a possible invasion of the *Yishuv* from Egypt by the German army in World War II, which was fighting in the Desert under Rommel.

Pauls Rolf - West Germany's first ambassador to Israel who submitted his credentials in 1965.

Peled Moshe - Division commander in the northern front in the *Yom Kippur* War.

Peres Shimon - Director general of the Ministry of Defense in the Fifties, under David Ben-Gurion. Prime minister from 1984 to 1986 in the rotation government with Shamir and after Yitzhak Rabin's assassination from November 1995 to May 1996. Served in various governments as minister of transport, finance, defense and foreign affairs. Winner with Yitzhak Rabin and Yasser Arafat of the Nobel Prize for Peace in 1994. He resigned in 1997 as leader of the Labor Party.

Peres Yoram - El Al pilot, killed in a terrorist attack in Zurich in 1969.

Peretz Amir - Labor party politician. Joined Haim Ramon in 1994 in the campaign against the *Histadrut*. Elected chairman of the *Histadrut* in 1995 instead of Ramon who returned to the Cabinet after Rabin's assassination.

Peretz Yitzhak - A religious minister who in 1990 refused to support the government headed by Shimon Peres and was consequently forced to leave *Shas*.

PLO (Palestinian Liberation Organization) - A Palestinian organization established for the liberation of *Eretz Israel*.

Pollard Jonathan - American Jew who spied for Israel while working for naval intelligence. Caught in 1985 and sentenced to life imprisonment.

Pope Paul VI - Visited Israel in 1964.

Porat Hanan - One of *Gush Emunim*'s leaders in 1974. An NRP member of *Knesset*.

Poraz Nir - *Sayeret Matkal* officer, killed in 1994 while trying to rescue kidnapped soldier Nachshon Wachsman.

Powers Gary Francis - Pilot of a U-2 spy 'plane, downed by the Soviets in 1960.

Rabin Leah - Yitzhak Rabin's much beloved wife.

Rabin Yitzhak - One of the commanders of the *Palmach*. The chief of staff who led the army to the Six-Day War victory and the liberation of Jerusalem. Israel's ambassador to Washington in the Seventies; Rabin was twice elected for premiership - in the Seventies and the Nineties. Nobel Prize for Peace laureate. Assassinated on November 4, 1995 whilst leaving a peace rally in Tel Aviv.

Rachamim Mordechai - Israeli security officer who was arrested in Zurich in 1969 after shooting a terrorist who tried to attack an El Al 'plane.

Radai Peleg - A high ranking officer in the GSS who demanded the resignation of the head of the GSS in 1986, but was himself forced to resign from the organization.

Ramon Haim - Labor party politician who defeated the Labor party in the campaign for the *Histadrut* in 1994. Minister in the governments of Rabin and Peres.

Red Rock (Petra) - A breath-taking site of an ancient city carved in rock in Jordan. Many youngsters were killed while attempting to reach the site.

Refugees - Palestinians who fled from Israel during the War of Independence.

Remez David - Minister of transport and education in Ben-Gurion's Cabinets.

Reparations Agreement - An agreement between Israel and West Germany which determined that Israel and its citizens would receive compensation for Nazi war crimes. Thus, the port of Ashdod was built with German money.

Reprisals - Military operations against infiltrators and Jordanian, Egyptian and Syrian military bases in the Fifties.

Riyad Abdul Munaim - Egypt's chief of staff, killed by an Israeli attack on the Suez Canal in 1969.

Rohan Dennis - Australian tourist who set the al-Aqsa mosque on fire in 1969.

Rokach Israel - Mayor of Tel Aviv during the War of Independence. He brought about the unification of Tel Aviv and Jaffa.

Rothschild Dorothy de - Widow of James de Rothschild. Placed the corner stone for the *Knesset* in 1958. She and her husband established the Rothschild Foundation which exclusively funded the erection of the *Knesset*, the Chief Synagogue and the Supreme Court building, as well as contributing towards the Israel Museum and other cultural establishments with great generosity and far-sightedness.

Rubinstein Amnon - Professor of law and member of *Knesset,* founder of Liberal *Shinui* party which merged with *Meretz*; he served as minister of education and culture and minister of communication and science in Yitzhak Rabin's government in the Nineties.

Rubinstein Elyakim - Legalist and top official in the past at the Ministry of Foreign Affairs. A judge, he was appointed attorney general in 1997 in the wake of the Bar-On Affair.

Sabena - Refers to a Belgian 'plane which was hijacked to Israel and rescued at Lod airport in a daring mission executed by *Sayeret Matkal*.

Sabra and Shatilla - Refugee camps near Beirut. The Christian *Phalangists* slaughtered the camps' Palestinian tenants in 1982 in revenge for the assassination of Bashir Jemayel.

Sadat Anwar - Nasser's successor as Egypt's leader. Sadat arrived on a historic visit to Israel in 1977 to make peace. He was assassinated in 1981 during a military parade because of his peace with Israel.

Saguy Uri - Major-General in the IDF. He served as head of military intelligence during the Tze'elim tragedy in 1992, in which five *Sayeret Matkal* fighters were killed.

Saguy Yehoshua - Head of military intelligence during the Lebanon War, he was discharged after the Sabra and Shatilla massacre.

Sapir Pinchas - Minister of finance and a powerful member of *Mapai* in the Sixties and Seventies. Died in 1975.

Sapir Yosef - A politician from the Liberal Party. He joined the National Unity Government as minister without portfolio in 1969.

Sarid Yossi - Labor party member of *Knesset*, who resigned from the party after the forming of the rotation government in 1984. One of the founders of *Meretz*, he later became its leader, serving as minister of the environment under Yitzhak Rabin.

Savir Uri - One of the people close to Shimon Peres. Director-general of the Ministry of Foreign Affairs and one of the architects of the Oslo Accords in 1993.

Sayeret Matkal - An elite IDF unit responsible for many operations against Israel's enemies. Most of the unit's operations are still kept secret.

'Secret Alliance of Zealots' - An ultra-Orthodox underground which attempted to attack the *Knesset* in 1951.

Sela Aviam - An outstanding pilot, commander of the Iraqi reactor team, he later became involved in the Pollard affair, acting as Jonathan Pollard's handler.

Shahak Amnon Lipkin - Paratroopers officer, former chief of military intelligence. He commanded Operation *'Aviv Ne'urim'* in Beirut in 1973 and was also a commander in Beirut in The Lebanon War. Appointed chief of staff in 1995.

Shahal Moshe - Labor party politician. Minister in the governments of Peres and Rabin.

Shalom Avraham - Head of the GSS in 1984, who gave the instruction to kill two captured terrorists in the No. 300 'bus hijacking. He claimed that he had acted on Prime Minister Shamir's order.

Shamir Yitzhak - *Lehi* commander, *Likud* politician and Israel's seventh prime minister.

Shapira Moshe - Minister of religious affairs in Ben-Gurion's Cabinet.

Shapira Ya'acov Shimshon - Minister of justice in Golda Meir's government, he resigned in 1972.

Sharansky Avital - Natan's wife who for many years fought for his release from the Soviet jail, having come to live in Israel during that time.

Sharansky Natan (Anatoly) - Famous *Prisoner of Zion*. In 1978, he was charged with espionage and sentenced in Russia to 13 years imprisonment; he was released in 1986 and came to Israel. He formed the new immigrant party *Yisrael be'Aliya* and was appointed minister of trade and industry in 1996.

Sharett Moshe - One of the original leaders of the Labor party. Minister of foreign affairs and Israel's second prime minister.

Sharon Ariel ('Arik') - Major-General who commanded 'Unit 101' set up to counter Arab attacks; he was minister of defense responsible for 'Operation Peace for Galilee' - The Lebanon War. The Kahan Commission recommended his dismissal as minister of defense. He is currently minister of national infrastructure, and has served in the past as minister of agriculture and housing, and Rabin's advisor on security.

'Shavit-2' - An Israeli missile that was successfully launched in 1961.

Shazar Zalman - Israel's third president from 1963 to 1973, he died in 1974.

Shetreet Bechor - Minister of police in Ben-Gurion's government.

Shkaki Fathi - Leader of the Islamic Jihad, he was assassinated in Malta in 1995.

Shomron Dan - Paratroopers' commander, who headed the Entebbe rescue operation; appointed chief of staff in 1987.

Shtarks Nachman - Yossele Shumacher's grandfather, who had the child kidnapped from his parents in 1960 and taken to New York.

Shukeiry Ahmed - The first chairman of the PLO, which was established in 1964.

Shumacher Yossele - The child who was kidnapped by *haredim* in 1960. He was discovered in New York two and a half years later by the *Mossad*.

Simhoni Assaf - OC of the southern front during Operation Sinai. Killed after the battles in an airplane crash.

Six-Day War - A war that broke out in 1967 between Israel on the one side and Egypt, Syria and Jordan on the other. The holy sites that were controlled by the Jordanians since the War of Independence, the Sinai Peninsula and the Golan Heights were all conquered by a victorious Israel.

Smadja Oren - Judoist. Won the bronze medal in the 1992 Olympic Games.

Sneh Ephraim - Labor party politician, and doctor, minister of health in the governments of Rabin and Peres; he presented his candidacy to head the Labor party in 1997.

Sovlan Robert - An American spy acting on behalf of the Soviet Union, he escaped from the US in 1962 and sought political asylum in Israel. He was deported and later committed suicide.

Stempel Moshe - Paratroopers officer who was commended after the Khan Yunis Operation; he was killed after the Six Day War in a chase after terrorists.

'Stinking manipulation' - The attempt by Shimon Peres in 1990 to overthrow Yitzhak Shamir's government.

Straits of Tiran - Sea straits in the southern part of the Sinai Peninsula, which are the maritime approach to Eilat. The closing of the straits by Egypt has provoked wars between Israel and Egypt.

Suez Canal - Water passage controlled by Egypt; IDF forces reached as far as the canal in two wars.

Szenes Hanna - Female paratrooper and Israeli heroine who was executed in Hungary towards the end of the Second World War.

Szenes Katarina - Mother of Hanna Szenes, who testified at the Kastner trial about her daughter's arrest in Hungary.

Talal Prince - Son of the Bedouin Hashemite King Abdullah, and his successor. Crowned in 1951 and dethroned after he was found to be mentally unstable; the title passed to his son, Hussein.

Tamari Nehemia - OC of the central region, who was killed in a helicopter crash in 1994.

Tamir Abrasha - Major-General who participated in the 1978 military talks with Egypt.

Tamir Shmuel - IZL activist and committed lawyer who represented many, including Kastner, against the *Mapai* establishment. In 1977, he was appointed minister of justice in Begin's government.

Temple Mount - The site where the Temple was located. Today the site of mosques.

Terner Ya'acov - Chief of police in the early Nineties. He claimed he was forced to resign after refusing to terminate the investigation against Minister of the Interior, Aryeh Deri.

Tichon Dan - Speaker of the 14th *Knesset*, from 1996.

Tubiansky Meir - Suspected of spying for Britain and executed by the *Haganah*. He was posthumously exonerated.

Uclik Otto, Dr. - A German scientist who was arrested in Switzerland in 1963 after threatening the lives of families of German scientists who were employed by Egypt.

Unit 101 - A commando unit formed in 1953 to fight infiltrators.

'Upheaval' - The change of governments in 1977, bringing the *Likud* to power with Menachem Begin as prime minister.

Vanunu Mordechai - A scientist at the nuclear reactor in Dimona who leaked Israel's atomic secrets; he was kidnapped in Rome in 1986 and brought for trial in Israel, after which he was sentenced to 18 years imprisonment.

Verdiger Avraham - *Agudat Israel* member of *Knesset* who refused to comply with the 'Council of Sages' instruction to support a government headed by Peres in 1990.

Wachsman Nachshon - IDF soldier kidnapped in 1994 by terrorists, who was then tragically killed during the failed rescue operation. A young man whose smile was described as "lighting up a room," the entire nation agonized in suspense as the deadline approached. His parents asked that everyone should light a shabbat candle to pray for him; most households complied.

Wadi Salib - A Haifa neighborhood, it became a symbol of Moroccan immigrants' battles against discrimination.

'Waiting Period' - the days before the outbreak of the Six-Day War, when IDF soldiers were drafted but the political echelon was still unsure as to whether or not to wage war.

War of Attrition - A state of static war along the Egyptian border, characterized by artillery shells and commando raids.

War of Independence - The war between Israel and its Arab neighbors which broke out immediately after the declaration of the State of Israel by David Ben-Gurion in 1948.

Weizman Ezer - Pilot, commander of the IAF, and minister of defense; currently the president of Israel since 1993.

Weizmann Chaim - Israel's first president, who died in 1952. Weizmann was a scientist, whose name is given to the country's internationally renowned scientific institute: The Weizmann Institute in Rehovot.

Western Wall - The holiest site for the Jewish people, it was liberated by the IDF in the Six-Day War.

Western Wall Tunnel - A Hasmonean tunnel in the vicinity of the Western Wall. Its opening in 1996 sparked running battles between Israel and the Palestinians, and claimed the lives of 26 Israeli soldiers.

'Who is a Jew' - Regulations passed in 1958, according to which every child may be registered as a Jew if his parents so declare. The regulations caused endless crises in Israel.

Ya'iri Uzi - Paratroopers officer holding the rank of colonel, who was killed while commanding the Savoy Hotel operation in 1975.

Yadin Yigael - IDF's second chief of staff. Famous archeologist, he formed *Dash* party in the late Seventies.

Yaguri Assaf - Armored battalion commander. The highest-ranked officer to be held captive by Egypt. Elected to the *Knesset* in 1977.

Yamit - Northern Sinai town, became a symbol for the struggle against the return of Sinai to Egypt. It was totally demolished in 1982, except for the synagogue.

Yariv Aharon - Major-General in the IDF. Israel's representative in the cease-fire talks with Egypt in 1973.

Yaron Amos - IDF commander in the Beirut area in 1982; following the massacre in Sabra and Shatilla, he was disqualified from positions of command.

Yasur - A type of helicopter that has been involved in the worst training exercises in the IDF's history: in 1977, a *Yasur* transporting 54 soldiers crashed and in 1957 two *Yasur* helicopters collided, killing 73 soldiers.

Yatom Danny - *Sayeret Matkal* fighter who participated in the rescue operation of the 'Sabena' plane in 1972. He was appointed the current head of the *Mossad* in 1996.

Yom Kippur War - A war between Israel, Egypt and Syria in 1973, which claimed the lives of many.

Yosef Dov - Austerity minister in Ben-Gurion's government, he headed the campaign against the Black Market and led the rationing policy during the country's first years.

Yosef Ovadia - Israel's chief *Sephardi* rabbi in the past, now mentor of Aryeh Deri and leader of the *Shas* party.

Yussuf Abu - Arafat's deputy who was killed in the operation 'Aviv Neurim' in Beirut in 1973.

Zamir Yitzhak - Attorney general during the GSS affair in 1986, he resigned in light of the affair and is today a supreme court judge.

Ze'evi Rechavam ('Gandhi') - Major-General and extreme right-wing *Knesset* member. Established the party *Moledet* which promotes the policy of 'transfer.'

Zeira Eli - Former head of military intelligence. Major-General who was discharged at the recommendation of the Agranat Commission in 1974.

Zelikovich Miriam - Married Prime Minister Levi Eshkol in 1964.

Ziad Tufik - An Israeli-Arab member of *Knesset* from Nazareth who was killed in a car accident in 1994 on his way back from welcoming Arafat to Jericho.

Zippori Mordechai - Brigadier-General in the IDF, deputy minister of defense, he participated in military talks with Egypt in 1978.

Zohar Uri - An Israeli entertainer who became newly religious; he headed a charity that supported Prime Minister Yitzhak Rabin in 1977.

Zorea Meir - Major-General who was head of the IDF manpower branch. He was discharged from duty after a badly coordinated mobilization of reserves drill in 1959 which nearly caused a war.